PRINCIPLES OF SMALL BUSINESS MANAGEMENT

McGRAW-HILL BOOK COMPANY

New York St. Louis Dallas San Francisco Auckland Bogotá Düsseldorf
Johannesburg London Madrid Mexico Montreal
New Delhi Panama Paris São Paulo Singapore
Sydney Tokyo Toronto

PRINCIPLES OF SMALL BUSINESS MANAGEMENT

William N. Macfarlane

WILLIAM N. MACFARLANE
Chief, Estimating and Cost Control Administration,
General Dynamics Corporation, Pomona (California) Division.

Lecturer in the Supervisory Training and Middle Management Curriculum,
Riverside City College, Riverside, California.

Head of Macfarlane and Associates Consulting Service.

Member, American Institute of Industrial Engineers, Inc.

Sponsoring Editor   Margaret Halmy
Senior Editing Supervisor   Linda Stern
Editor   Matthew Fung
Design Supervisor   Edwin Fisher
Designer   William Frost
Production Supervisor   Laurence Charnow

Library of Congress Cataloging in Publication Data

Macfarlane, William N   date.
    Principles of small business management.

    Bibliography: p.
    Includes index.
    1. Small business—Management. I. Title.
HD69.S6M23   658'.022   76-41237
ISBN 0-07-044380-7

2 3 4 5 6 7 8 9 0   DODO   7 8 6 5 4 3 2 1 0 9 8 7

Preface

No institution in the American economy offers greater opportunities to energetic, creative people than the small business.

There is hardly a major company operating today that did not begin as the result of the determination of a few individuals to own and operate a small business of their own. Those businesses succeeded because they were operated in accordance with sound management principles—principles clearly defined in William Macfarlane's book. To ignore these principles is to court disaster; to be guided by them is to embark with safety upon a rich, absorbing adventure.

> Edward A. O'Rorke, President
> New York Chamber of Commerce and Industry, Inc.

Principles of Small Business Management focuses on everything you need to know about small business in a unique question-and-answer format. It is written for those who have ever dreamed of owning a business of their own. For business people who will one day find themselves financially able to start or buy a business, it provides an overview of the major problems they will face and the pitfalls they must avoid if success is to be assured. For those who are already on the "firing line," it provides a means of self-evaluation and introspection which will help them find better ways of doing things. And for the student of business, it poses thought-provoking questions which stimulate analysis and understanding of business problems and builds a strong background for eventual business management.

THE FORMULA FOR SUCCESS

Business ownership is not without its problems. The chances of failure are high for those who go into business without adequate planning. Published statistics of business failures in the United States are appalling in their implications. Business data published by Dun & Bradstreet, Inc., for 1974 shows that 59.9 percent of all business that failed that year had been in existence 5 years or less. Attempts to analyze the reasons for these failures generally indicate serious deficiencies in the areas of planning, management, and administration which could have been avoided or at least minimized by attention to basic management principles.

Serious students of business management must ask themselves how it is possible, in the same business environment, for some businesses to fail while others, making the same product in the same geographical area, are successful. From the wealth of available information related to business failures, one may distill certain basic "truths" which appear to be associated with success. They may be summarized as follows:

1. There must be an awareness of the important factors in business success.
2. There must be a desire and capability to be a good manager.
3. There must be continual attention to acceptable standards and procedures.

OBJECTIVES

In business operations, experience has demonstrated that certain factors are critical in determining the course of action to take in making successful business decisions. If these factors are ignored or if the available facts are not interpreted correctly, the margin of failure increases. Major objectives of this book are to acquaint prospective managers with the basic principles of business management; to introduce the tools needed for effective planning, organization, leadership, and control; and to develop skill in analyzing management problems and controlling them.

ORGANIZATION

The principles of successful business management are presented in six parts:

Part I defines small business and provides statistics regarding the kinds and sizes of businesses in the United States. Data are provided for manufacturing, wholesale, retail, and service establishments. The material gives the reader an appreciation of why businesses exist, what problems they face, and how the manager's basic responsibilities affect the success of the business.

Part II introduces the critical activities associated with planning the new business, including such factors as form of organization, business location, financing the enterprise, and layout. Franchising is discussed as an alternative to the conventional ownership approach in starting a business.

Part III explores those techniques which will help the owners track the financial progress of their businesses and keep their finger on the "pressure points." Budgeting, forecasting, profit analysis, recordkeeping, insurance management, cost control, and credit management are stressed. Costs associated with absenteeism, accidents, overtime, labor turnover, procurement, theft, and inventories are highlighted as areas where sizable savings are possible.

Part IV treats the problems of marketing research, promotion, and advertising—all vital functions in any business. The points made are that merchandise incorrectly priced will result in either lost customers or leftover stock, that ill-timed sales promotions will bring less than expected sales and lost profit opportunities, and that ineffective advertising will add to owners' expenses without increasing their sales.

Part V deals with the importance of people and their attitudes toward their jobs in the successful operation of any business. It emphasizes that management practices in the area of employee relations directly affect the amount and quality of work done.

Part VI is focused on the major state and federal regulations which affect the operations of businesses. Laws relating to pricing, employment practices, credit management, taxes, and wage administration are emphasized.

LEARNING AIDS

Performance criteria, problems, and projects; related case studies; and self-check exercises accompany each chapter. They provide the student with a measure of his or her knowledge and understanding of the major principles as well as with an opportunity to correctly apply the subject matter presented.

An instructor's manual is available to provide supplemental materials and tests covering the contents of the text.

OVERTURE

Success in business by really trying is clearly the theme of this text. The question-answer strategy is designed to help the new business manager or owner to recognize and deal with potential shortcomings. Although the author does not guarantee that a business will succeed, this program points up the complexity of carrying on a small business and stresses the long hours of work and periods of uncertainty that accompany business success.

ACKNOWLEDGMENTS

The author gratefully acknowledges the support of the following organizations and publications for permitting the use of copyrighted materials: U.S. Small Business Administration; Bank of America; Dun & Bradstreet, Inc.; *Changing Times* magazine; National Retail Hardware Association; *Harvard Business Review*; Ideal System Company; California Institute of Technology; *Modern Manufacturing* magazine; Data Terminal Systems; and Sears, Roebuck and Co.

And finally, a special acknowledgment to my wife, Naomi, whose encouragement and loyalty helped make a dream become a reality.

William N. Macfarlane

Contents

CHAPTER

The Profile of Small Business

PERFORMANCE OBJECTIVES

After reading this chapter, you should be able to explain the various types of business which make up the United States business population, assess the importance of small business in the United States economy, and evaluate the criteria used to determine whether a business is considered "small." Specifically, you should be able to:

1. Discuss the growth of small business since 1900 and its relation to population trends.
2. Explain *small business* in terms of paid employees, sales, or another meaningful standard.
3. Defend the use of different size standards for different kinds of businesses serviced by the Small Business Administration.
4. Discuss the ratio of minority-owned businesses to the total business population, and describe the relationship of minorities in the United States population to the number of minority-owned businesses.
5. Judge what the statistical probability is that a new business will live to be 2 years old; 5 years old.
6. Explain small business trends in terms of annual starts, discontinuances, and net gains.
7. Analyze and discuss the major causes of business failures.
8. Distinguish which types of business have the best and worse survival records.

1

INTRODUCTION

Every year 250,000 new businesses are started in the United States. Most of them are "small" when judged either by the number of people they employ or by their annual sales. Many of them are operated by owners who are unable to cope with the problems which will cause half of them to fail by the end of the fifth year.

This chapter explores the composition of the 8.5 million businesses now operating in this country, provides comparative statistics about their size, and presents some insights into the causes of new business failures. The role of minority-owned firms in the American economy is examined briefly.

This overview of small business statistics is designed to acquaint the reader with the "big picture" of small business birth, growth, and survival and set the stage for subsequent chapters, which will treat the problems of starting and operating a new small business in detail.

HOW MANY SMALL BUSINESSES ARE THERE IN THE UNITED STATES?

There are approximately 5.5 million businesses which compose the so-called "visible" population—those with either paid employees or an established place of operation. In addition to these there are some 3 million businesses which operate as part-time activities from non-business locations or have no paid employees. The latter are often sidelines for people who are also on someone else's payroll. This makes a total of approximately 8.5 million businesses of all kinds.

HOW MANY OF THE EXISTING BUSINESSES ARE CONSIDERED SMALL?

Approximately 95 percent of the 5.5 million "visible" businesses are considered small by the U.S. Small Business Administration (SBA). These businesses employ about 40 percent of the civilian labor force. Of all businesses, 66 percent have annual gross sales of less than $100,000 and 71 percent employ fewer than ten people. Thus we can see that small businesses make up an important segment of the American business complex.

DO NEW BUSINESS "STARTS" FOLLOW POPULATION TRENDS?

Generally yes. The number fluctuates during business recessions, dropping to lower levels because of closings related to deteriorating business conditions. Over a long period of time, however, new businesses have grown at a rate which is slightly greater than the rate of growth in population. The ratio of businesses per 1,000 population is the criterion for following trends in new business incorporations. In 1900, there were 1,660,000 business firms in operation to serve a population of 76,130,000. The ratio was 21.8 per 1,000 of the population. By 1930, the ratio had increased to 24.0; it then dropped a little ten years later and was 23.8 in 1940. It hit an all-time high of

26.5 in 1950 as a result of the postwar boom. In 1972, our 8.5 million businesses were serving a population of 202,837,000 people, and the ratio was down to 24.6.

New business starts exceeded 20,000 per month in both 1969 and 1970. The current net growth is about 100,000 new businesses a year.

WHAT IS THE GENERALLY ACCEPTED DEFINITION OF A SMALL BUSINESS?

There is no hard rule here, although there are some good guidelines that have been developed which will serve as a point of departure. A problem immediately presents itself when we attempt to answer the question, How big is small? One would consider American Motors a "small" company when compared with General Motors or Ford; however, it would be considered large when compared with most of the businesses that you and I patronize. Most people would consider the independent druggist, service station owner, or local dry cleaner as "small" operators. Similarly, they would consider Mobil, Shell, or Exxon among the "big" businesses. The latter indeed appear on the listing of the 500 largest corporations, which collectively employed 76 percent of all United States workers in 1973. Where to draw the line between "big" and "small" is somewhat arbitrary, since there are several factors which relate to bigness or smallness, such as the number of employees, the type of business, the dollar value of sales or receipts, and the size of competitors.

The most widely used criterion is *paid employment*, or number of people on the payroll, although annual sales are commonly used in describing the relative size of retail and wholesale businesses.

The Small Business Act, passed by Congress in 1953, authorized the Small Business Administration to formulate size standards for defining which businesses qualified for assistance under its lending program because of their smallness. Retail and service firms, which compose over 40 percent of the total business firms in this country, are considered small by the SBA if their annual sales do not exceed $1 million to $5 million, depending on the type of business. Construction firms seeking SBA help are considered small if their annual sales do not exceed $7.5 million, averaged over a 3-year period. Wholesale firms with annual sales of $5 million or less are classed as small. In manufacturing, a firm with 250 employees or less is commonly recognized as small. If employment is between 250 and 1,000, a size standard for the particular industry is used. The definitions of small business undergo constant review by the SBA because the character of Amerian business is constantly changing. The trend in recent years has been to lower the size standard in order to effectively offer protection and assistance to those smaller firms which need such help in order to be competitive, and to limit assistance to those larger firms which do not actually need assistance in order to survive.

ARE THERE ANY CHARACTERISTICS OTHER THAN SIZE WHICH IDENTIFY SMALL BUSINESSES?

Yes. Many small businesses meet the definition provided by the Small Business Act previously cited, which defined a small business in more general terms as "one which is independently owned and not dominant in its field of operation." Such businesses are often owned and managed by the same person. Many of them have no paid employees. Initial financing typically comes from the owner's savings or from friends and relatives. The business serves a local market and most of the workers live in the home community. Both employees and patrons usually know one another—usually on a first-name basis. By these standards, most of the businesses we patronize each day qualify for the title "small."

HOW IS THE BUSINESS POPULATION DISTRIBUTED AMONG THE MAJOR INDUSTRIES?

Retail stores constitute the biggest grouping, composing over 40 percent of the 5.5 million "visible" businesses in 1970. Manufacturing made up the smallest group with 6.2 percent. Table 1-1 shows how these two groups, together with construction, service businesses, and wholesale trades, fit into the distribution. The "all other" category includes real estate, transportation, public utilities, communications, finance, and mining.

Retailing is characterized by merchants or owners who buy their products from wholesalers, distributors, jobbers, or other agents and provide them to the ultimate consumer where he or she desires them. Creation of the retail establishment is justified because

TABLE 1-1. DISTRIBUTION OF TOTAL BUSINESS POPULATION IN 1970

	Number (Thousands)	Percent
All industries, TOTAL	5,480	100.0
Contract construction	541	9.9
Manufacturing	340	6.2
Services	1,115	20.3
Retail trade	2,255	41.2
Wholesale trade	384	7.0
All other	845	15.4

Source: U.S. Small Business Administration, *Annual Report for 1970*, 1971.

retailing supplies a service to the customer which will provide the maximum in courtesy and service and make the transaction a pleasing one. For this reason, many retail establishments frequently spend sizable sums (often unnecessarily) to provide conveniences which cater to customers' desires. Examples of small retail businesses abound. They include eating establishments, bookstores, filling stations, grocery stores, garages, music stores, shoe stores, drugstores, and many others.

Service businesses almost defy categorization because of their wide diversity. Service firms provide services, often intangible, either at a specific business location or at the customer's home or business. The customer goes to the dentist for dental care but calls the pool service in to clean and vacuum the swimming pool at home. Many of the services with which we are familiar are discretionary in that they will not be demanded by customers until many of their more basic needs have been met. The demand for services increases during periods when spendable income increases. Familiar stereotypes of service firms are the accounting firms, advertising agencies, barber and beauty shops, cleaning and pressing shops, repair shops of all kinds, hotels and motels, travel agencies, and baby-sitters. There were 1,590,248 service establishments in 1972, employing 5.3 million workers, with sales of almost $113 billion.

A business is considered to be primarily engaged in wholesale trade when its principle function is buying or selling merchandise at wholesale, or acting as an agent or broker (middleman) in moving manufactured products between the manufacturer and the retailer. The term *at wholesale* includes marketing or selling merchandise to retailers; to other wholesalers; and to industrial, commercial, professional, and institutional users. Wholesale trade encompasses all types of establishments selling a wide range of products such as groceries; drugs; hardware; fruits, vegetables, and other farm products; industrial supplies; and petroleum products. The wholesale firm is in effect a service organization for small manufacturers who cannot economically store their products and distribute them to all the possible outlets which will sell them to the consumer.

Manufacturing businesses convert raw materials into the thousands of useful products needed by the ultimate consumer and by other industrial users. The conversion is accomplished through the procurement of materials, machines, and services and the coordination of these assets in a way that progressively changes the shape or form of the manufactured item until its conversion to the finished product. Because of the large investment required for equipment and machines, the average firm size in manufacturing tends to be larger than that in most other kinds of business. Most manufacturers pass their finished products on to wholesalers or distributors. Very few engage in the distribution process beyond the use of normal wholesale channels. Typical manufacturers include machine shops, bakeries, shoe factories, toy factories, cabinet shops, furniture manufacturers, and clothing manufacturers.

In 1972 approximately 4.2 million workers were employed in construction with an annual payroll of $40.8 billion. Of those workers, 35 percent worked for firms employing less than ten employees. The distribution of employees among the major classifications is shown below:

Classification		Employees (Thousands)	Percent of Total
General building contractors		1,177	28
Heavy construction		840	20
Special trade contractors		2,146	51
Plumbing, heating, air conditioning	460		
Electrical work	327		
Plastering and lathe work	180		
Masonry and stonework	171		
Roofing and sheet metal	160		
Concrete work	154		
Carpentering	125		
All other	569		
Subdividers and developers		62	1
		4,225	100

WHICH RETAIL BUSINESSES HIRE THE MOST WORKERS?

The Bureau of the Census has reported that retail firms had over 9 million employees in 1967 and more than 11 million in 1972. In 1969, the kinds of retail businesses which had the most workers were:

Eating places	2 million
Grocery stores	1.2 million
Department stores	1.1 million

These three business categories accounted for 44.3 percent of all retail employment in 1967.

Retail sales in billions for 1969 and 1972 are shown in Table 1-2.

ARE MOST RETAIL STORES "SMALL" WHEN MEASURED BY THE SMALL BUSINESS ADMINISTRATION DEFINITION?

If you use the $1 million of annual sales as the yardstick, 97 percent of them are small. In 1967, only 50,000 establishments out of 1,763,000, or 2.9 percent, exceeded this amount. If you use paid

TABLE 1-2. SALES OF RETAIL ESTABLISHMENTS BY KIND OF BUSINESS
GROUPS IN THE UNITED STATES

	Retail Sales (Billions)	
	1969	1972
Food stores	$70.3	$100.7
Automotive dealers	55.6	93.8
General merchandise	43.5	66.7
Miscellaneous retail stores	27.3	39.1
Eating and drinking places	23.8	36.9
Gasoline service stations	22.7	33.7
Building materials, farm equipment dealers, hardware	17.2	25.6
Apparel and accessories	16.7	24.7
Furniture, home furnishings	14.5	22.5
Drug and proprietary stores	10.9	15.6

Source: U.S. Department of Commerce, Bureau of the Census, *Census of Business—*
Retail, 1972.

employment as a measure of bigness, only 6,087 of these establishments had more than 100 employees. Table 1-3 shows data related to
the size of retail establishments in this country.

TABLE 1-3. EMPLOYMENT SIZE OF RETAIL ESTABLISHMENTS IN THE
UNITED STATES IN 1967

	Establish- ments as a Percentage of Total	Sales as a Percentage of Total	Employees as a Percentage of Total
Establishments with:			
Less than 4 paid employees	70.5	21.7	14.3
4 to 19 paid employees	24.4	31.8	36.5
20 to 49 paid employees	3.9	21.3	21.5
50 to 99 paid employees	0.9	11.3	10.8
100 or more paid employees	0.3	13.9	16.9
All establishments	100.0	100.0	100.0

Source: U.S. Department of Commerce, Bureau of the Census, *1967 Census of Business,*
Retail.

WHAT KINDS OF MANUFACTURING FIRMS EMPLOY THE MOST WORKERS?

In 1972 there were almost 19 million workers employed in manufacturing plants. Almost 60 percent of them were employed in the
following seven areas.

	Percentage
Food and kindred products	8.2
Transportation equipment	9.0
Electrical and electronic equipment	8.7
Machinery, other than electrical	9.9
Apparel and related products	7.2
Primary metals industry	6.0
Fabricated metal products	7.8

WHAT PERCENTAGE OF MANUFACTURING FIRMS HAVE FEWER THAN 250 WORKERS?

Almost all of them, according to the 1967 Census of Manufactures. Table 1-4 shows that only 4.5 percent (100.0 − 95.5 percent) of the total manufacturing firms had 250 or more employees; however, that segment was responsible for about 65 percent (100.0 − 34.9 percent) of the value added to manufactured products. Despite this lopsided relationship, the relative importance of small manufacturers should not be underestimated. They often supply critically needed materials to big firms and are considered an indispensable ingredient in any assessment of the nation's economic health. Without their output, the business community would be in serious difficulty. A large automobile manufacturer's existence depends upon the thousands of small firms who supply parts and assemblies to be used in the finished product. After the automobile is assembled, the manufacturer depends upon thousands of dealerships and other retail outlets to market the product. In this case, as well as hundreds of others, the industrial giant grows only through the services provided by small businesses.

TABLE 1-4.   1967 CUMULATIVE PERCENTAGES OF MANUFACTURING FIRMS FALLING INTO VARIOUS SIZE CLASSES, AND VALUE ADDED BY EACH FIRM

	Number of Establishments, %	Value Added by Manufacturing, %
1 to 4 employees	38.4	1.1
1 to 9 employees	51.3	2.3
1 to 19 employees	64.9	5.1
1 to 49 employees	80.9	12.1
1 to 99 employees	89.0	20.1
1 to 249 employees	95.5	34.9
1 to 499 employees	98.0	48.7
1 to 999 employees	99.2	62.0
1 to 2,499 employees	99.7	77.0
All establishments, TOTAL	100.0	100.0

Source: U.S. Department of Commerce, 1967 Census of Manufactures.

For convenience, wholesale trade can be divided into three major type-of-operation classifications, based upon the characteristics of each operation:

Merchant wholesalers

Manufacturer's sales branches

Merchandise agents and brokers

Table 1-5 shows the number of establishments and the sales figures for these groupings:

TABLE 1-5.   WHOLESALE TRADE BY TYPE OF OPERATION FOR 1972

Type of Operation	Number of Establishments	Sales in Billions of Dollars
All types, TOTAL	369,791	$695.2
Merchant wholesalers	289,974	353.9
Manufacturer's sales branches and sales offices	47,197	255.7
Merchandise agents, brokers	32,620	85.6

Source: U.S. Department of Commerce, Bureau of the Census, *Census of Business—Wholesale, 1972.*

Merchant wholesalers have consistently constituted the most important type of operation in terms of both establishments and sales.

HOW MANY WHOLESALE FIRMS QUALIFY AS "SMALL," BASED ON ANNUAL SALES OF $5 MILLION OR LESS?

About 90 percent of them. Less than 1 percent report sales of $20 million or more, and less than 2 percent fall in the $10 million to $20 million sales bracket. Table 1-6 shows the sales size of wholesale establishments in the United States in 1967.

DO WHOLESALE FIRMS EMPLOY A LOT OF WORKERS?

Despite the high dollar volume of wholesale activity, 42 percent of all wholesale firms had fewer than four employees in 1967. Many of those in the "1 employee" bracket actually had no paid employees.

TABLE 1-6. SALES SIZE OF WHOLESALE ESTABLISHMENTS IN THE
UNITED STATES IN 1967

Sales Size of Establishment	Establishment		Sales	
	Number	Percent of Total	Amount (Millions of Dollars)	Percent of Total
United States, TOTAL	311,464*	100.0	459,476	100.0
Establishments operated entire year with annual sales of:				
$20,000,000 or more	2,663	0.9	138,612	30.2
$10,000,000 to $19,999,999	3,993	1.3	54,126	11.8
$5,000,000 to $9,999,999	8,564	2.7	58,843	12.8
$1,000,000 to $4,999,999	59,977	19.3	125,572	27.3
$500,000 to $999,999	49,611	15.9	35,189	7.7
$200,000 to $499,999	73,643	23.6	23,944	5.2
Less than $200,000	105,200	33.8	10,170	2.2
Establishments not operated entire year	7,873	2.5	13,020	2.8

Source: U.S. Department of Commerce, Bureau of the Census, 1967 Census of Business, Wholesale Trade.

*The figures in this column do not add up to 311,464, but they have been reproduced exactly as shown in the source.

Table 1-7 shows comparative sales and payroll data for 1954 and 1967. A slight shift away from the smaller sizes of firms and toward larger establishments is apparent in both the sales and the payroll percentages shown in the table.

TABLE 1-7. EMPLOYMENT SIZE OF WHOLESALE ESTABLISHMENTS
IN THE UNITED STATES IN 1954 AND 1967

Employee Size	Number of Establishments in 1967	Sales as Percent of Total		Payroll as Percent of Total	
		1967	1954	1967	1954
United States, TOTAL	311,464	100.0	100.0	100.0	100.0
1 employee	63,679	3.3	5.2	1.7	2.0
2 to 3 employees	68,723	6.6	8.5	4.3	4.9
4 to 7 employees	70,013	11.8	13.7	10.2	11.2
8 to 19 employees	69,029	22.7	22.0	24.0	22.8
20 to 49 employees	29,464	24.1	23.1	25.5	25.5
50 employees or more	10,556	31.5	27.5	34.3	33.6

Source: U.S. Department of Commerce, Bureau of the Census, 1967 Census of Business, Wholesale Trade.

AREN'T MOST CONSTRUCTION FIRMS IN THE LARGE BUSINESS CATEGORY?

It might seem so to the outsider who associates the building of skyscrapers, bridges, and highways with bigness. Figure 1-1 indicates that just the opposite is true. There are thousands of general contractors today who operate on a modest scale. In addition to these, many more operate in specialized fields such as electrical, plumbing, and painting construction. Public construction of bridges, sewers, and streets attracts thousands more. According to Figure 1-1, about 98 percent (100.0 − 2.1 percent) of all United States firms engaged in contract construction in 1967 had receipts of less than $1 million. This indicates that it is small business people who are responsible for most of the construction in this country.

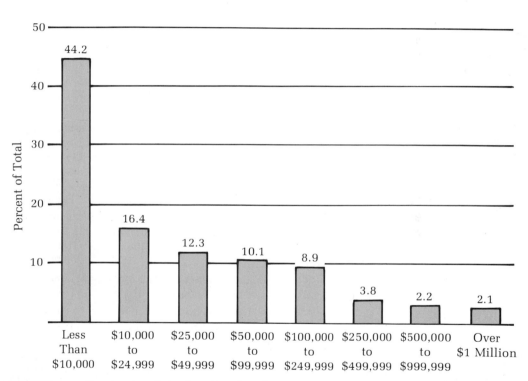

FIGURE 1-1. Construction firms, by size of total receipts in 1967. (*Source:* U.S. Department of Commerce, *Statistical Abstract of the United States 1974.*)

WHAT CHARACTERISTICS ARE UNIQUE TO SERVICE BUSINESSES?

The sheer number of service businesses and the variety of services they perform set them apart in the small business world. An examination of the yellow pages of your telephone directory will impress you with the number of hotels, beauty shops, laundries, repair shops, and similar businesses in existence today. Service firms exist solely to provide a service to their customers. Service is the only thing they have to sell. Their future, therefore, depends upon the promptness and quality of the service they render. If a service firm's service is substandard, the chances for success are minimal.

Most service firms have established a unique personal relationship with their customers. Customer preferences for their barbers, hairdressers, and automobile repair technicians are examples of the personal loyalties which often exist in this area of business. Good service causes customers to return and become a part of the permanent clientele of the business. Such rapport often causes customers to follow service personnel when the latter move from one business to another.

WHAT TYPES OF SERVICE FIRMS ARE MOST COMMON?

In 1972, there were over 1.5 million service establishments in the United States. The major categories and the number of paid employees are shown in Table 1-8.

TABLE 1-8. MAJOR CATEGORIES OF SERVICE ESTABLISHMENTS IN THE UNITED STATES IN 1972

Category	Number of Businesses	Number of Employees
Motels, hotels, trailer parks, and camps	79,685	726,577
Personal services	503,378	976,709
Business services	326,077	1,759,438
Auto repair, auto services, and garages	168,959	392,498
Miscellaneous repair services	148,925	206,842
Amusement and recreation services, including motion pictures	145,983	653,047
Dental laboratories	8,543	29,827
Legal services	144,452	267,656
Architectural, engineering, and land surveying services	64,246	292,587
	1,590,248	5,305,181

Source: U.S. Department of Commerce, Bureau of the Census, *1972 Census of Selected Service Industries.*

ARE MOST SERVICE FIRMS WELL MANAGED?

Good management is not by any means universal in the service trades. Because of the small amount of capital needed to start most service businesses, many owners start business on a shoestring and the business never progresses beyond the "marginal" stage. Service businesses are often started by owners who have little education and no prior management experience—a severe handicap for a struggling business. Failures during the first 5 years are higher in the service trades than they are in any other type of business except retail.

ARE THERE ANY STATISTICS REGARDING THE NUMBER AND KINDS OF BUSINESSES OWNED BY MINORITIES IN THIS COUNTRY?

A survey made by the U.S. Department of Commerce in 1969 indicates that minorities owned approximately 322,000 firms.[1] Roughly one-third of these businesses were retail firms, with restaurants and bars the most numerous (27,000). Food stores and building trades accounted for roughly 23,000 firms each. Food stores led in total receipts, with automobile dealers and service stations next.

When the minority sector is considered, the small business person's problems of capital acquisition, managerial know-how, and language barriers loom large in the picture of survival. Minorities compose 17 percent of the nation's population, yet own only one-hundredth of the nation's business assets and operate or own less than 4 percent of all the nation's businesses. In order to achieve "parity" in the business world, minorities would need 700,000 new full-time businesses worth $50 billion.

WHAT IS THE ETHNIC DISTRIBUTION OF MINORITY-OWNED BUSINESSES?

The study previously cited indicates that about 50 percent of the owners of minority-owned businesses are black, 30 percent are Spanish-speaking, and 20 percent are from other ethnic groups, including Chinese and Japanese. The major concentration of minority-owned businesses is in Los Angeles, which has 29,000. New York City has 16,000 and San Francisco 13,000, with Chicago running a close fourth with 12,000. Substantial numbers of minority-owned businesses are also found in Washington, Houston, Detroit, San Antonio, and Miami, with these cities ranked in descending order based on the number of minority-owned businesses in each.

WHAT ARE THE CHANCES FOR SUCCESS IN A NEW BUSINESS?

The infant mortality rate among new businesses is pretty staggering, especially during the first 2 years. One of the most revealing studies was conducted in the late 1950s by a team of investigators from

[1]Reported in *Nation's Business*, March 1972, p. 77.

Brown University in Providence, Rhode Island. The team selected 81 small businesses in the Providence area and followed their progress from inception for a 24-month period. Data for these small businesses were obtained through repeated interviews following their opening. The team's findings, published by the Small Business Administration, showed that almost half of the businesses failed during the first 2 years.[2] Almost half the 40 failures occurred within the first 6 months.

Other studies made by the U.S. Department of Commerce covering business starts and failures over several years indicate that the younger businesses tend to discontinue first. Of all new business firms started, about one-third are discontinued within 1 year; about 50 percent are discontinued within 2 years; and approximately two-thirds within 5 years. After 5 years, the failure rate drops significantly and chances for survival increase with each passing year.

Table 1-9 shows the ages of 9,915 businesses which failed in 1974.

[2]Kurt B. Mayer and Sidney Goldstein, *The First Two Years: Problems of Small Firm Growth and Survival,* Small Business Research Series, No. 2, U.S. Small Business Administration, Washington, 1961.

TABLE 1-9. AGE OF FAILED BUSINESSES BY FUNCTION, 1974

Age in Years	Manu-facturing	Whole-sale	Retail	Con-struction	Service	All Concerns
One year or less	1.7%	2.2%	2.1%	0.9%	1.9%	1.8%
Two	11.0	12.1	16.1	10.6	13.8	13.6
Three	17.2	16.7	22.3	17.5	16.6	19.3
Total—Three years or less	29.9	31.0	40.5	29.0	32.3	34.7
Four	14.6	12.6	15.6	15.2	14.7	15.0
Five	9.1	7.7	10.1	10.8	12.5	10.2
Total—Five years or less	53.6	51.3	66.2	55.0	59.5	59.9
Six	6.4	8.9	6.1	8.0	8.1	7.0
Seven	5.9	4.8	4.4	6.3	7.1	5.3
Eight	3.2	4.1	3.1	4.3	3.3	3.5
Nine	2.2	2.8	2.8	2.8	3.0	2.7
Ten	2.4	2.2	2.0	2.7	2.7	2.3
Total—Six–ten years	20.1	22.8	18.4	24.1	24.2	20.8
Over ten years	26.3	25.9	15.4	20.9	16.3	19.3
Total	100.0%	100.0%	100.0%	100.0%	100.0%	100.0%
Number of failures	1,557	964	4,234	1,840	1,320	9,915

Source: From *The Business Failure Record 1974,* compiled by Dun & Bradstreet, Inc., New York, c. 1975.

Business failures occur largely among small businesses. In 1970, there were 10,748 business failures reported by Dun & Bradstreet. In 1971, the figure was 10,326. Failures declined moderately to 9,915 in 1974. When compared with the early 1960s and the 1930s, these were relatively moderate years in terms of failures. Table 1-10 shows failure trends since 1920.

TABLE 1-10.   FAILURE TRENDS SINCE 1920

Year	Number of Failures	Failure Rate per 10,000 Listed Concerns	Year	Number of Failures	Failure Rate per 10,000 Listed Concerns
1920	8,881	48	1950	9,162	34
1921	19,652	102	1951	8,058	31
1922	23,676	120	1952	7,611	29
1923	18,718	93	1953	8,862	33
1924	20,615	100	1954	11,086	42
1925	21,214	100	1955	10,969	42
1926	21,773	101	1956	12,686	48
1927	23,146	106	1957	13,739	52
1928	23,842	109	1958	14,964	56
1929	22,909	104	1959	14,053	52
1930	26,355	122	1960	15,445	57
1931	28,285	133	1961	17,075	64
1932	31,822	154	1962	15,782	61
1933	19,859	100	1963	14,374	56
1934	12,091	61	1964	13,501	53
1935	12,244	62	1965	13,514	53
1936	9,607	48	1966	13,061	52
1937	9,490	46	1967	12,634	49
1938	12,836	61	1968	9,636	39
1939	14,768	70	1969	9,154	37
1940	13,619	63	1970	10,748	44
1941	11,848	55	1971	10,326	42
1942	9,405	45	1972	9,566	38
1943	3,221	16	1973	9,345	36
1944	1,222	7	1974	9,915	38
1945	809	4			
1946	1,129	5			
1947	3,474	14			
1948	5,250	20			
1949	9,246	34			

Source: From *The Business Failure Record 1974*, compiled by Dun & Bradstreet, Inc., New York, c. 1975.

TABLE 1-11. CAUSES OF 9,915 BUSINESS FAILURES IN 1974 (CLASSIFICATION FAILURES BASED ON OPINION OF INFORMED CREDITORS AND INFORMATION IN DUN & BRADSTREET REPORTS)

Underlying Causes	Apparent Causes	Percent					
		Manufacturers	Wholesalers	Retailers	Construction	Commercial Services	All
Neglect	Due to:						
	Bad habits	1.0	0.3	0.9	1.7	0.7	1.0
	Poor health	0.5	0.2	0.1	0.2	0.6	0.3
	Marital difficulties	0.3	0.4	0.2	0.3	0.1	0.2
	Other	0.5	0.3	0.4	0.2	0.3	0.4
Fraud	On the part of the principals, reflected by:						
	Misleading name	—	0.1	—	—	—	0.0
	False financial statement	0.1	0.9	0.4	0.3	0.5	0.4
	Premeditated overbuy	—	—	0.1	—	—	0.0
	Irregular disposal of assets	0.3	0.7	0.3	0.3	0.4	0.4
	Other	—	0.1	0.1	0.1	0.1	0.1

Lack of experience in the line
Lack of managerial experience
Unbalanced experience*
Incompetence

Evidenced by inability to avoid conditions which resulted in:

Inadequate sales	54.4	54.2	49.4	40.7	50.9	49.2
Heavy operating expenses	17.8	12.2	13.7	18.7	16.4	15.5
Receivables difficulties	16.2	14.6	3.3	14.0	6.5	8.8
Inventory difficulties	8.7	12.9	12.0	1.7	1.1	8.2
Excessive fixed assets	5.5	1.7	1.9	2.8	4.9	3.0
Poor location	1.2	1.9	6.8	0.6	2.7	3.8
Competitive weakness	18.4	18.2	22.9	29.9	19.7	22.6
Other	3.0	2.9	2.7	2.8	1.8	2.7

Disaster

Some of these occurrences could have been provided against through insurance:

Fire	0.3	0.5	0.6	0.1	0.1	0.4
Flood	—	—	0.1	0.0	—	0.1
Burglary	0.1	—	0.0	—	0.1	0.0
Employees' fraud	—	—	0.1	0.1	—	0.0
Strike	0.1	0.1	—	0.1	0.1	0.1
Other	0.6	0.2	0.3	0.1	0.3	0.3

Number of failures	1,557	964	4,234	1,840	1,320	9,915
Percent of total failures	15.7	9.7	42.7	18.6	13.3	100.0

*Experience not well rounded in sales, finance, purchasing, and production on the part of the individual in case of a proprietorship, or of two or more partners or officers constituting a management unit.

Source: Adapted from The Business Failure Record 1974, compiled by Dun & Bradstreet, Inc., New York, c. 1975.

Poor management is the most significant single cause of business failure. Some 90 percent of more than 1 million business failures analyzed by Dun & Bradstreet over a 100-year period were attributed to a lack of managerial experience and know-how. The statistics for 1974, reflected in Table 1-11, indicate that inexperience and incompetence are still major causes of business failure today. Competition claimed credit for 22.6 percent of the failures in 1974. Competitive weaknesses and inadequate sales take their toll in years characterized by business recessions. High employment and shrinking payrolls during these periods permit only those firms which are truly competitive to survive.

Even in times of prosperity, failures are frequent. Some statistics related to bankruptcies among small businesses during such periods have been reported by the Small Business Administration.[3] Ten companies which had failed during prosperous years were compared with ten concerns which had been highly successful in similar lines. All the bankrupt firms were in lines in which the successful companies, otherwise comparable, made money—at the same time and in the same metropolitan area. The failures fell into 18 specific and avoidable management "traps" which the successful firms somehow had avoided. All the bankruptcies stemmed from poor business management. Three kinds of management showed up repeatedly:

◻ Poor financial planning related primarily to inadequate records.
◻ Poor sales management, including inadequate product planning and poor market analysis.
◻ Poor general administration, culminating in expenses not covered by revenues.

Figure 1-2 shows the frequency with which the various "traps" were identified in the analysis of the bankrupt firms.

Here, briefly discussed, are the 18 management traps which the survey discovered:

1. *Inadequate Records.* Company A bid unsuccessfully on about 75 government contracts. Lacking the data with which to estimate closely, the managers first presented figures "high enough to be safe." Unable to get business this way, they then employed a consultant who turned out to be very expensive and who also got the company into a disastrous subcontract. A fraction of the money thus wasted would have been sufficient to establish an adequate bookkeeping system.

[3]A. M. Woodruff, *Traps to Avoid in Small Business Management*, Management Aids for Small Manufacturers, Annual No. 6, U.S. Small Business Administration, Washington, 1960, pp. 9–15.

Management Traps — Companies: A, B, C, D, E, F, G, H, I, J

Management Traps	Incidence
A. Poor financial planning	
1. Inadequate records	10
2. Cumulative losses	9
3. Neglected tax payments	5
4. Expansion beyond resources	4
5. Excessive fixed costs	3
	3
B. Poor coordination between manufacturing and selling	
6. Lack of product development	10
7. Lack of diversification	9
8. Lack of data on own customers	7
9. Contracted entire output to single buyer	5
10. Lack of market research	3
11. Continued policies of bankrupt predecessor	2
12. Legal problems	1
	1
C. Poor other general administration	
13. Family factors	7
14. Lack of administrative coordination	3
15. One-person management	3
16. Lack of technical knowledge	3
17. Absentee management	2
18. Internal conflict	1

FIGURE 1-2. Frequency of 18 management traps. (Source: Adapted from A. M. Woodruff, *Traps to Avoid in Small Business Management*, Management Aids for Small Manufacturers, Annual No. 6, U.S. Small Business Administration, Washington, 1960.)

Company E was a partnership with a good product. Neverthe-less, during bankruptcy proceedings, the accountants were un-able to reconstruct even the simplest form of income statement from the tangle they found. Office records consisted of masses of unsorted papers jammed into an old-fashioned safe.

2. *Cumulative Losses.* In several cases, serious losses were traced to a series of seemingly insignificant little leaks. Collectively, these dribbles amounted to the equivalent of a substantial breach in the financial dike. Management was unaware of the leaks at the time. Suitable reports were either nonexistent or too cumbersome for analysis, or too long delayed in reaching the proper desk.

3. *Neglect of Tax Requirements.* Company J, with yearly sales of about $400,000, was managed by technical people without administrative experience. These people were unconcerned about tax requirements, and took no interest in the tax aspects of depreciation. This firm was low bidder on a very substantial contract, but in figuring its bid omitted social security and un-employment taxes. Since no provision was made to pay these taxes, they became delinquent, with the inevitable conse-quences.

4. *Expansion Beyond Resources.* In most cases analyzed, trouble resulted from the growth of the business beyond the scope of the bookkeeping system which had been used while the firm was still small. In three cases, management deliber-ately tried to save money on recordkeeping. In another, the owner was unaware of any problems until events forcibly called his attention to them. By then it was too late.

5. *Inadequate Cost Analysis.* Company G had three operating departments. Two of them had skimpy cost data while the other had reports far too elaborate for ready analysis. Manage-ment was equally ignorant of costs in all three departments. It later was learned that one department had six identical opera-tions—all necessary. However, two cost about $10 per unit, two others nearly $25, and the other two in between. Such facts were in the cost reports but very hard to find.

6. *Lack of Product Development.* Late in the 1920s, Company B ran into mounting sales resistance to its line of wooden ice boxes in competition with steel ice chests. The owner refused to believe that any device for storing food would ever seriously rival his "time-tested line." By 1933, mechanical refrigeration was rapidly taking over the market. The owner of the firm, with no market study, ordered conversion from wooden ice chests to steel ice chests. In doing so, he shifted operations from one obsolete product to another. When the changeover to steel chests took all remaining capital in the firm plus the owner's entire personal savings, bankruptcy followed.

7. *Lack of Product Diversification.* All the unsuccessful companies lacked product diversification. Nine of them engaged in no product research at all. In contrast, nine of the ten successful firms surveyed emphasized product development as a means of having on hand ready alternatives in case of market trouble with any one product. The successful firms emphasized the importance of "keeping several balls in the air at one time."

8. *Lack of Customer Information.* When Company I became badly delinquent on a bank loan, the bank insisted on a review of the books by a local accountant. In the mass of confused data, the accountant unearthed an important source of trouble. Company I had been shipping to customers without any credit investigations. Its receivables were in bad shape. There was no systematic collection policy and most of the customer accounts were 90 or more days old. One customer was himself bankrupt and had made no payments for over a year. Yet Company I continued to ship to him.

9. *Lack of Market Diversification.* In order to avoid the problems of selling its product, Company A contracted all its output to one buyer. When the buyer canceled the contract, the company was left with no alternatives. And all its capital was tied up in that particular venture.

10. *Lack of Marketing Research.* Two companies undertook substantial ventures without any marketing research whatever. Three companies, in order to sidestep sales problems, adopted the seemingly easy solution of contracting the entire plant output to a single buyer. Later they found that this created very real hazards.

11. *Continuance of Policies of Bankrupt Predecessor.* Company D took over the assets of a bankrupt firm but continued all the same policies. Moreover, it engaged in a substantial tool-up, costing nearly $1 million, with no valid basis for believing that the expansion would be supported by sales. The new management was never able to get its sales up even to the point of profitable operation.

12. *Legal Problems.* Company H tried to save money on legal advice. When long-drawn-out patent infringement proceedings had to be undertaken, the firm was ill-equipped technically and financially. Foresight and competent professional guidance could have warded off much of the trouble.

13. *Family Factors.* There were three cases in which favoritism to members of the family contributed to eventual failure. Typically, company assets were depleted in order to carry idle and useless executives at high salaries. In one case, however, the owner's brother-in-law meddled so much in the active management that disaster resulted.

14. *Lack of Administrative Coordination.* Of the ten unsuccessful firms, seven were never able to coordinate selling and manufacturing. This was largely a by-product of the poor handling of records which management needed to determine what lines were selling and how profitably.

Trouble was also found in several concerns with regard to formulating policy and communicating it to those who had to carry it out. This was especially true in companies that expanded and found it more difficult to pay proper attention to administrative problems and to communicate effectively with new workers.

15. *One-Person Management.* One-person management destroyed Company C. The owner built up the firm from its start in a basement workshop to a value of over $220,000 in less than 5 years. Failing health forced him to sell out to a group of investors who did not realize that his technical genius had been the sole foundation of the company's success. When the plant failed 6 months later, the new owners suffered complete loss.

16. *Lack of Technical Knowledge.* A group of investors bought Company G. The new owners had little technical knowledge and lacked any background for selecting a good technical person as operating vice president. But, on the basis of the plant's previous reputation, they had no trouble getting a contract to supply gun parts. The first two shipments were rejected outright on the basis of quality. Ultimately, the contract was canceled. The new owners were bankrupt within 6 months. The lack of technical competence brought operations to a standstill and served to wreck the firm.

17. *Absentee Management.* Company B fell into the trap of management inattention. After a long period of profitable operation, the firm went through a series of years of absentee management. Financial records, which had never been good, were neglected, and with the owner away constantly, the bookkeeper failed to make several years' tax payments. In the end, the firm failed.

18. *Internal Conflict.* In Company E, bankruptcy was directly traceable to a 5-year fight between partners. The trouble centered on the subsidizing of relatives and allegations of various kinds of scandalous misconduct. Manipulation of partners' expense accounts and secret negotiations for sales contracts added to the problems which eventually resulted in failure.

The implications of these experiences for small business owners are clear. To stay competitive, managers must manage. This means planning, organizing, coordinating, and controlling— for the firm as a whole. It means thinking ahead to forestall potential trouble before it is too late.

WHICH FIRMS HAVE THE BEST SURVIVAL RECORD?

Wholesale firms seem to have the best record based on studies covering a number of years. Financial, real estate, construction, and manufacturing businesses usually do better than average. Service trades are below average, and retail businesses have the lowest survival rate of all. The data in Table 1-11 reflecting failures in 1974 seems to indicate this trend.

IN VIEW OF THE RECORD, ISN'T A FUTURE IN BUSINESS DISMAL?

Like any other area of human endeavor, freedom of opportunity gives everyone the chance to succeed or fail in her or his chosen field. The field of business probably offers more freedom and fewer restrictions to the would-be business owner than almost any other. Despite this freedom, many businesses are started each year "on a shoestring" with little more than money and ambition. Since freedom of opportunity does not guarantee success, thousands of new businesses fail each year. During the year, 100,000 more manage to survive than fail. Those that somehow manage to survive and prosper bring to their owners not only the monetary rewards that are vital to any business but also many intangible considerations such as independence, the freedom to "do their thing" the way they want to, the opportunity to live in the section of the country they prefer, and the feeling of being a vital part of the community in which they operate. To those with the stamina, ability, and know-how, operating a business can be a stimulating and challenging career.

This exercise is designed to test your understanding of the material presented in Chapter 1. Choose the response, *True* or *False*, which best fits each statement. Correct responses are presented in the back of the text.

SELF-CHECK OF KEY CONCEPTS

1. Small businesses employ about 40 percent of the civilian labor force.
2. Approximately 71 percent of all businesses hire more than ten workers.
3. It is possible for a manufacturing firm hiring 10,000 workers to be considered small.
4. Retail firms composed about 26 percent of all businesses in this country in 1970.

5. More than 20 percent of all retail firms' workers are employed by eating establishments.
6. In manufacturing, more than half of all firms hire fewer than ten people.
7. Minorities own about 17 percent of the nation's businesses.
8. Blacks own more small businesses than any other ethnic group.
9. Detroit has more minority-owned businesses than any other city in the United States.
10. Approximately 50 percent of all new businesses are discontinued within 5 years after they are started.

PERFORMANCE PROBLEMS AND PROJECTS

1. Consult your local library's copy of the *Reader's Guide to Periodical Literature* and list the articles which have been written within the last year on the following subjects. Prepare a bibliography to submit to your instructor.

> Big business
> Business conditions
> Business failures
> Manufacturers' statistics
> Retail trade
> Small business
> Wholesale trade

2. Statistically, there were 25 businesses for each 1,000 people in the United States in 1972. Make a list of small businesses you would expect to find in an average community of 5,000 people and indicate the number of each type of business you think would be found. How closely does your total number match the national average of 25 per 1,000 inhabitants?
3. List several businesses you believe would *not* be found in a community of 1,000 people.

A CASE IN POINT

HIDDEN PROBLEMS AT GREEN THUMB

Harry Stewart is the owner of a consulting firm which specializes in business management practices. Today he got a call from a potential customer who identified himself as R. G. Marshall, new owner of the Green Thumb Manufacturing Company, a local plant specializing in the manufacture of garden tools and lawn equipment. The plant employs approximately 200 workers.

"I have just acquired the plant from its former owner," Mr. Marshall explained, "who is retiring because of poor health. I know the plant has some temporary financial problems, but I feel that there is nothing wrong that can't be corrected. According to Ted Finney, the banker, your track record in helping businesses in trouble is pretty good. Can you find out what needs fixing at Green Thumb?"

"I'm flattered that Ted recommended us," Harry replied. "Did he provide any hints about the financial problems at the plant?"

"Only that the former owner had been absent a lot during the past year and that expenses had increased to the point that they had discussed a business loan with the bank. Finney indicated that it had been turned down because the company couldn't provide the financial information to justify the loan."

"Sounds familiar," Harry retorted. "When can we get together?"

"I have to be out of town tomorrow. How about the day after?"

"Fine. I'll meet you at the plant around 9 o'clock. That will give you a chance to get things started," Harry replied.

Two days later, as Harry drove to Green Thumb, he mused about the unique history of the business he had been asked to look at. Everyone knew that the former owner, Walter Eaton, had built up the business from its start in a small garage behind his house to a plant with a value of almost $1 million in 7 years. Failing health had forced his retirement when he was still less than 50 years of age. His technical ability and mechanical know-how were widely recognized. "Walt," as he was affectionately known to many of his employees, ran the company "single-handed" and, despite a limited education, was considered somewhat of a legend in Bloomfield.

Harry Stewart spent 5 days at the plant, talking to the new owner, visiting the employees, and looking at the operations with Frank DiVito, the person who had been unofficially in charge when Walt was away from the plant. Harry learned that Frank supervised the production and shipping operations and was also responsible for the office operations. Two employees handled the billing, payment of bills, payroll matters, and routine correspondence. Harry sensed an air of coolness on the part of the office employees when he was introduced to them.

After examining the plant's records, watching the workers on the job, and talking to two of Green Thumb's biggest customers, he drafted a report for the new owner listing his major observations:

☐ Despite the company's updated plant and modern facilities, office records consisted of masses of unsorted papers jammed into several four-drawer files. After Harry got over the initial shock, he asked about the availability of financial reports such as a balance sheet and profit-and-loss statement. "Mr. Eaton told us not to worry about lots of reports," one lady responded. "He said he could tell from his checkbook and his bank statement everything he needed to know," she said.

☐ Billing records and accounts payable were in somewhat better shape. Harry determined from a careful examination of accounts receivable that more than 25 percent were 90 days old or older and that no attempts had been made to collect them. Merchandise was being shipped to potential customers without any credit investigation because "nobody has time for that." One large delinquent account prompted Harry to find out more. He found that the customer himself was close to bankruptcy and had made no payments to Green Thumb in over 6 months.

Despite this fact, merchandise had been regularly shipped to the customer.

□ The ability of Green Thumb to pay its bills came under Harry's scrutiny. He discovered that operating cash was seldom available to take advantage of cash discounts. One of the office employees recounted how, in a discussion about using withholding funds set aside for income tax purposes for paying some of the bills, someone thought that was illegal and how they accordingly did not do it. A general pattern of hand-to-mouth operations was evident.

□ A check of sales during the past year showed that they were down about 15 percent from the previous year. No one knew exactly why. "Everyone has the same problem," ventured Frank DiVito. "It's just a general slowing down of business." Despite the sales decline, Harry found that the current head count at the plant was slightly higher than it had been a year earlier. To complicate things further, one of Green Thumb's biggest customers had told him that deliveries were often late and that they had been buying some of their merchandise from a competitor of Green Thumb's because the competitor delivered on time and at a lower cost on some items.

□ A conversation with a senior machine operator involved a new semiautomatic machine which was purchased 2 years ago. "It's a fantastic machine," the operator said. "Cuts about 50 percent from the time any other machine would take. That baby cost $80,000 but it's worth every cent of it!" Harry observed that it had not been in operation during the week he had been there. "We only run it a couple of times a month to make a special item," volunteered the operator. Harry later found out from Frank DiVito that it was purchased to enable the company to enter the market with a new revolutionary weed-cutting machine. The expected sales never materialized, however, and the machine was idle most of the time.

Harry presented his report to Mr. Marshall with the observation, "I really had no idea things were in such bad shape. It's going to take some doing to get things back in shape."

"It looks like we're going to have to bite the bullet," Marshall replied, with a trace of resignation in his voice. "What do you recommend?"

1. What are some of the things you think Harry Stewart will recommend?
2. What do you think was responsible for the problems found at Green Thumb?
3. Can you list some basic business principles which have been ignored at Green Thumb?

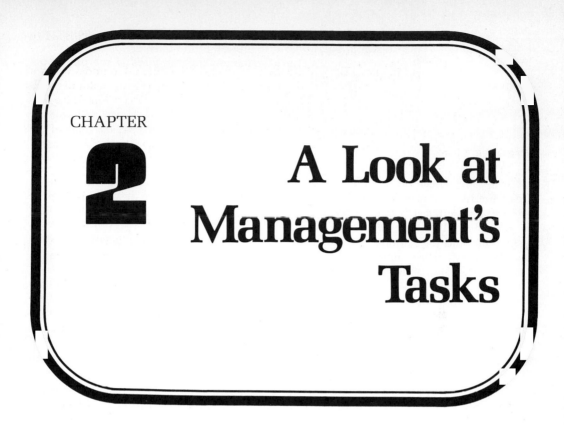

CHAPTER

2

A Look at Management's Tasks

PERFORMANCE OBJECTIVES

After reading this chapter, you should be able to develop a list of managers' most important functions and to determine the daily tasks characteristically performed by managers in carrying out their functions. Specifically, you should be able to:

1. Determine the assets available to managers in performing their jobs.
2. Weigh the significance of each asset in the overall success of the business.
3. Explain what managers do in the planning function of their jobs and predict the results of poor planning.
4. Defend the time spent in planning activities.
5. Differentiate between actions which *move* people and those which *motivate* them.
6. Assess the impact of monetary incentives in motivating workers.
7. Classify the traditional types of incentives into Herzberg's "motivators" and "hygiene factors" and predict the outcome of their application by a manager in a work situation.
8. Demonstrate the major steps required in the organizing function.
9. Sketch an organization chart for a small business in your community and explain the interrelationships between the various levels displayed on the charts.

10. Develop a list of mistakes commonly made in organizing and predict the impact of each on the operation of the business.
11. Explain the importance of management standards in the operation of a well-conceived control plan.
12. Create a list of conditions which could be responsible for loss of control in operating a business.

INTRODUCTION

Not everyone agrees on what a manager does. Hundreds of books and articles have been written on the subject of management and managing. The American Management Association and the National Management Association, which have memberships numbering in the thousands, are dedicated to the education and enlightenment of managers. Management training is offered in our community colleges and state institutions of higher learning everywhere. Each year, dozens of seminars, oriented to the peculiar tasks faced by managers, are offered to those who would improve their skills.

Despite this massive effort to train tomorrow's managers, it is difficult to define exactly what managers' responsibilities are. It is even more difficult to describe how managers should do their jobs.

This chapter attempts to expose you to several traditional concepts of management and to explore some of the basic functions of managers that almost everyone agrees with. The material will help you establish a mental image of the manager in the role of planner, organizer, motivator, and controller. The way the manager performs these tasks is naturally different for different businesses. Enough similarity exists, however, for the concepts presented here to be easily modified and adapted to any kind of business.

WHAT DO MANAGERS DO?

Basically, managers do those things that enable the business to attain its objectives. Since there are many different kinds of businesses, each with its own unique problems, managers approach their jobs in different ways. In reaching desired goals, a sales manager would take a route different from the one the manager of a production facility would. Despite this obvious fact, both managers have much in common. Both must rely upon the skills they have acquired and the expertise they have developed to manage the resources available to them. Workers must be acquired, trained, and organized into efficient work teams. Money must be obtained and accounted for in the financial management of the business. Materials must be ordered, stocked, accounted for, and issued. Both must be concerned with improving methods in order to remain competitive. Decisions regarding facilities and equipment must be made and followed up. The primary tasks for both managers deeply involve them in planning the direction of the business, organizing and motivating the employees, providing guidelines for their efficient operation, coordinating the total operation, and correcting those things that handicap the realization of their goals. All managers must be proficient in carrying out the recognized management functions. Figure 2-1 de-

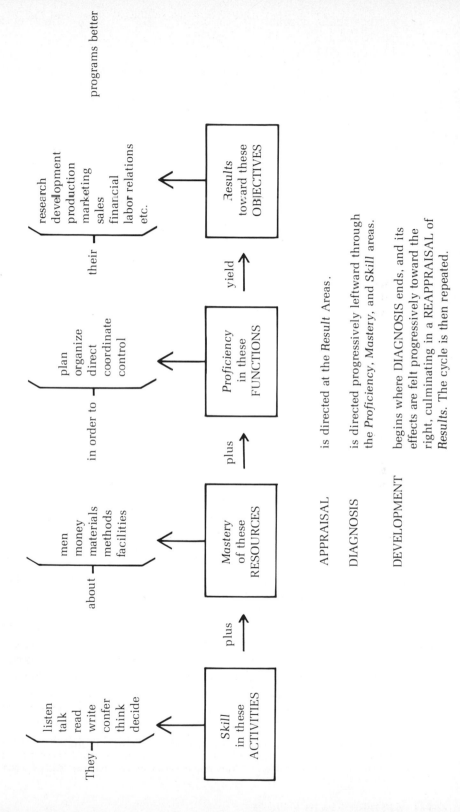

FIGURE 2-1. What do managers do? (*Source:* Reproduced by special permission from William Oncken, Jr., "Appraisal of Managerial Performance," in *Frontiers of Industrial Relations*, Industrial Relations Center, California Institute of Technology, copyright 1959.)

scribes them as planning, organizing, directing, coordinating, and controlling. Other bits and pieces of the total management job are highlighted in this illustration to dramatize the wide range of activities in which the typical manager becomes involved. In this chapter we will define the manager's job in terms of the things managers should do to assure the success of their businesses.

DOES EVERYONE AGREE ON THE LIST OF BASIC MANAGEMENT FUNCTIONS?

No. There has always been disagreement about the nature of the functions that should be included in the management process. Henry Fayol, the French engineer, included planning, organization, command, coordination, and control in his original list of administrative operations. A longer list has been developed and is described by the word POSDCORB, which represents planning, organizing, staffing, directing, coordinating, reporting, and budgeting. Such activities as forecasting, leadership, delegating, and investigating have also been included in the list of functions described by various writers. More recent statements of functional categories include the following:

☐ Harold Koontz and Cyril O'Donnell:[1] planning, organizing, staffing, direction, and control

☐ William H. Newman:[2] planning, organizing, assembling resources, supervising, and controlling

☐ George R. Terry:[3] planning, organizing, actuating, and controlling

☐ Henry H. Albers:[4] planning, communication, and motivation

Whether the functions which make up the management process are conceived as numbering three, four, five, or more, they all take place within a managerial or organizational structure. Some of the differences in the lists of functions are not as great as they appear to be. Fayol does not include staffing because he includes it in his term *organization*. The reporting function of POSDCORB could be called "control," and budgeting could be viewed as an aspect of planning. A major difficulty with some of the more traditional functional categories, such as those espoused by Koontz and O'Donnell, and also by Newman, is where to fit in modern be-

[1]Harold Koontz and Cyril O'Donnell, *Principles of Management*, 5th ed., McGraw-Hill Book Company, New York, 1972.
[2]William H. Newman, *Administrative Action*, 2d ed., Prentice-Hall, Inc., Englewood Cliffs, N.J., 1963.
[3]George R. Terry, *Principles of Management*, 6th ed., Richard D. Irwin, Inc., Homewood, Ill., 1972.
[4]Henry H. Albers, *Principles of Organization and Management*, John Wiley & Sons, Inc., New York, 1965.

havioral concepts. For example, where does motivation belong in the traditional lists? It is an outgrowth of planning and organizing, but is directly affected by the job and the actions of the supervisors.

DO THE MANAGEMENT FUNCTIONS NORMALLY OCCUR IN SOME ORDER?

Yes. The management process concept involves the idea of a sequence of actions through time. Planning comes first, then organizing, which is followed by staffing, directing, and controlling. Different sets of functions may be used in such sequencing. One function is assumed to lead logically to the next. Planning provides a basis for organizing, which in turn sets the stage for staffing, and so on. In some businesses, there may be significant departures from the sequence idea. For instance, changes in organizations are made sometimes without regard for particular plans. Staffing problems may actually lead to planning rather than the other way around. So we see that the sequence must be flexible and adaptable to the particular problems of the business.

WHICH MANAGEMENT FUNCTIONS ARE CONSIDERED ESSENTIAL FOR BUSINESS OWNERS?

A list commonly used by the National Management Association in its training programs consists of four functions: planning, organizing, motivating, and controlling. This list includes all the essentials and will be used as the basis for our discussion.

Planning involves looking ahead, anticipating problems, and devising actions which will prevent them or minimize their impact on the business. Planning involves all the resources available to the manager. It takes a lot of time if properly carried out. For this reason, it is often neglected by busy managers who prefer to spend their time on operating activities.

Organizing involves establishing the functions which will be required for the business to operate and attain its goals. Organizing includes assigning the responsibility for each function to a key individual so that all the important aspects of the business will get the proper attention. Making organizational decisions is similar to the problem faced by the baseball manager who must decide which player will be assigned to the various positions on the team. Each assignment must be considered in terms of the player best qualified to handle it. Once responsibilities are assigned, authority is then delegated to subordinates and operating employees so that they can carry out their assignments. The management group in the typical small business will consist of very few people at first. As the business grows, more people will be added to this group, and they should be selected carefully so that all the important functions will be carried out efficiently and profitably.

Motivating is the job of building enthusiasm and morale. Its primary goal is to get workers to want to work and to make their goals the same as management's. It is one of the most difficult jobs faced by managers, but one which they can do better than anyone else. Failure to properly motivate workers can cause serious repercussions throughout the organization.

Controlling consists of determining where things are not going right and deciding what corrective action to take. Baseball coaches use performance statistics and observations of their players to assist them in carrying out their control function. Business managers use the information from their records and reports to isolate problems and tell them whether performance is meeting management's standards. They then take whatever action is necessary to correct the cause of the problem.

IS MANAGING AN ART OR A SCIENCE?

Management has been referred to as an art by some writers because business is constantly changing and presenting new challenges, requiring managers to change their tactics often in seeking new solutions for new problems. The art is characterized as one in which the manager must constantly seek new remedies to cope with a business climate full of uncertainties. The art of management calls upon the manager to use judgment, experience, and insight to solve problems. It is not magic which allows managers to succeed but learned skills and behavior patterns established through training and experience.

There has also arisen over the last 50 years a body of business principles and concepts based on statistics, sound accounting practices, and mathematical approaches which lend to business operations an aura of the scientific approach. The scientific aspects of management address the quantitative factors which affect business decisions. An understanding of these principles takes much of the guesswork out of decision making and enables managers to base their decisions on factors which have a high degree of predictability. Thus we can see that management is both an art and a science. It consists of the ability to make rational decisions based on facts, without emotional bias or guesswork. The key phrase is "based on facts." The rational decision is best made when a manager is armed with carefully compiled facts.

Despite an occasional example of success which seems to result from "lucky breaks," a dependence upon chance in making decisions which will affect the future of a business is risk taking of the worst kind.

Most of us have read about people who seem to have achieved success without having consciously followed rigid guidelines or recognized business principles, and their success seems to deny the need for undue concern about the economic principles which often preoccupy many business planners today. Henry J. Kaiser was such a person. He was noted for his departures from the ordinary approach to business operations and for his lack of concern for detailed planning prior to making major decisions. He built a steel mill on the site of a horse pasture 30 miles east of Los Angeles over the objections of his closest technical advisers. With no previous experience in shipbuilding, he built and operated a vast shipyard on the West Coast during World War II, turning out 1,440 Liberty cargo ships and 50 baby aircraft carriers. During the 1960s he planned and built an "impossible" 600-acre, $350-million real estate development on former salt marshes and volcanic ash at the eastern end of Oahu island and then astounded skeptics by hauling sand with an enormous fleet of trucks around the clock for 40 days and nights to build one of the most beautiful beaches in Hawaii. In retrospect, one might conclude that these ventures were risky and that the chances for failure were greater than those a prudent entrepreneur should take. Fortunately, the pluses outweighed the minuses in these cases. Not so fortunate was Kaiser's attempt to penetrate the automobile market after World War II. Teaming with Joseph W. Frazer, a veteran in the automobile business, he manufactured and marketed two standard-sized automobiles and one compact car. Kaiser-Frazer lost $100 million in the ill-starred venture. Even by today's standards, the loss is one which few companies would be able to survive. One can only wonder how thorough the market analysis was that caused two seasoned veteran business people to gamble with such high stakes.

We must conclude from such examples that hard work alone is not enough to assure success. Something else is needed. In the chapters which follow, we will stress the use of time-tested tools and techniques used by successful business people who have learned that the probability of success based on a dependence on mere chance is far from promising.

Examination of the managerial techniques used by successful business people shows that the businesses they operate are successful because they "do things right." Business enterprises have the capacity to conform to well-known business principles, just as machines have certain well-defined characteristics which can be optimized by following guidelines of operation which are designed to produce the best performance. Automobile owners know, for example, that engines will last longer and give better service if proper attention is given to lubrication schedules and periodic maintenance recommendations. Tires and brakes will give maximum service only if properly adjusted and not abused. The manufacturer's warranty is based on the simple maxim that dependable mechanical performance and economical operation are best achieved only if well-known principles of good operation are observed.

In a similar manner, business enterprises possess certain well-defined characteristics which may be realized through sound decisions that conform to recognized business principles. Decisions are required every day which will determine how big the business will become, what kind of product it will manufacture, which items will be made and which purchased, and where the money will come from to finance the business. If the majority of the important decisions conform to sound business principles, the chances of success in the business will be greatly enhanced.

WHAT IMPACT DOES PLANNING HAVE ON BUSINESS SUCCESS?

Good planning is one of the most important and also one of the most neglected ingredients in business operations. Studies in one high-density business area provide some statistics which reflect the importance of planning. In the 11 southern counties of California, over 1,000 businesses fail each year. Planning Research Corporation, a Los Angeles–based research firm, estimates that roughly 50 percent of these failures are caused by a lack of sound and practical planning. They further state that many are managed by executives who believe they have an "instinct" for business and, therefore, ignore such fundamentals as profit planning, tax structures, traffic patterns, and personnel development. Their conclusion: If proper planning had been employed in the formative stages of many of these businesses, they would not have been formed at all.

The chances for success without a sound, continuing program of planning are slim. For newly formed businesses, the message seems clear: plan or perish.

WHAT IS THE NATURE OF THE PLANNING TASK?

Planning is essentially a form of decision making. In looking at the future, managers must ask themselves these questions:

☐ Why am I in business?

☐ What goods or services do I plan to make or sell?

☐ Where is the market for my product?

☐ Who is my competition?

- What will my sales strategy be?
- What merchandising methods will I use?
- How much money will I need to operate?
- How will I get the work done?
- What controls will I need to set up?
- Where can I go for help?

Although the answers to these questions might appear to be easy to find, they are not. There are several possible answers to each question, some more practical than others. They must be listed, each one evaluated, and the most practical ones retained for further consideration. A plan will be built around the one considered to be the best answer to the question. Decisions are required at every step of the planning process in order to assure that the best possible plan will result.

Planning is the first of the managerial functions because it is the cornerstone upon which everything else is built. The results of planning are felt throughout the entire organization. Good planning is essential to the future growth and health of the business.

HOW MUCH TIME DOES PLANNING REQUIRE?

It depends on the kind of job you have. Time spent by company presidents in planning activity will be quite different from that spent by first-line supervisors. Presidents will be concerned with company policies, public relations, financial matters, and future growth. They might spend as much as 80 percent of their time in pure planning related to events which will occur 1 to 5 years from now. First-line supervisors will be more concerned with short-term planning involving finding good employees, keeping machines operating, meeting schedules, operating within budget, and maintaining quality. The amount of time they spend on planning could be as little as 10 percent, although this is not enough for most supervisors. Studies have shown that a significant number of managers spend almost no time on planning activities.

ISN'T IT IMPRACTICAL TO TRY TO PLAN TOO FAR AHEAD?

We would be naïve if we did not admit that some of the plans you make will not turn out as well as you thought they would. Changing business conditions, unexpected problems, pressures from customers and bosses, and the unpredictability of workers have a way of knocking your plans into a "cocked hat." These are not good reasons for avoiding planning. Even a plan based upon assumptions which might never materialize is better than no plan. According to one author,[5] the planning of most supervisors does not extend beyond 6 months. Top-level planning often looks ahead 5 years. Many companies do long-range planning as far ahead as 10 years. Obviously, such plans will need to be reviewed periodically and updated in the light of new information. Table 2-1 shows the planning time spans reported by Terry at the various levels in the organization.

TABLE 2-1. PERCENT OF PLANNING TIME SPENT BY MANAGERS AT VARIOUS LEVELS WITHIN THE ORGANIZATION

Organizational Level of Manager	Period Covered by Plan				
	Current (Day to Day)	1 Month Ahead	6 Months Ahead	1 Year Ahead	5 Years Ahead
President	2%	5%	20%	25%	48%
Vice president	5	15	40	30	10
Middle manager	25	50	15	10	—
Department superintendent	50	30	15	5	—
Supervisor	80	15	5	—	—

Source: George R. Terry, *Principles of Management*, 6th ed., Richard D. Irwin, Inc., Homewood, Ill., 1972.

WHAT THINGS DO MANAGERS PLAN FOR?

The list is naturally different for the various kinds of businesses. For a manufacturing operation, this list would be minimal:

Production. What will be made? What alternative products are planned? Will the major thrust be toward commercial or defense products?

Sales. Who are the potential customers? How much firm business can you count on? How can you make your sales forecasts realistic? What percentage of the market can you expect to obtain?

Equipment. What kind and how much will be needed to meet projected sales levels? Should you buy or lease? What level of maintenance must be planned for?

Facilities. What kind of plant will you need? Will you rent, lease, or buy? Do you have ample space for expansion? What kinds of office areas, storage areas, and maintenance space should be planned?

[5]George R. Terry, *Principles of Management*, 6th ed., Richard D. Irwin, Inc., Homewood, Ill., 1972, p. 282.

Location.   How convenient is the plant for workers to get to? Are rail and highway transportation readily available? Will you select a metropolitan or suburban area? How close do you need to be to your customers? How close are your major competitors?

Methods.   Which processes will you use? What kinds of tools, work benches, and handling equipment will you need? Should you hire a methods specialist to take care of this area?

In addition to these six major areas, some planning attention must be given to getting money for your operation, selecting and hiring personnel, procuring materials, and dozens of other activities. No attempt is made here to indicate the order of planning activity since it is different for each business. Long lead times will probably be encountered on some kinds of equipment and materials. You will want to plan their procurement early in order to allow sufficient delivery time. The point is that each item requires conscious effort and hard work to plan for its eventual occurrence. A lot depends upon how well you do your planning job.

DON'T MOST MANAGERS ASSIGN PLANNING A PRETTY LOW PRIORITY?

Not intentionally. Many managers do not look at planning as a vital, life-and-death task. The general concept is so fundamental that most of them take it for granted—or think they are smart enough not to need it. Others do not really understand what it is or how to go about it, and so, at least consciously, they do not do much of it. Many never realize the value that planning has in shaping events which will happen in the future. A fresh insight into this subject is provided by an observation which is almost 200 years old. The author is George Washington, who was a successful businessman.

Take two managers and give to each of them the same number of laborers and let these laborers be equal in all respects. Let both these managers rise equally early, go equally late to bed, be equally active, sober, and industrious; and yet in the course of the year one of them, without pushing the hands that are under him more than the other, shall have performed infinitely more work. To what is this owing? Why, simply to contrivance resulting from that forethought and arrangement which will guard against the mis-application of labor.

Today's workers have their own way of expressing Washington's thoughts with a modern twist when they observe, "There's never time to do it right the first time, but there's always time to do it over." The challenge for managers is to recognize that it is not necessarily productive to move quickly, however efficiently, without first planning the move and its role in the total business plan. There is no justification for ever thinking that you do not have the time.

The nature of the average manager's day requires the manager to spend a lot of time on operating problems. Special projects and emergencies contribute their share to the hectic atmosphere. Since most managers readily admit their inability to get all their work done in a normal work day, they simply relegate planning to the bottom of the priority list—where it is likely not to get done at all. They complain of a lack of time for planning but seldom realize that good planning will save them time.

Many managers have a misconception of what planning is. They equate it with daydreaming or abstract thinking, totally unrelated to anything productive. Most of them do not look upon planning as "real work" and are critical of those who spend their time in seemingly idle activities.

Still others point out the futility of trying to plan and will offer convincing arguments that planning is a waste of time. These obstacles are real in the minds of most nonplanners. They will not be overcome except by deliberate efforts to train and indoctrinate workers in the techniques of planning. The company which makes planning a part of its daily routine by involving its workers in its future plans, which stresses the results-oriented approach to job performance, and which establishes clear understandable goals for everyone to work toward will be able to offer demonstrable proof of the benefits which result from good planning.

IS THERE A STEP-BY-STEP APPROACH TO PLANNING?

Since planning is often directed to solving problems, it utilizes the traditional approach to problem solving. The steps follow a logical sequence:

1. Identify the problem.
2. Gather all the pertinent information related to the problem.
3. Analyze the information and establish alternate solutions.
4. Select the solution which seems best.
5. Act upon the solution you select.

Let us see how these steps are carried out in practice. Step 1, problem identification, points up the importance of clearly stating the problem, goal, or objective which is the desired end product of the proposed planning. Planning should be directed toward specific rather than general goals. These goals should be written if possible. Remember the advice, "A problem well stated is half solved." Examples of clearly defined goals are:

- How can we increase sales by 5 percent next year?
- What merchandising ideas can we develop to reach more cus-tomers?
- How can we reduce absenteeism?
- How can we make our labor-supply forecasts more accurate?

Step 2, fact gathering, is carried out with the same thorough-ness exhibited by attorneys who want to win their cases in court. You should leave no stone unturned in finding all the facts which bear on the problem. Make sure your facts are really facts, not hear-say or unsupportable opinions. You cannot develop valid solutions if some of the facts are missing.

Step 3, analysis, requires evaluating the data you have found and listing as many practical solutions to the problem as you can. In the process of evaluation and analysis, you will find some of the facts you have gathered to be unusable in the solution and will have to discard them. You should keep in mind that the most obvious solution might not be the best one. Only after you have examined the advantages and disadvantages of each potential solution can you make a good decision. You will have to call upon your past ex-perience, the experience of others, and direct observation to help you make the best decision.

Step 4, making the decision, involves a final selection of the solution you believe is the best one and announcing your decision. This is a communications device which makes others who are affected by the decision aware of it. This step sometimes tests your ability to sell your decision to those who are likely to resist it.

Step 5, acting upon the decision, might generate the need for preparing new job procedures, modifying existing policies or rules, training employees, and coordinating with other departments.

WHAT IS THE PURPOSE OF ORGANIZING?

Whenever the job exceeds the limits of one individual, organi-zation is needed. Small business owners might personally be able to do all the ordering, recordkeeping, planning, decision making, and financial management required by their businesses when they are small. As their businesses grow, they will find it difficult to spread themselves thin enough to cover all the important day-to-day tasks. They might find it necessary to hire a part-time bookkeeper, additional salespeople, and some service technicians to repair the products they sell. They will need to establish the proper structure of authority and responsibility relationships so that everyone will understand who has what authority. The requirements of each job will need to be defined. These small business owners will need to delegate authority so that decisions will get made even if they are not there. And finally, they will need to designate who is accountable for the various parts of the operation. All these activities make up the process of organizing. Organizing enables owners to specialize the work and the people who do it. It is the means by which they can greatly multiply the amount of work that can be completed. It assures that all important jobs are covered and that the manager does not have so many jobs to do that he or she cannot exercise proper control.

Even in biblical times, the basic concepts of delegating responsibility, maintaining a reasonable span of control, and using the "exception principle" were understood and applied by leaders as a means of increasing their managerial efficiency.

WHAT ARE THE LOGICAL STEPS IN ORGANIZING A BUSINESS?

To answer this, let us look at the structure of an automobile dealer's agency which performs the normal services connected with selling new and used cars, plus repair and maintenance functions. Assuming the volume is great enough, we would need to first make some decisions about the organization itself.

Step 1. Decide on the structure.

- □ What will the major functions be?
- □ How many key people will you need?
- □ What reporting patterns will you use?

You decide that the business will be set up with four functions: sales, repair and maintenance, parts, and office functions. You decide to get four people with unique qualifications for these key functions and provide them with the authority to manage their functions as autonomous units. You want to keep the new and used car sales separate as reporting units but will place both under the sales manager. The body shop will be located away from the main agency a short distance. You decide to keep body shop and general repair activities separate, both reporting to the service manager. Such an organization would look like Figure 2-2. Next you need to look at the organization to see if you have covered all the tasks usually performed by an organization like yours. Some things like public relations, advertising, customer discounts, and the like should not be overlooked, and you will need to think about the best method of handling them. This brings us to step 2.

Step 2. Establish relationships within the organization.

- □ What are the limits of authority given to each manager?
- □ What are the specific functions to be performed in each area?

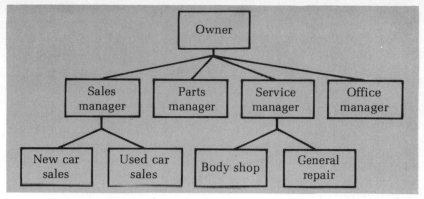

FIGURE 2-2. Theoretical organization of an automobile dealership.

    □ Are all the important functions covered?

    □ Is there any overlapping of functions or authority in the organization?

In this step the owner brings the organization down to earth and examines the practical aspects of operating the business. Owners must make sure that they will be able to provide all the services needed, that they have the best people assigned to manage the key areas, and that their organizations are structured to perform the required services as efficiently and harmoniously as possible. A "charter" for managers outlining their specific tasks, what authority they have, and what decisions they can make without prior approval must be prepared. The "charter," if properly prepared, will provide guidelines for the daily operation of the business.

Step 3.   Assign responsibilities.

    □ Who is responsible for what?

    □ Do all employees know what their jobs entail?

A division of labor within the organization is necessary in order to clarify responsibilities. You have written down a list of the major responsibilities for all the managers, and have told them that they should further subdivide these among their employees in the form of a job description for each specific task to be performed. This is your list:

Sales: Selling new and used cars.
              Advertising.
              Maintaining customer relations.
              Scheduling special sales events.
              Providing storage and security for all cars to be stored outside.

Service:	Preparing new cars for customers.
	Scheduling repair work on customers' cars.
	Training mechanics.
	Putting out service manuals, factory newsletters, and similar documents.
	Establishing a waiting area for customers or providing customer delivery service if requested.
Office:	Preparing payroll and distributing checks.
	Performing the cashier function.
	Handling general correspondence and filing.
	Keeping customer records.
	Keeping accounting records and preparing monthly profit-and-loss statements.
Parts:	Ordering and stocking new parts.
	Making special orders for customers.
	Pricing parts and materials.

Step 4. Delegate authority and responsibility.

☐ Where are decisions made?

☐ Do your policies clearly define the limits of each manager's authority?

Once you have told the managers what they are responsible for, you must now give them the authority to do their jobs. They will need to know where the decisions will be made about matters in their areas—whether you reserve the right to make them or whether you want them to make them. The sales manager will need to know how many new cars, and what models, to buy; what the budget for advertising is; what the discount policies are; and what can be offered customers for trade-ins. The office manager will want to know the policy on check cashing, credit limits, methods of record-keeping, and how thorough you want to be in establishing credit. Decisions regarding the handling of warranty parts and labor, how many people to hire, how many parts to stock, and many other matters will need to be faced, and policies have to be established on how the day-to-day problems will be handled. You might want to establish a number of written policies stating how such things should be handled and whose responsibility it is to make the decisions in each area.

Step 5. Establish accountability.

☐ Should you establish budgets for each manager?

☐ Will you want to look at profit contributions made by each manager's section?

☐ What is an equitable way to measure performance?

Concomitant with the power to manage is accountability for results. Managers who are assigned specific responsibilities for given functions must be accountable for the results. Thus the organization of a business is done in a way that responsibility, decision making, and accountability are shared by the owner with those reporting to him or her. In this way, the business can be expanded until it is rather large, and all functions will operate smoothly if the manager has done a good organizing job.

WHAT PRINCIPLES SHOULD BE OBSERVED WHEN ORGANIZING A BUSINESS?

The list of things to avoid is long. Listed below are a few of the hazards to avoid. Each of them is shown pictorially in Figure 2-3.

1. *Too many levels* leads to poor communications, slow decisions, and awkward salary administration. It is also costly to staff, often resulting in a superabundance of "chiefs." Responsibilities have to be cut so fine that operating can become a nightmare. The manager who wants to get things done in a hurry will avoid this structure and cut the number of levels down as much as possible.

2. *Duplication of responsibilities* can happen if your planning is poor or your thinking hazy about just what it is you want your organization to accomplish. In Figure 2-3, the duties of the maintenance specialist are not clear. You cannot tell who is responsible for maintenance performance and whom to call if you have a maintenance problem. It would be better to consolidate functional responsibilities by assigning the specialist to the maintenance department superintendent—as a staff assistant, for instance.

3. *Reporting to more than one boss* leads to conflicting orders, confusion over priority of assignments, and more than one source of appeal for worker problems. This is a mortal sin in organizing and should be avoided at all costs.

4. *Too many reporting to one* overloads key personnel by assigning them more subordinates than they can effectively control. There is no universally "right" number of subordinates since the type of work being done, the personalities involved, and the kind of training your subordinates have will all help determine the span of control which is right for your business. This kind of structure is dangerous because it dilutes the supervisor's attention, often resulting in snap decisions and problems in deciding what to attend to first.

5. *A one-over-one relationship* is not always bad, but it can result in the assistant becoming a messenger without any real authority. The assistant may also isolate the manager from others and

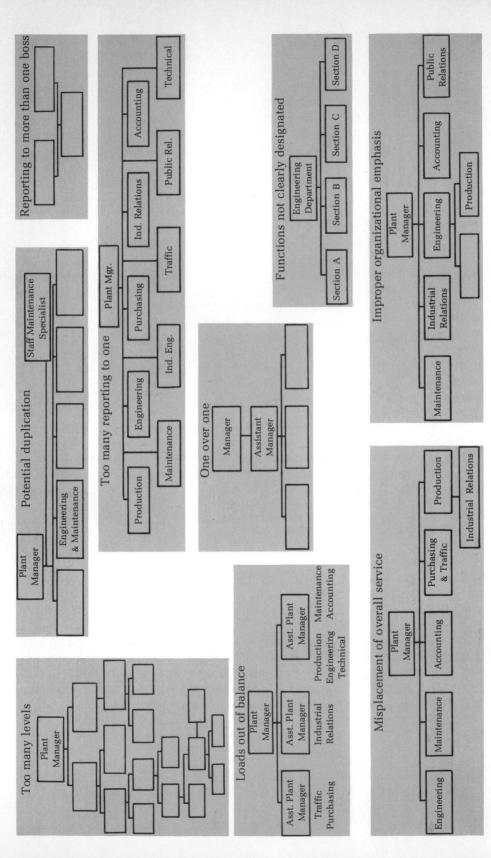

FIGURE 2.3. Hazards to avoid in organizing. (Source: Adapted from "12 Hazards in Organizing" and reprinted with permission from the November 1959 issue of *Factory*, a Morgan-Grampian publication.)

unintentionally slow down the decision process. If the assistants are staff aides, make them "assistants to—" and plainly spell out their responsibilities. If the top executive is gone a lot, the back-to-back arrangement can work. But it requires a clear statement of responsibilities to prevent confusion.

6. *Out-of-balance loads* should be avoided. This structure places the major share of the load on one individual and results in a lop-sided organization with morale problems. The idea of having three assistant managers is all right—if each has about the same work load. In Figure 2-3, the mix of work assigned to the assistant in charge of production does not make sense. The relative importance of the various functions is not reflected in their placement on the organization chart.

7. *Misplacement of an overall service* creates three problems. It restricts the subordinate department's ability to serve all other departments. It forces the manager to divide valuable time between his or her primary responsibility and the problems of other departments. And it imposes a "production orientation" on the industrial relations group in the example shown.

8. *Functions which are not carefully labeled* create hazy zones between the various functions, with resulting conflicts between department heads and employees. In our example, it is better to be specific in your titles by explaining what each section does—in this case, "drafting," "product design," "documentation," and so on.

9. *A major function that is too far removed from the influence of the plant manager* is a serious hazard. Decide what your major functions are and establish them on the same level. This keeps lines of communication as short as possible.

A final word about the organizing function. No organization is ever perfect despite the existence of a large body of knowledge about organizational techniques. Some managers seem to feel a compulsion to keep changing the organization to "make it more efficient." This process can be very costly in terms of morale and worker satisfaction. Should you be tempted to reorganize without a good reason, remember these words, attributed to Petronius Arbiter, written in the year 210 B.C.:

We trained hard . . . but it seemed that every time we were beginning to form up into teams we would be reorganized. I was to learn later in life that we tend to meet any new situation by reorganizing; and a wonderful method it can be for creating the illusion of progress while producing confusion, inefficiency, and demoralization.

It is difficult to measure the specific gains that result from a change in organization. Before it is made, it is useful to see what it is designed to accomplish over the short run and long run.

WHAT IS THE SIGNIFICANCE OF MOTIVATION TO A MANAGER?

Without motivated employees, the job of managing becomes difficult, if not impossible, to carry out effectively. In the final analysis, it is the workers who staff the offices and factories to produce the goods and services which keep American businesses operating. How they feel about their jobs affects the quality of the product, its cost, how much will be produced, and at what rate. Their attitudes and feelings are reflected in the products they make, which influence customers and their decisions regarding where they will buy the things they need. Examples of work done by unmotivated workers are all around us. Discourteous clerks who would rather visit than wait on customers, new products which do not perform their intended function because of faulty workmanship, billings that are incorrect, adjustments that take an inordinate amount of time and effort to consummate, unanswered correspondence, and endless buck-passing of customer complaints are all too familiar symptoms of workers who are not motivated to do their jobs in a way that supports management's goals. For business people, such problems can be disastrous unless the symptoms are recognized and the causes corrected. Nothing pervades a business environment so completely as worker attitudes. Motivation is one management function a manager can ill afford to ignore.

WHAT IS THE MEANING OF MOTIVATION?

The literal definition of a motive is any idea, need, or emotion which incites an individual to action. When we provide workers with a motive for actions we deem necessary, we are motivating them to *want* to do the job they have been assigned. Over the years, a great number of books, articles, and speeches have been directed at trying to unravel the puzzle of what motivates workers. The question "How do I get employees to do what I want them to do?" is not easily answered. The psychology of motivation is complex, and what has been learned about employee motivation is meager. Speculation about the "best" way to motivate workers abounds among managers who have tried different motivational techniques with varying degrees of success. Frederick Herzberg has indicated that the ratio of real knowledge to speculation about employee motivation is very small and that the market for what he calls "snake oil" in treating motivational problems is still brisk.[6] There is evidence that traditional theories about motivation need to be reexamined. Employees in some instances are less concerned with salary increases than with opportunities to participate more in decision making and with receiving recognition for work well done.

[6]Frederick Herzberg, "One More Time: How Do You Motivate Employees?" *Harvard Business Review*, January–February 1968, pp. 35–44.

There are several different theories, all widely recognized, which offer explanations of the major factors affecting an individual's will to work. Four of them are briefly described in Table 2-2.

TABLE 2-2.   FOUR WELL-KNOWN THEORIES OF MOTIVATION

Theory and Author(s)	Basic Premises
Basic need satisfaction A. H. Maslow, *Motivation and Personality*, Harper & Row, Publishers, Incorporated, New York, 1954.	All human effort is motivated by a striving to satisfy certain basic human needs. This striving follows a pattern whereby needs are satisfied in order of their importance to the individual. The strength of the behavior patterns exhibited depends upon the kinds and strengths of the needs.
Motivation-Hygiene theory Frederick Herzberg, B. Mausner, B. B. Snyderman, *The Motivation to Work*, John Wiley and Sons, Inc., New York, 1959.	Workers are motivated by an identifiable list of factors, called "motivators," which contribute to job satisfaction. Job dissatisfaction is related to a different list of factors called "hygiene factors." Motivation can be achieved only if the worker feels a sense of achievement on the job.
Theory X/Theory Y Douglas McGregor, *The Human Side of Enterprise*, McGraw-Hill Book Company, New York, 1960.	Theory X: The average human being has an inherent dislike for work and will avoid it if possible. Because of this, most people must be coerced, directed, or threatened to get them to produce a "fair day's work." Theory Y: People enjoy work and are capable of self-control and self-direction if they are motivated to achieve a goal. The average worker will not only accept, but also actively seek, responsibility.
Theory of meaningful work Chris Argyris, *Integrating the Individual and the Organization*, John Wiley and Sons, Inc., New York, 1964.	We have simplified and specialized jobs so much that we have removed much of the worthwhileness from them. The job itself must be made more meaningful and more challenging in order to satisfy worker needs. Jobs must include planning, doing, and controlling if they are to provide opportunities for growth and recognition.

DON'T ALL WORKERS HAVE THE SAME NEEDS?

If they did, they would all be struggling toward the same goals. Since this is not the case, the key to understanding workers' drives becomes that of finding out which needs they feel are most important to them. For simplification, the basic human needs have been categorized by Maslow into a hierarchy of five groupings: physiological needs, safety needs, social needs, ego needs, and the need for self-fulfillment. It is important to recognize that these needs have a relative order of importance in Maslow's theory. Most important are the physiological needs, followed by safety needs, and so forth. As one need category is satisfied, it loses its importance as a motivator and the worker concentrates efforts on other categories where needs are still unsatisfied. According to this theory, not all workers will be motivated by the same things. Discovering workers' unfulfilled needs theoretically determines what action a manager should take to motivate them. It would be well in reviewing the fulfilled and unfulfilled needs of a working force to give some thought to the composition of the force and the impact of their culture on what they consider to be their needs.

ISN'T JOB SATISFACTION JUST A MATTER OF ELIMINATING THOSE THINGS WORKERS ARE UNHAPPY ABOUT?

It is not that simple. A number of studies conducted by Herzberg and others in the area of job attitudes have led to the conclusion that the factors involved in producing job satisfaction are separate and distinct from the factors that cause job dissatisfaction. The Herzberg studies concluded that these two feelings are not opposites and that the one has no direct influence on the other. If you isolate a cause of worker dissatisfaction and eliminate it, the workers do not thereby become satisfied—only less dissatisfied. In order to achieve job satisfaction you must look at those things involved in the job itself and its potential for providing a feeling of achievement for the worker. Herzberg's research led to two lists—one containing factors related to job satisfaction which he termed *motivator factors*, the other containing factors related to job dissatisfaction which he termed *hygiene factors*. Here are the lists:

Motivator Factors	Hygiene Factors
Achievement	Company policies
Recognition	Supervision
Responsibility	Administration
Advancement	Working conditions
Growth	Salary
The work itself	Status
	Security
	Interpersonal relationships

In contrast to Maslow's theory, which suggests that one need must be satisfied before another becomes dominant, Herzberg's studies indicate that all needs are simultaneously pursued and that they come in no particular order.

WHAT IS THE SIGNIFICANCE OF McGREGOR'S THEORIES TO A MANAGER?

Theory X and Theory Y are at opposite ends of a continuum, and most managers' attitudes lie somewhere between the two extremes. McGregor suggests that the assumptions the manager makes about people will determine their behavior on the job. People who work for managers who lean toward Theory X, for instance, will become "maintenance seekers," stressing the pursuit of such things as better working conditions, salaries, job security, and status. Workers reporting to managers who basically believe in Theory Y will become "motivation seekers," striving for such things as added responsibility, recognition for good work, achievement, and growth. The role of managers is to integrate the goals of their workers with the goals of their departments so that the needs and desires of both are satisfied.

WHAT THINGS MAKE A JOB MORE WORTHWHILE?

In attempting to enrich a worker's job, management often reduces the worker's contribution to it, thereby removing the challenge and growth which come from doing new and more difficult tasks. Removing the more difficult parts of the job only leaves the worker free to accomplish more of the less challenging work. This approach is obviously not likely to motivate the worker. Sometimes the worker is rotated from one meaningless job to another in the name of reducing boredom and monotony. Herzberg has observed that substituting one zero for another is not only bad motivation but also bad arithmetic.

What is needed is the granting of additional authority to workers in their job activities, making them more accountable for their own work. This concept is carried out in some companies by involving workers in the product design phase, in laying out the work areas, and in many of the planning phases which precede actual production. When production begins, the workers make the parts, inspect them, and certify their quality. They become "experts" on the product and feel personal growth and achievement as a result. They automatically prepare themselves for new tasks, personal advancement, and an assured future. The conclusion is that it is the content of the job which produces motivation—and until the worthwhileness of a job is recognized by the worker, you will have a motivation problem.

DO MANAGERS REALLY UNDERSTAND WORKERS' NEEDS?

You would think the answer to this question would be an unqualified yes. However, studies have indicated that many supervisors do not really have their finger on the pulse of workers' feelings. It is pretty easy to find out what the workers believe their needs are by asking them. This can be effectively done with an attitude survey or through interviews. Not many managers use these simple tools—probably because they feel that they already know the answers or that they will not be able to do anything about the results anyway.

One of the most interesting answers to this question is reported by Boyd,[7] who cites the results of a survey published in *Foremen Facts* by the Labor Relations Institute of New York in 1946. From a number of different industries, 10,000 employees were asked to rank ten factors in the order of importance to them on the job. Simultaneously, the supervisors of these workers were asked to rank the items as they thought their employees would rank them. The results are shown in Table 2-3.

The strong influence of Herzberg's "motivators" is evident in the rankings made by the workers. The obvious reluctance of supervisors to become involved in "personal problems" of workers is also evident, although the workers ranked this item very high among the things that are important to them. If the results shown by this study are typical of business and industry in general, it is not difficult to tell why managers are unable to motivate workers.

TABLE 2-3.   THE EFFECT OF TEN JOB FACTORS ON WORKERS' ATTITUDES ABOUT THEIR JOBS

Employees' Ranking	Job Factors	Supervisors' Ranking
1	Full appreciation of work done	8
2	Feeling of being in on things	10
3	Sympathetic help on personal problems	9
4	Job security	2
5	Good wages	1
6	Interesting work	5
7	Promotion and growth in the company	3
8	Personal loyalty to employees	6
9	Good working conditions	4
10	Tactful disciplining	7

Source: Bradford B. Boyd, *Management-Minded Supervision*, 2d ed., McGraw-Hill Book Company, New York, 1976.

HOW EFFECTIVE ARE THREATS AS MOTIVATORS?

Most managers consider threats an inelegant way of motivating workers. Although threats work with some people to get them to move when you want them to, they are not permanently motivated by this technique. When you want them to move again, you have to

[7]Bradford B. Boyd, *Management-Minded Supervision*, 2d ed., McGraw-Hill Book Company, New York, 1976, pp. 152–153.

threaten them again. After a little of this, threats lose their power even to move people, much less motivate them. It is only when workers have their own generator that we can talk about true motivation. They then need no outside stimulation because they *want* to move since it is to their benefit to do so.

HOW IMPORTANT ARE WORK GROUPS IN MOTIVATING WORKERS?

Group influences are a fact of life and should not be ignored by managers. If workers want to be a part of the group, they must share the group's standards. Group standards are often lower than the individual's and this can cause workers some frustration and anxiety. However, group pressures are strong. Studies have shown that most college students, when told incorrectly that the group's opinion was contrary to theirs, quickly changed their opinion to conform to that of the group. The manager will be wise to be aware of group feelings and should try to use group influences to gain acceptance of plans and obtain cooperation.

WHAT IS INVOLVED IN THE CONTROL FUNCTION OF THE MANAGER'S JOB?

Control is the process of seeing that the operating results of a business conform as closely as possible to the business plan. It is really a means of keeping score on business operations. Since it lets the manager know whether or not things are working as planned, it is a vital function. The principal steps in a good control plan are:

☐ Establishing goals or objectives to be met.

☐ Developing a plan to accomplish the goals.

☐ Collecting information on actual performance.

☐ Comparing actual accomplishments with planned ones.

☐ Taking corrective action as required.

In the score-keeping process, variations from plan are bound to occur because planning deals with the future, which is uncertain. Besides, conditions assumed at the time the plans were made often change. The essence of control then is to identify the variances, establish their cause, and fix whatever is causing the variances.

HOW IS CONTROL IMPLEMENTED IN PRACTICE?

Control of special one-time projects usually requires a tailor-made control system designed to cope with the unique characteristics of the project. However, for routine recurring tasks, a logical five-step approach is effective.

Step 1. *Establish Your Goals.* Before a control system can be established, you need to determine what it is you want to accomplish in terms of goals, or objectives to be achieved or standards to be met. Goals should be specific and easy to understand. Here are some that are clear and concise:

- ☐ Earn a minimum annual net profit of 8 percent or more.
- ☐ Keep operating costs below 60 percent of total sales.
- ☐ Operate at 85 percent efficiency or better.
- ☐ Keep filing errors below 2 percent.
- ☐ Reduce absenteeism to 3 percent or less of scheduled hours.
- ☐ Install a new overhead budget system by January 1.

There is no vagueness about these objectives. Each one immediately suggests several possible approaches, which we will consider in the next step.

Step 2. *Develop Your Plan.* In this step you determine who the people are in the organization who can help you meet the goal by establishing a list of "action" items to be accomplished. Assign names to each item, indicating the individual who will be responsible for its completion. This should be a cooperative venture, involving all employees and departments which will be affected by the plan. Involvement at this step will generate support and help minimize resistance to any changes the plan might require. Your plan will show how or when something is to be done and by whom.

Step 3. *Gather Performance Data.* A plan is like a road map. You have to follow a prescribed course if you want to reach your destination. Checking from time to time tells you if you are still on course, how far you still have to go, and whether you will arrive at your destination when you planned to. You will need some intermediate checkpoints to tell you how you are doing. Here are some typical fact-gathering tools:

- ☐ Profit-and-loss statements will give you a feel for trends in operating expenses and profits.
- ☐ Ratios of operating expenses to total sales will tell you if sales will support your level of operation.
- ☐ Periodic audits of office practices will indicate whether your office employees are performing as you expect them to.
- ☐ Actual costs of products you make will tell you whether your bidding and pricing policies are realistic.

         ☐ Material usage reports will show whether you are using more material than you should.

         ☐ Production output reports could indicate potential schedule or delivery problems, poor utilization of personnel, or factors which are causing delays.

Step 4. *Compare Performance With Plan.* The moment of truth comes when you compare planned performance with actual. The picture brought into focus during the first few weeks is likely to shock you because there is something merciless about the way a control system shows up failures to reach planned goals. The initial reaction will probably generate ill-considered or even desperate action on the part of those who fell short. You will probably get some personal resentment too. As you examine the variances from plan, keep in mind that some of them might be beyond the control of the individuals you made responsible. Especially when a control system is new, review carefully your business resources in terms of money, equipment, and personnel to see if they are adequate for the goals you have set. If they are not, each individual goal should be reanalyzed and your entire plan recast if necessary.

When you start with a definite idea of what you want to control and what results you want to get, you do not have to wait until all the groundwork is done before seeing evidence of your progress. Movement toward many goals—attendance, performance, and cost goals, for instance—can be seen in the first 30 days after the basic decisions are made. The time depends upon how complex your control system is and what you have to start with. If your plan involves the design and installation of a new major system or procedure, results might not be measurable for several months.

Step 5. *Take Action.* No control plan is complete without this final step. This is where all your effort pays off in decisions which will get you back on course. Your analysis of variances will tell you where and how much you are missing your goals, but it might not tell you *why*. When you discover the reasons for the variances, the action which should be taken is often obvious. For instance, look at this list of "why's" and the corrective actions:

Reason for Missing Goal	Possible Corrective Action
1. Excessive "downtime" for equipment.	Check your maintenance practices. Establish an "uptime" record to show how much of the time equipment is operating and review monthly.

Reason for Missing Goal	Possible Corrective Action
2. Material cost per unit increased over previous period.	Check vendor prices; look for excessive scrap or adverse quality trends.
3. Turnover of personnel disrupted progress on the plan.	Indoctrinate and train new employees. Reestablish new target completion date if necessary.
4. Budget is inadequate to staff properly	Reassess tasks and budgets. Be sure the real reason is not inadequate training or substandard performance.
5. An affected department is resisting efforts to install the new system because of adverse effects on their operation.	Recheck your approach at step 2. Be sure to establish communications with all departments which will be involved in carrying out the plan.

WHAT PROBLEMS ARE ASSOCIATED WITH SETTING UP A CONTROL SYSTEM?

In devising effective controls for your business, you will have to cope with three basic problems.

First, to be of practical value, your system cannot be very costly, because a small company cannot afford to be burdened with excessive personnel and overhead charges. This means that your control system should be simple and sparing of personnel.

Second, you must face the fact that almost everyone resents the idea of being controlled or judged. More often than not, the targets of a control system are regarded as personal report cards. Standards and budgets can be highly unpopular. Many supervisors feel that they put too much pressure on employees and place too much emphasis on past performance. Therefore, you should expect some resistance to any plan which has not been put together with full participation of all concerned. These points suggest that your system should be installed with patience and tact so that it will be accepted by those who will have to use it. Otherwise, it might not be very successful.

Third, too much control is as bad as too little. "Full information" about job costs, for instance, might generate a volume of paper and reports that no one can assimilate. Maybe only summary-type information might be required for the decisions you need to make.

HOW LONG DOES IT TAKE TO GET AN ADEQUATE CONTROL SYSTEM WORKING?

The answer depends on how much control you already have. If your business can build on an existing foundation of good basic records plus some expertise in their generation and use, you will not have far to go. In that case, you can usually expect useful results in a matter of months. If, on the other hand, you have to establish a recordkeeping system, build up a backlog of useful historical information, and get experience in developing and implementing job procedures, some experts say you should not expect your system to be very effective until the third year.

This should not discourage you in your attempts to set up a control system. Every day you work at it, you are a little better off than you were the day before. The key to the problem is to start now to establish your control system. Plan to make adjustments as you go along, and watch developments very closely during the first year.

Do not attempt too ambitious a program at the start. The best approach is to insist that some progress be made continually, and that innovations be introduced and adopted at a rate which allows your organization to absorb each new technique.

WHAT DOES THE "BIG PICTURE" OF BUSINESS MANAGEMENT LOOK LIKE?

Business management is a dynamic, ever-changing interaction of four basic ingredients: getting money, spending money, operating, and marketing the product. This cycle provides the framework within which the manager's activities are concentrated. The basic management responsibilities in each of the four phases might be summarized as follows:

Phase 1. *Financing.* In new businesses, managers must identify the needs for capital and the various sources of capital which are available to help them get started. They must carefully estimate not only the funds necessary to promote and organize their businesses, but also the funds necessary to operate the businesses until they become self-sustaining. One of the common causes of business failure is inadequate capital. Most business people underestimate the amount of capital needed for a new business, and subsequently find that a lack of cash at critical times presents obstacles that cannot be overcome in time to save the business.

Phase 2. *Procurement.* There is an old axiom of business that most people in product development and marketing respect and follow: "To make money, go where the money is." There is a parallel to this in the world of procurement which is equally true and important: "To save money, watch where the money goes." In the average manufacturing concern more than 50 percent of every sales dollar is spent in procuring materials and services to support the production effort. Good practices in the procurement area can contribute significantly to the company's profits.

Phase 3. *Manufacturing.* In the competitive world of manufacturing, only the firms that are creative, flexible, and efficient in their production methods can survive. To keep operating competitively, managers must know the tools of production management and how to use them. They must keep up-to-date on product planning, plant layout, production methods, and quality control. In addition, they should know the advantages offered by production standards, incentive plans, job evaluation, and similar controls which are common in business. It is easy to forget that for each operation being performed there is a better and less costly way to do it. Cost-saving opportunities are abundant to the manager who knows where to look for them.

Phase 4. *Marketing.* The importance of the marketing function is often ignored by managers who prefer to spend their time on operating or financial problems. No matter how well the financing, procurement, and manufacturing functions are carried out, without customers there will be no business.

Marketing is not restricted to the art of selling goods or services to the customer. The sale itself is the result of a long series of events which includes market analysis, distribution, pricing, advertising, promotion, and sales training.

In the marketplace, business people compete with well-trained and well-organized competitors. Survival depends upon their ability to find market opportunities and to detect and react to changes in the market.

SELF-CHECK OF KEY CONCEPTS
This exercise is designed to test your understanding of the material presented in Chapter 2. Choose the response, *True* or *False*, which best fits each statement. Correct responses are presented in the back of the text.

1. There is a certain amount of luck associated with operating a business which can be exploited by taking chances now and then.
2. Most business failures are related to inadequate or incompetent management.
3. Data available regarding business failures indicate that better planning would have prevented many unsuccessful businesses from being formed at all.

4. Planning should be done first since it forms the basis for organizing and subsequent staffing and motivating.
5. Studies have shown that supervisors spend too little time on planning activities.
6. Planning for top-level managers usually does not extend beyond 6 months.
7. Many managers do not really know what planning consists of.
8. A one-over-one type of organization should be avoided.
9. In the minds of most workers, money is considered the most important factor in their job.
10. It is questionable whether most supervisors really understand their workers' needs.
11. The time required for a control plan to produce results can vary from 30 days to 3 years.
12. Workers resent the restrictions of a control system.

PERFORMANCE PROBLEMS AND PROJECTS

1. In the matrix below, the resources available to a manager are matched with the major managerial functions. Action points are indicated where each horizontal line intersects a vertical column. On a separate sheet of paper, indicate the appropriate actions the manager might take at each intersection point to satisfy the conditions imposed by the interaction of the resource and the function.

	Functions			
Resources	Planning	Organizing	Motivating	Controlling
Personnel				
Markets				
Machines			///////	
Materials			///////	
Methods				
Money			///////	
Minutes (Time)			///////	

2. The control process consists of five steps, starting with a goal or standard to be achieved, and ending with an action designed to eliminate any variance from plan in achieving the standard. Listed below are five items to be controlled. For each item indicate (a) what yardstick you would use as the standard and (b) suggested control action(s) you could take if performance does not meet the proposed standard:

> Maintenance efficiency
> Use of office supplies
> Production output
> Absenteeism
> Labor turnover

A
CASE
IN
POINT

THE CASE OF THE UNMOTIVATED WORKERS

The Excell-O Manufacturing Company is a manufacturer of automobile parts and accessories. It is a relatively new plant with modern equipment, employing about 450 workers. Borgen Industries, their primary competitor, is located 100 miles to the north. Borgen has been in the auto parts business for 15 years but has not modernized its equipment or methods since its opening.

The management of Excell-O have been disappointed in the production levels reached since the plant was opened a year ago and believe that they will lose business to their competitor unless they can somehow get their costs in line or increase their productivity.

From an attitude survey of their workers which was conducted by a consultant, they know that worker attitudes toward their work leave a lot to be desired. At the suggestion of the consultant, they have decided to hire a training specialist to come into the plant each week for 2 hours to present specially prepared material related to the human relations aspects of the supervisor's job, with special emphasis on the theories and techniques of motivating workers. The material will be presented to supervisory personnel.

Mr. Forbes, the instructor, has just spent the major portion of a session discussing the traditional theories of motivation and some of the newer emerging theories. At the conclusion of the presentation, he summarized as follows:

"You should be aware," he said, "that not everyone agrees on the best way to motivate workers. If you had to select the one most important motivator for the people who work for you, what would you list as your top choice?"

"That's easy," volunteered Al Wiley. "The primary motivator for employees is and always will be money. With it, the employees can satisfy their basic needs and be happier, better satisfied workers."

"Do you believe that a raise in pay would be followed by a raise in productivity?" asked Mr. Forbes.

"Sure," replied Al. "Everyone knows that if you want to get a worker to produce more, you pay him more. How else could you explain the success of all the incentive plans in use today?"

"That hasn't been true in my group," responded Tony Gonzales. "The average wage of the workers here at Excell-O is 15 percent higher than the average wage in the community according to the Wage and Salary Department. Yet our productivity is less than it was a year ago, in spite of the fact that all our employees get an automatic wage increase at the end of their first 6 months of employment. I believe that it takes something else besides money to get people to 'put out' for the company."

After some discussion of the two views, Mr. Forbes said, "It seems that the class is pretty evenly divided on this issue. Before our next session, I would like this half of the room to think about this theory of motivation and be prepared to list all the techniques you can think of for motivating employees by this method:

Group 1.   Monetary rewards are the primary means of motivating people.

The other half of the room will do the same for this thesis:

Group 2.   Recognition is a greater motivator than money.
Workers will produce more for psychological rewards than they will for tangible rewards.

"Be prepared to defend your choice and convince the other
group of the soundness of your approach," Mr. Forbes suggested.
"See you next week."

The next session was a lively one. As a result of the discussions the following items were listed on the chalkboard:

Group 1—Monetary Motivators	Group 2—Nonmonetary Motivators
Wage increases	Giving workers special assignments
Performance bonuses	Rotating work assignments
Incentive plans	Talking things over with workers
Piece rates	Giving credit when due
Contests with prizes	Group counseling
Suggestion awards	Use of performance charts
	Problem-solving sessions

Study these suggestions carefully and answer the following questions:

1.   To what extent do you think worker output would be affected
by the monetary motivators?
2.   Do you think the effects of monetary motivators are short-range
or permanent?
3.   Can you think of any disadvantages inherent in any of the monetary motivators listed?
4.   What cautions must be observed in giving employees special
assignments?
5.   What methods of "giving credit" can you list?
6.   Can you think of any advantages of group counseling over
individual counseling?
7.   What value comes from talking to employees about their jobs?
8.   What relationship can you see between productivity and getting workers involved in problem solving?

CHAPTER

3 Starting Your Own Business

PERFORMANCE OBJECTIVES

After reading this chapter, you should be able to explain the key steps required to start a new business and to assess the importance of each in assuring the future success of a new business. Specifically, you should be able to:

1. Defend the place of advance planning in evaluating a new business opportunity and explain some of the activities advance planning includes.
2. Predict what will happen if you misjudge the market for the product or service you plan to offer.
3. Evaluate the relationship of business success to managerial experience and offer suggestions for "filling the gap" where experience is marginal.
4. Judge the effect on your business of the people you hire and describe those characteristics which are considered desirable in your employees.
5. Evaluate the risks involved in starting business "on a shoestring."
6. Explain the kinds of records essential for a new business and describe how you would handle the recordkeeping in a proposed new business.
7. List and assess the importance of the major personal qualifications of a business owner.

8. Describe how you would go about finding a new business opportunity.
9. Classify some of the mistakes commonly made by new business owners under such headings as management methods, financing, recordkeeping, location, and personnel administration.
10. Explain what is meant by *goodwill* and discuss ways of putting a dollar value on it.
11. Discuss the various ways of establishing the fair price for a business you are considering to buy.
12. Construct a "composite" of the typical small business owner, including such things as age, experience, education, and motivation for business.

INTRODUCTION

Every year thousands of Americans, prompted by high hopes of success, take the step of becoming business owners. For many it will be the most important decision they will ever make, involving the investment of lifetime savings and a commitment to a world which is unforgiving of mistakes and weaknesses.

This chapter stresses an organized approach to business ownership characterized by a cautious look at all factors which can adversely affect chances for success. The advice of others who have experienced the disappointment of failure is offered to guide those who have not yet made the decision. Statistics from the Brown University study, mentioned in Chapter 1, of 81 small businesses in the Providence, R.I., area will serve to reinforce the premise that business ownership is not something to be entered into lightly.

WHAT ARE THE KEY STEPS IN STARTING AND OPERATING A BUSINESS?

People who have started businesses successfully suggest eight key steps to follow: First, make sure that your plans and objectives are reduced to writing and double-checked for completeness, clarity, and soundness. Second, study the market which the prospective business will seek to attract. Third, insist on the most efficient production facilities you need or can afford. Fourth, review the trade experience and technical know-how available to you and make sure both are adequate. Fifth, bring capable people into your organization. Sixth, obtain at an early stage firm commitments for the money you will need to start the business. Seventh, do not forget to make provision for keeping adequate records of your operations. And eighth, consider carefully whether you have the necessary personal qualifications to succeed. Let us look at each of these steps.

WHAT IS INVOLVED IN ADVANCE PLANNING? (Step 1)

Plans imply goals, procedures through which they are to be achieved, a time schedule, and recognition of any situation which might affect your plans. Sales planning will consider how much business (sales) you plan to do each month. Financial planning will tell you how much money you will need and when. Profit planning will force you to plan your expenditures and compare them each month with your expected sales. Clear objectives, diligently pursued, will give positive direction to your efforts. Unless objectives are written and checked frequently to indicate your progress, the risk is great that some of your energy and resources will be spent unprofitably on side activities. Subsequent chapters will show you how balance sheets, profit-and-loss statements, budgets, and cash flow forecasts can help you get the answers to your planning questions.

WHAT DO YOU NEED TO KNOW ABOUT THE MARKET? (Step 2)

Every new business should be based on a careful market study. You should have a thorough knowledge of the customers who will buy your product before attempting to produce it. It will be worthwhile to know how many customers are actually in the market for the product you will offer, who your first customers will be, what the most effective methods of advertising are, and how you expect to get the product to your customers. You must also be concerned with the long-range prospects for your business over the next 5 or 10 years. Try to foresee possible shifts in demand, because a new business in a declining industry will find many additional forces operating against it. Statistics show that the first companies to encounter difficulty during periods of decline seem to be the old marginal firms and the young unseasoned companies.

You should have a sound basis for believing that your business can operate as efficiently as a competing business. Your product must be able to meet existing competition and, if possible, outdo it. Consequently, you need as much knowledge as possible about the strengths and weaknesses of your competitors. You represent potential competition to them too, so it is reasonable to assume that they will not sit back and permit you to enter their market without a contest.

HOW CAN YOU EVALUATE PRODUCTION FACILITIES CORRECTLY? (Step 3)

Efficient production methods should be worked out and adequate facilities provided. The most efficient equipment you need and can afford should be acquired. Since there is almost an infinite number of ways to do any job, your ingenuity and background in making the product are important. If you lack the technical know-how for planning and laying out an efficient production line, you might need to get a specialist to help you.

A substantial edge on competition can often be achieved through strategic location. Many plants are used simply because they were available and the lease or purchase price was small. This factor alone is not enough for making a decision when selecting a site. Several other factors are of equal importance: accessibility to markets, sources of material and labor, power supply, cost of plant equipment, and local taxes are the more important ones.

HOW IMPORTANT ARE EXPERIENCE AND KNOW-HOW? (Step 4)

Ignorance of business practice is an obstacle which few but the most fortunate can overcome in time to save a business which has been started without it. All business owners should have sufficient experience to understand both overall business management and the specific requirements of their particular businesses. Some "experts" recommend 5 to 10 years of experience in the field before attempting to start a business of one's own. Others suggest working for someone else to gain the experience necessary to provide the know-how. The means of acquiring knowledge of up-to-date production techniques and trade practices will vary, depending upon the business. The point is that a business person must either possess the technical knowledge needed or employ the technical talent necessary to assure that this important area is adequately covered. Anyone can go into business, but a person who does not know the details of his or her particular line will soon be in trouble.

WHAT KINDS OF EMPLOYEES WILL YOU NEED? (Step 5)

Success or failure in business is almost always strongly influenced by people. Unless you are thoroughly trained in all phases of the business—and determined to operate a one-person business—you should obtain qualified people to provide the necessary skills. With incompetent employees, your chances for success are practially zero. Therefore, plan carefully how you intend to supplement your own experience and ability.

Loyal, energetic, and experienced employees are an asset. Whether you expect to employ a few people or many, you should be sure that workers with the necessary skills or aptitudes for training are available in your area. In addition to a competent staff, a trusted "second in command" who can be relied upon to share your problems and supplement your weak areas may well be one of your most valuable assets. New businesses might be limited in their growth potential if the owners spread themselves too thin to pay attention to all the important details.

HOW RISKY IS STARTING A BUSINESS "ON A SHOESTRING"? (Step 6)

Typically, the people who start businesses underestimate their financial needs. Too often, in their anxiety to get started they launch their business without enough money. Some shoestring starts have proved successful, but inadequate financing greatly magnifies the risks. The first setback usually spells insolvency. Therefore, every effort should be made to build adaptability into your business by providing reserve funds to meet unforeseen developments. While contingencies may be unforeseen, they are almost certain to occur.

Sufficient financing should be formally committed prior to the start of operations. Not only must buildings and equipment be acquired, but enough working funds must also be available to carry on operations until the business is able to generate its own flow of funds. Financial commitments must be firm since it is futile to depend upon vague plans or to seek additional capital when your "back is to the wall."

HOW ESSENTIAL ARE GOOD RECORDS? (Step 7)

It is not unusual for managers to get so involved with current operating problems that they forget to "keep score" on the trends of cash reserves, inventories, or accounts receivable. Or they do not have a yardstick which tells them when expenses are out of line. As a result, trouble is sometimes recognized only after it is too late for anything to be done. Having a competent accountant analyze the books regularly is important. In addition, records such as production schedules, sales quotas, cost targets, and return on the financial investment should be set up to keep you informed about what progress is being made toward planned goals. Although this task falls in the category of routine paperwork, its importance should not be underestimated. Critical decisions must often be based on the data reflected in your records. Good records, therefore, take much of the guesswork out of decision making and provide a sound basis for making good decisions.

WHAT PERSONAL QUALIFICATIONS SHOULD A BUSINESS OWNER HAVE? (Step 8)

While expert assistance can be hired, the judgment and leadership required to successfully start and guide a business must come from the owner. There is no precise list of the personal traits found in successful business people, but some of the important ones are:

Ambition. Do you have a burning desire to succeed? Is it strong enough to overcome the many obstacles and setbacks that are bound to occur? Will it last?

Tenacity. Are you ready and willing to work long, exhausting hours and to endure the personal sacrifices and frustrations your business will demand?

Enthusiasm. Is your enthusiasm intense and based upon an inherent enjoyment of planning and managing the type of business you have chosen?

Stamina. Can you give what your business will demand in mental and physical endurance? Is your family emotionally prepared for the continuing strain of your business demands?

Ingenuity. Are you a person with ideas? Do you have the required creative imagination and resourcefulness to overcome the obstacles which will be encountered?

Figure 3-1 is a rating scale for the most important personal traits prepared by the Small Business Administration.[1] It will give you an objective appraisal of your qualifications.

HOW DO YOU GO ABOUT FINDING THE "RIGHT" BUSINESS?

Once you have satisfied yourself that going into business is for you, finding a business which is compatible with your objectives and experience becomes the next order of business. There are several ways to go about this. Scan the "Business Opportunities" section of your local newspaper to see what is available in your community. If moving is no problem, or if you wish to consider opportunities in other areas, a subscription to newspapers serving those areas would be a good investment.

Trade journals representing the various industries are available at your public library. These are excellent vehicles for advertising for the kind of business you want. Researching old issues of trade journals will provide a lot of useful information on the field you have chosen, and will help you better understand the problems you will face.

The Small Business Administration has field offices in many cities. Their library of materials, much of which is free, is an excellent source of "how to" publications for the aspiring business person. In addition, they can provide assistance in obtaining small business loans, establishing credit, and solving production and management problems.

Chambers of commerce are anxious to help new businesses settle in the community. They are good sources of information about the community, the businesses already there, and what the community has to offer a new business.

Local banks can often provide useful information and be helpful to the new business. Because of their many business contacts, they can provide assistance aside from their normal banking functions which can help you find the kind of business you are seeking.

Keep in mind that many of the businesses which are for sale are in trouble. By talking to the owner you should be able to tell whether your chances of getting the business back in the black are

[1]Wendell O. Metcalf, *Starting and Managing a Small Business of Your Own*, The Starting and Managing Series, Vol. 1, 3d ed., U.S. Small Business Administration, Washington, 1973.

INSTRUCTIONS: After each question place a check mark on the line at the point closest to your answer. The check mark need not be placed directly over one of the suggested answers because your rating may lie somewhere between two answers. Be honest with yourself.

ARE YOU A SELF-STARTER?

I do things my own way. Nobody needs to tell me to get going.

If someone gets me started, I keep going all right.

Easy does it. I don't put myself out until I have to.

HOW DO YOU FEEL ABOUT OTHER PEOPLE?

I like people. I can get along with just about any-body.

I have plenty of friends. I don't need anyone else.

Most people bug me.

CAN YOU LEAD OTHERS?

I can get most people to go along without much difficulty.

I can get people to do things if I drive them.

I let someone else get things moving.

CAN YOU TAKE RESPONSIBILITY?

I like to take charge of and see things through.

I'll take over if I have to, but I'd rather let someone else be responsible.

There's always some eager beaver around wanting to show off. I say let him.

HOW GOOD AN ORGANIZER ARE YOU?

I like to have a plan before I start. I'm usually the one to get things lined up.

I do all right unless things get too goofed up. Then I cop out.

I just take things as they come.

HOW GOOD A WORKER ARE YOU?	I can keep going as long as necessary. I don't mind working hard.	I'll work hard for a while, but when I've had enough, that's it!	I can't see that hard work gets you anywhere.
CAN YOU MAKE DECISIONS?	I can make up my mind in a hurry if necessary, and my decision is usually o.k.	I can if I have plenty of time. If I have to make up my mind fast, I usually regret it.	I don't like to be the one who decides things. I'd probably blow it.
CAN PEOPLE TRUST WHAT YOU SAY?	They sure can. I don't say things I don't mean.	I try to be on the level, but sometimes I just say what's easiest.	What's the sweat if the other fellow doesn't know the difference?
CAN YOU STICK WITH IT?	If I make up my mind to do something, I don't let anything stop me.	I usually finish what I start.	If a job doesn't go right, I turn off. Why beat your brains out?
HOW GOOD IS YOUR HEALTH?	I never run down.	I have enough energy for most things I want to do.	I run out of juice sooner than most of my friends seem to.

FIGURE 3-1. Rating scale for personal traits important to a business proprietor. (Source: Wendell O. Metcalf, *Starting and Managing a Small Business of Your Own*, The Starting and Managing Series, Vol. 1, 3d ed., U.S. Small Business Administration, Washington, 1973.)

promising. If the problem is a poor location or oversaturation of the potential market, you might find that the business is no bargain at any price. Your thoroughness in pursuing all the angles before making your final decision will, as has been emphasized repeatedly, pay dividends.

WHAT HAS BEEN THE EXPERIENCE OF MINORITIES IN STARTING NEW BUSINESSES?

In 1972, the U.S. Department of Health, Education, and Welfare published the results of a study of 30 minority-owned businesses.[2] The study was designed to provide relevant information to minority adults about the problems associated with starting a business. The study focused on the business practices and procedures of these 30 businesses, 15 of which had failed. The 30 were selected from a broad spectrum of small businesses, including retail sales, service trades, manufacturing, and construction.

In response to the question "What do you wish you had known, but did not, prior to opening for business?" the following comments were offered. They deal almost entirely with mistakes to be avoided in the early stages of the venture. The recommendations stress the importance of that very crucial period between the generation of the idea for going into business and the actual start-up. Any mistakes made during this period can be fatal. Businesses may fail long after their doors have opened, but the problem which causes the failure is often born in the planning stages. Here are the responses to the question:

About the Management Skills Required. The most common response was one of regret that the business owners had not realized how complicated the job of managing a business would be. Once in business, they found themselves inadequately prepared to make the decisions required in those areas of the business in which they had had no previous experience or instruction. For example, although they might have known very well how to sell, they found that they did not know how to administer the work force, account for the flow of money into and out of the business, negotiate with suppliers, and so forth.

About the Specific Business. Many of the owners acknowledge that they knew much too little about the complexities of the specific type of business venture they undertook. In retrospect, they wished they had been a little less eager to get started and had spent more time learning about the business and what it took to make it succeed.

---

[2]*Minority Ownership of Small Businesses,* U.S. Department of Health, Education, and Welfare Publication OE-72-27, Washington, 1972.

About Lenders and Investors. If the business capitalization includes money from an outside lending or investing source, that source usually acquires a certain influence over the operation of the business. For example, a lender may place certain restrictions on the use of business assets or limit future borrowing, or an investor may get a controlling vote on the board of directors. Certain business owners lost control of their operations through just such means.

About Accounting. A lack of knowledge on how to keep the business books caused business owners more frustration than any other single item.

About the Location of the Business. Several of the business owners realized too late that the sites they selected for their ventures were inappropriate. They were either inconvenient for customers, too deteriorated for retail sales, or located in a high-crime area which caused problems with customer fear, employee retention, high insurance rates, and heavy thievery.

About the Selection of a Business Partner. A few of those who had chosen to open business with a partner later regretted the decision. They wished they had realized before entering business that their partners did not agree with their ideas of business goals, strategies, and policies.

About the Amount of Initial Financing Required. Many of the owners either underestimated the amount of money required to start their businesses or decided that they could somehow make do with less than what was needed. They wished they had studied the requirements more carefully, since an undercapitalized venture tends to start with difficulties which persist and defy later solution.

About Government Regulations and Requirements. Many of the owners admitted that they knew little of the complexities involved in even such basic requirements as withholding and paying employee taxes, making social security deductions, obtaining business licenses, and complying with local regulations.

About the Demands of Self-Employment on Them and Their Families. Nearly all the owners who were married wished they had known, prior to going into business, about the heavy work commitment and other strains which were in store for them. Some might not have undertaken the venture had they been aware of these burdens, and others would have at least forewarned their families of the strains they would have to endure. Most of them agreed that a venture which was to call upon the resources of the family as well as themselves should have been considered carefully by the total family.

This advice comes from the HEW publication previously mentioned:

☐ Before you actually commit yourself, be certain you are well prepared to do what you want to do. Take time to study the prospects. Know the business first.

☐ Consult with others in the business you are considering. Tap their brains. Benefit from their experiences.

☐ If possible, get some experience working in a similar business before you start yours.

☐ Be prepared to sacrifice. Expect the business to require long hours and more sweat and more worry than you think possible.

☐ Realize that you might make more money, for less effort, with less worry, by working for someone else.

☐ If possible, survey your potential customers. Ask them if they will buy. See if you can get some advance assurances of sales.

☐ Be certain your family approves of the venture and that it is prepared to live with the strains and problems certain to follow.

☐ Be careful of investing in a business selling a "fad" that will soon be out of style.

☐ If you take on a partner, be sure that you separate areas of responsibility and that these areas are well defined. Be certain that your partner's skills complement your skills and that his or her interests and goals are compatible with yours.

☐ Choose your location very carefully. Do not take the first thing that is available. Ask yourself why and how your intended customers would come to your location.

☐ After you plan your business strategy, be sure your financial resources match your plan. If available financing does not support the strategy, revamp the strategy.

☐ Expect suppliers to discriminate against you until you prove to be creditable. Be prepared to purchase your initial inventory needs with cash.

☐ Start with enough money to allow for a cash reserve to carry you if the business does not "take off" as quickly as you have hoped.

☐ Assume that local financial institutions will help. Apply at several and "shop" for the best deal.

☐ If you are offered a loan, check the terms and conditions carefully before accepting it.

☐ Do not accept a loan which is inadequate for your needs and which may prevent you from borrowing more money elsewhere.

- Get proper insurance coverage.
- Have a good accounting and bookkeeping system set up before you start.
- Be certain you understand the accounting system, even if someone else keeps the books.
- Pay your bills as they come due, especially tax payments. Do not let debts accumulate.
- Watch your costs closely. Plan an operating budget for a situation in which sales will be less than you expected and expenses higher.
- Hire good help.
- Be prepared to sell. In nearly all new business ventures, the owner-manager is the major, perhaps the only, salesperson. Be aggressive. Do not expect customers to come to you.
- Build your business cautiously. Anticipate certain problems, and invest in additional fixed assets when you are sure your sales growth warrants it.
- If a business opportunity still looks like a winner after careful analysis, go ahead and try it.

IS THERE ANY WAY TO FIND OUT WHAT IT COSTS TO GO INTO BUSINESS?

The answer depends on the kind of business you are considering, its size and location, and the competition.

One thing is sure: You will spend a lot of money before you get any back. Even the most profitable business does not make a profit for 3 or 4 months after it opens. Many businesses can be expected to take much longer.

If you are considering investing in a franchise, here are some rough estimates of the minimum investment required:

Dairy Queen	$ 20,000
Firestone Tire	25,000
Kentucky Fried Chicken	25,000
Midas Mufflers	20,000
Western Auto Supply	28,000
Holiday Inns	250,000–400,000

If you decide to go the ownership route, Table 3-1 shows estimates for ten different businesses compiled by *Changing Times*.[3]

---

[3]"What Going Into Business Costs," *Changing Times*, June 1971, pp. 25–29.

TABLE 3-1. WHAT GOING INTO BUSINESS COSTS

Business	Typical Range	What It Covers	Where to Get Other Information
Auto parts and accessories store	$10,000 to $17,000	Rent deposit, utility installation, office equipment, store fixtures, display cases, signs and opening inventory.	Automotive Parts and Accessories Assn., 1730 K St., N.W., Washington, D.C. 20006
Beauty salon	$10,000 to $18,000	Plumbing and electrical alterations, rent and utility deposits, reception furniture, salon supplies, down payment on equipment and cash reserve for a salon with four or five stations.	National Hairdressers and Cosmetologists Assn., 3510 Olive St., St. Louis, Mo. 63103
Coffee shop	$23,000 to $46,000	Renovation and equipment for a 25-seat shop, based on "rule of thumb" total capital requirement of $900 to $1,850 per seat.	Business Advisory Service, National Restaurant Assn., 1530 N. Lake Shore Dr., Chicago, Ill. 60610
Coin-operated self-service carwash	$22,000 to $27,000	Building, site preparation, equipment and utility installation for a four-bay operation. Does not include property costs.	National Carwash Council, Seven S. Dearborn St., Chicago, Ill. 60603
Coin-operated combination laundry/dry cleaner	$50,000 to $75,000	Equipment, installation, supplies, promotion, rent deposits and cash reserve for a store with six dry-cleaning units and 20 washers.	National Automatic Laundry and Cleaning Council, Seven S. Dearborn St., Chicago, Ill. 60603

Independent drugstore	$35,000 to $50,000	Store and pharmacy fixtures and initial inventory for a 3,000-sq. ft. store with projected annual gross sales of $150,000.	National Assn. of Retail Druggists, One E. Wacker Dr., Chicago, Ill. 60601
Gasoline service station	$10,000 to $15,000	Leasing a station, inventory of gasoline, oil, parts, accessories and tools, plus cash reserve for a medium-volume business.	National Congress of Petroleum Retailers, 2945 Banksville Rd., Pittsburgh, Pa. 15216
Mobile home park	$220,000 to $330,000	Architect's fees, construction, landscaping and utility installation costs for a 100-space community with swimming pool and other recreation facilities. Does not include property costs.	Trailer Coach Assn., 3855 E. La Palma Ave., Anaheim, Cal. 92806
Retail nursery	$40,000 to $60,000	Construction of buildings and parking lot, plus equipment, truck rental, opening inventory, lease deposit and cash reserve.	American Assn. of Nurserymen, Inc., 835 Southern Bldg., Washington, D.C. 20005
Preschool day-care center	$50,000 to $65,000	Building equipped to care for 30 children, with playground, kitchen and furnishings, plus cash reserve.	Day Care and Child Development Council of America, 1426 H St., N.W., Washington, D.C. 20005

Source: Reprinted by permission from *Changing Times*, The Kiplinger Magazine (June 1971 issue). Copyright 1971 by The Kiplinger Washington Editors, Inc., 1729 H Street, N.W., Washington, D.C. 20006.

Include in your expenses these major items:

Inventory	Depends on your business volume.
Equipment	Covers the costs of display cases, office machines, shelves, handling equipment, and similar items.
Prepayments	Includes rent, business licenses, and similar types of expense.
Remodeling	Get estimates from local contractors for painting, carpentry, electrical work, refinishing furniture and fixtures.
Operating capital	Enough cash is required to carry the business at least 3 or 4 months. Includes salaries, advertising, maintenance, rent, payments for loans, merchandise, and utilities.

WHERE DO NEW BUSINESS OWNERS GET THEIR MONEY TO GO INTO BUSINESS?

According to the Small Business Administration, the average new proprietor supplies over half the funds needed to get started from personal savings and cash. Another 15 percent comes from commercial lending institutions, and credit from suppliers accounts for about 6 percent. The rest comes from families, friends, and other sources. While it is comforting and reassuring to be able to borrow from families and friends, it is always a good idea to make your financial arrangements with them formal and businesslike. That way there is less likelihood for relationships to be jeopardized.

IS THERE ANY WAY TO TELL HOW MUCH MONEY A NEW BUSINESS WILL MAKE?

While your decision to go into business might not depend entirely upon the return you expect from your investment, it is one of the factors which will be important for you to consider. Frequently, people invest money in a business under the misapprehension that the financial return will be far greater than what they could expect from other investments. Investigation of annual average returns for the line of business in which you are interested is worthwhile.

Table 3-2 shows the percentage return on investment on 51 selected lines of business compiled by Dun & Bradstreet for 1974. The percentages are computed by dividing the amount of net profit before taxes by the tangible net worth of the line of business. Note that the *median* figures are shown for each line. This means that 49 percent of the businesses sampled had higher rates and 49 percent lower. Since the ranges from the highest to the lowest often show significant variances, the reader is invited to examine the source of the data for additional information.

TABLE 3-2. RETURN ON INVESTMENT FOR SELECTED LINES OF BUSINESS FOR THE YEAR 1974*

Type of Business (Number in Sample)	Net Return on Net Worth	Type of Business (Number in Sample)	Net Return on Net Worth
Retailing:		Manufacturing and construction (continued):	
Department stores (269)	5.22	Passenger cars, truck and bus bodies (59)	9.58
Discount stores (197)	9.44	Plumbing, heating, air conditioning (89)	10.69
Family clothing (102)	6.04	Soap, detergents, perfumes (65)	11.76
Furniture stores (163)	6.54	Soft drinks, bottled and canned (69)	13.36
Gasoline service stations (84)	21.71	Wholesaling:	
Grocery stores (133)	11.57	Automotive equipment (135)	10.83
Hardware stores (84)	7.45	Beer, wine, alcoholic beverages (92)	9.51
Household appliance stores (86)	8.66	Chemicals and allied products (48)	20.05
Jewelry stores (71)	7.93	Commercial machines and equipment (48)	6.80
Lumber and other building materials (156)	9.78	Confectionery (31)	9.55
Motor vehicle dealers (93)	7.68	Dairy products (39)	13.33
Paint, glass, and wallpaper stores (37)	9.23	Drugs and druggist sundries (87)	6.56
Shoe stores (86)	4.71	Electrical appliances, TV and radio sets (98)	8.24
Variety stores (69)	9.09	Footwear (56)	6.28
Manufacturing and construction:		Furniture and home furnishings (72)	9.94
Bakery products (54)	5.77	Groceries, general line (172)	11.45
Books: publishing and printing (55)	10.18	Hardware (161)	9.29
Communications equipment (78)	12.06	Industrial machinery and equipment (81)	12.40
Dairy products (103)	9.24	Lumber and construction materials (117)	11.06
Drugs (62)	16.29	Meats and meat products (44)	11.46
Electrical work (118)	11.94	Paints and varnishes (27)	11.03
Farm machinery and equipment (72)	16.74	Paper and paper products (111)	11.27
Heating equipment and plumbing fixtures (52)	8.51	Petroleum and petroleum products (86)	17.23
Household appliances (41)	8.14	Plumbing and heating equipment and supplies (143)	9.77
Iron and steel foundries (55)	13.38	Poultry and poultry products (40)	14.28
Motor vehicle parts (99)	11.25	Tires and tubes (42)	10.33
Paints, lacquers, varnishes, enamels (96)	9.00		

*Data represents profit on tangible net worth expressed as a percent. Tangible net worth is the equity in the business, obtained by subtracting total liabilities from total assets. Ratios are median figures (middle of the range) for the lines of business sampled. Half the businesses sampled will be higher than the median and half will be lower. Numbers in parentheses represent number of businesses sampled. Source: *Key Business Ratios* (1974), Dun & Bradstreet, Inc. Reprinted with permission.

There are pros and cons here. If you buy, you sometimes can get a business at a bargain price. This is true if the owner is retiring because of ill health or age. For personal reasons, an owner might be sufficiently anxious to sell an existing business to you at less than its worth. This approach can also save you time and effort in setting up your business and buying the equipment and stock necessary to operate it. If the owner has established a clientele who are accustomed to trading with the business, this is a plus. Steady customers are often difficult to acquire. If they come with the business, you save the initial waiting period to attract them while you are getting started. Finally, the owner might be able to give you valuable suggestions and advice on the operation of the business which could save you a lot later.

Some of the disadvantages are obvious. There is always the chance that you will pay more for the business than it is worth. This happens every day either because of buyers' inaccurate appraisals or because of former owners' misrepresentations. If the former owners did not enjoy a good relationship with their customers and suppliers, you might have to work hard to overcome the disadvantage. You can often overlook the fact that a business is not situated in a good location. This disadvantage is very difficult to overcome. The former owners' equipment and fixtures might be worn out or outmoded, requiring a large remodeling or replacement expense on your part. Their inventories could be made up of slow-moving or out-of-date items which will be difficult for you to sell. These are enough to warn you to "look before you leap" into buying an existing business.

WHAT IS MEANT BY TANGIBLE ASSETS?

These are the things of value you pay for when you buy a business. They include merchandise inventory, equipment and fixtures, and supplies. If the business you plan to purchase sells on credit, you will probably take over accounts receivable. In evaluating the value of tangible assets, look at the condition of the inventory you are buying. Is the stock of goods made up of timely, well-balanced selections of materials or merchandise? How much of it will have to be disposed of at a loss? The inventory should be appraised carefully and "aged" to show how old it is. Usually the older the inventory, the less value it has. Equipment and fixtures should be in working order. Find out their age and compare their asking price with similar merchandise offered by secondhand dealers. Office equipment should be checked to determine that it is efficient and in condition to do the job without breakdowns and delays. Repair parts for old equipment might be difficult, or even impossible, to obtain. To pay a high price for old equipment, no matter how good its condition, would be unwise. Your fair value for fixtures and equipment should give consideration to depreciation and obsolescence. Finally, determine how much money is tied up in these items and evaluate your needs. If there is a mortgage on any of the fixtures or equipment, find out before you buy, not after.

Things like accounts receivable should be "aged" to determine whether some of them are so old as to be uncollectible. Records and contracts involving favorable leases all have real value. You should make certain that these are included in the sale.

IS "GOODWILL" SOMETHING YOU CAN PUT A DOLLAR VALUE ON?

It is difficult, but you have to do it. It is made up of the firm's reputable name, capable personnel, high financial standing, good product or service reputation, favorable location, customer loyalty, and good relations with suppliers, creditors, and the community at large. From an accountant's standpoint, the ability of a business to make above-average profits as a result of all these factors is the value of *goodwill*. This term is not to be confused with *net worth*, which is the difference between the dollar value of the assets and liabilities of the business. When goodwill exists, it is a valuable asset.

You should be realistic in determining how much you will pay for goodwill. Since payment is for favorable public attitude, you should make some effort to check this attitude. Question customers, bankers, and others who you feel will give you an unbiased opinion. You must also consider the possibility that the goodwill will go with the seller, and not stay with the business. In this case, it is worth much less since you will have to establish your own.

A good way to judge the worth of goodwill is to estimate how much more income you will receive because of it than you would by starting a new business. You can also check similar businesses for sale and find out what they are asking as the value of goodwill.

This process of "shopping around" will give you an idea of not only the total prices asked but also the amounts asked over and above the reasonable value of net tangible assets.

HOW MUCH SHOULD YOU PAY FOR A BUSINESS YOU BUY?

In deciding how much you should pay for a going business, you should consider its profit potential. Tangible assets are important to future earnings and potential profit. If the seller is asking for something for the intangible asset of goodwill, take care to estimate how much it will add to your future profits. What you are concerned with is the future possibility of the business. Therefore, you should carefully estimate the sales and profits for the next few years. If you expect a 10 percent return on your investment, it will take 10 years to recover the investment. So you should be interested in trying to forecast sales and profits for 10 years.

Future profits will depend a lot on what has happened in the past, so you should examine the owner's books for at least 5 years back, or longer if the records exist. Compare the profits with those of similar businesses and see how the owner has performed. This can be done by comparing the business' "track record" with that of similar businesses, as shown in Table 3-3.

There are various formulas for pricing a business, but they differ according to the kind of business involved. Retail, wholesale, service, and manufacturing businesses are priced differently. Even in the retail category, retail hardware stores are priced differently from retail florist shops. Some formulas are based on the sum of 1 year's net profit plus the value of inventory at cost. Others establish a set amount for each $100 of net income per week. A formula which includes all the factors that we have discussed is shown in Table 3-4.

HOW ARE THE SELLER'S LIABILITIES HANDLED IN A BUSINESS SALE?

You should be sure that the seller pays off accumulated debts before you pay the money agreed to in the terms of the sale. The seller's liabilities are usually not carried over unless the buyer agrees to assume them. All the cards should be laid on the table concerning mortgages, back taxes, liens upon assets, or other creditors' claims. Obtain full information about any undelivered purchases. You should protect yourself in the purchase contract against false statements by the seller, inaccurate financial data, or undisclosed potential liabilities.

WHAT OTHER HINTS ARE OFFERED FOR PROSPECTIVE BUYERS?

In addition to the warranty against misleading information suggested above, be sure your purchase contract gives you a clear title to the business. Have a competent lawyer draw up the contract. A lawyer's expert guidance and knowledge of the intricacies of legal structure, laws, regulations, and contract terminology are essential. If you make the right decisions early in the game, you help ensure success. The contract should provide the buyer the profits and operating control as soon as the agreement is signed. This will prevent an unscrupulous seller from selling off the assets of the business or destroying the goodwill you agreed to pay for. Finally, do not hesitate to retain an accountant to check the books of the business and make recommendations. Resist the temptation to do it all yourself or to rely on a friend to check out the information for you. Make use of a lawyer and an accountant and consider the fee part of the purchase price of the business. The chances are that you will not have reason to regret it. This might be the best money you ever spent.

TABLE 3-3. PROFITABILITY FOR SELECTED LINES OF BUSINESS FOR THE YEAR 1974*

Type of Business (Number in Sample)	Net Return on Sales	Type of Business (Number in Sample)	Net Return on Sales
Retailing:		Manufacturing and construction (continued):	
Department stores (269)	1.72	Passenger cars, truck and bus bodies (59)	1.95
Discount stores (197)	1.47	Plumbing, heating, air conditioning (89)	2.05
Family clothing (102)	1.69	Soap, detergents, perfumes (65)	3.66
Furnitures stores (163)	2.16	Soft drinks, bottled and canned (69)	3.97
Gasoline service stations (84)	5.86	Wholesaling:	
Grocery stores (133)	1.00	Automotive equipment (135)	2.88
Hardware stores (84)	1.93	Beer, wine, alcoholic beverages (92)	1.19
Household appliance stores (86)	1.27	Chemicals and allied products (48)	3.07
Jewelry stores (71)	3.50	Commercial machines and equipment (48)	1.48
Lumber and other building materials (156)	2.93	Confectionery (31)	0.88
Motor vehicle dealers (93)	1.12	Dairy products (39)	1.32
Paint, glass, and wallpaper stores (37)	2.10	Drugs and druggist sundries (87)	1.00
Shoe stores (86)	1.60	Electrical appliances, TV and radio sets (98)	1.18
Variety stores (69)	2.25	Footwear (56)	1.52
Manufacturing and construction:		Furniture and home furnishings (72)	2.10
Bakery products (54)	1.47	Groceries, general line (172)	0.73
Books: publishing and printing (55)	4.02	Hardware (161)	2.21
Communications equipment (78)	4.13	Industrial machinery and equipment (81)	2.64
Dairy products (103)	1.23	Lumber and construction materials (117)	1.79
Drugs (62)	6.73	Meats and meat products (44)	0.67
Electrical work (118)	2.35	Paints and varnishes (27)	2.43
Farm machinery and equipment (72)	4.28	Paper and paper products (111)	1.84
Heating equipment and plumbing fixtures (52)	2.62	Petroleum and petroleum products (86)	2.65
Household appliances (41)	2.44	Plumbing and heating equipment and supplies (143)	2.43
Iron and steel foundries (55)	4.36	Poultry and poultry products (40)	1.29
Motor vehicle parts (99)	3.23	Tires and tubes (42)	1.78
Paints, lacquers, varnishes, enamels (96)	2.52		

*Data represents the net profit on sales obtained by dividing the net earnings of the business, after taxes, by net sales (the dollar volume less returns, allowances, and cash discounts). It is expressed as a percent. Ratios are median figures (middle of the range) for the lines of business sampled. Half the business sampled will be higher than the median and half will be lower. Numbers in parentheses represent number of businesses sampled. Source: Key Business Ratios (1974), Dun & Bradstreet, Inc. Reprinted with permission.

TABLE 3-4. FORMULA FOR PRICING A BUSINESS

1.	Adjusted tangible net worth *(appraised value of tangible assets less liabilities)*		$100,000
2.	Normal earning power at 7 percent *(what you could get by investing your $100,000 in corporate bonds)*	$ 7,000	
3.	Salary for owner-operator *(whatever you are making now)*	10,000	
4.	Your present earning power *(without buying the business)*	$17,000	
5.	Average net profit of the business *(over the past three to five years)*	25,000	
6.	Excess earning power of the business *(line 5 less line 4)*	$ 8,000	
7.	Goodwill *(as determined by this formula: for a well-established business, five times excess earning power; for a moderately well-established business, three times)*		40,000
8.	Fair price *(tangibles plus goodwill, or profit potential)*		$140,000

Source: Reprinted by permission from *Changing Times*, The Kiplinger Magazine (February 1971 issue). Copyright 1971 by The Kiplinger Washington Editors, Inc., 1729 H Street, N.W., Washington, D.C. 20006.

DO NEW BUSINESS OWNERS PAY ANY ATTENTION TO THE PRINCIPLES OF BUSINESS OWNERSHIP SUGGESTED IN THIS CHAPTER?

Only a small percentage of them go into business with a full and complete understanding of what problems they are about to face. The Brown University study previously mentioned provided new insights into, and important clues concerning, the entire process of small business formation, growth, and decline, and represents a new approach to the study of the problems faced by new business enterprises. It is a classic in its field.

From the wealth of information compiled in that study of 81 small businesses (started by 93 owners) in the Providence, Rhode Island, area, we will focus upon the following topics, which should be of considerable interest to anyone contemplating business ownership:

- The type of person who opens a new business
- The motivation for business ownership
- What determines the choice of business
- Critical location factors
- Financial planning

WHAT KIND OF PERSON OPENS A SMALL BUSINESS?

When we look at the occupational experience, educational background, age, and sex of the 93 owners involved in the Rhode Island study, some interesting things are apparent.

Data presented in Table 3-5 touches on the previous occupational experience of the business owners studied. Of the 64 enterprisers with manual work experience (49 with manual experience, 15 with manual and white collar experience), 21 (13 + 8) had also owned other businesses previously. Some of them had started their occupational careers as manual workers but had then consecutively operated a series of businesses. Others had changed back and forth between manual work and self-employment. The strong attraction of business ownership for manual workers is evident in the study. Two-thirds of the 93 owners had at some time been employed as manual workers. Of these 93 owners, 36 (40 percent) had done nothing but manual work prior to opening their new business.

TABLE 3-5. PREVIOUS OCCUPATIONAL EXPERIENCE OF BUSINESS OWNERS

Occupational Category	Previous Business Ownership	No Previous Business Ownership	Total
Manual	13	36	49
Manual and white collar	8	7	15
White collar	12	10	22
Business experience only	4		4
No previous occupational experience		2	2
TOTAL	37	55	92*

*No information on previous occupational experience was obtainable in one case.
Source: Kurt B. Mayer and Sidney Goldstein, *The First Two Years: Problems of Small Firm Growth and Survival*, Small Business Research Series, No. 2, U.S. Small Business Administration, Washington, 1961.

The educational background of the new owners is shown in Table 3-6. More than half of the total sample had less than a completed high school education. In fact, 18 did not go beyond the

TABLE 3-6.   YEARS OF SCHOOL COMPLETED BY BUSINESS OWNERS

Years of School Completed*	Number	Percent
8 years or less	18	19.4
9 to 11 years	31	33.3
12 years	20	21.5
12 years plus additional vocational training	5	5.4
13 to 15 years	7	7.5
16 years	6	6.5
More than 16 years	3	3.2
No answer	3	3.2

*Median years of school completed, 11.0.

Source: Kurt B. Mayer and Sidney Goldstein, *The First Two Years: Problems of Small Firm Growth and Survival*, Small Business Research Series, No. 2, U.S. Small Business Administration, Washington, 1961.

eighth grade. The largest single group, 25 (20 + 5) owners, completed their high school education with a diploma. Approximately 10 percent of the sample (9 out of 93) graduated from college (completed 16 or more years of school), while 7 more had some college training but did not receive a diploma. The median education of the whole sample was 11.0 years of schooling, which compared favorably with the 9.3 median attained by Rhode Island's population twenty-five years or older. The median educational level for the "proprietors, managers, and officials" category of the United States census in 1950 was 12.2 years of school. It appears the educational level of this sample is fairly typical of small business owners.

The ages of the business owners in this study are reflected in Table 3-7. The median age in the sample is 40.0 years. This indicates that the road to business ownership often must wait for the necessary money or experience, although a number of older owners in this

TABLE 3-7.   AGE OF BUSINESS OWNERS

Age*	Number	Percent
Under 20 years	1	1.1
20 to 29 years	16	17.2
30 to 39 years	29	31.2
40 to 49 years	26	27.9
50 to 59 years	16	17.2
60 years and over	5	5.4

*Median age, 40.0 years.

Source: Kurt B. Mayer and Sidney Goldstein, *The First Two Years: Problems of Small Firm Growth and Survival*, Small Business Research Series, No. 2, U.S. Small Business Administration, Washington, 1961.

sample went into business as an alternative to unemployment. Unable to find jobs because of the unwillingness of many employers to hire older workers, they tried to secure their future through self-employment. The median age would probably have been higher if the study had not been begun during a period of recession when young persons, as well as older ones, experienced difficulties in finding employment.

The percentage of female owners found in the study (18.3 percent) is significantly higher than the current national average. According to a U.S. Department of Commerce survey released in 1976, women owned only 4.6 percent of all businesses in 1972. The receipts of these businesses amounted to $8.1 billion, or 0.3 percent of the $2.4 trillion earned by all United States firms.

WHAT MOTIVATES PEOPLE TO GO INTO BUSINESS?

The reasons for going into business depend upon many factors, such as age, employment conditions, previous experience, education, and family considerations. In the Rhode Island study, the initial interview asked each owner, "Why did you go into business?" The results are shown in Table 3-8. Although monetary motives were

TABLE 3-8. MOTIVATION FOR BUSINESS OWNERSHIP

Reasons for Going Into Business*	Primary Reason	Secondary Reason
Immediate need for job:		
a. Lost job	16	
b. Fear of imminent loss of job	5	
To make a living through self-employment as alternative to working for others	32	2
To build up business for future:		
a. As replacement for current job	4	
b. As source of income and activity in retirement	1	
c. As business for children	2	
To supplement income:		
a. To supplement wages from another job	2	
b. To supplement pension or relief benefits	3	
To make "real" money	6	
To be independent	8	28
Others	2	

*Since the initial interview was conducted with only one owner in each business, the analysis of motivation factors is based on 81 cases. By contrast, data on the personal background were obtained for all 93 individual owners involved in the 81 firms.

Source: Kurt B. Mayer and Sidney Goldstein, The First Two Years: Problems of Small Firm Growth and Survival, Small Business Research Series, No. 2, U.S. Small Business Administration, Washington, 1961.

present, it was evident to the investigators that no real analysis of potential earnings from business ownership had even been attempted by most of the owners. Only 6 of the 81 business openings can be attributed primarily to a conscious desire to make a lot of money. Many of the respondents indicated that an income level comparable to what they could earn by working for someone else would be quite satisfactory. Most felt that the added benefits of being their own boss, assuring their own security, and obtaining higher prestige were important nonmonetary rewards which offset the money motive.

The picture uncovered in these cases deviates significantly from the image of the traditional business person. Many of the owners took the step of "going into business" with almost reckless abandon, little foresight or planning, and slim prospects for success. This approach is an almost certain invitation to failure.

WHICH FACTORS INFLUENCE THE CHOICE OF BUSINESS?

Closely related to the decision to enter business is the question of which business to enter. Many studies show that owners tend to buy businesses where they have had previous experience. The data from the Rhode Island study indicates that this is the single most important factor in determining the type of business established by the owner. The reasons given by the respondents in this study are listed below.

	Number of Cases
Experience or training	52
Liking of the line	8
Family business	5
Individual reasons	6
No particular reason	10

Table 3-9 shows the previous experience of the new business owners. Of the 52 cases listing "experience" (see table above), 23 were opened by owners who had previously owned and operated other businesses in the same line (see Table 3-9, the "same" and "same and different" columns). An additional 12 respondents had also owned businesses at some prior time, but in different lines. In all, 35 (20 + 12 + 3) of the 81 businesses were operated by owners who had been in business before. At one time or another, the 35 respondents had owned a total of 53 enterprises ([22 × 1] + [9 × 2] + [3 × 3] + [1 × 4]). This is by no means unusual.

Miscellaneous reasons given for the choice of business by the owners in this study included:

☐ Bought business because an apartment went with it.

☐ Business could be operated with no experience.

□ Business required minimum capital requirements.

□ Went into business purely for "kicks."

□ Wanted an investment for personal savings which would provide a working income.

Few of the owners approached business ownership as a result
of research and study of the business situation or an evaluation of
the problems which might result.

TABLE 3-9.   PREVIOUS BUSINESS EXPERIENCE OF CURRENT OWNERS

| Number of Previous Businesses | Type of Previous Business Compared to Present Business | | | |
	Same	Different	Same and Different	Total
Zero				46
One	12	10		22
Two	7	1	1	9
Three	1	1	1	3
Four			1	1
TOTAL	20	12	3	81

Source: Kurt B. Mayer and Sidney Goldstein, *The First Two Years: Problems of Small Firm Growth and Survival,* Small Business Research Series, No. 2, U.S. Small Business Administration, Washington, 1961.

WHAT FACTORS INFLUENCE BUSINESS OWNERS TO LOCATE WHERE THEY DO?

Many times new owners simply take over an existing business. In
the Rhode Island study 35 of the 81 new businesses involved changes
of ownership only. They were going concerns acquired by new
owners. The decision to take over an existing business is often influenced by chance factors since very few people decide beforehand to
look for a business which is for sale.

Sometimes a business location close to home is a deciding
factor. Although this method of selection seems irrational from an
economic standpoint, it often satisfies some personal need which is
considered more important than purely monetary rewards.

Strangely enough, competition in the area is seldom considered by a potential buyer although this factor carries considerable
weight in its effect on the long-range potential of the business. Such
factors as a "good street," low rent, easy accessibility, and the price
of the existing business for sale are often given more consideration.

In finding a location, the means used by the respondents in
this study to find specific locations were listed as:

Method	Number of Cases
Noticed vacancy	30
Told about it:	
By friend	12
By owner	7
By relative	1
By union	1
By customer	1
By oil company	3
Advertisement	9
Worked in same place	4
Family transfer	5
Own property	3
Other ways	5

On the whole, the data support what has already been pointed out about the businesses in this study. Factors of chance played an important role, with active, methodical planning being much less common. In finding a location, as in other factors, many of the owners took a passive rather than an active approach, stumbling more or less accidentally across a location, much as they drifted into the decision to go into business in the first place.

In summary, the data indicate that very little objective evaluation was given to important location factors. In fact, the figures shown probably overstate the actual attention paid to these factors; specific reference to these factors in the interviewer's questions probably evoked a positive response by some owners who had not actually considered these points.

HOW MUCH FINANCIAL PLANNING GOES INTO NEWLY FORMED SMALL BUSINESSES?

If the Rhode Island study is any criterion, not very much. The intense preoccupation with capitalization problems by writers and business experts has not benefited the type of business owners who were surveyed in this study. Literature which is designed to help prospective business owners estimate their capital requirements remains ineffective because most of the people with the type of educational and occupational background found in this study are unaware of its existence. Only 1 of the 93 in the sample had made use of this body of information, and he was a college-trained chemist. Even if the remaining owners had known about the availability of these aids and had tried to use them, the majority would have been completely baffled and frustrated. Most of the owners did not know enough about the type of business they had entered to enable them to make any reasonable estimates of their expectations.

In this study, the average capital investment amounted to just under $5,000. If this figure appears low, it should be recognized

TABLE 3-10. INITIAL CAPITAL INVESTMENT

Amount*	Number of Firms†	Percent
Under $500	8	10.0
$500 to $999	5	6.3
$1,000 to $1,999	17	21.3
$2,000 to $2,999	11	13.7
$3,000 to $4,999	14	17.5
$5,000 to $7,499	8	10.0
$7,500 to $9,999	6	7.5
$10,000 to $14,999	6	7.5
$15,000 to $24,999	3	3.7
$25,000 and over	2	2.5

*Average initial capital was $4,927.
†No information was available from 1 of the 81 firms.
Source: Kurt B. Mayer and Sidney Goldstein, *The First Two Years: Problems of Small Firm Growth and Survival,* Small Business Research Series, No. 2, U.S. Small Business Administration, Washington, 1961.

that the sample was intended to provide a cross section of newly established small business firms. None of the firms in the sample came even close to the $1 million in sales or receipts established by the Small Business Administration as the upper limits for a business to qualify as "small." More than half the concerns in the sample had an initial capital investment of less than $3,000. This heavy concentration at the bottom levels is by no means atypical of small businesses in the United States. Table 3-10 shows the amount and percent of capital reported by 80 of the 81 firms in the study. This table shows that more than one-third (30) of the firms had an initial capitalization of less than $2,000; one-half (39) had capital assets between $2,000 and $10,000. Only 14 percent (11 firms) exceeded $10,000. At the extremes of the range were $12 invested by an owner to take over a neighboring dry-cleaning outlet and $37,000 invested by an owner in a restaurant with a half-dozen employees.

The capital invested in gasoline service stations in the study ranged from $200 to $8,000. The wide range of investments in the same line of business represents the presence of two different types of owners. On the one hand, there are a small number of business people who realize that a business needs an adequate capital investment to begin operations. At the other extreme are those, with just a few dollars, who decide to go into business either as an alternate to unemployment or in a kind of reckless gambling spirit. These are people who, knowing nothing about business, open on a shoestring in the blind hope that they will be able somehow to make a go of it. They naïvely believe that enthusiasm and some good ideas will sustain them and substitute for hard cash.

The statistics published by Dun & Bradstreet for 1974 continue to reflect a high mortality rate among businesses which are less than 5 years old. In 1974, this group accounted for 60 percent of the failures. Among retail casualties, 66.2 percent of the failures were in the 5-years-and-under group. Nine out of ten failures were traceable to management failures or ineptitude. Roughly 30 percent lacked people with either prior management experience or any previous experience in the line of business.

Heavy operating expenses related to inflationary pressures and slow-moving inventories related to slack sales took their tolls of businesses which could not survive these stumbling blocks. Growth in receivables and slowdown in payments were special problems reflecting the condition of the economy.

In today's business environment we would be naïve to minimize the risks involved in starting a new business. Those who consider going into business without adequate experience or finances will likely join the 350,000 to 400,000 firms which are discontinued each year. The decision should be made only as a result of the most thorough evaluation of all factors which can affect the business and its operation. We have attempted to point out some of the pitfalls in this chapter.

SELF-CHECK OF KEY CONCEPTS
This exercise is designed to test your understanding of the material presented in Chapter 3. Choose the response, *True* or *False*, which best fits each statement. Correct responses are presented in the back of the text.

1. A substantial edge can be attained by competitors if they have a more desirable location.
2. If you do not have the technical knowledge required to run your business, you should seek a "second in command" who does.
3. Knowing how to sell is the most important skill needed for operating a successful business.
4. Working for someone else is sometimes a desirable alternative to ownership.
5. You can sometimes save money by shopping around for financial assistance.
6. Costs for going into business vary widely, even in the same line.

7. Financing of most new businesses is accomplished by borrowing from commercial banks.
8. Accounts receivable are considered a tangible business asset.
9. The value of the goodwill associated with a business is usually greater if the business is well established in the community.
10. It is a common practice for buyers to assume the liabilities of the businesses they buy.

1. After several months of searching, you have found a 24-hour liquor store for sale which is about the size you feel you can afford. It is located in a well-lighted shopping center which opened 3 years ago. Several people you know patronize the store and are regular patrons. The owner is asking $35,000 for it. He had owned it since its opening. It has been in operation since the shopping center opened. Your discussions with him have revealed the following information:

PERFORMANCE PROBLEMS AND PROJECTS

Appraised value of assets	$35,000
Outstanding liabilities	13,500
Average annual net profit (3-year average)	13,500

The owner's records show that the weekly net income for the past 6 months has been:

January	$1,950	April	$2,233
February	1,887	May	2,485
March	2,160	June	2,450

6-month average = $2,194 per week

Using the formula shown in Table 3-4, calculate the fair price of this establishment. For purposes of calculating the price, assume that corporate bonds are yielding 8 percent and that your present salary is $8,000 per year.

2. You decide to discuss the opportunity to purchase the liquor store with a friend of yours who is a business broker. He has been in business in this area for several years. He uses a formula which calculates a fair price based on the weekly net income of the business. The formula uses $1,200 for every $100 of weekly net income up to $1,000 per week; $1,500 for every $100 of weekly net income between $1,000 and $2,000 per week; and $1,700 for every $100 of weekly net income over $2,000 per week. Calculate the fair price using your friend's formula and compare it with the answer developed in Problem 1 above. How do these values compare with the asking price?

   a. Which method do you feel gave you the best answer?
   b. Based on the calculations in these approaches, do you feel that the asking price is fair?
   c. What factors will you need to give more thought to before making your final decision?

THE DREAM WITH THE UNHAPPY ENDING

Bill and Betty Odum had dreamed of owning a grocery store as long as they could remember. Now in their mid-thirties, they had saved about $8,000 over a period of 12 years and were anxious to have a business of their own. Bill had worked his way up through every job in the local "supermarket" and was confident that he knew enough about grocery stores to handle the operation of one. Betty had taken three night courses at the local community college in bookkeeping and business practices and planned to take care of the records of the business.

The Odums had been actively looking for a good business opportunity for the past year and had followed up many leads from the classified section of the local newspaper. In every case, they found the business too run down to salvage or too large to finance. They had also talked to a few real estate agents who specialized in business properties, but they had not been able to find anything that interested them.

One day a food sales representative dropped in. During the conversation he told the Odums, "I was just talking to Paul Smothers, who owns a small store on the other side of town. He told me that he was considering selling his store. It might be something you would want to consider."

After talking to the sales representative, the Odums called Paul to inquire about the details. They found out that the store had been established by Paul's father and had been in the same location 32 years. At first Paul was reluctant to sell it, but the long hours he was spending were beginning to become a real hardship. Besides, he added, he had been offered a paint-store franchise which would be less demanding, and he had decided to give the new business a try.

The Odums and Paul had several meetings to discuss the proposed sale. Paul's asking price was $25,000 cash and $300 a month rent for the 4,000-square-foot building in which the store was located. When asked about his sales, he stated that during the last 4 years business had declined from a high of $200,000 gross sales to around $100,000. The main reason for the decline in sales, in Paul's opinion, was the competition from several new supermarkets in his area.

"We would need to examine your books for the past couple of years before we make a decision," Betty said.

"I can't let you do that," Paul replied. "Most of my personal affairs are revealed in those books. Besides, I don't want to be giving away everything about my business to someone who might be a competitor someday."

"But we have to have something to go on," Bill protested.

"I'll answer any questions you have, so just fire away," Paul suggested.

The Odums found out that the fixtures and equipment had cost $30,000 new. Now 6 years old, they had a depreciated value of $15,000. The inventory had a wholesale cost of $10,000. Gross sales were running about $8,000 a month with gross margin between 14 and 16 percent. The store had achieved annual sales of $200,000 in

6 of the past 10 years. The layout was efficient and the store was clean and well-organized.

From their observations and their conversations with Paul, the Odums figured they could increase their sales to $20,000 a month within a year by more aggressive sales promotion—handbills, radio spot announcements, a new neon sign, and more personal service. This meant, in their opinion, that inventory would need to be enlarged to $12,000. To better the profit, which had been averaging 2.5 percent of gross sales, they believed the average markup should be raised from 18 to 20 percent. An additional increase in profit could be realized, according to their analysis, if they reduced the staff by one full-time and one part-time clerk.

In trying to arrange their financing, the Odums were unable to borrow the difference between their $8,000 savings and Paul's $25,000 asking price. Several banks turned them down before one agreed to loan them $10,000 at 8 percent interest with monthly payments spread over 5 years. They made an offer of $18,000 to Paul for the store, which Paul turned down. After some discussion Paul reduced the price to $23,000 and decided to carry an unsecured note for $11,000, payable monthly over 5 years at 8 percent interest. The balance was to be in cash. He also agreed to reduce the rent to $200 per month.

The Odums planned to use the $6,000 cash left from the bank loan to increase inventory and provide working capital.

The store changed hands 30 days after the agreement was reached. Bill and Betty discovered that the inventory was worth only $8,000 at wholesale cost. They immediately used $4,000 to increase their shelf stock. Sales during the first few months increased to $15,000 a month, and they felt sure they could reach their goal of $20,000 a month. Profit, however, was running only 2 percent of gross sales in spite of their attempt to increase their margins and reduce costs.

Six months later, the doors were closed on the Odums' store. The remaining inventory worth $6,000 was sold to a wholesale outlet for $5,400. The fixtures were sold for $8,200. Bill and Betty were trying to find a way to pay their debts and forget the loss of their life's savings.

1. What decisions do you believe contributed to the problems which spelled failure for the Odums?
2. What things did they overlook which contributed to their failure?
3. What signs were available which should have prompted them to proceed with caution?
4. Do you think their sales goals were realistic?
5. If they had reached their $20,000 per month goal, would they have been able to meet their payments to the bank and to Paul, assuming a profit of 2 percent of the gross sales?

CHAPTER

Deciding on a Form of Organization

PERFORMANCE OBJECTIVES

After reading this chapter, you should be able to describe the major legal forms of organization used by businesses in the United States and explain the advantages and disadvantages of each. Specifically, you should be able to:

1. Formulate some assumptions to explain why so many businesses are operated as sole proprietorships.
2. Explain the method of calculating income tax on net earnings from a sole proprietorship, a partnership, or a corporation.
3. Assess the risks involved in the proprietorship, partnership, and corporate forms of organization.
4. Judge the difficulty of acquiring capital in each of the forms in the previous question.
5. Draw some conclusions about the relatively low percentage of partnerships operating in the United States compared with other legal forms of organization.
6. Estimate the relative ease of forming a proprietorship compared with forming a corporation.
7. Describe the advantages of the Subchapter "S" corporation compared with the regular corporation.
8. Demonstrate what is meant by the "double taxation" feature of the corporation.

9. Illustrate some of the administrative problems encountered by the sole proprietor which are not characteristic of the corporation.
10. Defend the position taken by lenders who allow more lenience in making loans to partnerships than they do to proprietorships.

INTRODUCTION

Once you have decided to start a new business, your next consideration should be to determine what legal form of organization to choose. There are both legal and tax questions that will need to be analyzed before you make your decision. The advantages and disadvantages of the various legal forms of organization are not well understood by most business people. For this reason, you should get a good lawyer to help explain how each works. As your business grows and prospers, it will sometimes be to your advantage to change the legal form of your organization in order to take the fullest advantage of tax "breaks" that result.

Other factors which will enter into the decision to choose one form over another are: the risk or liability involved in meeting the obligations of the business; the ease or difficulty of obtaining additional capital after you start operations; whether you need technical assistance; and whether you want the business to continue if you should become unable to operate it.

A comparison of the principal types of business organization will enable prospective owner-managers to determine whether the sole proprietorship, the partnership, or the corporation best suits their needs and long-range objectives.

HOW MANY DIFFERENT LEGAL BUSINESS ORGANIZATIONS ARE THERE?

At least a dozen, including the sole proprietorship, the general partnership, limited partnership, corporation, pools, joint-stock companies, syndicates, investment trusts, joint ventures, and partnership associations. Some of these are specialized and are comparatively rare; therefore, our discussion will focus on the major types.

WHICH LEGAL FORM IS MOST COMMON?

In 1971, approximately 77 percent of American businesses were operating as proprietorships, 16 percent as corporations, and only 7 percent as partnerships. Despite the relatively small number of corporations, these enterprises claimed 72 percent of the receipts in 1971, with proprietorships claiming 22 percent and partnerships only 6 percent.

WHAT IS A GOOD DEFINITION OF THE THREE MAJOR LEGAL FORMS OF ORGANIZATION?

In a nutshell, here is a concise definition of each. The first two definitions are adapted from the 1975 edition of the *Tax Guide for Small Business*, published by the Internal Revenue Service.

Proprietorship.   This is a business run by one individual for his or her own benefit. It is the simplest form of business organization. Proprietorships have no existence apart from the owners. The businesses' liabilities are the personal liabilities of the proprietors and the businesses terminate upon their death. The proprietors undertake the risks of their businesses to the extent of their assets, whether used in the businesses or personally owned.

Partnership.   A partnership is the relationship existing between two or more persons who join together to carry on a trade or business, with each person contributing money, property, labor, or skill, and each expecting to share in the profits and losses of the business. If these conditions exist, a partnership exists, whether or not the members enter into a formal partnership agreement.

Corporation.   A corporation is a formal structure, operating under state law, whose scope of activity and name is restricted by its charter. Its business profits are taxed separately from the earnings of its owners. The corporation, not the owners and managers, is liable for its debts and taxes. It can sue and be sued, hold and sell property, and engage in those business operations stipulated in its charter. The corporation is a legal entity whose continuity is unaffected by death of the owners or transfer of stock shares by the owners.

HOW CAN YOU DETERMINE WHICH LEGAL FORM IS BEST FOR YOUR BUSINESS?

The decision depends on the type and size of your business, its earnings, the background of the owner, and other related factors.

If you have no capital problems, want to get into a business with a minimum of fuss and delay, and do not want to be encumbered with partners or governmental red tape, the sole proprietorship will be attractive. This form predominates in businesses operated in the United States. The success and continuity of the sole proprietorship is entirely dependent upon the skills, ability, and health of the owner. In this type of business, you are truly your own boss, making all decisions, keeping all profits, and assuming responsibility for all losses and debts.

If you need technical know-how or financial backing from others and do not mind an occasional disagreement with partners about running the business or what to do with the profits, you might find the partnership to your liking. It can be formed with a verbal agreement and a "handshake," although a written partnership agreement which spells out all the details is preferred. Such an agreement form can be obtained at any good stationer's. Start-up costs are low and the advantages of the broad management base the partnership provides make it attractive. It can offer tax advantages to sole proprietors whose incomes put them in high tax brackets. Finding suitable partners, however, can often be a headache, as can the division of authority between partners. As in the sole proprietor- ship, all partners are totally responsible for the debts and obligations of the business and each is legally responsible for the business ac- tions of all the other partners. When a partner dies or terminates association with the business, the partnership is dissolved unless a provision has been made in the agreement for the remaining part- ners to buy up his or her interest in the business.

Corporations offer the advantages of specialized management, limited liability, easy transfer of ownership, possible tax advantages, and perpetual life. In the eyes of the law, the corporation is a "per- son" and, as such, assumes responsibility for the debts and obliga- tions of the business. Its officers, directors, and owners (stockhold- ers) are responsible only to the extent of the value of the stock they hold. Their personal assets may not be seized by creditors to satisfy debts. Some of the unattractive features of the corporate form are related to the records and reports required, close government regu- lation, the expense of forming it, and its "double taxation" feature, which taxes corporate earnings separately from the dividends paid to stockholders. Its charter restricts it to operate in the state where it was issued. Operating in other states requires their permission and the retention of legal representation in each state to handle any legal problems which might arise.

WHICH FORM IS EASIEST TO GET STARTED?

The proprietorship is the easiest. The cost is quite low. Basically all you have to do is find out whether you need a license to carry on your business and whether you have to pay a state tax or license fee.

Partnerships are also started without difficulty. You can set one up by having the partners sign what is called a partnership agreement. A written document, however, is not necessarily a pre- requisite since an oral agreement is equally effective. The intent is what is important and the participation of those involved may be implied by their actions, even though no agreement, either oral or written, exists.

Limited partnerships are somewhat more difficult to set up. To form one, you file with the proper state official a written contract drawn according to legal requirements. This contract permits you to limit the liability of one or more partners to just the amount which they have invested. All limited partners must have actually invested in the partnership. These investments can be either cash or tangible property, but not services. Limited partners do not participate in the operation of the business or in establishing policies by which it operates.

Corporations are more complicated to form than any of the other types of organization. In creating one, you must strictly follow the legal procedures of the state in which the corporation is being established. The people who organize the corporation must file with the designated state official a special document called "articles of incorporation." They then must pay an initial tax and certain filing fees. Finally, various official meetings must be conducted to draft bylaws, deal with specific details of organization, and establish operating policies.

HOW BIG IS THE RISK FOR THE DEBTS OF A BUSINESS?

Regardless of legal structure, creditors are always entitled to be paid out of business assets. In cases where those assets are insufficient, the extent to which owners can be compelled to meet creditors' claims out of their own pockets varies with the type of organization.

Single proprietors are personally liable for all the debts of their businesses to the extent of their entire property. They cannot restrict their liability in any way. All members of a general partnership are fully responsible for all debts owed by their partnership without regard to the amount of their own investments in the business. In a limited partnership, the limited partners are protected; they risk only the loss of capital they have invested. But the general partners in a limited partnership are liable for all debts.

Corporations have an advantage over other legal structures where risk is concerned. Creditors can force payment on their claims only to the limit of the company's assets. Stockholders might lose all the money they have put into the company, but they cannot be forced to contribute additional funds out of their own pockets to meet business debts. This is true even if corporate assets are insufficient to meet creditors' claims.

WHAT FACTORS DETERMINE THE PERMANENCE OF A BUSINESS?

The continuity of proprietorships is dependent upon the health of the owners. Although proprietorships have no time limit on them established by law, they are not perpetual. Illness of the owners can seriously affect the operation of the businesses, and their death terminates the proprietorships.

Partnerships are terminated by death, incapacity, or withdrawal of a partner (except for a limited partner). Such an event necessitates liquidation or dissolution of the partnership and reorganization.

Corporations have the most permanent legal structure of all. They have a separate continuous life of their own. Their life is unaffected by the withdrawal, insolvency, injury, illness, or death of their owners, officers, or directors. Certificates of stock may be transferred freely from one owner to another with no effect on the concern's operations. This perpetual feature of the corporation is forcefully illustrated by one writer[1] who pointed out that "If all the stockholders of a given corporation died on the same day, the business would go on as a legal entity. Shares would pass to the heirs of the original owners of the stock and they would inherit a going concern."

WHAT ADMINISTRATIVE PROBLEMS ARE INHERENT IN EACH FORM OF BUSINESS ORGANIZATION?

The concentration of management in one individual in the sole proprietorship provides a flexibility for change and an ease of operation not found in the other types. It avoids the problems of divided responsibilities and the delays caused by opposing factions. The quality of decisions in this organization is dependent upon the capabilities of the owner. Needless to say, poor decisions can be disastrous.

In general partnerships, the partners typically have equal roles in administration, with the various operating functions divided among them. The combined talents of the partnership give it a distinct advantage over the proprietorship. But the division of responsibilities sometimes leads to policy disagreements. On the other hand, decisions can be made and changes adopted simply by oral agreement among the partners.

In corporations, the stockholders do not participate directly in either operations or policy formulation. Often these functions are centralized in a relatively small group of executives who own only a small percentage of the shares. If those in control have little or no direct financial interest in the business, there might be some risk of inefficient management.

HOW DO THE VARIOUS LAWS INFLUENCE THE OPERATION OF ORGANIZATIONS?

The laws regulating the legal rights and obligations of sole proprietors are clear in regard to their relationships with creditors and others with whom they deal in business. A private citizen carrying on a business in California can carry on business in Arizona without paying any greater taxes or incurring any more obligations in Arizona than local Arizona business people. The same is generally true of a partnership. Of course, a state might require the purchase of a license to carry on a particular kind of business. But the license will be equally available to business people of any state so long as they conform to prescribed uniform standards. The United States Constitution guarantees to citizens of each state "all the privileges and immunities" provided to citizens of the other states. Thus, the legal

[1]Dan Steinhoff, *Small Business Management Fundamentals*, McGraw-Hill Book Company, New York, 1974, p. 122.

structures of the proprietorship and partnership provide a freedom of action in all states. This is not true of the corporation.

Corporations owe their legal existence to the state in which they are organized. No other state is required to recognize them. In practice, other states allow out-of-state corporations to function inside their boundaries. This is permitted only if the corporation complies with special in-state obligations such as filing legal papers with the proper state officials, payment of specified fees and taxes, and appointment of a representative in the state to act as agent in its behalf. In order to comply with the laws of the various states, competent legal counsel is virtually indispensable. The unique feature of limited liability is preserved in every state.

HOW EASY IS IT TO BORROW MONEY TO FINANCE THE DIFFERENT LEGAL FORMS OF BUSINESS?

In proprietorships, owners may raise additional money by borrowing, purchasing on credit, or supplying additional amounts themselves. Their ability to borrow is influenced by their personal wealth. Since the owners are responsible personally for all the debts of their businesses, banks will consider their risk in terms of those owners' ability to stand unanticipated reversals and losses. For this reason, the funds they can obtain will always be limited by their own circumstances. This is not a major problem for small businesses; however, a business requiring large amounts of capital for successful operation should probably not organize as a sole proprietorship.

Partnerships can often raise funds with greater ease, since the financial resources of all the partners are behind the business. Since the combined personal wealth of the partners stands behind the business, and since they are personally liable for all the debts of the business, the risk to a lender in case of trouble is less than it would be with a sole proprietor. For this reason, a partnership can usually borrow more easily than a proprietorship and can often borrow on better terms than some corporations.

Corporations usually have the least difficulty in attracting capital. They can borrow money by pledging corporate assets or by selling securities to the public. Most stockholders will not invest more than they can afford to lose, and since this is the limit of their liability, they are willing to invest funds since they have the prospect of sharing in the profits of the business. Thousands of stockholders become part owners in corporations each year by loaning their money on the basis of this calculated risk.

WHAT TAX ADVANTAGES ARE ASSOCIATED WITH EACH FORM OF LEGAL ORGANIZATION?

Sometimes a tax advantage can be gained by changing to a different legal form of organization. Sole proprietors pay income taxes on the profits of their businesses in accordance with a progressive tax table provided by the Internal Revenue Service. As their net taxable incomes become larger, so do their taxes. The rates vary for the individual owner from around 15 percent for $1,000 of net taxable income to around 55 percent for $100,000 of income. The taxes payable by a married taxpayer filing an individual return on 1974 income are shown in Table 4-1.

TABLE 4-1.   NET TAXABLE INCOME LEVELS AND FEDERAL TAX
PAYABLE FOR 1974 FEDERAL INCOME TAX

Net Taxable Income (1974)	Tax Payable by Sole Proprietor Filing an Individual Tax Return
$ 1,000	$ 145
2,000	310
4,000	690
6,000	1,130
8,000	1,630
10,000	2,190
12,000	2,830
14,000	3,550
16,000	4,330
18,000	5,170
20,000	6,070
22,000	7,030
26,000	9,030
32,000	12,210
38,000	15,510
44,000	18,990
50,000	22,590
60,000	28,790
70,000	35,190
80,000	41,790
90,000	48,590
100,000	55,490

Source: Department of the Treasury, Internal Revenue Service, "1974 Federal Income Tax Forms," Schedule Y.

Corporations pay 22 percent on the first $25,000 of net taxable income and 48 percent on any income over $25,000. Small firms that operate as corporations can charge reasonable salaries to the businesses and these become the operating expenses of the firms. They may be deducted from gross income before arriving at net taxable income. It is then the remaining income which is taxed at 22 percent and 48 percent. The principals then file separate income tax returns and pay individual rates on the salaries they have drawn and charged to the corporation. Stockholders pay an individual income tax on any dividends paid on the stock they own.

Owners of small businesses which qualify as corporations can legally qualify members of their families (wives, sons, or daughters) as salaried employees and claim their salaries as business expenses, provided that they render services to the company. This expense is not allowable as a deduction in either the proprietorship or the partnership.

A comparison of the taxes paid by the three forms of organization on the same income is shown in Table 4-2. Our example assumes that all corporate income is shared equally by five principal stockholders, all of whom are married and filing separate returns. The chief officer draws a salary of $15,000 annually, which is deducted as an operating expense before calculating corporate taxes.

TABLE 4-2. SAMPLES OF FEDERAL INCOME TAXES PAID BY VARIOUS
LEGAL ENTITIES ON 1974 INCOME

Net Income	Single Proprietor Filing Individual Income Tax Return	Partnership (Two Partners) Sharing Profits Equally	Corporation—Assumes Income Is Shared Equally by Five Stockholders and That a $15,000 Director's Salary Is Paid		
			Corporation Tax	Individual Tax	Total Tax
$16,000	$ 4,330	$ 3,260	$ 220	$ 2,690	$ 2,910
20,000	6,070	4,380	1,100	3,450	4,550
32,000	12,210	8,660	1,540	6,150	7,690
50,000	22,590	17,060	10,300	10,950	21,250

Note: In the corporate example, the director's salary is first deducted from net income to arrive at taxable income for the corporation tax. Individual taxes, however, must be paid on the entire amount of net income since this amount was actually paid to principals.

WHAT IS A SUBCHAPTER "S" CORPORATION?

It is a special kind of small corporation which was created in 1958 by Subchapter "S" of the Internal Revenue Code to give small firms the advantages of the corporate form and at the same time provide a tax advantage not enjoyed by other corporations.

It is sometimes called a "tax option" corporation or a small business corporation because of the restriction on its size imposed by the Code. This provision allows closely held corporations with no more than ten stockholders, all United States citizens or resident aliens, to elect to be taxed as a Subchapter "S" corporation if all members agree to the election. No more than 20 percent of the corporate income may be derived from investments, and at least 20 percent of the corporate income must come from operations in the United States. Additionally, the corporation can have only one class of stock to qualify.

TABLE 4-3.   A COMPARISON OF THE MAJOR LEGAL FORMS OF ORGANIZATION

Factor	Sole Proprietorship	Partnership	Corporation
Start-Up Costs	Low. Only a license to operate is generally required.	Low. Partnership agreement and license to operate required.	Extensive. Incorporation fees, legal fees, and record retention requirements are extensive.
Liability for Debts	Unlimited. Owners and/or partners are personally responsible for all debts and obligations of the business. All personal assets are subject to claim by creditors of the business.		Limited to the value of the stock held by the owners (stockholders).
Distribution of Profits	All profits go to owner and are not shared.	Profits distributed to partners in accordance with a sharing ratio.	Profits may be retained or distributed at the discretion of the board of directors.
Tax Features	Owner reports all profits on individual income tax return and pays tax according to IRS schedules. Business losses are deductible.	Earnings are split between the partners and reported as business income by each individually.	Profit is taxed at the corporate level and again when dividends are distributed to individual stockholders.
Continuity of Business	Business ceases to exist when owner dies.	Business is usually discontinued if a partner dies or wants to get out of the business. This can be disruptive where several partners are involved.	Business is perpetual, with ownership passed from person to person through exchange of stock certificates.
Regulation From Outside Agencies	Greatest freedom from regulation.	Limited outside regulation.	Closely regulated. Charter is required and is recognized only in the state where issued. State and federal reports are numerous.
Capital Acquisition	Dependent on owner's personal wealth. Borrowing sometimes difficult because of unlimited liability and limited personal assets.	Pooling of income by partners makes borrowing less of a problem than in the proprietorship.	Relatively easy through sale of stocks, exchange of assets, etc. Borrowing of small corporations is made more difficult by limited liability of the corporation.
Authority to Operate	All decisions made by owner who is totally responsible for the operation of the business.	Danger of disagreement and willful abuse of authority can cause some problems. All partners legally bound by the actions of the others.	Vested in the board of directors who, in turn, acquire officers to operate the business. Management is concentrated although ownership is widespread.

If these stipulations are met, the corporate tax is waived and all income is taxed as partnership income to the individual stockholders. The corporate income is divided among the shareholders on the basis of a sharing ratio or other agreement and is then included in their individual income tax returns.

Although the requirements imposed by Subchapter "S" limit the flexibility of the corporate organization somewhat, the tax advantage makes it a very attractive variation of the corporate form.

WHAT CONCLUSIONS CAN BE DRAWN CONCERNING THE BEST LEGAL FORM OF ORGANIZATION?

Which is "best" will depend upon the circumstances in your particular case. Major points of comparison are start-up costs, liability for debts, distribution of profits, tax features, the continuity of the business, regulation from outside agencies, capital acquisition, and authority to operate. The three major legal forms of organization are compared using these factors in Table 4-3.

SELF-CHECK OF KEY CONCEPTS

This exercise is designed to test your understanding of the material presented in Chapter 4. Choose the response, *True* or *False*, which best fits each statement. Correct responses are presented in the back of the text.

1. Approximately 99 percent of all United States businesses can be classified either as proprietorships, partnerships, or corporations.
2. Percentagewise, the receipts of corporations closely match the percentage of such establishments in operation.
3. Corporations are more numerous in manufacturing than in retailing and service trades.
4. It is not necessary to have a written agreement for a partnership to be considered a legal entity.
5. In a partnership, each partner is equally responsible for a bad decision made by any one of the partners.
6. If a corporation goes bankrupt, the personal assets of the stockholders can be seized to pay its debts.
7. A corporation's charter enables it to operate in any or all of the states of the United States without restrictions.
8. The liability of limited partners is limited to their investment in the business so long as they refrain from becoming actively involved in the operation of the business.

9. If 50 percent of the stockholders in a corporation sell their stock, the corporation must be dissolved and reorganized.
10. Corporations usually have the least difficulty in raising capital.

1. Find a partnership agreement form at your local stationer's and assume that you and a friend have agreed to form a partnership to operate a 24-hour coin-operated laundry to be known as the A-1 Coin Laundry Service. Each of you will contribute $15,000 initially to purchase the business from its present owner. Fill in the rest of the form and discuss it with your classmates, asking for their suggestions regarding the completed instrument.

2. Obtain a current copy of the *Tax Guide for Small Business* from your Internal Revenue Office and carefully read the sections "Forms of Business Organization" and "Reporting Your Business Profits (Losses)." Find answers to the following questions:

   a. In the absence of a written partnership agreement, what method is used by the Internal Revenue Service to determine whether a partnership exists?
   b. What is required for a family member to be recognized as a business partner by the Internal Revenue Service?
   c. In the eyes of the IRS, what constitutes a business?
   d. What limitations exist for charitable contributions made by corporations, and how does one determine whether they are deductible for income tax purposes?
   e. What events can cause a Subchapter "S" corporation to lose its status and have its election terminated?

3. A business had a taxable net income of $70,000 in 1974. Using the data in Table 4-1, find the income tax which was due from a sole proprietor on these earnings. Then assume the business was owned by two partners whose agreement allowed them to share the income so that one got $32,000 and the other $38,000. Assuming that both had no other income and that each filed an individual tax return, how much tax did they pay on the income from the partnership? How much more of the $70,000 did the partnership retain after taxes than did the proprietorship?

HOW A REORGANIZATION SAVED THE TRAPANIS MONEY

In 1955, Sam and Martha Trapani started a small neighborhood grocery in a predominately Italian section of town, using their lifetime savings and a bank loan to get started. By 1975, their son and daughter were grown and both worked full time in the business along with them. Thanks to the promotional ideas of their son and their son-in-law, the small business was remodeled into a modern supermarket which still retained the personal family touch and friendly service. A separate coin-operated laundry was added and a large parking area surfaced. An advertising budget was established and weekly "specials" made their Foodmart one of the busiest places in town. Today the Foodmart employs 15 people and grosses around $450,000 per year.

Until lately the Trapanis had not thought much about the legal structure of their store. Their hard work had paid off and the volume of business made it necessary to have an accountant prepare their yearly income tax return. Last year they had their biggest year, making a gross profit of $32,000. After deducting $4,000 in business expenses, they reported $28,000 in taxable income and paid $10,090 in taxes.

The accountant suggested to Sam and Martha that they could reduce their tax by considering a different form of organization.

"With both of you, and your son and daughter all working full time in the business, you should consider changing to a corporation or a partnership. Both these legal forms of organization could save you a significant amount of tax," the accountant explained. "For instance, if your firm had been a corporation last year and Sam had taken a salary of $15,000, your tax bill would have been $6,050 instead of $10,090. That's a big enough saving to make a change worthwhile," he added.

"I don't understand how I could call my salary a business expense. I can't do that now," Sam replied.

"A sole proprietor has to pay taxes on his entire business profits," the accountant said, "but salaries are deductible in the corporate organization. There would be no objection from the Internal Revenue Service to a $15,000 salary for the president of a business the size of yours. Plenty of executives in similar situations are paid as much or more for the services they actually perform."

"That doesn't sound bad," Sam replied. "Even a partnership arrangement could enable Martha and me to start thinking of retiring and turning the business over to the kids. Why don't you look into the possibilities and let me know what you recommend."

1. In view of Sam's planned retirement, what suggestions could the accountant make to assure family control of the business?
2. How could the Trapanis save money on taxes by electing to organize as a Subchapter "S" corporation?
3. Can you think of any advantages which would result from reorganizing as a partnership?

CHAPTER

Financing the Small Business

PERFORMANCE OBJECTIVES

After reading this chapter, you should gain a better understanding of the role played by money and credit in the successful operation of a small business. You will be able to differentiate between those activities related to acquiring capital and those involved in allocating it where it will earn the greatest profit. Specifically, you should be able to:

1. Classify the various sources of capital available to a small business and predict the cost of borrowing money by the various means which are available.
2. Weigh the possible advantages of borrowing capital against the disadvantages.
3. Explain some of the factors a lender looks at in evaluating a borrower.
4. Explain what is meant by a *covenant* in a loan agreement.
5. Design a simple worksheet to be used in estimating the initial capital required to establish a bookstore.
6. Predict the consequences of starting a new business with insufficient capital.
7. Describe several methods of conserving cash in the operation of a business.
8. Analyze the operating ratios for a family of retail businesses and demonstrate how they can be used to estimate start-up costs for a new business.

9. Defend the time and effort required to evaluate and plan for the financial resources of a new business before starting it.
10. Explain why it is desirable for the owner's equity in a business to be as great as possible.
11. Assess the impact of excessive fixed assets on the ability of a business to operate efficiently.
12. Describe the financial manager's total job in terms of the specific activities involved.
13. Predict some of the results of excessive inventories in the operation of a business.
14. Explain why some business people are reluctant to use equity capital or venture capital in financing their businesses.

INTRODUCTION

One of the most common causes of failure among small firms is a lack of planning for the financial needs of the business. No new firm should be launched until the problems of providing adequate capital have been thoroughly examined and all the capital needs have been covered in the financial planning. One can find an occasional successful business that was grossly underfinanced when it started and somehow managed to survive and grow despite its "shoestring" start. But such cases are not common.

It is vitally important that business people carefully estimate not only the funds necessary to initiate the business, but also the funds which will be required to operate the going concern through its initial growth period. They must know when to extend credit, when to buy, what inventory levels to maintain, when to consider adding fixed assets, and when the money will be available to pay their bills. They must know not only where to get the money they need, but also how to use it wisely.

This chapter comments upon business people's role as financial managers, describes the kinds of funds they need, and lists the common sources of funds. It provides the reader with a tool for estimating initial capital requirements for a business, offers some suggestions for conserving cash, and emphasizes the importance of credit and borrowing in financing a business.

WHAT KINDS OF CAPITAL ARE NEEDED BY A SMALL BUSINESS?

There are basically two kinds of capital needed in the average business—*working capital* and *fixed capital.*

Some of the money, once acquired, is used to pay bills, buy inventory, finance credit sales, and take care of unexpected emergencies. Because of the uneven flow into and out of the business, such money circulates—that is, it is used to purchase goods which are then sold, returning revenues to the business, whereupon the cycle repeats. Due to the temporary nature of such funds, they are referred to as circulating capital or working capital.

Fixed capital is needed for buying the permanent assets of the business—those things which are not for sale. They include land and buildings occupied by the business, plus the tools, equipment, and facilities that are used in its operation. Money spent for such items is frozen in a sense because it cannot be used for anything else. The only way to make it available for other uses is to sell or *liquidate*

the asset. Most businesses plan carefully to ensure that the investment in fixed assets does not require so much capital that sufficient
working capital is not available.

You should keep working capital and fixed capital separate in
your planning. Although they are interdependent, their sources and
their effects on the long-range growth of the business are different.
Many companies maintain separate accounts for them. Some even
use different colored checks to highlight their separate nature.

Table 5-1 shows the relationship of working capital to fixed
capital and some of the common sources of each.

TABLE 5-1. FUNDS NEEDED BY A SMALL BUSINESS

	Working Capital	Fixed Capital
Kind and nature	Need is generated by the uneven flow of cash into and out of the business because of seasonal fluctuations and similar factors. Usually needed for less than 6 months.	Generated by the need for expansion, modernization, and purchase of fixed assets. Large sums are usually involved and financed for several years. Sources are often hard to find.
Required for	1. Financing credit sales 2. Buying inventory 3. Paying bills 4. Paying wages 5. Unexpected emergencies	1. Buying tools and equipment 2. Replacement of worn out facilities 3. Buying or expanding plant or store 4. Buying land 5. Starting another business
Sources of funds: Personal	1. Borrowing on life insurance 2. Loans from friends and relatives 3. Liquidating marketable investments	1. Mortgage loans on real property 2. Surrender of life insurance policies 3. Liquidation of personal assets
Loans	1. Short-term business loans 2. Lines of credit 3. Inventory loans 4. Accounts-receivable loans	1. Small Business Administration 2. Small business investment corporations 3. Regional business development companies 4. Institutional investors
Other	1. Revenue from current operations 2. Trade credit 3. Notes receivable	1. Venture capitalists 2. Retained earnings 3. Installment financing 4. Finding a partner 5. Sale of stock 6. Vendor loans 7. Sale-and-leaseback 8. Liquidation of business assets

Equity capital is the personal investment in the business of the owner or owners. Equity also includes the subsequent earnings which are retained in the business. Equity capital is sometimes called *risk capital* because those who furnish the capital are expected to take the primary risks of failure as well as reap the benefits of success. Equity capital provides a margin of safety for a lender. The greater the amount of equity capital, other things being equal, the easier it is to borrow. The primary source of equity capital is the personal savings of the owner of the business. Going concerns often add to their equity capital by taking in partners who supply additional money and become part owners of the business. This sharing of control with others is sometimes avoided by the sole proprietor who fears a loss of freedom of action from sharing ownership with others. Equity capital does not have to be repaid; therefore, it does not burden the business with fixed interest or repayment obligations.

Debt capital is money which you have borrowed and must repay. Few buyers have enough personal savings to finance the purchase of a small business without some debt financing. Owners may borrow money for the purchase of business by obtaining personal loans, borrowing against their insurance policies, or refinancing the mortgages on their homes. Banks are the principal sources of debt capital for small businesses.

If your company is pioneering in a new field, one of the estimated 600 organizations known as venture-capital companies might be a source of capital. These companies invest in relatively undeveloped industries that show good growth prospects. Their interests include new services, processes, and products in almost every commercial, industrial, and scientific industry.

Venture-capital companies finance their projects in a number of ways. The most common is a straight exchange of stock for the funds. In most cases, these companies demand voting stock for the risks they take. They become stockholders in your company. Whether or not the company buys a controlling interest, it prefers that the manager of the small company continue to run the business. Confidence in the manager is one of the criteria for investment. The investing company usually acts as adviser, providing support in such areas as financial management, administration, and marketing.

The venture company usually agrees to invest a certain maximum amount of capital.

WHAT IS MEANT BY THE STATEMENT "IT TAKES MONEY TO MAKE MONEY"?

This maxim is a simple way of saying that a business must have financial resources if it is to operate at a profit. If you are in wholesaling or retailing, you must keep a stock of goods on hand to be sold. You need to extend credit to your customers. A bank balance must be maintained to cover expenses such as payrolls and payments to suppliers. Funds are required to buy the land and buildings from which you operate. If you are a manufacturer, funds are also needed for equipment and machinery, for raw materials and supplies, for stock used in the manufacturing process, and for finished goods ready for sale. Financial resources are the basic ingredients which make possible the day-to-day operations of the thousands of businesses which supply our needs. It is handicapping yourself dangerously to start a business with less capital than your analysis shows you will need.

HOW GREAT IS THE RELATIONSHIP BETWEEN MONEY AND BUSINESS SUCCESS?

Business failure statistics for 1974 indicate that three out of four businesses failed for reasons related to the use or acquisition of money. It is a safe assumption that many of these failures could have been prevented with good financial management.

There was a time when the chief financial officer of a business was primarily concerned with *getting* the funds required to conduct the operations of the business. Despite success in this area, some businesses found that having money does not necessarily guarantee making a profit. You not only have to have money, you also have to use it well. The newer emphasis is on money management and it stresses the effective use of funds once they have been acquired. Responsible and effective control of costs is essential to the continuing prosperity of any business. Without it, costs become excessive, profits shrink, and it becomes impossible to continue profitable operations.

WHAT DECISIONS MUST BE MADE IN CONVERTING CASH OR CREDIT INTO BUILDINGS, PLANT SITE, EQUIPMENT, MATERIALS, AND SERVICES?

In the process of converting the money (or credit) we have acquired into the assets and services needed to launch the business, many problems must be faced and important decisions made. From the time the necessary funds are acquired, they are constantly being used to purchase all the things required for daily operations. The manager must decide upon the most economical way of providing a suitable plant or office; equipping it with tools, equipment, furniture, and fixtures; and hiring competent people to operate and maintain the facility. One of the most critical decisions involves the selection and purchase of a site. The efficiency of the procurement phase requires that each expenditure result in maximum value and that the proper balance be maintained for each expenditure in relation to the funds available. The manner in which this is done will have a great deal to do with the future operation of the business and its ability to maintain profitable operations.

Usually not, if you compare interest rates on commercial bank loans with leasing rates. Leasing rates are almost invariable higher. However, many companies with plenty of cash and good credit ratings are going the leasing route. Manufacturers of machine tools, photocopying equipment, furniture, machines, trucks, and data processing equipment are doing a brisk business in leasing their products.

Although there is no formula, companies that lease equipment expect to benefit financially in one or more of the following ways:

□ Leasing is a good way to meet seasonal peaks without committing long-term funds. Leasing eliminates insurance, depreciation, storage, and other equipment which is declared "surplus" during slow periods.

□ Leasing enables the leasing party to conserve its capital for more profitable uses. The trade-off here is determined by the amount of profit you can realize from the capital if it is not used to buy equipment.

□ Leasing saves taxes. Payments on a lease are tax-deductible. Most authorities agree that savings from leasing will offset depreciation and interest deductions for purchased equipment if the lease payments are scheduled so that they are higher in the early years of the lease than the sum of depreciation and interest.

□ Leasing eliminates worries about equipment becoming obsolescent. If you lease, you can exchange your machine for a later model periodically, and you do not have to worry about reconditioning and disposing of the obsolescent machine.

□ Maintenance costs are minimized since leased equipment is often maintained by the party supplying the equipment. This means that you can save the cost of training your own maintenance personnel and can do the job with fewer maintenance people. Full maintenance leases are most common with data processing equipment, photocopying equipment, and trucks.

HOW MUCH CAPITAL IS NEEDED TO START A BUSINESS?

The amount of capital needed to open the doors of a new business varies. It depends on the type of business and the sales volume you expect to attain. The costs to open a bookstore, for example, would be a fraction of the cost of starting a manufacturing facility. A large business would naturally require more inventory, personnel, and equipment than a smaller one. The capital needed must cover the initial costs of getting started—obtaining an office or plant, and the necessary equipment, tools, and supplies to get the business through the initial phase of "opening its doors." This cost can include promotional activity, remodeling, utility deposits, and similar items. Your available capital must exceed the initial requirements by a safe margin, because you must have enough in reserve to carry the business until its income exceeds expenses—or until it starts making a profit. This could be as long as 6 months. It could even be longer. Your planning must provide sufficient capital to:

- Pay your employees and keep the business running.
- Buy equipment and keep it operating.
- Take advantage of discounts offered by creditors.
- Grant customer credit if necessary to meet competition.
- Maintain an adequate stock of merchandise or materials to supply customers and build sales volume.
- Maintain your standard of living for you and your family.

Few owners of new businesses put up the entire amount of initial financing. A good rule of thumb requires that your "equity" in the business be at last 50 percent, preferably more, of the total amount. If you are not able to provide that much, you will find creditors unwilling to risk their money in your business.

HOW CAN YOU ESTIMATE YOUR SALES VOLUME?

Your volume will depend on the total amount of business in the area, the number and ability of your competitors who will be sharing the business, and your own capability to compete for the consumer's dollar. You can get some help in making your sales estimate from wholesalers, trade associations, your banker, and other business people. The advice of others can be compared with your own independent estimate of what you believe is needed to make the effort worthwhile to you. One approach for your independent estimate is to start with the income you desire and work backward. Suppose, for instance, that you hope to earn annual profits of $15,000 from operating a hardware store. Information available from the National Retail Hardware Association shows that the average profit for hardware stores is about 6.9 percent of sales (see Table 5-2). Then, to obtain an annual return of $15,000, sales of $217,000 ($15,000 ÷ .069) will be required.

In reaching your final estimate of sales do not be overenthusiastic. A new business usually grows slowly at the start. If you overestimate your sales, you are likely to invest too much in equipment and initial inventory and commit yourself to heavier operating expenses than your actual sales volume can justify. Take a conservative line. Review a final time your sales figures and cut them back enough to give you a cushion. Consider again whether the income figure you started your calculations with is a final one or a figure you would be willing to adjust downward.

		Percent of Sales
Net Sales		100.00
Cost of Goods Sold		66.05
Margin		33.95
Salary Expense:		
Owners and managers	7.15	
Salespeople, office, and other	9.60	
Total Salaries		16.75
Other Expense:		
Office supplies and postage		0.40
Advertising		1.55
Donations		0.05
Telephone and telegraph		0.30
Losses on notes and accounts receivable		0.15
Delivery expense (exclusive of wages)		0.50
Depreciation of delivery equipment		0.25
Depreciation of furniture, fixtures, and tools		0.35
Rent		2.70
Repairs to building		0.10
Heat, light, water, and power		0.80
Insurance		0.80
Taxes (not including federal income tax)		1.10
Interest on borrowed money		0.05
Unclassified (including store supplies)		1.20
Total Expense (not including interest on investment)		27.05
Net Profit		6.90

Source: The National Retail Hardware Association.

HOW CAN YOU BE SURE THAT ALL INITIAL EXPENSES HAVE BEEN CONSIDERED?

One method is to use a worksheet to guide you and assure that all items of initial expense have been covered. The Small Business Administration[1] has developed one which can be adapted to almost any kind of business. Figures 5-1, 5-2, and 5-3 show samples of a typical worksheet filled in for estimating the initial costs of starting a hardware store. The example has been based on an expected profit of $15,000, using the ratios for hardware stores shown in Table 5-2.

Each kind of business has its own set of ratios. The typical ratios for the kind of business you are considering are multiplied by your estimated sales volume and entered on Worksheet 1 in accordance with the instructions. We have entered the annual estimated

[1]Wendell O. Metcalf, *Starting and Managing a Small Business of Your Own*, The Starting and Managing Series, Vol. 1, 3d ed., U.S. Small Business Administration, Washington, 1973.

WORKSHEET 1

Estimated Monthly Expenses	Your estimate of monthly expenses based on sales of $217,000 per year*	Your estimate of how much cash you need to start your business (See column 3.)	What to put in column 2 (These figures are typical for one kind of business; you will have to decide how many months to allow for in your business.)
Item	Column 1	Column 2	Column 3
Salary of owner-manager	$1,293	$2,586	2 times column 1
All other salaries and wages	1,736	5,208	3 times column 1
Rent	488	1,464	3 times column 1
Advertising	280	840	3 times column 1
Delivery expense	90	270	3 times column 1
Supplies	72	216	3 times column 1
Telephone and telegraph	54	162	3 times column 1
Other utilities	145	435	3 times column 1
Insurance	145	6 Months 72	Payment required by insurance company
Taxes, including social security	199	796	4 times column 1
Interest	9	27	3 times column 1
Maintenance	18	54	3 times column 1
Legal and other professional fees	—	—	3 times column 1
Miscellaneous	362	1,086	3 times column 1

FIGURE 5-1. Estimated monthly expenses starting a retail hardware store. (*Source:* Adapted from Wendell O. Metcalf, *Starting and Managing a Small Business of Your Own*, The Starting and Managing Series, Vol. 1, 3d ed., U.S. Small Business Administration, Washington, 1973.)

*Use operating ratios shown in Table 5-2. Example for owner's salary: $217,000 × .0715 = $1,293 per month.

WORKSHEET 1, continued		
Starting Costs You Only Have to Pay Once	Column 2	
Fixtures and equipment	$12,600	Fill in Worksheet 2 on page 115 and put the total here
Decorating and remodeling	4,500	Talk it over with a contractor
Installation of fixtures and equipment	3,200	Talk to suppliers from whom you buy these
Starting inventory†	35,805	Suppliers will help you estimate this. For total amount use typical ratio to sales
Deposits with public utilities	50	Find out from utilities companies
Legal and other professional fees	125	Lawyer, accountant, and so on
Licenses and permits	80	Find out from city offices what you have to have
Advertising and promotion for opening	2,000	Estimate what you'll use
Accounts receivable‡	17,836	What you need to buy more stock until credit customers pay
Cash	3,500	For unexpected expenses or losses, special purchases, etc.
Other	1,000	Make a separate list and enter total
Total Estimated Cash You Need to Start With	$93,912	Add up all the numbers in column 2

FIGURE 5-2. One-time costs for starting a retail hardware store. (*Source:* Adapted from Wendell O. Metcalf, *Starting and Managing a Small Business of Your Own,* The Starting and Managing Series, Vol. 1, 3d ed., U.S. Small Business Administration, Washington, 1973.)

†Assumes stock turnover of four times per year: $217,000 ÷ 4 = $54,250.
Based on a margin of 34 percent, opening stock will cost $54,250 × 0.66 = $35,805.
‡Based on an average collection period of 30 days: $\frac{30}{365}$ × $217,000 = $17,836.

Leave out or add items to suit your business. Use separate sheets to list exactly what you need for each of the items below.	If you plan to pay cash in full, enter the full amount below and in the last column.	If you are going to pay by installments, fill out the columns below. Enter in the last column your downpayment plus at least one installment.			Estimate of the cash you need for furniture, fixtures, and equipment.
		Price	Down Payment	Amount of Each Installment	
Counters	$	$ 1,100.	$500	$ 50	$ 550
Storage shelves, cabinets		8,500	4,500	200	4,700
Display stands, shelves, tables		3,000	1,000	100	1,100
Cash register		550	225	50	275
Safe		3,500	1,000	100	2,100
Window display fixtures	1,800				1,800
Special lighting	1,575				1,575
Outside sign	500				500
Delivery equipment if needed	—				—
TOTAL FURNITURE, FIXTURES, AND EQUIPMENT. Enter this figure also in Worksheet 1 under "Starting Costs You Only Have to Pay Once."					$12,600

FIGURE 5-3. List of furniture, fixtures, and equipment. (*Source:* Adapted from Wendell O. Metcalf, *Starting and Managing a Small Business of Your Own*, The Starting and Managing Series, Vol. 1, 3d ed., U.S. Small Business Administration, Washington, 1973.)

sales of $217,000 ($15,000 ÷ .069) at the top of the first worksheet and have used the ratios shown in Table 5-2 to calculate each of the others. Costs of the fixtures and equipment are entered on Worksheet 2. These are based on prices supplied by equipment manufacturers and the credit policies they use in extending credit. Sometimes good used equipment is available that can be obtained at a significant savings. The totals for fixtures and equipment are entered at the top of Figure 5-2 and all the other items calculated or estimated in accordance with the marginal notes. You should verify and modify the estimates derived by this method by investigations within the market area where you plan to operate. Talk to your local trade association, chamber of commerce, banker, and anyone else who can help you arrive at the best estimate possible.

You should try to obtain typical ratios for the kind of business you are interested in. Among the sources for such information are trade associations, Dun & Bradstreet, Robert Morris Associates, The National Cash Register Company, and the Accounting Corporation of America. Information regarding the services they provide may be obtained by writing to the addresses shown:

Source	Ask for Information About
Dun & Bradstreet, Inc. Business Economics Department 99 Church Street New York, New York 10007	*Cost of Doing Business: Partnerships and Proprietorships*

Source	Ask for Information About
Robert Morris Associates Philadelphia National Bank Bldg. Philadelphia, Pennsylavnia 19107	Statement Studies (published annually)
The National Cash Register Co. Marketing Service Department Dayton, Ohio 45409	*Expenses in Retail Businesses*
Accounting Corporation of America 1929 First Avenue San Diego, California 92101	(Mail-Me-Monday) Barometer of Small Business

HOW DOES A MANUFACTURING BUSINESS DIFFER FROM A RETAIL TYPE IN ITS FINANCIAL REQUIREMENTS?

A manufacturing business is usually characterized by a heavy investment in fixed assets, which will use up a good portion of the initial capital. In addition, the investment in inventory is likely to be substantial, requiring good planning to keep it within reasonable bounds. Estimating your working capital requirements and investment in receivables is similar to the method used in retailing. Here are the things that make up the manufacturing estimate:

Fixed Assets. This includes the buildings, land, machinery, and equipment needed to produce the product. The amount you need will depend on the size of the business. The experience of equipment suppliers will be invaluable in estimating your requirements for production equipment.

When you have decided how big you expect to be (in terms of sales), this information must be translated into hardware items to be made each month, the number of machines required to maintain that level, and the number of employees needed to produce the hardware. Money values must then be calculated for all fixed assets. You should obtain only the minimum amount of equipment that will provide the most profitable and efficient operation. Be careful not to tie up capital in equipment you will use on a limited basis. The more fixed assets you have, the more inflexible you become. So move cautiously in this area.

Inventory Investment. The amount of cash you can expect to have tied up in inventories is dependent on the types and quantities of items to be kept in inventory. The amount is affected by the seasonality of sales, the length of the production cycle, and the frequency with which you "turn over" your inventory. The last item involves the relationship of the value of your inventory to your net sales. For instance, if the average value of your inventory is $50,000 and your annual sales are $250,000 you would have to replenish or "turn over" your stock five times during the year. After you have sold $50,000 from your inventory, you would have capital to produce the next increment of production. Expenses for things like material, wages, rent, sales, and office expense are calculated only for a period necessary for one stock turn. In the case shown above, $50,000 represents one-fifth of your annual production; therefore, one stock turn is equivalent to 2.4 months (one-fifth of 12 months).

In arriving at your investment in inventory, you must use operating ratios again. The 1973 issue of *Key Business Ratios*, published by Dun & Bradstreet, indicates that in the motor vehicle parts and accessories category of manufacturing, the average "net sales to inventory" ratio of 98 businesses was 5.2 for the year. This means that you would need an inventory of $48,077 to handle annual sales of $250,000 ($250,000 ÷ 5.2). If sales occurred equally over the 12 months, your inventory value each month would be roughly $4,000 ($48,077 ÷ 12). This figure is accurate enough for planning purposes if you arc considering this type of business.

Investment in Receivables. If you expect to sell on credit, you will need to provide for the financing of receivables. How much you need will depend on the amount of credit business you plan to do, the terms of payment, seasonality of sales, and general conditions which affect the ability of your customers to pay their bills on time. To get an idea of the investment necessary to finance accounts receivable, published ratios can again be helpful as guides. The average collection period in 1973 for manufacturers of motor vehicle parts and accessories was 46 days. This means that 46 days of sales were in the form of accounts receivable at any given time. Hence, if annual sales are forecasted at $250,000, the manufacturer, using the figure for the average collection period in 1973, should have $32,000 invested in accounts receivable at any given time. (46 days is 12.8 percent of 360 days; 12.8 percent of $250,000 is $32,000.) Obviously, this is a rough estimate, but it will provide an acceptable approximation until your history indicates a more accurate number.

In summary, the initial costs for starting a manufacturing establishment would be the cost of equipment, plus estimates for material, labor, rent, sales, and other expenses for a period necessary to produce one complete stock turn. Answers to questions such as these will be necessary before you can make a final estimate that will be realistic and close to the mark:

□   How many units must be produced each week to attain the desired volume?

□   How much machinery and equipment will be needed to maintain this level of production?

□   How much down payment on the equipment will be necessary?

□   How many operators will be needed?

□   What will material for this level of production cost?

Initial costs run anywhere from $5,000 (Budget Rent-a-Car) to over $250,000 (Holiday Inns), with the average somewhere under $15,000. Franchisors can provide very accurate estimates of initial costs based on historical information from their operating outlets. They sometimes help with financing and can provide good prices for equipment and fixtures through their volume purchase arrangements with their suppliers.

Whether you can get more for your investment dollar by operating a franchise or an independent business can only be determined by comparing them in terms of equity capital required, time needed to build up business volume, operating expenses, and potential profits. The disadvantages and advantages of franchising are discussed in detail in Chapter 8.

HOW MUCH CASH IS NEEDED TO KEEP A BUSINESS OPERATING EFFICIENTLY?

The answer to this question is important because cash is the fuel necessary for operating the business. In thinking about cash needs, many business people use an old rule of thumb that says a company's cash balance should be equal to at least one-fourth of the company's current debts. Another approach says that 5 to 10 percent of a firm's working capital should be in cash.

Forecasting cash needs is a part of financial planning. In a sense, planning consists of trying to anticipate what your financial situation will be on a certain date and how you plan to get there. A cash forecast will indicate whether your plan of operation is feasible. A budget will indicate the availability of cash at all points of operations. These tools are discussed in detail in Chapter 13.

WHAT CAN YOU DO TO CONSERVE YOUR CASH AND ASSURE AN ADEQUATE SUPPLY OF WORKING CAPITAL?

Planning, scheduling, and managing cash are some of the most important actions a business person gets involved in. Finding ways to conserve cash can often preclude borrowing and the costs associated with it. Here are a dozen ways in which smart managers watch their cash and take action to conserve it:

☐ Avoid excessive inventories and take steps to reduce surplus merchandise. Studies have shown that inventories in most businesses can be reduced more than 30 percent without affecting customer service. Keep in mind that inventories are not cash. But purchases must be paid for in cash. A supplier, of course, tries as hard to sell you as you try to sell your customers. A special-price purchase of more than you need can seriously upset your cash position.

- Avoid an excessive investment in fixed assets. Postpone the purchase of fixed assets unless you are convinced that they will "pay their way." Sell off idle assets that are not being used.

- Watch receivables closely. Any credit losses are direct deductions from profits. So grant credit with care, on terms that are fair and that are understood by the debtor. See that collections are in keeping with terms granted. Go after the delinquents.

- If your need for cash is great around the first of the month, your credit policies should encourage customers to pay you near that time. In many cases, offering a discount for prompt payment enables a company to keep its cash turning and thus operate with smaller cash balances.

- Defer payment for purchases to around the time when you will receive payment for finished goods. This will avoid depletion of ready cash. You might be able to make an agreement with your major suppliers which will allow you to stretch out your payment schedule so that you can always keep a certain level of ready cash on hand.

- Take steps to see that slow-moving items are not reordered.

- Look at your banking practices. By consolidating scattered accounts in one bank you can cut down on services charged for below-minimum-amount accounts.

- The owner's salary can offer a way to improve the cash position. By timing the drawing of your pay, you might be able to keep your cash balance high on critical days of the month. For example, if you pay for raw materials on the first of the month, you can draw your salary around the fifteenth, after funds have come in from some of your slow-paying customers.

- Teach your buyers to buy raw materials and other items at their best price. In delegating purchasing, make one person responsible to prevent waste which often occurs when several people buy items and none know what the others are doing.

- Leasing or renting equipment will make cash available that would otherwise be tied up in a fixed asset. Rental charges are considered a business expense and are tax-deductible.

- Avoid overtrading. To seek big volume by cutting prices might be enticing but it can lead to profit disaster and a cash squeeze. It is often better to take less volume and maintain margins. At times, competition can become so tough that it is good business to let your competition have the business—and the reduced profits that go with it.

- Set limits on expenses and do not exceed them. Scheduling cash and observing cash flow can do more to hold down operating expense than any other small business action. Effective control of expenses is attained by avoiding cost commitments.

Commercial banks provide most of the funds borrowed by businesses. There are a number of other sources, however, including commercial finance companies, insurance companies, factors, suppliers, small business investment companies, community development agencies, and the Small Business Administration.

Whichever of these sources you plan to approach, when you set out to borrow money or secure any type of credit financing, you should know how long you will need the credit. Short-term credit is generally considered credit extended for 1 year or less; intermediate-term credit, for more than 1 year but not more than 5 years; and long-term credit, for more than 5 years.

Keep in mind that the purpose for which the funds are to be used is an important factor in deciding the kind of money needed. But even so, deciding what kind of money to use is not always easy. It is sometimes complicated by the fact that you might be using some of various kinds of money at the same time and for idential purposes. A very important distinction between the types of money is the source of repayment. Generally, short-term loans are repaid from liquidation of the current assets they have financed. Long-term loans are usually repaid from earnings.

Short-term loans are usually sought for working-capital purposes—to pay for merchandise in time to take advantage of the discount, finance accounts receivable, cover payrolls, build up inventories for a seasonal increase in sales (during Christmas, for example), or cover unanticipated emergencies. It is expected that the loan will be paid out of ordinary operating income as the temporary need passes: for example, accounts-receivable loans, when the outstanding accounts have been paid by the borrower's customers; and inventory loans, when the inventory has been converted into salable merchandise.

Intermediate-term loans (often called term loans) provide small business people with capital for other than temporary needs without requiring them to yield business control. For example, suppose you need some new equipment to increase your output but do not have the money to pay for it. With an intermediate-term loan, you will be able to acquire title to the equipment immediately. During the life of the loan, the equipment will be helping to produce income from which you can repay the loan.

Long-term financing usually involves substantial sums to be repaid over a period of several years. Since most banks limit their loans primarily to working capital needs of going concerns, most loans are short-term types, with term loans being the exception.

If you decide that your need for long-term funds cannot be satisfied by the use of retained earnings, you should talk the problem over with your banker. Even if your banker is unable or unwilling to provide the funds you need, he or she might be able to suggest other sources. Perhaps your bank will agree to share a loan with one or more other financing agencies. In some communities there are community development agencies that usually confine their loans to firms whose credit may not be acceptable to commercial banks. There might also be institutional investors or individuals in the community who might be able to supply funds on terms that will suit your needs. Some federal agencies make or guarantee loans for business purposes.[2]

WHAT KIND OF FINANCING IS AVAILABLE TO MEET LONG- AND SHORT-TERM DEBT NEEDS?

Several different kinds of loans are available for debt financing. Among the best known are mortgage loans, vendor loans, life insurance company loans, equipment leasing, sale-and-leaseback of real property, state and regional development companies, Small Business Administration loans, small business investment corporations, and commercial banks. A brief description of each of these follows.

Mortgage Loans.   Long-term loans usually involve a mortgage on real estate. If you own mortgageable property you can use it as security for the funds you need. This gives your creditor a lien on your property. Mortgage debts are usually made for a long period of years.

Vendor Loans.   Manufacturers and distributors who are interested in strengthening their position with retailers who have growth potential will often help them by providing fixtures or outright loans. This approach helps the distributors by improving their marketing facilities. The repayment schedule is decided by mutual agreement.

Life Insurance Company Loans.   Insurance companies have shown an increasing willingness to make loans to small and medium-sized firms. Typically, these institutions grant loans for a period of not less than 10 years and not more than 20 years. The insurance companies are very interested in the repayment potential and in the collateral available to secure the loan. Terms for such loans usually cover minimum working capital, limits on the sale of assets, special reserves, and limits on certain types of borrowing.

Equipment Leasing.   It is increasingly common to lease equipment rather than buy it. This relatively new form of financing can be done in two ways: A firm may arrange for use of another party's property by paying a rental fee. Or a manufacturing firm which already owns the equipment may sell it and then lease it back for continued use for a given period of time. Leasing supplies you with new fixtures

---

[2]See *Loan Sources in the Federal Government*, Management Aids for Small Manufacturers, No. 52, U.S. Small Business Administration, Washington, D.C. 20416. Free from your nearest SBA field office.

or equipment at reasonable costs, and there is often an option which permits you to buy the equipment at the end of the lease period.

Sale-and-Leaseback. Most small business people are better off not having their funds tied up in fixed assets. One of the largest investments is usually that needed to buy or construct a building and pay for it. Some businesses sell their building to a financial institution, such as an insurance company, then lease the premises for an extended period, commonly 49 to 99 years. The same plan can be used to finance the building of a new store or branch. When the new construction is finished, the financial institution takes title to it and leases it back on a long-term basis. You avoid the large capital outlay and the rent you pay takes care of financing costs, including amortization, insurance, taxes, and similar payments which you would have to make if you owned the building.

State/Regional Development Companies. These organizations supply long-term funds to small firms which will strengthen the local economy by providing jobs and increased spending power in the local area. For their extended risk, they might receive common stock options as part of the financing. Since state laws usually cover this type of financing, the requirements will vary from state to state.

Small Business Administration Loans. The SBA has a varied program to provide small businesses with both intermediate- and long-term loans at modest prices. Whenever possible, the applicant is directed to available private sources of credit, and if no private source can be found, the SBA will consider making the loan, guaranteeing a loan, or participating in a loan with a bank or other lending institution. Direct loans are possible if you have sound collateral such as real estate. Generally the SBA may guarantee or participate up to 90 percent of the amount of the loan, but the SBA portion to any one borrower cannot legally exceed $350,000. Under law, the SBA cannot enter into an immediate participation agreement if a guaranteed loan is possible. SBA also has size limitations, with loans being limited to stores having sales of less than $1 million (retail stores) or $2 million (department stores).

If you need intermediate or long-term financing, inquire at the nearest SBA field office and get the details of the various programs they sponsor. Since the Small Business Administration is a public agency using taxpayers' funds, it has an unusual responsibility as a lender. It will not make loans to gambling enterprises, to firms in which 50 percent or more of the net sales are derived from the sale of alcoholic beverages, or to businesses involved in speculation in real or personal property.

Small Business Investment Corporations. The Small Business Investment Act of 1958 authorized the establishment of small business investment companies (SBICs), whose primary objective is to help finance small businesses by providing long-term loans and equity capital.

Small business investment companies, although licensed and regulated by the SBA, are privately owned, profit-motivated corporations. Their activities are restricted to providing financing and advisory services to small businesses. The SBA sets down guidelines for the operation of small business investment companies but it does not supervise the negotiations between you and the investment company. Any agreements you reach are strictly a private business arrangement with the SBIC.

Financing provided by an SBIC must be for a minimum of 5 years, and loans may be granted for as long as 20 years. Loans may be extended for 10 years if this will aid the small business in the orderly liquidation of the loan.

Commercial Bank Loans. As we have previously stated, commercial banks normally do not encourage term loans, but they can usually be persuaded to make them for a period of 5 to 8 years. The bank will require proof of your sound financial management, and it will want a good earnings record for the previous 5-year period. It might require the borrower to maintain a specific minimum of working capital, furnish financial statements from time to time, limit the amount of debt incurred, and limit salaries and employee bonuses.

Lines of credit are sometimes extended by banks. This is an informal understanding between business people and their banks in which the banks agree to grant loans as the business people request them so long as the loans do not exceed at any one time a maximum established in the agreement. The loans are usually unsecured, and are often granted automatically during the period of the agreement (usually a year) and up to the total specified. Credit lines are used most commonly by business people with a seasonal need for short-term funds.

WHAT ARE THE COMMON SOURCES OF BORROWED WORKING CAPITAL?

Growth generates the need for new working capital to finance larger inventories, meet larger payrolls, and to make it possible to grant credit or increase its availability to customers. Loans may be described on the basis of factors other than the time allowed for repayment. Some are described by the type of collateral required, others by the method of repayment, and some by the source of the loan. Some of the common sources are accounts-receivable loans, factoring, trade credit, and floor planning.

Accounts-Receivable Loans. When you obtain an accounts-receivable loan, you pledge or assign all or part of your accounts receivable as security for the loan. The agreement for the loan specifies what percentage of the volume of receivables you assign will be loaned to you. In the case of a bank loan, this will usually be from 75 percent to 80 percent of sound receivables. You assign accounts receivable to the lender as you need funds. Each time you prepare a schedule of assigned accounts and, if a loan is made, sign a note for the amount. Usually the lender stamps the assigned accounts in your accounts-receivable ledger.

Factoring.   In more and more companies, factoring companies are being used to convert accounts receivable into cash. In factoring, you enter into an agreement under which the factors buys all your accounts receivable as they arise. The accounts sold are no longer your assets. When you sell the accounts, you are no longer responsible for collection. The factor assumes all the risk and has no recourse if the account proves uncollectible. The factor typically makes a service charge of 1 or 2 percent on the face amounts of the accounts purchased. In addition, interest is charged between the time you receive the funds from the factor and the average maturity date of the receivables the factor purchases from you. Factoring is an expensive method of raising funds, but it does away with the need for a credit and collections department. It is often the quickest way for a small business to obtain cash. An obvious disadvantage lies in the lack of control over the methods used by the factor to collect slow-paying accounts. You could lose some customers because of this.

Trade Credit.   This is credit extended by a supplier to a buyer for goods purchased. It is the most commonly used form of short-term credit. If the goods purchased are paid for in time to take advantage of the discount, trade credit costs the buyer nothing. If not, it can be one of the most expensive types of financing. For instance, if you have an invoice for $1,000 with terms of 2/10, net 30, you need to pay only $980 if you pay the invoice within 10 days. If you do not have enough cash to pay the invoice within 10 days, you will have to pay the full amount within 30 days. The extra 20 days' credit will then cost 2 percent of the $1,000, or $20. If you borrowed the $1,000 from the bank on a 30-day note and paid the invoice within 10 days, you would pay the bank only about $10 interest, a savings of $10. If you do not take advantage of the cash discount, you are paying 2 percent to use the money for 20 days, or 36 percent a year. This is high interest.

Floor Planning.   If you sell major appliances or automobiles, you might be able to carry an extensive inventory of high-priced goods by entering into a floor plan arrangement with the manufacturers or their distributors. Flooring was originally developed to give dealers handling items of large value some method of financing enough of these items to put in a representative line of merchandise on their showroom floors. It enables the dealers to sell items right off the floor and replenish stock as sales are made. You sign a trust receipt for the assortment consigned to you. Title remains with the manufacturer, and you agree to make settlement as soon as you sell the merchandise—not on a settlement date as you would with other contract arrangements. The charge for financing floor planning paper is usually about 0.5 percent a month. It is not uncommon for the supplier to pay the interest charges to the financing agent for the first 90-day period so that the dealer has the inventory for 90 days at no cost. You might have to make a down payment, such as 10 percent, on the merchandise. In some cases you might be expected to buy outright any merchandise you have not sold within 90 days. If you cannot make payment, the manufacturer or distributor may accept another 10 percent payment on the cost value of your remaining stock and add a small carrying charge to the balance.

IS "GOING PUBLIC" A GOOD WAY TO RAISE CAPITAL?

Selling securities to the public is likely to be an expensive, involved, and uncertain way for a small business to raise money. The success of this method depends on the state of the market for securities, on the company's record, on whether it is a new or established company, and on many other factors.

If you decide to go this route, you must incorporate. The transaction is accomplished through the creation of printed forms or contracts of agreement called *stock certificates*, which are exchanged for cash or credit. These contracts give to their holders certain property rights in the assets of the business and certain rights to its earnings. The stock certificates may be sold to individuals or to lending groups who provide the company with funds through the purchase of stock directly from the company. The most common method of effecting this exchange is to sell the stock through a reliable investment house.

DOESN'T IT COST A LOT TO BORROW MONEY?

Depending upon the availability of money and upon your credit worthiness, the interest on borrowed funds fluctuates through a fairly broad range. When money is "tight" and interest rates are high, it can be expensive to borrow. If you decide to borrow, it will pay you to "shop around" and check the rates offered by several different lenders. But you should avoid excessive borrowing—and always be sure you borrow only what you need and can repay.

You should also be aware that there are some benefits associated with borrowing. Here are a few:

☐ Borrowed funds can sometimes earn more than they cost. The rate that lenders charge is generally lower than the rate of return you expect from your investment. As a result, borrowed funds, if they are used successfully, increase the return on your investment over what it would have been without the borrowing.

☐ Interest payments on borrowed funds are tax-deductible. Dividend payments or other returns to investors are not. These facts should be taken into account, along with other considerations, when deciding on borrowing policies.

☐ Some credit is a matter of convenience. Buying merchandise on open account is an example of credit for convenience. Even very small business people would find it difficult to operate on a pay-as-you-go, cash basis for all their operating expenses each day. The bookkeeping costs of doing business without credit would be enormous.

☐ Borrowing is more flexible than ownership. When business owners supply the entire investment, they might find that part of their capital is idle during off seasons. As a result, they might receive a lower average return than if they had invested some of their money elsewhere and used short-term borrowed funds during their companies' periods of peak needs. Business people can usually increase or decrease the amount of borrowed funds to correspond fairly well with their business capital requirements.

☐ Loan funds are easier to find than equity funds. The prospects of profits are often too uncertain to satisfy a potential owner-investor. Since lenders, as creditors, have prior claims to income and assets, loan funds are usually more plentiful than equity capital.

WHAT INFORMATION WILL A LENDER REQUIRE?

The lender—who more often than not is a banker—needs certain information on which to base a loan decision. Part of this information will be furnished by the borrower, and the rest will come from the banker's own credit files and from outside sources. Generally, this information is related to what is known as the "C's" of credit—character, capacity, capital, collateral, circumstances, and coverage (insurance).[3]

Character.   Banker must be satisfied that borrowers will keep their word and that they will do everything in their power to conserve their business assets and so ensure payment of their loans in accordance with the agreement.

Capacity.   This refers to the management skill shown by business people in using their investment. For those just starting a business or entering a new field, past experience might carry little weight. For

[3]Adapted from Jack Zwick, *A Handbook of Small Business Finance*, U.S. Small Business Administration, Washington, 1965.

example, experience as a machinist, salesperson, or bookkeeper alone—however successful—does not qualify a person to direct all the activities involved in operating a machine shop.

Capital.   Business people's investments in their own businesses are evidence of their faith in their future. They themselves must furnish the management and most of the capital until others have enough confidence in their businesses to be willing to invest in them.

Collateral.   Business people who have a high credit rating do much of their borrowing on an unsecured basis. Others are often roquirod to back up their credit standing with collateral. This is especially likely to be true of new small business people. If they own homes or other improved real estate, life insurance policies with a cash surrender value, or marketable securities, they might be able to use such assets as collateral for business loans.

Circumstances.   Some factors over which business people have no control might have a bearing on the granting of bank loans and their repayment. These include: the seasonal character of the business, long-run business changes, the level of community business activity, the competitive position of the firm, and the nature of the product.

Coverage.   Proper insurance coverage is very important. A going concern has little excuse for neglecting to establish and maintain adequate protection against such basic risks as fire, flood, explosions, tornadoes, death of the owner or partner, theft, embezzlement, and public liability not covered by workmen's compensation insurance. Your insurance broker can tell you what adequate coverage will cost.

WHAT KINDS OF LIMITATIONS ARE IMPOSED BY LENDERS ON BUSINESS LOANS?

A loan agreement is a tailor-made document covering all the terms and conditions of the loan. With it, lenders protect their positions as creditors and assure themselves of repayment in accordance with the terms of the agreement. Lenders reason that borrowers' businesses should generate enough funds to repay the loan while taking care of other needs. They consider that the cash flow into the business should be great enough to do this without hurting the working capital of the borrowers.

The actual restrictions in a loan agreement come under a section known as *covenants.* Negative covenants are things which the borrower may not do without prior approval of the lender. Falling in this category are such things as adding to the borrower's total debt, pledging of the borrower's assets to others, and paying of dividends in excess of the terms of the loan agreement.

Positive covenants spell out things which the borrower must do. Some examples are maintenance of a minimum net working capital, carrying adequate insurance, repaying the loan according to the terms of the agreement, and supplying the lender with financial statements and certain reports.

Loan agreements may be amended from time to time and exceptions made. Certain provisions may be waived from one year to the next with the consent of the lender. Before you sign a loan agreement, be sure you understand its limitations. You might want to get the advice of your associates and outside advisers. Try to get the terms you know you can live with. Once the loan is made and the agreement has been signed, you are bound by them.

WHAT SPECIAL PROBLEMS ARISE FROM FINANCING A BUSINESS?

The problems associated with financing are primarily related to the nature of the loan agreements entered into. We have already seen that much of the operating capital is derived from bank loans, sale of securities, and merchandise credits. The financial agreements entered into establish certain economic characteristics of the business and fix the nature of some of its financial obligations. For instance, a company might obtain the use of temporary funds which it uses for a short time. When it buys material on credit, agreeing to pay for it within 30 days, it has the use of funds equal to the value of the material it buys for a short period of time. As it pays for the materials used and buys additional materials, it creates a revolving fund. In this case, the company's statement of accounts payable represents money obtained through open-account credits on which it pays no interest. If the company borrows money from commercial banks to meet temporary requirements for funds, it gives its note for a specified period of time and pays interest at a rate of 8 percent or more per annum. Long-term loans are secured by bonds or mortgages and may run 5 years, 10 years, or 20 years or longer. Such bonds obligate the borrower to the payment of a fixed annual interest rate until the bonds are retired, regardless of earnings. The sale of stock certificates presents still another variation in the financing pattern. Those who buy the company's stock supply money or credit under the terms of the stock certificates. Such purchasers are known as the owners of the business and, as stated previously, may have certain rights on the earnings of the business. Each of these methods of raising money presents its own peculiar impact on the earnings of the business and poses a hazard to the assets of the business if certain conditions are not met. The basic problem is to obtain the capital for the business with a minimum of hazard to property rights and claims on the earnings of the business.

Other problems are associated with the *amount* of capital obtained. If you obtain too little, you might be unable to take advantage of cash discounts or pay your bills on time, thereby jeopardizing your credit standing. In addition, you might be unable to weather minor business reversals, maintain adequate inventories, or buy the machinery and equipment you need. Too much capital can sometimes result in loose credit policies, unwise expansion plans, and excessive inventories, all of which contribute to laxness and inefficiency. Good planning and accurate forecasting of cash requirements will help determine the adequacy of the capital the business needs. Each business must determine whether its capital is adequate for its current needs. At the same time, it must plan for future requirements. Finding the proper balance will be a compromise based upon risks and costs compared with expected advantages. Needless to say, estimates of the capital needs of a business can best be made when detailed records are kept and periodic analyses are prepared and considered in light of the economy.

This exercise is designed to test your understanding of the material presented in Chapter 5. Choose the response, *True* or *False*, which best fits each statement. Correct responses are presented in the back of the text.

SELF-CHECK OF KEY CONCEPTS

1. Short-term loans are usually repaid within 1 year.
2. Unless you have adequate insurance coverage, a banker will be reluctant to approve a business loan for you.
3. Factoring accounts-receivable is one of the least expensive ways to borrow money.
4. One of the advantages of renting equipment is that such rent can be listed as a tax-deductible business expense.
5. Generally, it is easier to borrow working capital than equity capital.
6. Venture capitalists usually want to assume control of a company as one of the conditions of loaning money.
7. The amount of equity owners have in their businesses affect their ability to borrow.
8. Most retailers have more merchandise in their inventory than they need.
9. Most commercial loans made by banks range from 1 to 5 years.
10. Trade credit is the most commonly used form of short-term credit.

1. You are planning to establish a household appliance store in a new shopping center and have been evaluating the initial costs and profit potential of such a business. You have a first-year net profit goal of $10,000 and believe that you could build the business up to a $15,000 level within 3 years.

PERFORMANCE PROBLEMS AND PROJECTS

Information on operating ratios shown in Dun & Bradstreet's *Key Operating Ratios* (1974) show the following for household appliance stores:[4]

Net profits on net sales	1.27 percent
Average collection period	28 days
Net sales to inventory ratio	5.0 times

Assuming that you could turn over your stock six times a year, calculate the following:

a. Annual sales required to provide a net profit of $10,000 a year when the net profit margin is 1.27 percent.

b. The value of your starting inventory, assuming a margin of 30 percent.

c. The amount you will need to finance accounts-receivable with a collection period of 28 days.

2. Assume that through inattention on the part of your office manager and lack of an aggressive collection policy your average collection period in Problem 1 actually turns out to be 45 days instead of 28. What additional capital will you have to provide to finance your accounts receivable?

3. Almost every small business will invest capital in buying a cash register. Contact your local distributor of cash registers and find out what kinds are available, what the prices are, and what the differences in the various models are.

4. The technique used in estimating initial capital requirements for a manufacturing firm differs from the technique used for a retail business in that a heavy investment in equipment, labor, and materials is characteristic of the former type of business.

Assume that you are going to establish a 6-person screw machine shop to manufacture a part for sales to a major automobile manufacturer, who will subcontract work for these specially machined parts to you. You have checked prices on the machines you will need and have current prices on them. The part will be priced at $1.50 each, including an 8 percent profit. The average labor rate for your machinists is $7.50 per hour. You expect to work a standard 40-hour week. You are renting space in a new industrial park for $1,500 per month. Your office force consists of a secretary and a combination buyer/scheduler. Their combined salaries are $1,500 per month. You have decided to limit your own salary to $1,200 per month until the business gets on its feet. Your objective is a net profit of $20,000 per year.

AJAX SCREW MACHINE SHOP
Estimate of Initial Capital

a. How much net profit do you   a. $_____
   expect to make the first year?

[4]*Key Business Ratios* (1974), Dun & Bradstreet, Inc., New York, 1975, p. 5.

b. At an 8 percent rate of net profit, what sales volume do you need to attain?

b. $_____

c. How many pieces do you need to make to net a profit of $20,000?

c. 8 percent of $1.50 = 12 cents on each piece made. The number of units required to net a profit of $20,000 is _____ units.

d. How many machines do you need and what will they cost?

d. 4 screw machines @ $11,000 each
1 multispindle drill @ $7,500
1 deburr machine @ $3,500
1 grinder @ $6,000
Total for equipment
$_____

e. Assuming a stock turn of four times per year, what is the value of material you will need in inventory?

e. "Net sales to inventory" ratio for this kind of business is 6.9.

$$\frac{\text{Annual sales}}{4} = \text{sales/quarter}$$

$$\frac{\text{Sales/quarter}}{6.9} = \text{inventory value for 1 stock turn}$$
$_____

f. How much in machinists' wages will be required for 1 stock turn (3 months)?

f. Assume 160 working hours per worker-month.
$_____

g. How much rent for 3 months?

g. $_____

h. How much for office expense, including wages, supplies, and telephone for 3 months?

h. $_____

i. How much do you estimate for utilities, insurance, maintenance and miscellaneous expenses for 3 months?

i. $_____

j. Owner's salary for 3 months

j. $_____

Total items d thru j
$_____

5. A supplier offers you trade credit on terms of 2/10, net 30. If you do not pay the invoice within 10 days and take advantage of the 2 percent discount, you must pay the full amount within 30 days. This means you are paying 2 percent interest to use the supplier's money for 20 days. To convert this to an annual effective interest rate, we would calculate the number of 20-day periods in a year (360 days) and multiply this number by 2 percent:

$$\frac{360}{20} \times 2\% = 36\% \text{ effective annual interest rate}$$

Two of your suppliers have offered you the following terms on merchandise you are buying from them. Calculate the annual effective interest rate for each:

a. 3/10, net 30
b. 2/20, net 60

A CASE IN POINT

THE CASH CRISIS AT RICHMOND ELECTRONICS

Bruce Richmond was the owner of Richmond Electronics Distributors, a very successful firm, with a net worth of $400,000, employing 32 employees. The success of the business was largely attributed to Bruce's energy and hard work. It seemed that he was everywhere. He supervised the outside sales force, the inside sales force, the warehouse operations, and his office of four workers. All his key people were hired for their willingness to put into the job whatever it required to keep things humming. Bruce prided himself on his ability to select and hire "go-getters" who would follow the pattern he had established. The business had made money every year, but the aftertax earnings had been shrinking for the last 2 years and Bruce found himself in an occasional bind for cash. He had not paid much attention to bookkeeping until his aftertax earnings dropped to $7,500 last year—down over 80 percent of what it was 3 years ago.

He decided to discuss the problem with his banker and his accountant. Both agreed that they would be willing to look at his financial situation but expressed mild surprise, as Bruce had seldom conferred with them since his business was established 5 years ago.

After a thorough examination of his books, a profit analysis, and a look at his methods of inventory control, they invited Bruce to a conference to discuss their findings.

"Your inventory is very high for a business the size of yours," they advised. "According to the annual sales of your company, the inventory is 40 percent higher than industry ratios indicate it should be. Some of your stock items are obsolete and have been replaced by most electronics distributors with more sophisticated electronic devices."

The banker added, "We have analyzed your accounts receivable and find that your average collection period is 83 days. The average for a business like yours should be around 43 days according to published operating ratios. Aging your accounts showed that roughly 25 percent of them were over 90 days old and that you are still shipping merchandise to most of them."

Both the banker and the accountant expressed surprise that the person who was responsible for ordering had never had any instruction in trade discounts. Consequently, they seldom paid their bills in time to take advantage of discounts. "Two percent discount doesn't seem like very much to get excited about," Bruce observed. "But I guess every little bit helps," he admitted.

Using the findings in this case, answer the following questions.

1. What action would you recommend to get the accounts-receivable problem under control?
2. What misconceptions does Bruce have about the nature of trade discounts?
3. What recommendations would you make to rectify the inventory problem?
4. Do you think Bruce knows which product lines are the most profitable? How can his accountant help him find out?

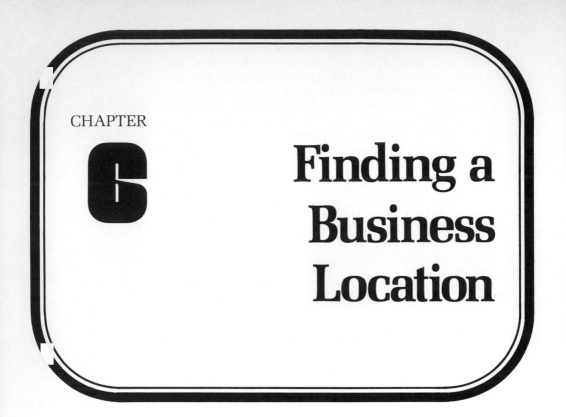

CHAPTER

6

Finding a Business Location

PERFORMANCE OBJECTIVES

After reading this chapter, you should understand the importance of thoroughly evaluating a proposed business location and site before making a decision to build, buy, or relocate. From the hundreds of factors which affect site selection, you should be able to assess the impact of the major ones on the potential volume of the proposed business. Specifically, you should be able to:

1. Evaluate the risk involved in selecting a site without making an analysis of the factors involved.
2. Predict the actions which could result from the inability of a potential customer to find adequate parking near your store.
3. Explain how you would find out the various age groups of the people living in Tempe, Arizona.
4. Construct a checklist of location factors to evaluate in seeking a location for a barbershop.
5. Conclude why it is unnecessary for a newsstand located in the lobby of a large hotel to spend a lot of money on advertising.
6. List some things to avoid in selecting a site for a beauty shop.
7. Prepare a rationale to explain the reciprocal relationship of occupancy cost to advertising cost.
8. Defend the position that two adjacent competing businesses are not necessarily incompatible, and give examples which support this position.

9. Explain the relationship that exists between per capita income and business volume.
10. Develop an interview sheet which could be conveniently used by a researcher to elicit from pedestrian shoppers the purpose of their shopping trip.
11. Predict the reaction of a community to a proposed steel-fabricating plant within the city limits.
12. Classify the factors which would be germane in deciding whether to locate a manufacturing plant near its source of raw materials or near its market.
13. List the characteristics of a drive-in food outlet which would make it incompatible with a cluster of apparel shops.
14. Explain the potential advantages of a retail business located in a growing community of young married couples, a high percentage of whom are college graduates.
15. Construct a composite of the "ideal" site for an equipment rental business, listing those things which are desirable and those things which should be avoided.

INTRODUCTION

There is an old adage familiar to many business people which says, "If you want to make money, go where the money is." This bit of sage advice stresses the importance of finding the right region, the right neighborhood, and the best area within a neighborhood when locating a new business. Business volume, one of the major ingredients in business prosperity and growth, is dependent upon the accessibility of your business to a large number of potential customers with money to spend. Where you decide to locate, therefore, is one of the most critical decisions you will have to make when you decide to start a business. The wrong location can easily mean the difference between success and failure. One authority has stated that "the difference between an acceptable and a superior plant location, let alone a poor one, can mean a difference of 10% to 15% in total operating costs for every year of a plant's existence."[1]

Existing businesses often find that area growth, population shifts, and competitive pressures indicate the need to relocate the business to a more favorable location. This

decision should be approached with the same thoughtfulness, thoroughness, and planning that characterized the selection of the original site.

This chapter discusses some of the major factors to be considered in selecting a business location and offers suggestions to assist small business people in eliminating undesirable sites and narrowing their list to a few with real potential. Collecting statistical data related to a particular market area can be an exacting and time-consuming task; however, selecting a business location without a knowledge of the potential customers in the proposed area, the number and sizes of competing stores, and the cost of occupancy in the various locations can cause problems which you might later have to correct by moving your business to a new location. You should not overlook the professional services offered by consultants and market analysts, whose expertise in the field will enable them to give you valuable assistance in collecting statistical information which could help you make the right decision when locating your store or plant. You may find that professional assistance can save you money in the long run.

[1]Leonard Yassen, "A New Ballgame in Plant Location," *Dun's*, March 1974.

WHAT IS THE DIFFERENCE BETWEEN A BUSINESS LOCATION AND A BUSINESS SITE?

Location generally refers to a state, county, region, or city where the market area for the proposed business exists. Site selection factors involve the specific area within the city which can be described by a street location and perhaps a certain address on that street, or even a particular side of the street. Even when the location of a new business is considered good, the advantages of a good location can be lost, or at least compromised, by the disadvantages of a poor site.

Deciding where to locate is generally the result of three logical steps: (1) selecting the town or city, (2) picking an area within the city, and (3) selecting a specific site in the area. This process often starts with one's hometown as a popular choice of locations. Some select a part of the country in which they would like to live and then narrow their choice to a city. While it is important to choose a spot where you will be happy, you should be sure that the community needs and will support a business like the one you propose to open.

WHAT CHARACTERISTICS OF A TOWN SHOULD YOU CONSIDER WHEN SELECTING A BUSINESS LOCATION?

You can spend a lot of time and money making a scientific evaluation of a new business location. Small business people with limited financial resources might not be able to afford an expensive evaluation, but they should be able to find out a lot about the town themselves. Chambers of commerce, banks, area development agencies, wholesalers, and distributors can be of assistance in providing information. Here are the factors to evaluate in narrowing your list of locations:

- □ The general economy of the area
- □ Population characteristics
- □ Competitive businesses already there
- □ Community support
- □ The labor force
- □ Taxes and government

WHAT DO YOU NEED TO KNOW ABOUT THE GENERAL ECONOMY OF THE AREA YOU ARE CONSIDERING?

Since your business will likely be supported by the people living and working in the community, you need to know what types of businesses and industries are providing the payrolls for your potential customers. Question the permanency of the existing businesses and ask about their long-range growth potential. Keep in mind that communities supported predominantly by space-age projects, defense-oriented activities, government contracts, and research businesses might lack the permanence and growth factors that would make an investment in the community on your part wise. It is not uncommon to hear of once-prosperous communities turned into depressed areas by the closure or departure of the major supporting business in the area.

The ideal community is one with a substantial percentage of permanent businesses, favorable trends in community payrolls, increasing new business starts, stability of existing businesses, all accompanied by healthy growth in population trends over the last 5 to 10 years.

WHAT POPULATION DATA IS SIGNIFICANT?

First, you will want to know whether the proposed market area is growing—and how fast. If population growth in the area is static or declining, it is unlikely that it will support any new businesses. If it is growing, the rate of growth is important. Census data for the last 20 years can give you an idea of how fast the area has grown. The chamber of commerce or other local sources such as a bank or newspaper can probably supply data for the years between census tabulations. A steady growth rate will affect your plans for expansion in the years ahead and will allow you to plan for this in your initial site selection.

You will want to know the composition of the population, including a breakdown by age, sex, marital status, and color or race. This information will tell you what percentage of the population is composed of young marrieds, older retired couples, women and men, and minority groups. It can be very helpful, depending on the kind of service or merchandise you propose to offer.

Next, you will need to know about the schooling, employment, occupations, and income of your potential customers. Unless you have information about incomes in the area, you will have no way to project your business volume and determine whether your business can operate profitably in the community. Generally, the higher the education level, the higher the income level is likely to be, with correspondingly greater capacity for goods and services. Trends in the level of education, particularly when correlated with income, may indicate future potential. Income is important in market analysis because changes in income are reflected in the demand patterns for goods and services. No business is free from this effect. For example, as barbershop prices increase, the interval between haircuts increases and the sale of hair clippers for home use rises.

Population and housing data is compiled as a result of the national census made every tenth year ending in "0." The following series of reports are available at depository libraries and are also for sale by the Superintendent of Documents by state:

□ 1970 Census of Population, Series PC(1)-A, titled *Number of Inhabitants*—lists population counts, including those of unincorporated places of 1,000 or more inhabitants, by state and United States summary.

□ 1970 Census of Population, Series PC(1)-B, titled *General Population Characteristics*—gives statistics on sex, age, marital status, color or race, and relationship to head of the household. One report for each state.

□ 1970 Census of Population, Series PC(1)-C, titled *General Social and Economic Characteristics*—includes years of schooling, occupations, and income.

□ 1970 Census of Housing, Series HC(1), titled *Detailed Housing Characteristics*—gives housing characteristics for places of 1,000 inhabitants or more. Included are housing units by tenure, vacancy status, number of rooms, number of persons, monthly rent, value of property, and condition.

□ 1970 Census of Housing, Series HC(3), titled *Block Statistics*—shows data for individual blocks on selected housing and population subjects. Also includes some data for communities outside urbanized areas.

In your analysis of the population, you will want to ask:

How many people live in the town or city?

How many are male? female?

How many fall into each age group?

How many households are represented?

How many homeowners? renters?

How many in each income group?

How many are employed? In what occupations?

WHERE ARE THE HIGH-INCOME AREAS IN THE UNITED STATES?

If family income is any indication of business opportunities in the United States, California leads the nation with the greatest number of rich cities. Among the 50 richest cities of 100,000 or more population, 14 are in California. It is followed by Michigan with 6; Indiana with 4; Illinois and Ohio with 3; and Connecticut, Wisconsin, Iowa, and North Carolina with 2. Here are the 10 richest, according to figures compiled by the U.S. Census Bureau in 1970:

City	Median Family Income
Livonia, Michigan	$15,216
Torrance, California	13,620
Stamford, Connecticut	13,571

City	Median Family Income
Warren, Michigan	13,452
Dearborn, Michigan	13,257
Huntington Beach, California	12,930
Fremont, California	12,659
Honolulu, Hawaii	12,539
Parma, Ohio	12,438
Yonkers, New York	12,151

The median income represents the middle of the income range for each city.

HOW CAN YOU FIND OUT WHERE PER CAPITA INCOME IS LIKELY TO BE HIGHEST IN THE YEARS AHEAD?

The U.S. Department of Commerce released the results of a study in 1974 showing the trends of personal income by state between 1973 and 1990. A comparison of the estimates of average income for 1990 and for 1973 shows these states will be the richest:

State	Income per Person		
	1973	1990	Increase, %
New York	$5,663	$9,312	64.4
Alaska	5,613	9,072	61.6
Connecticut	5,889	8,981	52.5
Illinois	5,753	8,846	53.8
Delaware	5,540	8,820	59.2
New Jersey	5,759	8,645	50.1
Hawaii	5,309	8,615	62.3
Massachusetts	5,233	8,571	63.8
California	5,438	8,542	57.1
Nevada	5,560	8,344	50.1

The study also showed that the Southeast and Southwest are likely to expand the most rapidly, measured by the rate of growth of personal income. The most conspicuous change is the replacement of the Far West by the Southeast as the fastest-growing area in both population and income.

HOW CAN YOU GET INFORMATION ABOUT YOUR COMPETITION?

If you want to know how many service stations, restaurants, or beauty shops there are in Podunk, the Census of Business will tell you. It will also tell you how much money they made in the census year. This information is published every fifth year ending in "2" or "7" in three series of area reports covering retail trade, wholesale trade, and selected services. Included are United States summary reports for these three major trade divisions and separate reports for each of the states. The information is by kind of business, county, city, and standard metropolitan area.

An analysis of the competition is highly desirable when considering a site in a proposed area. Attention should be given first to competitors about the same type and size as the proposed business, since they are on a more realistic level of competition. A small clothing store would concern itself with other small clothing stores rather than with a high-volume department store. In time, a small operation might grow to the point of competing successfully with major firms, but the immediate threat of competition will come from other businesses about the same size and description.

You should be concerned with not only the number of competing businesses in the area but also the extent and quality of their sales and promotion efforts, the physical appearance of their establishments, what price and style lines they carry, and what unique customer services, if any, they offer to attract and hold customers.

HOW CAN YOU TELL WHETHER THE AREA CAN SUPPORT ANOTHER BUSINESS LIKE YOURS?

When you have determined how many other competitors there are in your proposed market area, the relationship of the businesses to the total population can be determined. Table 6-1 shows how many inhabitants there are for each type of store in the United States. The data is based on the latest census information. It is of interest to note that there is one gasoline service station for every 914 inhabitants and one grocery store for every 905 inhabitants. On the other hand, there is only one sporting goods store for every 12,308 inhabitants. These are countrywide averages and might not be representative of the ratio in your area. They do, however, offer guidelines to indicate whether your local market is already saturated with stores like the one you plan to open.

Another good indicator is the number of competitive businesses that have gone out of business during the last year. If there has been a decline in the number of competitors, an attempt should be made to find out why. If the decline is significant, it might indicate that there are too many businesses of that type for the potential sales volume. If other areas of your site analysis tend to indicate a declining market, an exodus of competing businesses might help support those findings.

If general business conditions are such that other competitors are seeking to get out of the market by selling their business, you should know it. The reasons why competitors are leaving the market area should be learned. A decision to purchase assumes economic health in a market. A decision to sell could portend trouble ahead.

TABLE 6-1. NUMBER OF INHABITANTS PER STORE FOR SELECTED KINDS OF BUSINESSES BASED ON 1967 NATIONAL STATISTICS

Kind of Business	Total 1967 Establishments	Inhabitants per Store
Food stores:		
Grocery stores, including delicatessens	218,130	905
Meat and fish markets	17,943	11,005
Fruit stores, vegetable markets	8,890	22,211
Candy, nut, confectionery	13,981	14,123
Retail bakeries	19,598	10,075
Eating, drinking places:		
Eating places	236,563	835
Drinking places (alcoholic beverages)	111,327	1,774
General merchandise stores:		
Department stores	5,792	34,091
Variety stores	21,046	9,382
Apparel, accessories:		
Women's ready-to-wear	31,883	6,193
Women's accessories	10,297	19,176
Furriers, fur shops	2,343	84,275
Furniture, home furnishings:		
Furniture, home furnishings	55,207	3,577
Household appliances	20,806	9,490
Radio, TV, music stores	22,813	8,655

Kind of Business	Total 1967 Establishments	Inhabitants per Store
Gasoline service stations	53,722	914
Automotive groups:		
Motor vehicle dealers	62,023	3,183
Tires, batteries, accessories	29,189	6,765
Drugstores, proprietary stores	53,722	3,676
Building materials, hardware, farm:		
Building materials, supply stores	42,272	4,671
Hardware stores	27,162	7,270
Farm equipment dealers	16,739	11,796
Other retail stores:		
Liquor stores	39,719	4,791
Antique, second-hand stores	27,267	7,242
Sporting goods/bicycle shops	16,043	12,308
Jewelry stores	23,689	8,335
Fuel and ice dealers	22,258	8,871
Florists	22,451	8,795
Cigar stores, stands	5,560	35,514
Nonstore retailers:		
Mail order houses	5,948	33,197
Merchandising machine operators	10,888	18,135

Source: Number of establishments from *Statistical Abstract of the United States 1973*, U.S. Department of Commerce, Bureau of the Census. Number of inhabitants residing in the United States (excluding Armed Forces overseas) as of July 1, 1967 from same source.

DON'T SOME COMMUNITIES OFFER SPECIAL INDUCEMENTS TO GET BUSINESS TO LOCATE THERE?

Not all of them want more new businesses. There was a time when the city fathers would do almost anything to entice a new business into town, but those days went out with the advent of the environmentalists, who are preoccupied with your potential for creating noise, smoke, odor, and smog.

Whether the community you are considering wants your business is important. Some areas are eager to welcome new businesses and therefore eliminate some of the small problems which arise. Other communities' attitudes toward new business range from passivity to open hostility. Obviously, you should avoid a city or region that does not want new business.

AREN'T PROBLEMS OF THE LABOR FORCE ABOUT THE SAME EVERYWHERE?

Not by a long shot! Not only do labor rates vary significantly from one part of the country to another, but surpluses of labor still exist in some areas and shortages in others, despite the fact that labor is more mobile today than it has ever been. Companies with branches located in different parts of the country have also reported wide variances in productivity in different locations. Climate can be a big problem in getting people to move to your locality. To make matters worse, the serious lack of moderately priced housing in some areas makes it almost impossible for blue-collar and office workers to even consider living in the community, although they would prefer to. Unskilled people, in general, will move more readily than skilled people. Skilled workers, especially professionals, are reluctant to move at all unless things like good schools, libraries, and theaters are available.

The message that can be distilled from these trends is that unless the geographical area under consideration can provide at least five qualified candidates for every job you need to fill, you will likely have difficulty finding good workers.

The labor rates for major cities in the United States are published periodically by the Bureau of Labor Statistics. While these are available only for larger cities, the information provides an excellent starting point for estimating how much you will have to pay for labor in the area you select. Remember that labor costs tend to be higher in metropolitan areas. The difference could be as great as 10 percent. This fact might cause you to select a suburban area, with significant savings in operating costs. You should adjust wage estimates downward by 3 percent if labor is in great supply. Adjust them upward by at least 4 percent if you are considering an area where labor is not plentiful. Do not forget to include fringe benefits in your estimates. These can easily add 25 to 30 percent to your labor costs.

The importance of taxes has been overemphasized as a factor in selecting a business location. Between states, tax considerations have tended to level off. Whereas some states have gross volume taxes, and others have income taxes, the net collected from most businesses tends to be the same. On rare occasions, some significant differences occur because of the peculiarities of some companies, but these are not necessarily permanent, and successive legislatures can close loopholes and change regulations at will.

In considering your tax bill, be sure you look at the *total* bill, not just a part of it. This means that your analysis should include all the following taxes:

State franchise tax	Personal income tax
State corporate income tax	State/local sales tax
Gross receipts tax	State disability tax
Local real property tax	Workmen's compensation
Local personal property tax	insurance premiums
Unemployment compensation	

WHAT ARE THE UNIQUE LOCATION REQUIREMENTS OF MANUFACTURING AND WHOLESALE BUSINESSES?

In most manufacturing and wholesale businesses, the customer does not come to the business establishment. Customer accessibility, therefore, is not a critical factor. The costs of occupancy and the cost of operating in a given location would be more compelling factors than the location itself. Production efficiency, proximity to raw materials, utility costs, and transportation costs will become the critical factors in evaluating a manufacturing location. Customer orientation is of secondary importance unless customers come to your plant for reasons related to the transaction of business.

Radical changes in transportation modes during the past 15 years have made the problem of locating or relocating a factory much easier than it once was. The growth of air shipping makes sites near airports more attractive. Interstate highways have increased the popularity of trucks as a method of moving goods. More pipeline facilities are available. Railroads have adapted their services to provide mass transportation of truck trailers with their "piggyback" operations.

You should have a transportation expert furnish you shipping rates and delivery times to your major customers via the various modes of transportation. You might discover the preferable mode of transportation to be different from what you had expected.

The sources of raw materials can be marked on a map and distances noted. If they all come from one area, you should consider what advantages a competitor located adjacent to the source has over a more remote facility. It might be more important to be closer to raw materials than to your customers, or vice versa. Facilities should be available to bring the raw materials in rapidly and economically. Check to see if your supply is assured regardless of the season and if the supply seems assured for the foreseeable future. A consideration of the future cost and availability might cause you to select an alternate source of raw materials, which in turn could affect your planned location. What you want is flexibility, not a situation where you are locked into a single mode of transporting raw materials or a single source of supply.

WHAT SITE CHARACTERISTICS ARE IMPORTANT IN THE RETAIL BUSINESS?

Site location criteria are constantly changing on account of new methods of merchandising, the growth of shopping centers, and the increasing importance of advertising in generating sales. A site which would have been considered good 10 years ago might be inadequate by today's standards. Whether you are selecting a new site or relocating an existing business, these are the specifics to check, in addition to the "location" factors previously discussed:

☐ Parking facilities

☐ Compatibility of surrounding businesses

☐ Traffic density

☐ Street location

☐ Occupancy cost

☐ History of the site

HOW IMPORTANT ARE PARKING FACILITIES?

The use of the automobile as a means of getting shopping accomplished makes one wonder whether anyone ever walks "to the store" any more. The fact that we now have many families with two or more automobiles has created special problems in providing enough parking space to accommodate the customers we want to attract. Most of us can remember when parking was the least of our problems when we went "downtown" to shop. Concern about free parking and validation of parking tickets is the result of the mass movement of customers to shopping centers in outlying areas where parking is plentiful. We should remember that getting customers to our business is important. Assuring adequate parking facilities is a part of good planning. Parking area is related to the number of square feet of sales space which exists, to the average number of shoppers per car, and to the average length of their visit to the store. Get a traffic consultant to assist you in gathering these statistics and laying out an efficient parking area for your business.

The effect of neighboring stores on your success is more important than most business people realize. Whether the business next door hurts you, helps you, or has no effect on your business is a question which might have more to do with your success than any other location factor you could consider. *Compatibility* of two businesses often causes them to do more together than they would if separated. This concept is considered in the design of shopping centers and in the placement of stores within them. Placing a men's store in the midst of a group of stores which cater predominantly to women is an example of incompatibility. Mortuaries are highly incompatible with most retail businesses. In addition, they are heavy parking users and cause traffic congestion during funerals. Drive-in eating establishments, auto repair shops, service stations, and used car lots also show a high degree of incompatibility with other retail businesses. On the other hand, department stores are considered "good neighbors," as is evidenced by the clusters of small businesses that usually surround them. Large office buildings attract drugstores, restaurants, beauty parlors and barbershops, and similar retail businesses as compatible neighbors.

Compatibility of adjacent business results in customer interchange that would be nonexistent if they were located some distance apart. Even competitive stores can be compatible if they carry merchandise of different styles, lines, and prices, thereby increasing total patronage through cumulative attraction. Auto centers composed solely of all the major automobile dealers in a trading area have been very successful in many localities. Service stations and restaurants strategically located in these centers make it possible for customers shopping for new cars or waiting for repairs to do business in an atmosphere totally dedicated to their primary shopping objectives.

HOW CAN YOU RELATE TRAFFIC PATTERNS TO SITE POTENTIAL?

An analysis of automobile and pedestrian traffic around a shopping area can provide valuable information regarding potential shoppers. The volume of automobile traffic around a shopping center is significant. Many of our major shopping centers are located just off major highways or at intersecting arterial streets where accessibility is at its optimum. The key item, however, is to find out the number of passengers who become pedestrian traffic and are likely to come to your store.

It is desirable to make a count of pedestrians entering a shopping area during the various times of the day. Although this technique is inexpensive and effective, few business people bother to do it.

To be most useful, the count should separate the potential customers by sex and age. You would not, for instance, want to make the mistake of locating a store catering primarily to male customers in an area frequented primarily by female shoppers. The count should indicate the number of shoppers passing the site during every half-hour period in the course of each normal business day of the week. Pedestrian interviews, if kept short, can provide some insight into the reason why the shopper is in the area. Typical questions will draw out information about the shopper's destination, stores visited or to be visited, and the kind of goods or services being sought.

HOW IMPORTANT IS A "GOOD ADDRESS"?

Market research has shown the following factors to be significant to the location of a business. The ideal location on the street should be:

☐ On the side with the highest pedestrian count.

☐ On the side where the biggest business generators are located.

☐ On the side nearest the area of population growth.

☐ On the side offering the best protection from the weather.

☐ On the side which is shaded in the afternoon.

☐ On the side with fewest driveways and similar "interruptors" of pedestrian traffic.

It is generally believed that it is preferable to be at the "end of the line" on the better side of the street than to be centrally located on the other side. Researchers have found that pedestrians are reluctant to make right-angle changes in their direction of flow even to visit an attractive store across the street.

Other studies have claimed advantages for stores located on the right-hand side of the street leaving a downtown area, or for a location on the "going-home" side of a street used by workers leaving work at the end of the day.

HOW IS OCCUPANCY COST RELATED TO THE CHOICE OF A SITE?

The size of your store will indirectly determine the area to be chosen. Your investment might be so limited that it would be impossible to generate enough sales volume to pay the high rent of a downtown location. It would then be necessary to select an outlying area of a large city or to consider locating in a small town.

Occupancy cost or rent is a charge business people pay whether they lease a store from someone else or own the building themselves. In the latter case, owners charge themselves depreciation on the building and interest on their investment, as well as other costs like insurance, taxes, and maintenance which a landlord normally pays. In either case, the occupancy charge is expressed as *rent*.

Occupancy cost generally decreases as one moves from the center of the trade area toward the perimeter, or from a downtown location to one in outlying areas. Total occupancy costs are high for businesses with high markups and low advertising budgets. They tend to be low where markups are low and advertising budgets are high (discount stores, supermarkets). As a general rule, occupancy costs are the reciprocal of advertising costs. For example, discount houses and chain supermarkets are often found in low-rent areas away from the center of town, where ample parking and easy access are the rule. The location of such establishments is not critical since they rely on heavy advertising to attract customers to the site. Markups are low on the merchandise they sell and they rely on a high volume of business for their profits. The other extreme is illustrated by variety and specialty shops which require a good (high-rent) location near other stores upon which they depend for their customers. Markups are high and advertising costs are usually low for stores of this type.

Occupancy costs for second-floor or below-the-street locations are often as low as 50 percent of those for stores located at street level. Prime locations in well-established retail areas are recognized by landlords who set the rent they charge in relation to the volume the business enjoys because of its good location.

WHAT WILL THE HISTORY OF A SITE TELL YOU?

It might tell you to forget it. You should find how long the site has been vacant if it is not occupied. Also find out who the former tenants were, why they left, how long they stayed and any other information which might keep you from repeating the mistakes of others. Sites on which many businesses have failed should be avoided.

DOES A SHOPPING CENTER OFFER ANY ADVANTAGES OVER OTHER LOCATIONS?

Shopping centers offer customers an opportunity to drive in, park, and do their shopping with optimum safety and speed. Weather protection and air conditioning in some centers are a big plus during periods of inclement weather. As a result of the tenant selection procedure, you will usually have few or no directly competing businesses to worry about.

Do not forget that many shopping center developers give preference to well-known chains and big downtown department and specialty stores. With such tenants assured, the developers can obtain financing at lower rates. If you are accepted by the developer, you will have to pay your pro rata share of the budget for operating and maintaining the facility. You will be expected to keep store hours, light your windows, and place your signs in accordance with the established rules.

Experience has shown that shopping centers are ideal for stores that cater to mass demand—the big department store, the variety store, and the supermarket. Significantly, many of the smaller stores which have relocated from old locations often do not do well in a shopping center. Clientele from the previous location sometimes do not follow the business to the new location, and most of the mass shoppers at the center do not respond to the store's specialized appeal. If you are considering such a move, talk to others in businesses like yours who have relocated to a shopping center and use their experience to guide you in making a decision about relocating.

WHAT ARE THE DISADVANTAGES OF A DOWNTOWN LOCATION?

Congestion and parking problems, which have always been existent, are even more severe now. Parking lots and parking meters help, but the rates often deter potential shoppers who can enjoy free parking and easy access in the suburban shopping centers.

Downtown locations are less accessible to the former customers who have moved to the suburbs. This flight to suburbia has caused severe drops in sales volumes in many cities and has caused many merchants either to move to outlying areas or to open branch offices there in an attempt to compete effectively for the customer's dollar.

In some communities, new customer groups are replacing the old. For example, older people who have raised their families and now prefer the convenience of city apartment living are moving in from the suburbs. They can bring your business a well-to-do if somewhat conservative clientele. Also, keep in mind the growing number of middle-income, white-collar office workers who work downtown and live in the suburbs. They do much of their shopping downtown and pick up many of their convenience goods on their way to and from work. The time this group has for shopping is largely limited to lunch hours. So if you serve such customers, you might have to do half your day's business between 11:30 A.M. and 2:30 P.M.

WHAT THINGS SHOULD BE AVOIDED IN SELECTING A SITE?

This could be a very long list, but here are a few that can provide food for thought in your search for the "ideal" site:

□ Areas with vacant stores or unsightly vacant lots nearby.

□ Sites that are difficult to find or get to.

□ Sites on which many businesses have failed.

□ Areas of congested or metered parking.

□ Dark or isolated locations in which there is a low level of night or weekend activity.

- Businesses whose customers' parking time is extremely long.
- A location near an auditorium, convention hall, or theater where there is severe evening congestion and competition for parking space.
- Areas identified with noise, congestion, hazards, odors, or unsightliness.
- Businesses which generate heavy traffic either from vehicles or from pedestrians who are not shoppers.
- Areas with incompatible businesses.
- Areas which have been selected solely on the basis of personal preference, emotion, or friendship with the owner of the site.

WHAT OPTIONS ARE ASSOCIATED WITH BUYING OR LEASING AN EXISTING BUILDING?

This approach eliminates any choice you have about site selection since the location remains as it is at the time of the selling or leasing transaction. Buyers should evaluate the site as they would any other, keeping in mind the consequences of buying the building or leasing it just because it is available and cheap. Such a decision could lead to problems and make it necessary to relocate later, with additional costs for moving, building up a new work force, and attracting new customers.

If you are short of capital and need your funds for other investments, leasing might be preferable to buying. You can sometimes obtain a favorable lease from the owner with an option to purchase. Because of tax considerations, owners might prefer to lease their property rather than sell. In such case, they are likely to make the lease cost attractive.

A decision to buy should consider resale possibilities of the building. If you discover factors which would make resale difficult, leasing would be a better option.

WHAT FACTORS ENTER INTO THE FINAL LOCATION DECISION?

The factors discussed earlier are those associated primarily with the environmental and economic aspects of the community and specifically of the area under consideration. The emphasis was to offer a means of eliminating as many undesirable sites as possible, leaving a few good ones to be evaluated in detail. In the final analysis, a decision to locate or relocate a business, or to remain in the same location, must be based upon a comparison of the potential business volume with the cost of occupancy at each of the proposed locations. Obviously, location is not the only factor which affects business volume. Effective advertising, good management, skillful promotions, quality service, and good customer relations all contribute to success in their own unique way. Their contributions to the profit-and-loss statement can be largely wiped out, however, by high operating costs or low business volume caused by a poor location.

In evaluating the effect of business volume, business people attempt to determine what the effect will be if they find out through analysis that one site will produce 5 percent more volume at the same occupancy cost as another. Or they attempt to determine what potential profit is indicated by a comparison of two sites with the same volume, one of which has an occupancy cost 10 percent less than that of the other. Suppose a business has a volume of $1 million a year, and an analysis shows that a new site is available at an occupancy cost of $5,000 less a year, but that the business volume in the new location would be only $800,000. To determine whether moving to the new site is economically feasible, an estimate has to be made. If the business makes a 5 percent profit on its volume, it would cost the owner $10,000 a year in reduced profits (calculated at 5 percent of $200,000, the reduced business volume) to save $5,000 a year in occupancy costs. In that case a move would not be desirable.

WHAT IS THE METHOD OF DETERMINING BUSINESS VOLUME?

There are several methods, but some are too involved and complex for any but a consultant to use. One fairly simple way is to determine how many potential customers live in your trading area and measure their purchasing power. You can then calculate how much of their disposable income you are likely to get at your location. The following steps are usually followed in this method:

1. On a large map of your area, outline the prime trading area, based on the distance you believe people will travel to get to your store. You can use preselected travel time (say 10 minutes), or some other logical determinant of how far from your location you can expect to attract customers. Market surveys have indicated that people will not travel farther than 3 miles to patronize an equipment rental business. Large independence groceries find that most of their customers come from an area within a radius of 1 mile. On the other hand, customers will often travel several miles to eat at a good restaurant.

    Take into consideration the location of competitive stores situated between your business and the outer perimeter of your trading area. Customers will rarely pass through an intercepting store to get to one which offers the same product or services at about the same price.

2. Using available census data, or information from the chamber of commerce, determine how many families live in the area you have outlined. Determine their disposable income from census data or from other sources within the community.

TABLE 6-2. CONSUMER EXPENDITURES BY PRODUCT IN 1972

Product	Percent of Disposable Income
Food, beverages, and tobacco	21.7
Clothing, accessories, and jewelry	10.0
Personal care	1.5
Housing	14.5
Household operations	14.5
Medical care expenses	7.9
Personal business	5.7
Transportation	13.8
Recreation	6.6
Other	3.8

Source: *Statistical Abstract of the United States 1974*, U.S. Department of Commerce, p. 376.

3. Based on national norms, calculate how much of the disposable income would be spent in your trading area. The data in Table 6-2, for instance, shows that the average figure spent nationally for food, beverages, and tobacco in 1972 was about 22 percent. If your area has 1,000 families with an average disposable income of $8,000 per family, their food bill should approximate $1,760,000 annually (1,000 × $8,000 × 0.22).

4. Next, find out from your local trade association the amount of money actually spent on your product or service. Let us assume that the local retail grocer's association reports that retail grocery sales have amounted to $1,500,000 during a recent year, or an average of $1,500 per family. This would tell you that families in the area are spending only about 19 percent of their income for food at stores in the area, leaving a "vacuum" of $260,000 in potential business when compared with the national norm. By relating this potential volume to your estimated occupancy costs, you can get an approximation of the profitability of an additional grocery store in the area.

   There is no way of eliminating judgment in estimating business volume for a new business. In predicting the actions of customers faced with a new alternative represented by your proposed business, personal interviews to determine the likelihood of "switching" from their present store to a new one will take some of the guesswork out of the calculations. Interview techniques are time-consuming and tricky. You will likely need the services of a market consultant to assure reliable results.

   You can also compare the number of inhabitants in your area with the number of grocery stores in the area and compare the ratio with those shown in Table 6-1. If this preliminary check indicates that the area is already oversaturated with grocery stores, it is unnecessary to verify the need for another one.

At best, a checklist is a reminder of things to consider which might be detrimental to the future success of your business if overlooked. A thorough job of site selection for a manufacturing plant, for instance, would probably cover over 1,000 items. The risk involved in underestimating the importance of adequate research and analysis as a preliminary step in the site selection process is clearly stated by one of the country's foremost plant location authorities:[2]

The Utopian plant location is becoming ever more elusive. Lest management rues the day it cut the ribbon on the wrong plant in the wrong place at the wrong time, its ultimate decision on the site had best be determined by exhaustive research—and long before that first golden spade of earth is turned.

For small business people with limited financial resources, the following checklist for locating a retail store will be helpful. It was developed as part of a study funded by the Small Business Administration.[3] It can be adapted for use with other types of business.

CHECKLIST FOR LOCATING A STORE

I. City or town
  A. Economic considerations
    1. Industry
      a. Farming
      b. Manufacturing
      c. Trading
    2. Trend
      a. Highly satisfactory
      b. Growing
      c. Stationary
      d. Declining
    3. Permanency
      a. Old and well established
      b. Old and reviving
      c. New and promising
      d. Recent and uncertain
    4. Diversification
      a. Many and varied lines
      b. Many of the same type
      c. Few varied lines
      d. Dependent on one industry

    5. Stability
      a. Constant
      b. Satisfactory
      c. Average
      d. Subject to wide fluctuations
    6. Seasonality
      a. Little or no seasonal change
      b. Mild seasonal change
      c. Periodical—every few years
      d. Highly seasonal in nature
    7. Future
      a. Most promising
      b. Satisfactory
      c. Uncertain
      d. Poor outlook
  B. Population
    1. Income distribution
      a. Mostly wealthy
      b. Well distributed
      c. Mostly middle income
      d. Poor

[2]Leonard Yassen, "A New Ballgame in Plant Location," *Dun's*, March 1974, p. 38.
[3]Verne A. Bunn, *Buying and Selling a Small Business*, U.S. Small Business Administration, Washington, 1969.

2. Trend
    a. Growing
    b. Large and stable
    c. Small and stable
    d. Declining
3. Living status
    a. Own homes
    b. Pay substantial rent
    c. Pay moderate rent
    d. Pay low rent
C. Competition
    1. Number of competing stores
        a. Few
        b. Average
        c. Many
        d. Too many
    2. Type of management
        a. Not progressive
        b. Average
        c. Above average
        d. Alert and progressive
    3. Presence of chains
        a. No chains
        b. Few chains
        c. Average number
        d. Many well established
    4. Type of competing stores
        a. Unattractive
        b. Average
        c. Old and well established
        d. Are many people buying
            out of community?
D. The town as a place to live
    1. Character of the city
        a. Are homes neat and clean
            or run-down and shabby?
        b. Are lawns, parks, streets,
            etc., neat, modern,
            attractive?
        c. Adequate facilities
            available
            (1) Banking
            (2) Transportation
            (3) Professional services
            (4) Utilities
    2. Facilities and climate
        a. Schools
        b. Churches
        c. Amusement centers
        d. Medical and dental
            services
        e. Climate

II. The actual site
    A. Competition
        1. Number of independent
            stores of same kind as
            yours
            a. Same block
            b. Same side of street
            c. Across street
        2. Number of chain stores
            a. Same block
            b. Same side of street
            c. Across street
        3. Kind of stores next door
        4. Number of vacancies
            a. Same side of street
            b. Across street
            c. Next door
        5. Dollar sales of nearest
            competitor
    B. Traffic flow
        1. Sex of pedestrians
        2. Age of pedestrians
        3. Destination of pedestrians
        4. Number of passers-by
        5. Automobile traffic count
        6. Peak hours of traffic flow
        7. Percent location of site
    C. Transportation
        1. Transfer points
        2. Highway
        3. Kind (bus, streetcar, auto,
            railway)
    D. Parking facilities
        1. Large and convenient
        2. Large enough but not
            convenient
        3. Convenient but too small
        4. Completely inadequate
    E. Side of street
    F. Plant
        1. Frontage—in feet
        2. Depth—in feet
        3. Shape of building
        4. Condition
        5. Heat—type; air conditioning
        6. Light
        7. Display space
        8. Back entrance
        9. Front entrance
        10. Display windows
    G. Corner location—if not,
        what is it?

H. Unfavorable characteristics
   1. Fire hazards
   2. Cemetery
   3. Hospital
   4. Industry
   5. Relief office
   6. Undertaker
   7. Vacant lot—no parking possibilities
   8. Garages
   9. Playground
   10. Smoke, dust, odors
   11. Poor sidewalks and pavement
   12. Unsightly neighborhood buildings
I. Professional men in block
   1. Medical doctors
   2. Dentists
   3. Lawyers
   4. Veterinarians
   5. Others
J. History of the site

SELF-CHECK OF KEY CONCEPTS

This exercise is designed to test your understanding of the material presented in Chapter 6. Choose the response, *True* or *False*, which best fits each statement. Correct responses are presented in the back of the text.

1. An *acceptable* location can cost, per year, 10 to 15 percent more to operate than a *superior* one.
2. The advantages of a good location can be largely lost by selecting a poor site.
3. The principle of compatibility in selecting business sites indicates that competing businesses should never be adjacent to each other.
4. The fastest-growing area of the country in terms of population and individual income is the Midwest.
5. Admittance of a business to a shopping center virtually assures a high volume of business.
6. A retail location near a cemetery or a funeral home is not considered a wise selection.
7. If you locate in a low-rent section of the trading area, you will probably have to allow more money for advertising than you would if your store is in a prime high-rent area.
8. Sites that have been occupied by a series of unsuccessful businesses should be avoided.
9. Hourly workers are more reluctant to relocate than professional workers.

PERFORMANCE PROBLEMS AND PROJECTS

1. Al Richmond is considering the possibility of leasing a gasoline service station from a major oil company in a central Illinois community and is trying to determine which of three areas offered by the company shows the best potential in terms of customers he could expect to get. He has heard that some communities already have more service stations than

they can support, so he wants to be sure that the community he chooses can support another establishment and offers opportunity for future growth.

He has obtained the following from his local library:

National Statistics	1960	1970
United States total population	173,284,000	197,457,000
Gasoline service stations	206,755	216,059

Illinois Statistics

		1960	1970
1.	Decatur, Illinois, population	78,004	90,397
	Gasoline service stations	97	100
2.	Peoria, Illinois, population	103,162	126,963
	Gasoline service stations	114	132
3.	Springfield, Illinois, population	83,271	91,753
	Gasoline service stations	135	128

From this data make the following calculations:

a. How many inhabitants per station were there in 1960 in the United States?
b. How many inhabitants per station were there in 1970 in the United States?
c. From the data in b, calculate the percentage gain or loss in inhabitants per station between 1960 and 1970.
d. Make the same calculations you did in a, b, and c above for each of the three communities under consideration.

Answer the following questions:

(1) Which of the three communities has had the most rapid population growth between 1960 and 1970?
(2) How does the rate of growth for each city compare with the national average?
(3) Based on all the data examined, list the three cities in the order of their potential for supporting a new gasoline service station, with the most desirable listed first. Explain any pertinent data which influenced your decision.

THE CASE OF THE NEW LOCATION

A CASE IN POINT

Five years ago, Harriet Bryant bought a small hardware store from a retiring owner in Duncanville, Texas, a well-established suburb southwest of Dallas. The area had been built up over a period of 15 years by population expanding westward out of central Dallas. Duncanville was the center of a trade area of about 15,000 people. The store was situated in the Tyler Shopping Mall, a complex of 50 stores, including two large department stores.

Despite her location and a steady clientele during most of the year, her net profits were only 2 percent of her net sales. Operating expenses were pretty high in the center, and maintenance assessments were increasing since the shopping center was almost eleven years old.

By examining the Dun & Bradstreet net profit to sales ratios for hardware stores, Harriet found that the median figure for a recent year was 2.73 percent of net sales, but that the profit in the upper quartile of the stores sampled was over 5 percent. That meant, she correctly reasoned, that some stores had net profits in excess of 5 percent—maybe as high as 6 percent. This started her wondering.

She believed that she could at least double her net profits if she could find a larger location that would enable her to increase her volume substantially and at the same time permit her to reduce her rent and operating expenses.

She enlisted the help of Red Carpet Realtors, a firm which specialized in industrial and business properties. Her requirements for a store with approximately twice the area of her present store would enable her to carry a line of small household appliances and several items of convenience goods she did not have room to carry in her present store.

After 6 months of searching, Red Carpet called to tell her that they had located a vacant store in a small neighborhood shopping center at the western edge of Dallas in the Westlake area, a fast-growing area of middle-income families. One of the tenants in the center had estimated that about 1,500 people a day came to the center (Figure 6-1) to shop.

The shopping area contained a supermarket chain grocery, a coin laundry, a drugstore, an auto parts store, a dry-cleaning

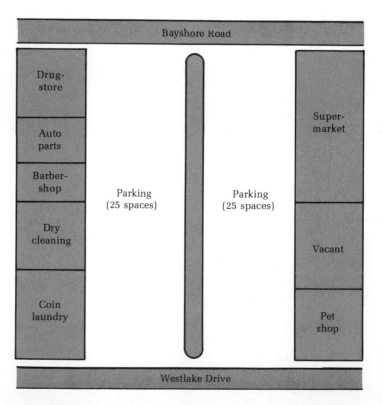

FIGURE 6-1. Sketch of the shopping area Harriet visited.

firm, a pet shop, and a barbershop. Harriet found out that a hardware store had previously occupied the empty space.

The Dallas Chamber of Commerce estimated Westlake's population at about 10,000 and stated that the area's population had been increasing about 15 percent a year for the last 3 years. This sounded encouraging, so she decided to examine the site.

On her first visit, she was impressed with the flow of traffic in and out of the area. The parking areas were crowded, but she was only in the area briefly after lunch. The vacant store was roomy and would need little refurbishing for her to move in. She counted 50 parking stalls, 25 on each side.

Based on the knowledge that about 75 percent of her present customers were women, she decided to hire a consultant to make a traffic count during the daytime and evening hours on all days except Sunday. Here is what the traffic count showed:

Day	Time of Day	Number of Cars	Total Shoppers	Female	Male
Monday	8:00– 9:00	32	80	25	55
	9:00–10:00	58	122	80	42
Tuesday	10:00–11:00	90	133	95	38
	11:00–12:00	84	100	56	44
Wednesday	12:00– 1:00	66	84	44	40
	1:00– 2:00	176	174	117	57
Thursday	2:00– 3:00	162	206	135	71
	3:00– 4:00	94	150	98	52
Friday	4:00– 5:00	58	64	25	39
	5:00– 6:00	30	38	20	18
Saturday	6:00– 7:00	76	144	67	77
	7:00– 8:00	64	136	50	86
	8:00– 9:00	56	100	43	57
			1,531	855	676

Customer Destinations

Drugstore	235
Supermarket	698
Auto parts store	112
Dry cleaners	157
Barbershop	57
Coin laundry	196
Pet shop	76
	1,531

1. Assuming that on the average the cars stayed in the parking lot 20 minutes, what conclusions can be drawn from the traffic count?
2. Based on your understanding of the principle of compatibility, can you foresee any problems?
3. Can you pinpoint any potential parking problems?
4. Do you believe that the move to the new location would be a good one? Give your reasons.

7 Planning and Implementing an Effective Layout

PERFORMANCE OBJECTIVES

After reading this chapter you should be able to explain how the physical layout of a business affects its operating costs. You should be able to differentiate between the various kinds of layout and describe the methods commonly used to plan and implement layouts, especially in retailing and manufacturing businesses. Specifically, you should be able to:

1. Demonstrate what the term *layout* means as it pertains to retailing, manufacturing, service businesses, and wholesaling.
2. Decide when it would become desirable to retain professional layout consultants in planning a layout.
3. Create a plan for evaluating the strong and weak points of several alternate layouts.
4. Explain the relationship of customer traffic inside a store to the placement of merchandise.
5. Sketch the generally recommended areas in a retail store where you should place impulse goods, convenience goods, utility goods, and staple items.
6. Demonstrate the "4–3–2–1 rule" as it applies to the value of floor space in a retail store.
7. Predict the consequences of a manufacturing layout charactertized by long hauls and excessive backtracking.

8. Develop a list of benefits associated with an effective manufacturing layout.
9. Demonstrate how manufacturing tasks are planned and how such planning can be used to determine how much floor area will be required.
10. Differentiate between a product-type layout and a process-type layout and explain where each is used.

INTRODUCTION

All across the country, small plants and businesses are engaged in a continual struggle to improve their operations, attract customers, and sell more merchandise.

Retailers often discover, sometimes by trial and error, that the location of merchandise in their stores can affect their sales. The physical arrangement, the accessibility of merchandise, the kinds and number of displays, and the appearance of the store front are all important factors in building and maintaining sales volume. Ignoring such factors can be costly.

In the manufacturing facility, managers are faced with an almost infinite number of ways to arrange equipment and machines within the physical boundaries of the production area. They are confronted with a challenge to find the "best" layout—one which will provide a smooth flow of material with a minimum of handling and wasted motion. The final arrangement they select is often a compromise made up of the strong features of several alternatives they have considered. They soon learn that there is no end to improvement and that the "best" layout is a continually sought-after goal which is never truly achieved.

The layout of an area determines the characteristics of the environment in which the firm's business will be conducted. This environment can become an aid or an obstacle, depending upon how effectively the layout is planned and implemented.

Achieving an effective layout of the physical facilities can contribute significantly to worker comfort, customer satisfaction, and increased sales.

This chapter explores layout principles and practices by emphasizing the importance of planning a layout before you implement it. The impact of layout on retailing and manufacturing operations is stressed since the principles applied to these businesses apply equally well in service trades and in wholesaling establishments, with minor modifications.

WHAT IS INCLUDED IN THE TERM *LAYOUT*?

For the retailer it encompasses the arrangement of merchandise in pleasing displays which attract customers and get them to buy the goods the store has to offer. It recognizes the principle that some areas of the store offer better exposure for certain kinds of merchandise than other areas. It also recognizes the relationship between customer traffic patterns through the store and the placement of merchandise along a theoretical path. It considers the cost of floor space in allocating goods to physical locations, reserving "high-rent" areas for those lines which will "pay their rent" in terms of gross profits returned to the owner. It also includes the physical characteristics of the store, including the appearance of the store front, lighting, air conditioning, decor, and similar factors which have a psychological effect on the customer.

In manufacturing, layout concerns itself with the efficient arrangement of machines and equipment in relation to the available floor space and to the workers who will be making the product. Layout is based on the premise that a smooth flow of materials over the shortest distance with the least amount of handling will be least expensive to operate with. Phenomenal reductions in manufacturing costs are often achieved by efficient layouts. A good layout also considers the optimum placement of supporting activities such as maintenance, shipping, and office functions.

To wholesalers who have to move hundreds of orders from their warehouses to waiting customers each day, the emphasis is on storage and retrieval methods, handling and transportation techniques, and efficient recordkeeping methods.

Layout to the service business stresses a pleasant atmosphere for customers, easy access to the store, and efficient handling of customer needs.

Any arrangement of display counters, machines, equipment, furniture, or shelves is a layout—just as any house plan is a plan. But some are better than others. We will concern ourselves in this chapter with the characteristics of "good" layouts and offer some guidelines for achieving them.

WHY BE CONCERNED ABOUT LAYOUT?

No successful business remains static for very long. As it grows and acquires more customers, the need for more space will eventually become pressing. Efficient utilization of existing buildings and floor space will delay the time when capital outlays for modernization or expansion will become necessary. This growth will eventually force the planning of additional facilities, more machines, equipment, utilities, and work stations for the people who will have to be hired. Accurate estimates of the capital requirements can be made only after a careful evaluation of the possibilities offered by several alternative layouts.

In manufacturing, where machine processes are already refined and cost reduction has been achieved through methods improvement, plant layout and the accompanying savings from reduced material handling might offer the only solution for further reductions in operating costs.

HOW CAN YOU TELL WHICH LAYOUT OF SEVERAL IS THE BEST ONE?

The layout engineer has developed several techniques for evaluating layouts. One technique is to compare the estimated costs associated with different layouts and decide which is most effective from a cost

TABLE 7-1.   COSTS TO BE CONSIDERED IN LAYOUT PLANNING

Investment	Operating

A. Initial cost of new facilities:
    Buildings
    Construction
    Machinery
    Equipment
	E. Material:
	    Production
	    Scrap or waste
	    Supplies and packing
	    Maintenance parts and
	      materials

B. Accessory costs:
    Tools—jigs, fixtures, tools
    Handling equipment
    Containers
    Benches and chairs
    Time clocks, water coolers,
      etc.
    Shelves, bins, racks
    Wiring and lights
    Piping and duct work
    Office equipment
    Engineering or design work
	F. Labor:
	    Direct
	    Overtime or extra shift
	      premium
	    Idle or waiting time
	    Clerical
	    Maintenance
	    Inspection
	    Handling and storerooms
	    Other indirect labor
	    Supervision

C. Installation costs:
    Building changes
    Machinery and equipment
    Services and supporting
      facilities
    Auxiliary service lines
	G. General:
	    Floor space
	    Power
	    Fuel
	    Taxes
	    Insurance
	    Rentals
	    Interest on investment

D. Depreciation and obsolescence costs	

Source: Richard Muther, *Practical Plant Layout*, McGraw-Hill Book Company, New York, 1955.

standpoint. A list of cost items related to a layout has been suggested by Muther[1] and is shown in Table 7-1. Costs are applied to each applicable item for each alternative layout under consideration and added to a total. This method is not precise because some of the items are difficult to obtain dollar values for and must be estimated.

Another method is to list the pros and cons for each layout and establish a relative point value for each item being considered. Table 7-2 shows how this method can be used to decide where in a new plant incoming materials are to be received. The evaluator first listed the advantages of both proposals and then used a weighting plan to assign an importance value to each item being considered. Notice that efficient utilization of otherwise "dead" space (basement area) in Plan A was given a high rating. No value was assigned to item 5 of Plan B since it offers a disadvantage which offsets the advantage recognized by the evaluator.

[1]Richard Muther, *Practical Plant Layout*, McGraw-Hill Book Company, New York, 1955, p. 250.

TABLE 7-2. ANALYSIS OF A RECEIVING LOCATION BY LISTING PROS AND CONS

Plan A. Receive at Rear of Building.

Advantages	Point Value	Reasons
1. Can utilize basement for raw-material storage.	3	Cannot use it effectively for much else.
2. Can use unloading dock for purpose it is best suited.	1	Can still use for stock room supplies, and paint storage.
3. Can receive by rail.	1	98% of shipments come in by truck.
4. Can easily install heavy machines.	2	The heart of the process.
5. Will have more room for expanding machine department.	1	Assembly operations can go to double shift; machine capacity is limited.
6. Can locate cafeteria near front office.	1	Office employees won't have to go through the shop.
7. Can use the present shop office where it is.	2	Moving it would be a long and costly job the way it is constructed.
8. Less construction cost to revamp receiving facilities	1	But facilities have to be revamped anyway.
TOTAL POINTS	12	

Plan B. Receive at Front Side.

Advantages	Point Value	Reasons
1. Requires no long haul for truck to back of building.	2	Narrow roadway into back of building; congestion with shipping and parking lot.
2. Will have a larger open area for location of assembly departments.	1	They are the ones most likely to be relaid out.
3. Can consolidate all receiving at one place.	2	Saves approximately 2 employees.
4. Majority of workers near parking lot.	1	But approximately 35% come by public transportation.
5. Machinery departments will be nearer engineering office.	0	But assembly will be farther from quality, production, planning and sales.
TOTAL POINTS	6	

Source: Richard Muther, *Practical Plant Layout*, McGraw-Hill Book Company, New York, 1955.

Other evaluation methods involve a ranking of items using a system tailored to particular requirements. For example, if you have certain well-defined objectives you hope to accomplish with a layout, you might rank these objectives in order of their importance and then compare each alternative layout by determining which ones best meet the individual objectives. Suppose you were planning a machine shop layout area and wanted to select the layout which best satisfies the objectives below. They are ranked in order of their importance:

Objective	Relative Weight	Objective Indicator
Minimum installation cost.	1	Estimated dollars to implement the layout.
Minimum material handling.	2	Number of material moves required in processing parts.
Minimum travel distance.	3	Distance in feet from start of first operation to part completion.
Straight-line flow.	4	Number of occurrences of backtracking and cross-tracking.
Maximum flexibility.	5	Ease of adding to or changing the layout.
Maximum space utilization.	6	Percent of total available area utilized for production activity.

Objective indicators provide criteria for evaluating how well each layout meets the objectives. They also provide a means of ranking each alternative on a 1–2–3 basis. All this is shown in Table 7-3.

The score on this evaluation results from multiplying the layout ranking for each item by the relative weight. The lower the score, the better the layout. It can be seen from Table 7-3 that Plan C is the best layout in this case.

This method can be adapted to any number of objectives and any number of layout possibilities. Its accuracy depends to some extent upon the elimination of subjective judgment and the use of meaningful objective indicators in ranking the alternatives.

TABLE 7-3.   EVALUATION OF ALTERNATIVE MACHINE SHOP LAYOUTS BY RANKING AGAINST DESIRED OBJECTIVES

Objective	Relative Weight	Plan A		Plan B		Plan C	
		Rank	Score	Rank	Score	Rank	Score
Minimum installation cost	1	2	2	1	1	3	3
Minimum material handling	2	1	2	2	4	3	6
Minimum travel distance	3	1	3	3	9	2	6
Straight-line flow	4	3	12	1	4	2	8
Maximum flexibility	5	2	10	3	15	1	5
Maximum space utilization	6	3	18	2	12	1	6
		TOTAL	47		45		34

Since a primary goal of retail selling is building sales volume, consideration must be given to the needs, desires, and habits of the customer. Pleasant surroundings, attractive merchandise displays properly located, and courteous service all contribute to the efficient operation of the retail store and help entice the customer back for repeat sales.

Customers coming into your store will often be looking for a specific item and will go directly to the area where it is sold without spending much time looking at other merchandise. Other customers come in to shop, compare quality and prices, and spend some time in the store. They will often buy items they did not come in to buy if displays are conveniently located and attractive. Studies have shown that most of these customers will turn right when entering your store and will work their way through the store counterclockwise. Based on these habits, high-margin impulse goods, which are bought as a result of visual merchandising, should be located near the front of the store. Convenience goods like tobacco, cosmetics, newspapers, and drugs are things the customer desires to buy with a minimum of effort and looking around. They are bought with frequency and in small quantities. For this reason, they should be placed in easily accessible locations at the front of the store, or along main aisles where they can be found and purchased quickly by the customer. To the extent that your displays lend themselves to self-service, the time needed to complete the transaction can be kept short. For customers who shop on the way to work or during their lunch hour, this can be important.

Necessities or staple goods are often placed toward the rear of the store. Some retailers believe that placing staple items at the rear will cause customers to pass displays of high-margin goods from which they will make impulse purchases. This is sometimes true. Placing the prescription department at the rear of a drugstore illustrates this principle. The rule is not infallible, however. Some customers with routine needs resent being obliged to go the full length of the store to get what they want and might simply look for another store where the goods they need are up front.

Window displays provide an important information link between the customer and your store. An effective window display will have about 10 seconds to "talk to" passing customers and influence their decision about coming into the store.

HOW CAN YOU TELL IF MERCHANDISE IS PROPERLY PLACED IN YOUR STORE?

The front 25 percent of the store area is often responsible for two-thirds of a store's total annual sales. This area should be used to display high-margin and high-volume merchandise. This space should be reserved for those goods that can "pay their way" in terms of their contribution to your total sales (and profits). You can calculate occupancy rates for the various areas of a store and compare them with the income rates on merchandise items to determine how much floor space you can allow each line of goods. In addition to the amount of space, rental rates will help you determine whether the merchandise should be placed in high, medium, or low rental value areas.

The decline in the value of space as you approach the rear of a store is sometimes described by the "4–3–2–1 rule," which assigns 40 percent of the rental value to the front 25 percent of the store; and 30 percent, 20 percent, and 10 percent to the remaining areas. A detailed analysis of how the rate per square foot is arrived at is shown in Figure 7-1 below.

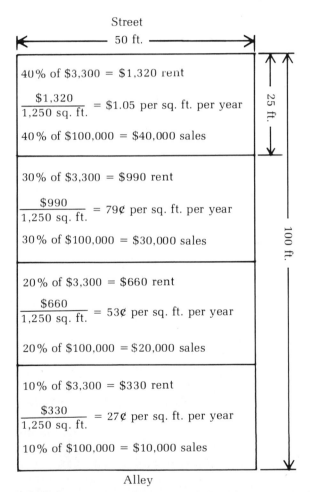

Street

|← 50 ft. →|

40% of $3,300 = $1,320 rent

$$\frac{\$1,320}{1,250 \text{ sq. ft.}} = \$1.05 \text{ per sq. ft. per year}$$

40% of $100,000 = $40,000 sales

30% of $3,300 = $990 rent

$$\frac{\$990}{1,250 \text{ sq. ft.}} = 79\cent \text{ per sq. ft. per year}$$

30% of $100,000 = $30,000 sales

20% of $3,300 = $660 rent

$$\frac{\$660}{1,250 \text{ sq. ft.}} = 53\cent \text{ per sq. ft. per year}$$

20% of $100,000 = $20,000 sales

10% of $3,300 = $330 rent

$$\frac{\$330}{1,250 \text{ sq. ft.}} = 27\cent \text{ per sq. ft. per year}$$

10% of $100,000 = $10,000 sales

25 ft.

100 ft.

Alley

The rent contracted by lease is $3,300 per year. Therefore 5,000 square feet divided into $3,300 = 66¢ per year. This is the average rent per square foot per year for the whole store.

Under the 4-3-2-1 rule, 40 percent of the total rent is assigned to the front quarter of the space; 30 percent of the total rent is assigned to the second quarter of the space; 20 percent of the total rent is assigned to the third quarter of the space; and 10 percent is assigned to the rear quarter of the space.

Typical rent or occupancy cost for a retail hardware store is 3.3 percent of sales, according to statistics published by the National Retail Hardware Association for 1974. So $3,300 = 3.3 percent of sales and 1 percent = $1,000. Therefore, 100 percent is equal to $100,000 of sales.

FIGURE 7-1. Use of the 4–3–2–1 rule in calculating rental costs. (*Source:* Modified from Leo V. Aspinwall, *Are Your Merchandise Lines Paying Their Rent?* Small Markets Aids Annual, No. 3, U.S. Small Business Administration, Washington, 1961.)

In this figure, our annual rent of $3,300 is divided into:

Front quarter of store	$1,320	(40% of $3,300)
Next quarter of store	990	(30% of $3,300)
Next quarter of store	660	(20% of $3,300)
Rear quarter of store	330	(10% of $3,300)
	$3,300	

If we rent a building for $3,300 a year to establish a retail hardware store, we can calculate how much our annual sales should be to pay this much rent or occupancy cost. The National Retail Hardware Association reported that hardware store occupancy cost in 1974 averaged 3.3 percent of sales. This means that we would have to sell $100,000 in merchandise ($3,300 ÷ .033) in order to pay $3,300 in rent—if we are a typical hardware store. We realize, of course, that some locations are more costly and others less costly than this reported average.

In a building 50 feet wide by 100 feet long, the average rent for the whole store would be:

$$\frac{\$3,300}{5,000 \text{ sq. ft.}} = 66¢ \text{ per sq. ft.}$$

However, merchandise placed in the front quarter of the store must pay 40 percent of the total rent since it occupies space worth $1.05 per square foot ($1,320 ÷ 1,250 sq. ft.). Unless your annual sales for merchandise in this area total $40,000 per year, the merchandise will not "pay its way."

Generally, the layout of a retail establishment should follow the pattern shown in Figure 7-2.

IS THERE A LAYOUT "STANDARD" FOR SERVICE BUSINESSES?

Because of their nature, service businesses vary widely in services they offer and in their approaches to the customer. Some uniformity can be found in the layout of barbershops, beauty shops, and doctors' offices. This is less true of travel agencies, quick-copy shops, and repair shops, where visual displays and literature designed to bring the customer in contact with the service are an integral part of "selling" the service. In businesses like pool servicing, lawn care, and rug cleaning, the layout is far less critical since the service is performed on the customer's premises.

Some service businesses specializing in repairs (TV shops and appliance repair shops) will be concerned with stocking of repair parts, adequate repair areas equipped with work benches and good lighting, convenient loading and unloading facilities, and office areas to handle the necessary recordkeeping functions. The layout must also consider telephone-service needs, location of service manuals and catalogs, and customer pickup areas. These businesses plan

Impulse Goods	Convenience Goods

Bought as a result of attractive displays conveniently located near the entrance in small stores or on main aisles in larger stores.
  Examples:
    ☐ Notions
    ☐ Candy
    ☐ Health aids
    ☐ Beauty aids
    ☐ Costume jewelry
    ☐ Pen and pencil sets
	Bought with frequency and in small quantities. Should be placed in easily accessible locations along main aisles or near the front of the store.
	  Examples:
	    ☐ Nonprescription drugs
	    ☐ Magazines
	    ☐ Newspapers
	    ☐ Tobacco products
	    ☐ Greeting cards

Necessities or Staple Goods	Utility Goods

Bought because of an actual need.
 	
  Examples:
    ☐ Clothing
    ☐ Food articles
    ☐ Prescription drugs
	Bought for home use.
	  Examples:
	    ☐ Paper dispensers
	    ☐ Wastebaskets
	    ☐ Bathroom accessories
	    ☐ Brooms
	    ☐ Small hand tools
	    ☐ Garden tools
	    ☐ Hangers
	    ☐ Miscellaneous hardware

Luxury and Major Expense Items

Bought after careful planning and considerable shopping to compare prices, quality, and style.
  Examples:
    ☐ TV sets
    ☐ Stereo sets
    ☐ Furniture
    ☐ Washers/driers
    ☐ Refrigerators
    ☐ Lawnmowers

FIGURE 7-2. Classification and arrangement of merchandise in small retail stores.

their layout around the number of customers to be serviced in the store, the number of service vehicles to be used for service outside the store, expected volume of telephone business, and similar factors. Since many items belonging to customers will be kept in the store during the repair period, consideration of fire-prevention devices, adequate storage space, and control of theft is important in planning the layout.

Wholesaling is characterized by the movement of large volumes of merchandise into and out of warehouses, heavy traffic in and out of the facility, and a need for physical protection and control of the goods being handled.

More than half of a wholesaler's cost is labor related to material handling. Any layout which reduces or eliminates handling, cuts moving distances, or speeds up the handling process will have a measurable impact on costs. Conveyors, belts, overhead hoists, pallet storage, and automatic handling devices are a few of the more common devices used to accomplish the handling job in the wholesaler's facility.

The volume of goods stored usually dictates a need for adequate, low-cost space with good access to the premises by truck and rail. Adequate parking areas must be provided. The kinds of merchandise stored will determine the need for protection from heat, sunlight, moisture, dust, and contamination of one kind or another.

Since the primary objective of wholesalers is to fill orders with speed and accuracy, the efficiency with which they store and retrieve merchandise to fill their orders is critical. A good layout can contribute measurably to an efficient low-cost operation.

WHAT PRINCIPLES GENERALLY APPLY TO AN OFFICE LAYOUT?

Here are a few that are often ignored or overlooked when laying out office areas:

- Desks should not face windows, walls, or entrances.
- Main lighting sources should be overhead and to the left of the user.
- Desks should not be back to back. When they are arranged in rows, there should be at least 6 feet between the front of one and the front of the next one.
- File cabinets should not open into aisles.
- If file cabinets are placed in long rows, 3 feet should be allowed between rows.
- Aisles should be 2 feet wide per person having to pass down them at one time, or a minimum of 4 feet wide.
- Average general office space per worker should be a minimum of 65 square feet.
- Layout should be built around major work flows and work centers.
- Paperwork should flow in a manner that reduces backtracking, double handling, and excessive distances.

The purpose of a production layout is to find the most economical arrangement of facilities and personnel in order to streamline the production flow, reduce effort, and cut the cost of manufacturing. A good layout is the result of identifying specific objectives, such as the ones below, and then responding to them:

☐ Reduction of handling costs through better methods of handling, more efficient handling equipment, and arrangement of the material flow in a "straight line" to reduce travel distance. Raw materials should be close to major areas of consumption.

☐ Increased production achieved by eliminating bottlenecks, reducing excessive handling of parts, changing inefficient methods, and reducing the manual labor required to make the product.

☐ Improvement of the working environment by eliminating excessive noise, heat, and odors. Judicious use of color, together with good lighting, improves worker morale and contributes to job satisfaction.

☐ Increased safety awareness resulting from planning for adequate fire protection, installation of safety devices, suitable storage areas, and elimination of hazards.

☐ Reduction of support labor so that a minimum amount of clerical work is required to control production. Place tool cribs and service areas in a central location. Locate small spare parts storage areas close to operating departments.

☐ Better utilization of space. Locate shop offices, laboratories, and maintenance and service facilities to serve the total plant to best advantage. Time clocks, cafeterias, first-aid stations, and vending machines should be strategically located. Plan working areas carefully to conserve space.

HOW CAN THE BENEFITS OF A NEW LAYOUT BE VERIFIED?

By checking the savings which result from lower operating costs and increased output. Output is an item that is easily plotted. A comparison of "before-and-after" production levels will tell you if an improvement was made and how much it amounted to. The cost to produce a unit of product should also decrease as the result of a layout improvement. Your accountants should be able to provide comparative figures to verify whether the expected reduction was in fact realized.

Other criteria for evaluating the benefits of a new layout are output per employee, output per square foot of plant space, or similar operating ratios. Use whatever ratio is most meaningful for your operation in evaluating efficiency on a "before-and-after" basis.

Since your production area will consist primarily of machines and storage space, predicting the number of machines you will need is the key to defining space needs. You can compare the machines you will need with the available space to determine whether your productive floor space is big enough to accommodate all the machines which will be required.

The machine work load is reflected in your future work schedules and customer orders. It is also influenced by how productive each machine is. Remember that a machine is nonproductive when it is being set up for a new run, when it is being repaired or serviced, or when the operator is away. Planning based on full utilization of machines is unrealistic. Experience indicates that machines can be expected to be operating between 70 and 80 percent of the available work time. This means that you should figure a machine's probable output at what it can turn out in 6 hours, not 8. You should figure the number of machines on that basis too. Other things to keep in mind when estimating your machine needs are these:

- Less production per operator is accomplished on night shifts than on the day shift. Efficiency drops at night.
- Productive output from extended work days and work weeks will be considerably less than it would on a normal 8-hour day, in a normal 40-hour week.
- You can increase machine production by scheduling work breaks and lunch periods so that the machine is run by relief operators during these times.

Here is a simplified procedure for estimating the number of machines you will need:

1. For each machine, calculate the "floor-to-floor" time for each operation. This time includes the time the machine is operating and the time taken by the operator to place the part on the machine and put the completed part back in its container.
2. Add some time to this cycle time to cover personal, fatigue, and delay factors which affect the operator. An allowance of 10 to 15 percent is not unreasonable, but the amount you add should be determined by the operating conditions in your plant.
3. Multiply this adjusted cycle time by the number of times the operation will be performed on that machine in a week. Do the same thing for all the other parts or products which will use that machine. If you use minutes, divide by 60 to convert the load to hours.
4. Finally, divide the total hours by the number of hours you expect to have the machine operating during the week (30 hours out of 40 would represent 75 percent utilization). This gives you the

total number of machines you need. If the total number exceeds the number you already have, you will need to plan space for additional machines and for any juggling or moving of existing machines to improve production efficiency.

A machine needs space for its electric motor, for its electrical control panel, for its operator, and for storage of material before and after the operation has been performed. The actual placing of machines is usually done after experimentally placing scale-model machine templates on a floor plan.

SHOULDN'T MACHINES BE ARRANGED SO THAT THE PRODUCT BEING MADE FLOWS LOGICALLY FROM ONE MACHINE TO THE NEXT?

If you are making a single product—or only a few—and the same sequence of operations is required on all of them, it is much more economical to establish a production line and flow the materials from machine to machine. In such arrangements, the machines are often permanently "set up" to do a specific job and never have to be converted to any other kind of work. Where you are making lots of parts, this method will sometimes permit you to reduce your product flow time from weeks to days and cut manufacturing costs dramatically. The obvious advantages of this pattern of operation are reduced handling time, more accurate scheduling of parts through the line, tighter control over machines and operators, and a steady flow of material in a straight line.

Since machines and equipment are only used for certain operations, this plan can result in a higher investment in fixed assets. In addition, a high volume is necessary for you to keep profits above the break-even point of your costs. Some problems can result from machine breakdowns since the entire line can be affected by such occurrences. For this reason, very tight supervision is required and immediate response from your maintenance people is essential to get things going again after a stoppage.

WHAT IF YOU WANT TO MAKE A VARIETY OF PRODUCTS WITH THE SAME EQUIPMENT?

You have to use a different arrangement of machines. This process is called job-lot manufacturing. It is typical of many small specialty machine shops which do work for many different customers. When you have to manufacture a number of different products using the same machines, you usually place all the lathes together, all drills in one area, and so forth. This pattern is called a process-type layout. You route each product to those machines required to manufacture it. New products can be introduced or old ones modified or discontinued without affecting the layout. This flexibility is important to the small plant owner.

The process-type layout offers some potential for problems in routing and scheduling the various jobs since they will all be competing for time on the same machines. The cost of transporting the material can be high since the separation of machines into similar groups makes it necessary to move the parts frequently. Backtracking and excessive handling of parts is common. More storage space is required, too. In-process materials have to be stored between operations while waiting for the next machine to become available. Inspection is more difficult and control over operations is harder to attain. Inefficient utilization of some equipment is inevitable since some machines will be used less often than others. Effective cost control is very difficult to achieve without constant attention and detailed cost collection systems.

AS LONG AS THE PARTS GET TO SHIPPING, WHAT DIFFERENCE DOES IT MAKE HOW THEY GET THERE?

The distance traveled by materials moving through the various operations affects not only material handling costs but total production costs as well. It takes twice as long to haul a load of parts 200 feet as it does 100 feet. Any way you look at it, it translates into costs. If the total travel of a part can be reduced from 1,500 feet to 300 feet, you will benefit from reduced handling costs, less congestion, smaller inventories, and reduced hazards associated with transporting materials. If your layout results in a congested mess through which production must fight its way, your costs will be greater than they should be.

WHAT SPECIAL LAYOUT REQUIREMENTS SHOULD BE CONSIDERED?

Operations which have objectionable fumes or other objectionable characteristics should be isolated from other manufacturing operations. Such conditions are hazardous to workers' health and can cause damage to materials.

Excessively noisy areas and those which have vibrations from heavy machines should be insulated from office areas or other areas where precision work is done. Use of shock absorbers or special foundations separated from the rest of the structure should be considered when making the layout.

In some plants special hazards related to moving equipment, fire, or explosion must be recognized. Special ventilation should be planned for areas where paint spray, toxic fumes, or gases are present. Sometimes state laws or local fire laws require special fire walls to isolate hazardous operations from other areas.

Moving or rerouting of utilities such as electricity, compressed air, or vacuum is more expensive sometimes than moving the equipment itself. The cost of moving such utilities must be considered when any major changes in layout are made.

This exercise is designed to test your understanding of the material presented in Chapter 7. Choose the response, *True* or *False*, which best fits each statement. Correct responses are presented in the back of the text.

1. The "best" layout is usually imperfect because it is based on compromises.
2. One of the major objectives of a good layout is maximization of sales.
3. The front 25 percent of a store area is responsible for about 65 percent of the store's total annual sales.
4. The area at the very center of a store is considered a prime location for impulse goods.
5. More than 50 percent of a wholesaler's cost is composed of labor related to recordkeeping.
6. In an office, main lighting sources should be overhead and to the right of the user.
7. It is possible to determine whether a new layout has benefited business operations.
8. Planning based on the premise that machines will be operating 100 percent of the time can introduce errors in calculations of machine requirements.
9. The output per worker on a night shift is lower than it is during the day.
10. A layout for job-lot manufacturing is not affected by product production rates or by the number of different products being made.

Figure 7-3 shows a typical planning sheet for manufacturing a machined item. Column 12 indicates the time an average operator should need to perform each operation.

1. Based on the data shown on the figure, convert the time shown as "Std. Hrs. per Unit" to minutes for Operations 10, 15, and 25 by multiplying "Std. Hrs." by 60.
2. From the converted times, calculate how many parts per hour you could turn out at Operations 10, 15, and 25. How many pieces could you turn out in 8 hours at each operation?
3. If you assume that operator delays, machine downtime, setup and similar factors limit machine operating time to 75 percent of the total time available, recalculate the number of pieces from Problem 2 to show the output for each operation for an 8-hour day.
4. Assuming a drop in output of 20 percent for a night shift operation, how many pieces per 8-hour shift could you expect from each operation, using the data developed in Problem 3?

PART NAME — DINGLEWIDGET (1)	CHG. NO (7)	PLANNER (8) H. T. Smith	DRAWING NO. (9)	PART NO. (10) 300512
MATERIAL IDENTIFICATION — P/N 001-613-215 Aluminum Alloy (2)	1		150623	REPLACES (11)
SIZE & SPEC. — Per Drawing No. 150623 (3)				
LOT SIZE (4) 100	FLOW DAYS (5) 13	CONTRACT (6) 440		

STD. HRS. PER UNIT (12)	SET UP TIME (13)	DEPT. (14)	MACH. GROUP (15)	OPER. NO. (16)	OPERATION (17)	TOOLING AND MATERIAL HANDLING EQUIP. (18)
.000	.000	2/100		5	Furnish 001-613-215 6061-T6 aluminum alloy casting	No. 241 Handling Rack
.500	1.500	30/07	10	10	Face, turn, and bore Note: Protect both ends with CAP 000-923-253	Ser 4455 Turning Fix Ser 0015 Tool Bit 000-923-253 Cap
.120	1.000	30/07	10	15	Face to 1.550 machine start dimension and finish bore 1.500 plus .005 minus .000 diameter	Ser 4455 Turning Fix Ser 0015 Tool Bit
.000	.000	45/18		20	Inspect per quality assurance tech instruction no. 88	
.360	2.000	30/09	23	25	Tumble deburr per manufacturing process spec 10.02	
.000	.000	45/18		30	Inspect	
.003	.000	18/15		35	Degrease and bag per manufacturing process spec 15.08	
					Forward to stock	
.980	4.500				Department 30 (machine shop)	
.003	.000				Department 18 (processing)	
.983	4.500				Total	

FIGURE 7-3. Operation and route sheet.

174

5. Calculate how many machines would be required to produce 5,000 dinglewidgets per month based on the following:
   a. Scrap rate will be 5 percent.
   b. Work will be done on a standard 8-hour day with no overtime.
   c. Machine utilization will be 75 percent of capacity.
   d. Assume a 20-day month (working days).
   e. Ignore the requirements for Operation 35 (Figure 7-3).
   Operations 10 and 15 require lathes; Operation 24 requires deburr machines.
6. Based on the data developed in Problem 5, determine how much floor space you would need to accommodate the necessary machines. The floor space requirement for each type of machine, based on its physical dimensions, is:
   Machine Group 10 (lathe) 8 × 10 feet = 80 square feet
   Machine Group 23 (deburr) 5 × 10 feet = 50 square feet
   Add 25 percent to your calculations for storage space and aisles.
7. What options are open to you if your physical machine shop area is only 2,500 square feet?

THE CASE OF SOL COHEN'S HOME IMPROVEMENT CENTER

A year ago Sol Cohen purchased a retail hardware store in a neighborhood shopping center serving a residential area of about 10,000 people. There were no other hardware stores within a 5-mile radius of Sol's location. After checking the location thoroughly, Sol decided to buy the business.

In examining the previous owner's books, Sol noticed that the net profit for the last 3 years had hovered around 3 percent. He knew from studying the literature he got from the National Retail Hardware Association that this profit level was below the average for stores of this kind. He believed, however, that more aggressive advertising and some well-planned promotional events could result in a substantial improvement in profits. He also had some ideas about adding a new line of sporting goods which he felt could improve sales volume. After his first year of operation, the profit picture had improved somewhat but still was short of the 6 percent goal he had set for himself.

One day he received some literature concerning a 1-day seminar in merchandising methods offered by a university in a neighboring town in conjunction with the Small Business Administration. The agenda included some topics which interested Sol, so he decided to attend.

Sol found the seminar very worthwhile. It introduced him to some concepts which were unfamiliar to him. He was impressed by one speaker's remarks about the importance of store layout—a topic he had thought very little about. As he drove home he remembered the principal points the speaker had made: "Make convenience goods easy for the customer to find . . . The front of your store should be used for your high-margin merchandise and fast-moving convenience goods . . . Most shoppers will turn right when entering your store. Locate fast-moving impulse goods at that spot." Sol wondered whether his store's layout matched the ideal arrangement. He decided to find out.

First, he examined his annual sales for the previous year and broke them down by product category. This what he found:

	Total Sales	Percent of Total
Lawn and garden supplies	$ 8,750	12.5
Sporting goods	6,580	9.4
Hand and power tools	7,070	10.1
Electrical supplies	5,040	7.2
Housewares	13,440	19.2
Farm and home hardware	5,600	8.0
Plumbing and heating supplies	6,860	9.8
Paint and paint supplies	13,020	18.6
Major appliances	3,640	5.2
	$70,000	100.0

Using some literature he picked up at the seminar, Sol next made a floor plan of his store showing where each type of merchandise was located. Then, using the "4–3–2–1 rule," he calculated how much of his $2,400 annual rent should be charged to each of the areas. In each block he showed the sales which would be necessary to "pay the rent" for that area, and he also entered "last year's sales" in each block. When he finished, it looked like Figure 7-4.

Sol had figured what his sales would have to be to pay the $2,400 rent, assuming that the average cost of occupancy for retail hardware stores was 3.3 percent of sales. He got this figure from literature from the National Retail Hardware Association.

$2,400 ÷ .033 = $72,727 per year (sales needed to pay $2,400 rent)

His sales almost made it last year. He believed that, with a little change in the layout, he could get his occupancy cost below 3 percent. It was worth a try.

1. What problems in layout seem to be indicated by the data shown in Figure 7-4?
2. What changes in layout can you make to get related lines closer together?
3. Do you have any recommendations for the low-profit lines Sol is carrying?
4. Sol needs to sell $80,000 in merchandise next year to get his occupancy cost to 3 percent of sales. What lines offer the best potential for added profits?
5. Make a new layout for Sol's store showing where you would locate the various lines of merchandise.

6. Based on the material presented in Chapter 6, is the population of the area in which Sol is doing business large enough to support a hardware store?

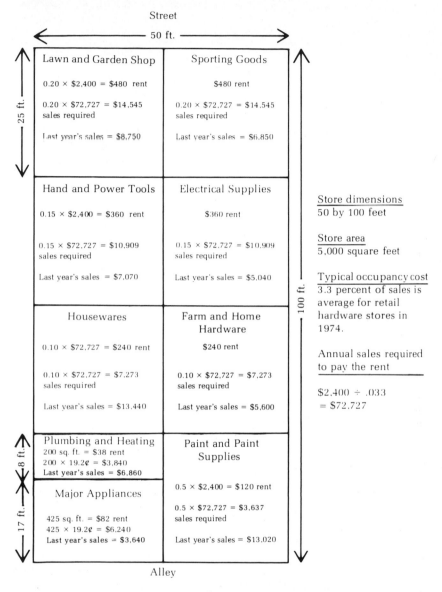

Street

← —————————— 50 ft. —————————— →

Lawn and Garden Shop	Sporting Goods
0.20 × $2,400 = $480 rent	$480 rent
0.20 × $72,727 = $14,545 sales required	0.20 × $72,727 = $14,545 sales required
Last year's sales = $8,750	Last year's sales = $6,850

25 ft.

Hand and Power Tools	Electrical Supplies
0.15 × $2,400 = $360 rent	$360 rent
0.15 × $72,727 = $10,909 sales required	0.15 × $72,727 = $10,909 sales required
Last year's sales = $7,070	Last year's sales = $5,040

Housewares	Farm and Home Hardware
0.10 × $72,727 = $240 rent	$240 rent
0.10 × $72,727 = $7,273 sales required	0.10 × $72,727 = $7,273 sales required
Last year's sales = $13,440	Last year's sales = $5,600

Plumbing and Heating	Paint and Paint Supplies
200 sq. ft. = $38 rent	
200 × 19.2¢ = $3,840	
Last year's sales = $6,860	

8 ft.

Major Appliances	
	0.5 × $2,400 = $120 rent
425 sq. ft. = $82 rent	0.5 × $72,727 = $3,637 sales required
425 × 19.2¢ = $6,240	
Last year's sales = $3,640	Last year's sales = $13,020

17 ft.

100 ft.

Alley

Store dimensions
50 by 100 feet

Store area
5,000 square feet

Typical occupancy cost
3.3 percent of sales is average for retail hardware stores in 1974.

Annual sales required to pay the rent

$2,400 ÷ .033
= $72,727

FIGURE 7-4. Sol's Home Improvement Center.

8 Evaluating Franchise Opportunities

PERFORMANCE OBJECTIVES

After reading this chapter, you should be able to describe the importance of franchising in the American economy and to evaluate some of the good and bad features of franchising as it exists today. You should be able to point out the things to look for in evaluating a franchise opportunity and discuss some of the pitfalls of franchising. Specifically, you should be able to:

1. Explain how franchising benefits both franchisor and franchisee.
2. Describe some of the practices which have given franchising a bad reputation in the eyes of some observers.
3. Relate some of the corrective measures which have been taken at federal and state levels to control fraudulent franchising practices.
4. Identify some of the risks faced by a potential franchisee deciding to sign a contract for a franchise.
5. List some questions you should ask when evaluating a franchise.
6. Develop a rationale to explain the relatively low failure rate of franchises compared with nonfranchised businesses.
7. Assess the difficulties that might arise from buying a nonexclusive franchise.
8. Relate how it is possible to determine the income and sales for a franchise before it is opened.
9. Explain the importance of obtaining information about franchise failures and the reasons for them when evaluating a franchise.

INTRODUCTION

Franchising is a modern term for a method of wholesale and retail product distribution which is more than one hundred years old. Although most of us are aware of the great growth of franchises during the last 20 years, automobile manufacturers, brewers, soft drink bottlers, and oil companies have been franchising their products for many years. Now franchising has expanded to almost every conceivable kind of product or service, including food, pets, lodging, clothing, education, and many other activities.

In the past several years franchise companies have received much attention from the business community, not only because of the performance of franchise stocks, but also because so many of the blue chip companies have entered the franchise field.

Franchising can be an answer for you if you want to go into business for yourself with a minimum of expense and with the backing of a nationally recognized trade name and the goodwill associated with it. One of the biggest mistakes you can make, however, is to be in a hurry to get into a franchise business. You might be "pressured" into a franchise that is not suited to you, or you might find out that other franchises would have been more profitable if you had taken the time to evaluate them.

This chapter will stress the information-gathering and evaluation activities that should precede any decision to buy into a franchise. Properly pursued, an organized approach to franchise evaluation will enable you to weed out the bad risks from the field of prospects and to focus your attention on those prospects that are right for you.

WHAT IS FRANCHISING?

Franchising is essentially a system of distribution under which an individually owned business is operated as though it were part of a large chain. The trademarks, symbols, design, equipment, services, and products are standardized in all franchise outlets so that they present essentially the same company image regardless of location. Franchising can be used for almost any type of business.

Under the right circumstances it is an attractive way of doing business for both franchisors and franchisees. Franchisors are able to expand a chain of outlets for their brand of products or services with relatively little capital outlay of their own. Franchisees are able to gain many of the advantages of big business yet remain small. They are their own bosses, in a position to profit directly from their own investment and efforts, while at the same time they benefit from such things as national advertising, large-scale purchasing, and expert management consultation.

WHY ARE FRANCHISES SO POPULAR?

Franchises have caught the imagination of small investors by providing them with the opportunity to become self-employed with a minimum of risk of failure. It affords them a chance to become a part of a large organization, often with a worldwide reputation, and yet retain their individuality. They can get expert management assistance, special training, marketing help, and promotional expertise as part of the service they contract for. While franchising has been around for a long time, only recently has it blossomed into a "boom" with annual sales exceeding $100 million.

Franchising began to flourish after World War II because opportunities were offered to small investors to operate franchised roadside businesses, primarily drive-in food and ice cream stands. When such drive-ins began to spread, franchising became a magic word. Today hundreds of companies market many products and services through franchised outlets. Some of the best-known names in American industry are using franchised stores to expand into new markets with new or established products.

WHERE ARE THE RISKS IN FRANCHISING?

Although it is difficult to list all of them, unsatisfactory or negative answers to these questions might be a tip-off that you are assuming more risk than a prudent business person should:

- What are the risks of your franchisor? The greater the franchisor's risk, the keener his or her interest in your success.
- Does your franchise give you exclusive territorial rights?
- Are minimum sales or purchase quotas required? Are these quotas based on realistic minimums instead of optimistic projections?
- How do you handle defective or obsolete merchandise you receive from the franchisor?
- In your selected area, has the franchisor done any feasibility studies, promotion, or publicity?
- What indications of market demand and ability to pay exist?
- How many franchises are being sold in this area by the franchisor?
- Are products or services of the repeat type or "one-shot"?
- Is the product or service seasonal? If so, what happens in the off-season?
- What is the franchisor's name worth in your area?
- How competitive is the franchise?
- Do you have enough managerial experience to run the business? What outside help can you depend on?
- How much training will you get from the franchisor?
- Could you survive if the franchisor fails?
- If you have to liquidate, could you get back your investment?
- Will you have the option of renewing the franchise agreement? When? What will it cost to renew?

- What are the provisions for termination of the franchise by either party?
- Can franchisors delay or prevent resale of the franchise? Can they cancel it? Must a release fee be paid to them or anyone else?

The questions presented here should be given serious consideration by all prospective franchisees. Moreover, prudence suggests that you discuss the investment with your attorney, accountant, banker, or business adviser before committing a substantial sum of money to buying a franchise.

WHAT OPPORTUNITIES ARE AVAILABLE TO A PROSPECTIVE FRANCHISEE?

Since the introduction of franchising by the Singer Sewing Machine Company shortly after the Civil War, hundreds of new companies have joined the franchising movement. Many such as McDonald's, Holiday Inns, Howard Johnson, Denney's, Sambo's Restaurants, and Kentucky Fried Chicken have had outstanding success. For every successful franchise, there are many ill-conceived, poorly run, or inefficient ones that have failed. These failures, regardless of the reason, have served to strengthen the sound franchises and have resulted in a higher quality of service to the public.

Classification of franchises by kind of business finds automobile dealerships and service stations at the top of the list in the retail category. The 30,000 franchised car dealerships and 150,000 franchised service stations in the United States together account for over half the total sales of all franchises.

Distributorships are sometimes franchise operations. Wholesale distributors might be franchised to sell a manufacturer's product in given areas. The distributors might own their own warehouse facilities and inventory and distribute the product under a licensing agreement with the manufacturer.

Food service operations are the franchises which are most recognizable by the general public. The distinctive, easy-to-recognize business of the McDonald's or Dairy Queen chains is familiar to consumers throughout the country. With their limited menus and takeout service, they have literally taken over the "eating out" business and have grown to an estimated 30,000 franchised outlets operated by 236 fast-food companies.

Retail stores have long used franchising methods to distribute products to the public. As early as 1900, drugstore and variety-store chains were in existence. Later additions to the retail family included auto parts, convenience food, and apparel.

Service businesses, spearheaded by the hotel and motel industries, have now proliferated to include income tax and business services, correspondence schools, printers, beauty salons, day-care centers, and employment agencies.

Manufacturing franchises are less common than the other types. The franchisee generally buys a license to produce and sell the franchisor's product within a certain area.

IS THERE A QUICK METHOD FOR EVALUATING A FRANCHISE?

Checking out a franchisor's program can cost you a lot in time, trouble, and frustration. A quick test of practices which often betray the disreputable franchisor can help you eliminate some franchisors without spending too much of your time in a lengthy evaluation. Here are some things to look for:

□ Promises of high profits in exchange for minimum efforts. There is no legitimate franchisor who can assure you a $10,000 return on a $1,000 investment or guarantee you a chance to get rich by working part time.

□ Pressure to get you to sign a contract at once or lose the opportunity. Most reputable franchisors encourage potential franchisees to take their time before signing a contract. They often require time to check your background as well.

□ Reluctance to give specific and direct answers to your questions. This approach is indicative of the salesperson whose primary job is to sell franchises. It could indicate a superficial knowledge of the company's operations.

□ Hedging or reluctance to provide a list of references for you to talk to.

□ Any attempt to discourage you from having your attorney review the contract before you sign it.

If the franchisor gets a clean bill of health on these five points, a visit to an operating franchise is in order. You can observe first-hand the operations of the business and find out what the franchisee thinks about the franchisor's competence and integrity. This should tell you whether it would be worthwhile to pursue the opportunity further.

WHAT SHOULD YOU KNOW ABOUT THE FRANCHISED PRODUCT?

Be sure that the product or service being offered is reputable. Customers will buy the first time on a promise of quality, but they will not return if they do not get what they were promised. Stale doughnuts and soggy french fries are not the way to win and keep customers in a fast-food franchise. If the product or service is one with which you are unfamiliar, talk to customers of the franchisor who are familiar with the product and get their reactions. Check it yourself by writing to the Better Business Bureau of your city and that of the city of the franchise headquarters. Ask the people at the nearest Small Business Administration field office about the product. Your primary concern is to be sure that the product or service is needed in your area, that there is a demand or market for it, and that it is not a passing fad or luxury item that few can afford.

WHAT DO YOU NEED TO KNOW ABOUT FRANCHISORS?

You should find out enough about them to be sure that they are reputable, financially strong, and recognized leaders in their fields. Your success will in large part be determined by their ability to assist you.

You should find out whether the franchise company is part of a larger company. Ask for the name and address of the parent company and evaluate it along with the franchisor. Remember that being part of a larger company can be a very important asset to you in terms of financial stability.

If the parent company is a publicly owned corporation, you can get a stock report from your stockbroker which will give you much valuable information about its operations and financial structure. Look for rising trends in sales, profits, and earnings per share. You can also get copies of the parent firm's quarterly and annual reports by writing to the company. Often product literature is also available. If you do not have access to a stockbroker, go to your local library and ask for assistance.

Write to your state consumer agency to find out whether there are laws requiring franchising companies to disclose fully their financial conditions. Some require the franchisor to supply a prospectus to the potential franchisee.

IS A NATIONAL FRANCHISE PREFERABLE TO A REGIONAL OR LOCAL ONE?

There are many excellent regional franchises with high income potential. There is a direct relationship, however, between the franchise fee and the reputation of the franchisor. Chances are that a franchise that is now only local or regional is in the beginning of a test stage and will go national once the test has proved successful. The national and international franchises are usually older and better established. They are also better known. The latter point is important if your product is a consumer one such as that in the fast-food or motel field.

ARE PART-TIME FRANCHISES CONSIDERED GOOD BUSINESS VENTURES?

This depends on what you are looking for. There are very few successful part-time franchises. Those that are successful involve a lot of hard work and effort. Many franchisors prefer that your whole family share in the enterprise. It is not unusual for a fast-food franchisee to work 60 or more hours in a week, with the spouse and children contributing an additional 25 to 30 hours. It is highly doubtful that you can sit back, as some part-time franchises profess, make some mailings, and watch the money roll in. There are a few franchises in the personal-service field that can be started on a part-time basis and later developed into an operation that you can conduct on a full-time basis.

HOW DO FRANCHISE FAILURES COMPARE WITH THOSE IN OTHER BUSINESSES?

The statistics here are a bit sketchy, but indications are that they run less than 10 percent. One report from the Conference Board, a private business-research organization, indicated that 75 percent of the franchising companies reported business failure rates of less than 5 percent a year.[1] Some of the very successful chains like McDonald's claim that they have never had a failure. The statistics are impressive when compared with the fortunes of small business people in other segments of the business community. But one must be careful when looking at these statistics. One of the major problems in franchising lies in the determination of whether the franchisor or franchisee was at fault. In addition, failures often do not include franchises that have been relocated or bought out. This would cause the failure statistics to reflect a favorable bias.

The number of failures is not as important as the franchisor's opinion of the reasons for the failures. A satisfactory answer to this question is a must. Ask the franchisor for the reasons of the failures in order of importance. Then ask for the names and addresses of franchisees who have failed. Contact them and ask the same question. Finally, check the Better Business Bureau in the city where the franchise failed and ask the same question. If the answers all agree, find out from the franchisor if the factors within his or her control have been corrected. If the answers do not agree, try to find out from the franchisor why they do not. Keep in mind the probable bias on the part of each party you talk to. Then draw your own conclusions about failures and the reasons for them.

HOW CAN YOU FIND OUT ABOUT COMPETITION IN THE AREA YOU ARE CONSIDERING?

One of the easiest ways is to look in the yellow pages of your telephone book. You can quickly determine the numbers and locations of other franchises dealing in a similar service or product. Make a list of them with addresses and telephone numbers. Visit several of the bigger ones and observe appearances, traffic in and out, and the

---

[1]See "A Changing Pattern for the Franchise Boom," U.S. News and World Report, April 24, 1972, pp. 88–89.

quality of service offered. Attempt to draw some general conclusions. If you are impressed and the franchise looks particularly good, talk to the manager and get the name of the franchisor. Write for the franchise package and compare it with the one you are evaluating. It might be better than the one you are considering. The thing you want to accomplish by such an approach is determine whether the area will support another business like the one you are considering and what kind of problem you will have in competing with those who are already established in the area.

ARE ALL FRANCHISES INDEPENDENTLY OWNED?

A number of franchisors still own a substantial number of their franchised outlets. *Barron's*[2] reports that the largest operator of coffee shops, Howard Johnson Co., has 900 shops in operation, but that only 290 of them are run by licensees. Next largest in the coffee shop business is the Marriott Corporation with its Bob's Big Boy chain, of which 115 are company-owned and 718 franchised.

McDonald's owns about 800 of its own units versus roughly 1,200 run by independent owners. Early in 1972 Pizza Hut had 496 franchisees and 359 company-owned units. This mix was a significant departure from the ratio 5 years earlier which showed only 5 company-owned outlets out of 296. This turnaround in company ownership stems partly from the success of the independently owned and operated franchises, whose profits are often three to four times those of the company-owned outlets. The trend is for the larger companies either to build new units and operate them or to buy out their more successful outlets. This encroachment by the parent company is viewed by some independent operators as a threat, and they fear that they may be pressured into selling out.

If you are considering a franchise, you should find out whether the outlets are independently owned. If you find out that the parent company has bought back a significant number of franchises within the last 5 years, find out why. If the parent company reserves the right to repurchase a franchise, find out what the repurchase agreement is. Contracts sometimes permit the parent company to buy back the franchise at the original purchase price, allowing nothing for appreciation and the goodwill that has been built by the franchisee. If you find out that franchises have been taken over for contract violations, this could be a plus, indicating franchisor interest and an effective policing program to identify poorly performing franchises and get them back under closer corporate control. The performance of an individual franchisee can favorably or adversely affect the business of other franchisees. A constructive policy program can do much to safeguard the reputation of the company and thereby benefit all franchisees of the company.

[2]"Coffee Shops Perk Up," *Barron's*, August 11, 1975.

DO YOU HAVE AN EXCLUSIVE RIGHT TO OPERATE IN THE AREA WHERE YOU BUY A FRANCHISE?

This depends on whether your franchise is exclusive or nonexclusive. Contrary to what some people think, franchises are not always exclusive as far as territory is concerned. In some cases both the distributor and the franchisor retain the right to sell direct in the franchise territory. Also, they retain the right to sell more than one franchise in a given territory. There is nothing unlawful about the nonexclusive franchise as long as you are aware of the provision before you buy the franchise and do not mind working this way. The obvious disadvantage of a smaller sales potential could mean the difference between success and failure. This item should be spelled out in the contract before you sign it.

CAN A MARKET ANALYSIS ASSURE SUCCESS IN ESTABLISHING A FRANCHISE?

No, but a thorough feasibility study will greatly reduce the chances of failure on account of poor location, insufficient sales volume, wrong kind of customer, and similar factors critical to the success of the franchise. If your franchise requires that customers come to your place of business, such a study is the best way to determine in advance whether those factors are likely to be a stumbling block once you have opened for business. Such a study should be done by franchisors. Their experience in setting up successful franchises in other areas similar to yours will uniquely qualify them to provide this service. They will check the traffic count at various location possibilities, the average income of the area from census data, the number of target prospects in the area (some franchises do better in areas with a high concentration of young families), and other factors. You should make sure that any money advanced for such a feasibility study will be returned to you in the event the results of the study are negative.

WHAT IS INCLUDED IN THE TOTAL COST OF A FRANCHISE?

This varies widely from company to company. To start any business, independent or franchised, takes capital for equipment, supplies, store site, labor, operating funds, and, in the case of a franchise business, a franchise fee. What you are paying for in the franchise fee is the right to use and promote a name and identification program. This fee usually covers, in addition to the use of the name and trademark, some amounts for training and home-office assistance to get you started. It might cover other things too.

If you find out that a franchise fee is required, you should find out specifically what the fee covers and make a list of all the things you will get for your money. Some franchisors will provide a list of services, which you should analyze carefully, item by item. Then ask your lawyer and accountant to look it over to see if you are getting true value for the fee.

While it is important to determine whether the fee is justified, it is equally important to find out whether it is only a "down payment," with additional costs to be assessed later in the form of royalties. These royalties often run as high as 5 to 10 percent of your gross profit and can prove to be disastrous in a business operating on a tight margin. In some instances, promoters fail to clearly spell out the total cost of the franchise. The promotion might only refer to the cash outlay that is needed to purchase the franchise, with no mention being made that it is only a down payment or that other charges may be levied which are incidental to the operation of the franchise.

Changing Times reports that one survey of franchisees showed that the cash investment required just to open the doors ranged from $2,000 to $180,000, with about half the respondents stating the amount as $15,000 or less.[3] This did not include operating capital or long-term debt. Another study showed the range for the franchise purchase fee alone was from about $6,000 to $11,500.

When you analyze franchise costs, get answers to the following questions:

☐ Is there a franchise fee? If so, how much?

☐ What does the franchise fee include? How is it to be paid?

☐ What portion of the fee goes for intangibles such as services? When do these services begin? Are they mandatory? Who performs them? Are they for a limited period or continuing?

☐ What is the total price of the franchise package, including site location, accounting, prepaid rent, fixtures, inventory, equipment, training, and promotion?

☐ What credit arrangements are available on inventory purchases?

☐ What advertising and sales aids are offered? How are they paid for?

☐ Who pays for shipping charges on products? Are they absorbed by the franchisors in the sales price or billed separately by them or the carriers?

☐ What is the minimum capital needed?

☐ How much insurance do you need? If a loss occurs, who gets the proceeds?

☐ What remedy do you have if the franchisor fails to perform services on a timely, adequate basis?

☐ How are future disputes to be settled? Can either party compel arbitration?

[3]"Franchises—One Way to a Business of Your Own," in the Changing Times Family Success Book, *Changing Times*, Washington, 1974.

The franchisors have a better answer to this question than anyone else. The experience of successful franchises provides them with a wealth of information which they can use to predict future income for new franchises prior to opening. One word of caution about sales forecasts: Do not be overpowered by an enthusiastic promoter who provides "blue-sky" projections that are characteristic of only well-established flagship operations. Most new franchises do not make much profit for the first year or two, so it is better to stay on the conservative side in projecting sales.

A good sales forecast should relate closely to the market you expect to serve. If the forecast is based on other franchises, they should serve a market equal in size and composition to yours. The forecast should be compatible with the profile of your proposed market in terms of average age of potential customers, income, race, family size, property values, and similar factors.

HOW IS THE FINANCING OF FRANCHISES HANDLED?

The primary source of funds for franchisors are loans from banks or insurance companies, going public and selling stock, selling franchises, and servicing franchises. Capital shortages sometimes make it difficult for franchisors to borrow the money they need. During times when money is scarce, it is not only difficult for franchisors to borrow but also hard for them to sell franchises to investors who are also having a hard time raising money for a down payment.

Franchisees are not much different from other business people in the problems they face in raising capital to buy a franchise. The typical approaches of using personal savings, borrowing from friends and relatives, soliciting help from banks or lending institutions, and selling personal items of value are characteristic of the methods used to raise the "equity capital" to buy a franchise. Some franchisees receive financial help from the franchisor, and many can qualify for loans from the Small Business Administration.

Banks and other lenders generally evaluate loans for franchises in the same way as any other loan. The three C's—character, capital, and capabilities—of the loan applicant are of major concern to a lender. The lender will also want to know how the loan will be repaid. The terms of the contract will be examined closely as will the financial background of the applicant.

Well-established franchises stand a better chance of being considered favorably for a loan than a new franchise just starting up with an unknown name and untested product. If lenders feel that there are oppressive or unfair provisions in the agreement, or that the franchisees will be unable to operate successfully because of their debt load, they will be reluctant to make the loan.

HOW ARE FRANCHISED PRODUCTS OR SERVICES SOLD?

There are different methods of selling. For example, a franchise like Avon would require a door-to-door canvass until the business becomes self-supporting from repeat sales; a technical school franchise would probably require in-home presentations on an appointment basis; a bill-collecting agency would be operated by a combination of direct mail and telephone solicitations. The sales of fast-food and other retail businesses would be in-store sales. In short, the nature of the franchise would dictate the method of selling.

WHAT KIND OF ADVERTISING SUPPORT SHOULD A FRANCHISEE EXPECT?

If your franchisor is a national chain, you will want to know what kind of national program the chain supports which promotes the products you will be selling. The visibility of the product or service, and its trademark are important aspects of the business. They are a part of the franchise fee you pay. For this reason, you have a right to know the extent of radio, television, newspaper, magazine, and outdoor advertising planned by the franchisor. Samples of national advertising should be available to prospective franchisees. You might want to ask for a written guarantee that you will get adequate advertising in your market area as well. This includes local advertising and promotion programs in support of your franchise in your market area. It is an extension of the national program. In it the franchisor supplies packaged programs for your use, including ad mats, radio spots, TV commercials, direct-mail programs, point-of-purchase material, sample publicity releases, and so forth. A good example of such advertising is the package supplied by the franchisor for your opening. Often sample kits are available for your inspection. You will be paying for these services from your gross profits. Be sure you are paying for an effective continuing program which will keep your product or service in the public eye.

WHAT KIND OF TRAINING IS OFFERED BY A FRANCHISOR?

The more reputable franchisors know that your success in operating a franchise depends upon knowing the particular skills and procedures which have worked for successful franchisees in your line. Consequently, many franchisor agreements include provision for some training in the operation of the new franchise outlet. The amount of training involved depends on the nature of the business. Training periods of 1 to 6 weeks of special training at the parent company's training center are common. Instruction is usually free, but most franchisees pick up the tab for their transportation and lodging expenses unless these costs are included in the franchise fee. A few companies give franchisees a salary while they are being trained. Others include as part of the training a period of time during which franchisees actually work in an operating outlet.

When franchisees return to operate their businesses, field support from the parent company should provide them with assistance and advice through company coordinators, who periodically visit their businesses to provide on-the-job training, information on new products and techniques, and training aids such as newsletters, filmstrips, and tapes. Sometimes refresher courses are provided by the franchisor to update the training of the franchise owners.

The amount and kind of training should be clearly spelled out in the agreement you sign with the franchisor. This service is vital if you are lacking in experience in the line you propose to operate.

WHAT PROFITS CAN BE EXPECTED FROM A FRANCHISE?

Since anticipated profits are frequently the major reason for entering a franchise business, promoter representations concerning earnings potential should be carefully checked. Ask to see certified profit figures of franchisees operating on a level of activity you can reasonably expect. In addition, you will be wise to personally contact franchisees and quiz them regarding the profits they have made in their respective businesses. Always remember to evaluate the comments of such individuals in the light of the territory and size of operation you have under consideration.

There is no question that many franchise arrangements provide excellent income-producing opportunities. It would be a mistake, however, to assume that a franchise will provide an easy "road to riches." Most franchises probably make an average net profit of less than $20,000 a year and an estimated 30 percent average less than $15,000. While some franchise promoters would have you believe that you can become successful through a minimum or part-time effort, experience has proved otherwise. Franchisees can only expect to succeed by hard work and full-time effort. Plans based on less than this generally produce only modest results.

WHAT LEGAL PROTECTION DOES A POTENTIAL FRANCHISEE HAVE AGAINST UNSCRUPULOUS FRANCHISORS?

Not much in most states, although some progress has been made in some dozen states. Led by the state of California, these states have enacted franchise-investment laws which require full disclosure of all the facts by the franchisor. Under California law, franchisors cannot sign an agreement with you or accept any money from you until 48 hours after they give you a prospectus. This includes so-called "good faith" deposits. Several other states have similar legislation pending. A major objective of the states is to end one of the worst abuses of the 1960s by forcing franchisors to disclose information on how all the outlets in the chain are doing—not just a few with unusually high returns.

Legislation has been hastened by hearings held by the U.S. Senate Select Committee on Small Business in 1970. Stories presented to this committee telling of franchise deception, gouging, deceit, and misrepresentation have set the stage for action at both the federal and state levels.

Along with the new laws, some court decisions have been important in setting precedents and nullifying old practices considered oppressive to the franchisee. The common practice of some franchise companies of forcing franchisees to buy merchandise from them alone has been questioned. The possibility of class-action suits against franchisors to recover damages for illegal practices was enhanced by an amendment to the Federal Rules of Civil Procedure in 1966. This amendment makes it possible for actions brought by a single franchisee to apply to all other franchisees similarly situated. In addition, if it can be shown that franchisors are violating the antitrust laws, franchisees can bring suit for treble damages in their own behalf and in behalf of all other franchisees in the system.

These laws will not help those who have lost life savings in franchise swindles to get their money back, but they do represent a move toward improving the lot of franchisees in their fight to get fair treatment and consideration of their grievances.

WHAT STEPS CAN PROSPECTIVE FRANCHISEES TAKE TO PROTECT THEMSELVES?

Because of the impact of franchising on the American economy and the alarming number of complaints to the Federal Trade Commission and other consumer protection agencies, it is obvious that the franchise industry will continue to be the subject of regulation by federal and state agencies. An important step in governmental regulation was the issuance of a consumer bulletin on franchises by the Federal Trade Commission.[4] This bulletin has had wide circulation and is considered invaluable to the prospective franchisee who wants to avoid the pitfalls into which other less fortunate investors have fallen. Following is a summary from this bulletin:

□ Do not be rushed into signing a contract or any other documents relating to a franchise promotion. Be wary of pressure for an immediate contract closing. Do not make any deposits or down payments unless you are absolutely certain you are going ahead with the franchise agreement. Remember, reputable firms do not engage in high-pressure tactics.

[4]*Advice for Persons Who Are Considering an Investment in a Franchise Business*, Consumer Bulletin No. 4, Federal Trade Commission, Washington, 1970.

- Find out all you can about the franchise. Resolve all areas of uncertainty before making a decision. Ask the franchisors for the names and addresses of their franchisees and discuss all aspects of the operation with the latter. Find out from the franchisees whether the franchisors have fulfilled all their promises and met their contractual obligations.

- Check with your local Better Business Bureau. Ask for a business responsibility report on the franchisor-promoter.

- Be sure that all terms of the agreement are set forth in a written contract which is not a handicap on you and not weighted unfairly in favor of the franchisor.

- Consult a lawyer and have him or her review all aspects of the agreement before you sign the contract or any papers relating to the franchise. This may turn out to be the soundest investment you make.

- If you have any complaints about deceptive franchising practices, report to your local or state consumer protection agency or the Federal Trade Commission. The Commission may not be able to recoup your losses, but it will be able to prevent other prospective franchisees from being deceived.

DO MINORITY FRANCHISEES HAVE ANY SPECIAL PROBLEMS?

Of an estimated 500,000 franchises operating in the mid-1970s, less than 1.5 percent were minority-owned. The difficulties faced by minority business people in obtaining adequate financial backing have been mentioned in an earlier chapter. A lack of business know-how is a serious obstacle for many minority business people. It is believed by many that franchising, properly applied, can help in creating viable business opportunities for people from minority groups. With little or no previous experience required and continuing management assistance offered, franchising may present a solution to some of the problems involved in this area.

The U.S. Department of Commerce's Office of Minority Business Enterprise (OMBE) has directed a major part of its efforts toward the idea of opening up more franchising opportunities for minorities with the financial support of the Small Business Administration, which would make, or guarantee, loans to minority franchisees. The OMBE has also attempted to obtain "pledges" or "commitments" from groups of franchisors to open up more of their franchises to minorities. However, only a few franchisors have established special programs providing training and financing geared to the special needs of minority applicants. McDonald's, Kentucky Fried Chicken, and Shell Oil are among the major franchisors who have active programs which are directed toward assisting minorities in their efforts to get into a franchising business.

□ An increase in the number of franchises in the "services" group and slower growth of product-related franchising appears to be taking place. *Dun's Review* reports that in 1971 and 1972 the fields of recreation, entertainment, travel, and business services have displaced fast-food franchises as the fastest-growing areas of the business.[5] Some writers state that the 1970s will see $2 of sales for services to every dollar of sales for products.

□ There will be an overall slowdown in the growth rate for some franchisors. Marginal or poorly operated franchises will have trouble surviving. Those that do survive will have to be responsive to changes in consumer tastes and needs. Some franchisors are already feeling the effects of saturated markets at home, and some, like McDonald's, are testing overseas markets as a means of expanding their operations. Franchisors like H. & R. Block, who are willing to operate in smaller communities, will be able to expand their operations, although many franchisors are unwilling to risk operating in markets where the volume of business is limited.

□ Many franchisors, either voluntarily or under the pressure of threatened class-action suits, will likely modify their franchise agreements to make the "partnership" relationship more equitable for franchisees. Franchisees, with more support from the courts and newly acquired interest in forming their own groups, will be having more say in how the "partnership" is defined. Resolution of the many legal problems and human relations problems will undoubtedly serve to strengthen the image of franchising and prove what many already believe—that franchising still represents one of the best ways for small business people to get into business.

□ Recruitment of franchisees will be toned down from previous levels, where exaggerated claims and half-truths led many investors into franchises that were doomed to failure. Full disclosure of all information—both good and bad—by the franchisor will become more general as more states adopt franchise-investment laws. An overall upgrading of minority franchise operations will result from improved selection and training of minority franchisees.

□ Franchising is clearly booming again after a severe shakeout in the late 1960s. One expert predicts franchise sales growth of $10 billion to $15 billion a year, and 40,000 new franchised outlets annually during the 1970s. The trend indicates that franchising has become as American as apple pie and that more and more businesses will be operating as franchises in the years to come.

[5]Thomas J. Murray, "The Cautious Boom in Franchising," *Dun's Review*, November 1972, pp. 45–49.

This exercise is designed to test your understanding of the material presented in Chapter 8. Choose the response, *True* or *False*, which best fits each statement. Correct responses are presented in the back of the text.

1. Total receipts from franchise businesses in the United States exceed $100 billion a year.
2. Franchising started after World War II, when roadside businesses like ice cream stands first employed the idea of franchise chains.
3. Franchising is limited primarily to retail businesses.
4. Not many franchises can be operated successfully on a part-time basis.
5. Failure rates among franchise businesses are lower than they are for nonfranchised enterprises.
6. Big franchise companies own and operate most of their outlets in order to maintain control.
7. Most franchises average less than $20,000 a year.
8. All states have now enacted franchise-investment laws to protect potential investors in franchises.
9. Talking to owners of operating franchises is a good way to get information about profits, operating problems, and relationships with the franchisor.
10. Minorities operate approximately 8 percent of the franchises in the United States.

PERFORMANCE
PROBLEMS
AND
PROJECTS

1. Check the reference collection of your local library for copies of franchise directories which describe the franchise companies, the services offered, and the requirements for ownership. Find the data for the following companies:

   Dairy Queen
   H & R Block
   Kentucky Fried Chicken
   Western Auto Supply

   Prepare a chart comparing the following data for each of those companies:
   a. How long the company has been in business.
   b. The number of franchise outlets operating.
   c. The cash outlay required to become a franchisee.
   d. Training and background requirements.
   e. Any available information relative to royalties, fees, and profits.[6]

[6] A good treatment of profits with sample profit-and-loss statements appears in Robert Metz, *Franchising: How to Select a Business of Your Own*, Hawthorn Books, Inc., New York, 1969.

2. Write to the following franchisors and ask for their franchise "package" for prospective franchisees. Prepare a report which discusses similarities in the franchises and areas where they are unique in their requirements. Based on the information you have, explain which franchise appears to be the best investment.

   a. American Dairy Queen Corporation
      7110 France Avenue South
      Minneapolis, Minnesota 55435

   b. H & R Block Franchise Headquarters
      4410 Main Street
      Kansas City, Missouri 64111

   c. Kentucky Fried Chicken Corporation
      P. O. Box 13331
      Louisville, Kentucky 40213

   d. Western Auto Supply Company
      2107 Grand Avenue
      Kansas City, Missouri 64108

3. Visit your local bank and inquire whether they have a small business advisory service. If so, find out what kinds of literature or other material are available on the subject of franchising. Report your findings to the class.

RON SIZEMORE'S EQUIPMENT RENTAL SERVICE

A CASE IN POINT

Ron Sizemore had been a high school teacher ever since his graduation from college. He had provided modestly for his wife and two sons, who were both ready to enter high school. The Sizemores lived in a new neighborhood of middle-income families in a fast-growing section of Albuquerque. With Ron's limited income, they lived on a strict budget and worried a lot about educating their two sons. Ron had been looking for over a year for a new field to enter—one that would permit him to expand his income. One of the opportunities he had investigated was a franchise with one of the country's largest equipment-rental franchisors, whose headquarters were near his home.

A careful investigation revealed a growing market potential composed primarily of young families who would prefer to rent the equipment they need rather than buy it. He noted that the nearest competitor was 11 miles away from the neighborhood where he lived. After reading the franchisor's literature, Ron was convinced that the potential was there. But he was concerned with his lack of background for running such a business. He found out, however, that the franchisor's training program was designed to overcome just such preliminary doubts. An intensive 4-week program consisting of 3 weeks of classroom instruction at the parent company's headquarters covered store operation, inventory control, use of rental contracts, maintenance control procedures, telephone selling, and the planning and use of advertising and publicity materials, with emphasis on merchandising and grand-opening procedures. The fourth week would be spent in an operating franchise outlet actually doing the work and getting a feel for all phases of the operation. The end result of the training was to familiarize the franchisee with all aspects of the equipment-rental business.

At the franchisor's suggestion, Ron selected several names at random from a list of the company's franchisees and visited several of them at his convenience. Each one seemed pleased with his own business and encouraged Ron to seek his own franchise with the company. With the minimum cash outlay, Ron estimated that his first year would permit him to earn around $20,000 before taxes. Two franchisees told him that their second year was about 25 percent better than the first in terms of business volume and profits. This was quite a bit more than Ron was making teaching school.

Further inquiry indicated that the location for the new proposed franchise could be right in his area. The tentative location selected by the franchisor was in a location that boasted 20,000 families according to the latest census data. Projections for growth over the next 10 years by the Albuquerque Chamber of Commerce were optimistic for the area.

The initial cash investment that would be required for the franchise was $8,000 (with the balance to be carried on credit) plus an additional $5,000 for working capital, and the franchisor was ready to aid Ron in securing the financing. This arrangement would provide initial rental, about $35,000 in parts and equipment inventory, outdoor signs, utility deposits, and office supplies.

Continuing assistance offered by the franchisor included monthly conferences for all area franchise operators to review various phases of operations, sales progress, and business proficiency.

The initial requirements Ron had to meet—besides his initial cash investment—were a strong desire to earn more money and an ability to work with the public and communicate with people.

1. List the advantages you can see in the franchisor's offer.
2. List the principal disadvantages you can see in the franchisor's offer.
3. What additional information should Ron get before he makes his final decision?
4. How can Ron verify the net profit figures of the operating franchises?
5. What course of action would you recommend for Ron based on what you know at this point?

CHAPTER

9

Fundamental Business Records

PERFORMANCE OBJECTIVES

After reading this chapter you should develop an appreciation for the importance of good records to the smooth operation of a business. You should be able to judge the impact of business records on the success of a business and to cite specific examples of business failures which are related to a lack of adequate records. Specifically, you should be able to:

1. Demonstrate how good sales records can minimize chances of failure due to inadequate sales volume.
2. Explain the primary reasons for keeping business records.
3. Describe the basic differences between the single-entry and double-entry bookkeeping systems.
4. Develop a list of basic records which would be needed as a minimum by a small retail hardware store.
5. Explain the nature of the sales information which the business owner's records should document.
6. Demonstrate a method of checking cash each day as a control device.
7. Explain the actions which could lead to a cash shortage or overage at the end of a business day.
8. Discuss the purpose of a monthly bank reconciliation and describe how the reconciliation is accomplished.
9. Differentiate between purchases of goods for resale and purchases of supplies used in operating the business.

INTRODUCTION

Good business records and reports are the foundation upon which sound financial management is based. The reports used by the manager can be no more accurate than the records they summarize. Bad decisions can be made (and often are) because of a lack of meaningful cost information which good business records can supply.

Business records may be simple or complex, depending upon the size and nature of the business. Regardless of the system used to capture significant management information, records should always be well-organized and consistent.

For new businesses, experience clearly indicates that good records increase chances for survival. For established businesses, a good recordkeeping system increases the chances of growing and earning larger profits.

This chapter describes some of the basic business records in use today for recording the vital information related to sales, expenses, purchasing, cash management, personnel, equipment, and credit. Some of the more important records required for the preparation of various tax reports are emphasized; willful negligence in this area can be both costly and embarrassing.

Emphasis is upon a simplified record system which business people or their employees can maintain without difficulty. The growing popularity of the various one-book record systems in use today is evidence that adequate record systems can be established and maintained at moderate cost to the small business owner.

WHAT IS THE RELATION BETWEEN BUSINESS FAILURE AND BUSINESS RECORDS?

Statistics compiled by Dun & Bradstreet related to the causes of business failures in retailing and service trades during 1974 reveal that almost 80 percent of the failures resulted from the inability to avoid certain conditions which adequate records would have disclosed in time for early corrective action. The conditions found were:

Cause of Failure	Percent of Failures	
	Retailing	Service Trades
Inadequate sales volume	49.4	50.9
Heavy operating expenses	13.7	16.4
Receivables difficulties	3.3	6.5
Inventory difficulties	12.0	1.1
Excessive fixed assets	1.9	4.9
	80.3	79.8

WHAT PURPOSES DO RECORDS SERVE?

There are three main reasons for maintaining good records: better management control, proof of credit worthiness, and support for tax reports.

For the manager, records document significant facts for future use. One of the most important aspects of financial management is the ability to analyze the past in such a way as to throw light on the future. This ability is critical for a business that wants to grow. For example, sales reports which analyze sales by area, type, and customer are necessary for making sound marketing decisions. Production records which show the unit cost of a product are essential for preparing future estimates for similar products. Records of past performance establish the criteria which guide the production manager in compiling realistic forecasts for the future. Good records enable the manager to substitute informed judgment for guesswork and intuition in making business decisions.

In the area of cash management, it is practically impossible to negotiate a business loan from a lending institution without properly prepared financial statements. It is even difficult to obtain credit in any form without such statements. Bankers and other credit granters need to study the balance sheet and income statement in order to decide whether credit should be extended. Sometimes audited financial statements are required. The record system must provide the basis for these statements.

Probably as important as the management and credit aspects of financial records is the requirement by federal and local government agencies for adequate records to support tax payments. The responsibility for keeping such records and proving their accuracy falls on the taxpayer, so the importance of keeping substantiating records is obvious.

WHAT KINDS OF RECORD SYSTEMS ARE IN GENERAL USE?

There are two basic types of recordkeeping systems you can use. The double-entry system requires that you record each item in two different ways—identifying them as *debits* or *credits*. For example, when a customer pays $10 on his or her account, it will be credited (reduced) by $10 on your books. At the same time, the store's cash will be debited (increased) by a like amount. In this system, a single item shows up in two places in the business' books. All other transactions are recorded in the same way, providing two sets of figures which must balance to the same totals. If the totals do not balance, you know that a mistake has been made. This safety factor is a big advantage and is responsible for the use of the double-entry bookkeeping system in many businesses.

The other system requires you to record each item only once, and results in only one set of figures. In their early years, most small businesses find such a system ideally suited to their requirements. It is economical to use and does not require an accountant to maintain it. This approach has made many "one-book" systems commercially available. Because of their simplicity and convenience, they are used by many business owners who want to become personally involved in the records of the business. As the business grows, more sophisticated systems will perhaps become necessary to keep track of the dozens of items which find their way into the records of a business.

HOW CAN YOU TELL HOW MANY RECORDS YOU NEED TO KEEP?

What kinds of records and how many you need will depend on the kind of business you are in. Teenagers selling hot dogs at ball games or newspapers on routes have little need for inventory records since they buy and sell their entire stock each day. On the other hand, a dress shop or a shoe store will need records of sizes and styles on hand in order to satisfy customer demands and provide a basis for reordering. Such records may also be used for determining which items are not selling well.

Every record you use should provide information which is important to you in operating your business efficiently. It should be as simple as possible to maintain.

In a small service or retail firm, bits of information flow in daily reflecting sales data, cash flow, equipment information, purchases, payroll, accounts payable, and, if credit is offered to customers, accounts receivable. A recordkeeping system for such a business should include the following "basic" records:

Cash receipts	Used to record the cash which the business takes in each day.
Sales	Used to record and summarize the income of the business.
Purchases	Used to record the purchases of merchandise bought for processing or resale.
Cash disbursements	Used to record the firm's expenditures.
Accounts receivable	Used to record the balances which customers owe the firm.
Accounts payable	Used to record what the firm owes its creditors and suppliers.
Payroll	Used to record the wages of employees and their deductions, such as those for income tax and social security tax.
Inventory	Used to record the firm's investment in stock. This information is used in arriving at the firm's profit and for income tax reports.
Equipment	Used to record the firm's capital assets, such as equipment, office furniture, and motor vehicles.

Not all records are used for financial control or accounting purposes. Some aid in better management control; still others are necessary for carrying out the day-to-day functions related to office activities, maintenance, and the like. Here are a few common records of this type:

☐ INSURANCE REGISTER. Shows the policy numbers of your insurance policies, the companies representing the insurer, kinds of coverage and amounts, expiration dates, and premiums. Such records are helpful when filing claims for losses and when reviewing insurance coverage with your insurance agent.

☐ MAINTENANCE RECORDS. Document the types and locations of all machines and equipment, what is spent to maintain them, and how often they are serviced or checked. Records are also used to keep track of the costs of maintaining buildings and grounds, rearrangement costs, costs of utilities, equipment accountability, and facilities planning.

☐ QUALITY CONTROL. Includes statistical records related to product quality, reasons for rejections, functional and environmental testing, chemical analysis, disposition of discrepant hardware, and vendor-related information.

☐ OFFICE RECORDS. Are related to incoming and outgoing correspondence, personnel records, mailing lists, invoice forms, receipts, sales books, stationery, and service records.

WHO SHOULD KEEP THE BOOKS FOR YOUR BUSINESS?

There are several possibilities. The public accountant who helps you set up the books might keep them and thereby provide the greatest accuracy. You will have to weigh the cost since the accountant will have to charge you for his or her time and operating expense. A good accountant can often save you more than he or she costs.

A second possibility is to keep the books yourself. If you have the time, background, and inclination, you can save money this way. Or a friend or relative might be able to help, even on a part-time basis.

Accounting firms often have part-time bookkeepers available on whom you can depend for occasional help during busy seasons and vacation periods. Look in the yellow pages of your telephone book under "Employment, Temporary."

Finally, there are free-lance bookkeepers who work full time but divide their time among several businesses.

Sales slips and cash register tapes are common sources of sales data. Sales slips will provide information about price, department where sold, salesperson, quantity sold, the date, and information about the customer. Sales slips can be retained indefinitely, destroyed at predetermined times, or microfilmed to provide a permanent record of your sales transactions and income. Modern cash registers do an excellent job of summarizing sales data. Some can be equipped with tape-punch attachments which provide a punched tape to be sent to a service bureau for processing and printing of several different kinds of reports for management analysis. Others record information which can be used for inventory control and reordering.

Great strides in improved cash control have been made with the introduction of electronic cash registers. These stand-alone units range in price from $450 to around $4,500. They offer such features as these:

□ Sales totals by department

□ Cash-in-drawer total

□ Tax-collected total

□ Paid-out total

□ Received-on-account total

□ Automatic computation of tax

□ Multiple quantity price extension

□ Split pricing

□ Void error correction

□ Automatic change computation

Industry studies indicate that it takes about 7 minutes to total out a mechanical cash register, plus approximately 2 hours of the store manager's time to reconcile totals and cash, and to account for all cash flow. An electronic cash register can do the same job in 30 seconds and provide a printed record of the day's business in a form similar to Figure 9-1.

These devices have taken much of the work out of record-keeping and have resulted in greater accuracy, faster customer processing, and improved cashier performance.

There are many one-book record systems on the market today which provide an easy convenient way for small business people to keep their business records in a way that will help them prepare their tax reports, calculate their profits, and make intelligent decisions concerning future actions. Figure 9-2 shows how sales information can be summarized each day, using a standard form from such a system.

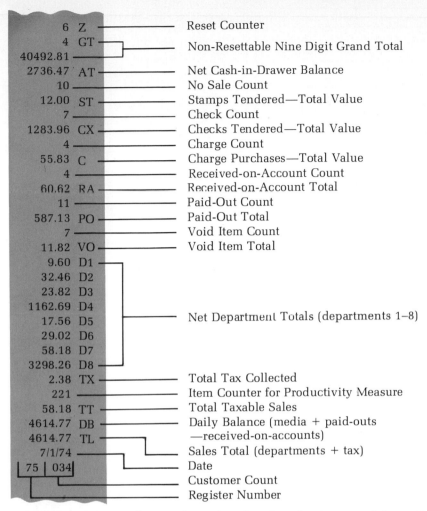

6 Z	Reset Counter
4 GT	Non-Resettable Nine Digit Grand Total
40492.81	
2736.47 AT	Net Cash-in-Drawer Balance
10	No Sale Count
12.00 ST	Stamps Tendered—Total Value
7	Check Count
1283.96 CX	Checks Tendered—Total Value
4	Charge Count
55.83 C	Charge Purchases—Total Value
4	Received-on-Account Count
60.62 RA	Received-on-Account Total
11	Paid-Out Count
587.13 PO	Paid-Out Total
7	Void Item Count
11.82 VO	Void Item Total
9.60 D1	
32.46 D2	
23.82 D3	
1162.69 D4	
17.56 D5	Net Department Totals (departments 1–8)
29.02 D6	
58.18 D7	
3298.26 D8	
2.38 TX	Total Tax Collected
221	Item Counter for Productivity Measure
58.18 TT	Total Taxable Sales
4614.77 DB	Daily Balance (media + paid-outs
4614.77 TL	—received-on-accounts)
7/1/74	Sales Total (departments + tax)
75 034	Date
	Customer Count
	Register Number

FIGURE 9-1. A printout from an electronic cash register showing a complete record of the day's transactions. Such information can be provided at any time during the day. (*Source:* Data Terminal Systems, Maynard, Massachusetts.)

HOW CAN YOU KEEP CONTROL OF THE CASH YOUR BUSINESS HANDLES DAILY?

You can make a daily reconciliation of your cash transactions by using information from your cash-register tapes or other sources of cash-receipts information. The information can be reconciled from beginning-of-day and end-of-day changes in the cash position. Not all businesses bother to make daily summaries of such information, but such a report is a useful tool in checking how your business is doing each day. Whether you use a cash register or sales slips or both, every cash receipt and every charge sale is recorded. At the close of each day's business, the actual cash on hand is counted and

FIGURE 9-2. Sales and cash receipts. (Source: *The Merchant's Bookkeeping and Tax Record*, marketed by Ideal Systems of Berkeley, California. Used with permission.)

THE IDEAL SYSTEM, REG. U. S. PAT. OFFICE MADE IN U.S.A.

SALES AND CASH RECEIPTS

FACSIMILE PAGE
ILLUSTRATING THE USE OF THIS IDEAL SYSTEM FORM.

DISTRIBUTION OF SALES
IDEAL SYSTEM FORM 21
(REPLACES FORMS 41, 131, 141)

Line	Date 19__	Memoranda	1 Cash Sales	2 Credit Sales	3 Merchandise Returned or Allowances	4 Total Sales (1+2−3)	5 Cash Received to Apply on Credit Sales	6 Other Cash Received	7 Total Cash Received (1+5+6)	8 Dept A	9 Dept B	10 Dept C
1	Mar 1	Days Business	123 00	14 00		137 00	10 00		133 00	80 50	38 50	18 00
2	2	" "	161 20			161 20	16 50		177 70	103 50	36 20	21 50
3	3	" "	118 50			118 50	4 25		122 75	54 80	41 70	22 00
4	4	" "	134 00	8 25	6 25	136 00			134 00	78 20	39 80	18 00
5	5	" "	128 50	16 00		144 50			128 50	94 40	27 00	23 10
6	6	" "	160 60			160 60	26 50		187 10	91 10	43 50	26 00
7	8	" "	128 50			128 50			128 50	80 50	38 20	9 80
8	9	" "	142 00	20 00	10 00	152 00	12 50		154 50	80 10	41 50	30 40
9	10	" "	134 20			134 20	8 10		142 30	75 20	37 50	21 50
10	11	" "	119 00	2 50		121 50			119 00	61 10	39 80	20 60
11	12	Deposit refund Gas Co						25 00	25 00			
12		Days Cash Sales	182 00			182 00			182 00	114 50	67 50	
13	13	Credit Sales R.A. Smith		21 10		21 10					21 10	
14		" Lou Warnke		80 00		80 00				80 00		
15		Recd on acct R.A. Smith					10 00		10 00			
16		Mdse retd Ed Morgan			3 20	(3 20)						(3 20)
17	15	Days Cash Sales	148 00			148 00			148 00	94 00	32 50	21 50
18		Credit Sales J. Brown		16 50		16 50					16 50	
19		" " Tom Jones		18 10		18 10				18 10		
20		Recd on Acct. Geo Riley					9 20		9 20			
21												
22												
23												
24	Mar 25	Days Business	130 00	21 00		151 00			130 00	94 90	56 10	
25	26	" "	120 26	16 50		136 76	24 50		144 76	105 26	31 50	
26	27	" "	142 90			142 90			142 90	80 70	62 20	
27	28	" "	165 74	8 10	6 00	167 84			165 74	96 44	71 40	
28	29	" "	143 50			143 50	9 00		152 50	97 50	16 25	29 75
29	30	" "	129 40	9 25		138 65			129 40	83 65	20 75	34 25
30												
31												
32												
33		TOTALS	2511 30	251 30	25 45	2737 15	135 55	25 00	2671 85	1644 45	779 50	293 20

YOU MAY EITHER SUMMARIZE THE ENTIRE DAYS SALES AND CASH RECEIPTS ON ONE LINE EACH DAY ~ IN WHICH CASE YOUR ENTIRE MONTHS ENTRIES WILL BE ON ONE PAGE ~ OR YOU MAY USE AS MANY LINES DAILY AND AS MANY PAGES MONTHLY AS ARE NEEDED TO ITEMIZE EACH TRANSACTION EACH DAY.

WHEN MERCHANDISE THAT HAS PREVIOUSLY BEEN ENTERED IN THIS SECTION IS RETURNED TO YOU FOR CREDIT -- ENTER AND CIRCLE THE AMOUNT (OR ENTER IN RED) ~ AND DEDUCT THE AMOUNT FROM THE COLUMNS CONCERNED.

COLUMNS WITH BLANK HEADINGS MAY BE USED TO KEEP TRACK OF ANY PARTICULAR CLASS OF SALES YOU WISH. FOR EXAMPLE: REPAIR DEPT.; APPLIANCE SALES; RETAIL SALES; WHOLESALE; LABOR; MATERIAL SALES; ETC; ETC;

TRANSFER ALL OF THE MONTHLY TOTALS TO FORM S-21 SUMMARY (LAST PAGE OF THIS SECTION). THIS GIVES YOU A MONTH BY MONTH COMPARISON OF YOUR SALES - IN EACH DEPARTMENT OF YOUR BUSINESS ~ SHOWING YOU EXACTLY HOW YOUR BUSINESS IS PROGRESSING.

THE MONTHLY TOTAL OF COLUMN 4 (TOTAL SALES) IS TO BE ENTERED ON LINE 1. (UNDER THE PROPER MONTH) ON THE SUMMARY OF BUSINESS AND STATEMENT OF INCOME FORMS

THE IDEAL SYSTEM REG. U. S. PAT. OFFICE

"balanced" against the total of the receipts recorded for the day. This data is then recorded on a daily summary similar to that shown in Figure 9-3.

DAILY SUMMARY OF SALES AND CASH RECEIPTS

Date_____

Cash Receipts

1. Cash Sales $345.00
2. Collections on Account 80.00
3. Miscellaneous Receipts 10.00
4. Total Receipts to Be Accounted For $435.00

Cash on Hand

5. Cash in Register:
    Coins   . . . . $ 18.00
    Bills 402.00
    Checks 76.00

       Total Cash in Register $496.00
6. Petty Cash Slips 34.00
7. Total Cash Accounted For $530.00
8. Less: Change and Petty Cash Fund:
    Petty cash slips . . . . $ 34.00
    Coins and bills 66.00

       Change and Petty Cash Fund (fixed amount) . . 100.00
9. Total Cash for Deposit $430.00
10. Cash Short (Item 4 Less Item 9) . . . . $ 5.00
11. Cash Over (Item 9 Less Item 4) . . . . None

FIGURE 9-3. A daily summary for controlling the cash handled by a business.

The top section of Figure 9-3 records all cash taken in during the day from all sources. This is the cash that must be accounted for over and above the change in the cash register and cash in the petty cash fund at the start of the day. "Cash sales" is the total on the cash register tape or the total of all the sales slips.

"Collections on account" are summarized either from the cash register tape or from the customer receipts you have written. After these are recorded, you set them aside for later posting to the accounts-receivable record, which is discussed later.

"Miscellaneous receipts" covers such items as refunds from suppliers, collections of rent, and similar income which cannot be classified as cash sales or collections on account. A sales slip or a memo should be used to document each miscellaneous receipt of cash.

"Cash on hand" is the sum of cash in the register and the slips in the petty cash drawer. These slips represent cash that has been paid out. The total is added to the amount of cash in the register to arrive at "Total cash accounted for." This total will include the day's receipts and the amount that was on hand at the beginning of the day—the change in the register and the cash in the petty cash fund.

Item 8 represents the petty cash slips on hand and the cash needed to make up the balance of the fixed amount carried in the petty cash fund. In our example, the fixed amount is $100. Subtracting $34 for petty cash slips from this amount leaves $66 in coins and bills in the fund. Since the petty cash fund will be kept intact and used again tomorrow, its fixed amount is subtracted from item 7 to arrive at the amount available for deposit at the bank. When the bank deposit has been made, a duplicate deposit slip should be attached to the daily summary for filing as a permanent record.

By comparing item 4 with item 9, we can determine whether we have more cash or less at the end of the day than our sales receipts indicate we should have. Any shortages or overages should be checked to see if the error can be traced to lost sales slips, incorrect recording of payments, incorrect change, or other reasons.

At least once a month your cash records should be reconciled with the bank records. You or some trusted employee who does not have access to your cash receipts or checks should get the monthly bank statement and prepare the reconciliation. The bank balance should be reconciled with both your bank book and your account which shows cash in the bank. Figure 9-4 illustrates the data used in such a reconciliation.

HOW CAN YOU KEEP TRACK OF MERCHANDISE PURCHASED FOR RESALE?

Set up a separate record for such items since they will become a part of your "cost of merchandise sold" when you prepare your financial statement at the end of the month. You should enter all merchandise purchases on the record, whether paid for or not. Be careful to exclude from this record any supplies purchased for use in operating your business, such as office supplies, brooms, mops, wrapping paper, and stationery. Since these items are not purchased for resale, they are recorded as operating supplies and become a part of your cost of doing business. In the "one-book" system we have described, separate monthly totals for purchases and operating supplies are developed and transferred to the monthly summary.

WHAT CATEGORIES ARE USED TO RECORD BUSINESS EXPENSES?

Commonly used categories include payroll, payroll taxes, income taxes, license fees, supplies, utilities, rent, insurance, car expense, losses, depreciation, and bad debts. Most businesses use some of these and add others which have significance to the particular busi-

```
                         BANK RECONCILIATION
                          December 31, 19___

Balance per Bank Statement . . . . . . . . . . . . . . .    $543.22
Add Deposits Not Credited:
    December 29 . . . . . . . . . . . . . .    $157.33
    December 30 . . . . . . . . . . . . . .     202.25     359.58
                                                          ─────────
                                                           $902.80
Deduct Outstanding Checks:
    No. 113   11/20 . . . . . . . . . . . . .   $ 15.18
        129   12/15 . . . . . . . . . . . .        5.10
        135   12/25 . . . . . . . . . . . .      132.80
        139   12/30 . . . . . . . . . . . .       75.30
        140   12/30 . . . . . . . . . . . .       69.80
        141   12/30 . . . . . . . . . . . .       55.33     353.51
                                                          ─────────
Adjusted Balance per Bank Statement . . . . . . . . . .    $549.29
                                                          ═════════
Balance per Checkbook . . . . . . . . . . . . . . . . .    $544.54
Add:
    Check No. 120 entered as $28.30 should be
        $23.30   . . . . . . . . . . . . . . . . . .    $  5.00
    Deposits of Dec. 1 recorded as $298.60
        should be $299.60 . . . . . . . . . . . .          1.00       6.00
                                                                   ─────────
                                                                   $550.54
Deduct Bank Service Charge . . . . . . . . . . . . . . .              1.25
                                                                   ─────────
                                                                   $549.29
                                                                   ═════════
```

FIGURE 9-4.   A bank reconciliation.

ness. A manufacturing business would modify these classifications to segregate manufacturing, selling, and administrative expenses in order to permit an analysis of costs by major cost category.

WHAT IS THE SIMPLEST RECORD SYSTEM THAT WILL PROVIDE DATA FOR A PROFIT-AND-LOSS STATEMENT AND INFORMATION FOR TAX REPORTS?

A "barebones" record system for the small retailer was developed by the U.S. Department of Commerce in the late 1960s. It features a daily cash report to provide a record of cash receipts and payments plus a summary and classification of cash received and paid out each day. This information is recorded on the front and back side of a single form as shown in Figure 9-5.

A cumulative one-book summary is used to record the daily information from the daily cash report. Such items as cash transactions, credit transactions, and payments are posted onto a single record and summarized at the end of the month. See Figure 9-6.

These two records replace all journals and ledgers except accounts receivable, employee records, and records of fixed assets.

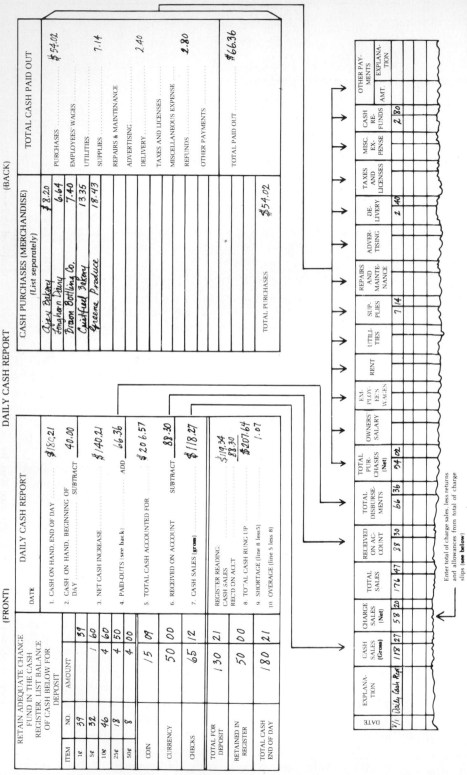

FIGURE 9-5. Daily cash report. (Source: Clifford M. Baumback, Kenneth Lawyer, and Pearce C. Kelley, *How to Organize and Operate a Small Business*, 5th ed., Prentice-Hall, Inc., Englewood Cliffs, N.J., 1973. Reproduced with permission.)

CUMULATIVE ONE-BOOK SUMMARY

DATE	EXPLANATION	CHECK NO.	CASH SALES (GROSS)	CHARGE SALES (NET)	TOTAL SALES	CASH RECEIVED ON ACCOUNT	TOTAL DISBURSEMENTS	PURCHASES (NET)	OWNER'S SALARY	EMPLOYEE'S WAGES	RENT	UTILITIES	SUPPLIES	REPAIRS AND MAINTENANCE	ADVERTISING	DE-LIVERY	TAXES AND LICENSES	MISC. EXPENSES	CASH RE-FUNDS	OTHER PAYMENTS AMT	OTHER PAYMENTS EX-PLANATION	LINE NO.
1	Daily Cash Rept.	x	118 17	58 20	176 47	88 30	66 36	54 02					7 14			2 40			2 80			1
1	Wholesale Supply	46					142 60	142 60														2
1	City Electric Co.	47					10 14					10 14										3
2	Daily Cash Rept.	x	81 74	45 87	127 63	112 60	117 70	110 20						4 50	3 00							4
2	John Doe	48					50 00													50 00	Drawings withdrawal	5
2	Hill Garage	49					12 50									12 50						6
2	Dixon Supply	50					116 50	116 50														7
3	Daily Cash Rept.	x	93 19	69 27	162 46	237 80	100 76	94 16					4 60					2 00				8
3	City Telephone Co.	51					9 62					9 62										9
3	Brown Realty	52					80 00				80 00											10
3	Ajax Co.	53					60 00													60 00	counter display	11
4	Daily Cash Rept.	x	132 46	79 20	212 16	321 42	126 07	109 27						5 20	5 00	5 00		1 60				12
4	John Doe	54					75 00		75 00													13
4	Smith Poultry	55					32 40	32 40														14
4	First Nat'l Bank	56					103 00											3 00		100 00	note payable	15
4	Col. of Taxes	57					10 00										10 00					16
5	Daily Cash Rept.	x	221 97	104 19	351 16	135 15	211 49	127 92		76 30			3 27						4 00			17
5	Jones Bros.	58					85 14	85 14														18
5	Col. of Int. Rev.	59					20 80			10 40							10 40					19
5	Col. of Int. Rev.	60					37 50			37 50												20
7	Etc.																					21
																						22
31	Total, Aug.		3,531 93	1,945 38	5,477 31	1,686 27	5,169 03	4,061 65	300 00	353 10	80 00	19 76	23 25	17 65	10 00	52 38	20 40	8 64	12 20	21 00		80
			(A)	(B)	(C)	(D)	(E)	(F)	(G)	(H)	(I)	(J)	(K)	(L)	(M)	(N)	(O)	(P)	(Q)	(R)		

NOTE: To insure accuracy of entries and additions the column totals should be cross-checked as follows:

Column (B) should equal the total of columns (F) to (R), inclusive.
Column (C) should equal Column (A) plus Column (B).

FIGURE 9-6. Cumulative one-book summary. (Source: Clifford M. Baumback, Kenneth Lawyer, and Pearce C. Kelley, *How to Organize and Operate a Small Business*, 5th ed., Prentice-Hall, Inc., Englewood Cliffs, N.J.: 1973. Reproduced with permission.)

The daily cash report does not provide a record of charge sales or returns and allowances. These must be figured separately either from the cash register tape, from the sales slips, or from a separate record maintained to accumulate the data. The same is true of cash received on account. If the cash register does not have a means of identifying such payments, a separate record of such receipts will have to be kept.

The monthly or quarterly totals supplied by this system will provide almost all the information needed to prepare the income statement. The annual totals may be used for the preparation of the owner's income tax return and for making an annual profit-and-loss statement for the business.

HOW CAN YOU KEEP TRACK OF WHAT YOU OWE AND WHAT OTHERS OWE YOU?

You can set up a simple record of accounts receivable showing who owes you, how much has been paid, and what is still owed. Recording the date on which the charge was incurred will enable you to tell how long the charge has been on the books. A card for each customer, or a loose-leaf notebook with a page for each customer, can provide an adequate record for this purpose. The information for accounts receivable is posted to this record each day from your sales slips.

A similar record can be maintained for the amounts you owe creditors.

WHAT BASIC PAYROLL RECORDS DO YOU NEED TO MAINTAIN?

Usually an earnings record card or sheet is set up for each employee on which the information is recorded. Every wage payment to the employee, all amounts withheld or deducted, and the net amount paid the employee are shown.

A record of the hours worked is also required for all nonexecutive personnel to prove your compliance with the law on minimum wages and overtime. This record is useful in keeping track of costs associated with vacations, illnesses, tardiness, and other absences.

A number of payroll records systems are available commercially. Some are based on the multiple-copy principle, where a single writing of the check or payslip to be given to the employee makes a carbon copy on the employee's earnings card and on a payroll summary. Most one-book systems have a payroll section with sheets similar to Figure 9-7.

If you have only one or two employees, you might not need a payroll system. Payroll information can be entered in your cash disbursements record and summarized from that when required for tax reporting. If you do not want to enter individual employees' wages in the cash disbursements record you can prepare individual earnings cards which contain the necessary data.

FIGURE 9-7. Individual payroll record. (Source: The Merchant's Bookkeeping and Tax Record, marketed by Ideal Systems of Berkeley, California. Used with permission.)

FACSIMILE PAGE   INDIVIDUAL PAYROLL RECORD FOR YEAR ENDING December 31, 1960

NAME OF EMPLOYEE John Doe
ADDRESS 1800 Central Street   CITY Metroville
PHONE Taylor 5-8306   DATE OF BIRTH 8-12-20
SOCIAL SECURITY NO
MARRIED [x]   SINGLE [ ]
NUMBER OF EXEMPTIONS CLAIMED ON FORM W4 2
DATE EMPLOYED Jan. 1, 1950
DATE TERMINATED
REASON
IDEAL SYSTEM - FORM Q-812

THE IDEAL SYSTEM COPYRIGHT U S PAT OFFICE

WEEK ENDING	REG TIME	OVER TIME	RATE	PER	REGULAR TIME EARNINGS	OVERTIME EARNINGS	OTHER COMPEN-SATION	TOTAL EARNINGS (A)	STATE UNEMPL INS %	FEDERAL OLD AGE INS %	FEDERAL WITHHELD INC TAXES	OTHER WITHHELD INC / FEES	OTHER DEDUCTIONS	TOTAL DEDUCTIONS	NET AMOUNT PAID EMPLOYEE (COL A LESS COL B)	CHECK NO	
Jan. 4	40		1.80	hr	72.00			72.00	.72	1.80	8.50			11.02	60.98	60	1
11	40		1.80		72.00			72.00	.72	1.80	8.50		5.00	16.02	55.98	93	2
18	32		1.80		57.60			57.60	.58	1.44	5.70			7.72	49.88	128	3
25	40		1.80		72.00			72.00	.72	1.80	8.50			11.02	60.98	167	4
Feb. 1	40	4	1.80		72.00	10.80		82.80	.83	2.07	10.30			13.20	69.60	194	5
8	36		1.80		64.80			64.80	.65	1.62	7.10		10.00	19.37	45.43	221	6
15	40		1.80		72.00			72.00	.72	1.80	8.50			11.02	60.98	263	7
22	40	8	1.80		72.00	5.40		77.40	.77	1.94	9.20			11.91	65.49	297	8
Mar. 1	40		1.80		72.00			72.00	.72	1.80	8.50			11.02	60.98	329	9
8	39		1.80		70.20			70.20	.70	1.76	8.20		5.00	15.66	54.54	359	10
15	40		1.80		72.00			72.00	.72	1.80	8.50			11.02	60.98	391	11
22	40		1.80		72.00			72.00	.72	1.80	8.50			11.02	60.98	421	12
29	40	5	1.80		72.00	13.50		85.50	.86	2.14	10.70			13.70	71.80	453	13
TOTAL 1ST QUARTER					912.60	29.70		942.30	10.15	23.57	110.70		20.00	163.70	778.60		14
Apr. 5	40	6	1.80	hr	72.00	16.20		88.20	.88	2.21	11.20			14.29	73.91	487	15
12	40		1.80		72.00			72.00	.72	1.80	8.50		5.00	16.02	55.98	515	16
19					off this week illness												17
26	38		1.80		68.40			68.40	.68	1.71	7.80			10.19	58.21	545	18
May 3	40		1.80		72.00			72.00	.72	1.80	8.50			11.02	60.98	609	19
10	40		1.80		72.00			72.00	.72	1.80	8.50			11.02	60.98	634	20
17	40		1.90		76.00			76.00	.76	1.90	9.20		10.00	21.86	54.14	672	21
24	40	4	1.90		76.00	11.00		87.00	.87	2.18	11.00			14.05	72.95	705	22
31	36		1.90		68.50			68.50	.69	1.71	7.80			10.20	58.30	737	23
June 7	40		1.90		76.00			76.00	.76	1.90	9.20			11.86	64.14	769	24
14	vacation with pay		1.90		76.00			76.00	.76	1.90	9.20		5.00	16.86	59.14	801	25
21	40		1.90		76.00			76.00	.76	1.90	9.20			11.86	64.14	832	26
28	40	2	1.90		76.00	5.50		81.50	.82	2.04	10.00			12.86	68.64	866	27
TOTAL 2ND QUARTER					880.90	32.70		913.60	9.14	22.85	110.10		20.00	162.09	751.51		28
																	29
																	30
																	31
																	32
																	33

(Annotation — OTHER DEDUCTIONS column) ENTER SUCH ITEMS AS ADVANCES, INS-URANCE, COST OF MEALS GIVEN TO EMPLOYEE IN LIEU OF WAGE, ETC.

(Annotation — TOTAL EARNINGS column) TAX DEDUCTIONS ARE TO BE CAL-CULATED ON THE AMOUNTS IN THIS COLUMN.

(Annotation — OTHER COMPENSATION column) MAY BE USED FOR ANY MERCHANDISE, MEALS, LODGING, ETC. SUPPLIED TO EMP-LOYEE AS PART OF WAGE.

(Annotation — quarterly totals) EACH QUARTERLY TOTAL OF EACH COLUMN IS ALSO TO BE ENTERED AT THE BOTTOM OF THE REVERSE SIDE OF THIS FORM ON THE LINE FOR THE PROPER QUARTER. THIS GIVES YOU EACH EMPLOYEE'S INDIVIDUAL TOTAL EARN-INGS, WITHHOLDING TAX, ETC. FOR YOUR FINAL WITHHOLDING TAX RETURNS.

(Annotation — bottom left) TRANSFER THE QUARTERLY TOTALS OF EACH EMPLOYEE TO FORM 5-BIL PAYROLL SUMMARY. THIS GIVES YOU YOUR COMBINED INDIVIDUAL QUARTERLY PAYROLL FOR YOUR PAYROLL TAX RETURNS.

THE IDEAL SYSTEM   REG. U.S. PAT OFFICE

DO YOU NEED TO KEEP RECORDS SHOWING BAD DEBTS OR UNCOLLECTIBLE ACCOUNTS?

If you grant credit, you will sooner or later be faced with collection losses or "bad debts." These can be deducted as a business expense for tax purposes if they are properly documented in your records.

The amount of such losses varies with the type of business, your credit and collection policies, and the economic environment in which your business operates. You should try to find out what the experience for businesses like yours is. Your trade association might be able to supply such information. The National Retail Hardware Association, for instance, published statistics for 1974 which showed that bad debts amounted to 0.33 percent of sales in hardware stores during that year.

Your customer accounts should be reviewed from time to time, and a determination should be made as to which will be written off. Some businesses keep an accounts-receivable aging list which shows the length of time customers are delinquent. Such a list helps you determine which ones might become bad debts. This record lists in one column the receivables dating from the past month to the current month and shows the total balance for each customer. The portions of the total that are from the previous month, the month before that, and so on are shown in appropriate columns. These highlight potential bad debts by showing those receivables which have been on the books a long time.

IS THERE A SIMPLE WAY OF KEEPING TRACK OF YOUR FIXED ASSETS?

An equipment record can be established for this purpose. This record is used to show the purchase of capital items such as furniture, fixtures, business vehicles, tools, machines, buildings, and the like. Items such as these are not an expense in themselves, but depreciation (wear and tear) on them is. This record shows the nature of each piece of equipment, the date you acquired it, its cost, its estimated life, and the method of depreciation you intend to use. One-twelfth of the annual depreciation should be charged off each month as expense in order to get a true profit-and-loss picture for the business each month.

WHAT RECORDS SHOULD YOU KEEP REGARDING YOUR TAX LIABILITIES?

All business people are required to maintain records that will enable them to prepare complete and accurate returns and insure that they pay their proper taxes.

The law does not require any particular kinds of records. You may choose any system suited to the purpose and nature of your business that will accurately reflect income. Regardless of your bookkeeping system, your permanent books of account or records must clearly establish not only your gross income but also your deductions and credits. This means you must maintain whatever records or data as may be required to support the entries on your tax return. Paid bills, canceled checks, and similar records that substantiate entries in your records should be filed in an orderly manner and stored in a safe place. For most small businesses, the business checkbook is the prime source of entries for business records.

Here is a list of records needed for income tax purposes:

- The amounts and dates of all wage payments subject to taxes.
- The names, addresses, and occupations of employees receiving such payments.
- The periods of their employment.
- The periods for which they are paid while absent because of sickness or personal injuries, and the amount and weekly rate of such payment.
- The social security numbers of your employees, which are also their taxpayer identifying numbers.
- Employee income tax withholding allowance or exemption certificates.
- Duplicate copies of quarterly and annual returns filed and the dates and amounts of deposits made for taxes.

You should keep such records for at least 4 years after the date the tax to which they relate becomes due or is paid, whichever is later.

WHAT HAPPENS IF YOU FORGET TO WITHHOLD INCOME TAX FROM YOUR EMPLOYEES' WAGES?

You are required by law to deduct and withhold tax from the wages and salaries of your employees, and you are liable for the payment of that tax whether you collect it from your employees or not. If you for any reason deduct less than the correct amount of tax, you are liable for the full amount of the correct tax.

CAN YOU BE PENALIZED FOR FAILING TO KEEP ADEQUATE RECORDS TO BACK UP YOUR TAX REPORTS?

If your records do not reflect your true taxable income or do not prove adequate in enabling you to defend your income tax returns during an audit, you will be warned by the Internal Revenue Service to correct the deficiencies. You will also be warned of the penalties for willful failure to keep records as required by tax laws and regulations.

If a follow-up investigation the next year still reveals inadequate records, you may be taken to court and charged with willful negligence (a misdemeanor). If found guilty, you can be fined up to $10,000 or imprisoned up to 5 years, or both; and you will have to assume the court costs. A civil penalty of 50 percent of the underpayment is added to the tax.

The Internal Revenue Service is not the last word in determining either the extent to which records must be kept or the tax liability of the taxpayer. The actions of the service are subject to review by the courts.

HOW LONG SHOULD YOU KEEP RECORDS FOR INCOME TAX PURPOSES?

There is no clear-cut answer. You are required to keep the books and records of your business available at all times for inspection by Internal Revenue officers. Your records must be retained as long as their contents may become material in the administration of the Internal Revenue law.

Records that support an item of income or deduction which appears on a return should be retained until expiration of the statute of limitations for that return. Ordinarily, the statute of limitations for an income tax return expires 3 years after the return is due to be filed or 2 years from the date the tax is paid, whichever occurs later.

If you are an employer, you must maintain all records pertaining to your employment taxes for a minimum of 4 years after the due date of the return.

Some experts advocate keeping your general ledgers, or at least a reproduction of them, forever. With the availability of microfilm, some businesses are copying their essential records and saving storage space. Such records are acceptable to the IRS and are admissible in a court of law. Before installing such a system, however, you should compare the expense of storing records for 7 to 10 years with the cost of microfilming.

WHAT ACCOUNTING PRACTICES WILL KEEP YOU OUT OF TROUBLE WITH THE TAX PEOPLE?

Failure to understand basic accounting procedures causes most of the problems in the tax world. These are the ones most often overlooked or ignored by business people:

□ To keep effective books you should deposit all receipts in a special place. Establish a petty cash fund for small expenses—well documented to make sure that such expenditures are strictly for business purposes.

□ A well-kept checkbook is a good basic business record, but for ease in accumulating data about your business, the use of journals and ledgers is preferred. Although many single-entry books are satisfactory for the small business, the larger business will find many advantages in a well-kept double-entry set of records.

☐ Whenever possible, all disbursements should be made by check. Unless a check is drawn for personal expenses, it should not be written to "cash" or the "proprietor." If this practice is followed, an adequate explanation should be placed in the file at the time the check is written.

☐ As a matter of sound practice, your bank statement should be reconciled with your records at least monthly.

☐ Intelligent classification of expenditures into understandable, acceptable groupings is recommended for ease in understanding and using your records. Such classifications as purchases, office supplies, machinery repair, maintenance, and advertising are examples. If expenditures are not properly classified, tax agents might suspect that an attempt has been made to bury an improper item in an account.

The importance of good records is emphasized by the fact that almost half of all small businesses have difficulty with the IRS at one time or another. Studies have also indicated that two out of three small business overpay their taxes.

HOW CAN YOU PREVENT "WASTED MOTION" IN YOUR RECORDKEEPING PROCEDURES?

So far we have been discussing the kinds of records found in business and the kinds of facts they provide for the business owner. The efficient handling of the records you decide to keep is sometimes a problem because it is easy to get in the habit of keeping too many records or of keeping records you do not really need. Sometimes duplication of activities between different records increases your recordkeeping costs unnecessarily. If your goal is to record the basic facts about your business as quickly and accurately as possible, you should be continually questioning your recordkeeping procedures to be sure that you are not doing a lot of unnecessary things that are costing you money.

The following questions[1] are designed to help you check your methods of handling records. As you study them, they might suggest others that could be helpful in finding and eliminating any wasted motion in your recordkeeping.

☐ Are you handling payroll data more than once? Do you, for example, record payroll data in a payroll journal, then write it on a payroll check stub, and finally write it again on an individual

[1]Adapted from William L. Raby, *Keeping Score With Effective Records*, Small Marketers Aid No. 94, Annual No. 9, U.S. Small Business Administration, Washington, 1967, pp. 18–19.

employee record? The use of an inexpensive one-write system will enable you to handle the payroll journal, check stub, and employee ledger in one operation.

☐ Do you maintain unnecessary ledger records of your accounts payable? Many small business people have found that a file of unpaid bills works just as well and requires less clerical effort. Check with your accountant on the advantages of the voucher system for handling payables.

☐ Are you missing the boat in the use of punched-paper (cash register) tape in sales and other analyses? Punched-tape attachments for cash registers and adding machines are helping to bring electronic recordkeeping within the reach of small business people. This tape, which is a by-product of regular operations, can be processed by a service bureau to give you back a variety of reports.

☐ Are old records cluttering up your storage space? Not all records need to be saved forever. Work out a record-retention system with the help of your accountant; then destroy your records in accordance with that program. You might want to check out the possibilities of putting some records—those that the law requires—on microfilm.

SELF-CHECK
OF KEY
CONCEPTS

This exercise is designed to test your understanding of the material presented in Chapter 9. Choose the response, *True* or *False*, which best fits each statement. Correct responses are presented in the back of the text.

1. Inadequate financial records can be a factor in failing to obtain a loan at a bank.
2. During 1974, approximately 80 percent of the retail and service business failures resulted from conditions which adequate business records could have disclosed.
3. If you are qualified to do so, you should keep your own books.
4. Cash payments should be made by check or from the petty cash fund, never from the cash register.
5. Errors are difficult to detect in the double-entry bookkeeping system.
6. At least once a week your cash records should be reconciled with the bank records of your account.
7. Bad debts may be written off as a business deduction if they are properly documented.

8. An electronic cash register can print out and reconcile the day's transactions in less than a minute.
9. Unless you charge off some depreciation each month, your business expenses will be understated.
10. You should keep tax records for at least 10 years.

PERFORMANCE PROBLEMS AND PROJECTS

1. Find the name of a major supplier of cash registers in your telephone book and write to the supplier, requesting information relative to the kinds of equipment available, what the capabilities are, and what the prices are.
2. Talk to a public accounting firm in your community and find out what services it provides and what it charges for them.
3. Visit your local stationer and see what is available in one-book recordkeeping systems. Examine the types of records they contain, get prices, and list the systems which are available for proprietors of service stations.
4. Sol's Home Improvement Center started the day with a petty cash fund of $100. It sold $660 (including sales tax) worth of merchandise for the day. Of this amount, $435 was for cash sales and $225 was taken in for charge sales. During the day, Sol paid $14 by check for a COD package. At the end of the day, his petty cash fund contained $33.53 worth of petty cash slips and $66.47 in coins and bills. When he counted his cash and checks at the end of the day, he had $477.47. Prepare a daily cash summary to see what he should have had. Is his cash position over or short? What could have happened to cause the discrepancy?

MINICASES IN POINT

1. Paul Kirby owned and operated a medium-sized neighborhood grocery store in a predominantly rural community. During the summer and fall, he bought fresh produce from many of the farmers who were good customers of his. He often paid for such items in cash directly from his cash register drawer. Since most of the money would be spent in his store, he figured that this method of handling the transaction was the simplest for everyone concerned.

   a. What problems do you think this practice will cause?
   b. What method would you recommend for handling such transactions?

2. Ruth Hardesty is the bookkeeper for a ladies' ready-to-wear store in a busy shopping center. She has just finished posting the last of the month charge sales to the accounts-receivable control sheet and has totaled the month's charges to $852.67. When she adds up the daily postings on the daily sales records, the total comes to $837.40 for charge sales made during the month.

   a. Where will Ruth look to reconcile the difference?
   b. What specific actions should she take to find the error(s)?

3. Mike Wong just bought a TV and appliance repair store with two service trucks. He has two service technicians who work in the store and one person who handles maintenance jobs, ordering and stocking of parts, and similar tasks.

His investment in parts is sizable, and he is concerned about the lack of good records to show how many parts are used, what repair orders they were used on, what the high usage parts are, or what the value of the inventory is. He feels that this lack of control can lead to losses through scrap, pilferage, and negligence.

a. What kind of procedure do you think Mike needs to establish better control of his inventory?
b. What records does he need for accumulating the information vital to efficient management?

4. When Yolanda Domico opened her flower shop, she discussed her insurance needs with an insurance agent in her community. In addition to buying coverage for direct losses from such perils as fire, floods, and wind, she listened with interest as the agent explained how "business-interruption" insurance would enable her to keep paying salaries, rent, taxes, interest, utilities, and similar consequential losses while she was rebuilding after a disaster. The policy would provide indemnity for as long as it took to restore the damaged property and get back into business, the agent explained. One of the provisions of the policy was that the insured must be able to show that if the business had not been damaged it would have continued to earn at least enough to pay its fixed expenses.

a. What responsibility does such a policy place on Yolanda in the event a disaster closes her business for 2 months?
b. If you were Yolanda, what kinds of records would you establish to protect your interest?
c. What problems would Yolanda have if all her records were destroyed in the disaster?

10 Understanding the Nature of Costs

PERFORMANCE OBJECTIVES

After reading this chapter, you should be able to determine the costs found in business and industry and demonstrate how they are analyzed and eventually applied in the pricing of finished products. Specifically, you should be able to:

1. Explain what direct costs are and give specific examples.
2. Describe indirect costs, distinguish them from direct costs, and explain why they are termed *indirect*.
3. Assess the differences in behavior between fixed and variable costs and give examples to illustrate how their behavior changes as volume increases or decreases.
4. Explain why fixed costs contribute less to the price of the finished product as the number you make increases.
5. Determine how much control first-line supervisors in manufacturing can exercise over their fixed and variable costs.
6. Define the term *overhead* and judge its significance in the cost of manufactured products.
7. Interpret a chart of accounts and defend its purpose.
8. Explain how overhead pools are used in accumulating costs.
9. Allocate plantwide overhead costs to production departments.
10. Sequence the flow of costs from the time workers enter their work charges on their time cards until the cost of their labor is incorporated into the cost of the product.

INTRODUCTION

An understanding of costs and their impact on business operations is essential if the owner is to make sound decisions. Tomorrow's plans are invariably tied to yesterday's history, and the owner finds it necessary to look backward in order to plan forward. The past, with all its mistakes, is still one of the best criteria to use for forward planning. Historical costs, properly accumulated and accurately recorded, provide owners a unique insight into the inner workings of their businesses. They will often "flag" activities that require management attention and permit the proverbial "stitch in time" to be taken expeditiously.

The classification and flow of costs are best understood by studying them in a manufacturing context. The traditional areas of manufacturing, sales, and administration provide a wide range of cost behavior and enable us to understand the basic concepts and apply them in other areas such as retailing and wholesaling with only minor changes.

This chapter describes the kinds of costs found in a typical manufacturing operation, explores their interrelationships, and examines their flow from inception to the finished product. There is a deliberate emphasis on overhead costs.

WHAT KINDS OF COSTS ARE USUALLY FOUND IN MANUFACTURING?

Figure 10-1 shows a typical company cost pattern for a manufacturing operation. Although the percentages vary from company to company, this classification is readily understood by those involved in estimating, accumulating, or analyzing manufacturing costs.
The various "wedges" of the pie include the following:

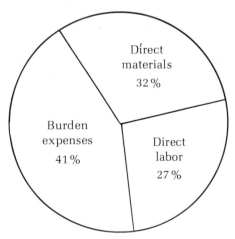

FIGURE 10-1. A typical manufacturing company cost pattern.

Materials (Direct). Includes all raw materials and purchased parts which become a part of the finished product. Since these materials are directly and easily identifiable to the product, they are termed *direct materials* in order to differentiate them from items which are needed in manufacturing the product but which do not become a part of it. The latter kind of materials is termed *indirect material* and is treated differently in cost analysis and financial control. The costs of items you buy from someone else, like subassemblies such as pumps, valves, and so forth, which you assemble into the final product in your plant, are considered a part of your material costs.

Labor (Direct).   Labor costs generated by workers who are assigned to make the product are collected here. Workers who handle the product and change its form, shape, or add value to it and contribute to its progress through the manufacturing cycle are termed *direct workers*. This classification differentiates their costs from those of office workers, janitors, supervisors, managers and similar groups who support manufacturing but do not work directly on the product.

Burden (Indirect).   Burden costs are often called *overhead costs*. They represent those expenses which are generated by support personnel, both in the manufacturing area and in other departments, who do not work on the product but who provide services of various kinds which are vital to the manufacturing operation. The materials used by these groups which do not become a part of the finished product are also included in burden costs. The factory area generates its own unique category of burden expense from those indirect employees assigned to the factory and from the indirect materials they use. Collectively, these costs are called *factory burden*. The sources of factory burden are the supervisors, clerks, expediters, inspectors, stock clerks, and similar classifications who are assigned to the factory and identified in this manner by the payroll and accounting departments. Burden also includes costs associated with indirect employees in departments outside the factory, such as maintenance people who keep factory equipment operating, plant security personnel, people who buy material items, accounting personnel who track and record costs, industrial engineers, payroll personnel, and many others. These people and the costs associated with them are often referred to as *administrative burden*. Factory burden and administrative burden are normally separated in accounting for the purpose of cost collection and control. Together, the costs in these two areas often account for as much as half the total cost of the product.

These broad general subdivisions of costs are found in all manufacturing organizations. For cost analysis, they are much too large to use for any purpose other than a "broad-brush" look at the total operation. We shall see how smaller pieces of these costs can be much more useful to the manager.

WHAT IS MEANT BY FIXED COSTS AND VARIABLE COSTS?

Fixed costs are those which do not change when the sales volume goes up or down. They are constant in total amount whether you make 100 gizmos or 10,000. Some examples are building rent, insurance, property taxes, and depreciation. Since these costs are fixed, their contribution to the unit cost of the product becomes less as sales volume increases; their contribution becomes more as sales volume drops. At low sales levels their impact on the cost of each unit can be great.

Variable costs are those which change with the number of units you make. Direct material is a good example. If you pay $1.50 for the material needed to manufacture a carpenter's hammer, your material costs would be $1,500 if you made 1,000 hammers and $7,500 if you made 5,000. The total material costs would vary in a predictable way, changing in direct proportion to the number of hammers made. Direct labor will also vary with the number of hammers made, although changes made in the manufacturing process which make the work easier and the improvement in the workers' skill as they make more and more hammers will cause the labor cost to decrease over the long haul, so that hammers made later in the production process will cost less for labor than the earlier units. Nonlabor expenses such as telephones, gas, water, and power will vary with volume although each of these has a "minimum charge," which modifies their variability characteristic to some degree. We will see later that few costs are "pure" in the sense that they are 100 percent fixed or variable. It is important that we recognize the general characteristics of these two concepts since this will be helpful later in understanding break-even curves and in making profitability analyses.

CAN ALL COSTS BE CLASSIFIED AS VARIABLE OR FIXED?

As we have already seen, some costs exhibit characteristics of both fixed and variable expenses. The electricity in the factory on weekends when the plant is closed would be required only to operate lighting and air-conditioning systems. It would, therefore, during this period act like a fixed cost. During the week, the consumption would rise in relation to the number of machines you operate. This characteristic represents the variable portion of the power bill. So the power bill is a mixture of both fixed and variable costs. There is also a "gray area" between fixed and variable cost-behavior patterns as exhibited by some costs which increase with volume but not in direct proportion. These are called *semivariable* costs. And finally, there are costs which are fixed only for a small range of volume and increase abruptly when the volume exceeds the limit. The new level is again fixed for a narrow range and might again increase when a new volume level is reached. Plotting such costs results in a chart which looks like a flight of steps. These costs are called *semifixed*. In summary, all costs exhibit some of the characteristics of both fixed and variable expenses. Quantifying how much of each type exists in a given cost is a special technique which we will discuss in the chapter on profit planning.

The features we have been discussing are easier to see if we plot the cost-volume relationship for a few everyday examples such as those in Figure 10-2. These cost expenditure curves merely reflect the various "flavors" that costs come in. They are by no means intended to represent all the possible combinations but only a few you will recognize.

WHAT IS OVERHEAD?

Overhead is a term used to describe those activities and related expenses which cannot be charged directly to a manufactured product. Overhead is probably the most often discussed element of cost in the entire area of financial control. As you have already seen in Figure 10-1, the contribution of overhead to product costs is significant, often exceeding the combined expenses attributable to labor and material. For this reason, overhead costs get a lot of management attention. The term *burden* or *indirect expense* is sometimes used to describe overhead expenses.

WHAT THINGS MAKE UP THE OVERHEAD COMPONENT OF MANUFACTURING COSTS?

Indirect labor claims the lion's share of overhead costs in most companies. Wages for workers performing supervisory duties, clerical operations, and support functions predominate. The last group includes departments such as cost accounting, quality assurance, purchasing, industrial engineering, and production control. There are many workers in these support areas who charge to overhead accounts on a full-time basis. By nature, their jobs require that they work on many different projects or products. Charging directly to a product is not feasible for these workers because of the great number of different tasks performed during the day and the impossibility of relating their efforts to any specific product.

Other major items carried in the overhead expense category are maintenance materials, depreciation, expendable tools, office supplies and equipment, utilities, communications, and travel.

HOW DO YOU KEEP TRACK OF OVERHEAD EXPENSES?

Once you have identified those expenses you want to keep track of, group them into similar groups and have your accountant assign a unique account number to each of them. This requires that you set up a chart of accounts like the one shown in Table 10-1 so that everyone knows what the account numbers represent. For convenience in analyzing costs, accounts can be grouped into categories such as indirect labor, employee benefits, taxes, employment, communications, travel, administration, facilities, and the like. This

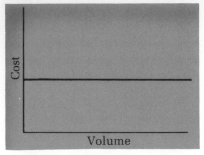

A. Fixed cost. The cost remains fixed regardless of changes in the volume. Examples are rent and insurance.

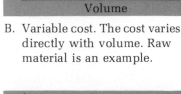

B. Variable cost. The cost varies directly with volume. Raw material is an example.

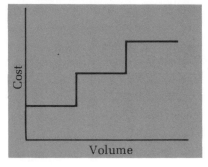

C. Semifixed cost. The cost is fixed for limited ranges of volume.

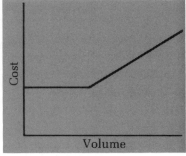

D. Fixed variable model. Example is a power bill consisting of a flat fixed charge, plus a variable cost after a certain number of kilowatts have been used.

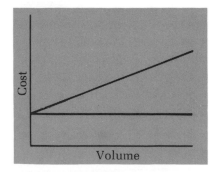

E. A portion of this cost is fixed at all levels. The remainder varies at some constant rate.

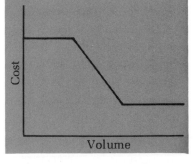

F. A mixed cost. Example is a rental agreement calling for $10,000 per month, less 10 cents for each direct-labor hour worked in excess of 100,000, with a $2,000 minimum.

FIGURE 10-2. Typical cost expenditure curves.

TABLE 10-1.   A CHART OF ACCOUNTS FOR OVERHEAD EXPENSES

Departmental Expenses		Administrative Expenses	
Account Name	Basic Account	Account Name	Basic Account
Labor:		Supervision (Executive Payroll)	11
Supervision	11	Vacation & Holiday Pay	31
Administrative	12	Payroll Taxes & Insurance	35
Clerical & Office	15	Retirement Plans	36
Stock Handling	16	Group Insurance	37
Janitors	18	Savings Plans	38
Plant Protection	19	Miscellaneous Benefits	39
Tooling Labor	21	Office Supplies	42
Maint. Labor—Grounds & Bldgs.	22	Plant Rearrangements	47
Maint. Labor—Machinery & Equip.	23	Utilities	49
Maint. Labor—Other Equipment	24	Depreciation	51
Plant Rearrangements	25	Property & Other Insurance	53
Special Tasks—Direct Labor	26	Property Taxes	54
Training—Direct Labor	27	Franchise Taxes	55
Unassigned—Direct Labor	28	Sales & Use Tax	56
Other Indirect	29	Telephone Expense (Special)	61
Overtime Premium	32	Telegraph & Teletype	62
		Postage	63
Other Overhead:		Freight	67
Employee Awards	33	Professional Service (Special)	71
Miscellaneous Benefits	39	Memberships Organizations	73
Operating Supplies	41	Contributions	77
Office Supplies	42	Miscellaneous Credits	78
Perishable Tools	43	Miscellaneous Expense	79
Minor Plant Equipment	43	Bidding & Proposal	81
Maint. Material—Grounds & Bldgs.	44	Research & Development	82
Maint. Material—Mach. & Equip.	45	Service Transfers	83
Maint. Material—Other Equip.	46	Expense Transfers—In	84
Plant Rearrangements	47	Expense Transfers—Out	85
Material Adjustments	48	Corporate Office	87
Property Rentals	57	Interdivision Transfers	89
Data Processing Equip. Rentals	58		
Other Equipment Rental	59		
Telephone Expense	61		
Photo & Print Expense	64		
Publications	65		
Travel Expense	66		
Professional Services	71		
Organization Memberships	73		
Public Relations	74		
Advertising	75		
Educational Contributions	77		
Miscellaneous Expense	79		

method will allow you to use a series of account numbers for each grouping which easily identifies it. With such a list, you can add or delete accounts as required.

Further breakdowns within an account are possible by using subaccounts and identifying them with dash numbers. For instance, basic account 39, "Miscellaneous Benefits," can be expanded as follows:

-1   Sick leave, hourly employees

-2   Sick leave, salaried employees

-3   Jury duty

-4   Bereavement pay

-5   Military pay differential

-6   Other paid absences

As expenses are accumulated each week from the time cards, they can be readily grouped into meaningful categories.

WHAT IS MEANT BY AN *OVERHEAD POOL?*

This term describes a device for collecting overhead charges in such a way that the expenses of the major overhead functions are grouped together. Administrative pools are commonly used to collect the costs generated by the financial, procurement, marketing, legal, contract, and industrial relations activities. Plant engineering expenses can be collected into a pool and later reassigned to those departments which benefited from the services. Pools related to geographic locations are not uncommon. For example, sales managers might want to see their sales expenses grouped by state, groups of states, or some similar arrangement.

Figure 10-3 shows the functions normally found in four major overhead pools in manufacturing plants. There are more than 15 different kinds of pools in common use by manufacturers today. Segregation of these activities into pools permits an analysis and the development of a "rate" which can be used to cost that kind of service. An analysis might show that engineering costs are running $10 per direct-labor hour worked in the factory, and that administrative departments "cost" $8.50 per direct-labor hour worked in the factory. This information is of great interest to managers.

DO RETAILERS AND WHOLESALERS HAVE AN OVERHEAD DISTRIBUTION PROBLEM LIKE THAT OF FACTORY MANAGERS?

Yes, but their problem is considerably less complex than the one which exists in manufacturing. If they are only interested in looking at their total costs, they have no allocation problem. The profit-

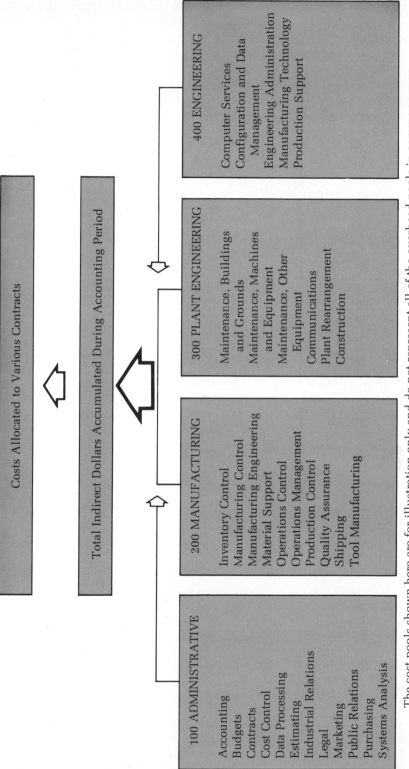

The cost pools shown here are for illustration only and do not represent all of the overhead pools in common usage. Quality Control and Tool Manufacturing are often separately identified for the accumulation of indirect costs. In addition, material handling pools, off-site (geographical) pools and pools of fringe benefit costs are also in common use. Plant Engineering is sometimes identified as a "service center" whose costs are distributed to other "user" pools based upon identification of the using departments.

FIGURE 10-3. Functions assigned to typical overhead pools.

and-loss statement for Ernie's Ranch Market shown in Figure 10-4 certainly provides a wealth of cost information, and it meets the requirements for tax reporting. Despite the accuracy and completeness of this statement, there are some unanswered questions aggressive managers would want answers to. The statement does not tell them whether their profit is acceptable in terms of what other markets like theirs are earning in the same area. It does not tell them whether some departments of the market are contributing more to profits than others—or even whether some are "losers." To find answers to these questions, they would have to work out a profit analysis by department. This means identifying the major activities in the market and keeping their costs separately. If they decide to segregate their sales and expenses for the meat department, the produce department, and the grocery section (everything else), they would have a much more enlightening report. Figure 10-5 shows the total expenses broken down by "department." There is now no doubt now where the "winners" and "losers" are.

PROFIT-AND-LOSS STATEMENT
Ernie's Ranch Market
Year Ending 31 December 19___

Gross Sales			$50,000
Cost of Goods Sold:			
Opening Inventory		$ 5,000	
Purchases		30,000	
	Total	$35,000	
Closing Inventory		6,000	
	Total Cost		29,000
Gross Profit			$21,000
Expenses:			
Payroll		$ 7,000	
Payroll Tax		140	
Licenses		115	
Supplies		600	
Utilities		900	
Insurance		300	
Car Expense		800	
Rent		1,200	
Depreciation		350	
Bad Debts		40	
			11,445
Net Profit			$ 9,555

FIGURE 10-4. A simplified profit-and-loss statement for a small retail market. (*Source:* Adapted from Fred G. Harris, *Fundamental Records for Small Marketers, Small Marketers Aids,* No. 19, U.S. Small Business Administration, Washington.)

	Groceries	Produce	Meats		Totals
Gross Sales	$30,000.00	$10,000.00	$10,000.00		$50,000.00
Cost of Sales:					
Opening Inventory	$ 3,000.00	$ 1,500.00	$ 500.00	$ 5,000.00	
Purchases	15,000.00	9,000.00	6,000.00	30,000.00	
Total	$18,000.00	$10,500.00	$ 6,500.00	$35,000.00	
Closing Inventory	3,500.00	2,000.00	500.00	6,000.00	
Total cost	$14,500.00	$ 8,500.00	$ 6,000.00	$29,000.00	29,000.00
Gross Profit	$15,500.00	$ 1,500.00	$ 4,000.00		$21,000.00
Expenses:					
Payroll	$ 4,500.00	$ 1,000.00	$ 1,500.00	$ 7,000.00	
Payroll Tax	90.00	20.00	30.00	140.00	
Licenses	91.00	12.00	12.00	115.00	
Supplies	400.00	100.00	100.00	600.00	
Utilities	500.00	100.00	300.00	900.00	
Insurance	200.00	50.00	50.00	300.00	
Car Expense	600.00	50.00	150.00	800.00	
Rent	800.00	200.00	200.00	1,200.00	
Depreciation	250.00	50.00	50.00	350.00	
Bad Debts	40.00	—	—	40.00	
Total	$ 7,471.00	$ 1,582.00	$ 2,392.00	$11,445.00	11,445.00
Net Profit	$ 8,029.00	(−$82.00)	$ 1,608.00		$ 9.555.00

FIGURE 10-5. A profit analysis by department for Ernie's Ranch Market. (*Source:* Adapted from Fred G. Harris, *Fundamental Records for Small Marketers*, Small Marketers Aids, No. 19, U.S. Small Business Administration, Washington.)

Once you break down the cost data to departments, you are faced with the problem of allocating expenses like rent, insurance, and license fees. These items are general expenses which are not related to a specific area of operation. Another problem would be the distribution of payroll costs for checkers and box boys, who handle items from all three areas.

Allocating these costs is not unlike that faced by the accountant who assigns general overhead costs to the operating departments in the factory. In the market example, the manager must decide how the burden is to be divided among his three areas. Each must be charged with some part of the rent, insurance, license fees, and labor costs generated in the check-out area. Logic suggests that rent might be assigned to each area in proportion to the floor space it occupies. Check-out labor could be allocated on the basis of total sales rung up for each area. Today's cash registers code sales in a manner that will permit this type of segregation. Methods of allocating other general expenses must be decided by the manager and consistently applied.

We will see later how expense data becomes a part of the financial information used to prepare income statements and profitability analyses.

IN MANUFACTURING, WHAT IS THE DIFFERENCE BETWEEN A PRODUCTIVE DEPARTMENT AND A SERVICE DEPARTMENT?

In manufacturing, it is a common practice to group similar machines or operations together and to designate these groups as departments or cost centers. In a company which manufactures steel filing cabinets, we might find a sheet metal shop, a machine shop, an assembly area, and a paint shop. These are known as *productive* departments and are established in terms of the types of operations, the machines, and the skills peculiar to each. Costs associated with each department are easy to identify through time cards and other documents it processes.

In addition to productive departments, manufacturing plants have some *service* departments. Their function is to help the factory do its job by assisting them in their primary mission—production. In an average-sized manufacturing plant you might find these service departments: a maintenance department, a toolroom, a production control department, a shipping department, an accounting department, and a personnel department.

The primary difference between productive and service departments boils down to the fact that productive departments make the product and service departments offer their own unique services in support of the production effort. The cost of both must eventually find their way back to the finished product and must be paid for by the customer.

HOW DO COSTS FLOW THROUGH A MANUFACTURING ORGANIZATION?

Figure 10-6 is a greatly simplified flow chart showing how direct and indirect costs flow from the source where they are generated to their final absorption in the cost of the completed product.

Direct expenses originate when employees record appropriate cost data such as contract number, accounting job order number, part number, department, employee number, and work times and quantities on their time card. The time card becomes the vehicle for transmitting direct labor charges to the accounting system. Charges are related to the contract by the assignment of a unique accounting job order number for each major task which will be done on the contract. This identification ties the contract to all cost records. Job order numbers, once assigned, authorize labor charging during the life of the contract and are retired when the contract is completed. Departmental information permits the employee's labor to be accumulated along with other employees' in the same department and results in a performance measurement when compared with the pieces produced.

The basic information which should be documented includes employee identification, work department, part number or job number on which the labor was expended, and the elapsed time charged

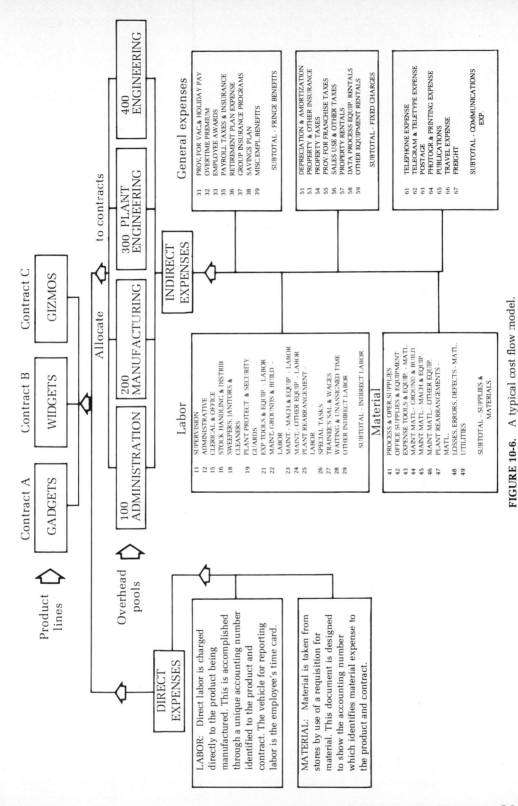

FIGURE 10-6. A typical cost flow model.

Part Number				Part Description		
Deliver to					Qty. Needed	Qty. Delivered
Department	Function	Building	Room/Col.			
Issued by		Date Filled			Job Order No.	Account No.
Originator's Signature					Phone Ext.	Location
ACCOUNTING DATA						
Using Contract	Qty. Issued	Unit Value	Extended Value		Matl.Cont.Approval	

FIGURE 10-7. A sample material stores requisition.

to each job or part number. It is often useful to require information to be entered showing pieces completed so that unit costs can be calculated later by accounting personnel.

Material costs are documented on the purchase invoice and become a part of the accounting cost system when the parts are received from the vendor. After they are inspected, they are placed in stores to await processing by the factory. They are later withdrawn by the production departments as required by manufacturing schedules. The document used for this transaction is a *material stores requisition*. A sample is shown in Figure 10-7.

All the information needed by Accounting to accumulate material costs into "direct" and "indirect" accounts is provided on the form. The using department and contract are also identified. Again, format is a matter of individual preference. The use of individual preprinted, multicopy forms for each part withdrawn from stores provides all the information needed for Accounting to price the part and charge it to the proper contract.

Information for factory overhead expenses comes from a number of sources. Indirect materials and expendable tools, for instance, will be reported first on purchase invoices and then on material requisitions just like direct material. Indirect labor, inspection labor, and maintenance labor plus all the other labor in overhead-type departments will be reported on various kinds of time cards. Utilities and outside services are tied to their respective invoices and get into the cost system when the bills are paid. Essentially, all cost information flows from its source to cost records through some variation of the forms we have discussed. More and more manufacturing companies have gone to the use of data processing equipment to accumulate the cost information from prepunched cards which provide computers the raw data from which various kinds of reports are produced, thereby saving time in manually manipulating the hundreds of transactions performed each day. In retailing, super-registers now automatically record each transaction, subtract the sales from inventory, and provide a wealth of information about the movement of goods into and out of the store. Small retailers collect their costs from a series of standard forms which were discussed in Chapter 9.

HOW DO OVERHEAD COSTS GET REFLECTED IN THE PRICE OF THE FINISHED PRODUCT?

Since overhead costs are a part of the cost of doing business, they must eventually find their way back to the product. The problem then becomes one of getting the overhead costs out of the burden pool where they accumulate and into the cost of the product. To accomplish this it is necessary to allocate some portion of the overhead expense to each production department so that you eventually end up with a departmental cost which includes:

□ Departmental direct labor costs

□ Departmental direct material costs

□ Departmental indirect labor costs

□ Departmental indirect nonlabor costs

□ Indirect costs of service departments

Costs related to the various departments can be identified through cost data provided by time cards, material requisitions, utility bills, and so forth. Take this data and spread it as follows:

1. First, charge directly those overhead costs which can be identified to a department, both productive and service.

2. Second, allocate the indirect costs to all departments, both productive and service, which benefited from their incurrence. Distribute these costs on the basis of some reasonable measure of the benefit received by each. The distribution of the power bill, for instance, might be related to the numbers and types of machines and equipment using electricity in each department.

3. Third, distribute the total cost of each service department to all the other departments which use its service, until all service department costs have been assigned to productive departments. Use whatever basis of distribution that is equitable and appropriate (e.g., maintenance costs on the basis of the maintenance hours worked in each department as reflected by a "location code" recorded on the maintenance worker's time card at the time he or she does the work).

4. The sum of items 1 through 3 now represents the total overhead cost of operating each department.

HOW DOES ALL THIS HELP YOU DETERMINE THE SELLING PRICE OF THE PRODUCT?

At this point you now have accumulated at the department level all costs, both direct and indirect, which must be reflected in the cost of the finished product. Let us suppose that Department A's direct workers last year worked 1,000,000 direct hours and were paid $5,000,000 in direct-labor wages. This comes to an average of $5 per hour. Next, suppose the department's overhead costs, as computed above, were $7,500,000. This means that the overhead cost is 150 percent of the direct-labor cost ($7,500,000 ÷ $5,000,000 = 150 percent). For every direct-labor hour spent in Department A, an overhead cost of $1.50 must be absorbed. If the departmental direct-labor rate is $5 per hour, the department's total rate becomes $12.50 when we add 150 percent for overhead. This figure represents a total rate, including all overhead charges.

With this information, it is now possible to determine how much a product made in Department A will cost. If the workers turn out 100,000 widgets and spend 40,000 hours making them, the cost of making widgets in Department A is 40,000 hours × $12.50 per hour or $500,000. Each widget, therefore, costs $5 to produce in Department A. If you add the cost of material, you will have the total cost of a widget.

This approach must be repeated for each department which makes widgets because direct-labor rates vary from department to department. For this reason, the cost contributed by each department to the total cost of a widget will be different.

Although this method sounds complex, it is an accurate way to arrive at the true cost of a manufactured product. It provides a predetermined rate which will be accurate as long as the direct-labor base in the manufacturing departments remains relatively constant. It will need to be recalculated periodically if there are significant changes in the overhead costs or in departmental direct-labor costs.

ARE THERE ANY STANDARD FORMULAS FOR ALLOCATING SERVICE-DEPARTMENT COSTS TO PRODUCTIVE DEPARTMENTS?

Unfortunately, no. The allocation of indirect costs is largely a matter of common sense and logic. The basic idea is to get the costs back to departments which benefit from the overhead services. For those expenses which are too general to relate to a productive department, the manager must use discretion in finding a fair way to make the allocation.

Table 10-2 shows how the total allocation process provides an overhead rate for each department in a theoretical manufacturing plant which has three productive departments and one service department (maintenance).

TABLE 10-2. LITTLE WONDER MANUFACTURING COMPANY: CALCULATION OF DEPARTMENTAL OVERHEAD RATES IN JANUARY, 19___

Step	Type of Cost	Basis of Allocation	Plant Total	Machine Shop	Assembly Department	Paint and Package	Total Maintenance
1	Department indirect labor	(Actual charges)	$11,000	$ 5,000	$ 3,000	$ 1,000	$ 2,000
2	Departmental inspection labor	(Actual charges)	5,500	3,000	2,000	500	—
3	Factory indirect material and supplies	(Actual charges)	3,950	2,500	500	500	450
4	Factory rent	Square feet of floor space in each area	3,800	1,500	1,200	800	300
5	Machinery depreciation	Acquisition cost of machinery	2,600	1,200	700	500	200
6	Factory management	Number of employees in each department	3,500	2,000	1,000	200	200
			$30,350	$15,200	$ 8,400	$ 3,500	$ 3,150
	Distribution of Maintenance Costs						
7	Maintenance expense	Worker-hours of maintenance worked in each department		2,300	700	150	(3,150)
	TOTAL OVERHEAD IN PRODUCTION DEPARTMENTS		$30,350	$17,500	$ 9,100	$ 3,650	—
8	Direct-labor worker-hours spent		8,600	2,300	3,800	2,500	—
9	Overhead rate (dollars per direct-labor hour)		$3.53	$7.61	$2.39	$1.46	—

The direct departmental costs are first assigned based on actual recorded charges in steps 1, 2, and 3. Factory rent is then allocated in step 4 based on the number of square feet used by each department. The machinery depreciation total of $2,600 is allocated on the basis of the equipment and machinery used in each department. Its cost when acquired becomes the basis for the allocation. In step 6 the cost of factory management is spread to each department based on the number of workers it has.

The service department costs must now be spread to the three production departments. In step 7 this is accomplished by examining the number of maintenance worker-hours each production department required and allocating the total maintenance costs so that they now reside in the production departments.

In step 8 we have shown the direct-labor hours worked in each production department and in step 9 have calculated a departmental overhead rate which must be added to the cost of each direct-labor hour worked in order to obtain a fully "burdened" rate. This method of calculating the overhead rate gives you an answer in dollars instead of percent. Either approach will give you the same answer.

IS A LOW OVERHEAD RATE AN INDICATION THAT MANAGEMENT IS DOING A GOOD JOB OF COST CONTROL?

Not necessarily. The popular misconception that a low overhead rate can be used to determine the efficiency of a manufacturing operation has been debunked by a number of authors,[1] who point out that the overhead rate is the result of an interaction of two independent variables—direct-labor costs and overhead expense. The overhead rate will go up if you do nothing except reduce your direct-labor costs; yet this reduction might occur as a result of management's decision to add an overhead-type employee to the payroll who does something which enables manufacturing to reduce its costs. We can illustrate this interaction easily with some theoretical examples:

Example 1.   A small manufacturer had an annual direct-labor cost of $750,000 and overhead expense of $600,000. His overhead rate, calculated on a plantwide basis, was 80 percent ($600,000 ÷ $750,000).

Example 2.   The manufacturer decides to hire a topflight industrial engineer (overhead) to analyze his work flow, plant layout, work methods, and similar factors. After 1 year, new ways of doing work had reduced manufacturing costs to $600,000 a year. The engineer's salary had in-

[1]See Phil Carroll, *How to Control Production Costs*, McGraw-Hill Book Company, New York, 1953, Chap. 3.

creased overhead costs by $18,000 per year. The overhead rate is now 103 percent ($618,000 ÷ $600,000). Note, however, that the *total* costs have been reduced by $132,000 ($1,350,000 − $1,218,000—see the table in Example 3).

Example 3. During his second year, the engineer was able to reduce the cost of some high-cost operations by installing some automatic equipment, making it possible to reduce annual direct-labor costs to $500,000. Simultaneously, overhead costs increased to $640,000 per year because of added depreciation, maintenance, and related expenses. The overhead rate is now 128 percent ($640,000 ÷ $500,000), but the total plant operating cost has dropped again, by $78,000 to $1,140,000.

	Example 1	Example 2	Example 3
Direct labor	$ 750,000	$ 600,000	$ 500,000
Overhead cost	600,000	618,000	640,000
	$1,350,000	$1,218,000	$1,140,000
Overhead rate	80%	103%	128%

Thus we see that by increasing the overhead we have been able to effect a reduction in total costs of $210,000 (16 percent). One could say that we have made money by raising our overhead. Lest we jump to any wrong conclusions, we must realize that this is possible only if the things responsible for the increased overhead help us reduce direct expenses more than enough to pay for them.

HOW DOES THE ACCOUNTING DEPARTMENT KEEP TRACK OF ALL THE COSTS?

We have already seen how overhead costs can be tracked by relating them to overhead areas and identifying them from a chart of accounts.

In order to provide the cost detail needed by the various supervisors to monitor their costs, the accounting department often breaks costs down below the job-order and department levels. In getting a product's costs, they have to deal with the things you spend your money for—labor, materials, services, travel, tooling, and overhead. What you spend your money for are called *elements of cost*. Table 10-3 shows how some typical cost elements relate to the functions they measure.

The accounting department collects information about what you spend your money for; then they can give you cost data on what you want information about—products, operations, and areas of functional responsibility. Areas of functional responsibility can include manufacturing, test equipment manufacturing, tool manufacturing, shipping, production engineering, quality assurance, and engineering.

TABLE 10-3. MAJOR ELEMENTS OF COST IN MANUFACTURING

Element of Cost	Function

1. Direct material:
    Purchased parts
    Raw materials
 	
2. Direct labor
 	
3. Factory burden:
    Indirect labor
    Indirect material
    Miscellaneous indirect expenses
	Manufacturing

4. Selling expense:
    Commissions
    Wages
    Advertising
    Warehousing
    Travel
	Sales

5. General and administrative expense:
    Executive salaries
    Office salaries
    Office supplies
	Administration

HOW CAN A KNOWLEDGE OF COST BEHAVIOR HELP BUSINESS OWNERS?

Financial management is one of the most important areas that require the attention of business owners. Unless they have the skill and understanding necessary to control their costs, they are likely to fail in attaining the profit objectives of the business. Here are a few financial problems which are directly related to the impact of costs on the operation of the business.

Income Determination. Owners must know what their incomes and expenses are in order to tell whether their businesses are making profits. Their understanding of the cost data available to them will determine the course of action they take.

Profit Planning. Planning next year's profits requires a knowledge of profit-volume relationships and an understanding of the ways in which fixed and variable costs affect the amount of profit the business will retain after it pays all its expenses.

Inventory Valuation. The business' financial condition is reflected in the relationship which exists between its assets and its liabilities. The value of finished goods in inventory must be accurately determined since it is a major portion of the company's assets. The owner must, therefore, know how to establish and maintain a cost system which reflects the true cost of the product.

Cost Control. A company's actual costs are the yardstick by which it measures its performance against the standards established by management. Any variances from standard performance must be analyzed and explained. This requires an orderly cost collection system which gathers costs and groups them by responsible supervisor, who is held responsible for the variances.

Cost Estimating. Managers' success in acquiring additonal business depends largely on their ability to estimate future costs accurately. The availability of good historical cost information is absolutely essential to managers in preparing estimates and bidding successfully against their competitors.

This exercise is designed to test your understanding of the material presented in Chapter 10. Choose the response, *True* or *False*, which best fits each statement. Correct responses are presented in the back of the text.

SELF-CHECK OF KEY CONCEPTS

1. The typical cost pattern for manufacturing shows costs about equally split between labor, material, and overhead.
2. "Direct" employees can be differentiated from "indirect" workers by the type of work they do.
3. If you buy a lot of your parts preassembled from someone else, your material bill will be higher than it would if you made the subassemblies yourself.
4. Factory burden and administrative burden are usually separated in the cost records.
5. Direct material costs are about as close to a "pure" fixed cost as you can get.
6. There is no standard formula for allocating overhead expenses to production departments.
7. Window area should be used as a basis for allocating custodial expense only if the custodians perform the window-cleaning service.
8. A certain amount of inaccurate information on the time cards is acceptable since managers can make an allowance for it.
9. A telephone bill is a mixture of both fixed and variable costs.
10. When your overhead rate increases significantly, it is a signal that something is wrong.

1. Describe the steps you go through when allocating overhead costs to a manufactured product.
2. Indicate what basis for allocating you believe would be appropriate for each of the following overhead costs:

    a.   Electricity
    b.   Plant manager's salary
    c.   Machinery depreciation
    d.   Workmen's compensation taxes
    e.   Purchasing expense

3. On charts such as those illustrated below, draw a line which graphically portrays the cost behavior described:

    a.   Electricity bill, which is a flat fixed fee up to 10,000 kilowatts, plus a variable additional cost after 10,000 kilowatts.
    b.   Taxes paid at a rate of 3.5 percent on the first $8,700 of each employee's wages in a plant where the labor force is constant and the average annual salary is $10,000 per worker. (Assume that there are five employees earning $6,000; $8,000; $10,000; $12,000; and $14,000, respectively.)
    c.   Wages of gasoline station attendants where one attendant is required for the first 10,000 gallons pumped. A second is required from 10,000 to 20,000 gallons, and an additional attendant for each additional 10,000 gallons.
    d.   Cost of a car rental, which is charged at a rate of 10 cents per mile for the first 500 miles, 7 cents per mile for the next 500 miles, and 5 cents per mile for each mile in excess of 1,000 miles.

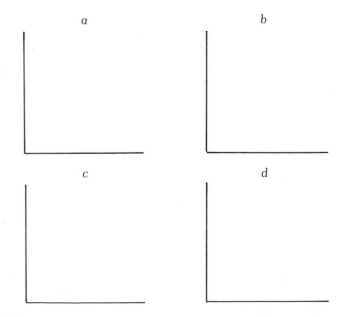

4. You have been retained by Ernie's Ranch Market to prepare a profit-and-loss statement each month showing how much

profit he made after expenses that month. Ernie also wants to know how much each of his major departments contributed to the overall profit. The gross sales and gross profit are shown on the accompanying worksheet. In addition, other pertinent information is shown below:

Departmental Information

Grocery Section:
    10 employees at $5 per hour.
    Each employee worked 160 hours last month.
    Sacks and operating materials cost $180.
    Floor space is 76,000 square feet.
    Equipment is valued at $150,000.

Meat Section:
    2 employees at $6.25 per hour.
    Both employees worked 160 hours each last month.
    Wrapping materials and sawdust cost $150.
    Floor space is 15,000 square feet.
    Equipment is valued at $130,000.
    Repairs to the walk-in cooler cost $320 last month.

Produce Section:
    2 employees at $6 per hour.
    Each employee worked 160 hours last month.
    Operating supplies cost $8.
    Floor space is 9,000 square feet.
    Equipment is valued at $20,000.

General Expenses:

Custodial services	$ 250
Payroll tax	200
Rent	350
Insurance (equipment)	80
Store manager's salary	1,500
Utilities	300

Calculate the profit contributed by each section of the market for the month by identifying those expenses that each generated. General expenses will need to be allocated to the productive departments on the basis of some plan you consider fair and equitable. Indicate the basis you use for the allocation in worksheet format that matches the statement on p. 242.

THE CASE OF THE OUT-OF-LINE OVERHEAD

Jack Williams, plant manager of the J. C. Transformer Company, had been supplying transformers to Everett Radio Corporation for several years. Everett manufactured radios, stereo components, and several items of electronic gear for the Department of Defense. Jack knew that Everett also bought transformers from American Electronics, a major competitor, but only considered it good business for a manufacturer as big as Everett to maintain several sources of supply for the things it bought.

A CASE IN POINT

PROFIT-AND-LOSS STATEMENT
Ernie's Ranch Market
March, 19___

	Grocery Section	Meat Section	Produce Section	Totals
Gross Sales	$20,000	$ 8,000	$ 5,000	$33,000
Cost of Sales	8,500	4,500	3,500	16,500
Gross Profit	$11,500	$ 3,500	$ 1,500	$16,500

Departmental Expenses:
Salaries and Wages _____ _____ _____ _____
Operating Supplies _____ _____ _____ _____
Repairs _____ _____ _____ _____

Allocation of General Expenses: Basis
Payroll Tax _____ _____ _____ _____
Rent _____ _____ _____ _____
Custodial Costs _____ _____ _____ _____
Insurance _____ _____ _____ _____
Store Manager's
  Salary _____ _____ _____ _____
Utilities _____ _____ _____ _____

                      Totals

Total Expenses
  (Rounded) _____ _____ _____ _____
Net Profit/(Loss) $_____ $_____ $_____ $_____
Profit as a Percentage
  of Departmental Sales _____% _____% _____% _____%

Everett Radio was preparing a proposal to bid on a large order for the National Aeronautics and Space Administration involving some new products never manufactured before. Because of the nature of the program, it invited both J. C. Transformer and American Electronics to visit its plant and examine drawings of the new items and to prepare bids as subcontractors for the devices they felt qualified to manufacture.

At lunch on the day of Jack's visit, he ran into Stan Norman, the purchasing agent for Everett Corporation. They chatted about the new product and during the conversation the problems of subcontracting out part of the work came up.

"Jack," said Stan, "our management feels that the nature of this job is such that we will probably award the transformer subcontract to a single source. The decision will be a tough one because we have been happy with the quality and delivery of transformers from both you and American Electronics. We have noticed though that your plant overhead rate is about 50 percent higher than American's. If I were you, I'd sharpen my pencil on this bid and take a hard look at my overhead costs."

Jack was pretty upset by the time he had driven back to his plant. He immediately called in Bob Oliveros, his controller, and laid it on the line.

"I couldn't believe it when Stan Norman dropped this one on me, but the guy has been doing business with both us and American for years and he knows what he's talking about," Jack said. "American's plant is no newer than ours, it's about the same size, and our wage rates can't be that far apart. I just don't understand how our overhead can be so far out of line. I need an answer by tomorrow, Bob, telling me what we can do to reduce the overhead figures we put into our bid. I'd hate to arbitrarily cut the rate by 50 percent, but I'd sure hate to lose that contract to American."

1. Do you think Jack Williams understands his overhead costs?
2. If you were Bob Oliveros, what would you look for in preparing an answer to the boss's request?
3. What risk will Jack run if he arbitrarily cuts his overhead figures by 50 percent in his bid?

11 The Importance of Financial Reports

PERFORMANCE OBJECTIVES

After reading this chapter, you should be able to explain how the records of a business can be used to prepare the reports needed for understanding the financial aspects of business management. You should be able to demonstrate how a lack of timely financial information can adversely affect business operations and to judge the consequences of operating with inadequate financial data. Specifically, you should be able to:

1. Describe the accounts which are shown on the balance sheet of a business.
2. Demonstrate the difference between current assets and fixed assets.
3. Construct a simple balance sheet to show how the various accounts "balance."
4. Predict what can happen to an owner's equity in the business if liabilities exceed assets.
5. Assess the probability of success in a business whose owner has limited interest in accounting and financial reports.
6. Defend the amount of time a business owner must spend to prepare and analyze financial reports.
7. Describe the kinds of financial ratios which can be developed from the financial records of a business.
8. Discuss some of the symptoms of poor financial management and describe actions the owner can take to prevent them.

9. Demonstrate how failure to charge some depreciation off each month can inflate earnings on the profit-and-loss statement.
10. Explain how retailers arrive at the value of "cost of goods sold" on their profit-and-loss statement.

INTRODUCTION

If one thing is constant in our ever-changing business world, it is the all-consuming interest in money and financial control. Students of business administration, practicing supervisors, and business people alike have a need to know how to manage their financial assets.

The need is emphasized by the fact that an average of more than 1,000 businesses are formed each day in the United States, and roughly 930 businesses are discontinued, many having failed as a result of poor financial management.

This chapter explores the increasing importance of money management. It explains the basic financial reports which can help managers and owners measure the financial health of their businesses and take decisive action to keep them financially sound.

Five key business ratios which measure the ability of a business to pay its bills are discussed and illustrated. The importance of financial management to business success is emphasized as a key skill which is a fundamental ingredient in successful business management.

IS THE TYPICAL SMALL BUSINESS OWNER COMPETENT IN THE FINANCIAL ASPECTS OF BUSINESS OPERATIONS?

Most of them experience difficulty in managing their financial assets at one time or another. Setting up adequate records requires technical skill and background that many business owners lack. The mechanics of constructing a balance sheet or income statement intimidates many owners. The mere language of finance and accounting is foreign to many, who feel that anything so academic is best left to the professional accountant.

It is safe to assume that financial management is the most neglected of the business owner's many responsibilities. Without financial control, many firms find their way into the business failure statistics. Most small business owners are not accountants, but they should understand the tools of financial management if they are to operate successfully. Responsibilities to themselves and to others make it imperative that owners be acquainted with the function and purpose of the balance sheet and the profit-and-loss statement. If they are going to stay in business, they must have a reasonable knowledge of these tools.

WHAT DOES FINANCIAL MANAGEMENT INCLUDE?

Financial management includes the following functions:

☐ Seeing that the assets of business are used in such a way as to bring the highest possible return on the money invested.

- Obtaining funds to finance the addition of new assets or expansion of existing ones.

- Managing both new and old assets so that each contributes its full share toward the profitable operation of the business.

- Repaying borrowed funds from profits generated from the use of those funds.

One of the most important aspects of financial management is to keep the assets of the business working hard and productively. Often it seems that the opportunities to spend money are unlimited. The office manager needs new equipment to speed up the handling of the paper avalanche. The production manager wants newer and faster machines, better tools, larger stocks of raw materials to reduce production costs and improve manufacturing time. The sales manager wants more lines of finished goods, more liberal credit terms, and larger inventories to improve service to customers.

The aim of financial management is to make certain that new or increased assets pay their way. You must be constantly aware that bigger does not necessarily mean better. You must be sure that the added profits these new assets bring in exceed the cost of the assets.

WHAT FINANCIAL TOOLS DO BUSINESS OWNERS HAVE TO WORK WITH?

If they are going to do a good job of managing the financial aspects of their businesses, they need well-organized accounting records, regular financial reports, and some techniques for analyzing the reports. These tools will enable them to replace guesswork with facts and reach sound decisions based on tested principles of business management.

The importance of good records was emphasized in a previous chapter. The reports with which a business owner works can be no more accurate than the records they summarize.

There are a number of financial reports that can be helpful in financial management. The most useful ones are the balance sheet and the profit-and-loss statement. These financial reports are examined by your creditors when they are faced with decisions about lending you money or extending credit. They become the basis for reports required by state and federal laws. And they become your road map that tells you where your business has been and where it is going.

Owners' financial decisions concerning return on invested funds, applying for bank loans, securing supplier credit, raising additional capital, and similar actions can be more successful if they develop an understanding of the balance sheet and the profit-and-loss statement.

In spite of what might appear to be complicated practices or "big business" rituals, the balance sheet and profit-and-loss statement merely tell you what you did and how you stand. They are simply a summary of what you have been recording in your books all year. These financial reports allow you to view your business in the same way you view a map—with everything spread out in front of you, ready to be analyzed.

HOW CAN FINANCIAL REPORTS HELP MINIMIZE CHANCES OF BUSINESS FAILURE?

The statistics on business failures show that a large number of failures are associated with financial mismanagement. The financial reports of a business are like a pressure gauge. When sales are high, operating costs are in line, credit and collections are under control, and fixed assets and inventories are properly balanced, the pressure gauges will reflect these conditions in favorable earnings. When sales fall off, operating costs go up, poor credit and collection policies tie up cash, fixed assets and inventories become excessive, the buildup of pressures that these "failure points" exert on the business is registered in the financial reports of the business.

By watching the potential failure points and comparing trends from month to month, you will be in a position to step in and stop adverse trends before they become catastrophic.

WHAT ARE SOME OF THE SYMPTOMS OF POOR FINANCIAL MANAGEMENT?

Undercapitalization is one of the most common. It is the result of starting with too little capital, tying up too much capital in fixed assets, or exercising poor control of credit. It is a problem which requires an abnormal amount of owners' time, diverting their efforts from more important things.

Slow-moving or excessive inventories are also symptomatic of financial mismanagement. Quantity purchases of stock that cannot be sold quickly contribute to the problem. Storage of slow-moving merchandise ties up funds that could be used more effectively elsewhere. Excessive inventory should be sold off and stock control measures instituted to minimize the cash investment in inventories.

Spending money on the wrong things is an easy habit to fall into. Many of the activities that require the owner's time and money contribute little to the financial health of the business. Activities which promise to yield the highest returns should be emphasized. Those which are unprofitable should be curtailed or eliminated. Your financial reports will help you identify the "losers."

Failure to take advantage of cash discount can cost a business hundreds of dollars a year. Most suppliers offer a discount between 2 and 5 percent on bills paid within a certain period, usually 10 days. A 2 percent saving on a $10,000 order amounts to $200. By exploiting purchase discounts, you can improve your cash position.

Lax credit and collection policies get many businesses into hot water. If a business is to pay its own bills and make a profit, it must receive prompt payment for the goods and services it sells. The antidote for this malady is to develop a firm policy concerning credit extension, terms, limits, and collection. Delinquent accounts should be pressed for payment, and further credit or extensions to slow payers stopped.

WHAT IS THE DIFFERENCE BETWEEN THE "BOOKS" AND THE FINANCIAL REPORTS OF A BUSINESS?

The "books" are a running chronological record of business operations. They consist individually of the expense records, cash records, accounts receivable, accounts payable, depreciation records, and all the other statistical records needed to measure the activities in which the business is engaged.

Periodically, the statistics reflected in the "books" are compiled into financial reports, which are required by lenders when making a loan and by business owners when making out their annual tax return.

Financial reports are like photographs of the business. The balance sheet is a "still" picture of the business, showing its assets, liabilities, and owner's investment in the business on a given date. It is usually prepared as of the close of business on the last day of the month. It tells how the business stands financially at that time.

The profit-and-loss statement (also called the income statement) measures costs and expenses against sales and revenue over a period of time such as a month or year to show the profit or loss of the business over the entire period. In this regard, it is like a "moving" picture which periodically gives owners a look at their financial condition based on the activities which have occurred during the period covered by the report. The "bottom line" on the profit-and-loss statement shows whether the business made or lost money during the period covered by the report. Figure 11-2 shows a simplified profit-and-loss statement for a small retail firm whose balance sheet is shown in Figure 11-1.

HOW DOES THE BALANCE SHEET GET ITS NAME?

From the fact that the total assets balance with, or are equal to, the total liabilities plus the net worth of the business. The balance sheet represents an equation:

Assets = liabilities + net worth

A business with assets of $20,000 and liabilities of $15,000 would have a net worth of $5,000, net worth representing the difference between total assets and total liabilities. If the liabilities of a

THE JOHNSTON CITY DISCOUNT STORE
Balance Sheet
December 31, 19—

Assets			Explanation
Current assets:			Cash in the bank, United States government
Cash	$10,000		securities, money in the till, and petty cash
Accounts			fund.
receivable	20,000		Accounts receivable and amounts owed the
			company by its customers and others.
Inventories	22,500		Merchandise, raw materials, and
			work-in-process items owned by the
Total current			company.
assets.....	$52,500		
Fixed assets:			
Machinery,			Land, buildings, and equipment owned by
equipment	$20,000		the company which are not for resale. They
Building	28,000		are shown at their cost, less depreciation for
Land	10,000		wear and tear.
Total fixed			
assets.....	$58,000		
TOTAL			
assets ...	$110,500		Everything the company owns.

Liabilities and owner's equity

Current liabilities:			
Notes payable	$10,000		Principal payments on bank loans that fall
			due within 1 year.
Accounts payable	15,000		Money the company owes its suppliers.
Accrued liabilities	3,000		Wages, interest, and other amounts owed
			but not yet paid.
Taxes payable	2,000		Amounts owed for real estate, social
Total current			security, and income taxes.
liabilities..	$30,000		
Owner's equity:			
Owner's capital	$56,000		Amount owner has invested in the business
(Jan. 1, 19—)			at the beginning of the year.
Profit for the period	24,500		Undistributed profits for the year, before
Total equity (Dec. 31,			taxes.
19—)	$80,500		
TOTAL liabilities and			
equity ...	$110,500		

FIGURE 11-1. A simplified balance sheet.

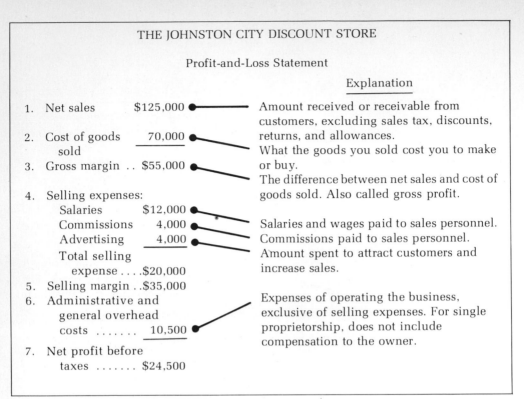

FIGURE 11-2. A simplified profit-and-loss statement.

business exceed its assets, the net worth would be a negative amount. In this case, our equation could be written:

$$\text{Net worth} = \text{assets} - \text{liabilities}$$

A pictorial representation of the balance sheet is shown in Figure 11-3.

WHAT IS THE DIFFERENCE BETWEEN CURRENT ASSETS AND FIXED ASSETS?

Current assets consist of cash and assets that are expected to be converted to cash during the normal operating cycle of the business. This period is usually no longer than a year. Current assets include notes receivable, accounts receivable, marketable securities, and inventories. Fixed assets are those acquired for long-term use in the business. They include land, buildings, plant, machinery, equipment, furniture, fixtures, and so on. These assets are typically not for resale, and they are recorded on the balance sheet at their cost to the business, less depreciation.

A fixed asset is treated as a long-term cost, with the cost allocated as depreciation over the working life of the asset. Thus, the

BALANCE SHEET
This is how the business looks on a specific date.

ASSETS	LIABILITIES
What the business itself owns.	This side of the balance sheet shows the claims on the assets—by both creditors and owners of the business. The claims of creditors are debts of the business—the LIABILITIES. The owner's claim is his investment in the business—the NET WORTH.

CURRENT ASSETS: In varying states of being converted into cash—within the next 12 months.

 CASH: Money on hand, in the bank.

 ACCOUNTS RECEIVABLE: What the customers owe the business for merchandise or services they bought.

 INVENTORY: Merchandise on hand:
1) ready to be sold
2) in some stage of production
3) raw material

FIXED ASSETS: Used in the operation of the business. Not intended for resale.

 REAL ESTATE: Land and buildings used by the business. Listed at original cost.

LEASEHOLD IMPROVEMENTS: Permanent installations— remodeling or refurbishing of the premises.

 MACHINERY, EQUIPMENT, VEHICLES: Used by the business. Listed at original cost.

 Less Accumulated Depreciation: These assets (except land) lose value through wear, tear and age. The business claims this loss of value as an expense of doing business. The running total of this expense is the accumulated depreciation.

NET FIXED ASSETS: Cost of fixed assets less depreciation = Present Value.

CURRENT LIABILITIES: Debts owed by the business to be paid within the next 12 months.

 NOTES PAYABLE: IOU Bank or Trade Creditors.

 ACCOUNTS PAYABLE: IOU Trade & Suppliers.

 INCOME TAXES: IOU Government.

LONG-TERM LIABILITIES: Debts owed by the business to be paid beyond the next 12 months.

 MORTGAGE: On property.

NET WORTH: Owner's (or stockholders') claim on the assets of the business; his investment. His equity in the business.

 For Proprietorship or Partnership: MR. OWNER, CAPITAL: Owner's original investment plus any profit reinvested in the business.

For Corporation:
CAPITAL STOCK: Value assigned to the original issue of stock by the directors of the corporation. If the stock sold for more than the as- signed value, the excess will show as:

SURPLUS, PAID IN: The difference between assigned value and selling price of the original issue of stock. (The subsequent selling price of the stock does not change the as- signed value.)

RETAINED EARNINGS: Profits reinvested in the business AFTER paying dividends.

BALANCE SHEET EQUATION: ASSETS = LIABILITIES + NET WORTH

FIGURE 11-3. A pictorial representation of a balance sheet. (*Source:* Reprinted with permission from *Small Business Reporter*, Vol. 7, No. 11, "Understanding Financial Statements," Bank of America, c. 1971.)

value of the fixed asset shown on the balance sheet is not necessarily the same as the resale value of the asset. Inventories that will not be used within a year and notes receivable or accounts receivable that will not be collected within a year should be shown as fixed assets on the balance sheet.

The same distinction is true for liabilities. Current liabilities are those due for payment within a year. Long-term or fixed liabilities are debts that are not due for payment within a year.

IN MAKING OUT THE BALANCE SHEET, HOW CAN YOU TELL
HOW MUCH YOUR INVENTORY IS WORTH?

You have to have an accurate count of what is in your inventory. This is accomplished by a physical count. Be sure to get an accurate description and count of all items. The inventory should be valued according to an accepted method. The one generally used is "cost or market, whichever is lower." The market value of an asset is defined as its replacement cost. The cost of manufactured products is normally made up of raw materials plus other production costs such as direct labor and overhead.

If manufacturers want to know what is a fair value to place on their ending inventory of finished goods, they would extract the total cost to manufacture them from their records. Assume the following costs have been incurred during the current year to manufacture 10,000 units of Product A:

Direct material	$ 50,000
Direct labor	35,000
Factory overhead	55,000
	$140,000

The cost to produce each item is $140,000 ÷ 10,000 or $14 each. If you still had 2,000 units of Product A in inventory at the end of the year, its value would be 2,000 × $14 = $28,000.

HOW IS THE EFFECT OF DEPRECIATION SHOWN ON THE BALANCE SHEET?

Depreciation and other factors reduce the value of some assets. Because it is important that the balance sheet reflect true values of the assets, it should be set up to show that provision has been made for such reduction in value. This is done by using valuation accounts to show value reductions because of "bad debts," inventory losses, and depreciation. Figure 11-4 shows the adjustments in each of these accounts.

Accounts receivable are analyzed according to the length of time the money has been owed. An estimate is then made as to what part of them will turn out to be uncollectible. Then the allowance for bad debts is computed for a given accounting period either as a per-

THE JOHNSTON CITY DISCOUNT STORE
Balance Sheet
December 31, 19___

Assets

Current Assets:

Cash		$10,000	
Accounts Receivable	$20,000		
Less Allowance for Doubtful			
Accounts	1,600	18,400	
Inventories	$22,500		
Less Allowance for			
"Shrinkage"	2,500	20,000	
Total Current Assets			$48,400

Fixed Assets:

Buildings	$28,000		
Less Allowance for			
Depreciation	6,000	$22,000	
Land		10,000	
Machinery and Equipment	$20,000		
Less Allowance for			
Depreciation	4,000	16,000	
Total Fixed Assets			$48,000
TOTAL ASSETS			$96,400

Liability and Owner's Equity

Current Liabilities:

Accounts Payable	$15,000	
Accrued Liabilities	3,000	
Notes Payable	10,000	
Taxes Payable	2,000	
Total Current Liabilities		$30,000

Owner's Equity:

Owner's Capital (Jan. 1, 19___)	$56,000	
Profit for Period	10,400	
Total Equity		$66,400
TOTAL LIABILITIES AND EQUITY		$96,400

FIGURE 11-4. A balance sheet showing valuation accounts.

centage of the average balance of receivables or as a percentage of the net credit sales for the period. The balance sheet shows it as a deduction from the asset "accounts receivable."

Reductions in inventory values might occur as a result of pilferage, price changes, physical deterioration, or style changes. If such losses are likely to occur, an estimate of possible shrinkage should be made. This estimate appears on the balance sheet as a deduction from the value of the inventory.

A periodic charge for depreciation should be made and shown on the balance sheet as a deduction from the value of the asset. This decline is caused by wear and tear from normal usage, obsolescence, or other causes. All fixed assets other than land decline in value over time.

WHAT IS MEANT BY THE TERM *EQUITY*?

Equity refers to the owner's or stockholders' claims on the assets of the business. For a proprietorship or partnership, it consists of the owner's (or owners') original investment plus any profit reinvested in the business. The equity is often referred to as *owner's equity* or *owner's capital*.

If your business is a corporation and has raised funds through the sale of stock, the stockholders become the owners of the business. Their equity is the value of the stock which was issued to them in exchange for the money they supplied to the business, plus any undistributed earnings retained in the business after dividends are paid.

By definition, the assets of a business minus its liabilities equal the equity.

HOW DOES THE BALANCE SHEET OF A MANUFACTURER DIFFER FROM THAT OF A RETAILER?

The differences are primarily in the inventory accounts. The balance sheet of a manufacturer typically shows three types of inventories—raw materials, work in process, and finished goods. The value of each must be carefully determined and entered on the balance sheet. The balance sheet of the retailer will show only merchandise (finished goods) and supplies as the items making up the inventory account.

WHAT IS MEANT BY *COST OF GOODS SOLD* ON THE PROFIT-AND-LOSS STATEMENT?

To retailers and wholesalers, it represents the total price they paid for the products they sold during the accounting period, plus in-transportation costs. This term is sometimes called *cost of sales*. Service station operators who pay 45 cents a gallon for gasoline and sell 10,000 gallons during the month show $4,500 as their cost of goods sold. If they sell this amount for 60 cents a gallon, their total sales become $6,000 and their gross margin $1,500. Most small retail and wholesale businesses compute the cost of goods sold by adding the cost of goods purchased during the accounting period to the beginning inventory, and then subtracting the value of the inventory at the end of the accounting period.

```
                    IDEAL TRANSFORMER COMPANY
                  Statement of Cost of Goods Manufactured
                        Year Ending December 31, 19__

Work-in-Process Inventory (Jan. 1, 19__)                              $ 1,800
Raw Materials:
   Inventory, Jan. 1, 19__                          $15,420
   Purchases                                         26,800
   Freight In                                           920
   Cost of Materials Available for Use              $43,140
   Less Inventory on Dec. 31, 19__                   16,300
      Cost of Materials Used                                           26,840
Direct Labor                                                           15,300
Manufacturing Overhead:
   Indirect Labor                                   $ 2,400
   Factory Heat, Light, and Power                     8,950
   Factory Supplies Used                              2,210
   Insurance and Taxes                                  810
   Depreciation of Plant Equipment                    3,530
      Total Manufacturing Overhead                                     17,900
Total Work in Process During Period                                   $61,840
Less Work-in-Process Inventory on Dec. 31, 19__                         4,260
            Cost of Goods Manufactured ...............                $57,580
```

FIGURE 11-5.   Calculations for determining the cost of goods manufactured.

Because small manufacturers convert raw materials to finished goods, their method of accounting for cost of goods sold
differs from the method used by wholesalers and retailers. As in retailing and wholesaling, computing the cost of goods sold during
the accounting period involves beginning and ending inventories,
and purchases made during the accounting period. But in manufacturing it involves not only finished-goods inventories but also
raw-materials inventories, goods-in-process inventories, direct labor,
and overhead costs.

To avoid a long and complicated profit-and-loss statement,
the cost of goods manufactured is usually reported separately. Figure 11-5 shows a statement of cost of goods manufactured for a small
manufacturing plant making transformers.

WHAT IS THE DIFFERENCE BETWEEN GROSS PROFIT, OPERATING PROFIT, AND NET PROFIT?

We have defined gross profit as the difference between sales and the
cost of goods sold. Gross profit does not take into account the sales
expenses incurred or the administrative or general expenses which
are incurred to produce the profit. These operating expenses are

deducted from the gross profit to arrive at operating profit. This profit is sometimes called *income from operations*. To convert operating profit to net profit, the following is required on the profit-and-loss statement:

1. Deduct any interest expense incurred.
2. Deduct amounts for such things as doubtful accounts, losses on the sale of fixtures or equipment, and discounts granted (if not already deducted from sales).
3. Add income from all sources other than operations.

The result is net income before taxes. This is the amount on which the owner pays income tax.

In Figure 11-2, the Johnston City Discount Store had a gross profit of $55,000 on sales of $125,000, or about 44 percent. This indicates that the goods sold cost the company about $56 per $100 of sales. After selling expenses have been deducted, the profit becomes 28 percent (i.e., $35,000 ÷ $125,000). The net profit of the business is the final profit after all costs and expenses for the accounting period have been deducted. For this firm, it is 19.6 percent.

HOW CAN FINANCIAL REPORTS BE USED TO DETERMINE THE FINANCIAL SOUNDNESS OF A BUSINESS?

Various relationships exist between the figures found on the balance sheet and on the profit-and-loss statement which can be helpful in interpreting the data. These indicators are comparative measures (usually expressed as ratios) of the ability of a business to pay its bills, or to liquidate its assets quickly if it has to. They are more useful than dollar amounts for analyzing business operations and spotting trends in the direction of better or poorer performance. They also make it possible for you to compare your company's performance with the average performance of similar businesses. It is well to keep in mind that there is much to be learned, at no cost, from such comparisons, and it would be a costly oversight to neglect this avenue of investigation.

Typical ratios for retail, wholesale, and manufacturing firms are published regularly by many trade associations. Dun & Bradstreet, Inc., publishes annually a series of ratios for 125 lines of business. Most public accounting firms have access to standard ratios for many different businesses and can advise small business owners regarding the significance of their firms' ratios.

From a list of a dozen "key" business ratios, we have selected five measures of liquidity—the ability of a business to pay its bills—which are significant indicators of financial condition. These reflect primarily balance-sheet relationships. Additional ratios designed to help you measure profitability are discussed in Chapter 12.

Ratio	How Calculated
Current ratio	$\dfrac{\text{Current assets}}{\text{Current liabilities}}$
Acid-test ratio	$\dfrac{\text{Cash} + \text{receivables} + \text{government securities}}{\text{Current liabilities}}$
Average collection period	$\dfrac{\text{Receivables}}{\text{Average daily sales}}$
Inventory turnover	$\dfrac{\text{Cost of goods sold}}{\text{Average inventory}}$
Debt to tangible net worth	$\dfrac{\text{Current liabilities}}{\text{Tangible net worth}}$

WHAT IS THE SIGNIFICANCE OF THE CURRENT RATIO?

This ratio is one of the best-known measures of financial strength. This test of solvency measures the liquid assets available to meet all debts falling due within a year's time.

Current assets are those normally expected to become cash in the course of a merchandising cycle. Such assets include cash, notes, accounts receivable, and inventories. In Figure 11-1, the Johnston City Discount Store's balance sheet shows current assets of $52,500 and current liabilities of $30,000. Its current ratio is:

$$\frac{\text{Current assets}}{\text{Current liabilities}} = \frac{\$52,500}{\$30,000} = 1.75$$

A current ratio of 2 to 1 or better is considered good. If your ratio is much lower than this, you can raise it by paying some debts, reinvesting profits, or increasing your assets through loans with a maturity of more than 1 year.

A gradual increase in the current ratio is usually a healthy sign of improved financial strength. Ordinarily, a current ratio of more than 4 or 5 to 1 is regarded as unnecessary, and is likely the result of an insufficient volume of business to produce a desirable level of earnings.

HOW DOES THE ACID-TEST RATIO GET ITS NAME?

This ratio is the most exacting measure of a firm's liquidity, since it considers only the most liquid of a firm's assets (cash and accounts receivable) in calculating the ratio. By not including inventories, it concentrates on those assets whose values are fairly certain. It is sometimes called the *quick ratio*. Our theoretical discount store's balance-sheet data develops the following acid-test ratio:

$$\frac{\text{Cash} + \text{receivables}}{\text{Current liabilities}} = \frac{\$10,000 + \$20,000}{\$30,000} = 1.0$$

This ratio answers the question, If all cash income from sales suddenly stopped, could my business meet its current obligations with readily convertible funds on hand?

A ratio of 1 to 1 is considered satisfactory if the pattern of accounts-receivable collections does not lag much behind the schedule for paying current liabilities and if there is no danger of anything happening to slow up the collection of accounts receivable. A ratio of somewhat higher than 1 to 1 will carry a measure of safety and give your creditors a warm feeling about your firm's condition.

HOW CAN YOU TELL IF YOUR AVERAGE COLLECTION PERIOD IS TOO LONG?

The rule of thumb is that your average collection period should not exceed the net maturity indicated by selling terms by more than 10 to 15 days. If you offer 30 days to pay, your average collection period should be no longer than 40 to 45 days. If it is longer, you should examine the reasons for the delay in collections since money tied up in accounts receivable curtails your working capital and could make it difficult for you to meet your obligations.

The average collection period, or number of days tied up in accounts receivable, can be computed from the balance sheet and the profit-and-loss statement for our discount store in the following manner:

$$\frac{\text{Net sales for the year}}{365 \text{ days}} = \frac{\$125,000}{365} = \$342 \text{ average daily sales}$$

$$\frac{\text{Receivables}}{\text{Average daily sales}} = \frac{\$20,000}{\$342} = 59 \text{ days of sales tied up in receivables}$$

Knowing the average collection period tells you how well your credit department is handling the collection job and gives you a means of interpreting the importance of the acid-test ratio. If our discount store offers 30-day credit terms, the 59-day collection period is excessive and should be looked into. If your store does not sell merchandise 365 days a year, fewer days (representing business days you are open) can be used to develop the data.

WHAT DOES AN INVENTORY RATIO OF 4 TIMES TELL YOU?

It tells you how fast your merchandise is moving. It gives you an idea of how much capital was tied up in inventory to support the company's operations. It is important as a guide to whether or not your business is investing too heavily in inventories.

It is computed for the Johnston City Discount Store from its balance sheet and its profit-and-loss statement as follows:

$$\frac{\text{Cost of goods sold}}{\text{Average inventory}} = \frac{\$70,000}{\$22,500} = 3.1 \text{ times}$$

Although this example uses the inventory value from the balance sheet as of December 31, a more accurate method is to add the January 1 and December 31 values and divide by 2 to get a yearly average.

Because inventories are a significant part of a merchandising firm's assets, this ratio is especially important. A high ratio means that your company has been able to operate with a relatively small investment in inventory. This indicates a good quality of merchandise and correct pricing policies. A downward trend in the ratio could be a warning signal of poor merchandising policy or obsolete or "stale" merchandise on the shelves. Such a warning should prompt action that will not only correct the merchandising policy but also move the merchandise that has been in the house too long. What that action should be will depend on how much obsolete or stale merchandise is on hand.

There is no universal ideal inventory turnover ratio which is suitable for all businesses. The desirable ratio depends upon your line of business, level of business activity, and your method of valuing inventories. A study of the turnover rates of businesses similar to yours will help you decide on the ratio which is right for your business.

Like the average collection period, inventory turnover should be computed each month in order to avoid seasonal fluctuations.

WHAT DOES A DEBT-TO-WORTH RATIO TELL YOU?

This ratio compares what is owed to what is owned. Total debt reflects the interest of creditors in your business since it is their money you are using to finance your inventories, equipment, and other business assets. Tangible net worth represents your original investment in the business plus any profits you have not withdrawn. The balance sheet of the Johnston City Discount Store shows the following values, which are used to calculate the ratio:

$$\frac{\text{Total debt}}{\text{Tangible net worth}} = \frac{\text{current} + \text{fixed liabilities}}{\text{capital}}$$

$$= \frac{\$30,000}{\$80,500} = 37\%$$

As this ratio approaches 100 percent, the creditor's interest in the business approaches the owner's. If it exceeds 100 percent, the business is probably undercapitalized. This is often a signal for management to restrain its purchases of inventory, property, and machinery, which would tend to lower the ratio.

This exercise is designed to test your understanding of the material presented in Chapter 11. Choose the response, *True* or *False*, which best fits each statement. Correct responses are presented in the back of the text.

1. The balance sheet cannot balance if the total liabilities are greater than total assets.
2. Information shown on the balance sheet is valid only for the point in time indicated on the report.
3. Business owners cannot determine their profit from the information shown on the balance sheet.
4. The inventory turnover rate is more significant than the size of the inventory.
5. A current ratio of at least 4 to 1 is considered a minimum for a well-run business.
6. A note which is due for payment 2 years from today is shown as a fixed liability on the balance sheet.
7. When equipment is kept in good repair, it can be depreciated over a longer period of time.
8. Taxes payable are shown on this year's balance sheet despite the fact that they will be paid next year.
9. Amounts owed by customers which you feel will be uncollectible are shown as "accrued liabilities" on the balance sheet.
10. The term *liquidity* refers to the ability of a business to pay its bills.
11. The current ratio can be increased by paying some of your debts or increasing your working capital by means of an intermediate-term loan.
12. In calculating the acid-test ratio, only cash and accounts receivable are used in the "assets" calculations.
13. The average collection period of a store which offers 30-day credit terms should not exceed 45 days.
14. A business with a high inventory turnover rate runs the risk of an occasional inventory shortage.
15. The debt-to-worth ratio should be kept as low as possible.

1. Jay's Appliance Repair Shop had a balance sheet at the end of last year as shown on the next page. Study the data shown there and calculate the following ratios. Assume net sales for the year (365 days) to be $325,000.

Current ratio	Average collection period
Acid-test ratio	Debt-to-worth ratio
Inventory turnover	

State the conclusions that may be drawn from the ratios.

JAY'S APPLIANCE REPAIR SHOP
Balance Sheet
December 31, 19___

Assets			Liabilities	
Cash	$ 875		Notes Payable	$ 3,500
Notes Receivable	2,160		Accounts Payable	69,976
Accounts Receivable	59,465		Accruals	1,785
Inventory	58,025		Total Current	
Total Current			Liabilities	$ 75,261
Assets	$120,525		Mortgage	4,000
Depreciation	8,350		Total Liabilities	$ 79,261
Equipment/Fixtures	1,886		Owner's Equity	52,000
Prepaid Expenses	500		Total Liabilities	
Total Assets	$131,261		and Owner's	
			Equity	$131,261

2. Prepare a profit-and-loss statement for a small retail business whose books reflect the following data for a recent year:

Gross sales	$190,000
Wages paid	25,000
Depreciation	3,600
Returns and allowances	2,500
Cost of goods sold	140,000
Miscellaneous expenses	2,000
Federal, state, and local taxes	5,800

a. What is the pretax profit this business made this year?
b. What percent of net sales does pretax profit represent?
c. What is the net profit after taxes, expressed as a percent of sales?

CHAPTER

12

Profit Planning and Control

PERFORMANCE OBJECTIVES

After reading this chapter you should gain a better understanding of the importance of profit planning to small business owners and of the tools which are available to help them in controlling those factors which affect profits. Specifically, you should be able to:

1. Define the term *profit* in simple understandable terms.
2. Discuss the major factors which affect profits and explain their impact on profit level.
3. Explain how a business with high sales volume can operate at a loss.
4. Defend the philosophy that a business is entitled to all the profit it can make.
5. Discuss the effect of price controls on the financial structure of a business.
6. Assess the effect on profits of a dollar saved through cost reduction, as compared with a dollar earned from sales.
7. Demonstrate how the net profit ratio is calculated.
8. Assess the effectiveness of the net-return-on-investment ratio as a measure of profitability.
9. Develop a list of business practices which can lead to profit leaks.
10. Explain the difference between fixed costs and variable costs and give examples of each.
11. Construct a sample break-even chart and explain its significance.

262

12. Demonstrate the effect that changes in variable costs have on the break-even point.
13. Explain what courses of action are open to a business operating below its break-even point.
14. Demonstrate how a semivariable expense like power can be broken into its fixed and variable components.

INTRODUCTION

Profits provide incentives to owners, give them a measure of managerial performance, and tell them whether the resources of the business are being effectively utilized. Without profits, small businesses would lack the motivational force necessary for them to struggle and grow. Going into business would no longer spark the imagination of would-be business owners, who envision a world where profits are the rewards for their creativity and ingenuity.

Despite the significance of profit in the success formula of the modern business, many small business owners are ill-informed about the factors that affect profit levels and are not aware of the actions they can take to assure profitable operations. What is needed is a means for owners to use the data from their record system to predict their future profits under various operating conditions.

This chapter discusses the key ratios that you can use to measure profitability and compare your experience with that of similar businesses. It introduces you to some basic tools that will assist you in profit planning and control. A careful study of these tools will enable you to find many practical uses for the concepts and techniques that are presented.

WHAT IS THE MEANING OF THE WORD *PROFIT*?

There are many different definitions for this term. To business people, it is most often considered to be the earnings on the capital that they and others have invested in the business. To the accountant, it is what is left after all costs and expenses for the accounting period have been deducted from the income for that period.

Profit is the result of careful and thorough planning. It is the incentive that motivates managers to strive for improvement. Although some businesses appear to make a profit without much planning, the profit level can be improved significantly by sound planning based on the information from your records.

WHAT THINGS SHOULD BE CONSIDERED IN PROFIT PLANNING?

An analysis of the following factors will be helpful:

Profitability of Similar Businesses. Table 3-3 of Chapter 3 shows the profitability of selected retail, manufacturing, and wholesale businesses based on data compiled by Dun & Bradstreet, Inc. for the year 1974. Although the statistics are based on a limited sample and show results for a single year, they provide guidance to profit planners who are interested in the profits of similar businesses.

Wholesale Price Index. Figure 12-1 shows the Wholesale Price Index for a 7-year period ending in November 1975. A study of the economic trends in this chart will assist the profit planner in forward pricing since they reflect the average prices for industrial commodities over a long period of time and are, therefore, beneficial in projecting what is likely to happen to operating expenses in the period ahead. Sharp rises in this index can significantly affect profits unless offsetting cost reductions can be made in operating expenses to maintain the profit level.

Labor Contracts. Consumers are painfully aware of the tendency of business to pass along costs resulting from increased wages and fringe benefits awarded in newly negotiated contracts with labor unions. To the extent business people decide to absorb these costs, their profits will be affected. With competition, consumer resistance, and government monetary policies all operating to keep prices down, business people are faced with serious decisions in their struggle to maintain a reasonable profit level.

Sales Potential. Without sales there would be no profit to plan for. Even with moderate sales, some businesses fail to earn enough to pay the costs of keeping the doors open—the so-called "fixed" costs

The wholesale price index fell 0.4 percent in November (no change after seasonal adjustment). Prices of farm products and processed foods and feeds dropped 2.3 percent (1.2 percent seasonally adjusted). Industrial commodity prices were up 0.4 percent (0.6 percent seasonally adjusted).

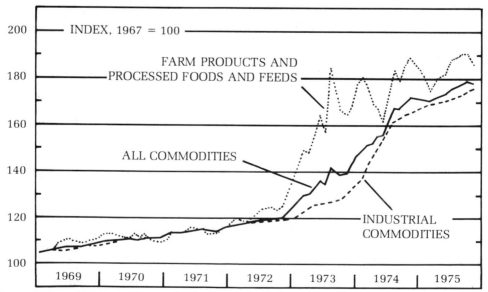

FIGURE 12-1. Wholesale Price Index for a 7-year period. (*Source:* Department of Labor, Council of Economic Advisers.)

of doing business. In order to make a profit, planners must know what their total costs are and how many units they need to make and sell to break even. Additionally, their sales planning must allow for some sales above this point to generate a reasonable profit for their effort. If this level of sales cannot be reached and maintained, the business will operate with meager profits or none at all. Profits are the result of effective sales planning and a continuing cost-control program. Both are items which must be addressed in effective profit planning.

HOW MUCH PROFIT IS ENOUGH?

No business person should be satisfied with a little profit. In a period of rising costs and growing shortages, business people can find themselves in serious trouble unless they have been farsighted enough to find ways of maintaining their profit level in spite of increasing costs. The generation of profit assures continued employment and allows the manager to provide efficient equipment and facilities, and pay for employee benefits which are often taken for granted by employees who do not realize that without profits none of these things would be possible. Our free enterprise system imposes no limit on the amount of profit a progressive business can make. Profits are the rewards of creativity and ingenuity in managing a business. Managers who are able through hard work and planning to keep their expenditures at the lowest possible level earn the right to a fair profit. The profit motive underlies our entire economic system and is the driving force behind any effective cost-reduction program, which has as its primary objective the maximizing of profit.

The long-range welfare of any business and its employees requires a growing profitable organization. To this end, both management and its employees must recognize their joint responsibilities to do everything possible to reduce operating expenses and at the same time to provide a quality product priced within the customer's ability to pay.

HOW CAN BUSINESS PEOPLE COUNTERACT THE EFFECTS OF RISING COSTS?

Figure 12-1 shows what happened to the cost of goods and services between 1969 and 1975. During periods of inflation, business people see the cost of the things they buy rise significantly. Simultaneously, they see the difference between their income and expenses shrink alarmingly. Faced with such a dilemma, they must examine the courses of action which are open to them. They have three options:

- ☐ Pass cost increases along to the customer.
- ☐ Absorb cost increases and accept less profit.
- ☐ Offset rising costs by reducing their operating expenses.

WILL THE CUSTOMER STAND STILL FOR MORE PRICE INCREASES?

This option will work only so long as the customer is willing to pay the new price and so long as your competitors are not selling their products at a lower price than you are. Prudent business people are aware that there is a limit to the price increases customers are willing to absorb. Nationwide protests and boycotts of selected products are not uncommon. Such actions reflect the mood of consumers and indicate that their patience is not unlimited. This fact, made more complex by the possibility that your competitors might *not* raise their prices, makes the risk of this approach even less attractive. Every sales representative can tell you stories of accounts that "dried up" because the customer was able to buy just as good a product cheaper elsewhere.

WHAT IS THE DANGER IN ABSORBING COST INCREASES?

This option is all right as long as you are satisfied to make less profit each year as costs go up. Eventually you will be operating your business with zero profit—or at a loss. It is obvious to even the most naïve that there many other investments which provide returns of more than 5 percent on the investor's capital—without any of the headaches that go with managing a business. In addition, this approach is not likely to be popular with stockholders, if you have any. They will find more profitable ways to invest their money.

WHAT IF YOU ARE ALREADY OPERATING AS EFFICIENTLY AS YOU CAN?

No system or approach to business management is ever perfect. The basic premise of work simplification is that there is always room for improvement; that no matter what method is being used today, there is a better way to do any job; and that the *best* method is never truly achieved. This philosophy makes it possible for two manufacturers making identical products to generate costs that are significantly different. Attention to such factors as motion economy, work measurement, efficient handling techniques, enlightened purchasing practices, and better work methods makes the difference. For modern managers, the methods, techniques, and tools of financial control are as much a part of their basic knowledge as scheduling, personnel administration, human relations, and quality control. A systematic analysis of the various factors which contribute to cost will provide managers with the facts they need to implement effective controls. Figure 12-2 illustrates the impressive contribution to profits which result from the systematic control and reduction of operating expenses.

The chart shows the effect on profits of a dollar of sales compared with a dollar saved as a result of a cost-reduction effort. Assuming a net profit from sales of 5 percent, business people must

Sales Dollar   Cost-Reduction Dollar

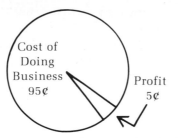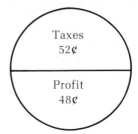

FIGURE 12-2. The effect on profits of a dollar earned through sales compared with a dollar saved by an effective cost-reduction program.

spend 95 cents of every sales dollar for wages, materials, advertising, selling costs, and other items known collectively as the "cost of doing business." After these expenses are deducted, they retain 5 cents of each dollar as a return for their total effort. The cost-reduction dollar, on the other hand, immediately becomes a dollar in the profit column. Assuming that they must pay 52 cents of this dollar for taxes, they keep 48 cents as net profit. Thus, the return from a dollar saved is almost ten times the return realized from each dollar of sales. This comparison dramatically shows the benefits to be realized from a well-planned and continuing cost-reduction program.

WHY IS PROFIT PLANNING IMPORTANT?

Businesses today are failing at an alarming rate. For those businesses that are fortunate enough to survive, it is becoming increasingly difficult to make a profit and remain solvent. Profit is directly contingent upon the degree to which the business is effectively managed. Since nearly all companies pay about the same for the goods and services they buy, the real basis for competition between similar businesses lies in the managers' skill in finding new ways to reduce operating costs in the face of increases in the price of the goods they buy—ways that enable them to maintain their profit level even in lean times. It is a good understanding of the principles of financial management that provides a distinct advantage in the battle for survival.

Profit planning is a part of everyday life for business people. It is the inevitable condition of progress in an industrial economy. It is a by-product of sound management, without which there can be no effective sustained control over costs. Increasing competition, growing consumer resistance, and rising prices are all potent factors acting to increase operating costs and reduce profits. Only those businesses that fully understand the factors which impact their costs and take steps to control them will succeed.

There are several profitability ratios which can be developed from the information shown on your balance sheet and your profit-and-loss statement. The most common of these are: net profit on sales, return on the owner's equity, and return on investment. In addition to these measures of profitability, the break-even analysis, the profit-volume analysis, and the return-on-investment analysis are techniques which will enable you to measure how well you are meeting your profit goals.

WHAT DOES THE NET PROFIT RATIO MEASURE?

It measures the difference between what your business takes in and what it spends in the process of doing business. It shows how much of every sales dollar is profit. The higher this percentage, the more efficient your operation. This is one of the most commonly used measures of business operations. The ratio depends on two factors—operating costs and product prices. If your net profit on sales decreases, for instance, it might be because you have lowered the price of your product to stimulate sales. Or it could be caused by increases in your operating costs while prices remain the same. Net profit on sales is obtained by dividing the net earnings of the business, after taxes, by the net sales (dollar volume less returns, allowances, and cash discounts). Based on the data reflected in Figure 12-3, the net profit ratio for the Johnston City Discount Store would be:

$$\frac{\text{Net profit}}{\text{Net sales}} = \frac{\$18,000}{\$125,000} = 14.4\%$$

THE JOHNSTON CITY DISCOUNT STORE
Profit-and-Loss Statement
Year Ending December 31, 19__

Gross Sales	$126,500
Less Returns and Allowances	1,500
	$125,000
Cost of Goods Sold	70,000
Gross Margin	$ 55,000
Operating Expenses	20,000
Operating Profit	$ 35,000
Administrative/General Overhead Expense	10,500
	$ 24,500
Estimated Income Tax	6,500
Net Profit After Taxes	$ 18,000

FIGURE 12-3. Condensed profit-and-loss statement.

This ratio is useful in profit planning when you compare it with businesses similar to yours. Such a comparison is afforded by Table 3-3 in Chapter 3. The ratio may also be used to compare the net profit on sales for the various departments in a store, or to compare the profits made on individual products or product lines.

HOW CAN YOU TELL IF YOUR BUSINESS IS PROVIDING A REASONABLE RETURN ON YOUR INVESTMENT?

By dividing the net income from the profit-and-loss statement by the owner's equity shown on the balance sheet. This relationship reflects the return on the owner's equity. Expressed as a percentage, it is one of the most significant of all financial ratios. It supplies the answer to the important question, How much is my business earning on my investment? Naturally, a large or increasing ratio is favorable. If the ratio shows that you are earning less than you could by investing your money, say, in a savings and loan association, you should have serious questions about the financial health of the business. Statistics previously shown in Chapter 3 (Table 3-2) indicate that some retail stores averaged less than 6 percent return on the owner's investment in 1974. This seems meager compensation for the problems faced by most business people.

The Johnston City Discount Store earned 22.3 percent on the owner's investment in 19__. This is calculated as follows:

$$\frac{\text{Net profit (Figure 12-3)}}{\text{Owner's equity (Figure 11-1)}} = \frac{\$18,000}{\$80,500} = 22.3\%$$

In computing the ratio, the average equity is customarily used—the average of the 12 individual months if it is available, or the average figures from the beginning and ending balance sheets.

Broad economic forces may change the general direction of this ratio. A higher rate may be due to general prosperity and a decline to a recession or less favorable economic conditions, or to higher taxes.

You can divide the percentage reflected by this ratio into 100 to see how many years it will take to get back the total investment in the business. In our case it is:

$$\frac{100}{22.3} = 4.5 \text{ years}$$

HOW DOES THE RETURN-ON-INVESTMENT RATIO DIFFER FROM RETURN ON OWNER'S EQUITY?

The rate of return on investment compares net profit with total assets. It is probably the most useful measure of profitability for the small business owner. Our hypothetical discount store's ratio is:

$$\frac{\text{Net profit (Figure 12-3)}}{\text{Total assets (Figure 11-1)}} = \frac{\$18,000}{\$110,500} = 16.3\%$$

In calculating the rate, be consistent in determining which numbers you will use as your "profits" (before taxes, after taxes, etc.) and your "assets."

HOW CAN THE PROFIT-AND-LOSS STATEMENT HELP YOU FIND PROFIT PROBLEMS?

By reducing the values on the profit-and-loss statement to percentages of net sales, you can compare your expenditures with other similar businesses and spot those areas where your costs seem out of line. For instance, Figure 12-4 is the profit-and-loss statement for a small appliance repair store. The owner's net profit before any withdrawal for salary was only $3,600 for the entire year—hardly enough to justify continuation of the business. The reasons for the low profit are not obvious on the profit-and-loss statement. However, if we

---

Profit-and-Loss Statement
for
OK Appliance Repair Company

Gross Sales		$70,000
Cost of Sales:		
Opening Inventory	$13,000	
Purchases	25,000	
Total	$38,000	
Ending Inventory	14,000	
Total Cost of Sales		24,000
Gross Profit		$46,000
Operating Expenses:		
Payroll (Not Including Owner)	$26,000	
Rent	3,000	
Payroll Taxes	1,500	
Interest	600	
Depreciation	1,400	
Truck Expense	5,500	
Telephone	2,400	
Insurance	1,000	
Miscellaneous	1,000	
Total		42,400
Net Profit (Before Owner's Salary)		$ 3,600

FIGURE 12-4. A profit-and-loss statement for a small appliance repair store. (*Source:* Adapted from Irving M. Cooper, *Accounting Services for Small Service Firms,* Small Marketers Aids, No. 126, U.S. Small Business Administration, Washington, 1967.)

have set up our books to capture sales and expense information by category, we can then prepare our statement to show how much was related to the "parts" activity and how much was related to "service." Furthermore, we can show in each of these categories what percentages of each sales dollar was spent for the various expenses incurred. Our profit-and-loss statement would then look like Figure 12-5.

We now have a way to compare our financial data with that of other time periods or with the data of other businesses like ours.

In Figure 12-5, there are two problem areas. The profit of $1,000 on parts worth $24,000 shows that the parts were grossly

OK Appliance Repair Company
P-and-L Statement Showing
Expenses as Percentages of Sales

	Total		Parts		Service	
	Amount	Per-cent	Amount	Per-cent	Amount	Per-cent
Gross Sales	$70,000	100.00	$25,000	100.00	$45,000	100.00
Cost of Sales:						
Opening Inventory	$13,000		$13,000			
Purchases	25,000		25,000			
Total	$38,000		$38,000			
Ending Inventory . . .	14,000		14,000			
Total Cost of Sales	$24,000	34.29	$24,000	96.00		
Gross Profit	$46,000	65.71	$ 1,000	4.00		
Operating Expenses:						
Payroll	$26,000	37.14			$26,000	57.78
Rent	3,000	4.28	$ 1,500	6.00	1,500	3.34
Payroll Taxes	1,500	2.14			1,500	3.34
Interest	600	.86	300	1.20	300	.66
Depreciation	1,400	2.00			1,400	3.11
Truck Expense	5,500	7.86			5,500	12.22
Telephone	2,400	3.43	1,200	4.80	1,200	2.67
Insurance	1,000	1.43	400	1.60	600	1.33
Miscellaneous	1,000	1.43	500	2.00	500	1.11
Total	$42,400	60.57	$ 3,900	15.60	$38,500	85.56
Net Profit (Loss)—	$ 3,600	5.14	$ (2,900)	(11.60)	$ 6,500	14.44
(Exclusive of Owner's Salary)						

FIGURE 12-5. The same profit-and-loss statement showing departmental performance data and expenses as a percentage of sales. (*Source:* Adapted from Irving M. Cooper, *Accounting Services for Small Service Firms*, Small Marketers Aids, No. 126, U.S. Small Business Administration, Washington, 1967.)

underpriced. If we assume a 30 percent discount on the parts when purchased from the wholesaler, the $24,000 worth of parts should have been sold for $34,286 (i.e., $24,000 ÷ 0.70), giving the owner a profit of $6,386 ($10,286[1] minus operating expenses of $3,900). This would have turned a $2,900 loss into a net profit.

The other problem which needs analysis is the high percentage of payroll costs to sales. When 58 percent of service income is spent for payroll, it could indicate that service labor is underpriced or that service labor is being used in an inefficient manner. This problem suggests a detailed analysis of the manner in which jobs are priced, the way overtime is reflected in the billing, the methods used to perform the services, the methods of estimating the cost of labor and parts, and similar factors.

The point is this: The profit-and-loss statement can tell you where to look for profit leaks if it is properly constructed.

WHICH BUSINESS PRACTICES ARE LIKELY TO GENERATE PROFIT LEAKS?

From a list that is almost endless, here are a few of the more likely ones:

Purchasing Expense.   In most businesses, merchandise bought for resale and operating supplies make up a sizable portion of your costs. Buying only what you need and can justify should be a habit. If you are not buying from the most economical source, find out why. Also check to see what discounts you are losing and what they are costing you.

Shrinkage.   Shrinkage of your inventories due to normal breakage and damage is expected. Losses due to pilferage, shoplifting, or theft can put you out of business if not controlled. Find out what makes up your shrinkage, get an idea of how big the problem is, then develop a plan to combat it.

Payrolls.   Excessive overtime, too many people, and personnel turnover are all symptoms of operating inefficiencies. Overtime can get to be an expensive habit that is difficult to break. Excessive personnel indicates a basic lack of planning plus an absence of job and performance standards. Turnover is more expensive than you think. Find out why people are voluntarily leaving your company. This effort could pay big dividends.

Unbalanced Insurance Coverage.   You could be "insurance poor" from excessive coverage. A review of your insurance coverage and your requirements should be made at least once a year. If your policies are covering more than you need, find out if you can make combinations that will give you what you need for less dollars than you are now paying. It pays to "shop around" when buying insurance.

[1]This figure is obtained by subtracting $24,000 from $34,286.

Inventory Costs.   The aim of any business is to keep inventories balanced and prevent sales losses from carrying an insufficient supply of goods. This can cause you to stock more than you need just to be sure you have enough on hand. Many studies have shown that most inventories can be reduced by 25 percent without appreciable effect on customer service. Try to carry items that turn over fast and drop slow-moving items as soon as you can.

Taxes.   It is generally believed that more than half of all business people pay more taxes than they should. Review your tax bills at all levels to be sure you are paying the right amount for your business. A tax adviser can often help you save money on taxes through legitimate deductions you are not aware of.

Wasted Sales Efforts.   Be sure you are expending your sales efforts on those customers who are contributing most to your profits. A hard look at your product lines will almost always show unprofitable lines that are costing you money to handle. There are both customers and product lines that you would probably be better off without. In reevaluating customers and products, list why they are unprofitable and decide what needs to be done.

Out-of-Line Overhead.   Expenses like rent, heat, telephone, supplies, and indirect labor have a habit of growing to the point where you must question their reasonableness. Planning the expenditures of these items and tracking them against a well-planned budget will provide you with a means of control. Reducing heat or air conditioning on weekends, using letters instead of long-distance telephone calls, and establishing rules concerning the use of business telephones are examples of approaches that can save money.

DOESN'T SELLING A LOT OF MERCHANDISE ASSURE THE EXISTENCE OF A PROFIT?

Volume offers no guarantee of a profit. You could be selling merchandise "like hotcakes" and still be going broke simply because the selling price is too low. The selling price selected by the manufacturer, for example, must account for all the costs involved in making and selling the product. These costs include:

Variable Costs.   These are made up primarily by direct labor and direct material used in making the product. These costs vary with the number of items made. If you are not making anything, they are zero. Freight and packaging expense are included in these costs. In the average business, 60 to 65 percent of all costs are variable.

Fixed Costs.   Costs which remain the same regardless of the volume of production are called *fixed costs*. Costs such as rent, insurance, depreciation, property taxes, and certain executive salaries are incurred whether you are producing anything or not.

Selling Costs.   Salaries and commissions you pay to the employees who sell your product plus any advertising and promotion costs make up this category.

Profit.   The difference between sales revenue and the sum of all your costs is profit. The selling price must be high enough to provide a reasonable profit.

Assuming that the product is properly priced, we must then sell enough to overcome incurred costs before any profit is assured.

HOW CAN YOU BE SURE YOUR PRICE IS HIGH ENOUGH TO RETURN A REASONABLE PROFIT?

First, determine what your production volume will be, based on past sales, market surveys, or sales forecasts. An accurate forecast of production or sales is necessary before you can do any profit planning. Let us assume that you are the owner of the Ideal Transformer Company, which makes and sells 6,000 transformers a year.

Next, determine what it costs you to make a transformer. Your accounting records can provide this information. Develop a cost of goods manufactured similar to that shown in Figure 11-5 of Chapter 11. The following data has been extracted from that illustration:

Cost Category	Annual Amount
Direct materials	$26,840
Direct labor	15,300
Manufacturing overhead	17,900
	$60,040

From this information, it can be seen that it costs Ideal $10 to manufacture each transformer during a year ($60,040 ÷ 6,000). The cost of a single unit is made up of the three cost elements in the following amounts:

	Unit Cost	Kind of Cost
Material	$26,840 ÷ 6,000 = $ 4.47	Variable
Labor	$15,300 ÷ 6,000 = 2.55	Variable
Overhead	$17,900 ÷ 6,000 = 2.98	Fixed
	$10.00	

If we assume that there are no other expenses to be considered, we can experiment with several different prices. If we add 10 percent to the cost of each unit for profit, the selling price would be $11 per unit. The annual profit before taxes would be $6,000 if we sell 6,000 transformers and make $1 of profit on each one. Use this planned profit to figure the return-on-investment ratio and compare it with the ratios of other manufacturers of similar products. Adjust the price until a reasonable return is assured, based on your expected sales volume of 6,000 units per year. If the market will not support this price, you will have to find a way to make it for less and still earn a reasonable profit.

WHAT IS MEANT BY THE BREAK-EVEN POINT?

This term describes the point where income just equals total costs, leaving no profit or loss. The relationship can be illustrated graphically by a chart. For the Ideal Transformer Company, it would look like Figure 12-6. The data displayed is based on fixed costs of $18,000 (6,000 units × $3 each), variable unit costs of $7.02 ($4.47 + $2.55), and a unit selling price of $11.

A careful examination of this chart reveals that above the break-even point, increasingly greater profits are earned as sales volume increases. The reverse is true below the break-even point, where increasingly greater losses are incurred as sales volume decreases.

The break-even point will be lowered by decreasing fixed costs, decreasing variable costs, increasing the selling price, or a combination of all three.

Any of these actions causes the total-cost line to intersect the total-sales line sooner, permitting the generation of profit on less volume than before.

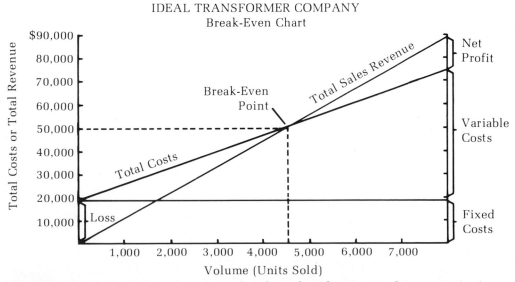

FIGURE 12-6. The break-even chart shows the relationship of costs to profits at various volumes.

By knowing what your variable and fixed costs amount to, you can calculate the point at which revenue from sales covers all your costs. For example, if Ideal Transformer Company sets a selling price of $11 each and its total overhead (fixed) costs amount to $18,000, the following relationships would exist:

Total fixed costs = $18,000

Total variable costs = Variable cost per unit times the number of units. Material is $4.47 per unit and direct labor is $2.55 (total $7.02). Therefore, the variable costs would be $7.02 times the number of units produced.

Total costs = total fixed costs + total variable costs

Table 12-1 shows the relationship which exists between volume and costs in this case: Ideal cannot afford to produce less than 4,523 units per year at a selling price of $11 each because if it does it will not recover its total costs. When operating at its forecasted volume of 6,000 units, its profit is $5,880 (8.9 percent of sales).

Before deciding on a final price, Ideal should examine the relationship between profit and volume at various selling prices. Once it has selected a pricing policy that considers labor and material costs, trade discounts, overhead expense, and similar factors, it should periodically reevaluate the price charged to determine the effect of inflation and competition on the profit level.

CAN YOU FIND THE BREAK-EVEN POINT WITHOUT DRAWING A CHART?

You can determine the break-even point mathematically by a formula whose components are variable expenses and fixed expenses. The formula will provide an answer in "units to be sold" to break even. For the Ideal Transformer Company, the calculations are:

$$\text{Units to be sold} = \frac{\text{fixed expense}}{\text{unit sales price} - \text{unit variable expense}}$$

$$= \frac{\$18,000}{\$11.00 - \$7.02}$$

$$= 4,523 \text{ units}$$

When Ideal sells 4,523 transformers, its income and expense are equal:

Income = 4,523 × $11 = $49,753

Expense = (4,523 × $7.02) + $18,000 = $49,753

TABLE 12-1. BREAK-EVEN MATRIX FOR IDEAL TRANSFORMER COMPANY

Production	1,000	2,000	3,000	4,000	4,523	5,000	6,000	7,000	8,000
Total fixed costs	$18,000	$18,000	$18,000	$18,000	$18,000	$18,000	$18,000	$18,000	$18,000
Total variable costs	7,020	14,040	21,060	28,080	31,753	35,100	42,120	49,140	56,160
Total costs	25,020	32,040	39,600	46,080	49,753	53,100	60,120	67,140	74,160
Total sales revenue	11,000	22,000	33,000	44,000	49,753	55,000	66,000	77,000	88,000
Profit or (loss)	(14,020)	(10,040)	(6,600)	(2,080)	0	1,900	5,880	9,860	13,840

Thus we can see that only after Ideal has sold $49,753 worth of transformers will it begin to make any profit. If the output or sales is below the break-even point, three courses of action are open if the business is to become profitable: reduce expenses, increase sales, or do both at the same time.

WHAT GUIDELINES CAN YOU USE TO CLASSIFY YOUR EXPENSES AS FIXED OR VARIABLE?

By definition, fixed costs include such things as rent, insurance, property tax, depreciation, and executive salaries. Equally easy to categorize are the "almost pure" variable costs like direct material, direct labor, sales commissions, and small tools. These vary with volume.

Some expenses do not fall neatly into the pattern of fixed and variable costs. Your telephone expense, for example, has a fixed monthly instrument and service charge which is the same each month. In addition, your bill includes an amount for toll charges which varies somewhat with production and sales levels. You can easily separate the fixed and variable components of telephone expense by examining your billing. This type of cost is called a semi-variable cost for obvious reasons. Expenses such as supplies and utilities would also be semivariable, with some expense being generated even when volume is zero. Power, for instance, would be at a low (constant) level during periods when the plant is not operating. During the normal workweek power usage would vary with activity in the factory, being affected by the number of machines operating, the number of hours per day being worked, the number of shifts, and similar factors.

TABLE 12-2. UTILITY COSTS COMPARED WITH FACTORY DIRECT-LABOR HOURS IN A SMALL MANUFACTURING FIRM

Month	Cost of Utilities	Factory D/L Hours
January	$ 830	450
February	650	350
March	675	325
April	850	500
May	690	400
June	800	525
July	600	300
August	865	551
September	750	425
October	705	375
November	750	475
December	610	275
	$8,775	4,951

It is necessary for you to be able to separate your semivariable costs into their fixed and variable components before you can make a break-even chart. One method of doing this is to prepare a scattergram. In a scattergram, a relationship is set up between the semivariable expense (utilities, for example) and another variable. The semivariable is scaled on the vertical axis; the other variable on the horizontal axis. The paired values of the two series are plotted on these scales on a time basis.

The utility bill for Ideal Transformer Company when compared with factory direct-labor hours last year looks like Table 12-2.

If these two variables are plotted on a monthly basis, the 12 points will fall in a pattern shown on Figure 12-7. After the points are plotted, a *line of best fit* is drawn through the points. This line passes through some of the points, but others are either above the line or below it. In drawing the line, we have tried to make it pass through the theoretical center of the plots, allowing as many points to fall above the line as there are below it. If you extend the line until it reaches and intersects the vertical axis, the intersection point indicates the fixed portion of the semivariable cost. In our case, the intersection point is $345 per month, which says that we pay out that much each month for utilities just to keep the doors open. This

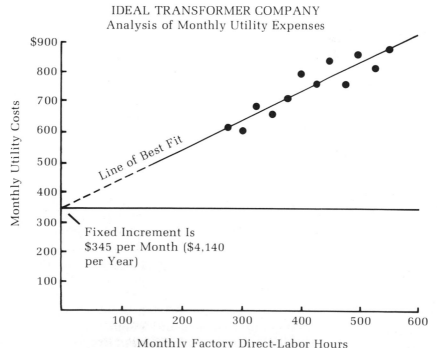

IDEAL TRANSFORMER COMPANY
Analysis of Monthly Utility Expenses

FIGURE 12-7. A sample scattergram of two-variable costs.

means that about 48 percent of Ideal's utility bill was fixed last year and not subject to much control in terms of reducing it.

When we examine the behavior of each expense, we can classify them as shown in Table 12-3.

TABLE 12-3. CLASSIFICATION OF EXPENSES:
Ideal Transformer Company

Type of Expense	Total	Variable	Fixed
Direct material	$26,840	$26,840	—
Direct labor	15,300	15,300	—
Utilities	8,590	4,450	$ 4,140
Supplies	210	210	—
Insurance/taxes	810	—	810
Depreciation	3,530	—	3,530
Indirect salaries	4,400	1,600	2,800
	$59,680	$48,400	$11,280
Percentage	100.0	81.1	18.9

In classifying expenses for making a break-even analysis, estimates can be used for costs that cannot be precisely identified as fixed or variable. Accuracy is necessary only to a point that permits you to reach sound decisions. Keep in mind that roughly 60 percent of your expense accounts are responsible for less than 20 percent of your costs. Determine whether these costs are predominantly fixed or predominantly variable. After you have made a careful examination, classify them as one or the other.

WHAT ARE THE ADVANTAGES OF A BREAK-EVEN ANALYSIS?

A break-even analysis allows you to see the total effect of both price and volume on profits and provides you with a means of determining profit under a wide range of assumed conditions. It tells you if your selling price is realistic and how much you have to change it to provide a reasonable return. You can use it to determine the effect of specific managerial actions on the profit you will make. Graphic presentations of the break-even analysis provide you with an easy-to-read reporting device which summarizes the data contained in the income statement. As a management aid, the break-even chart has these specific uses:

☐ It indicates potential pricing problems by showing you which products are profitable and which are not, enabling you to make decisions regarding which products to push and which to de-emphasize or discontinue.

- It will tell you if sales are falling short of your goals and enable you to undertake a program of corrective action early enough to be effective.

- It will enable you to assess the impact on profit of such things as proposed methods improvements, new equipment, and wage increases.

- It visualizes the probable effects on profits of price changes in combination with other changes.

AREN'T SOME OF THE ASSUMPTIONS IN A BREAK-EVEN ANALYSIS QUESTIONABLE?

Any reporting device has its limitations. The break-even chart is no exception. Keep in mind that cost and revenue information often change after you have made your break-even analysis, introducing variables which you could not have foreseen. For instance, one of the assumptions you must make in a typical forecast of income is that the selling price will remain constant over the entire range of output. This assumption is often made invalid by changes in list prices, changes in product mix, and changes in distribution methods, which often throw such an assumption out of line with reality. Some problems can result from attempts to separate and classify costs as fixed and variable since fixed costs often do not remain truly fixed and variable costs have a habit of exhibiting fixed characteristics at some volume levels.

Finally, competition and the changing nature of the economy often cause shifts in cost and income data that upset the assumption of static conditions. Despite these limitations, the advantages of break-even analysis far outweigh the disadvantages.

WHAT CAN YOU DO TO KEEP THE BREAK-EVEN POINT AS LOW AS POSSIBLE?

Reduce your costs, increase your sales, or both. Although increased sales are necessary to maximize profits, the break-even point responds dramatically to reductions in variable expenses. To illustrate this point, we can examine what would happen if Ideal Transformer Company found a way to reduce variable costs by $1 per unit. Case 1 below reflects the data previously shown in Figure 12-6. Case 2 shows the effects of a reduction in variable expense on profits:

	Case 1	Case 2
Fixed expenses	$18,000	$18,000
Unit sales price	$11.00	$11.00
Unit variable expense	$7.02	$6.02
Break-even volume	4,523	3,634
Profit on 4,523 units	None	$4,523

Profit is the difference between sales income and total expense (fixed costs + variable costs) at the 4,523 volume level.

$$\text{Profit} = \text{sales} - (\text{fixed costs} + \text{variable costs})$$

$$= \$49{,}753 - (\$18{,}000 + \$27{,}230)$$

$$= \$49{,}753 - \$45{,}230$$

$$= \$4{,}523$$

In this example, each expense dollar saved becomes a profit dollar. If Ideal has a profit margin of 10 percent, it would have to increase its sales by $45,230 to make the same amount of profit.

HOW CAN THE RELATIONSHIP BETWEEN COST, VOLUME, AND PROFIT BE SIMPLY SHOWN?

Table 12-4 shows a convenient way to display these three variables in such a way that their interrelationship can be clearly demonstrated. The "actual" column in this figure shows sales, costs, and managerial information for a business selling 60,000 units of a product at $20 each, whose fixed costs are $400,000 and variable costs are $12 per unit. The effects of changing unit prices, variable expenses, and volume individually and in combination may be seen in the ratios and other information at the bottom of the chart.

WHAT IS THE SIGNIFICANCE OF RATE OF RETURN ON INVESTMENT TO A BUSINESS OWNER?

The rate of return on investment (ROI) is probably the most important of all management guides for profit planning. It takes into account all the various items that go into a balance sheet and income statement. Figure 12-8 shows graphically a structural outline of the relationship of these items to the rate of return on investment and to each other.

The various terms used in the calculation of ROI must be defined and used consistently. The following definitions will be helpful:

Sales.   You can use either billed sales or net sales in your computations, but not both. Be consistent in your use and stay with one or the other.

Profits.   The term *profit* in the ROI formula is ordinarily taken to denote profit after taxes. Sometimes *net income before taxes* is used to eliminate the effect of changes in tax rates during periods you are comparing. This is advisable where the rates of return are being compared during a period of fluctuating tax rates.

TABLE 12-4. COST-VOLUME-PROFIT ANALYSIS UNDER CONDITIONS OF CHANGING SALES PRICE, VOLUME, AND VARIABLE EXPENSES

	Actual	Unit price changes — 10 percent increase — Case A	Unit price changes — 10 percent decrease — Case B	Variable expense changes — 10 percent increase — Case C	Variable expense changes — 10 percent decrease — Case D	Volume changes — 10 percent increase — Case E	Volume changes — 1 percent decrease — Case F	Volume changes — Case G[a]	Volume changes — Case H[b]
Sales:									
60,000 @ $20 per unit	$1,200,000								
60,000 @ $22 per unit		$1,320,000							
60,000 @ $18 per unit			$1,080,000						
60,000 @ $20 per unit				$1,200,000					
60,000 @ $20 per unit					$1,200,000				
66,000 @ $20 per unit						$1,320,000			
54,000 @ $20 per unit							$1,080,000		
63,000 @ $18 per unit								$1,134,000	
57,000 @ $22 per unit									$1,254,000
Less variable expenses:									
60,000 @ $12 per unit	720,000								
60,000 @ $12 per unit		720,000							
60,000 @ $12 per unit			720,000						
60,000 @ $13.20 per unit				792,000					
60,000 @ $10.80 per unit					648,000				
66,000 @ $12 per unit						792,000			
54,000 @ $12 per unit							648,000		
63,000 @ $10.80 per unit								680,400	
57,000 @ $13.20 per unit									752,040
Marginal income	480,000	600,000	360,000	408,000	552,000	528,000	432,000	453,600	501,600
Fixed expenses	400,000	400,000	400,000	400,000	400,000	400,000	400,000	400,000	400,000
Net profit (loss)	80,000	200,000	(−40,000)	8,000	152,000	128,000	32,000	53,600	101,600
Managerial information:									
Net profit ratio[c] (in percent)	6.66	15.15	(−3.7)	0.666	12.66	9.7	2.96	4.7	8.1
P/V ratio[d] (in percent)	40	45.45	33.33	34	46	40	40	40	40
Break-even sales[e]	$1,000,000	$880,000	$1,200,000	$1,176,470	$869,565	$1,000,000	$1,000,000	$1,000,000	$1,000,000
Percent change in net profit	[f]	150	(−150)	(−90)	90	60	(−60)	(−33)	27
Percent profit on investments[g]	8	20	(−4)	8	15.2	12.8	3.2	5.36	10.16

[a] Sales price decrease, 10 percent; variable expenses decrease, 10 percent; volume increase, 5 percent. [b] Sales price increase, 10 percent; variable expenses increase, 10 percent; volume decrease, 5 percent. [c] Net profit divided by sales. [d] Marginal income divided by sales. [e] Fixed expenses divided by profit-volume ratio. [f] Actual equals 100 percent. [g] Assuming an investment of $1 million.

Source: B. La Salle Woelfel, Guides for Profit Planning, Small Business Management Series, No. 25, U.S. Small Business Administration, Washington, 1960.

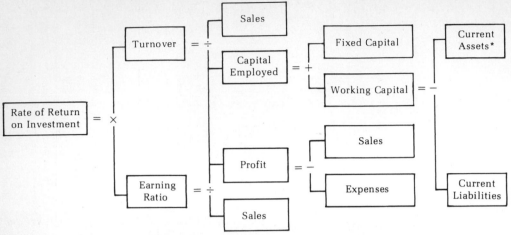

*Includes cash, accounts receivable, and inventory.

FIGURE 12-8. Relationship of balance sheet items and return on investment formula. (*Source:* B. La Salle Woelfel, *Guides for Profit Planning*, Small Business Series, No. 25, U.S. Small Business Administration, Washington, 1960.)

Capital Employed. When attempting to define this term for ROI calculations, we encounter the greatest area of differing opinions. Among the various opinions concerning what assets should be included in *capital employed*, these two are most generally considered acceptable:

- Total assets (current + fixed).
- Total assets less current liabilities. This concept combines net working capital (current assets − current liabilities) with permanet capital (fixed assets).

CAN RETURN ON INVESTMENT BE REDUCED TO A SIMPLE FORMULA?

The basic formula for the ROI rate contains two components:

$$(1) \quad \text{Turnover} = \frac{\text{sales}}{\text{capital employed}}$$

$$(2) \quad \text{Percent profit on sales} = \frac{\text{profit}}{\text{sales}}$$

Turnover is a measurement of movement of assets in relation to sales during a period of time. It is a measure of the general efficiency of management because the larger volume of business that you can do on a given investment, the more efficient you are. Percent profit on sales provides a description of your earnings. Together these measurements describe the amount of money earned on the dollars invested in a business. This relationship is expressed by the formula:

$$\text{ROI rate} = \text{turnover} \times \text{percent profit on sales}$$

$$= \frac{\text{sales}}{\text{capital employed}} \times \frac{\text{profit}}{\text{sales}}$$

Mathematically, the "sales" figures in the formula cancel each other, leaving

$$\text{ROI rate} = \frac{\text{profit}}{\text{capital employed}}$$

If we look at the balance sheet (Figure 11-1, Chapter 11) and the profit-and-loss statement (Figure 12-3) for the Johnston City Discount Store, we find the following relationships:

Net Sales	$125,000
Less: Total Expenses (Cost of Goods Sold + Operating Expenses + Administrative and General Overhead Expense + Tax)	107,000
Net Profit	$ 18,000
Working Capital (Cash + Accounts Receivable + Inventory – Current Liabilities)	$ 22,500
Fixed Assets (Excluding Land)	48,000
Total Capital Employed	$ 70,500

Substituting these values in our formula, we find that

$$\text{ROI rate} = \frac{\$18,000}{\$70,500} = 25.5\%$$

To keep the ROI rate as high as possible, a business should attempt to increase sales while maintaining its operating profit and simultaneously employing its resources in such a manner that it consistently increases its earnings on capital employed.

WHAT IS CONSIDERED NORMAL FOR AN ROI RATE?

We can only look at the experience of operating businesses to answer this one. Dun & Bradstreet's *Key Business Ratios* (1974) shows these *median* figures for the kinds of businesses listed:

	ROI Rate, %
Retail:	
Department stores	7.01
Discount stores	11.06
Grocery stores	25.60

	ROI Rate, %
Hardware stores	10.07
Motor vehicle dealers	11.33
Variety stores	10.28
Wholesale:	
Dairy products	25.48
Lumber and construction	12.46
Meat products	15.51
Tires and tubes	10.46
Manufacturing:	
Bakery products	16.51
Communications equipment	14.71
Drugs	25.03
Household appliances	9.12
Petroleum refining	66.90
Soft drinks	38.44

SELF-CHECK OF KEY CONCEPTS

This exercise is designed to test your understanding of the material presented in Chapter 12. Choose the response, *True* or *False*, which best fits each statement. Correct responses are presented in the back of the text.

1. Passing cost increases along to the customer is considered the best solution to the problem of rising costs.
2. Theoretically, it is impossible to operate a business at 100 percent efficiency.
3. A cost reduction dollar contributes more to the profits of a business than a sales dollar.
4. Rate of return on investment and rate of return on owner's equity are different terms for the same thing.
5. A business begins to make a profit only after it passes its break-even point.
6. When you are not making or selling anything, variable costs are zero.
7. The break-even point is raised by a reduction in fixed expenses.
8. Advertising costs would be an example of a variable expense.
9. Fixed costs are incurred whether or not the business is making or selling anything.
10. There is nothing wrong with making a lot of profit.

1. The relationship between profit and volume (number of items sold) can be expressed as a percentage by dividing profit by sales:

$$\frac{\text{Net profit}}{\text{Net sales}} = \frac{\$5,000}{\$135,000} = 3.7\% \text{ return on sales}$$

In this example, if the manufacturer increases his volume (sales), his profit will increase at a rate of 3.7 cents per additional dollar of merchandise sold, all other cost factors being assumed to remain constant.

An effective cost-control program also contributes to profits. Each dollar saved in this instance becomes a dollar in the profit column because it reduces expenses, automatically adding the full amount saved to the profit column of the financial reports of the business.

In the table below, calculate the increased sales which would be needed in each instance to match the money saved by a $10,000 cost improvement:

If Profit on Sales Is	You Would Have to Sell This Much to Match a $10,000 Cost Improvement
1%	$_____
2%	_____
5%	_____
10%	_____
20%	_____

2. The Excello Wholesale Company is preparing its operating budget for next year and is analyzing its fixed and variable expenses in order to project a profit-and-loss statement.

Excello's telephone expenses, compared with its sales volume on a monthly basis for last year, are shown in the following:

EXCELLO WHOLESALE COMPANY
19__ Telephone Expense

Month	Telephone Expense	Sales Volume
January	$ 970	$15,000
February	780	12,000
March	900	14,000
April	820	15,000
May	810	12,000
June	730	11,000
July	990	14,000
August	870	13,000
September	720	10,000
October	1,170	20,000
November	1,030	17,000
December	1,020	16,000

From this data prepare a scattergram and answer the following questions:

a. How much of the monthly telephone expense is fixed?
b. If Excello expects to average $18,000 per month in sales next year, how much should it budget monthly for telephone expense?
c. How much of the amount in b is variable expense?
d. If Excello finds a way to reduce the variable portion of its telephone bill by 25 percent next year, what will its telephone bill amount to in a month when sales are $15,000?

3. Figure 12-9 shows the break-even chart for a manufacturer who makes power lawnmowers for a major mail-order house. The manufacturer's plant has a capacity of 2,500 mowers a year and he can sell all he makes. His break-even chart shows that his present break-even point (2,000) is 80 percent of his capacity. He would like to lower his break-even point in order

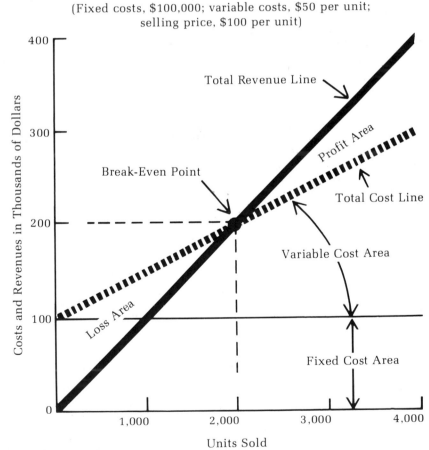

(Fixed costs, $100,000; variable costs, $50 per unit; selling price, $100 per unit)

FIGURE 12-9. Volume break-even chart. (*Source:* Jack Zwick, *A Handbook of Small Business Finance*, Small Business Management Series, No. 15, U.S. Small Business Administration, Washington, 1965.)

to improve his profit level. To attain this goal, he begins by evaluating the following actions in terms of their impact on the break-even point:

a. Reduce fixed costs from $100,000 to $80,000. No change in selling price or variable costs.
b. Reduce variable costs from $50 per unit to $45 per unit, with no change in fixed costs or selling price.
c. Raise the selling price from $100 per unit to $105 per unit, with no change in fixed or variable costs.
d. Simultaneously reduce fixed costs to $80,000, reduce variable costs to $45 per unit, and raise the selling price to $105 per unit.

For each of the alternatives shown above, calculate the new break-even point in units and the profit the owner would make on 2,500 mowers.

THE STORY OF ELAINE'S FIRST YEAR IN BUSINESS — A CASE IN POINT

Elaine Washington's Home Improvement Center has completed its first year of business. When Elaine bought the store, she set the following goals:

☐ A net profit of 6 percent of sales.

☐ Sales volume of $125,000 per year.

☐ Occupancy cost of 3 percent or less.

Soon after she started, Elaine sensed the need for adding a line of rental equipment for the do-it-yourself trade. She invested heavily in such items as power tools, lawn and garden equipment, painting equipment, and similar items. She had to rent space adjacent to her store to handle the additional merchandise. By the end of the year Elaine knew that this new line was a money maker. Approximately 40 percent of her sales came from the equipment rentals. Elaine was not sure how much profit her equipment rental generated because she did not segregate her expenses by department.

Just after she opened, she instituted a vigorous advertising campaign and was pleased with the response. A rough check of the year-end figures indicated her volume of business at $155,000 for the year. She was sure that her other goals had been met, but she asked an accountant to summarize her year's activity, analyze the financial data, and suggest any changes that would improve the operation of the store. She also threw a holiday party in December for her six employees and their spouses to celebrate a successful year.

The accountant made a balance sheet for Elaine's store. This balance sheet is shown in Figure 12-10.

Next he prepared a profit-and-loss statement which showed that Elaine's net profit before taxes was less than 5 percent last year. This revealing information, which Elaine had never had prepared for her before, is shown in Figure 12-11.

ELAINE'S HOME IMPROVEMENT CENTER
Balance Sheet
December 31, 1975

Current Assets:
Cash	$ 5,800	
Receivables	8,500	
Inventory	25,000	
Total	$39,300	

Fixed Assets:
Fixtures	$ 7,200	
Rental Equipment	88,000	
Total	$95,200	
Total Assets		$134,500

Current Liabilities:
Accounts Payable	$ 6,000	
Notes Payable	2,000	
Total	$ 8,000	

Fixed Liabilities:
Equipment Loans	$70,000	
Total	$78,000	
Owner's Equity	$56,500	
Total Liabilities and Owner's Equity		$134,500

FIGURE 12-10. Balance sheet of Elaine's Home Improvement Center at the end of 1975.

TABLE 12-5. FINANCIAL PERFORMANCE OF 350 RETAIL HARDWARE STORES IN 1974 COMPARED WITH THAT OF ELAINE'S HOME IMPROVEMENT CENTER IN 1975

Areas of Performance	350 Retail Hardware Stores, 1974 Experience	Elaine's Home Improvement Center, 1975 Experience
1. Profit on investment	25.65%	5.4%
2. Active owner's return	40.12%	11.1%
3. Current asset ratio	5.07	4.91
4. Quick asset ratio	1.87	1.80
5. Total debt to tangible net worth	38.93%	138.0%
6. Stock turn times	2.68	4.23
7. Sales to inventory ratio	4.12	6.20
8. Net sales to accounts receivable	16.58	18.23
9. Net sales to total assets	1.77	1.17
10. Net sales to net worth	2.47	2.74
11. Net sales to net working capital	2.97	4.95
12. Sales per person employed	$36,095	$25,833

Source: The data on the 350 retail hardware stores is provided by the National Retail Hardware Association.

From his files, the accountant obtained a sheet showing the operating ratios of 350 retail hardware stores for the previous year. These are shown in Figure 12-12.

He then compared Elaine's financial-performance data with data on 12 key items provided by the national trade association for hardware dealers. The comparison is shown in Table 12-5.

After studying the data carefully, answer the following questions:

1. How does Elaine's net profit on sales compare with that of other hardware stores?
2. Which items on the profit-and-loss statement look out of line with the experience of other hardware stores?

ELAINE'S HOME IMPROVEMENT CENTER
Profit-and-Loss Statement
Year Ending December 31, 1975

	Amount	Percent
Net Sales	$155,000	100.00
Cost of Goods Sold	105,726	68.21
Gross Margin	$ 49,274	31.79
Operating Expenses:		
Owner's Salary	$ 9,998	6.45
Employees' Wages	17,437	11.25
Employee Benefits	651	.42
Payroll Taxes	1,240	.80
Total Payroll/Personnel	$ 29,326	18.92
Rent	$ 3,333	2.15
Utilities	1,085	.70
Repairs	185	.12
Total Occupancy Costs	$ 4,603	2.97
Taxes	$ 697	.45
Interest on Loans	806	.52
Advertising	2,635	1.70
Insurance	698	.45
Depreciation	620	.40
Telephone	465	.30
Bad Debts	1,395	.90
Office Supplies	465	.30
Donations	155	.10
Other (Miscellaneous)	155	.10
Total Costs of Doing Business	$ 8,091	5.22
Net Profit	$ 7,254	4.68

FIGURE 12-11. Profit-and-Loss Statement of Elaine's Home Improvement Center at the end of 1975.

3. Which of the 12 key financial-performance factors in Table 12-5 show a need for further analysis and possible corrective action?
4. Based on your analysis of the data, what recommendations would you make to Elaine for improving next year's operations?

Net Sales Volume:	$269,994
Current Year's Sales versus Previous Year	+12.66%
Net Sales	100.00%
Cost of Goods Sold	64.92
Margin	35.08
Payroll and Other Employee Expense:	
Salaries—Owners, Officers, Managers	5.85
Salaries—Other Employees	9.04
Federal and State Payroll Taxes	.82
Group Insurance	.20
Benefit Plans	.32
Total Payroll and Other Employee Expense	16.23
Occupancy Expense:	
Heat, Light, Water, Power	.67
Repairs to Building	.29
Rent or Ownership in Real Estate	2.27
Total Occupancy Expense	3.23
Other Cost of Doing Business:	
Office Supplies and Postage	.40
Advertising	1.49
Donations	.08
Telephone and Telegraph	.24
Bad Debts	.30
Delivery (Other Than Wages)	.47
Insurance (Other Than Real Estate and Group)	.66
Taxes (Other Than Real Estate and Payroll)	.46
Interest on Borrowed Money	.61
Depreciation (Other Than Real Estate)	.57
Unclassified (Including Store Supplies)	1.59
Total Costs of Doing Business	6.87
Total Operating Expense	26.33
Net Operating Profit	8.75
Other Income	1.65
Net Profit (Before Federal Income Taxes)	10.40

FIGURE 12-12. Summary of operating ratios of 350 retail hardware stores in 1974. (*Source:* National Retail Hardware Association. Used with permission.)

CHAPTER

13

Cash Management and Budgeting

PERFORMANCE OBJECTIVES

After reading this chapter, you should gain an appreciation of the part played by effective cash management in protecting the profit a business can realize. Specifically, you should be able to:

1. Explain what is included in the term *cash planning*.
2. Discuss the specific activities which contribute to the cash flow in a typical retail operation.
3. Enumerate the circumstances which might justify doing cash planning "in your head."
4. Predict some of the consequences of failure to do effective cash planning.
5. Explain the difference between a forecast and a budget.
6. Discuss the assumptions normally made in preparing a cash budget.
7. Demonstrate the concept of "flexible budgeting" with examples which illustrate how the technique is applied.
8. List the questions which are addressed by a cash budget and demonstrate how the budget provides answers to each question.
9. Develop a listing of expense-control techniques for a retail business and explain how each item impacts profits.
10. Describe the importance of an accurate sales forecast in preparing operating budgets for a manufacturing firm.

INTRODUCTION

Despite respectable sales volumes, many owners of small firms run into financial trouble. Their concern with the operations side of the business causes them to neglect the financial planning required to provide the necessary funds at the right time. Knowing where your cash is coming from and where it will be spent, forecasting cash needs, planning to borrow at the right time, and planning how the borrowed funds will be repaid are all critical to the survival of the business.

Good financial management requires that you know in advance what cash problems you anticipate and that your planning is thorough enough to provide the cash needed to pay your bills. Cash management is essential if a business expects to operate successfully. Your cash position at any given time is an index of your firm's ability to grow. Even though your balance sheet shows total assets to be adequate, there is no substitute for cash for paying your obligations. One of the crucial management functions in any business is that of being prepared at all times to meet the cash demands placed upon the operation.

As your business grows, there will be times when you will need additional funds. You must be able to plan for these requirements. To do this, you need to be familiar with forecasting tools. This chapter offers suggestions for cash planning and control, including the development of budgets which allow you to look ahead and anticipate your financial needs.

WHAT IS MEANT BY CASH PLANNING?

This term refers to the management practice of estimating for some future time period all the sources of cash available to a business and the uses to which this cash will be put. It attempts to pinpoint in a time framework the flow of cash into and out of the business in order to determine in advance whether you will have problems in meeting your cash needs. It generally carries the connotation of committing your financial plans and forecasts to a paper report of some kind, although this is not always done.

The term *cash flow* is used to describe the volume of cash that comes into and goes out of your business during an accounting period. A major element in your cash flow is the volume of cash you realize from normal operation. For this reason, an accurate forecast of sales and a good estimate of money expected from payments on account are very important ingredients in preparing a cash forecast. Unless you have a realistic cash forecast, you might find yourself in continual "hot water" because of insufficient cash. If you do not have money to make payments, you can lose discounts. Some of your suppliers might even curtail credit or services. It is a good idea to forecast the cash flow for your business several months ahead.

IS IT PRACTICAL TO FORECAST CASH NEEDS VERY FAR INTO THE FUTURE?

For businesses using cash forecasts it is unusual to find planning periods in excess of 1 year. One study of 28 small manufacturing companies in the Los Angeles area showed that 35 percent of them prepared cash budgets for 6 months to 1 year ahead, 25 percent for 3 to 6 months, 30 percent for 1 to 3 months, and 10 percent for periods of less than 1 month.[1] The problem with longer periods lies in the fact that changing conditions cause the difference between expectations and actual results to become significant, requiring frequent modifications to make the forecast usable as a planning tool.

WHAT IS INVOLVED IN MAKING A CASH FORECAST?

The important thing to keep in mind about a cash forecast is that it is not a complicated procedure. A simple form like the one shown in Figure 13-1 should be designed. The format is not fixed; it should be designed to meet the specific needs of each business. The forms can be typed, mimeographed, or prepared by hand.

Cash balances at the beginning of the first month are first entered on the form. Next add the receipts which you expect from all sources. Disbursements are usually shown in some detail. These are totaled for the first month and subtracted from "total cash available" to arrive at the cash balance at the end of the month. This figure becomes the cash on hand at the beginning of the second month.

If it appears that the cash position for a particular month will be a negative amount (cash disbursements exceed receipts), you will need to plan how you will meet this shortage in order to avoid a "cash crisis."

By watching cash receipts each week, you can determine whether the forecasted receipts look realistic and, if not, what actions you will need to take to meet the month's financial obligations. Waiting until the crisis is upon you indicates a lack of sound cash planning, which can be avoided. Keep in mind that more businesses fail for lack of cash than for lack of profit.

DOES EVERYONE AGREE ON THE NEED FOR CASH PLANNING?

There are two schools of thought on this subject. One holds that planning for the future is far better than an attitude of "wait and see." Advocates of this view point out that many small businesses do not have sufficient cash or liquid assets to survive repetitive cash crises, which can be minimized by advance planning. According to them, even though many aspects of business operations are subject to chance happenings, chance favors the prepared mind. They feel that cash planning is basic for survival.

Opposed to this theory of required cash planning are those who believe that there is a very low correlation between business success and cash planning. They present rather persuasive arguments to demonstrate that financially healthy companies do not

[1]Joseph C. Shabacker, *Cash Planning in Small Manufacturing Companies*, U.S. Small Business Administration, Washington, 1960.

	January		February		March	
	Estimated	Actual	Estimated	Actual	Estimated	Actual
Cash Balance at Beginning of Month						
Receipts:						
Accounts Receivable Collections						
Cash Sales						
Bank Loans Received						
Other Sources						
Total Cash Available						
Disbursements:						
Accounts Payable Payments						
Hourly Payroll						
Salaried Payroll						
Selling Expenses						
Repair and Maintenance						
Income Taxes (Local, State, Federal)						
General Expenses						
Bank Loan Repayment						
Total Disbursements						
Cash Balance at End of Month						
Less Minimum Balances						
Estimated Cash Available						

FIGURE 13-1. Sample cash forecast form.

have a need for cash projections, that if operations are healthy, there will always be sufficient cash on hand to take care of future financial needs.

In the study previously cited,[2] the chief executive officers of the 28 respondent manufacturing companies, the bankers serving each, and the accountants used by each were asked for opinions relating to the importance of cash planning in business success. Their responses are shown in Table 13-1. Over 50 percent of those responding believe that cash planning contributes more than "mildly" to business success. Roughly half of the presidents responding in this study felt that cash planning was both essential and desirable, another 35 percent felt that it was desirable but not essential, and the balance felt that it was impractical for the small business for a variety of reasons.

TABLE 13-1.   CASH PLANNING IN RELATION TO SUCCESS IN 28 MACHINERY-MANUFACTURING FIRMS

Percent of Total Respondents

Cash Planning	Presidents	Bankers	Accountants
A. Crucial to success	9.4	10.3	4.8
B. Quite important	21.9	24.1	19.0
C. Generally important	46.9	27.5	28.6
Total of top three	78.2	61.9	52.4
D. Mildly contributes	18.7	10.3	23.8
E. Has no bearing	3.1	13.9	19.0
F. No opinion	0.0	13.9	4.8
Total	100.0	100.0	100.0

Source: Joseph C. Shabacker, *Cash Planning in Small Manufacturing Companies*, U.S. Small Business Administration, Washington, 1960.

HOW DOES CASH PLANNING COMPARE WITH OTHER FACTORS WHICH AFFECT SUCCESS IN MANUFACTURING?

Not too well, according to the presidents, bankers, and accountants of the 28 manufacturing firms involved in the Los Angeles study. It ranked a poor fifth behind production efficiency, sales activity, product development, and personnel performance. The ranking of all items contributing to success, based on this limited study, is shown in Table 13-2.

We have no comparable data for retail firms, but we could logically assume cash planning to be more important in an environment where production efficiency and product development are not factors to be considered.

[2]Ibid., p. 126.

TABLE 13-2. RANKING OF ACTIVITIES IN THE ORDER IN WHICH THEY
CONTRIBUTE TO BUSINESS SUCCESS AS REPORTED BY INTERESTED
PARTIES FOR 28 MACHINERY-MANUFACTURING FIRMS

	Activity	Percentage of Time Ranked First, Second, or Third		
		By Presidents	By Bankers	By Accountants
A.	Production efficiency	25.9	34.4	30.0
B.	Cash planning	10.1	9.3	3.3
C.	Sales activity	23.6	26.5	30.0
D.	Product development	14.6	14.1	20.0
E.	Personnel performance	19.0	12.5	13.3
F.	Decisions of big business	0.0	0.0	1.7
G.	Government tax policy	3.4	1.6	1.7
H.	Other	3.4	1.6	0.0
	Total	100.0	100.0	100.0
	Total responses	89	64	89

Source: Joseph C. Shabacker, *Cash Planning in Small Manufacturing Companies*, U.S. Small
Business Administration, Washington, 1960.

IS A WRITTEN PLAN NECESSARY FOR EFFECTIVE CASH PLANNING?

There is no statistical data to indicate what percentage of all small
businesses use formal cash planning which culminates in a written
plan, although less than 30 percent of the manufacturing firms in the
Los Angeles study felt that a written plan was required. Most of the
respondents felt that a mental awareness of cash requirements is
sufficient. In most small businesses, much of the owner's day is concerned with making sales, collecting receivables, and paying bills.
Despite the absence of written plans, most of them are aware of their
future cash needs and do what they perceive to be adequate cash
planning "in their heads." And there is no doubt that many individuals are able to keep the pertinent figures in mind, consider the
actions that may be required, and take the necessary steps at the
right time.

There are special situations where a written cash plan is important to a small business. When owners plan to approach a lending institution for a loan, their success might well depend on their
ability to demonstrate through a detailed cash plan how and when
they expect to pay back the loan. Bank loan officials readily admit
that they are more inclined to make a marginal loan when a cash
forecast is presented as a part of the request.

In any event, it would seem that a written plan which permits
a comparison of last year's performance with this year's or a comparison of this month's planned cash outlays with actual cash expenditures is certainly better than reliance on memory.

WHAT ARE THE RISKS FOR THE OWNER WHO CHOOSES TO IGNORE CASH PLANNING?

This is like asking, How sick should you be before you see a doctor? One author's opinion, based on 2½ years of research on the cash-planning practices of small manufacturing firms, is summarized below:[3]

Decisions to do cash planning then should follow the same line of reasoning which one applies to doctor visits and the use of medicines. If the patient is ill, the sooner and more thorough the diagnosis and the prescription, the higher the probability that he will return to normal health in time. Let the medical care be postponed for too long a period, then no amount of even the best advice and care will save the patient. And, just as an occasional checkup at the doctor's is preventive medicine for a healthy man, the periodic use of a cash plan may easily bring to light some underlying difficulty existing in an otherwise healthy business.

WHAT IS THE DIFFERENCE BETWEEN A FORECAST AND A BUDGET?

A forecast is an estimate of what will happen in the future. It is a first step in the planning process. Forecasting provides a prediction or assumption upon which planning decisions are later made. Economic and financial forecasts are often expressed in terms such as these:

Sales are expected to increase by 5 percent next year.

The prime interest rate is expected to drop to 7 percent during the next quarter.

The cost-of-living index will continue to increase at its present rate.

Spendable income will increase at a rate of 2 percent per year for the next 2 years.

We will maintain our present share of the market for the next year.

Like a weather forecast, each of these statements is an assumption upon which future plans can be based, but the predictions themselves are not plans. The future success of any plans is greatly dependent upon the validity of the assumptions made in the forecast.

A budget is a collection of estimates or a plan concerning action to be taken in the future. The estimates are often stated in monetary values but they need not be. The estimates which make the budget are influenced by the assumptions made in the forecast. If the budget is to bear any relationship to reality, it must be based on some forecast of what the future holds.

[3] Ibid., p. 139.

Budgets are usually prepared for some specific period of time and most of them involve some prediction of costs, income, or profit. For example, a sales budget will project the dollar income expected from sales; a production budget estimates the costs associated with making the product; a selling-expenses budget predicts the cost of selling merchandise.

The budget becomes, in effect, a standard of performance to be accomplished. Once established, management can compare actual experience with the standard represented by the budget and gauge the progress being made. Appropriate action can then be taken to bring performance into line with the budget or to explain the variance.

WHAT GUIDES ASSIST BUSINESS PEOPLE IN MAKING A BUDGET?

Your sales forecast will give you an idea of the amount of merchandise or material you will have to buy. Past experience will tell you what the relationship between sales and material purchases is. If your practice is to pay your bills in time to take advantage of discounts, payments for merchandise will be made in the month after the merchandise is received. Collections on accounts will depend upon your collection policies and your past collection experience. Some portion of credit sales will be collected within 30 days, with smaller amounts becoming cash receipts in the second and third months after the sales are made. Labor costs will be based upon your personnel forecast for the periods covered by the budgets. All other activity contributing to cash inflow or cash expenditures can be examined in the same manner and a determination made as to the month in which the activity will occur. Figure 13-2 shows a sample cash budget for a 3-month period, along with some explanations of where the various figures come from. Since this is a cash budget, credit sales are excluded from consideration. Payments on account, however, are considered cash and are included as part of the data.

The 3-month period used in the illustration represents the last quarter for a firm whose business is seasonal, with sales and related expenses increasing during the holiday season. This period also coincides with the length of the traditional 90-day bank loan. We have shown such a loan, which is needed to cover cash shortages in October and November. It is repaid in December when cash receipts provide a cash surplus large enough to repay the loan.

The significant figures for the manager are the "cash available" or "cash needed" amounts shown on lines 19 and 20. An excess of cash can be invested or used to pay off outstanding liabilities. An alert manager will not allow such funds to remain idle. Cash shortages can be quickly spotted and their magnitude determined in time to arrange for additional funds to be acquired. In this event, the cash budget can be the document offered to the lender to demonstrate both the need for funds and a plan for repayment.

CASH BUDGET

For 3 Months Ending December 31, 19___

Line		October	November	December	Basis of Projection
	Expected Cash Receipts				
1	Cash Sales	$10,000	$12,500	$15,000	Sales forecast.
2	Collections on Accounts Receivable	2,200	2,000	2,500	Base on collection pattern for your business.
3	Other Income	—	—	—	List if applicable.
4	Total Cash Receipts	$12,200	$14,500	$17,500	Sum of lines 1, 2, and 3.
	Expected Cash Payments				
5	Merchandise or Material for Resale	$ 8,500	$10,000	$ 9,000	Forecast. Assume payment in month after delivery.
6	Payroll	2,500	2,500	2,800	Personnel and applicable labor rates.
7	Plant and Equipment	—	250	—	Anticipated repairs purchases, or payments on equipment.
8	Advertising	250	400	400	Your best estimate.
9	Selling Expense	330	400	450	Wages and commissions on expected sales.
10	Administrative Expense	500	500	500	For general office support.
11	Loan Repayments	—	—	1,500	Assume 90-day repayment period for loan.
12	Interest Expense	80	50	50	Your estimate.
13	Other Payments	625	200	200	Utilities, insurance, taxes, etc.
14	Total Cash Payments	$12,785	$14,300	$14,900	Sum of lines 5 through 13.
15	Expected Cash Balance at Beginning of Month	$ 500	$ 1,415	$ 1,615	Last month's ending cash balance.
16	Cash Increase (Decrease)	(585)	200	2,600	Line 4 minus line 14.
17	Expected Cash Balance at End of Month	(85)	1,615	4,215	Line 15 plus line 16.
18	Desired Cash Balance	1,500	1,500	1,500	Your policy.
19	Short-Term Loans Needed	1,500	—	—	Line 18 minus line 17, if line 18 is larger.
20	Cash Available for Short-Term Investment	—	115	2,715	Line 17 minus line 18, if line 17 is larger.

FIGURE 13-2. Sample cash budget with explanatory notes.

You have to prepare the cash budget by the month or quarter since many cash transactions are normally completed within a short time cycle. Some assumptions used in preparing the cash budget are:

1. Sales will not develop evenly over the year since most businesses have seasonal "peaks" and "valleys." Using last year's experience, find out what percentage of your annual sales occurred in each month and use this pattern as a guide in projecting monthly sales for next year.

2. Inventory levels will have to be established to support the monthly sales pattern. If you want enough material in inventory at the end of each month to supply next month's sales, your expenditures for purchased materials and direct labor needed to produce the end item must be related to a production budget which precedes sales by 1 month. If your experience indicates that you need only 35 percent of next month's sales in inventory at the end of this month, your cash budget will use this pattern in time-phasing disbursements for labor and materials.

3. Assumptions relating to accounts receivable will be based on the experience pattern for your business. If you feel that you ordinarily have a collection period of 60 days, the assumption is made that receivables at the end of any given month are equivalent to the sales for the preceding 2 months. Your collection period is the key that tells you when receivables will be converted to cash.

4. Monthly purchases represent a major portion of your cash outflow. In order to time-relate cash expenditures, an assumption must be formulated which describes how you expect to pay your bills. If you intend to take advantage of all cash discounts, this would require you to pay for all merchandise in the month following purchase. The cash budget will be set up to show this pattern.

5. Assumptions regarding planned borrowings will involve the amount to be borrowed, the interest rate, and the length of the loan. Interest on a loan is usually paid monthly or quarterly, with the principal payable in 60 or 90 days in accordance with the loan agreement.

6. Patterns for advertising, selling expense, overhead expense, and payrolls can be estimated from past experience. Your records will yield data that will enable you to make such assumptions as:

    a. Commissions will be calculated at 10 percent of sales.

    b. Gross profit averages 30 percent of sales; therefore, the cost of goods sold is 70 percent of sales.

    c. Overhead expense will run 12 percent of sales.

Whatever assumptions are used in making the cash budget, they should be as realistic as possible. Your past experience will provide a benchmark for forward planning of cash flow; however, you might wish to modify what past experience shows if you believe that there is a likelihood of improved performance in the period ahead. In modifying, it is wise to be conservative and not make too many assumptions about the degree of improved performance.

WHAT QUESTIONS ARE ANSWERED BY A CASH BUDGET?

There are five basic questions which can be answered by a well-prepared cash budget. Here is how the cash budget helps you do a better planning job:

Question	How a Cash Budget Helps
1. Will I need additional money?	If the answer is yes, the cash budget will tell you in time to develop a sound borrowing program and to plan for the implementation of money-saving approaches. If the answer is no, it might indicate the existence of surplus cash, which you can plan to invest.
2. When will I need it?	A cash budget will indicate the time period when cash outflow exceeds income and give you time to plan for alternate courses of action instead of responding to a "crisis" when it happens.
3. How long will I need it?	The duration of the cash emergency is shown in a cash budget. This will tell you whether short-term or intermediate-term funds are needed.
4. How much cash do I need?	The cash budget allows you to look ahead several months and determine total cash needs. This allows you to borrow just what you need without incurring excessive indebtedness. You can accurately anticipate seasonal business needs and talk to your banker in terms of specific amounts, not generalities.
5. How can I repay borrowed cash?	The cash budget will indicate the time when cash surplus will be sufficient to repay all or part of the loan, allowing you to show a workable plan of debt repayment to a prospective lender.

WHAT IS SUGGESTED BY THE TERM *CASH MANAGEMENT*?

Cash management consists of setting up controls which prevent questionable practices in the receipt and disbursement of business funds. It suggests safeguards to prevent theft or misuse of funds while they are being used in the day-to-day operation of the business. It includes, but is not restricted to, the following practices:

- Cash receipts should be deposited daily during banking hours or in a night depository. It is considered bad practice to keep large sums of money in your store overnight.

- Never make cash payments out of cash receipts. Use prenumbered checks to pay bills, and be sure all checks are accounted for, whether issued or voided. Voided checks should be kept and filed.

- For safety purposes, have all incoming mail—in which there might be checks, cash, or money orders—opened by someone other than the person responsible for handling the store's money. In this manner, employees will know that all money will pass through more than one person's hands before being deposited. In a very small firm, temptation is minimized since the owner is often personally involved in cash control.

- The practice of drawing checks to "cash" and predating or signing checks in advance are symptoms of lax cash management. Nothing is more vulnerable to abuse than cash. It should be rigidly controlled. Checks should be drawn to the order of the firm or a responsible employee, and blank checks should not be signed in advance of use.

- The amount of money kept in the petty cash fund should be kept reasonably small and should be used only for making small expenditures not exceeding a stated amount. Only enough cash should be in petty cash to cover needs of a week or two. Never deposit "surplus" cash in petty cash rather than deposit it in a bank. You should set up your petty cash fund by drawing a check on your bank funds. Replenish it the same way when necessary.

HOW CAN BUDGETING HELP YOU DO A BETTER JOB OF FINANCIAL MANAGEMENT?

Budgeting replaces guesswork with meaningful data which has resulted from thoughtful consideration of the unique variables making up your business. Well-prepared budgets ensure profitability by providing "early-warning" signs of trouble, permitting you to take action before it is too late. Budgets enable you to measure actual performance against a standard and exercise control by identifying profit leaks and eliminating them.

The importance of budgeting is often overlooked by small business people who prefer to spend their time on business operations. One author has warned of the possible effects of such a course of action:[4]

Few, if any, techniques are more vital to the sound management of a manufacturing enterprise than budgeting. But many smaller companies unwisely neglect or ignore this simple, effective tool. Yet, smaller compa-

[4]Howard Ellsworth Sommer, *Budgeting in the Small Plant*, Management Aids for Small Business, No. 23, U.S. Small Business Administration, Washington.

nies have a great need for it because of a pressing need for profitable utilization of working capital, and for the development of sound plans for meeting future competition and for expanding.

There seems to be a high degree of correlation between business failure and the inability or unwillingness of business owners to exercise proper control over the financial aspects of their businesses. Budgeting provides assurances that:

☐ You have a safety signal which quickly tells you where you are out of control.

☐ Responsibility for efficient performance is assigned to those who spend the money.

☐ Profit is protected since spending is kept within the limits of income.

☐ All phases of your business have been subjected to close scrutiny to be sure that profit leaks are minimized.

☐ You are prepared to talk to your banker about loans, with a definite plan for repayment outlined.

HOW MANY DIFFERENT KINDS OF BUDGETS ARE THERE?

Some sources list at least 30 different kinds of budgets commonly found in manufacturing companies. Only very large manufacturers will normally spend the time and money to develop all of them. We can condense this number to a dozen basic budgets:

1. The sales budget
2. Cost-of-goods-sold budget
3. Selling-expenses budget
4. Administrative-expenses budget
5. Budgeted income statement
6. Budget of collections of accounts receivable
7. Production budget
8. Budget of direct material purchases
9. Payment-on-purchases budget
10. Direct-labor budget
11. Manufacturing-overhead budget
12. Cash budget
13. Budgeted balance sheet

Normally, a retailer will not even use all of these budgets. Budgets 7, 8, 10, and 11 are peculiar to manufacturing firms. This would leave nine remaining budgets which are applicable to retail operations. Some businesses will use only a cash budget.

WHAT CAN BE DONE TO KEEP THE PROFIT-AND-LOSS STATEMENT "HEALTHY"?

A good start is the maximization of sales and the minimization of expenses. We have pointed out previously that volume in itself carries no guarantee of profits. What is needed is a careful examination of the expenses to determine which ones can be controlled and execution of the steps necessary to establish some standards of performance, supplemented by reports which show how well your performance measures up. Some of the expenses reflected in the profit-and-loss statement which are subject to control are shown in Figure 13-3.

TABLE 13-3. COMPARISON OF SALES AND NUMBER OF EMPLOYEES
FOR THE JOHNSTON CITY DISCOUNT STORE

Month	Sales	Employees
May	$ 50,000	25
June	40,000	21
July	60,000	30
August	70,000	38
September	50,000	23
October	90,000	46
November	80,000	42
December	100,000	51

HOW CAN YOU DESIGN A BUDGET TO RESPOND TO WIDE VARIATIONS IN VOLUME?

It is not always possible to know what level of volume will be attained during the year. Seasonal variations in retail firms often cause wide fluctuations in the sales volume, characterized by peaks during December, for example, followed by a significant drop in January when the traditional "white sales" are promoted to bolster the dropping volume. A fixed budget would not be realistic in such cases. To have a meaningful standard, we need a budget with some flexibility—one which can be adjusted to any volume level. Such a budget would allow business owners to determine whether their companies are operating within the budget during the seasonal peaks as well as the seasonal valleys.

The development of a "flexible budget" depends upon the fact that some expenditures show a close correlation with volume,

Item on Profit-and-Loss Statement	Suggestions for Improvement	
1. Sales	*a.*	Train clerks and salespeople in sales techniques.
	b.	Provide incentive or bonus plans for sales personnel.
	c.	Maintain effective promotions and advertising.
	d.	Push high-margin merchandise.
	e.	Drop low-volume, low-margin items.
2. Cost of Goods Sold	*a.*	Get competitive bids on merchandise you buy.
	b.	Take advantage of cash discounts.
	c.	Look for better terms on special-quantity purchases.
	d.	Keep a cash reserve which will enable you to take advantage of special cash "buys."
	e.	Use the most economical means of transportation.
3. Employees' Wages	*a.*	Set up a good training program. Increased productivity will give you more for your wage dollar.
	b.	Be more selective in hiring people.
	c.	Establish an acceptable ratio of sales to wages paid.
	d.	Consider part-time help for busy periods.
4. Occupancy Expense	*a.*	Check for heat losses. Insulate to keep them down.
	b.	Turn down heat and air conditioning before the end of the day, on weekends, and at night.
	c.	Use light-colored ceilings and walls.
	d.	Investigate costs of various lighting systems.
	e.	Keep store size appropriate for sales volume.
5. Advertising	*a.*	Use the best medium for the best response.
	b.	Use free supplier displays which fit in with your merchandising plan.
	c.	Investigate cooperative advertising.
	d.	Check with your postmaster on bulk-mail rates.
6. Insurance	*a.*	Consult your agent about variable coverage—special rates for off-season coverage.
	b.	Review your coverage at least annually to reduce duplication of coverage or excessive coverage.
7. Selling Expense	*a.*	Learn what territories and/or products are most profitable. Concentrate on these.
	b.	Wherever possible, have sales representatives document travel expenses by means of a credit card. This prevents expense-account "padding."
	c.	Establish records showing "sales dollars per call" or similar performance standards.
	d.	Cut out customer "extras" you cannot afford.
8. Bad-Debt Losses	*a.*	Select credit customers carefully.
	b.	Establish a well-defined, effective collection policy. Be firm with delinquent accounts.
	c.	Keep your ratio of credit to cash sales within reasonable limits for your type of business.
	d.	Send out monthly statements on time. Send reminders to customers with past-due accounts.

FIGURE 13-3. Expense control for items affecting the profit-and-loss statement.

which permits us to establish budgets for different levels of operation. We can illustrate this concept by examining the number of employees in a retail firm and comparing the number, month by month, with sales. Such a comparison is shown in Table 13-3. It is apparent from the data that when sales increase, more employees are needed and the budget should be increased. During the slowest month (June), 21 employees were on the payroll and sales were only $40,000. The biggest month was December, when sales were 2½ times those in June, and 51 employees were needed. We can describe the relationship between the high and low months in the following manner:

Month	Sales	Employees
December (high)	$100,000	51
June (low)	40,000	21
Difference	$ 60,000	30

$$\frac{\$60,000}{30} = \$2,000 \text{ of sales per employee}$$

The relationship between sales and employees required is assumed to be constant for all months in using the "high-low" method to establish the sales-per-employee ratio. We can convert employees to dollars and establish a labor-dollar budget at any level with the information we have developed. Assuming the average employee makes $400 per month, we can establish the following flexible budget:

TABLE 13-4.   FLEXIBLE LABOR BUDGET FOR THE
JOHNSTON CITY DISCOUNT STORE

Monthly Sales Volume	Number of Employees	Monthly Payroll Budget
$ 10,000	5	$ 2,000
20,000	10	4,000
30,000	15	6,000
40,000	20	8,000
50,000	25	10,000
60,000	30	12,000
70,000	35	14,000
80,000	40	16,000
90,000	45	18,000
100,000	50	20,000

Flexible budgets can be developed for other variable expense items in the same manner. This technique is not used for fixed costs since they have no variable component.

A factory illustration provides an ideal situation for showing the usefulness of the flexible-budgeting technique as a management tool. Significant variations in manufacturing activity from month to month make a static budget impractical.

Preparing a flexible overhead budget requires that you first decide on a reasonable, normal level of production on which to base the assignment of overhead costs. You then estimate overhead costs for that level of activity, sometimes called the *control volume,* and for other levels of activity lower than the control volume. It is necessary that you identify your overhead costs as fixed or variable.

The control volume for assigning overhead costs will be somewhere below the theoretical maximum level of activity. If, for example, the factory operates on a 40-hour week, and 47 workers are needed to keep every machine operating at full capacity, the total regular worker-hours expended each week will be 40×47 or 1,880 hours. Annually this would amount to 97,760 hours (assuming a 52-week year). We know that machine breakdowns, delays, personal time, and absences of employees will make it impractical for us to base our "normal activity level" on the theoretical maximum. We must, therefore, reduce the maximum to a realistic planning number. In examining our production records, we find that the absentee rate averages around 5 percent of scheduled hours. Another 3 percent of scheduled hours is lost because of delays, and an additional 2 percent is needed for setup time (getting the machines ready for producing parts). We can subtract this 10 percent nonproductive time from the total and get 87,984 hours per year as our normal activity level. We will identify this level as our control volume and assign a value of 100 percent of normal capacity to it.

We now estimate the overhead costs for the factory when it is operating at control volume. Fixed costs are based on known values and remain the same at all volume levels.

Next we must determine, either from past history, use of scattergrams, or our knowledge of the cost behavior of the variable items, how much to budget for each activity level. Payroll taxes and payroll insurance are assumed to vary in exact proportion to changes in production levels. Other costs, because they are semivariable, do not vary exactly as production levels do because their fixed component causes them to decrease at a slower rate than volume decreases.

In Table 13-5, we can see the relationship between direct-labor hours and total overhead costs at all levels of activity. This relationship is described by the "overhead rate per direct-labor hour" appearing at the bottom of the table. We can see that our overhead costs are $1 per direct-labor hour at the control volume, but that overhead costs become proportionately higher as volume decreases, because the fixed component of the overhead does not change with changes in volume.

TABLE 13-5.   OVERHEAD BUDGET FOR THE YEAR 19___

	70	80	90	100 = Control Volume
Percent of Normal Maximum Direct-Labor Hours	61,589	70,387	78,986	87,984
Fixed Costs:				
Depreciation	$15,000	$15,000	$15,000	$15,000
Supervision	18,125	18,125	18,125	18,125
Rent	6,700	6,700	6,700	6,700
Insurance	2,750	2,750	2,750	2,750
Taxes	4,245	4,245	4,245	4,245
Total Fixed	$46,820	$46,820	$46,820	$46,820
Variable Costs:				
Indirect Labor	$17,000	$18,750	$20,625	$22,500
Supplies	2,388	2,622	2,938	3,250
Small Tools	2,875	3,050	3,622	4,000
Power	2,688	2,800	3,150	3,500
Maintenance	2,250	2,525	2,812	3,075
Payroll Taxes	2,188	2,500	2,812	3,125
Payroll Insurance	1,050	1,200	1,350	1,500
Total Variable	$30,389	$33,447	$37,309	$40,950
Total Budgeted Overhead	$77,209	$80,267	$84,129	$87,770
Overhead Rate per Direct-Labor Hour	$1.25	$1.14	$1.05	$1.00

SELF-CHECK OF KEY CONCEPTS

This exercise is designed to test your understanding of the material presented in Chapter 13. Choose the response, *True* or *False*, which best fits each statement. Correct responses are presented in the back of the text.

1. Cash planning does not always culminate in a written plan.
2. Most cash forecasts are prepared for 1 year ahead.
3. Operating executives, bankers, and accountants are in agreement regarding the importance of cash planning.
4. In manufacturing, production efficiency is considered more significant than cash planning in its contribution to business success.

5. A cash budget and a cash forecast are the same thing.
6. Credit sales are not included as sales income in the cash budget.
7. Blank checks should not be signed in advance of the time they will be used.
8. A "flexible budget" is practical only for retail firms since they show the widest variations in volume of any type of business.
9. Bank loan officials are more inclined to make a marginal loan when a cash forecast is presented as a part of the request.

1. The Whiz-Bang Toy Company has hired you to prepare a cash budget by quarter for next year. Its manufacturing activities are heavy in the second and third quarters in anticipation of Christmas sales. Selling and administrative expenses are incurred throughout the year on a relatively uniform level. The sales forecast for the coming year shows:

First quarter (January–March)	$150,000
Second quarter (April–June)	250,000
Third quarter (July–September)	400,000
Fourth quarter (October–December)	85,000
	$885,000

The beginning balance of receivables from the last quarter of last year is $30,000, which is expected to be collected in the first quarter of the following year. Subsequent collections are made 50 percent in the quarter in which the sales are made and 50 percent in the quarter following.

Direct labor is incurred and paid in each quarter as follows:

First quarter	$ 40,000
Second quarter	75,000
Third quarter	60,000
Fourth quarter	45,000
	$220,000

Material purchases are scheduled as follows:

First quarter	$ 70,000
Second quarter	70,000
Third quarter	60,000
Fourth quarter	40,000
	$240,000

Factory overhead is paid in cash in the quarter in which it is incurred. This expense is basically fixed except for indirect supplies. Expenditures by quarter are:

First quarter	$ 47,500
Second quarter	53,000
Third quarter	51,500
Fourth quarter	48,000
	$200,000

Selling and administrative expense is planned in the amount of $20,000 per quarter throughout the year. Taxes, insurance, and rent total $62,000 for the year and are paid in four equal quarterly amounts.

The company plans to maintain a minimum cash balance of $5,000. Any amounts borrowed are to be in multiples of $1,000. Loans will be repaid as soon as cash is available, provided that the minimum cash balance is not affected. Interest is at 8 percent. Assume that any borrowing is made at the beginning of a quarter, and the repayments made at the end of a quarter.

The beginning cash balance is $6,000. Complete the cash budget for the Whiz-Bang Toy Company.

CASH BUDGET
Whiz-Bang Toy Company

	1st Quarter	2d Quarter	3d Quarter	4th Quarter
Cash Balance	$6,000			
Cash Receipts:				
Accounts Receivable (last year)	$30,000			
Current Sales				
Previous Quarter Sales				
Total Receipts				
Cash Available				
Less Expenditures:				
Material				
Direct Labor				
Factory Overhead				
Selling/Administration				
Rent/Insurance/Taxes				
Total Expenses				
Ending Balance				
Add Cash Borrowed				
Less Loan Repayment				
Less Interest Paid				
Ending Cash Balance				

FIGURE 13-4. Cash budget for the Whiz-Bang Toy Company.

2. Harriet's Gift Shop offers a selection of specialty items during the Christmas season. Last year she offered Christmas stockings filled with 1-ounce chocolate bars (foil-wrapped) which

were purchased in bulk from a candy manufacturer. Each stocking contained 32 bars (2 pounds) and sold for $2.50. An identical stocking filled with 2 pounds of mixed unshelled nuts sold for $1.50 each. The sales last year were brisk in these items, so Harriet is planning to offer them again this year during November and December.

It is near the end of October, and pre-Christmas forecasts indicate that consumer spending is up about 8 percent over last year. Statistics from trade association publications show that retail sales for the first 9 months are up 6 percent over a similar period a year ago. Based on her best feel, Harriet believes she can sell 10 percent more of these specialty items than she did last year. She needs to order the merchandise in order to have it in stock by November 1. Here are the statistics she has to work with:

Selling price per pound:
Candy $1.25
Nuts   0.75

Purchase cost:
Candy   0.60 per lb.
Nuts   0.40 per lb.
Stockings   0.10 each

Last year's sales:

	November	December	Total
Candy (pounds)	2,000	3,000	5,000
Nuts (pounds)	1,500	1,000	2,500

Based on the information given above, calculate the following:

a. Budgeted sales of candy in pounds and dollars for November and December.
b. Budgeted sales of nuts in pounds and dollars for November and December.
c. Total pounds of candy to be ordered and its cost.
d. Total pounds of nuts to be ordered and their cost.
e. The cost of stockings needed for both items.
f. The gross margin Harriet will realize if she sells everything she buys.

1. Ever since Tom Dawson read about break-even analysis in a Small Business Administration booklet he bought, he has been excited about using this tool in his business. "This is the greatest thing since the wheel was invented," he excitedly told a business associate who was unfamiliar with its use. "As long as you stay above the break-even point, everything is okay," he said, "because the break-even concept covers all the financial aspects of sound business operations."

a. What do you think of Tom's theory?
b. Can you think of anything he has overlooked in the financial control of his business?

2. Sam Owens has been doing business with Midvale Bank for all of the 8 years he has been in business. He is miffed because his banker refused to approve a business loan without more detailed information about Sam's financial condition. Sam felt that the Schedule C from his federal income tax return told the whole story about the financial condition of his business.

   a. What information do you think the banker needs?
   b. Do you think Sam's attitude is justified?

3. Jenny Donovan operates a successful small business and is planning to buy some new equipment and expand her operations. Both her accountant and her banker have suggested making a cash budget for a 1-year period to be sure she is not taking on more than she can handle. Privately, Jenny cannot see the reason for such an exercise. "My profits for the last 2 years have been above the average for businesses like mine," she reasons, "so why do I need to spend money to prove it? Success speaks for itself."

   a. Do you agree with Jenny's thinking?
   b. What problems could Jenny be inviting?

CHAPTER

14

Risk Management and Insurance

PERFORMANCE OBJECTIVES

After reading this chapter, you should be able to develop a list of risks faced by small business owners which could result in losses to the business, and decide the courses of action open to them to minimize the losses associated with the risks. Specifically, you should be able to:

1. Defend a business owner's decision not to insure some risks.
2. Explain the differences between eliminating risks, minimizing them, shifting them, and absorbing them.
3. Determine which risks are speculative risks and which are pure risks.
4. Explain the problems related to the self-insurance concept for small business owners.
5. Assess the possible effect of erroneous statements made on an application for insurance.
6. Demonstrate the principle of indemnity and explain how it keeps the insured from making a profit on his or her insurance.
7. Defend the principle of coinsurance in fire insurance policies.
8. Evaluate the significance of the risks which are covered by business interruption insurance.
9. Outline a program of risk management for a small business, indicating various ways of obtaining adequate coverage while keeping the costs reasonable.

INTRODUCTION

Risk is as much a part of running a business as it is in our personal lives. Each of us takes risks in driving to work, traveling on public transportation, eating at a restaurant, performing our assigned jobs, and working around our homes. Each year more than 100,000 people are accidentally killed in the United States, and for each death ten additional persons are injured. We are constantly reminded by daily newspaper stories of the losses which result from the risks we take each day. To minimize the losses from such occurrences, we drive carefully, observe laws, employ safety devices of various kinds, utilize reliable and safe transportation, keep our cars repaired, and buy insurance.

Business risks are just as common as the personal risks we have enumerated. They consist of potential losses, damages, and injuries that can be disastrous to businesses if not insured against. Such risks as fire hazards, burglary and theft, accidents to customers and employees, losses from bad debts, interruptions to the business, and loss of key personnel are always present. They cannot be ignored any more than profit leaks, poor quality, or substandard performance can.

Risk management consists of identifying the kinds of risks present and evaluating the courses of action which are open to eliminate them, minimize them, shift them, or absorb them. This chapter will discuss the different kinds of insurance available, explore just what insurance is, and explain what insurance can and cannot do for small business owners.

WHAT IS MEANT BY THE TERM *RISK* IN THE BUSINESS SENSE?

Risk can be defined as uncertainty. Two major types of risks have been identified—pure and speculative.

Pure risk exists when a person is faced with a situation in which there is only the possibility of loss. Thus the occurrence of a fire, windstorm, a flash flood, the death of a key employee, or a lawsuit brought by a customer cannot be determined with any degree of certainty and generally causes nothing but loss. Since it is most unusual for these perils to bring about a gain, they may be classified as pure risks. In general, you can do nothing about pure risk. It exists whether you like it or not. Just by owning a gun, you are confronted with the risk of having an accident. Just by owning a building, you are similarly confronted with the possibility of a fire or damage from any one of the elements.

Speculative risk exists when a person is faced with a situation in which there is the possibility not only of loss but also of gain. Investments in common stock, real estate, or a small business are examples of situations that can produce either a profit or a loss. In speculative risk, you can choose whether or not you will "take the chance," and you decide how much risk you wish to assume. The risk is something over which you can exercise some degree of control. For this reason, you usually cannot obtain an insurance policy against such risk. Otherwise, no matter how poorly you ran your business, you could insure yourself against the risk of losing your capital and thus obtain a guarantee against failure.

HOW DOES INSURANCE REDUCE THE RISKS FACED BY A BUSINESS?

The main value of insurance lies in its reduction of the pure risk you face in your business operations. Purchasing insurance gives you the opportunity to trade a large but uncertain loss for a small but certain loss (or expenditure) called a *premium*. You trade uncertainty for certainty; that is, you reduce your risk. Insurance reduces worry, stimulates initiative, frees funds for investment, prevents loss, and makes credit easier to obtain. But all these values come from one central value—risk reduction.

WHY COULDN'T YOU SET ASIDE ENOUGH FUNDS TO COVER YOUR RISKS?

One way to appreciate just what insurance does for you is to imagine what steps you would have to take to handle pure risk if insurance were not available. For example, suppose you were told that every year one building in a thousand burned to the ground. Assume that you want to take some steps to prevent such a loss and guarantee that you will be able to continue in business if your building should be the one that burns.

Now let us assume that the value of your property and its contents is $25,000. This amount would include your inventory and equipment. How much money should you set aside each year to replace any loss by fire? $500? $1,000? $2,000? If the figure is $500 per year, it would be 50 years before your fund would be big enough to make a full replacement. Assuming you have a full loss, this amount would probably not be adequate to replace the loss. Even if it were adequate, what guarantee would you have that a similar loss would not occur the next month? The so-called "law of averages" does not protect you against such a possibility. The loss can strike anywhere at any time. If the loss occurs the second or third time, your fund would be exhausted several times over. In most locations, commercial insurance protects you against a $25,000 fire loss for less than $200 annually.

ARE THERE SOME SITUATIONS WHERE INSURANCE IS IMPRACTICAL?

There are certain situations in which business people should not use commercial insurance even if it is offered. For instance, if the potential loss is trivial, even if the peril should occur, there is no point in insuring it. What is trivial depends upon the financial resources of the business. For a very big business a loss of $1 million might not be a severe financial loss because the firm might have more than $1 billion of exposed values. Such a firm might properly self-insure its first $1 million of loss. On the other hand, a small business firm might feel that a loss of even $1,000 might be too much to bear. Such a firm would need outside protection even if the probability of loss is very small.

If the cost of purchasing commercial protection is so high that the premium constitutes a substantial proportion of the value of the exposed property, the question arises whether the insurance should be purchased. It is surprising how often this seemingly simple point is overlooked. Many people with old automobiles often insure them against collision at a cost ranging up to 20 percent of the replacement value. In addition, many owners purchase $50-deductible collision insurance when they could save $35 annually by purchasing $100-deductible coverage. The owner is paying $35 for $50 of extra coverage or 70 percent of the possible recovery in the event of a single collision during the policy term. This is very high insurance.

ARE THERE OTHER WAYS OF DEALING WITH RISK BESIDES BUYING INSURANCE?

Yes. Besides insurance, there are at least four recognized ways of dealing with risk:

- □ Doing nothing about it (noninsurance)
- □ Loss-prevention programs
- □ Transfer of risk to others
- □ Self-insurance

Although noninsurance sounds risky, most businesses find that they must inevitably assume some pure as well as speculative risks. Trying to acquire coverage against every possible contingency is impractical for most businesses. Yet it is foolhardy to assume large risks when reasonably priced commercial coverage is available. You should assume the risk only when the severity of the potential loss is low. Noninsurance should be restricted to risks that are more or less predictable, preventable, or largely reducible. It is ideally suited to risks which are essentially "business risks."

Loss-prevention programs are designed to reduce the probability of loss, thereby indirectly reducing the risk. Programs to prevent theft, prevent fire, keep workers from getting injured on the job, provide better building construction, and protect health usually reduce the cost of operating a business. A loss-prevention program seldom eliminates all losses, but it does reduce their frequency substantially and permits commercial insurance to be purchased at reasonable costs.

Transfer of risk to persons other than commercial carriers is often both feasible and economical. For example, you can transfer to others the result of loss resulting from automobile accidents by leasing all your vehicles under an agreement whereby the lessor maintains all the insurance. The lease device can also be applied to personnel, buildings, equipment, and other property. The same principle applies when you purchase the services needed for your operations instead of hiring your own personnel. By this method, you eliminate the direct costs of personal insurance such as hospitalization, workmen's compensation insurance, and group life and group health insurance which are ordinarily provided for employees carried on your payroll.

In self-insurance you set aside funds which are adequate for certain losses as they occur. If a separate fund is not set aside, the working capital of the business should be large enough to meet losses without causing the business to resort to borrowing. Under this plan accounting reserves should be established for expected losses. Self-insurance is not the solution for an underfinanced firm trying to save money which it would otherwise pay out for commercial insurance premiums. Responsibility and authority to supervise the self-insurance program is usually centered in one person, who supervises the loss-prevention programs, keeps records of losses, supervises payment of losses to those departments suffering them, and decides when it is more cost-effective to buy commercial insurance to cover risks rather than to provide self-insurance. Note that self-insurance differs from noninsurance in that in noninsurance you assume a risk and do nothing about it.

WHAT HAPPENS IF YOU MAKE INACCURATE STATEMENTS ON YOUR APPLICATION FOR INSURANCE?

A statement given by the person seeking insurance coverage is called a *representation*. Discovery of false or inaccurate representations considered to be material to the risk permits the insurer to void the contract. Failure of the insured to divulge material fact is called a concealment and also permits the insurer to void the contract when it is discovered.

Statements made on your application for insurance are of great importance to the insurer because they are the chief source of information used by the insurer to decide whether or not to accept you as a risk. Complete honesty on the part of the insured is required, and breach of this standard can endanger your coverage.

CAN YOU COLLECT INSURANCE FOR A BURGLARY IF YOUR ALARM SYSTEM WAS NOT WORKING ON THE NIGHT OF THE BURGLARY?

If a statement that the burglar alarm would be kept in good repair is made by the insured and incorporated into the written policy, it then becomes a warranty, breach of which allows the insurer to void the contract. If the breach of warranty is proved after the burglary occurs, the insurer can refuse to pay the claim. This is true even if the burglary was not aggravated or caused by the inoperative alarm system. It suffices for the insuring company to prove on examination that a warranty was breached.

HOW CAN YOU TELL IF YOUR INSURANCE POLICY IS CANCELED BY THE INSURER?

Insurance contracts may either be canceled or not renewed upon given notice to the insured, or they may not be canceled except for nonpayment of premium. In general, most property and liability insurance contracts are cancelable at the option of the insurer upon due notice, but life insurance policies are not cancelable once they are in force. This helps to explain why life insurance agents usually are not given authority to bind coverage, although property and liability agents are given such authority. In accident and health insurance, some policies are cancelable, and some are noncancelable.

WHAT HAPPENS TO THE INSURANCE ON A BUILDING WHICH IS NO LONGER OWNED BY THE INSURED?

If you are the owner of a building and hold property insurance on it naming you as the insured, and later sell the building to someone else, you no longer have an insurable interest in the building. If the policy is not transferred to the new owner, he or she cannot collect if the building burns because the insurance was never transferred and issued to him or her personally. Thus, you should be especially careful about how the insurance policy is issued, who is named as the insured, and who is named as beneficiary of the proceeds if the beneficiary is someone other than yourself.

CAN YOU INSURE A BUILDING WORTH $10,000 FOR $20,000?

Yes, but in the event the building is totally destroyed you can collect only your actual cash loss, and not the amount named in the policy as the policy limit. This is known as the *principle of indemnity* and works like this: Actual cash loss is generally determined by applying a reasonable allowance for depreciation against the current replacement cost of the building. A building costing $10,000 to replace with new materials might be thirty years old. If the building has depreciated to only 20 percent of its original useful life, the building would be worth only 20 percent of its replacement value. If the structure were completely destroyed, only $2,000 could be collected. Otherwise, the insured would be obtaining "new for old" and would be profiting by the insurance. It is possible for you to purchase "replacement cost" insurance which gives you "new for old," but at a higher premium price.

HOW IS THE VALUE OF A LIFE DETERMINED FOR A LIFE INSURANCE POLICY?

It has never been considered feasible to determine the actual cash value of an insured life for the purposes of insurance. Therefore, the insurer must pay the entire face value of the policy upon the death of the insured, without regard to the "value" of that individual. Courts in the United States have for many years taken the position that a person may place any value on his or her life for purposes of insurance. A person's life is irreplaceable, and it is assumed that no great hazard exists that an insured will take his or her own life for purposes of collecting insurance. If this should happen, however, the suicide clause applies, and the insurer's only obligation is to return the amount of the premiums the insured had paid. If one person negligently takes the life of another, the insurer cannot proceed against the former under any subrogation rights because the life insurance policy does not provide this right. From the above legal principles, it can be seen that for purposes of life insurance bought for a legitimate business reason, a business firm may place any value that it wishes upon the life of a key employee.

IS IT POSSIBLE TO TAKE OUT LIFE INSURANCE ON THE LIFE OF A BUSINESS PARTNER?

A partner or stockholder in a business firm can take out insurance on the lives of other partners or stockholders in any reasonable amount, depending upon the specific circumstances.

CAN YOU BUY TWO POLICIES TO INSURE A LOSS AND COLLECT ON BOTH?

No, you cannot. Often you will have more than one type of policy which applies to a given loss. If these policies happen to be contracts of indemnity (as most property and liability insurance contracts are), each will contribute to the loss in the proportion that the applicable coverage of each contract bears to the total coverage. Thus, if you have five policies of $10,000 each insuring a $50,000 building, each policy will contribute one-fifth of any loss up to $50,000.

The pro rata liability principle reinforces the indemnity principle. If it were not for the pro rata liability clause, it would be possible to overinsure a building by purchasing several policies whose total value would exceed the actual loss and to collect several partial losses in excess of the total loss.

WHAT PURPOSE IS SERVED BY DEDUCTIBLES ON AN INSURANCE POLICY?

Many insurance contracts use deductibles. The deductible may take the form of a percentage of loss or a specified dollar amount. In some contracts, the deductible may take the form of waiting periods. In others, it is subtracted from the loss settlement that would otherwise be payable or from the value of the insured property. Deductibles serve definite purposes. One purpose is to discourage overinsurance. In general, they permit you to bear part of the loss yourself in return for a reduction in premium. The reason for the savings made possible by deductibles lies in the fact that they often exclude small losses which are very costly to adjust and which are very frequent. Insurance is often not a suitable device for handling such small, frequent losses.

IF YOU CARRY $30,000 INSURANCE ON A BUILDING WORTH $50,000, WHAT HAPPENS IF A FIRE CAUSES $10,000 DAMAGE?

In fire insurance and related lines, the coinsurance clause is widely used. It requires you to carry a specified amount (percentage) of insurance, based on the value of the insured policy, or bear part of a partial loss yourself. The required amount is usually 80 to 90 percent of the actual cash value of the property. This does not mean, as is commonly supposed, that if you are required to carry 80 percent "to value" and fail to do so, you must bear 20 percent of the loss. It means that if you carry, for example, 60 percent to value when you are required to carry 80 percent, the insurer will pay six-eighths of any partial loss and you will pay two-eighths of the loss.

WHAT PERILS ARE COVERED AND EXCLUDED IN THE STANDARD FIRE INSURANCE POLICIES?

Fire insurance is standardized throughout the United States. The basic policy is nearly identical in every state. The standard fire policy contains an insuring clause; 165 lines of stipulations and conditions that govern both your basic insurance contract and the additions—called extensions or endorsements—that are commonly attached to the policy; and an attachment, known as the *form*, which describes the property being insured.

The standard fire policy, excluding any endorsements, insures you for only three perils: fire, lightning, and losses to goods temporarily removed from your premises because of a fire. You must pay for any additional perils by adding extensions to the basic policy.

The policy excludes theft, actions resulting from war or orders of civil authority, and negligence by the insured in using all reasonable means to save property after a loss. Coverage is suspended if the hazard to your business is increased by any means within your control, if your property is vacant for an extended period, or if an explosion or riot occurs, unless fire results, in which case the loss from the fire is covered. Thus the policy suspends your coverage if you increase the hazard by running a dry-cleaning plant in your basement or if you change the basic nature of your business to one more hazardous. If you have occasion to change the basic nature of your business and have the slightest doubt that the new business activities are covered by your policy, it would be well to check.

The individual states regulate fire insurance rates and license organizations known as rating bureaus to inspect most business properties for which insurance is sought. The rating bureaus, representing individual insurers, develop a rate for each building which is generally followed by the insurer. Things like sprinkler systems which make your building more fire-resistant earn you extra credit in the rating. If your building is exposed to another less fire-resistant structure or if your stock is especially susceptible to loss by fire, you will be required to pay additional charges, called *exposure charges*.

Loss experience in given territories determines fire rates. All cities having more than 25,000 population are surveyed periodically and rated in classes—in descending order from 1 to 10—according to adequacy of water supply, fire departments, alarm systems, hazard ordinances, and the like. In each city, the rates charged correspond roughly to the rating class assigned.

CAN YOU GET BUSINESS INSURANCE COVERAGE FOR RIOTS AND CIVIL COMMOTION?

Yes, you can get this with an extended coverage endorsement to the basic fire insurance policy. This endorsement does not add to the face amount of the policy but merely extends the perils covered by the policy—windstorm, hail, explosion, riot, riot attending a strike, and civil commotion. Aircraft damage, vehicle damage, and smoke damage may also be covered in the endorsement. The endorsement further defines the limits of each of these perils. For example, smoke loss refers only to that caused by sudden, unusual, and faulty operation of any heating or cooking unit. It excludes smoke damage from a fireplace or from industrial apparatus.

IF A CUSTOMER FALLS AND INJURES HIMSELF OR HERSELF IN YOUR STORE, ARE YOU LIABLE FOR DAMAGES?

In conducting your business, you are subject to the rules of common and statutory law governing negligence to customers, employees, and anyone you do business with. Negligence may be defined as failure to exercise the degree of care required under the circumstances. For example, your firm is expected to maintain a safe place for customers to enter. If one of your customers falls on a slippery floor, you may be held liable for damages even if you have posted signs warning of the danger. It is not a defense to say that your failing to exercise due care was unintentional. Generally, in accidents on business property or accidents arising out of business operations, there is a strong presumption that negligence exists. Failure of business people to recognize the danger they face by not carrying liability insurance can be one of the most serious errors they could make. One liability judgment could easily wipe out the entire assets of a firm and cause its liquidation.

WHAT LIMITATIONS ARE IMPOSED ON PAYMENTS FOR LIABILITY POLICIES?

Liability policies limit payments in several ways. The comprehensive general liability policy contains a limit per person and a limit per accident. For instance, a contract may specify that it will pay $100,000 per person injured, or a total of $300,000 for any one accident. If two persons are injured in a single accident and are awarded judgments of $150,000 each, the policy will pay a total of only $200,000 because of the limit of $100,000 per person. Other policies have a single limit which applies to both bodily injury and property damage. There is usually an aggregate limitation of products liability that applies to any one batch of bad products. If a business owner who carries a $25,000 policy on products may be responsible for the sale of spoiled food resulting in 50 claims of $1,000 each, his or her policy treats this as a single "accident" and will pay only $25,000, the limit of liability stated in the policy.

WHAT KINDS OF INSURANCE ARE AVAILABLE FOR THE VEHICLES USED IN A BUSINESS?

There are two basic kinds—liability insurance and physical damage insurance.

The basic principles of liability insurance apply to the liability small business people may incur in owning and maintaining or using an automobile. Business firms are often legally liable for the use of trucks and passenger cars even though they do not own any. This happens when employees or subcontractors use their own cars on behalf of their employers. You are usually liable for an accident that occurs when your employees use rented or leased vehicles, or when an employee is operating a car belonging to customers. The various kinds of automobile liability policies provide protection for specific business uses.

Almost all automobile owners carry insurance for damages from collision, fire, theft, and other physical perils. Insurance for physical damage is of several kinds. You can usually insure collision damage separately from other types of losses. Collision insurance does not cover glass breakage and damages from falling objects, flying missiles, windstorm, hail, malicious mischief, and vandalism. You can insure all types of physical loss except collision by taking out a "comprehensive" policy. It excludes only losses from wear and tear; loss to tires (unless owing to fire, malicious mischief, or vandalism, or arising from a collision); loss from radioactive contamination; and loss from freezing or from mechanical or electrical breakdown. You are covered if any of these losses results from theft.

If you do not want to buy automobile comprehensive insurance, you can cover separate perils. For example, you can buy fire and theft insurance at rates somewhat below those for comprehensive insurance. Theft insurance not only covers loss of your car by theft, including all damage done by thieves if the car is later recovered, but also pays you $10 per day for loss of use, with a limit of $300. Coverage for loss of use begins after a 3-day waiting period and ceases when the insurer offers to settle with you for the lost vehicle.

WHAT INSURANCE DO YOU NEED TO COVER YOUR EMPLOYEES?

Common law requires that employers provide their employees a safe place to work, hire competent fellow employees, provide safe tools, and warn their employees of any existing danger. If they fail in these duties, they are liable under both common law and workmen's compensation laws for damage suits brought by an employee. Every employer, therefore, needs protection for both kinds of liability.

Under a workmen's compensation and employer's liability policy, the insurer pays all sums you are legally obligated to pay because of your common law liability; and it agrees to pay all compensation and other benefits that the applicable workmen's compensation law requires you to provide.

State laws determine the kind of benefits payable under workmen's compensation policies. The insurer does not determine the level or type of benefits. Most such laws provide medical care to the injured worker; lump sums for dismemberment and death; benefits for disablement by occupational disease; and income payments for a disabled worker or his or her dependents. In some cases, the income payments might last as long as the worker is disabled, even if it is for life.

Premiums for workmen's compensation are based on the insured's payroll, as determined by audit at the end of the policy year. Rates vary from 0.1 percent of the payroll for "safe" occupations to about 25 percent of payroll for very hazardous occupations. In most states, employers can lower their premium cost by reducing their accident rate below average by means of safety and loss-prevention measures.

HOW CAN BUSINESS OWNERS PROTECT THEMSELVES AGAINST THEFT AND EMBEZZLEMENT?

Each year, thefts by employees probably amount to several times the loss from burglary, robbery, and larceny. Embezzlers often steal small amounts over a period of years, eventually draining large sums from their employers. Small business people should consider the use of fidelity bonds to protect themselves against this unpredictable hazard.

Fidelity bonds protect you against a most serious potential loss, one which most small business people can seldom afford. Requiring your employees to be bonded often discourages stealing, which might otherwise occur. The character investigation conducted by the bonding company sometimes discloses unfavorable facts about an employee's honesty, enabling you to take steps to prevent potential losses.

Fidelity bonds differ from insurance policies in two major ways. First, the insurance policy covers only two parties: the insured and the insurer. The fidelity bond concerns three: the employee who is bonded, called the *principal*; the person or firm protected, called the *obligee*; and the licensed bonding corporation or insurance company, called the *surety*. Second, if the principal steals, the surety must immediately pay the obligee. The surety, however, has the right to attempt to recoup its losses.

CAN YOU GET INSURANCE AGAINST CRIMES SUCH AS BURGLARY AND ROBBERY?

Burglary insurance, covering your safes and inventoried merchandise, is the most basic protection you can get against crime losses from "outsiders." It covers only those cases in which visible marks of the burglar's forced entry are left. It does not cover your losses from sneak thieves who come in through an open window and leave no trace of their burglaries. The policy also covers damage incurred in the course of a burglary. It excludes loss of such property as manuscripts, accounts, or fur articles in a showcase window.

Robbery insurance protects you from loss of property, money, and securities by robbery either on or off your premises. Robbery is defined as taking property from a person in charge of it by force or threat of violence. Typical policies also cover property on your premises that is damaged by robbery. You can select different limits of liability for robbery outside or inside your premises and for robbery of your payroll or other money.

To most business people, crime insurance is the least familiar of the various types of insurance. Available figures indicate that business losses from criminal acts exceed all property losses from fire each year. Thus, the peril to your firm caused by crime is very serious. In some instances, robbed firms unprotected by insurance have had no alternative but liquidation.

HOW CAN YOU BE SURE THAT ALL YOUR MAJOR RISKS ARE COVERED BY INSURANCE?

By buying an "all-risk" policy. This type of insurance was developed and offered after World War II. It offers considerably improved protection to the typical purchaser of fire insurance and related lines. All-risk policies cover all perils except those specifically excluded by name. Such a policy prevents the duplication which sometimes results from purchasing several different named-peril policies. By thus eliminating overlapping coverage you can save money and get better service since only one agent will be handling your business. In addition, the time you spend in supervising your insurance program is reduced because you handle all coverage in one action.

Usually, all-risk policies do not cover buildings but offer various forms of protection for personal (movable) property. Three basic types of policies are available for business firms:

□ The commercial property insurance policy gives most retail and wholesale firms all-risk protection on stocks of goods.

□ The industrial property insurance policy gives manufacturing establishments all-risk protection on stocks of goods.

□ The inland marine floater policy is designed for specialized types of retailers and wholesalers such as jewelers, furriers, launderers, and equipment dealers.

CAN YOU INSURE AGAINST LOSSES AND EXPENSES INCURRED WHILE YOUR BUILDING IS BEING REPAIRED AFTER EXTENSIVE DAMAGE?

If you have had the foresight to buy business interruption insurance and the interruption is caused by property loss from an insured peril, the answer is yes. Such indirect losses are frequently even more severe in their eventual cost than direct losses from such perils as fire. Consider what can happen if you are forced to close your business for 2 or 3 months following a serious fire. You might have full insurance on losses to raw materials, goods in process, finished goods, furniture and fixtures, and machinery and buildings. But while rebuilding, you must continue to pay salaries of key employees and such scheduled expenses as taxes, interest, depreciation, and utilities. Without earnings from production and sales, you would be in serious difficulty. Business interruption insurance was developed for this kind of situation. All small business owners should find out about the type of protection it offers them.

WHAT KINDS OF SPECIAL-PURPOSE INSURANCE ARE AVAILABLE?

Listed below are the principal types of special-purpose insurance:

Power Plant Insurance. This type of insurance is sometimes called boiler and machinery insurance. It protects you against losses caused by explosions of furnaces, steam boilers, engines, and electrical equipment. The standard fire policy generally excludes explosions of this type, and the potential for such losses often goes unrecognized until an accident takes place.

Glass Insurance. Insurance against the peril of glass loss has increased in recent years. Property covered includes plate-glass windows, glass signs, motion-picture screens, glass bricks, glass doors, and insulated glass panels. The comprehensive glass policy is used for most business firms. It provides all-risk coverage on glass— excluding only fire, war, and nuclear destruction. It is assumed that the firm's fire insurance policy will cover any loss to glass from fire. The insurer generally elects to replace glass losses immediately instead of making a dollar settlement. In this way, you are quickly protected against other property damage that might result because the glass is broken.

The comprehensive glass policy covers damage to glass and its lettering or ornamentation by breakage, repair or replacement of frames when necessary, installation of temporary plates or boarding up of windows when necessary, and removal or replacement of any obstructions used in replacing the glass. Loss in all but the first is generally limited to $75 per occurrence. No dollar amount of liability is stated.

Credit Life Insurance. Credit life insurance is generally used by retail firms selling goods on credit to final consumers. The amount of life insurance is automatically adjusted to the size of the outstanding debt. Therefore, the amount of the policy is sufficient to repay the debt if the customer dies before repaying his or her loan. Coverage on an individual account expires as soon as the individual debt is repaid. Credit life insurance is a suitable and desirable form of coverage if you sell on installment terms, and it is an inexpensive way to handle the risk of death among your debtors. It is also a service to your debtors because it relieves the debtor's estate of the obligation to repay the debt.

Rent Insurance. Several different kinds of rent insurance cover loss of use of real property damagd by fire or other peril. If you rent a building and your lease calls for continued payments even if a fire makes the building untenantable, you can obtain coverage for this loss. On the other hand, if the lease calls for canceled or reduced rental payments, the owner can cover his or her loss of income with a different kind of insurance policy.

Sprinkler Leakage Insurance. Most business firms can reduce their fire insurance rates substantially by installing an automatic sprinkler system. But sprinklers introduce a new hazard: accidental leakage or discharge of water from the sprinkler heads or broken pipes. Such a loss can happen without a fire or other insured peril having occurred. Depending on the type of goods exposed, it can cause substantial damage.

You can apply sprinkler leakage insurance to your own property or to the property of employees or customers in the building covered. The exposure to loss by sprinkler leakage is not considered as serious as the fire peril because the loss is usually confined to a smaller area. Coverage is suspended when the building is vacant or unoccupied and during the completion of repairs or alterations involving walls or supports of a floor or roof.

WHAT ARE SOME OF THE WAYS OF REDUCING THE COST OF ADEQUATE INSURANCE COVERAGE?

First, formulate and write down a clear statement of your insurance philosophy. This will help clarify your thinking in regard to what you will insure and what means you will take to plan for the common risks. After you have done this, decide which of the different kinds of risk protection will work best for you. Investigate methods such as loss prevention, self-insurance, and noninsurance to see if they offer better approaches to your needs than buying commercial insurance coverage.

Second, cover your largest loss exposure first, the less severe as your budget permits. Use your premium dollar where the protection need is greatest. For instance, it is unwise to insure your business vehicles for collision and neglect to buy liability insurance. Liability judgments can bankrupt a firm; collision losses seldom are large enough to cause bankruptcy.

Third, make proper use of deductibles. In many lines of insurance, full coverage is not economical because of the high cost of covering the "first dollar of loss." But if you cannot afford a $1,000 loss, do not select a deductible of this amount. Reduce the deductible to the amount you can afford.

Fourth, check the market occasionally to see if you are getting your insurance for a reasonable price. You should not switch insurers each time a lower price is quoted, but you should be aware of the "going rate" for the kinds of coverage you require.

Fifth, analyze insurance terms and provisions. When an insurer offers to sell you coverage for less than you are paying, find out why. Often you will discover that the hazard you want to insure is not covered because of a technicality or that the insurer can only reduce the premium by reducing the services and settlement policy.

Sixth, insure the proper exposure. One firm purchased coverage by bonding its employees who handled cash but did not bond those who handled material. One in the latter group stole large amounts of materials, causing serious and extensive financial loss, which was not covered by insurance, to the company.

Finally, do everything possible to keep your losses down. This will give you the advantage of lower insurance rates. Although you might be fully covered, the noninsurable indirect losses resulting from the occurrence of any peril can be a severe drain on your funds. Invariably such losses come at the most inconvenient times, and they often exceed the initial estimate of the amount of business lost and the extent of interruptions in normal business activities.

SELF-CHECK
OF KEY
CONCEPTS

This exercise is designed to test your understanding of the material presented in Chapter 14. Choose the response, *True* or *False*, which best fits each statement. Correct responses are presented in the back of the text.

1. Pure risk exists when a person is faced with the possibility not only of loss but also of gain.
2. You usually cannot obtain an insurance policy against speculative risk.
3. In most locations, commercial insurance protects you against a $25,000 fire loss for less than $200 per year.
4. Noninsurance should be restricted to risks that are predictable, preventable, or reducible.
5. Self-insurance and noninsurance are different names for the same thing.
6. Life insurance policies are not cancelable once they are in force.
7. It is not possible to purchase insurance coverage which will replace an old building, if it is destroyed, with a new one.
8. A person may place any value on his or her life for purposes of insurance.
9. Basic fire insurance policies are standardized throughout the United States.
10. The standard fire policy insures you for only three perils: fire, lightning, and loss of goods removed from your premises because of fire.
11. You cannot collect on burglary insurance unless there is evidence of forced entry.
12. The deductible on an insurance policy you buy should not exceed the amount you can afford to lose if the loss occurs.

PERFORMANCE
PROBLEMS
AND
PROJECTS

1. Under the provisions of a coinsurance clause, the insured business owner agrees to carry insurance equal to some specified percentage of the value of the property in return for a lower rate. Payment for loss is made under the coinsurance provision on the basis of the following formula:

$$\frac{\text{Amount of insurance actually carried}}{\text{Amount the insured is required to carry}}$$

$$\times \text{ amount of loss} = \text{amount paid}$$

If you own a business building with a current depreciated value of $100,000 and insure it with a 70 percent coinsurance provision, you must have coverage equal to 70 percent of the actual cash value at the time the loss occurs in order to collect the full value of the loss. Knowing this, you insure the building for $70,000.

Five years later, a shopping center has caused the value of your building to increase to $140,000. Before you can sell the property, a fire causes a loss of $50,000 to the building.

- ☐ How much can you collect from your insurance?
- ☐ What kind of insurance should you have bought to protect your $140,000 property to its full value?
- ☐ What lessons can be learned from this illustration?

2. Talk to a local fire and casualty insurance agent in your community and discuss with the agent the kinds of insurance he or she offers to small business people. Find out what problems are most frequently encountered, and what kinds of insurance he or she recommends to clients.

3. Contact two or three business people in your community and discuss their insurance coverage with them. Find out why they buy the kinds of insurance they do. Ask if they have had any loss not covered by insurance. Report your findings to the class.

4. Listed below are several risks which are often faced by small business owners. A good loss-prevention program can *eliminate* some of them. Losses from others could be *absorbed* by the business. Others should be covered by *insurance* because of their potential for causing severe financial hardship if a loss occurs. For each risk, indicate what action you could take to minimize or eliminate it by using the terms *Eliminate, Absorb, Transfer,* or *Insure.* If you show that the risk can be eliminated, tell how you would accomplish this. If you can transfer the risk to someone else, state how you would get another party to assume the risk.

 a. Fire
 b. Faulty wiring
 c. Theft by employees
 d. Machinery obsolescence
 e. Delivery truck accidents
 f. Damage to window glass
 g. Accidents to customers
 h. Loss of inventory value because of falling prices
 i. Loss of records
 j. Loss of market because of population shifts

1. Roberto Ruiz acquired an auto repair business 10 years ago with an appraised value of $100,000. He bought a fire insurance policy with an 80 percent coinsurance requirement and bought coverage for $80,000. Business properties appreciated in value about 5 percent per year each year since Roberto started his business.

 a. If he were to have a serious fire now, would his insurance cover the loss?
 b. What could Roberto have done to preclude the possibility of becoming a coinsurer to a serious extent?

MINICASES IN POINT

2. Tim Higgins was a mechanic in Roberto Ruiz's garage. His specialty was sports cars. Last month, while overhauling a car, he needed a rebuilt carburetor which was available from the parts department of a sports car dealer whose shop was located a couple of miles across town.

"Roberto, I need to use the garage truck to pick up a carburetor for the job I'm working on," Tim said as he strode into Roberto's office.

"Sonny took it over to Central City to pick up a new transmission," Roberto replied. "I doubt if he will be back until after lunch. Why don't you take your car and we'll reimburse you for the gas."

"Okay," Tim said. "Be back in a half hour."

On the way Tim swerved to avoid hitting a dog in the road and piled his hot rod into a light pole, throwing him from the vehicle. Police at the scene called an ambulance to take Tim to Mercy Hospital's emergency ward where he received treatment for shock, a dislocated shoulder, and a broken arm. Subsequent treatment was required and Tim's total bill came to $746. He was unable to pay it.

a. Who is legally responsible for Tim's hospital expenses?
b. Are there any circumstances under which an employer can be held liable?

3. Frieda Schneider was the secretary to Larry Greene, owner of a successful manufacturing firm. She was entrusted with a $300 petty cash fund and was solely responsible for its safekeeping. Every Friday before closing she unobtrusively removed $100 from the fund and used it to bet on the horses during the weekend at the local track. She had every intention of replacing the money but often after a bad weekend found it impossible. Unable to stop the practice, she continued until a routine audit by an independent firm 3 years later disclosed the irregularities. After questioning by Mr. Greene and the auditor, she tearfully told the whole story. The auditor was able to estimate the loss at $7,300.

Was there any way that Mr. Greene could have protected himself from such a loss? Explain how.

4. Acme Fiberboard Products manufactures boxes, cartons, liners, and special-order containers for commercial users. Until this year they were having trouble getting enough business to assure a profitable operation. After a long search they hired a new sales manager, Ken Whitman. He had a good record as sales manager with a firm selling similar products. The $45,000 salary they paid him was quite a bit more than what his predecessor was making, but he soon put to rest any questions about his ability to produce. Within a year he had captured three big new accounts for the firm and through many personal contacts had doubled sales by the end of the second year.

The company was elated. The board of directors elected Ken to a vice-presidency. Plans for a plant expansion were under way when he unexpectedly suffered a fatal heart attack. During the next year, a 25 percent drop in sales caused cancellation of any expansion plans. It took 18 months to find a suitable replacement.

Is there any way a company can protect itself against such a disaster?

15

Managing Credit Sales and Collections

PERFORMANCE OBJECTIVES

After reading this chapter you should understand the significance of credit-granting and credit-collection policies and their effect on the profit a business can realize. You should be able to explain how a firm's credit policies affect its collection procedures and to appreciate the amount of planning required to establish a workable approach to credit management. Specifically, you should be able to:

1. Evaluate the importance of promptness in collecting overdue accounts.
2. Discuss the relationship between a firm's credit policies and its collection policies.
3. Evaluate the logic in arranging the steps to be used in a collection procedure in a specific sequence.
4. Discuss the growth of consumer credit during the past 10 years and explain its impact on small business owners.
5. List and discuss some of the problems inherent in the collection process.
6. Differentiate between collection approaches which can be used with customers who are "good risks" and those who are "poor risks."
7. Discuss the concept: The longer an account is on the books, the harder it is to collect.
8. Discuss the advantages which credit cards offer to the small business owner.

9. Explain the difference between open-end credit and closed-end credit.
10. Illustrate the cost to merchants of carrying installment sales on their books.

INTRODUCTION

The wide use of customer credit in operating today's business has made it almost impossible for small business people to ignore credit as an inducement for building a clientele. Credit to customers can help build a business in many ways. Yet offering credit privileges to customers is not without its risks. Judgment and experience must enter into every decision.

Extending credit and making collections from credit customers are activities which fall into an area generally termed *credit management.* Owners must not underestimate the necessity of becoming knowledge-able in the techniques of extending credit, determining credit limits, "aging" accounts receivable (finding out how long they are outstanding), handling late payments, and collecting overdue accounts. They must train themselves in credit and collection management and understand the effect of such management upon their current and long-range business activities.

This chapter explores some of the problems associated with credit management and provides suggestions which will be helpful in placing this important facet of business management into proper perspective.

WHAT IS CREDIT?

Credit is the privilege extended by a seller to a buyer to provide goods and services in exchange for the promise to pay a specific amount on some future date. Sometimes a limit is placed on the amount of credit a seller is willing to grant. The terms of repayment are usually stipulated in a written agreement which is signed by the debtor. Consumer credit is extended by retailers to their customers, whose purchases occur over an extended period of time, making it necessary for the retailers to keep accurate records indicating who owes them money, how much is owed, and how long it has been owed. Business credit is extended by wholesalers and manufacturers to their customers, which are other business firms that buy supplies or services from them.

Credit implies trust that the payment will be made. The element of risk is that customers will not pay, or will be so slow in paying that their creditors must find other sources of working capital. This is unprofitable for the creditors.

Credit is a part of the characteristics of individuals that cause you to trust them to do whatever they promise, so far as they are capable. It is this habitual making good on promises which develops into the valuable personal trait of credit worthiness. If customers possess this trait, merchants and bankers will ordinarily trust them to perform as they promise, although they might not know them personally.

Owners of small firms, whether retail, wholesale, or manufacturing, must understand the part played by credit in running their businesses. It is estimated that about 90 percent of all sales made by manufacturing and wholesale firms are credit sales. Almost half of all retail sales are on credit. Since working capital is vitally important to the operation of a business, large amounts of capital tied up in accounts receivable can cause severe cash problems if collections are slow. Therefore credit management is particularly important.

Through trade credit extended by the supplier, a small business is allowed to buy merchandise on credit and pay for it later—without paying interest on the amount involved. This practice of "borrowing" against future sales income literally keeps small businesses alive and makes it possible for them to borrow with impunity for short periods of time.

Between 1950 and March of 1974, the amount of outstanding consumer credit in this country grew from $21.5 billion to $177.6 billion, an eight-fold increase. During this same period, the percentage of disposable income used for consumer credit jumped from 10.4 to 19.1 percent (almost doubled). The most rapid growth in the use of credit by consumers has been in installment buying. Table 15-1 shows the growth for each year from 1950 to 1974 and breaks down the installment and noninstallment categories into their components.

IS IT BETTER TO BUY ON CREDIT OR TO BORROW MONEY AND PAY CASH?

Most people have definite opinions about this. Many openly boast that they "pay cash for everything" and are convinced of the merits of their choice. To be fair, however, we should point out some contrary attitudes held by customers and merchants which indicate that the answer to this question is not an easy one.

To begin with, consumers have shown that they do not always consider cost in itself the most important reason for deciding to buy something on credit. If they habitually shop in the area, it might be more convenient to go back to the store when they make a payment rather than make a separate trip to a lending institution. Visits to the store serve the purpose of cementing their acquaintances with the store, which is important if they plan to make additional purchases there. The record of their prompt payments there creates an atmosphere of mutual trust and friendship, which they find satisfying and pleasing.

From the merchant's viewpoint, it is commonly believed that repeat visits from credit customers paying their bills will cause them to buy additional merchandise and continue to patronize the store where they have established their credit. This characteristic is not always found in customers who pay cash. They are not tied to the

TABLE 15-1. CONSUMER CREDIT: 1950 TO 1974*

Type of Credit	1950	1955	1960	1965	1968	1969	1970	1971	1972	1973	1974 Mar.
Credit outstanding	21.5	38.8	56.1	89.9	110.8	121.1	127.2	138.4	157.6	180.5	177.6
Ratio to disposable personal income (percent)	10.4	14.1	16.0	19.0	18.7	19.1	18.4	18.6	19.8	20.5	19.1
Installment:	14.7	28.9	43.0	70.9	87.7	97.1	102.1	111.3	127.3	147.4	145.8
Automobile paper	6.1	13.5	17.7	28.4	32.9	35.5	35.2	38.7	44.1	51.1	50.3
Other consumer goods paper	4.8	7.6	11.5	18.5	24.6	28.3	31.5	34.4	40.1	47.5	46.5
Home improvement loans	1.0	1.7	3.1	3.7	4.2	4.6	5.1	5.4	6.2	7.4	7.4
Personal loans	2.8	6.1	10.6	20.2	25.9	28.7	30.3	32.9	36.9	41.4	41.5
Noninstallment:	6.8	9.9	13.2	19.0	23.0	24.0	25.1	27.1	30.2	33.0	31.8
Single-payment loans	1.8	3.0	4.5	7.7	9.5	9.7	9.7	10.6	12.3	13.2	13.2
Charge accounts	3.4	4.8	5.3	6.4	7.2	7.4	8.0	8.4	9.0	9.8	7.9
Service credit	1.6	2.1	3.3	4.9	6.3	6.9	7.5	8.2	9.0	10.0	10.7
Installment credit:											
Extended	21.6	39.0	50.0	78.7	100.0	109.1	112.2	124.3	143.0	165.1	13.2
Repaid	18.4	33.6	46.1	70.5	91.7	99.8	107.2	115.1	126.9	145.0	13.4
Net change	3.1	5.3	3.7	8.2	8.3	9.4	5.0	9.2	16.0	20.1	-0.2

*In billions of dollars, except percent.
Source: *Statistical Abstract of the United States 1974*, U.S. Department of Commerce, Bureau of the Census.

store with a credit account and are not so likely to return unless persuaded by costly advertising and promotion to do so. It does not cost as much in advertising to bring back credit customers. Cash customers sometimes complain that credit customers seem to get preferential treatment—an observation which is often true. Merchants know from experience that once customers have established credit and have learned for themselves the treatment they can expect, they are likely to return. No retailer cares to lose a good credit customer to a competitor through some failure to give satisfaction.

HOW CAN YOU TELL WHETHER IT IS PRACTICAL TO OFFER CONSUMER CREDIT?

The kinds of goods you sell must be considered in any decision you make about selling on credit. If your merchandise is mostly small, low-value merchandise or merchandise which is nondurable (i.e., will last only a short time), credit sales are not practical. Most customers do not want to be bothered with using credit for small sales. They also resent having to continue payments over a long period of time after the merchandise is worn out and discarded. If you are selling a repair service such as air conditioning, TV or auto repair, your customers might prefer to pay for such services by the month. Installment purchases of major consumer goods is also popular because customers can enjoy the merchandise while they are paying for it.

The second thing to consider is the amount of capital you will need to finance credit sales, especially installment purchases. When you offer installment selling, you are offering long-term credit for 90 days or longer. Even though the customer pays for this privilege in a service charge, carrying installment purchases might cost more money than you can afford. Unless you can get the money to carry you until the income from installment accounts is received, you might run short of cash.

If your competitors are offering customer credit, you might have to do it too. There is no doubt that credit terms attract customers. If you have no choice, try to make your plan as attractive as possible.

One last item to check. Some states have regulations regarding installment selling. Check your state's laws to determine what kinds of merchandise are covered and how the law will affect your business.

WHAT ARE SOME OF THE PROBLEMS ASSOCIATED WITH GRANTING CREDIT?

Merchants who decide to extend customer credit should be aware of some of the problems they will face:

☐ Granting too much credit, causing financial problems related to insufficient working capital.

- Bad credit risks resulting from failure to evaluate the credit standing of new customers.
- Credit customers' abuse of the returned-goods privilege.
- Added cost of borrowing because of too liberal a credit policy.
- Added costs associated with operating the credit and collection systems. The true cost of credit can greatly exceed the income from finance charges.

Bad-debt losses can develop even when the best efforts have been made to evaluate the risks. Unsound decisions in credit and collection management can be a step on the road to bankruptcy.

WHAT KINDS OF CONSUMER CREDIT ARE OFFERED TO BORROWERS?

Credit transactions can be classified by type of credit and by type of lender.

Type of credit generally includes single-payment loans and installment loans. You may arrange a single-payment loan for a small or large sum of money. You promise to repay the entire loan, with interest, in one payment according to the terms of the contract, which may specify repayment in 30, 60, or 90 days or longer. Installment loans are generally used for large items of durable goods such as automobiles, boats, major household appliances, and the like. The items under normal use will last a number of years beyond the repayment period. Repayment terms are typically offered up to 36 months. Longer periods are usually granted for such items as mobile homes. Such loans are paid in weekly or monthly payments. Some loans are made on the borrower's signature; others require the borrower to pledge assets of some kind as collateral to secure the loan.

Type of lender covers two major types, retail firms and financial institutions, which are subdivided as shown in Figure 15-1.

Installment-credit loans shown in Figure 15-1 can be either open-end arrangements, where the customer can go on making new purchases under the original agreement, or closed-end, where the customer is granted credit for a fixed amount over a fixed period of time. In open-end transactions, new purchases are added to the outstanding balance up to a ceiling the lender has prescribed. A finance charge may be imposed on the unpaid balance in the manner spelled out in the agreement. Open-end accounts are often called *revolving* or *option* accounts. Closed-end arrangements are normally used for big-ticket items.

WHAT ARE THE STEPS INVOLVED IN GRANTING CREDIT?

Every firm should have a procedure which it follows in granting credit. Since a customer who uses credit is using the firm's capital, it is assumed that customers will be willing to comply with reason-

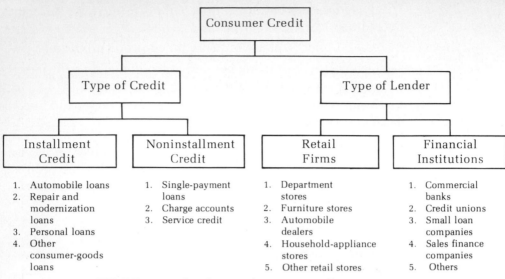

FIGURE 15-1. Classification of consumer credit transactions.

able rules governing the extension of credit. Granting credit is a serious responsibility. It should be approached with the objective of protecting the interests of both the creditor and the debtor. The following guidelines will provide such assurance.

1. Have all credit solicitors submit a credit application. Figure 15-2 shows a sample form used by a large retail merchandiser.

2. Check the applicant's credit history with the local credit bureau, or with other stores the applicant has done credit business with. The applicant's bank should also be contracted for any information regarding his or her character or financial background. If an applicant is denied credit based on a credit-bureau report, you are required under Public Law 51-508 to give the customer the name and address of the credit bureau.

3. Based on the information obtained in steps 1 and 2, evaluate the applicant's potential as a credit risk. Willingness to pay must be judged by evaluating the character of the applicant, whose ability to pay will depend upon his or her earnings, his or her other debts, and the prevailing economic conditions. Buyers have credit worth related to their willingness and ability to pay. Sellers must determine the extent to which they are willing to take the risk that credit applicants might be unable or unwilling to pay their accounts when they are due.

4. If you are convinced of the applicant's potential for paying his or her bills, you next need to determine how much credit to ex-

SEARS, ROEBUCK AND CO.
CREDIT ACCOUNT APPLICATION

INSTRUCTIONS: IF YOU ARE APPLYING FOR AN INDIVIDUAL ACCOUNT IN YOUR NAME AND A SUBSTANTIAL PART OF THE INCOME ON WHICH YOU ARE RELYING AS A BASIS FOR CREDIT IS DERIVED FROM YOUR SPOUSE OR FORMER SPOUSE, PLEASE OBTAIN THE WRITTEN AUTHORIZATION OF YOUR SPOUSE OR FORMER SPOUSE IN ORDER TO ALLOW SEARS TO INVESTIGATE HIS OR HER CREDIT RECORD. A SPACE FOR THIS AUTHORIZATION IS PROVIDED BELOW IN THE BLOCK HEADED "INFORMATION ON APPLICANT'S SPOUSE OR FORMER SPOUSE". THIS AUTHORIZATION IS A REQUIREMENT OF THE FEDERAL FAIR CREDIT REPORTING ACT. (NOTE: IF YOU ARE PRESENTLY MARRIED AND YOUR INCOME IS DERIVED **SOLELY** FROM THE INCOME OF YOUR SPOUSE, THIS APPLICATION SHOULD BE COMPLETED IN THE NAME OF YOUR SPOUSE.)

NAME AND ADDRESS OF CREDIT APPLICANT – NAME IN WHICH ACCOUNT IS TO BE CARRIED

COURTESY TITLES ARE OPTIONAL

☐ MR.   ☐ MRS.   ☐ MS.   ☐ _____

PLEASE PRINT

First Name _____ Middle Initial _____ Last Name _____

Street Address _____

City _____ State _____ Zip Code _____

If applicant's spouse and/or others are authorized to buy on the account, print names here.

AUTHORIZED BUYERS

SPOUSE: _____

First Name   Middle Initial   Last Name

OTHERS: _____

First Name   Middle Initial   Last Name

First Name   Middle Initial   Last Name

INFORMATION ON CREDIT APPLICANT

MARITAL STATUS: REQUIRED ONLY IF APPLICANT'S SPOUSE IS AUTHORIZED TO BUY ON THE ACCOUNT OR IF APPLICANT RESIDES IN A COMMUNITY PROPERTY STATE. COMMUNITY PROPERTY STATES INCLUDE: ARIZONA, CALIFORNIA, IDAHO, LOUISIANA, NEVADA, NEW MEXICO, TEXAS, AND WASHINGTON.   ☐ MARRIED   ☐ UNMARRIED   ☐ SEPARATED

Phone No:
Home _____
Business _____ Age _____ Soc. Sec. No. _____

Number of Dependents _____ (Excluding Applicant)

How Long at Present Address _____   Own ☐   Rent-Furnished ☐   Rent-Unfurnished ☐   Board ☐   Monthly Rent or Mortgage Payments $_____

Name of Landlord _____ Street Address _____ City and State _____

Former Address (if less than 2 years at present address) _____ Street Address _____ City and State _____ How long _____

Employer _____
How long _____ Occupation _____ Net Income $_____ Monthly ☐ Weekly ☐

Former Employer (If less than 1 yr. with present employer) _____ How long _____

Other Income, If any: Amount $_____ **Note: Income from alimony, child support or maintenance payments need not be disclosed unless relied on as a basis for credit.** Source of other income _____

Name and Address of Bank _____ Savings ☐ Checking ☐ ☐ Loan Acc't No. _____

Previous Sears Account ☐ Yes ☐ No   At What Sears Store _____   Account No. _____   Is Account Paid in Full ☐ Yes ☐ No   Date Final Payment Made _____

Relative or Personal Reference Other than Spouse _____
(Name)   (Street Address)   (City and State)   (Relationship)

CREDIT REFERENCES

Charge Accounts Loan References Store/Company Address	Name Account Carried In	Account Number	Balance	Monthly Payments	Comments

SEARS IS AUTHORIZED TO INVESTIGATE MY CREDIT RECORD AND TO VERIFY MY CREDIT, EMPLOYMENT AND INCOME REFERENCES.

SIGNATURE OF APPLICANT _____ DATE _____

INFORMATION ON APPLICANT'S SPOUSE OR FORMER SPOUSE

ONLY PROVIDE THE FOLLOWING INFORMATION IF APPLICANT'S SPOUSE IS AUTHORIZED TO BUY ON THE ACCOUNT OR IF APPLICANT IS RELYING, AS A BASIS FOR PAYMENT: ON INCOME FROM SPOUSE ☐; ON ALIMONY, CHILD SUPPORT OR MAINTENANCE PAYMENTS ☐; OR ON COMMUNITY PROPERTY IF APPLICANT RESIDES IN A COMMUNITY PROPERTY STATE ☐. COMMUNITY PROPERTY STATES INCLUDE: ARIZONA, CALIFORNIA, IDAHO, LOUISIANA, NEVADA, NEW MEXICO, TEXAS, AND WASHINGTON.

Name of spouse (or former spouse) _____ Address _____ City and State _____ Age _____

Employer _____ Street Address _____

How long _____ Occupation _____ Soc. Sec. No. _____ Net Income $_____ Monthly ☐ Weekly ☐

Name and Address of Bank _____ Savings ☐ Checking ☐ ☐ Loan Acc't No. _____

AUTHORIZATION TO INVESTIGATE CREDIT RECORD OF APPLICANT'S SPOUSE OR FORMER SPOUSE. SEE THE INSTRUCTIONS AT THE BEGINNING OF THIS APPLICATION.

SEARS IS AUTHORIZED TO INVESTIGATE MY CREDIT RECORD AND TO VERIFY MY CREDIT, EMPLOYMENT AND INCOME REFERENCES. _____

(Signature of Applicant's spouse or former spouse)   Date

FIGURE 15-2.   A credit application used by a major merchandiser. (Source: Courtesy of Sears, Roebuck and Co.)

tend. This will depend on his or her debt position, income level, and financial resources. The credit limit is set so that the customer will not buy beyond capacity and by so doing jeopardize his or her credit standing.

5. Establish terms of payment with the customer, stipulating the amounts to be repaid and when payment is expected. The time for which credit is extended on open accounts is frequently 1 month, with payments due by the tenth of the month for the previous month's purchases. Periodic review of credit limits should be made and the limits revised when necessary.

WHAT FACTORS ARE IMPORTANT IN EVALUATING A CREDIT RISK?

Creditors use different standards in evaluating potential credit customers. Generally, occupation and permanence of employment are ranked high on any list of standards to be used in evaluating risk. Correlations between occupations and credit rating have shown that consumers in professional occupations are the best credit risks, followed by skilled workers, clerical and office workers, and unskilled labor groups, in that order.

Permanence of employment would seem to reflect on the applicant's stability and continued earning power. Stability of income is considered by many raters as more important than size of income. This would tend to give an edge to permanent members of the Armed Forces, civil service workers, postal employees, and school teachers. The irregularity of employment in such occupations as construction, entertainment, and mining would be considered a minus when evaluating risk.

A customer's past payment record can also be an important factor in evaluating risk. Since habits seldom change significantly, payment records which show past delinquency and slowness are an indication that your experience with the applicant will probably not be much different from that of other creditors.

WHERE CAN YOU GET BACKGROUND INFORMATION ABOUT CREDIT APPLICANTS?

Because of the tremendous growth of credit, it is almost impossible for retailers and lending agencies to verify the background information on every person who applies for credit. In order to serve the need for such services, credit bureaus or credit-reporting agencies have been established.

Credit bureaus collect information about credit users—employment, income, residence, past debt performance, assets, court records—and sell the information to creditors. This information is collected from employers, credit managers of stores where the credit users have done business, lending agencies, police and court records, newspapers, and sometimes neighbors.

A credit bureau serves its members by providing a summarized report of an individual's credit experience to the merchants, who use the information to evaluate the credit worthiness of the applicant. If the local bureau is affiliated with the National Retail Credit Association or the Associated Credit Bureaus of America, it can obtain an individual's credit record even when the applicant has moved several times.

Credit bureaus do not offer opinions regarding the suitability of applicants for credit. They merely supply the information on which merchants base their decisions. The format in which this information is recorded and filed is shown in Figure 15-3.

Information about an applicant's employment history and income is often solicited on a credit-application form.

Manufacturers and wholesalers often use the services of mercantile credit agencies to obtain credit information about business firms. Credit ratings supplied by these privately owned and operated agencies are based upon the observed experience of the reporting firms. Among the general mercantile agencies, Dun & Bradstreet is the best known. Dun & Bradstreet offers its reference book, credit reports, and other special information to firms that buy its services. The reference book includes credit ratings, evaluation of financial strength, and other vital credit information.

HOW ARE CONSUMERS PROTECTED AGAINST INCORRECT OR MISLEADING INFORMATION SUPPLIED BY A CONSUMER REPORTING AGENCY?

Consumer reports often involve interviews with a third party about your character, reputation, or mode of living. In order to protect consumers against the circulation of inaccurate or obsolete information and to assure that consumer-reporting agencies exercise their responsibilities in a manner that is fair to consumers, Congress enacted the Fair Credit Reporting Act in April of 1971. Its provisions give consumers certain rights.[1] These are the most important:

□ The right to be told the name and address of the consumer-reporting agency responsible for preparing a consumer report that was used to deny you credit, insurance, or employment or to increase the cost of credit or insurance.

□ The right—at any time and for any reason—to be told the nature, substance, and sources of the information (except medical) collected about you by a consumer-reporting agency.

□ The right to be told who has received a consumer report on you within the preceding 6 months (or within the preceding 2 years if the report was furnished for employment purposes).

[1]Condensed from *Your Rights Under the Fair Credit Reporting Act,* Consumer Bulletin No. 7, Federal Trade Commission, Washington, 1972. For sale from the Superintendent of Documents, Washington, D.C.

If you took a look at what your local credit bureau has about you in its files, you would find a lot of identifying information—name, address, birth date, where you work and so on. The heart of the report will be a summary of your bill-paying record, plus any information bearing on your credit that may appear in public records, such as a judgment or a bankruptcy. Often the information will appear in this form:

CREDIT HISTORY (Complete this section for all reports)

KIND OF BUSINESS	DATE REPORTED OR VERIFIED	DATE ACCOUNT OPENED	DATE OF LAST SALE	HIGHEST CREDIT	AMOUNT OWING	AMOUNT PAST DUE	TERMS OF SALE AND USUAL MANNER OF PAYMENT	
491DC2872	11/74							R3
491BB21875	06/74	03/67	10/71	5345	987	200	26M–$200	
LATE PAYMENTS/NOTICES		30 DAYS–11/60 DAYS–15/90 DAYS–3						
491BB21580	06/74	05/55	09/73	2345	1234	600	12M–$200	
LATE PAYMENTS/NOTICES		30 DAYS–11/60 DAYS–15/90 DAYS–3						
491BB75433	04/74	08/70		6789	4321	345	$345	I1
491BB75442	05/74	02/72		5000	3245		$213	
LATE PAYMENTS/NOTICES		30 DAYS–00/60 DAYS–10/90 DAYS–0						
491DC5008	03/74	09/67	11/73	300	200		$5	R1
491DC8028	03/74	02/42	12/73	342	43			I1

The letter-number code in the last column—the closest thing to a rating—is based on a creditor's actual experience with your account over a period of time. The letter identifies the type of account: "O" is for 30- to 90-day open accounts; "R" for revolving accounts; "I" for installment accounts. The number indicates the usual manner of payment: "1" for paying up within 30 days or as agreed; "2" for paying in more than 30 days but not more than 60 days or one payment past due; to a "9," which indicates bad debt or placed for collection. Some bureaus are adopting a report form that cites the number of times you were issued 30-, 60- and 90-day overdue notices on accounts, as in lines 3, 5 and 8 of the example above.

Nowhere does the credit report give an over-all rating of your credit worthiness, nor does it recommend to the creditor using it how to treat your application. The creditor must make those judgments for himself from the information provided and the basis of his own criteria.

Investigative reports—the kind more likely to be made when you apply for an insurance policy or for a job with a new employer—usually contain no information at all on how promptly you pay your bills. But as the article explains, they do go into your character, reputation and personal behavior. For example, the "drink habits" section of a typical investigative report form might look like this:

8. DRINK HABITS
A. Use of intoxicants:
   If frequent user,
   (1) How often?
   (2) How many drinks taken on these occasions?_____
   (3) What?
   (4) Where?
B. Use(d) intoxicants excessively?
   (IF "YES," SEE OVER.)

Total abstainer?
Frequent user?

If "yes" is checked for part B, a detailed section—like the one shown below—would also be completed by the investigator.

As in the case of the credit report, the investigative report does not rate you or recommend what action should be taken on the basis of whatever material the report provides.

DETAILS OF DRINKING HABITS: Give these additional details to show drinking habits as definitely as possible:

ANSWER ONE OR MORE.

	How often?
18. Describe excessive drinking: ☐ Present ☐ Past	
A. Getting "drunk," stupefied, unable to control usual faculties?	A. ☐ A. _____
B. Loud, boisterous, or obviously under influence, although still in possession of most of faculties?	B. ☐ B. _____
C. Mild excess, just getting "feeling good"; exhilaration or stimulation?	C. ☐ C. _____
19. How long do (did) these occasions last?	
20. How long has (had) applicant been drinking to this extent?	
21. WHEN WAS THE LAST OCCASION OF THIS SORT?	
22. Does (did) applicant drink and drive?	
23. Has applicant ever received treatment for use of intoxicants? If so, when?	
24. Tell how applicant drinks, if social or solitary, whether ever arrested, and details to give clear picture of drinking habits; if habits have changed, tell how and how long since change. If reformed, what led to reformation?	

FIGURE 15-3. How credit bureaus record your credit history. (*Source:* Reprinted by permission from *Changing Times,* The Kiplinger Magazine, August 1975 issue. Copyright 1975 by The Kiplinger Washington Editors, Inc., 1729 H. Street, N.W., Washington, D.C. 20006.)

- The right to have incomplete or incorrect information reinvestigated and, if the information is found to be inaccurate or cannot be verified, to have such information removed from the file.

- The right to have the agency notify, at no cost to you, those you name who have previously received the incorrect or incomplete information and to have the agency declare that the information has been deleted.

- The right to sue a company for damages if it willfully or negligently violates the law and, if successful, to collect attorney's fees and court costs.

- The right not to have most adverse information reported after 7 years. One major exception is bankruptcy, which may be reported for 14 years.

HOW EXPENSIVE IS IT FOR A MERCHANT TO CARRY INSTALLMENT PURCHASES?

It depends on the terms offered, the down payment, and the regularity with which customers pay their bills. In a theoretical business that does $5,000 worth of installment business a month, with 10 percent down, 6 months to pay, and a service charge of 1 percent per month on the unpaid balance, we can calculate the outstanding receivables at the beginning of each month, assuming that all customers pay one-sixth of their original purchases each month. This data is shown in Table 15-2.

TABLE 15-2. MAXIMUM DOLLAR AMOUNTS TIED UP IN
INSTALLMENT RECEIVABLES

Month	New Installment Business Written	Installment Payments	Month-End Installment Receivables
1	$4,770*	$ —	$ 4,770
2	4,770	795	8,745
3	4,770	1,590	11,925
4	4,770	2,385	14,310
5	4,770	3,180	15,900
6	4,770	3,975	16,695
7	4,770	4,770	16,695
8	4,770	4,770	16,695
9	4,770	4,770	16,695
10	4,770	4,770	16,695
11	4,770	4,770	16,695
12	4,770	4,770	16,695

*Represents installment sales of $5,000 per month, less down payments of 10 percent, plus $270 in finance charges based upon the beginning unpaid balances (1 percent per month or 6 percent for 6 months).

Installment receivables for a given month are equal to installment receivables of the previous month, plus new installment business written during the given month, minus installment payments received during the month. With smaller down payments, your maximum dollars tied up in accounts receivable would increase.

From this analysis we can see that the merchant has over $16,000 in receivables when the peak is reached in the sixth month. This represents the amount of cash he has tied up that cannot be used. In his financial planning, it represents an additional $16,000 he must make available to cover outstanding receivables.

For some firms, accounts receivable represents up to 75 percent of the firm's assets. When collections begin to fall off on these accounts, capital reserves must be drawn upon in order to continue in business. Attempts to recover unpaid accounts through professional collectors can help, if started in time. As overdue accounts continue to age, chances for collection decline rapidly.

WHAT CRITERIA GOVERN INSTALLMENT CREDIT?

If you plan to offer installment credit, here are some guidelines that will be helpful:

Credit Investigation. Since sales of big-ticket items can represent high dollar values spread out over several months or years, it is very important that your credit investigation be thorough. You want to be convinced that your customers can and will pay as agreed since your profit from installment sales comes as they finish their contract and make their last payments. Do not allow the possibility of repossession to influence your decision to grant credit because you do not make profit on repossessing merchandise.

What Goods to Offer. Confine your installment sales to high-volume lines of durable goods. Be sure it is a major purchase for a customer. This means you will have to consider your customer's spendable income and buying habits before deciding what goods to offer on installment terms.

Down Payment. This can vary from "no money down" to a figure calculated as a percentage of the purchase price. It can also be stated as a minimum amount. The down payment should be small enough to permit customers to buy the item, but large enough to give them a sense of ownership. This strategy motivates them to continue making their payments to assure ownership at the completion of the contract. Without a sense of ownership, they can become discouraged and stop making their payments. The down payment should typically be 20 percent or more. You should keep in mind that "no money down" plans or very low down payments pose a risk if you should have to repossess merchandise, since your repossession expenses and losses will be greater with lower down payments.

Amount of Scheduled Payments.   You have some flexibility here in relating the amount of payment to your customers' income and their other obligations. The time of payment is usually set at a time of month which is most convenient for them. Installment contracts should be set up so that the unpaid balance is never greater than the resale value of the merchandise.

Installment Terms.   Make the terms of your contract bear some relationship to the expected life of the merchandise. Terms of 24 or 36 months are reasonable for automobiles, refrigerators, and television sets, since the customer will continue to use the article long after the contract is paid off. Terms on nondurable goods such as clothing should be relatively short—in the area of 4 to 6 months. Generally, you should try to keep terms as short as possible.

Carrying Charges.   Comparisons of your carrying charges with those of your competitors are now possible for potential credit customers. Although installment customers expect to pay a finance charge to offset your costs of extending credit, they can now see the exact charges and determine whether you are competitive with others, thanks to the Truth in Lending Act.

You should explain your finance charges to potential customers so that they understand the method to be used and agree that it is reasonable for the "service package" you are offering. In some states, laws have established the maximum a merchant may charge for carrying credit accounts. Competition sometimes forces a merchant to ask less than the law allows for fear of losing customers who "shop around" for the lowest charges.

Excessive carrying charges drive away potential customers; on the other hand, very low charges make cash customers feel that they are being exploited. Some merchants use a dual pricing system with one price for credit customers and a lower one for cash customers, the difference representing carrying charges.

ARE CASH DISCOUNTS A FORM OF CREDIT?

When you buy merchandise from suppliers and have 30 days to pay them, they are granting you credit without a charge for that period of time. Cash discounts are simply an incentive for you to pay them sooner. The terms of sale they extend have significant effects on their cash needs. It sometimes is cheaper for them not to be so liberal with cash discounts and to borrow the funds they need to supplement their working capital. Normal credit-sales terms are shown in Table 15-3.

One of the problems arising from the use of cash discounts is the tendency of some customers to take them after the expiration of the discount period. You will have to decide whether you will permit this practice and, if not, what your policy will be. Possible approaches are to send an additional billing for the amount due with

TABLE 15-3. COMMON BUSINESS CREDIT-SALES TERMS

Term	Explanation
3/10, 1/15, n/60	3 percent discount for first 10 days; 1 percent discount for 15 days; bill due net on 60th day.
MOM (middle of month)	Billing will be on the 15th of the month (middle of the month), including all purchases made since the middle of the previous month.
EOM (end of month)	Billing at end of month, covering all credit purchases of that month.
CWO or CIA (cash with order, or cash in advance)	Orders received are not processed until advanced payment is received.
CBD (cash before delivery)	Merchandise may be prepared and packaged by the seller, but shipment is not made until payment is received.
COD (cash on delivery)	Amount of bill will be collected upon delivery of goods.
SD—BL (sight draft—bill of lading)	A negotiable bill of lading, accompanied by the invoice and a sight draft drawn on the buyer, is forwarded by the seller to the customer's bank. The bill of lading is released by the bank to the customer only upon his honoring the draft.
2/10, n/30, ROG (receipt of goods)	2 percent discount for 10 days; bill due net on 30th day— but both discount period and 30 days start from the date of receipt of the goods, not from the date of the sale.
2/10, n/30, MOM	2 percent discount for 10 days; bill due net on 30th day— but both periods start from the 15th of the month following the sales date.
2/10, n/30, EOM	2 percent discount for 10 days; bill due net on 30th day— but both periods start from the end of the month in which the sale was made.
8/10, EOM	8 percent discount for 10 days; bill due net on 30th day— but both periods start from the end of the month following the sales date.

Sales date is the day that the shipment was made. It will generally be the same date shown on the invoice. In consumer credit, the sales date is the day the sale was made and may or may not coincide with the date of shipment.

Source: Harvey O. Krentzman, *Managing for Profits*, U.S. Small Business Administration, Washington, 1968, p. 101.

an explanation, return the check and request a correct one, or add the amount to the next billing. Small sums might not be worth the additional collection cost. Your policy will have to spell this out. The individual decisions you make may be influenced by the importance of the customer, your cash position at a given time, or the rigidity of the policy that you have announced beforehand.

WHAT DOES IT COST TO MAKE A CREDIT PURCHASE?

When merchants offer credit terms to buyers, they are offering a "package" of credit service, to which a dollar value is attached. That there is some cost to merchants who offer credit is obvious. It is reflected on the customer's billing as a service charge, and it covers the following costs:

Credit Rating. The firm with which customers deal must spend time and money on a credit report. Additional time is required to establish a credit limit and establish a payment schedule.

Bookkeeping and Billing. The retailer or lender must open new bookkeeping accounts for the record of credit transactions. Each time a purchase or payment is made there is a cost for entering the transaction on the record. Additionally, there is the cost of mailing bills or statements.

Collection. Human frailties, sickness, temporary financial difficulty, family emergencies, and forgetfulness cause delays in some payments. Every credit office knows in advance that a modest reserve must be kept for taking action to keep collections current and arrange for the necessary adjustments where changed conditions make old commitments difficult to keep.

Interest. Money has an interest value and everyone expects to make his or her fair payment for using it. Some people think that interest on the money used to finance credit is the ruling factor in setting the cost of smaller loans and credit purchases. Actually, it is one of the less significant ingredients in the total.

Insurance. Merchants or lenders may purchase credit life insurance protecting the accounts of all customers, treating the cost as they would any credit-department expense. They may insure each customer separately and include the modest premium as a part of their credit service charge. Often, however, it is an optional addition to the installment transaction, listed in the contract, the premium being paid by the customer.

Customers must decide whether the service charge is reasonable by considering such things as courteous treatment, quick service, a shorter trip to make their payments, a long time to pay, and dependable repairs.

DO MERCHANTS HAVE TO STATE HOW MUCH THEY ARE CHARGING FOR EXTENDING CREDIT?

The Consumer Credit Protection Act (Public Law 90-321, also called Truth in Lending Act) enacted in 1969 requires merchants and lenders who extend credit to provide customers with full disclosure of credit costs and terms. The purpose of this "truth in lending" legislation is to make it easier for the consumer to shop intelligently for credit.

The Truth in Lending Act requires merchants and lenders to provide customers and borrowers with the amount of the finance charge and the annual percentage rate of the charge.

With such information, the customer can decide whether to establish credit, save enough to pay cash and eliminate the finance charge, make a larger down payment and reduce the finance charge, or shop for better terms.

WHAT RESTRICTIONS ARE PLACED ON ADVERTISING BY THE TRUTH IN LENDING ACT?

After considering the problems of consumers because of misleading advertising, Congress included in the act provisions against the use of misleading words or phrases that promise different down payments or installment amounts than are in fact available.

If an advertisement includes any details of a credit plan, it must also include as disclosures substantial information on finance charges, rates, cash price, down payment, and other information that may be included in the specific regulations that will be used to enforce the law.

WHAT ARE THE PENALTIES FOR VIOLATING THE TRUTH IN LENDING ACT?

If creditors knowingly and willingly violate the act, they are subject to criminal penalties. Fines up to $5,000, imprisonment of up to 1 year, or both, are provided for. Debtors can sue for twice the amount of the finance charge (but not more than $1,000 or less than $100), and, if they win the suit, their creditors are required to pay attorney's fees and court costs. The debtors, however, must still repay their debts, including the finance charges.

ARE CREDIT CARDS WIDELY USED AS SOURCES OF CREDIT?

Today one out of every two families uses at least one credit card. If a family uses a credit card, it generally uses several. Among families with annual incomes over $15,000, it is estimated that 75 percent use credit cards. The most popular cards among such users are store and gasoline cards, with bank cards ranking third. Travel and entertainment cards are the least popular among all income groups.

Half of all credit card users take advantage of the debt feature of their cards. Many families who use the debt feature treat the debt line as an installment loan, making a small payment each month.

Sellers like credit cards. They build up brand and company loyalty. Cash customers are anybody's customers. Studies show that credit customers buy more frequently and buy more expensive merchandise than cash customers do. Oil companies report that only about 40 percent of their cash customers fill their tanks, but 75 percent of their credit customers do.

HOW DO CREDIT CARDS HELP THE SMALL BUSINESS OWNER?

Credit cards make it possible to eliminate the costs related to bookkeeping and billing. These are handled by the firm that issued the card. It also assumes the responsibility for collecting credit card accounts. Credit plans give retailers access to a larger number of potential credit customers than they would have if they ran their own credit departments.

WHAT FACTORS AFFECT COLLECTION POLICIES?

The nature of the business, the type of clientele, the margin of profit, and your competitors' practices must all be considered.

Creditors selling on open account are generally more lenient in their collection policies than those selling on the installment plan. When successive installment payments fall due and are not met, cumulative deficiencies can result in serious cash problems for the creditor. Businesses offering a service such as telephone or utilities must be firm in their collection policies since customers are continuing to use the service during periods of delinquency.

Clientele using credit may have different collection policies applied to them. Debtors in your "good-risk" category will pay their bills promptly in most cases. They are sensitive to pressures regarding delinquencies and will exert every effort to keep their accounts current. Your collection approach to this group should be low-key, mild, and courteous. Customers who are considered "fair risks" make up the largest group of a retail store's credit accounts. Occasional delinquencies are expected, but most customers are basically honest and require a little patience from the credit manager. The collection procedure should allow reasonable "slack" in the time between the various steps in the collection plan. "Poor risks" will require special handling. Since some will not pay until forced to, your approach must be firm and positive. Keep credit purchases for these customers within the limits established. Since persuasion and tact often fall on deaf ears with this group, your collection procedure must move rapidly toward the strongest action included in your collection policy. There is little to be lost in a firm approach once the intentions of a chronic delinquent have been substantiated.

The margin of profit has some bearing on collection policies since a business operating on a narrow margin cannot allow many accounts to become delinquent. In general, the higher the margin of profit, the more lenient the collection process can be.

What your competitors are doing about collections affects your policies. You are competing with them in terms of customer service as well as price and quality. If you are facing strong service competition, your collection policy might have to be modified to allow for this condition.

WHAT PROBLEMS ARE INHERENT IN THE COLLECTION PROCESS?

For a small business which extends credit, survival might well depend on its ability to collect accounts payable from its credit customers. Too many slow accounts cause a hardship to the owner. The risks inherent in collecting debts may be summarized in a list of problems which would not exist except for the existence of consumer credit:

Nonpayment of Accounts. Some customers will fail to pay their bills. These accounts represent a total loss and will have to be written off as bad debts. Industry experience will tell you what is "normal" for bad-debt losses for your type of business. Such losses range from 0.5 to over 5 percent of net sales—enough to make the difference between profit and insolvency.

Slow-Paying Customers. The retailers in this country lose substantially more from slow bill payers than from totally bad debts. Money tied up in slow-paying accounts can cause you to have to borrow money to pay your own debts. In addition, you are losing revenue you could have earned on the money owed you. Effort spent in trying to collect money due takes time away from other more important activities. The firm extending credit must be continually alert to the relationship of credit sales to collections. When collections for a period of time are significantly less than credit sales for the same period, this is a signal that indicates trouble. Promptness and tact in approaching slow-paying customers will often keep them from becoming nonpaying customers.

Lost Customers. Once an account is past due, the objective of business people becomes one of collecting the money without losing the customer. As you approach the problem of collection techniques, it is helpful to think in terms of why your customers have not paid. Sometimes accounts are past due because of conditions over which your customers have little or no control. In this case, no amount of pressure from you would be effective in getting them to pay their accounts. Whether the customers are the victims of unexpected misfortune, their own poor management, or simply "dead beats," it would be better to explore the reason *why* they are unable to pay rather than *when* they expect to. Remember that a patient and understanding approach is not coddling when it helps keep the debtor—who needs your product—on your company's list of active accounts.

Special Collection-Policy Problems.   Whether to charge interest on overdue accounts or to suspend sales to delinquent accounts often presents special problems for the creditor.

The charging of interest on overdue accounts depends on the amount involved and how long the payment is expected to be delayed. Usually no attempt is made to collect interest on open-end accounts that are past due a short time. When it is the intent of a creditor to charge interest for overdue accounts, the customer should understand the policy. Words to this effect may be printed on the statements or on stickers attached to bills.

Suspension of credit for delinquent customers is designed to speed collections by making it impossible for those customers to buy more merchandise until they have paid for that already bought. It is common practice to grant a grace period of 30 to 90 days before taking such action. The length of the period will depend upon the rate of consumption or sale of the goods for which payments are in arrears.

WHAT ARE THE COMMON METHODS OF HANDLING OVERDUE ACCOUNTS?

An effective collection system depends upon the kinds of collection devices to be utilized, the frequency or time interval between steps, and the length of time you can afford to wait for the entire collection process to evolve. The sequencing of the collection steps suggests the use of milder approaches first, followed by more stringent measures as required to obtain the desired results. Table 15-4 shows the various elements of a general collection system.

WHAT INTERNAL RECORDS ARE NEEDED TO MAINTAIN CONTROL OF CREDIT ACCOUNTS?

We have already discussed in a previous chapter the accounts-receivable record for each customer. This record shows how much each customer owes, when the purchases were made, and when he or she made payments. An inspection of these records by the credit manager will provide a visual means of determining which accounts are in trouble. This method requires a periodic screening of all accounts to find those which need special collection attention. This is time-consuming and disruptive to the records section. For these reasons, it is likely to be neglected and done on a hit-and-miss basis.

A better method is to make up a card for *only* the delinquent accounts, on which the collection action taken and the dates can be documented. Cards are placed in a tickler file by the date on which the next collection action will be taken. It is then examined at each step to see whether the customer has responded to your last inquiry. If not, the next step is taken and the card moved to a new date for subsequent checking. When the account is paid, the card is removed

TABLE 15-4.   A GENERAL COLLECTION SYSTEM

Stage of System	Collection Devices Available for Use	Debtors Involved
Impersonal routine	Statements—1st, 2nd, 3rd, etc. Statement inserts and stickers Notes on statements Form letters of reminder type (Note: These refer only to devices used after expiration of credit period.)	Those awaiting notice Honestly overlooked Temporarily financially embarrassed Careless or procrastinating debtor

Impersonal appeals	Form letters appealing to:
	  "Anything wrong" tone
	  "Tell us your story" tone
	  Pride in credit responsibilities
	  Sense of fair play
	Seeking reply from debtor:
	  Telephone
	  Telegram
	  Special letters:
	    Registered
	    Special delivery
	    Trick reply
		Honestly overlooked
		Careless or procrastinator
		Temporarily embarrassed
		Overbought
		Accident or misfortune
		Disputed account

Personalized appeals	Personal collector:
	  Telephone
	  Telegram
	  Personal interview
	Personal letters to:
	  Debtor
	  Employer
	  Credit bureau
		Overbought
		Eventual insolvents
		Accident or misfortune
		Frauds—no intent to pay
		Disputed account

Drastic or legal action	Extension agreement Composition arrangement Assignment of accounts receivable Collection agency Garnishment or wage assignment Repossession Attorney Suit Other actions	Same as debtors shown in the *Personalized appeals* (all should have assets)

Source: Reproduced with permission from Robert H. Cole and Robert S. Hancock, *Consumer and Commercial Credit Management*, rev. ed., Richard D. Irwin, Inc., Homewood, Ill., 1964, p. 296.

from the file, leaving those which still have problems. Although this method duplicates some of your existing records, it saves the credit manager time by allowing him or her to apply the "exception" principle to the collection process.

HOW DOES AGING OF ACCOUNTS RECEIVABLE HELP IN CREDIT MANAGEMENT?

A list of aged accounts tells you how efficient your collection procedure is and which accounts are likely to turn out to be uncollectible. Under normal circumstances, more than half of your credit customers will pay what they owe promptly. Other customers will have to be nudged or pushed to pay on time, if at all. You need to know which debtors need collection attention. A list of aged accounts will highlight the potential troublemakers. The longer accounts remain uncollected, the more difficult they are to collect. A business associate of mine has his own theory about this relationship. He says, "When an account hasn't paid for a year or longer, you have two chances of collecting—slim and none!"

At least once a quarter your accounts receivable should be aged by classifying them as current, 30 to 60 days old, 60 to 90 days old, 3 to 6 months old, 6 to 9 months old, 9 to 12 months old, and over 1 year old. You have to analyze each account and determine how long the various credit purchases have been on your books. If Tom Smith's accounts-receivable record looks like the following illustration, we age it as shown in Figure 15-4.

Month	Credit Purchases	Payments on Account	Balance Owed
January	$75.00	—	$75.00
February	—	$50.00	25.00
March	49.50	—	74.50
April	25.00	—	99.50

On Figure 15-4, Mr. Smith's balance of $99.50 is entered in the "total amount" column, and his April purchases of $25 in the "current" column. Since all his March purchases are included in the balance owed at the end of April, the $49.50 is entered in the "30 to 60 days" column. This leaves $25.00 of the current balance still to be accounted for. He made no purchases in February, so no entry is made in the "60 to 90 days" column. The remaining $25.00 represents purchases made in January, which are now entered in the "3 to 6 months" column. When all accounts are aged in this manner and the column totals are related to the total as percentages, we arrive at the summary which is Figure 15-4.

Aging thus brings to your attention accounts that are slow. You might want to press some for payment or suspend credit privi-

Customer	Total Amount	Current	30 to 60 Days	60 to 90 Days	3 to 6 Months	6 to 9 Months	9 to 12 Months	Over 1 Year
T. Smith	$ 99.50	$ 25.00	$49.50		$25.00			
T. Anke	87.00	87.00						
J. Brown	23.00	23.00						
R. Cortez	55.00	55.00						
I. Cox	14.25					$9.50	$4.75	
B. Farmer	9.75	9.75						
R. Ihne	37.00	22.00		$15.00				
J. Jiminez	10.00							$10.00
A. Nero	12.00	7.50		4.50				
Total	$347.50	$229.25	$49.50	$19.50	$25.00	$9.50	$4.75	$10.00
Percent	100	66	14	6	7	3	1	3

FIGURE 15-4. Aging of accounts receivable.

leges on others. Two accounts in Figure 15-4 (Mr. Cox's and Mr. Jiminez's) are in danger of becoming uncollectible. Together they represent 7 percent (3 + 1 + 3) of the outstanding receivables. If 75 percent of your total sales are credit sales, the two accounts represent about 5.5 percent of your total sales for the 4-month period.

This exercise is designed to test your understanding of the material presented in Chapter 15. Choose the response, *True* or *False*, which best fits each statement. Correct responses are presented in the back of the text.

SELF-CHECK OF KEY CONCEPTS

1. In 1974, approximately 20 percent of the spendable income of American workers was spent for credit purchases.
2. The cost of carrying accounts receivable is reduced when repayment terms are shortened from 6 months to 3 months.
3. In evaluating a customer for credit, the level of income is more important than regularity of income.
4. A strong collection system will overcome shortcomings in the credit-granting process.
5. Credit cards help small business owners by relieving them of the responsibility for granting credit and collecting overdue accounts.
6. Roughly 90 percent of all retail business consists of credit sales.
7. An interest rate of 1.5 percent per month is the equivalent of 18 percent per year.
8. About half of all American families use at least one credit card, probably more.
9. It is sometimes cheaper to borrow money to pay your bills than to extend credit terms that are too liberal in hopes of increasing your working capital.
10. The maximum amount of finance charge that a merchant may charge is fixed by law.

1. List all the common collection methods that can be used by a retailer selling on a regular 30-day, open-end, charge-account basis.
2. Obtain credit applications from several large retail businesses and compare the kinds of information requested from the credit applicant. Prepare a comparison chart showing the names of the stores across the top, and the data requested down the left margin. Then, under each store write *yes* or *no* beside each data item, indicating whether the application form does or does not ask for it.

PERFORMANCE PROBLEMS AND PROJECTS

3. Check your local library for pamphlets or similar publications which discuss the Truth in Lending Act, and find answers to the following questions:
   a. Does the act regulate the amount a creditor can charge for financing credit?
   b. Is real estate credit covered under the act?
   c. Does a customer have the right to cancel a credit transaction he or she has consummated with a creditor? Under what conditions?
   d. What restrictions are placed on credit advertising by the Truth in Lending Act?
4. Using the data shown in Table 15-2, calculate the maximum amount a merchant will have tied up in accounts receivable if he reduces the payment terms from 6 months to 3 months. Assume all other data is unchanged.
5. Collection letters can be very mild in their approach or very strong. Check several sources of information on credits and collections and prepare a brief report for the class on the use of letters in collecting overdue accounts. Include in your report samples of "mild," "firm," and "strong" collection letters. You will find the following sources helpful:

> Chapin, Albert F., and George E. Hassett, Jr., *Credit and Collection Principles and Practices*, McGraw-Hill Book Company, New York, 1960, Chap. 26.
>
> Cole, Robert H., and Robert S. Hancock, *Consumer and Commercial Credit Management*, Richard D. Irwin, Inc., Homewood, Ill., 1964, Chap. 17.
>
> Ettinger, Richard P., and David E. Gottlieb, *Credits and Collections*, 5th ed., Prentice-Hall, Inc., Englewood Cliffs, N.J., 1962, Chap. 18.

A
CASE
IN
POINT

HOW LOOKING AT THE WRONG THING GOT PHIL IN TROUBLE

Phil Esparza opened a large sporting goods store in January. He had talked to his accountant, Jerry Browning, about operating costs and had asked him to set up a recordkeeping system that would give him current information about costs and profits. As an inducement to customers, Phil wanted to extend credit to selected customers.

"That makes sense," Jerry agreed. "Your competitors are offering 30-day open-end credit and you need to be competitive in service as well as price."

"How much of my total sales should I plan as credit sales?" Phil wondered out loud.

"That depends on what you can afford," Jerry replied. "If you are shooting for sales of $10,000 a month, and half of those sales are credit sales, you will have about $5,000 tied up in accounts receivable at any given time—if your customers pay their bills on time. You will have to allow for this in planning your cash requirements."

After some thought, Phil decided to offer credit terms to carefully screened low-risk customers and to try to limit credit sales to $5,000 a month. He and Jerry prepared a cash budget for the year which showed that he could afford such a plan without causing problems in meeting his other obligations.

The expected credit sales materialized and each month Phil checked to be sure he was not overextending himself. At the end of the year his credit sales totaled $60,755, but he was in trouble. His profit for the year was far below what he had planned. In midyear, he had to borrow $5,000 from the bank in order to pay his current bills.

"I don't understand what went wrong, Jerry," Phil explained. "We carefully screened all credit applicants for income levels and job stability. We kept credit sales at the planned levels, but I ran into trouble in midyear."

"How are your collections in relation to your credit sales?" queried Jerry.

"Okay, I guess," replied Phil, not sure he understood the question. "Most of my customers eventually pay what they owe. We don't have to spend a fortune on collections. And my bad-debt losses are almost negligible. I don't think that could get me in the kind of trouble I'm in."

"But if your collections are lagging sales by a significant amount, it means that the $5,000 you planned for carrying your credit sales might not be enough," Jerry pointed out. "Better let me analyze your collections to see if there is a problem," he concluded.

Jerry Browning's analysis of Phil's credit and collections system looked like the data in Table 15-5.

Analyze the data in Table 15-5 below. Then answer the questions on p. 360.

TABLE 15-5.   DATA FOR PHIL'S SPORTING GOODS STORE

Month	Credit Sales	Collections	Accounts Receivable
January	$ 4,800	—	$ 4,800
February	5,200	$ 4,080	5,920
March	4,950	3,815	7,055
April	5,480	4,275	8,260
May	5,515	4,770	9,005
June	6,125	4,300	10,830
July	5,960	5,360	11,430
August	5,565	5,580	11,415
September	5,230	4,735	11,910
October	4,580	4,310	12,180
November	4,150	3,885	12,445
December	3,200	3,550	12,095
Total	$60,755	$48,660	

1. Can you pinpoint the month when Phil's accounts receivable first deviated from his plan?
2. If all of Phil's customers had paid their bills within 30 days after receiving their statements, what is the maximum amount Phil would have had in accounts receivable at the maximum point?
3. What steps do you think Jerry will recommend to Phil to rectify the situation?
4. Is something missing in Phil's credit-screening method?
5. How could Phil have got reliable data on the average collection period for his type of business?

16

Where to Look for Cost Savings

PERFORMANCE OBJECTIVES

After reading this chapter you should become aware of some of the major profit leaks in operating a business and gain a better appreciation of the effect that these leaks can have on the success of the business if not controlled. Specifically, you should be able to:

1. Assess the impact of prolonged overtime on output and demonstrate how inefficiencies related to overtime affect manufacturing costs.
2. Recommend ways of keeping the extra costs related to overtime to a minimum.
3. Develop a method of recording and measuring absenteeism in a small business.
4. Explain why it costs so much to replace skilled workers when they terminate their employment.
5. Develop guidelines designed to control theft and pilferage in a retail establishment.
6. Explain some of the ways in which enlightened purchasing practices can save money.
7. Show how a 20 percent reduction in a $100,000 inventory saves a firm money.
8. List the direct and indirect costs associated with job-related accidents.
9. Explain why material-handling costs are lower in a retail business than they are in a manufacturing concern.

10. Relate the poker player's philosophy "Trust everyone—but cut the cards" to the business owner's evaluation of employee honesty in regard to theft.

INTRODUCTION

There are many opportunities for cost reduction in the business world. Waste and inefficiency become so commonplace that we often develop a tolerance for them and rationalize their existence as a necessary part of "getting the job done." We seldom look upon absenteeism and labor turnover as significant cost problems. We justify excessive overtime as a means of meeting customer deliveries, unaware of the price we are paying for it. We know that crimes against business have become commonplace, yet we are naïve enough to believe that someone else's employees, not ours, are the ones who need watching. We tolerate purchasing inefficiencies, excessive material handling, and "balloon" inventories as though we have come to accept less than optimum performance in these areas.

This chapter looks at eight major "cost generators" which add billions of dollars of unnecessary expense to the profit-and-loss statements of the nation's businesses. Each represents a gold mine of potential savings to the owner who recognizes their importance and designs policies to control them. These are the areas covered: the inefficiency of overtime, absenteeism, the high cost of accidents, turnover costs, theft and pilferage, material handling, purchasing, and inventories.

WHY IS OVERTIME WATCHED SO CLOSELY BY EXPERIENCED MANAGERS?

Because it is so expensive and inefficient. The expense is related to the provisions of the Fair Labor Standards Act, which requires employers in most businesses to pay their workers 50 percent more for each hour worked on overtime than is paid for a regular hour. This provision is commonly called the "time and one-half for overtime" provision of the act. The basic 40-hour pay for workers earning $4 an hour would be $160 a week. When you work them on Saturday, they must be paid $48 for that day instead of the $32 that they make on a regular day. A six-day week, including Saturday, results in a weekly paycheck of $208 for each of these workers. Their hours have increased by 20 percent, but their pay has increased by 30 percent. This additional pay buys you some additional output, but most studies indicate that output does not increase in proportion to the increased hours. For each Saturday hour worked you pay an extra $2, but you get no more for the $6 hour than a $4 hour worked on Wednesday.

Working prolonged overtime is like smoking, a habit that is easy to form but difficult to break. Although the judicious use of overtime is necessary to meet unexpected schedule demands or unforeseen emergencies, prolonged overtime results in excessive costs, worker fatigue, and reduced production. What can happen is that, almost before anyone is aware of it, a pattern of overtime is established and taken for granted. Repeated need for overtime work calls for an analysis of its cause and profitability.

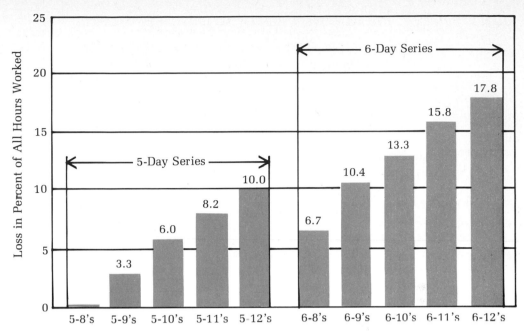

FIGURE 16-1. Efficiency loss related to length of workweek (light work, operator controlled). (*Source:* Compiled from data shown in U.S. *Department of Labor Bulletin*, No. 917, "Hours of Work and Output.")

HOW INEFFICIENT IS OVERTIME?

In 1947, the U.S. Department of Labor published the results of a study of the effects of long working hours.[1] The study covered several years and resulted in a report consisting of 78 case studies covering 2,445 men and 1,060 women in 34 different plants performing a variety of manufacturing jobs. The objective of the study was to determine the effects of fatigue, induced by long working hours, on worker efficiency, absenteeism, work injuries, and level of output. Various patterns of weekly schedules based on 5-, 6-, and 7-day workweeks were studied and the related data compiled statistically into a series of tables.

Figure 16-1 summarizes the effect of long hours on efficiency for a series of 5-day and 6-day workweeks. The basic 5 × 8, or 40-hour, standard workweek is used as the index against which other patterns are compared. If we call the efficiency of the 40-hour week 100 percent, we can read from the chart the loss of efficiency as we increase the work hours.

The effect of long hours on workers is related to the type of work performed, whether it is machine-controlled or operator-controlled, the shift being worked, and the attitudes of workers toward management.

[1]*Hours of Work and Output*, Bulletin No. 917, U.S. Department of Labor, Bureau of Labor Statistics, Washington, 1967.

HOW IS THE EXTENDED WORKWEEK REFLECTED IN WORKER OUTPUT?

The ultimate criterion of the effectiveness of longer hours is the level of output. Although output increases in total as the workweek is extended, the increase in weekly hours is rarely matched by a proportionate increase in output. The studies of workers on various 6-day patterns show that the ratio of the equivalent of output hours gained to additional hours worked is about 0.6 or 0.7, indicating that 3 hours of work are required to produce the output of 2 hours on shorter workweek schedules. In terms of labor cost, at overtime rates, this means about 4½ hours' pay for 2 hours of additional output.

WHAT IS THE RELATIONSHIP OF OUTPUT TO THE SHIFT WORKED?

Day-shift production is higher and less costly than that done on night shifts. Since many new workers are assigned to night-shift work, the skill level is lower than that of day-shift workers. Night-shift workers often come to work tired, either from insufficient sleep or overexertion; all this cuts efficiency and boosts costs. The night shift is likely to be 10 to 15 percent less efficient than the day shift. To make matters worse, most plants pay their night-shift workers a "shift differential" of 15 cents or so above their basic hourly rate. Assuming that this adds up to 5 percent of their hourly wage, you will find that products made on night shifts will cost 15 to 20 percent more than products made on the day shift.

HOW LONG DOES IT TAKE FOR THE EFFICIENCY LOSS TO BE NOTICEABLE WHEN OVERTIME IS PROLONGED?

It depends on the overtime pattern used and the length of time the overtime is continued. Occasional days of overtime do not have significant effects on either efficiency or output. When the overtime is prolonged, however, a measurable relationship between overtime and output can be established.

As a result of a 2-year study to establish the general patterns of "deterioration" when overtime is prolonged, Fuller[2] found that it was possible to predict the day after inception of overtime when efficiency would start to deteriorate. Further, he found that efficiency would continue to deteriorate, if the pattern was continued, to the point at which output for the overtime pattern was no greater than it would be for a standard 40-hour workweek. He called this the *point of no return* (PNR) and defined it as the *working* day after the inception of overtime which first showed no increase in productivity over the regular 8-hour day.

[2]Don Fuller, *Organizing, Planning, and Scheduling for Engineering Operations,* Industrial Engineering Institute, Boston, 1962.

Pattern	Hours in Week	Point of No Return, Days
5 × 9	45	21
5 × 8 + ½*	45	18
5 × 9 + ½	50	15
5 × 10	50	12
6 × 8	48	10
6 × 9	54	8
7 × 8	56	4

Source: Don Fuller, *Organizing, Planning, and Scheduling for Engineering Operations*, Industrial Engineering Institute, Boston, 1962, p. 13-5.
*By this, Fuller means five 8-hour days plus 5 hours on Saturday.

The seven patterns studied by Fuller are shown in Table 16-1. He found that efficiency gains were essentially flat for two-thirds of the days, with deteriorating efficiency most pronounced during the last third of the PNR cycle. This condition is shown in Figure 16-2.

It is significant to recognize from Figure 16-2 that efficiency does not begin to drop significantly until two-thirds of the PNR span is reached. If overtime can be confined to this part of the span and stopped before the final third of the cycle is complete, the effect on output would be minimal.

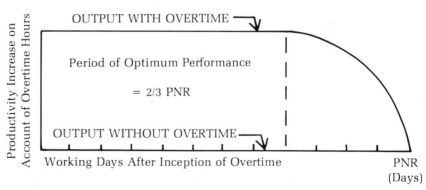

FIGURE 16-2.   Point-of-no-return concept when working prolonged overtime hours. (*Source:* Don Fuller, *Organizing, Planning, and Scheduling for Engineering Operations*, Industrial Engineering Institute, Boston, 1962, p. 13–6.)

IF YOU STOP OVERTIME AND RESUME IT LATER, DOES THE DETERIORATION PATTERN REPEAT?

Fuller's studies showed that 4 days without overtime allowed "recovery" from its effects and permitted repetition of the cycle. Best results were obtained by stopping the overtime on a Wednesday so as to take advantage of the weekend. Optimum patterns for inter-mittent overtime were also found in the study:

Overtime Required	Best Days
1 day	Wednesday
2 days	Wednesday and Thursday
3 days	(Best) Wednesday through Friday
	(Second best) Tuesday through Thursday

WHAT MAKES ABSENTEEISM SO EXPENSIVE?

It is estimated that over 2 million workers are absent without pay every working day. For every dollar these workers do not take home because of absenteeism, business loses another $1 to $2 because of:

□ Scrap caused by inexperienced substitute workers.

□ Disrupted schedules and inconvenienced customers.

□ Overtime pay to maintain schedules with fewer workers.

□ Idle machinery and unused equipment.

□ Extra people on the payroll to take the place of those who are absent.

□ Higher inventories caused by delayed shipments.

A business with 50 employees would have an annual payroll of $400,000 a year, if we assume an average wage rate of $4 an hour and no overtime. If absenteeism runs 5 percent of scheduled hours, the absent employees would lose about $20,000 in pay. In addition, the business would lose an additional $20,000 to $40,000. You would have to sell a lot of merchandise to make that much profit.

CAN LOSSES FROM ABSENTEEISM BE PREVENTED?

Nationally, absenteeism runs from 3 to 5 percent of all scheduled hours. It is generally believed by most authorities that absenteeism can be cut in half and that 1.5 to 2.5 percent is a realistic goal. Many companies maintain this lower average with programs designed to zero in on "avoidable" absences.

Avoidable absences are those provoked by whim or attitude of the employee. These psychological absences are not related to sick-ness, fatigue, or physical problems but to the way the worker is treated at work. Only about 10 percent of absences are caused by industrial accidents or disease. Another 45 percent are attributable to respiratory illness such as the common cold and flu. The remain-ing 45 percent include personal business, death in the family, mar-riage, and "other causes." The other causes are obviously of interest to management. Many are related to such reasons as "My job bores me to death," "My boss is a tyrant," "I don't think my work group likes me," or "I hate my job, my boss, and the company." These attitudes cause employees to feign illness when they are not really sick. Such absences have their roots in human relations problems. Many of them can be prevented with proper analysis and planning.

WHAT FACTORS ARE RELATED TO ABSENTEEISM?

Statistics related to absenteeism make fascinating reading. With some exceptions, here are a few general statements which are usually true, regardless of the type of business:

- Businesses or departments with predominantely female workers will have the highest absentee rates.
- Office employees have slightly better attendance records than those who work in the shop.
- Skilled employees are absent less than unskilled or semiskilled workers.
- There are more absences on night shifts than day shifts.
- Emotional factors are involved in 25 percent of all absences.
- Most of the absenteeism is concentrated in a small segment of the work population, with 45 percent of the absenteeism caused by a group constituting about 10 percent of the work force.
- About 30 percent of employees are never absent.
- Long-service, older employees are absent less than the "under 25" group.
- A bad attendance record does not necessarily correlate with poor performance.
- Studies show that over 50 percent of all 1- and 2-day absences precede or follow otherwise legitimate time off for holidays or weekends.
- There is a high correlation between employee "illness" and major sports events.
- Absenteeism gets worse with high levels of employment and prosperity.
- Absenteeism is reduced with good supervision, high morale, and satisfying work.
- Absenteeism increases with prolonged overtime and extended workweeks.

Business owners can discover the reasons behind the statistics reflected in these statements. The influence of motivation, morale, job satisfaction, and job involvement is evident in explaining why employees do not go to work. It is these areas that offer the greatest opportunities for improvement.

WHAT CAN YOU DO ABOUT ABSENTEEISM?

A basic approach is to keep good records on absences, study them to ascertain the reasons for absences, and discuss them with your workers. Find out what they say about the reasons for being absent. You will sometimes find that employees are surprised when they see their 6-month record of absences and are shown how their record compares with that of the other members of the work group. Emphasize the use of attendance records in determining wage increases, promotions, and layoffs. Remember that absences and tardiness are a reflection of morale. You should concern yourself with finding the causes of such absences.

Techniques for reducing absences have been reported by various companies. Here are some of the more common ones:

□ Do not pay for 1-day absences.

□ Do not pay for holidays when the employee is absent on the day before or after the holiday.

□ Base sick-leave accumulation and merit increases on months of perfect attendance.

□ Give bonus days off for a specified number of months of perfect attendance.

□ Do a better job of screening new employees and do not hire those with questionable attendance records with other companies.

□ Establish a written policy for absenteeism, defining its limits and the disciplinary action which will be taken if it becomes excessive.

The worst thing you can do about absenteeism is ignore it. A systematic approach designed to find the causes and build an atmosphere where good morale is a reality will be effective in reducing absenteeism.

HOW CAN YOU MEASURE YOUR ABSENTEE RATE?

Find the total number of scheduled hours which were not worked during the month and divide by the total number of hours of work which were scheduled to be worked during the month. Multiply by 100 to get the percentage of absenteeism. Scheduled hours may be found by multiplying the average number of employees on the payroll for the month by 8 hours per day and then by the number of working days in the month. A plant with 50 employees would generate $50 \times 8 \times 21 = 8,400$ scheduled hours in a 21-day month. If the records show that there were 50 worker-days of absences during the month ($50 \times 8 = 400$ hours), the absentee rate will be:

$$\frac{400}{8,400} \times 100 = 4.7\%$$

The average number of employees can be determined by adding those on the payroll on the first day of the month to the number on the payroll on the last day of the month, and dividing the sum by 2. It is a common practice to exclude scheduled vacation hours from the calculations since they are a planned activity and are not subject to change or reduction.

DOES THE 4-DAY WORKWEEK REDUCE ABSENTEEISM?

One of the main reasons why the "four-forty" sprang into vogue in the early 1970s was the expected benefit of reduced absenteeism. Although the early experience in most companies was reflected by significant drops in absenteeism, after the initial impact wore off absenteeism returned to the old levels. Earlier starting hours increased tardiness in many companies, and staffing for vacations complicated planning. As a result, one in every dozen companies that have tried the 4-day workweek has gone back to the standard 5-day week.

A newer trend using "flexible work hours" is showing some promise for reducing both tardiness and absenteeism. The plan permits employees to come to work at any time (within reason) and go home 8 hours later. The major advantage is that such a plan permits employees to take care of personal business without using sick-leave time or other paid company time and still put in a full day's work.

It is too early to tell what effect "flexible hours" will have on absenteeism, but the concept allows a degree of freedom employees have never had before. It holds promise of improving management-employee relations and creates a condition which is conducive to good morale.

HOW EXPENSIVE ARE ACCIDENTS?

For Americans under the age of thirty-five, accidents are the leading cause of death today. During 1974, a typical year, 105,000 men, women, and children in this country were killed by accidents, and more than 11 million were injured. Every 5 seconds, someone was injured; every 5 minutes someone was killed. The total cost was $40 billion, including lost wages, medical expenses, administrative and claim settlement cost of insurance, "indirect" costs, and property damage. The fatality toll, as reported by the National Safety Council, is shown in Table 16-2.

TABLE 16-2.   THE NATIONAL ACCIDENT FATALITY TOLL IN 1974

Category	Total Deaths	Disabling Injuries (Millions)
All accidents	105,000	11.0
Motor vehicle	46,200	1.8
Public*	24,000	3.0
Home	25,500	4.0
Work	13,400	2.3

*Includes recreation, transportation except motor-vehicle, public building accidents, etc.
Source: Accident Facts, 1975 Edition, National Safety Council, Chicago, 1975, p. 3.

WHAT CAUSES ACCIDENTS?

Accidents are caused by hazardous physical conditions, improper attitudes toward safety, and human physical defects. Many employees of small businesses are injured by falls, slipping, tripping, improper lifting, and by striking some part of the body on other objects. Hand, foot, and back injuries are common.

A careful analysis of accidents reveals that almost 90 percent of them are caused by unsafe acts—by people doing something they should not, or failing to do something they should. The reason can be traced to ignorance of the proper procedure (caused by improper training), failure to observe hazards, inattention and carelessness, or poor mental attitude toward safety ("Accidents never happen to me"). Whatever the reason, the significant fact is that most accidents can be prevented because they are created by people. They can be prevented by a strong safety program which trains employees and enforces safety rules. It is management's responsibility to see that this is done.

WHAT STEPS CAN A SMALL STORE OWNER TAKE TO PREVENT ACCIDENTS?

The first step is to look for, identify, and eliminate all the physical safety hazards you can find. Some will be easy to find, others will require more effort. Tripping hazards, wet or slippery areas, poorly lighted stairways, improper stacking, and unsafe accumulations of waste are easy to spot. Your local fire department can help you spot fire hazards. Others can be spotted by use of a checklist like the one shown in Table 16-3.

TABLE 16-3. CHECKLIST FOR LOCATING HAZARDS IN A SMALL STORE

Look for the following kinds of danger spots when you check your store for hazards which can cause accidents.

Falls

Highly polished floors
A single stairstep in an unexpected location
Dark stairs
Unanchored or torn rugs
Wet or slippery floors
Unused display fixtures
Projecting objects, such as open drawers behind counters
Wastebaskets, stock cartons, and ladders
Loose wires

Stockroom Hazards

Check for improper storage, or improper use of papercutters, scissors, and razor blades. (Be sure that employees use proper knife for opening cartons.)

Dollies, carts, and other materials handling equipment
Goods improperly stacked, especially on high shelves
Ladders in bad repair

Aisles

Narrow, or crowded, aisles are dangerous, especially when employees are in a hurry. For one-way traffic, an aisle should be 2 feet wider than your widest stockcart. For two-way traffic, the aisle should be 3 feet wider than twice the width of your widest cart. Eliminate wherever possible sharp inclines, narrow passageways, and low ceilings. Even when you have taken these precautions, you have to be on the lookout for the following hazards:

Obstructions in aisles
Protruding valves and pipes
Blind corners

Fire Hazards

Even though your local fire department may inspect retail stores periodically, include fire hazards in your check. Thus you can be sure that the recommendations of the fire department are in force. Look for the following:

Accumulations of waste paper, rags, and so on
Smoking in areas containing flammable materials
Insufficient ash trays for smokers
Unmarked fire exits
Blocked fire exits
Fire doors which need repairs
Wrong size electrical fuses
Frayed or exposed electrical wires
Fire hose which has been weakened by rot
Extinguishers which need recharging (A store should have one for paper fires and another for electrical fires.)

Miscellaneous Hazards

Loose overhead plaster
Loose overhead light fixtures
Elevators (If you have one, has it been inspected recently?)

Source: S. J. Curtis, *Preventing Accidents in Small Stores*, Small Marketers Aids, No. 104, U.S. Small Business Administration, Washington, 1974.

When you check for hazards, you will find some which you cannot remove. The next best thing is to mark them with bright colors, signs, or posted rules which govern their use. Such approaches can be used for cutting and grinding equipment, open drawers, electrical hazards, overhead pipes, and protruding valves. A list of rules or reminders can serve as a discussion guide for short 10- to 15-minute accident-prevention discussions held as often as possible. Such a list is shown in Table 16-4.

TABLE 16-4. FIFTEEN SAMPLE RULES FOR PREVENTING INJURIES

The best rules for preventing injuries are those which are specific. Keep in mind that employees are more willing to observe your rules when they know the reason behind them. Here are 15 rules that will apply to practically all small stores:

1. If you smoke, smoke only in authorized areas and use an ashtray. Don't throw matches or ashes into the wastebasket or into an empty carton.
2. Open doors slowly to avoid hitting anyone coming from the other side.
3. When moving tanks and carts, watch out for customers and fellow workers.
4. Don't stand in front of a closed door.
5. Clean up liquid spilt on the floor immediately.
6. Use handrails when going up or down stairs. Never carry anything so heavy or bulky that you don't have one hand free to hold the railing. Carry so you can see where you are going.
7. Don't run—walk.
8. Never indulge in horseplay.
9. Never stand on an open drawer or climb on stock shelves.
10. When using a ladder, make sure that it is steady.
11. Don't leave drawers or cabinet doors open.
12. Remove staples with a staple remover.
13. Open cartons with the proper tool.
14. Keep selling and nonselling areas neat at all times.
15. When a repairman is working in your area, move out of his way and warn customers.

Source: S. J. Curtis, *Preventing Accidents in Small Stores*, Small Marketers Aids, No. 104, U.S. Small Business Administration, Washington, 1974.

Enlist the cooperation of your employees in finding and correcting hazards. Plan regular meetings where hazards are discussed, first-aid techniques are demonstrated, and emergency procedures are outlined. Emergency numbers to be called should be prominently posted, and a first-aid kit should be provided for minor injuries.

Finally, be alert to unsafe practices. If you see some of your employees working unsafely, stop what you are doing and go over the situation with them. Good enforcement which results in training and discussion of the reasons for working safely will pay dividends. Above all, resist the temptation to criticize, belittle, or embarrass employees who occasionally "forget" the rules. Impress on your employees the notion that you are interested in their well-being and are concerned about their safety. Properly handled, the safety program can be a motivator and a morale builder.

CAN YOU GET INTO TROUBLE BY IGNORING SAFETY IN YOUR BUSINESS?

If your place of business has hazards that are likely to cause death or serious personal harm to your employees, you are probably violating the 1970 Occupational Safety and Health Act. This act carries penalties up to $10,000 or jail terms for repeated and willful violations of its standards. It is important that employers be aware of their obligations under the act.

Many states have now adopted the provisions of the federal Occupational Safety and Health Act and have enacted legislation of their own, with central enforcement authority for all occupational safety and health standards placed in state agencies whose primary function is the administration of industrial safety.

Practically all workers, except domestic and household workers, and those in mining, who fall under the jurisdiction of other legislation, are covered by the 1970 law.

WHAT IS TURNOVER?

Turnover refers to the mobility of people coming to work for a company or leaving the company for some reason. It includes all the new hires, those who are rehired after temporary layoffs, and those coming in from another division of the company. These are called *accessions*. Turnover also includes all employees laid off because of a reduction in force, those who are discharged for cause, and those who voluntarily quit, retire, or leave the payroll for other reasons such as military service, death, and so forth. The latter group are termed *separations* when calculating the turnover rate.

When the number of people falling into all these categories is divided by the total number of people on the payroll for a specified period and multiplied by 100, you get the turnover rate. If you hire three new workers during the month, if one retires and two quit, and if your average labor force during the month is 75, your turnover rate is:

$$\frac{3 + 1 + 2}{75} \times 100 = 8\% \text{ per month}$$

The average work force is determined in a manner similar to that used in calculating the absentee rate. The rate is usually calculated monthly and the percentage compared with that of other businesses like yours. Such data is published by the Bureau of Labor Statistics.

Turnover rates vary between companies and between departments in the same company. The national average for all businesses in the United States is about 7 percent a month or 84 percent a year. It is not unusual for some businesses to experience turnover rates in excess of 100 percent per year. The costs associated with such rates are significant.

The turnover rate can be influenced by your decision to include all accessions and separations without exception, or to exclude from the calculations unavoidable separations such as retirements, deaths, and employees leaving for military service.

CAN YOU PUT A PRICE TAG ON TURNOVER?

Depending on the job being considered, it costs anywhere from $150 to several thousand dollars to replace a single worker who leaves. One source puts turnover cost at "500 times the hourly pay rate" for the employee being replaced. This means that it would cost about $2,000 to replace a worker making $4 an hour.

Turnover costs involve costs for advertising, agency fees, brochures, booklets, and the time of recruiters. Selecting and hiring costs include the costs of screening and processing application letters, answering letters, interviewing applicants, providing medical examinations, checking references, testing, making security checks, providing travel expenses, and making credit investigations, and similar costs. Keep in mind that several potential applicants must be processed to fill a single job, so the costs of all recruiting, selection, and hiring are charged to filling the one opening. When the number of applicants is large in relation to the number actually hired, the cost per person hired becomes impressive.

WHAT CAN YOU DO ABOUT TURNOVER?

Turnover is almost always related to poor morale. An examination of your management practices, especially those which affect job satisfaction, will reveal areas for improvement. In addition, here are some specific suggestions:

1. Screen new workers carefully to be sure they are qualified to do the job for which you plan to hire them.

2. Plan an orientation program designed to integrate them into the work group and give them a feeling of "belonging." The sooner you can do this the better.

3. Follow up with a training program aimed at increasing the employee's skill and sense of accomplishment.

4. Pay attention to grievances, either real or imagined. Put rumors to rest and listen for signs of job discontent.

5. Try to find out the real reasons why employees are voluntarily leaving your business. This will give you a clue to improved job relations and help you correct the causes of job turnover.

HOW MUCH STEALING GOES ON IN BUSINESS?

According to the U.S. Department of Commerce, crimes against business totaled a whopping $20.3 billion in 1974. This is the combined total of shoplifting, employee theft, highjacking, and similar offenses. This represents a 30 percent increase over 1971. It is estimated that 75 percent of these crimes are committed by employees.[3]

Insurance company statistics indicate that United States businesses lose $10 million every day because of employee theft and embezzlement—most of it in the form of small thefts by relatively honest persons.

WHAT CAUSES EMPLOYEES TO STEAL FROM THEIR EMPLOYERS?

Many are tempted to steal because of debts they cannot pay or because they habitually live beyond their income. Some employees steal in an attempt to "get even" with employers for real or imagined grievances. Others do it because it is easy and because management seems unconcerned about security. They view what they are doing not as stealing but rather as taking and rationalize that the company has so much of whatever they take that it will never miss it.

The climate for dishonesty is often inadvertently created by management. If you trust too many people with keys, cash, safe combinations, and critical records and do not take active steps to prevent in-plant pilferage, you are making it easy for some "trusted" employee to steal your business right from under your nose. There are few businesses where dishonest employees are not busily at work. Such employees are protected by management's indifference as they continue to steal more and more.

The owner who does not exercise tight control over invoices, purchase orders, material requisitions, and credits is asking for embezzlement, fraud, and theft. Dishonest office workers and production and maintenance personnel thrive on sloppily kept records, unwatched inventories, and haphazard physical security.

To control theft, you must have an active program of loss prevention, and it is important that evidence of such program be demonstrated by security checks, spot audits, periodic inventories, lock changes, testing of alarms, and systems audits.

[3]See "More and More Businesses Stolen Blind," *U.S. News & World Report*, June 16, 1976, pp. 28–29.

Haphazard physical security is high on the list of invitations to theft. If you are careless about key and lock control, you are inviting dishonest employees to take advantage of the situation and enter your business after work.

The more doors a plant has, the more avenues of theft it offers. A business designed for maximum security will have a minimum number of active doors, with a guard or supervisor stationed near each door. A supervisor should be present when materials or finished goods are being received or shipped or when trash is being removed. Central station alarm systems should be used to protect a plant after hours. This system will provide the only indication of possible theft when an employee hides inside and leaves the building after closing hours. The use of "deadbolts" which require a key to open the door is effective if local regulations do not prohibit the use of such a lock.

Windows and skylights afford easy access to buildings, especially if they are located in alleyways or on little-traveled streets. Windows accessible from the street or adjoining buildings should contain heavily wired glass and be securely locked from inside. If possible, bars or a heavy screen should cover each of them to delay attempts to enter.

Burglar alarm systems can give protection for all accessible openings. While an alarm system does represent an expense, you will probably find that one of the many types of alarm systems can be adapted to your building at a reasonable cost.

Fire-resistant, burglar-proof safes should be used for all valuable records and cash. At night, they should be illuminated by an overhead light and placed where a guard or police officer can observe them.

Safe combinations should be changed once a year or oftener if personnel having them leave the company.

Locked cash registers and cash drawers are open invitations to burglars. At night, leave them empty and open. In this way you can avoid both the loss of cash and damage to the container.

Each business has its own peculiarities which dictate potential areas where thefts are most likely. However, certain general approaches can be used almost universally.

Here are a few general rules that can help reduce pilferage:

☐ Inspect every lunch box, bag, or package as employees leave the plant.

☐ Snap all padlocks shut on hasps when not in use to prevent switching of locks.

☐ Never leave the key hanging on a nail near the lock where a "crooked" worker can borrow it and have a duplicate made.

- Do not allow trash to accumulate or be picked up near storage sites of valuable goods.
- Supervise trash pickups and inspect trash receptacles at irregular intervals if you have reason to suspect collusion between employees and trash collectors.
- Do not allow trucks to approach the loading platform until they are ready to load or unload.
- Do not allow drivers to load their own trucks by taking goods from stock.

HOW CAN YOU TEST YOUR CONTROL PROCEDURES TO SEE IF THEY WORK?

One effective method is to input deliberate errors. Put more goods on the shipping platform than the shipping order calls for. Withhold an invoice from your bookkeeper and accounts-receivable clerk. Wait to see how your employees respond to such obvious errors. Unannounced inspections are another way of checking your procedures. Do not forget to cover the second and third shifts with your audits. Thieves are delighted when you consider it inconvenient to check on night-shift operations. Incidentally, you should keep the means of testing the controls secret. Employees should know that there are controls, but they should not know what specific checks and reviews are used. This technique keeps dishonest employees off balance and keeps them from developing the feeling that they can beat your system. The use of surprise elements in your loss-prevention program will go a long way in keeping employees honest.

HOW EXPENSIVE IS MATERIAL HANDLING?

It has been estimated that 25 cents of every dollar spent by American industry goes for material handling. In some businesses, material handling claims as much as 80 percent of the expense dollar. Material handling is responsible for 50 percent of the cost of the average manufactured product. One out of every ten industrial workers is employed full time in moving, handling, and storing materials.

Many informed people, even in business and industry, find the statistics about material-handling costs hard to believe, probably because they have never seriously looked at the enormous potential for saving money which exists in this area.

WHAT FUNCTIONS CONTRIBUTE TO THE HIGH COST OF MATERIAL HANDLING?

In following raw materials through production to the finished product, there are six definable material-handling functions. Each adds something to the cost of the product and each represents a potential area for cost reduction. Here they are.

1. *Transportation of Raw Material.* Each delivery of a material to a plant by truck, rail, air, or water generates cost.

2. *Receiving.* Most activities that occur at the receiving dock, such as unloading and moving materials to their assigned places, constitute material handling. The physical inspection to verify quantities and quality involves additional handling. The handling often takes more time than the inspection itself.

3. *Storage and Warehousing.* Stocking, order picking, assembly of orders, packing, and shipping are material-handling operations. Material or parts may be stored at the workplace in bins or on pallets.

4. *In-Process Handling.* All movements of material, parts, or products between departments and to individual workplaces add to the cost of handling. It is not uncommon for pieces of material to be moved as many as 50 times, manually or mechanically, as they are combined with others in a load.

5. *Handling at the Workplace.* In some small plants this is the costliest and least recognized of all material-handling operations. Manual feeding of single pieces of material into a machine and disposal of the pieces can account for more than 50 percent of the operations in a work cycle. This is a phase of material handling that offers great opportunities for reducing labor costs.

6. *Distribution.* Labeling and packaging of finished goods represent the final phase of material handling.

WHAT IS THE PAYOFF FROM A WELL-DESIGNED MATERIAL-HANDLING SYSTEM?

Cost-reduction experts believe that with a little ingenuity and application of a few basic principles, material-handling costs can be cut in half. In a manufacturing company spending 50 cents of the payroll dollar just to move things around, such a reduction can amount to 25 percent of the total payroll.

Material handling is wholly a service function but it directly affects costs and profits. Improvements in material handling will accomplish some or all of the following objectives.

Reduce Waste. Modern material handling reduces waste by keeping to a minimum spoilage caused by rough handling and improper stacking.

Improve Working Conditions. Efficient material handling makes for safe working conditions; it reduces employee fatigue and plant accidents. Your workers will be more productive when their personal comfort is improved.

Increase Productive Capacity. Material-handling methods can smooth out work flow and eliminate delays and bottlenecks. In so doing, they can increase productivity per worker-hour, increase machine efficiency by reducing downtime, and improve production control.

Reduce Costs.   Modern material handling will reduce your costs of space by utilizing it to better advantage. In addition, inventories can be better controlled, and, through planned package handling, pilferage can be cut.

WHAT GUIDELINES ARE AVAILABLE FOR PLANNING MATERIAL-HANDLING REQUIREMENTS?

The principles followed in analyzing and improving material-handling procedures utilize the "common sense" and "question-asking" techniques developed by work simplification advocates in their systematic approach to job improvement. Table 16-5 lists some of the principles which apply to material handling.

WHAT ARE THE SYMPTOMS OF INEFFICIENT MATERIAL HANDLING?

To control costs effectively in material handling, you need to know where to look for waste and inefficiency. Some handling operations are themselves inefficient. Others affect production operations in such a way that costs are increased there. In order to see the entire problem, a cost analysis must look both at the services rendered by the material-handling function and at the areas being serviced. Thus, by studying the entire production process, costs attributable to material handling can be brought into perspective.

One of the most noticeable symptoms of poor material handling is idle machine time. Interruptions of the production flow because of a lack of material can shut down entire lines, causing additional costs from rescheduling and extra setup time. Large inventories are often the result of slow movement of materials. Usually, the more efficient a material-handling system, the smaller the inventory required. Breakage and damage to materials being moved can be traced to poorly trained material handlers. Maintenance costs for material-handling equipment represent a double loss—the cost of the time and parts spent for corrective action, plus the loss of the equipment's useful time. Improper use of material-handling equipment is the major contributing factor in such avoidable costs.

HOW MUCH OF THE SALES DOLLAR IS SPENT BY THE PURCHASING DEPARTMENT?

Depending on the nature of your business, the amount spent by the purchasing department amounts to somewhere between 35 and 75 cents of every sales dollar. In manufacturing, it is slightly more than

50 cents. In plants doing primarily packaging or assembly operations, it will run on the upper side of the range. In service industries, it will tend toward the lower side.

TABLE 16-5. THE 20 PRINCIPLES OF MATERIAL HANDLING

1. *Planning Principle.* Plan all material handling and storage activities to obtain maximum overall operating efficiency.
2. *Systems Principle.* Integrate as many handling activities as is practical into a coordinated system of operations covering vendor, receiving, storage, production, inspection, packaging, warehousing, shipping, transportation, and customer.
3. *Material Flow Principle.* Provide an operation sequence and equipment layout optimizing material flow.
4. *Simplification Principle.* Simplify handling by reducing, eliminating, or combining unnecessary movements and/or equipment.
5. *Gravity Principle.* Utilize gravity to move material wherever practical.
6. *Space Utilization Principle.* Make optimum use of the building cube.
7. *Unit Size Principle.* Increase the quantity, size, or weight of unit loads or their flow rate.
8. *Mechanization Principle.* Mechanize handling operations.
9. *Automation Principle.* Provide automation that includes production, handling, and storage functions.
10. *Equipment Selection Principle.* In selecting handling equipment, consider all aspects of the material handled—the movement and the method to be used.
11. *Standardization Principle.* Standardize handling methods, as well as types and sizes of handling equipment.
12. *Adaptability Principle.* Use methods and equipment that adapt to the widest variety of tasks and applications except where special purpose equipment is justified.
13. *Deadweight Principle.* Reduce ratio of deadweight of mobile handling equipment to load carried.
14. *Utilization Principle.* Plan for optimum utilization of handling equipment and manpower.
15. *Maintenance Principle.* Plan for preventive maintenance and scheduled repairs of all handling equipment.
16. *Obsolescence Principle.* Replace obsolete handling methods and equipment when more efficient methods or equipment will improve operations.
17. *Control Principle.* Use material handling activities to improve control of production, inventory, and order handling.
18. *Capacity Principle.* Use handling equipment to help achieve desired production capacity.
19. *Performance Principle.* Determine effectiveness of handling performance in terms of expense per unit handled.
20. *Safety Principle.* Provide suitable methods and equipment for safe handling.

Source: Educational Committee of the Material Handling Institute, Inc., *Improving Material Handling in Small Business,* Small Business Management Series, No. 4, 3d ed., U.S. Small Business Administration, Washington, 1969.

It is obvious from these statistics that procurement activities can contribute significantly to the company's profits. The potential for savings through smart buying was expressed well by the old Yankee merchants who said, "Goods well-bought are half sold."

You should not overlook the fact that it requires many dollars of sales to earn the dollar that can be saved at the source in purchasing.

ISN'T FINDING THE LOWEST COST THE ESSENCE OF PROFITABLE PURCHASING?

Not necessarily. Some people would be quick to point out that you get what you pay for. But the answer to this question goes deeper than that. Perhaps John Ruskin said it best:

It's unwise to pay too much, but it's unwise to pay too little, too. When you pay too much, you lose a little money . . . that is all. When you pay too little, you sometimes lose everything because the thing you bought was incapable of doing the thing it was bought to do. The Common Law of business balance prohibits paying a little and getting a lot . . . it can't be done. If you deal with the lowest bidder, it is well to add something for the risk you run, and if you do that, you will have enough to pay for something better.

HOW CAN YOU SAVE ANY MONEY BY JUST PLACING ORDERS?

Purchasing is more than just placing orders. Although the purchasing department's main job is to get things which are needed to run the business, most purchasing personnel feel that management expects too little of them. Here are some areas where the purchasing department can make major contributions to profit improvement:

Vendor Efficiency.   Good buyers know that they must be interested in a vendor's problems. Their responsibility does not end when the order is placed, for there are schedules to be met and quality levels to be maintained. If a vendor gets into trouble, it is not uncommon for the purchasing department to request special assistance from the buyer's technical staff to help resolve the problems and assure on-time delivery and acceptable quality.

Value Buying.   The true measure of value in buying is how effectively and economically a purchased material or product serves the purpose for which it is purchased. There have been many instances where the purchasing department found better products which could do the job for less. Obviously, a material inadequate for the purpose is no bargain at any price. On the other hand, overspecification and the money paid for a product which is better than what is needed is wasteful. The purchasing department is in a unique position to save costs by evaluating the need and finding the best way of satisfying it. Better materials at the same cost, equivalent materials at a lower cost, or a material that is readily available to replace one whose supply is unpredictable are examples of value buying.

Better Cost Analysis. The purchasing department's contribution to profit through negotiating prices with vendors is commonly recognized. Savings in such areas as tooling costs, freight charges, cash discounts, and quantity discounts are often substantial. Cash discounts of 2 percent are commonly offered if cash is paid within 10 days. Quantity discounts often make it possible to save up to 50 percent of the cost by buying 10 percent more.

New Buying Sources. Savings in this area can be sizable. You can sometimes find differences of 100 percent between prices quoted by different vendors for the same product. Savings are possible particularly on the less obvious items like factory supplies and office supplies.

Standard Materials. By standardizing materials and getting better parts specifications from the engineering department, it is often possible to buy less costly materials or to increase the number of vendors to choose from. Standard products cost less than custom-made "specials," and they are more widely available. Since they do not have to be purchased in production lots or stored in such large quantities, they can lead to savings in inventory costs.

HOW CAN YOU MAKE AN OBJECTIVE EVALUATION OF YOUR SUPPLIERS?

The only sensible way to evaluate your suppliers is with some sort of vendor rating. To establish an objective evaluation, you have to select criteria which you feel are important and determine a method of grading each individual criterion in a logical manner.

Some of the important criteria you will want to consider are quality, price, delivery, and service. Once you have decided on the relative importance of each criterion, assign point values to them so that they total 100 points. Give more points to those you feel are more important. You might end up with a plan like this:

Criterion	Points
Quality	40
Price	30
Delivery	20
Service	10
	100

Next, develop some meaningful way of comparing vendor performance on each criterion. For example, you can obtain a numerical rating on quality by dividing acceptable lots from a vendor by the total number of lots he or she has delivered and multiplying this quotient by the point score for that criterion. A vendor who has had 2 lots rejected out of 10 delivered would get:

$$\frac{8}{10} \times 40 = 32 \text{ points for quality}$$

In a similar manner, numerical values for the remaining criteria can be developed. Price performance might consist of the lowest quoted price divided by the vendor's price and the quotient multiplied by the price points. Delivery could relate on-time deliveries to total deliveries in the same manner. Service would be concerned with the competence of the sales representative, the handling of invoices and credits, and the promptness with which complaints are handled.

Such a system requires good records of delivery performance and price information from quotations sent to vendors. It is fairly complex, but it will provide a good numerical rating for each vendor.

WHAT IS MEANT BY INVENTORY?

Inventory is the raw materials, goods to be resold, parts, shop and office supplies, and machinery and equipment needed by the business to perform its function. Such items represent money spent to accumulate enough of everything to maintain production schedules and satisfy the demands of your customers. Since you have money tied up in inventory, your working capital is less by the value of the inventory. Inventory shows as an asset on the balance sheet but, unlike working capital, you cannot spend it. To make matters worse, it becomes worth less the longer you hold it.

When you look at the cost of your inventory and compare it with sales, the ratio normally runs 80 to 85 percent for a wholesaler, 60 to 65 percent for a retailer, and between 30 and 50 percent for a manufacturer. Even a small reduction in inventory will release cash for you to use for reinvestment or paying your bills.

WHAT IS THE IDEAL AMOUNT OF INVENTORY?

That amount which permits you not to run out of anything and lose sales or customers, but which does not unnecessarily tie up the capital you need for other things. If this sounds contradictory, it makes the point that inventory is neither easy to describe nor easy to control. To retailers, who must have the "right" sizes, colors, and styles on hand to satisfy the anticipated needs of their customers, deciding what to carry in stock can be a nightmare. If they guess wrong, they will have too much of some items and will be forced to mark them down in order to move them; on other items, they will have too little and will experience shortages. Their unhappy customers will buy at other stores. If manufacturers miscalculate the amount of spoilage their operation will generate, they can run out of some materials and experience costly delays. If they have too much in inventory, they might have to borrow to remain solvent. Effective inventory control is the only answer to such problems.

When business owners carry a larger inventory than they need, they not only tie up money unnecessarily but also subject their businesses to carrying charges on the unnecessary inventory. Carrying charges are the expenses connected with keeping inventory on hand. Some of these expenses are:

- Rent for storage space.

- Shrinkage and obsolescence.

- Physical damage (or its prevention).

- Manual and clerical labor to store inventory items and keep track of them.

- Insurance and taxes.

- Interest that could be earned on the money tied up.

- Taking of physical inventories.

- Material handling associated with inventories.

Inventory carrying charges can be high. The average for manufacturers is about 12 percent of the average inventory value. This means that for every $100 worth of inventory you carry for a year you spend $12 just keeping it on the shelf. Its value also decreases because of obsolescence or physical damage while it is in storage. So you lose two ways.

You can cut your carrying charges by increasing the turnover of your inventory. For example, if your average inventory value is $25,000 and you sell $50,000 worth of merchandise (or use $50,000 worth of material) each year, this means that you turn over your inventory twice a year. At 12 percent, your carrying charges would be $3,000 (12 percent of $25,000).

If you could increase your turnover to four times, you would have a total of only $12,500 tied up in inventory rather than $25,000, and your carrying charges would be only $1,500.

In view of the unnecessary costs which result from excessive inventory, it is a major objective of inventory control to reduce the investment tied up in inventory to the barest practical minimum. Some caution is advised about going overboard in this regard, because too rigid control can cause you to order too little too often. This practice can increase procurement costs and create a lot of unnecessary paperwork and handling.

WHAT ARE THE COMMON APPROACHES TO INVENTORY CONTROL?

Most small retail businesses control inventories through observation, physical checks, perpetual inventory records, or a combination of these.

Observation and memory may be sufficient in a very small store where the variety of merchandise is not large, the rate of sales is consistent, and the owner is in very close contact with the merchandise. This method is not very accurate, however.

A physical inventory check of the entire stock requires a great deal of time for an accurate count and must be done during nonworking periods. The frequency of such checks will vary according to the rate of sale and the value of the merchandise. The physical check is normally made by two people going from item to item, with one person calling off the name of the item, the number on hand, and the value of the item, while the other person records the information. The data accumulated from such an inventory can be compared with the previous inventory and with merchandise ordered during the period between inventories.

Perpetual inventories, which seek to keep a running tally on the current stock of each item, are used by many small businesses. In the perpetual inventory, a record is kept of each item of merchandise as it is brought into the store, stocked, and sold. Because of the amount of expense involved, perpetual inventories are difficult to justify from a cost standpoint. They are most successful in the control of high-dollar items which need strict control. Such items receive a great deal of management attention. Hence, the organization is disciplined to keep close watch on them and the control is likely to be more accurate. The advantage of such a record is that it tells you at all times the amount of goods on hand, its value, and the sizes and styles in stock.

Inventories may be controlled by the use of turnover ratios supplied by trade associations or by agencies such as Dun & Bradstreet. By comparing your ratio with those of successful businesses like yours you can determine whether your inventory is too high. If the ratio is lower than the average, it could indicate excessive inventory or poor sales volume. It is best to have a turnover ratio a little above the average for your type of business.

Although various kinds of inventory records are kept on highvalue items, the low-value, "nuts-and-bolts" items are often controlled with simple records or no records at all. Some examples of "no record" control are:

Bin Tag Control. Under this procedure, records are maintained at the bin location. Entries reflecting withdrawals or additions to stock are entered on a bin card. Hand-calculated balances are used to determine when to reorder.

Level Control. The stock bin has a marked level. When the stock falls below that level, a predetermined order quantity is ordered.

Dual Bin Control. Two bins of the material are kept. When the first is emptied, the order is placed. At that time the second bin of material is used until the new order arrives.

Barrel Peeping. This procedure uses no benchmarks or level controls. It utilizes a physical check of the item to determine whether there is enough for current needs. It is adaptable to such items as tape, gases, solder, and other items for which measures of consumption are not normally kept or for which predictions of usage may be difficult to obtain.

SELF-CHECK OF KEY CONCEPTS

This exercise is designed to test your understanding of the material presented in Chapter 16. Choose the response, *True* or *False*, which best fits each statement. Correct responses are presented in the back of the text.

1. Most accidents are caused by people and can be prevented with proper training.
2. Absenteeism can be reduced by 50 percent by a well-planned program of control.
3. Of all American industrial workers, 25 percent are employed full time in material handling.
4. In manufacturing, over 50 percent of every sales dollar is spent by the purchasing department.
5. It is impossible to determine the causes of 30 percent of the accidents that happen at work.
6. According to statistics published by the National Safety Council, more people are killed accidentally at home than at work each year.
7. The labor turnover rate can be calculated by dividing the number of people on the payroll for a given period by the total number of terminations for the same period.
8. After you work overtime consistently for a while, you will reach a point where your output is no more than it would be for a normal 8-hour day.
9. One of the principles of material handling states that you should use gravity wherever possible.
10. Large inventories are desirable since they assure having in stock anything the customer wants.

PERFORMANCE PROBLEMS AND PROJECTS

1. Turnover annually runs about 84 percent for companies in the United States. Examine the turnover statistics for the following companies and determine whether their records are better or worse than the national average.

Annual Turnover Statistics in 19__

Category	Company A	Company B
Voluntary quits:		
Retirement	2	4
Military service	1	3
To accept other employment	6	17
Moving out of area	0	6
Going into business	1	0
Marriage	2	7
Other	3	26
	15	63
Involuntary separations:		
Reductions in force	2	13
Disciplinary terminations	0	2
Other	0	1
	2	16
Accessions:		
New hires	23	13
Transfers from other divisions	0	2
Recalls from layoff	2	4
	25	19
Employment:		
January 1, 19__	50	318
December 31, 19__	58	258
Annual turnover rate	__%	__%

2. You are the owner of a small machine shop employing ten workers. You have just estimated a job for the Tru-Val Manufacturing Company to provide some machined parts. Based on their need date, you estimate the job as follows:

80 hours of labor at $8.50 per hour (straight-time)	$ 680.00
Material, including 2 percent for scrap	536.00
Shipping costs (motor freight)	35.50
	$1,251.50

Your plan is to work 10 days of 8 hours each with no overtime. This will leave 2 days to pack and ship the parts so that they will reach the customer on time.

The day before you are ready to start the job, you get a call from Tru-Val stating that their schedule has changed. This change will require delivery 2 days earlier. The purchasing agent asks for a new price for the expedited deliveries. After a quick check, you decide that 8 days of 10 hours each will enable you to meet the new requirements. You will not have to work any Saturday or Sunday hours. To assure on-time delivery, you decide to use air freight instead of motor freight. This means of transportation is 20 percent more expensive.

a. How much will the overtime hours add to your labor costs?
b. Examine Table 16-1 and determine whether your efficiency loss will be significant. If so, add something for efficiency loss.
c. Calculate the new shipping cost.
d. What will your new estimate to Tru-Val be?

3. As office manager of a small office employing six workers, you have been checking the monthly expenses for postage and note that postage stamp usage has doubled during the past 6 months. The volume of correspondence has remained about the same. There has been no accountability for stamps in the past. You now want to set up a control to check the usage. What system would you install?

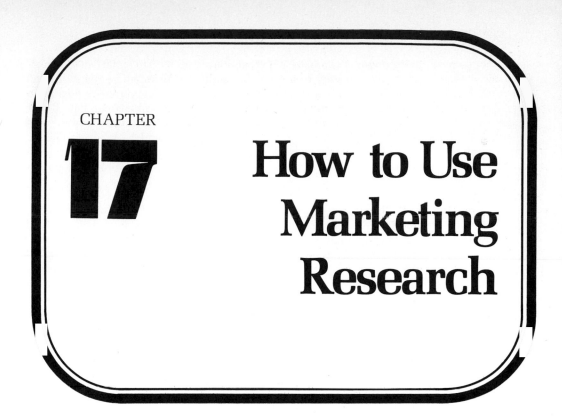

CHAPTER

17

How to Use Marketing Research

PERFORMANCE OBJECTIVES

After reading this chapter you should be able to evaluate the importance of marketing research in the planning efforts of small business owners and to relate the cost of such activity to the benefits to be gained. Specifically, you should be able to:

1. Differentiate between the terms *market* and *marketing*.
2. Explain how data gained from marketing research helps business people make better decisions.
3. Discuss the primary uses of marketing research.
4. Describe the kind of statistical data provided by Bureau of the Census publications.
5. Assess the probable results of carrying out a research study without first having clearly defined the problem.
6. Describe how sales managers can use marketing research techniques to evaluate the performance of their sales forces.
7. Explain how the validity of data collected by personal interviews can be affected by bias and other factors.
8. Evaluate the effectiveness of telephone interviews as a means of collecting marketing data.

INTRODUCTION

Today's business environment is character-ized by change. Markets have shifted from downtown areas to outlying shopping cen-ters, leaving many "ghost towns" in their wake. Customers are more mobile, more af-fluent, and more unpredictable than ever before. There have been significant changes in distribution methods and handling tech-niques, all designed to satisfy ever-increas-ing customer demands for goods and ser-vices. Night-time and Sunday shopping have become commonplace. The advent of the discount store and the supermarket has revolutionized merchandising techniques. And television has made it possible to reach millions of potential customers simul-taneously, providing advertising oppor-tunities never before possible.

What this all adds up to is the fact that busi-ness people today must be aware of the changes taking place and remain flexible in their planning. They must keep their finger on the pulse of trends toward newer ways of doing business and be ready to change when it is to their advantage. They must be alert to the impact of national affairs on their industry as a whole.

An understanding of marketing research will enable them to find answers to many of their marketing questions. This chapter dis-cusses the basic objectives of marketing re-search and provides examples of the various uses to which the tools of marketing re-search can be put in collecting and analyz-ing marketing information.

WHAT DOES THE TERM *MARKETING* INCLUDE?

Marketing includes just about every activity you can think of that is related to the effort required to move goods from the producer to the consumer in a way that creates optimum satisfaction of consumer demands. No one agrees on a definitive list of marketing functions. There are at least 25 or 30 distinct functions which may be readily identified as "marketing" activities, including selling, merchandis-ing, promotion, transportation, advertising, storage, pricing, market analysis, distribution, product planning, and display techniques. These, in turn, may be subdivided into dozens of other activities which total over 100.

The term *market* is often confused with *marketing* in the mind of people outside the profession. *Marketing* is a broader term than *market:* it covers the entire distribution process.

The term *market* refers to the aggregate demand of the poten-tial buyers for a product or service. In the American economy, it is used in a wide variety of ways. For example, we speak of buying food or other items in a supermarket; we buy or sell a house on a real estate market; we buy or sell wheat on a commodity market, common or preferred stocks on a stock market, and bonds on a bond market. We differentiate between the urban and rural markets and speak of regional or metropolitan-area markets. We may also refer to larger geographic markets, such as the West Coast market and, in terms of international trade, the Common Market.

Additionally, business people use the word *market* when they speak of special groups of persons as potential customers. For exam-ple, they refer to the teenage market, the senior citizens market, the leisure market, and the ethnic-group food markets, such as the Spanish-American and the Jewish markets.

So we can see that the term *market* has come to mean far more than the physical location of a marketplace.

WHAT IS MARKETING RESEARCH?

Marketing research is the means by which information about the various elements that make up buying and selling is obtained and evaluated. The technique is characterized by a systematic gathering, recording, and analyzing of data which is related to the marketing of goods and services. Business people who want to know how many potential customers are in their proposed trade area, or whether they should start a bookstore in a shopping center, or how they can increase sales by 10 per cent, or what customers think about product X need information which can be obtained through marketing research.

Marketing research is primarily a fact-finding and compiling activity which provides data on which the manager can make decisions or decide upon the proper courses of action to take regarding marketing problems.

WHO NEEDS MARKETING RESEARCH?

Anyone who is planning to offer a product or a service can benefit from marketing research. In order to make intelligent decisions and plans for such a step you need accurate and current information about your "buying public" and the means you will employ to make your goods or services available to them. The basic questions answered by marketing research are these:

☐ Who is likely to buy my product or services?

☐ Where do these potential customers live in relation to my place of business?

☐ How often will they buy and in what amounts?

☐ What styles, colors, and sizes will they want?

Marketing research can obtain the answers to these questions and others which you will need when deciding how to plan the movement of products or services to the point of ultimate sale.

Because the acceptance or rejection of a consumer product is dependent not only upon consumers' needs, wants, and preferences but also upon their buying motives, tastes, and habits, producers annually spend thousands of dollars to discover how best to satisfy the demands of consumers. And since consumer demands are constantly changing, marketing research must be continuous.

Changes in marketing habits have highlighted the need for a means of keeping up with the rapidly changing complexion of the market.

City people used to shop downtown and depended upon public transportation. Population shifts to the suburbs and the great increase in automobile ownership have caused the suburban shopping center to become the dominant retail outlet in many parts of the country. This mobility and the general availability of larger and better home freezers and refrigerators have changed the food-buying habits from daily purchases at the neighborhood store to large-scale purchases, at lower prices, on a once-a-week or longer basis.

In a similar manner, new living patterns coupled with shorter working hours have created an interest in convenience products, do-it-yourself goods, and sporting equipment. The increased purchasing power of our affluent society has resulted in increased demands for luxury products and services. The growth of television as a promotion and advertising medium has revolutionized the methods of selling to a mass market. This, in turn, steps up the rate of changing habits even further.

What it all adds up to is the need for a business to remain flexible. The very speed with which changes continue to occur increases the risks of doing business. Marketing research is one way of minimizing such risks.

WHAT IS ACCOMPLISHED BY MARKETING RESEARCH?

There are many marketing problems that can be solved with well-planned research. A knowledge of customer needs, preferences, and desires is vital to the operation of a modern business.

Customer reactions to the introduction of proposed new products are needed for predicting the probable success of penetrating the market and capturing a profitable share. Test marketing of new products enables the researcher to determine the degree of customer acceptance before large expenditures are committed to an all-out marketing effort.

Marketing research can provide valuable information regarding the size and makeup of the market in your area. Such information as family size, income level, type of occupation, age, and sex of your potential customers will weigh heavily in your decision to locate a store or plant. Once a good location is found, the merchant must be aware of the changes in market geography caused by the introduction of new shopping centers that lure customers from one geographic area to another. Business people must be aware of such market trends and be prepared to cope with them. This often involves changing location or building branch stores in order to remain competitive.

Other marketing research addresses the problems related to distribution of products from manufacturers to ultimate users. Finding the most economical and efficient marketing channels is necessary if customer demands are to be met in a timely manner and at lowest cost.

Marketing research is sometimes directed toward planning sales territories, forecasting sales, and establishing sales quotas. Questions associated with such planning activities must be answered accurately in order to prevent costly mistakes. An intelligent analysis of marketing data will provide the manager with such assurances.

The "pulling power" of advertising can be determined by marketing research. Thus, business people can find out which media are reaching the customers needed to assure profitable operation.

Business people must be keenly aware of marketing, advertising, and distribution trends, for it is only through such awareness that they can improve their companies' positions in the marketplace. Marketing research is the tool which will enable them to keep abreast of rapidly changing buying habits, distribution patterns, and customer preferences.

CAN YOU PERFORM MARKETING RESEARCH AS A DO-IT-YOURSELF PROJECT?

The small manufacturer can make periodic collection of certain basic marketing facts—such as the distribution of company sales by salesperson, by type of customer, by order size, and the like. Company personnel may be able to get data on competitors' products, prices, and methods of sale. They might also handle other fact gathering, involving tabulations of sales or the collection of marketing data from trade sources.

Most small businesses do not have people on their full-time staff with the talent to do a thorough marketing research job. A good researcher should know techniques which come from many disciplines, including economics, statistics, accounting, psychology, industrial engineering, and mathematics. Especially important marketing problems are best handled by specially trained company personnel or by outside organizations and consultants. Good research is costly but poor research is even more costly when the answers obtained lead you to the wrong decisions.

WHERE CAN YOU GET ASSISTANCE IN DOING MARKETING RESEARCH?

If you do not have trained personnel for marketing research, you can secure assistance from professional marketing research firms, management consultants, or advertising agencies.

The marketing research firm is an organization which specializes in the field of individual problems for clients. Such an organization has both the experience and facilities for studying the problem, planning the approach, gathering data, conducting interviews, tabulating and compiling the results, and presenting the findings in a written report. The firm charges a fee for its services which is largely determined by the nature and scope of the job to be done. The fee is often quoted as a flat charge based on estimates of time, personnel, and facilities required for the job. It may be on a more variable basis such as a charge per interview, the final cost to be determined by the number of interviews obtained.

Professional management consultants provide services very similar to those of the professional marketing research firm. The basic difference is that the management consulting firm does not restrict its activities to marketing research. Fees charged by consultants for their services are generally based on a fixed rate per day for the personnel involved, with the final quotation determined by an estimate of the time required to do the job. Travel and out-of-pocket expenses are usually extra.

Advertising agencies often have marketing research services available for their clients. These may range from consultation and advice on marketing problems to the gathering and compilation of marketing data or the planning and execution of a survey. In some instances, certain services may be available to small manufacturer clients at no extra cost. In other cases, where the research job involves substantial out-of-pocket expenses, the client is expected to pay for all the expenses.

In addition to these groups, there are many college teachers of marketing who are available to carry out individual research assignments for a reasonable fee.

WHAT STATISTICAL DATA IS AVAILABLE TO MARKETING RESEARCHERS?

Because the geographical location of any given market is a primary consideration in the preparation for marketing research, the researcher has to consider not only the number of people in the area but also the population characteristics. These data include such items as number of households, sex, age, ethnic classification, marital status, and income.

Most of this data can be found in the Census of Population, which was authorized by Congress in 1787. It has been taken every 10 years since 1790. The Bureau of the Census, a part of the U.S. Department of Commerce, collects population data and publishes them for the United States as a whole, with separate volumes for each state. Typical census tables reflect per capita income, median family income, and population shifts for selected metropolitan areas. Population data can be helpful in pinpointing areas where population is increasing and also in identifying those areas where population is trending downward. Such information can be helpful in establishing or expanding markets and in searching for a site location.

In applying census statistics to your market analysis you should keep in mind that the Census Bureau compiles descriptive data. You have to do the interpreting. Interpretation starts with questions. Suppose some California manufacturers of automobile accessories want to add new sales territories in their state. Their first question would be, Where are the high concentrations of automobiles? The latest Census of Housing covering seven large counties in California would provide statistics on the number of automobiles available in each county. With this information, the manufacturers would logically think of the next question, Which geographic areas have concentrations of auto supply stores? These are the types of retail outlets that do the best job in selling your type of product. You can find this information in the Census of Retail Trade. Typical data is shown for every city in California with 500 retail establishments or more. For example, we can find that in 1970 there were 27 auto and home supply stores employing 289 people plus 21 miscellaneous automotive dealers with 127 employees in the city of Riverside. A check of the Yellow Pages would reveal their exact locations and the nature of the establishments.

If your questions relate to family size, income, or occupation, you can find information in the Census of Housing for areas as small as census tracts located in 240 different metropolitan regions throughout the United States. A census tract contains about 4,000 people.

Census tracts are further broken down into "blocks" and the following data is provided for each block:

Population statistics:

Total inhabitants in the block

Percentage of black population

Percentage of under-18 population

Percentage of over-65 population

Housing units:

Number of one-unit structures

Structures of 10 units or more

Average number of rooms

Average value

Average rent

Number of units owned

Number of units rented

Data regarding plumbing facilities

General characteristics of the population in each census tract may be found in the Census Bureau publication *Census Tracts*. This publication gives the population makeup by race, age, sex, number of children, and the marital status of all residents in the tract.

Small business owners can use census data to help them decide how to allocate their advertising budget and get the most for their advertising dollar. Effective use of advertising dollars is a matter of finding answers to two questions: (1) In what areas should I advertise? and (2) Which media reach the right audience (the one that contains my customers)? For example, if your product is a cosmetics line, you would want to gather data regarding age groupings of the female population. From the census figures, you can learn where groups of potential customers are located. You can then place advertising in the proper media (radio, magazines, newspapers, television, etc.) to reach the members of the groups. Finally, you must assure that the advertised products are stocked in retail outlets throughout the geographical areas saturated by your advertising.

WHAT APPROACH WORKS BEST FOR MARKETING RESEARCH STUDIES?

Marketing research studies follow various patterns. They may be similar in that they are geared to finding answers to one or more specific marketing problems, but they are likely to be different in the manner in which they are carried out.

The traditional problem-solving approach of stating the problem, gathering factual data, evaluating the data, and reaching a conclusion works well in marketing research, with a few frills which are unique to marketing added to the basic pattern. Here are the basic steps:

1. Defining the problem.
2. Making a preliminary investigation.
3. Planning the research.
4. Gathering factual information.
5. Interpreting the information.
6. Reaching a conclusion.

Let us look at each step in more detail.

HOW CRITICAL IS PROBLEM DEFINITION IN MARKETING RESEARCH?

Almost everything else you do in the research approach depends upon your ability to state accurately and clearly the problem or question that needs an answer. This is important because the nature of the problem determines the issues that are involved in the research, what questions to ask, and what types of solutions are needed. It is a crucial step and should not be rushed just to get on with the research. Remember the advice offered by our most effective problem solvers: "A problem well-stated is half solved." Time and money spent on determining the exact nature of the problem frequently save time and money later by eliminating false starts and the collection of data not relevant to the problem.

WHY SPENT TIME AND MONEY ON A PRELIMINARY MARKETING SURVEY?

The purpose of a preliminary survey is to develop a sharper definition of the problem and hopefully come up with a set of tentative answers. These tentative answers are developed by talking to people who are knowledgeable about the problem and by examining internal factual data related to the problem. If manufacturers propose to survey the market to determine how they can expand the market for a product, they can get a preliminary feel of the market by having research teams talk to distributors and retailers of the product. Wholesalers can quickly determine from their own records what people are buying in their broad geographical territory and how much these people are spending. Retailers can provide valuable information on sales trends for the product in their local area. All of them can tell from what leaves the shelves what their customers are buying.

Experience has taught that while all kinds of retailers should be queried, it is best to concentrate inquiries on the larger stores because of the greater volume of potential sales. It is common practice for researchers to look about the retail outlets they visit in order to observe the store's advertising methods and product-display practices and to discover whatever they can about competing products. Special notes of anything significant become a part of the study.

The talks with wholesalers and retailers are supplemented by talks with consumers who may or may not be purchasers of the product in question. To obtain the widest consumer-opinion coverage, the consumers interviewed are selected from different kinds of communities—urban, rural, large, small, and medium-sized. Within such communities consumers are picked to represent various age, race, and income groups.

Some preliminary activity will involve an examination of your own records to determine the volume of sales of the product over a period of time, the areas or regions where sales are greatest, what the trends have been, and who the biggest customers are.

WHAT CONCLUSIONS CAN BE REACHED FROM A PRELIMINARY SURVEY?

The preliminary survey helps define the direction the formal research study will take. The researcher will be able to determine, after looking at the results of the preliminary study, what facts are needed to resolve the identified problem and what facts are available. He or she compares the factual information available at this point and makes plans on how to gather the remaining data. Once the basic research plan has been formulated, the fact-gathering phase is launched. The techniques to be used will be determined by the plan and the available sources of information. Some of the techniques which may be used are personal interviews, mail interviews, telephone interviews, market measurement, questionnaires, and motivation research.

WHAT IS THE NATURE OF A FORMAL MARKETING SURVEY?

After the preliminary investigation is completed and the data is analyzed, the research will recognize certain patterns in the data which focus on areas requiring an exploration in depth. These areas will determine the purpose and plan of the formal survey, which is much broader in scope than the preliminary survey. It will cover a broader area, include more people, and ask more questions than the preliminary survey.

The questionnaire method, one of the most frequently used in formal surveys, may employ questions aimed at factual, opinion, or interpretative answers. For example, in a factual survey, the respondent may be asked, "What brand of breakfast food do you use?" In an opinion survey, the question is asked differently. The respondent may be asked, "Which of these three package designs do you like best?" The response requires an opinion, which may then be pursued by further exploratory questions to determine why the particular choice was made. In an interpretative survey, the respondent may be asked a question such as "Why do you use Brand X?" or to complete a sentence beginning with "I like Brand X because ..." The factual and interpretative questions may be mailed, or they may be used in a telephone survey. The opinion questionnaire, where varying objects must be visualized, obviously demands the presence of a personal interviewer.

Many steps are involved in the planning and execution of a formal marketing survey. But when it has been finished, and the final report is available, it will be up to the manager to decide whether to follow all the report's recommendations, some of them, or none of them. Since marketing research is likely to touch in some way every segment of a company's operation, the more skillfully it is planned, executed, and acted upon, the more widespread will be the benefits to the company.

HOW CAN MARKETING RESEARCH HELP IN MEASURING SALES PERFORMANCE?

An objective of any sales organization is to realize the maximum amount of sales per sales-expense dollar. For manufacturing firms, a small proportion of the territories, customers, orders, or products is responsible for the bulk of the sales (and profits). It is not unusual to find 90 percent or more of a company's sales coming from 20 percent or less of its customers. This means that a large part of the sales effort is wasted on customers who generate only a small portion of the company's profits.

To find out how effective the sales effort is, a cost analysis which compares the cost of selling with the related sales and profits for the different segments of the business can be made. Greatly increased efficiency and significant cost reductions in selling expenses often result from such an analysis.

WHAT LIMITATIONS ARE POSED BY HOME INTERVIEWS?

The home interview is the most useful and the most expensive kind of marketing survey technique. In this method, a carefully planned questionnaire is in the hands of an interviewer who talks to the customer. A great many questions can be handled by such a technique and a large amount of information recorded. The survey may also include observed data such as the apparent socioeconomic status of the family, possessions of the consumer, attitudes toward a variety of subjects, and the use or presence of certain products. The personal nature of such an interview yields a high percentage of response and can handle sensitive subjects better than other methods.

The quality of a home interview depends heavily on the effectiveness of the interviewers. Most of them are employed temporarily or work on a part-time basis. Even when you are very careful in choosing and training them, the possibility still remains that they will lack motivation, may not ask the same essential questions each time, or might incorrectly record the answers. Because the nature of the work prevents direct supervision and observation, great care should be taken to hire only the most reliable interviewers. They should also receive adequate training on the questionnaire to be used.

Another limitation is the inability of the respondent to give factual answers to the questions asked. If questions cannot be answered with a specific fact, the results might be misleading. If consumers do not know the correct answers, they might give replies which they think seem reasonable and will make them appear to have keen judgment. This same desire might cause your respondents to give false answers. It is not unusual to have people reply that they use fashionable, big-brand names from prestige stores, when in fact they use unknown brands from budget stores. All questions should be designed to prevent opportunities for such responses.

WHAT TYPES OF QUESTIONS SHOULD BE ASKED IN PERSONAL INTERVIEWS?

Generally speaking, the best questions are those that cannot be answered with a yes or no. Although such questions might be very helpful in getting respondents into an interview mood or to develop simple statistical data, the answers give no facts and they often fail to reveal the actual basis for a belief or preference. For example, you will probably get an affirmative answer if you ask an automobile owner the question, Do you like your present car? After all, the customer picked out the car, and must have had some good reason for selecting it. But you are more likely to get factual information and attitudes if you ask, What do you wish your car had that it does not?

Another type of question that often reveals significant facts is one which asks the respondent to complete an open-end statement. For example, the interviewer says, "Please tell me how you would complete this statement: 'The best method for cleaning windows is _____.' " The response to such a question requires some effort on the part of the respondent. The answer is likely to be useful in determining reasons or motivations that prompt the respondent.

The wording of questions and the method of asking them are important in determining the validity of the answers. The introduction of a single word may suggest bias on the part of an interviewer and thereby influence the answers given. For instance, if I ask you to compare the qualities of wool and cotton for winter clothes, that is one thing. But if I ask you to compare warm wool with cotton, the word *warm* has introduced a basis for bias which will affect the statistical average of the answers. All survey questions must be carefully constructed, examined for bias, and tested for validity. It is all too easy to elicit answers which you want to hear and which seem to confirm views you already have. That kind of interview will yield data you can tabulate, but they are not worth very much.

WHAT KINDS OF INFORMATION CAN BE OBTAINED IN STORE INTERVIEWS?

This technique is designed to get answers to such questions as how often customers shop, where they live, why they frequent this store, or why they selected specific brands or products from among several. Usually such questions are limited in number so as not to take too much time. The information is recorded on an easily marked card so that a permanent record is made.

A variation on the point-of-sale survey technique is to offer a premium to customers participating. There is always the danger of the customers' trying to give the answer they believe the interviewer wants just for the reward, particularly if the premium is a product connected with the survey.

An increasingly popular point-of-sale type of survey is a contest entry blank which contains the questions to be answered. The customer fills it out along with the necessary name and address information. Questions must be limited in number in this method. Care must also be taken to avoid erroneous results from entries filled out by children or from multiple entries. This method has the advantage of being low in cost and of yielding quick results. It lacks the touch of the skilled interviewer who can evaluate the response.

The accuracy of marketing research depends largely upon how representative your sample is. A sample is a portion of the total number of people who could be contacted if you wished to have 100 percent coverage. For example, you would not find it feasible or necessary to talk to all automobile owners in doing a marketing survey to determine what brand or style of tire they prefer.

The professional survey designers use the term *universe* for the total population about which a marketer wants information. This universe has to be specified by trade area, geographic location, age group, sex, or some other classification. Then, the marketing researcher breaks down that universe into units from which samples may be taken. In a local trade area, the researcher will often use one sample per block, giving as even a geographic and economic representation as possible. Care must be taken to assure that the choice of units is truly representative. Selection of names at random from a phone book does not offer such assurance, since the sample selected would not include people without telephones, those with unlisted numbers, or those who are new and have not got a telephone yet.

The number of respondents in a sample is considered to be less important than true representation and the quality of information obtained. As a rule of thumb, a sample should be as small as it can be and still be representative of the general universe it represents. Use care to be sure that the universe really represents the market in which you are interested. Misleading and inaccurate information is useless and is worse than no information at all. This is a good reason for considering the use of trained research specialists, who can better select a representative sample.

WHAT ADVANTAGES ARE OFFERED BY MAIL SURVEYS?

Mail surveys are cheaper than personal interviews and easier to tabulate. This method utilizes a self-administered questionnaire sent by mail with a letter of explanation and a request to return the questionnaire (in a stamped or postage guaranteed envelope). Sometimes the survey can be used as a promotional device suggesting that the sender is truly interested in the opinions of the consumer. Being asked for an opinion satisfies customer desires for recognition and status. Except in unusual circumstances, only about 10 percent of such questionnaires are ever returned.

Often people become "judges" and "opinion givers," and such status can make their responses unreliable. This can also happen in a direct interview, but the interviewer can clarify or evaluate the response and guard against some erroneous information.

A disadvantage of mail surveys is that they are generally inflexible, but they are relatively inexpensive and often represent the only way to reach certain high-income groups.

There seems to be more resentment toward this type of survey than others. Respondents are often irritated because of the unwanted interruption in their routines. This attitude is reflected in the increased use of unlisted telephone numbers. Still, the technique is valid. Telephone questionnaires should be made simple, direct, and brief. It is better to find out the name of the party to be interviewed prior to the call if possible. This establishes a firmer, more business-like relationship.

Telephone interviews have the advantage that a single interviewer can handle more respondents than in a home interview and the overall cost is considerably less. But generally the results are not as accurate and fewer questions can be handled.

WHAT ARE THE COMMON CAUSES OF NEW PRODUCT FAILURES?

According to the National Industrial Conference Board, the following are the primary ones:

☐ Inaccurate appraisal of the need for a product, or the extent of its market, or the competition it is likely to face.

☐ Introduction of products before they have been officially developed for the market or before they have been adequately tested under market conditions.

☐ Poorly planned or inadequate introductory marketing campaigns.

SELF-CHECK OF KEY CONCEPTS This exercise is designed to test your understanding of the material presented in Chapter 17. Choose the response, *True* or *False*, which best fits each statement. Correct responses are presented in the back of the text.

1. The term *marketing* is synonymous with personal selling of merchandise at the retail level.
2. The Census of Population is taken every 10 years.
3. In conducting personal interviews, it is best to use questions which can be answered yes or no in order to minimize bias in the answers.
4. A return of 25 percent of the questionnaires sent out on a mail survey could be considered a good return.
5. Telephone interviews sometimes generate resentment because they intrude on the respondent's privacy.

6. An analysis of sales statistics in manufacturing firms shows that most of their sales come from a relatively small percentage of their customers.
7. If you were doing marketing research on the kinds of car batteries automobile owners prefer, your "universe" would be all people who own automobiles.
8. Since customer demands are constantly changing, marketing research must be continuous.
9. It is not unusual to find that 80 percent of a company's customers are responsible for only 20 percent of its sales.
10. The home interview is the least expensive of the marketing survey techniques.

1. You have just been promoted to a position as manager of marketing in an organization that employs 1,800 people in a firm manufacturing small tools and lawn and garden equipment. These products generate sales of approximately $4 million a year to the following retail outlets:

PERFORMANCE PROBLEMS AND PROJECTS

Customer	Approximate Sales
Builders' Hardware	$1,000,000
A-1 Home Supply Centers	800,000
Green Front Stores	600,000
Imperial Hardware Chain	600,000
Town & Country Garden Shops	300,000
Small hardware retailers	700,000

You have a sales force of five people. Through interviews with them, you have been able to get basic data regarding the customers they service, number of personal contacts made last year, the number of orders obtained, and total sales for each customer. Your accounting department has supplied expense information for each sales representative and the amount of profit each customer is responsible for. The following matrix summarizes all the data you have collected:

SALES-INCOME-PROFIT DATA FOR 19___

Sales Representative	Customer	Calls Last Year	Total Orders	Total Sales Produced	Net Profit Made
Yarbrough	Builders' Hardware	415	320	$986,000	$34,510
Yarbrough	Green Front Stores	300	255	623,000	18,067
Jackson	A-1 Home Supply	435	185	795,000	23,850
Brink	Imperial Hardware	325	195	610,000	19,520
Brink	Town & Country	285	210	298,000	4,470
Simpson	Territory A	450	150	250,000	7,000
Rivera	Territory B	600	485	450,000	11,250

SELLING COSTS IN 19___

Sales Representative	Annual Compensation	Annual Expenses	Total Annual Cost	Allocation to Customers*
Yarbrough	$18,500	$ 8,800	$20,748	76% to Builders' Hardware
			6,552	24% to Green Front Stores
Jackson	17,000	7,200	24,200	100% to A-1 Home Supply
Brink	15,600	5,800	11,342	53% to Imperial Hardware
			10,058	47% to Town & Country
Simpson	13,800	10,500	24,300	100% to Territory A
Rivera	12,500	10,200	22,700	100% to Territory B

* Allocation of sales-representative cost based on total calls to each customer.

From the information shown, calculate the information required in the table below. The first line is completed as a sample.

SALES-PERFORMANCE DATA

Sales Representative	Territory	Average Order Size, $	Orders per Call Ratio, %	Cost to Sales Ratio, %
Yarbrough	Builders' Hardware	$3,081	77.1	2.1
Yarbrough	Green Front Stores			
Jackson	A-1 Home Supply			
Brink	Imperial Hardware			
Brink	Town & Country			
Simpson	Territory A			
Rivera	Territory B			

You should also be able to analyze each customer's contribution to your company's profits and calculate what each profit dollar costs in terms of sales dollars by calculating the data required to complete this chart:

Customer	Sales Representative's Cost	Profit Dollars Contributed	Sales Representative's Cost per Profit Dollar
Builders' Hardware			
Green Front Stores			
A-1 Home Supply			
Imperial Hardware			
Town & Country			
Territory A			
Territory B			

Answer the following questions from your analysis of the data:

a. Which sales representative has the highest ratio of sales per call?

b. Which sales representative has the largest average order size?

c. Who is the most expensive sales representative you have in terms of cost to sales ratio?

d. Which customer is providing the greatest volume of business for your company?

e. Which company is contributing most to your total net profit each year?

CHAPTER

18

The Pricing of Products and Services

PERFORMANCE OBJECTIVES

After reading this chapter, you should understand the importance attached to the responsibility of business owners for correctly pricing their products and services. Unless this function is understood and properly carried out, there is no assurance that revenues will cover expenses or that established prices will be acceptable to the customer. Your understanding of this concept will be demonstrated by your ability to:

1. Identify the specific items that are covered by the price of an item of merchandise sold at retail.
2. Define *price* from the viewpoint of the customer.
3. Relate the criteria likely to be used by the consumer in determining the fairness of a price.
4. Justify the differences in price for the same product sold by different merchants.
5. Construct a model showing the relationship between cost of goods sold, selling price, gross margin, and markup.
6. Explain the difference between a markup based on cost of goods and one based on sale price.
7. Develop a hypothetical example to demonstrate how a service firm develops a "rate" to use in pricing its services.
8. Assess the soundness of legislation which attempts to prevent a merchant from selling an item below cost.

9. Explain what is meant by the "loss leader" concept in pricing and defend its application in small business.
10. Defend the use of markdowns and discuss the conditions under which they might be used.
11. Explain the technique of "skimming" pricing for new products and tell how it differs from "penetration" pricing.
12. Explain why the price of a popular new product declines over time after it has been introduced to the market.
13. Determine the kind of analysis which must be made before establishing a pricing structure for a business.
14. Predict the problems which can result when pricing policies are not established prior to the time goods or services are offered for sale.
15. Explain the advantage of offering a range of similar products at different price levels.

INTRODUCTION

The pricing function is not well understood by most business people. Although pricing arithmetic is not difficult to understand and apply, the reasons for establishing a specific price are often vague and are based on hunches or observations of what others are charging.

Since most people are in business to make a profit, the established prices for goods and services must bear some relationship to the merchant's costs. If operating costs are to be ultimately reflected in the price charged the customer, it is obvious that a business cannot operate inefficiently and pass along the cost of such inefficiency to the customer. Even when operating costs are in line, the actions of your competitors and the attitudes of the customer cannot be ignored as very persuasive factors to be reckoned with in setting prices.

The effects of existing legislation, distribution costs, and customer sensitivity to prices must be simultaneously understood and considered when a price is established. Not all goods can be priced for profit, but aggregate prices charged for all items should yield a profit. This goal requires a flexible system of pricing which recognizes the need to consider all factors which affect price.

This chapter will discuss the various factors which directly or indirectly influence price. It will touch on the psychological barriers which must be overcome in order to establish the "right" price. Some attention will be directed to pricing arithmetic, to the special pricing requirements of new products, and to providing guidelines designed to improve your skills in establishing prices for your products.

DOES PRICE MEAN THE SAME THING TO EVERYONE?

The term *price* generally includes the cost of the goods or services you sell, plus some amount to cover your administrative and selling expenses, plus the profit you want to make. Price to a manufacturer means something different from what it means to a wholesaler. The price charged by a service firm carries still a different connotation, as is illustrated below.

For the *manufacturer,* price will be composed of:

1. Material and supplies used in making the product, plus
2. Labor applied to making the product, plus

3. Overhead expenses of operating the plant, plus
4. Administrative and selling expenses, plus
5. Profit.

For the *wholesaler*, price will be composed of:

1. The cost paid for the goods to be resold, plus
2. The cost of selling the goods (sales personnel's salaries, advertising, and promotion), plus
3. General overhead (utilities, office supplies, office salaries, and management salaries), plus
4. Profit.

For the *service firm*, price will be composed of:

1. Materials used or goods purchased for use in providing the service, plus
2. Labor performed in providing the service, plus
3. General overhead, plus
4. Profit.

To the consumer, price represents an amount of money paid by the buyer to the seller of a product or service. It is the monetary value of such goods and services in the marketplace. In the mind of customers, price and value must be compatible; that is, the product or service must be worth the price paid, or they will refuse to buy or will look elsewhere. This definition is easy to understand. Although there are more sophisticated definitions of price, none are more significant to business people than one which reflects the customer's viewpoint. How the customer feels about your price is critical in building sales volume, without which your success will be limited. Henry Ford expressed this relationship clearly when he stated, "The only thing that makes anything not sell is too high a price."

DO MOST SMALL BUSINESS OWNERS PRICE THEIR PRODUCTS WELL?

To the contrary, most business people do not understand the factors which affect the price they should charge. Only a small percentage of even large companies have written price policies. An understanding of pricing arithmetic by small business owners is comparatively rare. Some small firms establish prices which do not even cover their costs. Insolvency is the inevitable result. Many businesses fail to distinguish between getting business and operating profitably, forgetting that volume carries no guarantee of profit. Only carefully established prices can assure a measure of protection against operating "in the red."

The traditional concept of pricing is based upon the recovery of costs and the generation of a predetermined profit percentage. This full-cost approach is reflected in the widespread use of cost-plus pricing wherein the price of the product is established to cover all the costs of the product. When this method is used, all costs, including labor, materials, overhead, and selling expenses, are determined and a profit percentage is added. Because of other operating variables, full-cost pricing sometimes results in a price which is too high to be competitive. It must then be modified to a price that will be acceptable to the customer. This is accomplished by using full cost as a base or reference point to which flexible markups are added.

Gross-margin pricing is another approach which is widely used by retailers. This method adds a set markup to the wholesale price. Although the markup can be computed as a percentage of wholesale cost, it is more often computed as a percentage of selling price. Since expense items on the profit-and-loss statement are historically analyzed in relation to sales, this approach makes the analysis of markup compatible and facilitates the analysis of data related to profit. Most firms using this method do not apply the same markup to all items, but they do strive to achieve an aggregate average for all items. For example, if your markup goal is 35 percent of sales, your markup could range from 30 to 40 percent and achieve the overall average. If you use this method, you should check total costs and retail prices from your invoices each month to be sure the target is being achieved.

Suggested prices provided by manufacturers or wholesalers are often used by retailers. Their use obviates the need for calculating a markup and provides a standard price likely to be found in most other stores.

Although all of these methods are widely used in pricing, they are sometimes not responsive to changing conditions. Good pricing must respond to changes in customer attitudes, capitalize on developing opportunities, and offer a practical approach to the pricing policies of competitors. To do a good job of pricing, you must understand more fully the factors which affect price.

WHAT FACTORS INFLUENCE THE PRICE OF A PRODUCT OR SERVICE?

Despite the simple concept of price in their minds, consumers are often unaware of the many factors which influence the price of a commodity.

They might not know, for example, that their state has established minimum prices for milk, liquor, and haircuts; or that a "fair-trade" law prevents merchants from selling an item to them at a price lower than that established by law; or that a suggested retail price established by the manufacturer must be observed by merchants under pain of being penalized by the supplier of the merchandise.

Some of the more obvious price determinants are easier to detect. For example, when customers pay a $350 "destination charge" on their new automobiles, they see how distribution costs become a part of the price. They understand the use of "loss leaders" as they search their newspaper for grocery bargains each week and are secretly grateful that the existence of several supermarkets in their shopping area tends to keep prices down. They also know that they can influence prices by refusing to buy those items which are priced too high for the value received. Consumer boycotts of meat and sugar have been instrumental in reducing prices at various times.

Not so well understood are the effects of economic conditions on prices, or how purchasing practices or selling expenses affect price. Consumers might be vaguely aware of the part played by timing when they defer the purchase of a new product until "prices come down."

Some of the factors which influence prices are shown in Table 18-1.

WHAT IS MEANT BY THE TERM *PRICING POLICY*?

Setting prices is one of the most critical planning activities a merchant undertakes. As such, it should be conducted in accordance with certain guidelines, preferably written, which determine the policy to be followed.

The pricing policy of manufacturers must consider their actual costs, their methods of distributions, their discounts to be offered to customers, the kinds of customers to be served, and the quantities to be made.

Typical retailers or wholesalers sell something produced by someone else—goods or merchandise which are bought and later sold in the same form. Their pricing policies will be concerned with finding a reliable low-cost source of merchandise and with calculating markups which consider customer sensitivity to price. Guidelines will be needed to cover such activities as markups, discounts, markdowns, establishing price lines, multiple pricing, and repricing.

Service firms must establish pricing policies for pricing service labor, which may be wholly controlled by the seller. Placing a value on a "service hour" or on the service provided is critical, since competition from others offering almost identical service is likely to be intense. Service prices are largely dependent upon the methods of the sellers, the skills of those they employ, and the level of services they provide. Unless the service firm's pricing policies are sound and are the result of efficient operations, customers will seek out those firms which offer the most "service per dollar."

Unless business people have sound pricing policies, sales forecasts will be in jeopardy because it will be difficult to build their volumes by attracting new customers. Their profit forecasts will be unreliable because they will not know how much business is being

TABLE 18-1.   SOME OF THE FACTORS WHICH INFLUENCE PRICES

Factor	How Prices Are Affected
1. Competition	Operating efficiencies, better buying practices, and better cost control all help reduce operating expense, making it possible for you to meet the challenges of your competitors. Effective promotions and advertising increase volume, providing a cost advantage which helps keep you competitive.
2. Legislation	Statutes at both national and state levels affect price fixing, price control, and price cutting. The effect is to limit the actions which can be taken by businesses in establishing prices for their products.
3. Production Costs	The price of manufactured products must cover labor, material, overhead, and selling costs. Inefficiencies in these areas will be reflected in price unless competition acts to eliminate inefficient producers.
4. Distribution Costs	Over half the cost paid by the ultimate consumer is attributable to the cost of distribution. The more "middlemen" who handle a product, the more expensive it becomes.
5. Economic Fluctuations	"Good times" permit higher markups in anticipation of escalating labor and material costs, which will make replacement costs for manufactured goods higher. During recessions, margins must be cut to retain a share of the market.
6. Type of Merchandise	High-volume convenience goods normally carry lower markups than low-volume shopping or fashion goods. Standard and well-advertised products frequently support a higher price because of their "image."
7. Marketing Strategy	Use of "loss leaders," penetration and skimming pricing, advertising and promotion, and personal services to customers all affect the price at which the product is sold.
8. Purchasing Practices	Careful selection and evaluation of vendors, volume buying, and quantity discounts help keep procurement costs in line and prices low.
9. Selling Costs	Costs of advertising and maintaining physical facilities for selling, sales expense, and delivery costs must be absorbed in the selling price.
10. Value	The worth of a product in the customer's mind establishes a sensitivity to prices. Advertising and promotion can help overcome buyers' attitudes.
11. Timing	Most new products are sold at a higher price when first introduced to the market. Television sets and panty hose are examples.

lost to competitors through poor pricing approaches. They will learn the hard way that weak pricing policies will cost them business and profit.

HOW CAN YOU TELL WHAT THE BEST PRICE FOR A PRODUCT IS?

Because of the variables involved, you will seldom find a price which maximizes revenue or minimizes costs in an ideal manner. You will find it a mistake to assume that an established price on a product is necessarily the best price, or that the product is priced "right." You must assume that the "best" price is never truly achieved and that constant effort is required to arrive at a "better" one than you now have. This thought is expressed well in the following statement:[1]

The best price for a product is not necessarily the price that will sell the most units, nor is it always the price that will bring in the greatest number of sales dollars. Rather, the best price is one that will maximize the profits of the enterprise. The best selling price should be oriented to cost as well as customer. Costs tend to establish price floors, and demand tends to establish price ceilings. In general, prices should be high enough to cover costs and help make a profit but low enough to attract customers and build sales volume.

You must be willing to experiment with prices and to change them when necessary, always being consistent with your established policies and the need to maintain customer goodwill.

SHOULD YOUR PRICE REFLECT ALL THAT THE TRAFFIC WILL BEAR?

This approach assumes that consumers are unaware of price differences between competing businesses, or that they will pay a premium price for such extras as convenient credit or free delivery. Although there is some truth in this assumption, increasing prices to the limit of the customer's willingness to pay is a dangerous practice. Today television and newspaper advertising constantly remind customers of the products and services which offer the most value for the money. Grocers have long known that there are approximately fifty items to which customers are price-sensitive. They must be competitive on these or lose business to competing stores. If your prices are consistently found to be higher than those of your competitors, customers will soon learn what it would cost them to shop at your store.

Following the pattern of grocery marketers, it is important that you determine what your customers know about your products, what type of pricing pattern they expect, and what products are available from competitors. Keep in mind that customers will often be

[1]John V. Petrof, Peter S. Carusone, and John E. McDavid, *Small Business Management: Concepts and Techniques for Improving Decisions*, McGraw-Hill Book Company, New York, 1972, p. 153.

willing to pay a little extra if they are aware of the extras you provide that are not offered by others. For example, a small retail store might develop a successful business by offering credit and delivery services to customers who do not mind paying extra for the added convenience. It might in this way continue to price above its larger competitors and still attract a profitable share of the market.

SHOULD YOU LET A COMPETITOR'S PRICE INFLUENCE YOUR PRICING POLICY?

Obviously, you cannot consistently charge more than your competitors and stay in business. You cannot ignore competitors' prices, especially if the prices are for identical products. So you must recognize the nature of your competition, look at their pricing policies, and develop marketing strategy which will allow you to compete successfully. Your entry into the market will not go unnoticed. You should expect some response from competition as a result of your move to take away some of their business. If your pricing policies parallel theirs, their reaction is likely to be to look upon you as "one of the boys" and to learn to live with another competitor. If you decide to price your products below theirs, you can expect retaliatory action of some kind, including price cutting, and a dedication to continue it until such time as you are no longer a threat. You should try to avoid head-on price competition with others who are better able to achieve a lower pricing structure.

Offering something extra in the way of service, location, or merchandising is one way to assure survival until your competitors know that you are here to stay. This assumes, of course, that your business methods are as efficient as those of your competition and that you do not have an efficiency problem masquerading as a pricing problem. In such case, your competitor's prices are not the real problem and will have little bearing on your ability to compete.

HOW DO FAIR-TRADE LAWS AFFECT THE PRICE OF A PRODUCT YOU SELL?

Some states have "fair-trade" laws which allow manufacturers to establish a price floor on trademarked items or those uniquely identified with the manufacturer. The purpose of such legislation is to protect the image of the product and to discourage price cutting which restricts competition. Prices may be set by the manufacturer by means of national advertising, price agreements, or by law. Such prices can be enforced by exclusive or selective distribution to those dealers who agree to sell at the suggested price.

Strong opposition to the fair-trade laws by consumers and many retailers has caused courts to rule against them and has been responsible for their repeal in several states. Some large companies which had previously attempted to enforce them have become less aggressive, thus aiding the momentum for their repeal. Whether you are affected by such legislation will depend upon what the laws of your state say about fair-trade practices. Your trade association or attorney can advise you on this matter.

WHAT IS THE ADVANTAGE OF SELLING A PRODUCT BELOW COST?

The primary purpose of carrying "loss leaders" is to attract customers to the store who may make other purchases while there, thus building volume. In this sense, selling below cost is a promotional device, similar in its objective to advertising.

Some states have passed laws to prohibit below-cost selling because such practice tends to limit or eliminate competition. Anti-loss leader laws which prohibit selling an item at less than cost have been passed in some states. These laws generally define cost as invoice cost plus a fair share of the cost of doing business (arbitrarily defined as 5 or 6 percent).

WHAT IS THE SIGNIFICANCE OF A "SUGGESTED RETAIL PRICE"?

These are prices set by the manufacturer or distributor and imposed on the retailer as a condition of handling the product as an exclusive sales outlet. Goods carrying such prices are not fair-traded, but the merchant is expected to use and follow the established pricing structure. There is no legal penalty if sellers choose not to comply, but they run the risk of being dropped from the list of exclusive dealers, with the resultant loss of that particular product from their lines of merchandise.

WHAT DO DISTRIBUTION COSTS ADD TO THE PRICE OF A PRODUCT?

Goods must flow from manufacturers through any one of several "middlemen" to retailers and then to the ultimate consumer. The flow of a product from the place of production to the consumer is called a marketing channel. Since most manufacturing plants do not sell directly to the consumer, they must depend upon agents, brokers, wholesalers, retailers, and similar groups to perform this function. These middlemen each performs a function which adds cost to the product in the form of a markup before the product moves to the next step in the distribution chain. By the time the product is in the hands of the consumer, approximately half its cost can be attributed to marketing.

The costs of distribution are high, but no one has found a way to eliminate the channeling process. An obvious approach would be for the retailer to buy from a source which is as close to the manufacturer as possible, thereby eliminating the costs associated with additional handling by middlemen.

WHAT IS DIFFERENT ABOUT PRICING NEW PRODUCTS?

New products that are unique require a different pricing policy because they are distinctive. No one else sells quite the same thing. For this reason, the initial demand will be greater and the price higher when they are first introduced on the market. One of the best examples of this occurrence is the history of prices on black and white television sets. The initial price was high. The dramatic drop in price over the next 10 years put them in practically every American home. The pattern was repeated with the introduction of color television. Ladies' panty hose cost almost $5 a pair when they were first introduced. Within 3 years, they were available in the local supermarket for less than a dollar a pair.

The distinctiveness of a new product soon wears off as competitors bring out imitative substitutes. The market will eventually have an ample supply of comparable products and prices will come down. The speed with which this happens will depend on the investment required for competitors to manufacture and distribute a competing product, and on their alertness in responding. By establishing the "right" price for a new product initially you can slow the speed with which competitive products are placed on the market. Finding the "right" price is not easy, however. Past experience is no guide because there is nothing similar with which to compare. If competitive products are already on the market, they are usually significantly different in function or quality, offering no valid basis for price comparison.

In pricing a new product there are three objectives which must be satisfied:

□ Getting the product accepted. Despite its distinctiveness, it still must carry a price tag which customers will accept.

□ Maintaining your market in the face of growing competition. This will require constant reappraisal of your price and close attention to advertising and promotion techniques.

□ Making a profit. A new product should never be introduced to the market at a price less than cost. It is easier to reduce prices later than to increase them after the product is on the market.

WHAT ARE THE CHOICES IN PRICING A NEW PRODUCT?

There are two choices, representing the extremes of pricing policy. Although there are a number of in-between positions, they represent various combinations of the two we will discuss.

For new and highly distinctive products, a policy of high price coupled with an intensive promotional program in the early stages of market development is often used. This is called "skimming" pricing. It appeals to those customers who are not sensitive to price and enables you to build volume during the period before competition becomes a factor. The experience gained in this early phase will be helpful when you later shift your approach to a lower-price, mass-market technique. Skimming pricing will provide you with the funds you need for financing expansion plans when you begin producing for a larger mass market.

If no elite market exists for your product and you suspect that the product will be faced with strong potential competition soon after introduction, you should start with a lower price and develop an entering wedge into mass markets early. This is especially true if you can achieve substantial economies in costs by operating at large volumes. Low initial prices are often called "stay out" prices because they discourage competitors from investing large amounts of capital to produce an item with a low profit margin. This technique of pricing is known as "penetration" pricing. Penetration pricing can be employed at any stage of market development, even after skimming pricing has made its initial impact on the market.

The ease and speed with which competition can bring out substitute products is probably the most important consideration in making a choice between skimming and penetration pricing.

HOW IMPORTANT IS PRICING IN DEVELOPING A SHARE OF THE MARKET?

When coupled with a good advertising program, pricing is very effective in developing a share of the market. Since the market for any given product or service is only so big, the only way a new business can get a share of the market is to take it away from someone else. Nothing has been found to be more effective than good advertising and reasonable prices for getting customers to buy. If reducing prices increases the volume of business, you might want to experiment with prices until you feel that additional volume and market share represent the limit of your potential.

Some service organizations and large supermarket chains will often use a pricing program featuring prices below the level of their competitors when opening a new store. The objective is to build a clientele and establish a foothold before unobtrusively raising prices.

WHAT IS MEANT BY THE TERM *MARKUP*?

Markup is the amount added to the cost of goods procured by a retailer to cover selling and other operating expenses, anticipated pilferage, shortages, markdowns, employee discounts, and a margin of profit. It represents the difference between the cost of goods and the selling price.

A markup of $3 on an item costing $7, for example, produces a selling price of $10. If we assume that there are no subsequent price reductions, the gross margin is also $3. We can illustrate this relationship as shown in Figure 18-1.

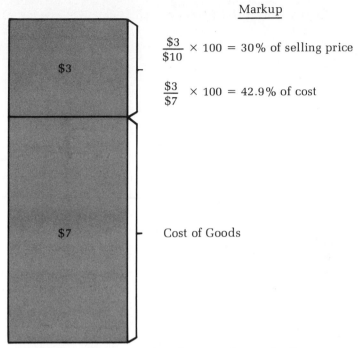

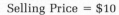

Selling Price = $10

Markup

$$\frac{\$3}{\$10} \times 100 = 30\% \text{ of selling price}$$

$$\frac{\$3}{\$7} \times 100 = 42.9\% \text{ of cost}$$

$3

$7 — Cost of Goods

FIGURE 18-1. The relationship of cost, markup, and selling price.

We can also use formulas to show the relationships which exist between cost of goods, markup, and sale price:

(1) Dollar markup ÷ cost = percent markup on cost
(2) Dollar markup ÷ selling price = percent markup on price
(3) Gross margin = sale price − cost of goods sold

From these examples, it can be seen that markup can be expressed either as a percentage of cost or as a percentage of sales. Most retailers prefer to state markup as a percentage of sales. For those who prefer to use the "percentage of cost" method, a conversion from one price to the other can be readily made by using the formula:

Percentage markup on cost

$$= \frac{\text{percentage of markup on retail}}{100 - \text{percentage markup on retail}} \times 100$$

On our $10 item, the 30 percent markup on price is converted to percentage markup on cost as follows:

$$\frac{30}{100 - 30} \times 100 = \frac{3,000}{70} = 42.9\%$$

TABLE 18-2. MARKUP TABLE

Markup as a Percentage of Selling Price	Markup as a Percentage of Cost	Markup as a Percentage of Selling Price	Markup as a Percentage of Cost
20%	25.00%	36%	56.25%
21	26.58	37	58.73
22	28.21	38	61.29
23	29.87	39	63.93
24	31.58	40	66.67
25	33.33	41	69.49
26	35.14	42	72.41
27	36.99	43	75.44
28	38.89	44	78.57
29	40.85	45	81.82
30	42.86	46	85.19
31	44.93	47	88.68
32	47.06	48	92.31
33	49.25	49	96.08
34	51.52	50	100.00
35	53.85		

A markup table is often used to make the conversion quickly. Table 18-2 gives the values between 20 and 50 percent markup on selling price and the corresponding markup on cost.

If you were pricing a product which you wished to markup at 35 percent of sales, you would add 53.85 percent (from Table 18-2) to the invoice price. When the product is sold at the resulting price, the gross profit on the sale would be 35 percent.

Example. You have just received a gross (144) of ballpoint pens and the invoice cost is $172. You want to add a 35 percent markup based on sale price. What would the price per pen be?

35% of sales would be 53.85% of cost (from Table 18-2)
$172 × 53.85% = $92.62 (total markup amount)
$172 + $92.62 = $265 (total retail value, rounded)
$265 ÷ 144 = $1.84 per pen

IS THE SAME MARKUP PERCENTAGE APPLIED TO ALL MERCHANDISE?

It is not desirable to establish the same markup goal on everything. Pricing is still an art, and you must always weigh volume possibilities against customer acceptance, probable costs, and expenses. Some items will need a low markup to sell. You will have to make up this reduced profit by using a higher markup on others, thereby maintaining your average.

For items that are highly speculative, or those that move slowly, or that carry the risk of large markdowns later, you will want to use a markup which is higher than your average goal. Examples of such items are high-fashion goods and similar items with an unpredictable market; seasonal or novelty goods which cannot be held over another year; goods which are easily soiled or damaged; and goods which are easily pilfered.

On the other hand, you might decide to price other merchandise using a below-average markup. This policy would apply to goods where competition is keen, or where the risk of carrying the item is low.

Fast-moving goods carried as a convenience for your customers are often priced with low markups, especially if they are widely distributed and found in a great many outlets. They do not contribute greatly to your profits, but their availability attracts customers into your store, where they buy other high-margin merchandise.

Clothing items are often popular one year, only to be replaced next year by something more popular. Since you will likely be faced with substantial price reductions late in the season, your markup should be high to offset the anticipated loss.

Specialties and novelty goods are usually short-lived, and volume will drop quickly as competitive substitutes are introduced into the market. Novelties such as the "Hula-Hoop" are examples of fads which quickly fade from the market when the novelty wears off. The prospect of being left with quantities which cannot be sold without substantial markdowns should prompt a high initial markup. As the demand drops, you will have to make weekly or even daily price adjustments in order to move them.

Larger items such as automobiles, furniture, and major appliances constitute the "shopping goods" category. Buyers are generally more selective when buying them and prefer to shop around before buying. Their high cost causes buyers to be more deliberate in making a choice, often shopping for several weeks before making a final decision. This pattern results in a slow turnover, creating higher inventory and merchandising costs. Such costs must be offset with higher markups.

WHAT PURPOSE IS SERVED BY MARKDOWNS?

Markdowns are designed to maintain volume in the face of declining demand or in the event of competing products being introduced. Markdowns are reflected in "2-for-1" sales, "cents-off" sales, and other special promotional sales which keep buyers interested in buying. In fashion goods, price changes are a particularly acute problem because delays in taking markdowns can lead to heavy losses at the end of the season. In most stores, it is best to take markdowns early at a time when many customers are still in the market. A relatively small markdown early in the season will draw buying attention to the merchandise, but if you wait too long even deep cuts may fail to attract many shoppers. Thus, the timing of markdowns is critical. Planning of markdowns should be done so that you will not wait too long. Such action can be taken as a part of special promotional events like back-to-school sales, after-Christmas sales, and other planned "clearance" sales.

WHAT IS MEANT BY MULTIPLE PRICING?

In pricing articles commonly bought in sets or multiples, you can stimulate volume by offering the customer a "deal" for buying more than one. A price of "55 cents each, 2 for $1" is an example. In this case your handling and overhead expense is no more for a $1 multiple than for a 55-cent unit. You more than compensate for the slight loss in markup by the increased dollar value of the sale. You can review your regular merchandise to determine where multiple pricing would materially stimulate your sales volume by offering the customer an inducement to buy two or three at a time.

HOW DOES THE PRACTICE OF PRICE LINING WORK?

When customers are looking for shopping goods, they often have a predetermined amount in mind to spend. If all your prices are higher than what they can afford, they will go elsewhere to shop. For this reason, it is good business to stock merchandise in several different price ranges or price lines. The hardware store might carry lawn mowers in "good," "better," and "best" categories, for example. Each category differs from the others in some features, and prices vary according to the quality and performance of the item. Automobile prices are established so that there is something for everyone —from the budget-minded buyer who wants a minimum of accessories and is looking for the "basic car" to the customer who wants the top of the line and is willing to pay for expensive extras. Dresses might run from $19.95 to $69.95, with several intermediate prices between the lowest- and highest-priced styles.

How many price lines to carry is up to you. A policy of concentrating on three prices within a range suited to the income levels of your potential customers is a common pattern, although six or seven price lines in a major merchandise classification or large department is not uncommon. You can use different prices for special promotions or special sales, but when the sale ends, merchandise prices should return to the established price lines.

Price lining will make it necessary for you to plan your merchandise purchases by price line. Knowing the price at which the goods will sell, you can plan your shopping trips and purchase your stock with these retail prices in mind. Your sales records will tell you how many items in each line to buy. You will need to break down your buying plan by types, materials, colors, and sizes, depending on the nature of the goods you carry.

Price lining simplifies buying, pricing, and stocking of merchandise by eliminating those goods falling outside the lines you want to carry. It establishes the selling price as the criterion for buying and allows you to buy for the known preferences of the customers you are serving.

Price lining is seldom used for convenience goods because of their low price and the fact that customers often buy them on impulse or in a hurry. Since they do not represent a large investment for either the buyer or seller, establishing price lines would serve no useful purpose.

WHAT FACTORS AFFECT THE PRICING POLICIES OF SMALL RETAILERS?

Small retailers are concerned primarily with the nature of their market, the effect of competition, the movement of a certain volume of goods, and the efficiency of their internal operations.

Customers are retailers' most important consideration. If they do not know their customers' preferences, sensitivities to price, spendable income, and buying habits, they will not be in a position to offer acceptable price lines which appeal to them. They will find it difficult to establish prices which will be "right" for the clientele they hope to attract, and they will have to be satisfied with moderate volume and low profits.

Not only are retailers faced with competition from other stores like theirs, but their merchandise is also likely to be sold by supermarkets, drugstores, and mail-order houses. They must be aware of both the prices and the services offered by their competitors and evaluate their prices and those of their competitors in these terms. They must stress value in order to convince the customer that they offer more than anyone else.

Volume is important to retailers because it is from selling merchandise that they obtain revenue to pay their bills and make a profit. The break-even chart will not allow them to become complacent about promoting their merchandise and cultivating good customer relations through courteous and friendly treatment. Their pricing should have as its principal objective that of moving merchandise. Any pricing policy which ignores the importance of sales promotion is headed for trouble.

Their own efficiency in planning, organizing, training, buying merchandise, advertising, and selling will determine whether they can offer competitive prices and services. They cannot expect their customers to pay for inefficiencies which are reflected in excessive markups.

The biggest problem of manufacturers is to control their cost of production. The general price of each product is closely related to this cost. The cost of the materials they buy often amounts to 50 percent or more of the final cost of the manufactured product. It is important that they find reliable low-cost suppliers if they are to produce a competitive product. The balance of their costs depends on how well they manage their personnel, materials, and machines to convert the raw materials to the final end product. The opportunities for influencing the cost of the product are almost endless.

If manufacturers make more than one product, accurate pricing of each will be more difficult than it is in a single-product plant. Since they do not know what the volume will be over a period of time, prices will be difficult to determine for customers who want "quotations" from them in advance. They will establish low prices on some items to meet competition or solicit business while maintaining high margins on those products that are not price-sensitive. By so doing, they will work for a gross margin which is a composite resulting from a wide range of prices.

It should be remembered that volume can be increased as well, and often better, by advertising, promotion, packaging, and personal selling. This fact suggests that price is only one way for manufacturers to expand their market. Lowering prices should be considered only if that is a more effective way to attract customers.

Manufacturers must consider the prices of competing products and the effect of volume discounts which are customary in their lines. In selling to large customers, they must be careful to comply with the provisions of the Robinson-Patman Act, which makes it illegal to price a product to a large buyer so low that it does not carry a proportionate share of plant overhead costs. The legal restrictions on pricing are discussed in Chapter 21.

HOW DO SERVICE FIRMS COME TO GRIPS WITH A WORKABLE PRICING POLICY?

The sheer number of service establishments and the variety of services they perform make pricing more complex than it is for the retailer. Customers are often amazed at the various prices charged for the same services by different establishments and wonder what "magic" is used to arrive at the price. As a matter of fact, many services are priced on the spot by business people who charge what they think is fair under the circumstances. This practice will almost certainly alienate some customers and make sales forecasting difficult.

Every service establishment should have a bookkeeping system which accurately reflects operating expenses and the cost of all materials used by the business to perform the service. Since labor and material are the most easily identifiable cost items affecting price, you should know what your average direct labor rate is and what each item of material costs. Indirect costs related to the operation of the business should be recorded and allocated in some equitable fashion to each unit of service. Let us look at a theoretical TV repair shop (Bill's). The annual expenses and costs for last year looked like Table 18-3. Bill's costs last year amounted to $7.33 for every productive hour worked. In order to use this data for pricing, you need to add profit. To do this, determine the percent of net operating profit you want on sales. Subtract this figure from 100. This is your cost complement. Now divide this into your cost per unit of service and multiply by 100 to get your unit selling price. Based on information he obtained from his trade association, Bill had planned 10 percent profit. His unit selling price would then be:

$$\frac{\$7.33}{90} \times 100 = \$8.14 \text{ per service hour}$$

This example assumes that the material used does not vary from customer to customer. If this is not the case, you will have to recalculate the cost per service hour without material. Then you add to that figure the actual cost of material used plus a reasonable markup to determine your selling price on a specific job. By excluding material costs, Bill's direct labor cost would be $5.33 per productive labor hour. A 2-hour job would be priced as follows:

Labor 2 hours × $5.33	$10.66
Material cost (actual)	7.80
Markup at 10%	1.84
Total	$20.30

During periods when labor rates are escalating or when material costs are increasing, the price per service hour should be calculated at least quarterly. Otherwise, you will be underpricing labor and profits will suffer.

TABLE 18-3. ANNUAL EXPENSES AND COSTS FOR BILL'S TV REPAIR SHOP

Indirect expenses:		
Rent	$2,400	
Manager's salary	7,200	
Clerical wages	2,400	
Other overhead	3,600	
Direct expenses:		
Labor	15,600	
Material	14,400	
Advertising	7,200	
Total costs	$52,800	
Productive hours worked		7,200
Cost per productive working hour		$7.33

The nature of some service businesses is such that prevailing price schedules are used by all businesses of a certain kind. For example, you are likely to find the labor cost for standard auto repairs to be priced similarly by most garages. This is possible through the use of "rate manuals" which establish standard times for specific operations. The standard is multiplied by the hourly rate to obtain the price to be charged for the service. This method of pricing assures that the same repair job will cost about the same wherever you get it done. Such standard operations as wheel balancing, changing points and plugs, minor tune-ups, and similar services lend themselves to pricing by this method.

Sometimes manufacturers publish suggested repair prices for use by the company agencies who represent the manufacturers.

It should be remembered that "standard" times represent the time required by a competent service technician working under average conditions. There is no guarantee that the price based on such standards is "fair," since wide variations are found in worker skills and in the conditions under which the service is performed. A repair that needs to be made after hours, on a weekend, or over a holiday period may with good reason cost more than the suggested price. In the same way, a repair that must be done on the spot, without regard to other priorities, may be priced somewhat higher.

WHAT CAN MANAGERS DO TO SHARPEN THEIR PRICING SKILLS?

The management practices of a business may be subjected to analysis in the same manner that financial practices may be examined and their impact on the financial health of a business determined. Since successful managerial procedures are largely the result of the business attitudes of small merchants themselves, it is important to analyze pricing practices from time to time to determine whether they are responsive to changing conditions.

In today's competitive climate, a small business can prosper only if it is following well-established principles and practices which are known to contribute to success. Here are some questions in the area of pricing designed to help business people determine how well they "measure up."[2]

1. Do you figure markup as a percentage of retail price rather than as a percentage of cost?
   Comment: Using selling price, you can more easily compare your markup with that of other stores and with your own store expenses

[2]From John W. Wingate, *Management Audit for Small Retailers*, Small Business Management Series, No. 13, 2d ed., U.S. Small Business Administration, Washington, 1971, pp. 19–21. The comments have been abridged to capture the basic response.

(which are usually expressed as a percentage of retail). Because most of the difference between cost and selling price represents expense, it is preferable to express markup as a percent of the retail price. You should set a markup goal not only for your store but also for each department and for each type of merchandise.

2. Do you set price lines and/or price zones?
   Comment: Setting price lines will give you good assortments at the price levels you want, and you will have a minimum inventory investment. Using price lines also helps you to aim all merchandise categories at specific groups of customers. Price lines should be determined only after you have studied the income levels of your customers. They should be revised as income level and buying desires change.

3. Do the prices you set provide for as much markup as possible within the limits of competition?
   Comment: Carelessly set prices often throw away markup without appreciable advantage to your customers. You should aim for maximum markup—that is, the highest profit you can obtain without losing sales.

4. In pricing new items, are you guided by what you think the typical customer will consider good value and will readily pay, rather than by the cost?
   Comment: Value is a subjective concept toward which objective pricing should strive. Following is a good way to judge the reasonableness of a cost price quotation: Estimate the retail price for an item and from that subtract the markup you have set for similar goods; the amount remaining would be the reasonable cost for the item.

5. Do you practice the technique of averaging markup rather than aiming for the same markup percentage throughout your store?
   Comment: Sound pricing indicates that you should take larger markup on goods whose risk and handling costs are high in order to offset the low markups you would take on competitive merchandise. The pricing mix, by which you achieve an average desired markup, is more important than the markup on individual items.

6. Do you keep a record of all your markdowns, and do you analyze them by cause?
   Comment: Using markdown records, you can calculate a retail book inventory in dollars that you can use both for merchandise and for shortage determinations. Analysis of markdowns by cause will help you to eliminate or reduce major causes, such as reordering too late in the season or holding too many special sales.

7. When you have clearance merchandise, does your first markdown normally move at least 60 percent of it?
   Comment: Usually, two or even three markdowns are required to dispose of an entire lot of clearance merchandise. If you sell out everything at the first markdown, you may have taken an unnecessarily large loss. On the other hand, if you use a very small markdown that moves less than half of the goods, you are likely to carry the goods into the next season, when there will be very little demand for them.

8. Before you mark down goods for clearance, do you consider alternate or supplementary ways of moving them—such as special displays, repackaging, and including them in a deal?
   Comment: In stores handling fashion and seasonal goods, clearance markdowns are one of the heaviest costs. Ingenuity and imagination often make it possible to move goods without markdown; and using other promotion devices allows you to take a smaller markdown.

This exercise is designed to test your understanding of the material presented in Chapter 18. Choose the response, *True* or *False*, which best fits each statement. Correct responses are presented in the back of the text.

1. Following the manufacturer's suggested retail price is considered the most acceptable method of pricing retail merchandise.
2. Prices are arrived at by the manufacturer, the wholesaler, and the retailer in the same way.
3. Most customers are not aware of the "hidden" factors which affect the price charged for a product.
4. If you are going to charge more for your product than your competitors, you must provide something extra which the customer recognizes.
5. Distribution costs constitute about half the cost of a retail product.
6. If you want to keep competitors out of the market with a competitive new product, you should start with a low initial price rather than a high one.
7. A 25 percent markup on cost is the equivalent of 20 percent of the selling price.
8. Markups are usually higher on merchandise that is subject to intense competition.
9. Your pricing policy should never permit pricing an item below your cost.
10. If you wait too long to take markdowns, you might not be able to move the merchandise at all.
11. The objective of multiple pricing is to stimulate volume.
12. Generally, the more price lines you have, the lower your inventory costs will be.
13. Customer sensitivity to price is the single most important factor to be considered by retailers.
14. Without good records, it is almost impossible for a service business to establish a realistic price for its services.
15. The use of "standard" prices takes all the guesswork out of setting accurate prices.

PERFORMANCE
PROBLEMS
AND
PROJECTS

1. Green's Fashion Store carries four price lines of ladies' dresses —$10.95, $17.95, $29.95, and $49.95. It has been customary to use a markup of 40 percent on dresses to cover expenses, profit, and markdowns. An order of two dozen dresses has just arrived and the invoice price is $250. At what initial price should they be offered?
2. Bring to class a half dozen newspaper advertisements which show how price is used as an inducement to stimulate sales.

Comment on them in terms of (a) their impact on you as a potential customer, and (b) their potential for increasing sales volume.

3. Check with four local TV repair shops and get their labor costs for the following services:

   (a) Changing picture tube (color set).
   (b) Adjusting color and focus on color set.
   (c) Service call to home (if separately priced)

   Discuss any differences in price and see if you can determine whether they were independently established or whether there is any indication of using "standard" pricing for any services.

4. You employ a five-person crew which performs janitorial services in office buildings at night when the offices are empty. Your cost per productive working hour is $6.75, including all wages and materials. If you want to make 10 percent profit, what would you charge a business which requires your entire crew 4 hours each night, 5 nights a week? Calculate the weekly charge for your services in this case.

THE CASE OF THE DISAPPEARING PROFIT

Λ CASE IN POINT

Tom Stafford had been saving money to buy a bicycle or motorcycle shop if the right opportunity came along. He was impressed with magazine articles he had read which told how many people were buying bicycles to ride as a part of their physical fitness program. The market for such products seemed almost inexhaustible.

After watching the ads for almost a year, he found a shop which had a brisk business. It was for sale by an owner who was moving to another state. A careful examination of the books showed consistent sales, with expenses running around 23 percent of sales. Expenses included a salary for the owner of $500 a month.

Tom reasoned that a 30 percent markup on cost would provide a profit margin of 7 percent, which seemed a fair return. With sales averaging around $15,000 a month, Tom figured his profit at around $1,000 ($15,000 × .07) a month. This plus the $500 salary seemed a good return for the venture.

Tom continued the advertising policies of his predecessor and was pleased to see the sales figures riding slightly above his expectations. Despite this obvious prosperity, Tom found that profits were not enough to enable him to take advantage of cash discounts. There never seemed to be any extra cash.

At the end of the first 3 months, he had an accountant prepare a profit-and-loss statement to see if he could pinpoint the problem. The accountant found that profits and expenses were just about offsetting each other, leaving Tom very little net profit.

"I don't understand it," Tom protested. "My expenses are almost exactly 23 percent as I planned. My markup is 30 percent. Where did the 7 percent profit I planned disappear to?"

1. Can you explan the disappearing profit?
2. What will Tom have to do to cause the profit to reappear?
3. How could Tom have prevented this problem from developing?

19

Effective Sales Promotion and Advertising

PERFORMANCE OBJECTIVES

After reading this chapter you should understand the importance of an effective advertising and promotion program in assuring the growth of a business. You will realize that advertising is the result of careful planning, and that haphazard, ill-conceived advertising is wasteful and ineffective. You should be able to relate business growth to the amount and kind of advertising used. Specifically, you should be able to:

1. Distinguish between sales promotion and advertising.
2. Explain what is meant by projecting the right store image and give examples of image-making devices used in advertising.
3. Discuss some of the reasons why people buy and show how these reasons help determine what you advertise.
4. Defend the theory that "some advertising is necessary for the business just to stay even."
5. Offer some guidelines for determining how much to spend for advertising.
6. Assess the likely result of a radio "spot" advertisement designed to reach teenagers, which is aired at 10 A.M. weekdays.
7. Explain why radio advertisements in the 6 A.M. to 10 A.M. period are more expensive than those slotted in the 7 P.M. to midnight period.
8. Discuss some of the pitfalls inherent in preparing your own advertising copy.

9. Judge the effectiveness of a newspaper advertisement which does not show the store's location or business hours.
10. Explain the advertising importance of the following slogans:

Good to the last drop
The pause that refreshes
It's mountain-grown
Ask the man who owns one

INTRODUCTION

No business should underestimate the value of a good advertising and promotion program. Since the ultimate objective of all businesses is to sell goods and services, it is imperative that merchants find a way to attract customers to their stores. A good location is an advantage, but only a small percentage of the people passing a retail establishment as street traffic are prospective buyers. Unless they have some knowledge about your business, and unless they know that you want them as your customers and that you have something they need, even the best location will not be enough to assure the volume of traffic you need to ensure a profitable operation.

Merchants must find an effective way to issue special invitations to prospective customers who might otherwise never enter their stores, or who do not pass their store regularly. Advertising is the best way any-body has found for reaching large numbers of potential customers in a short time at relatively low cost.

This chapter will emphasize the importance of advertising and promotion in helping business people meet their sales goals and add new customers. A well-planned, continuous program based on tested approaches will be outlined. Some of the principles of ad preparation will be examined. A comparison of the various advertising media will be made and their usefulness in meeting sales objectives explored. Finally, several means of measuring the effectiveness of advertising will be discussed. Checklists for evaluating the effectiveness of personal selling, window displays, and the total promotion program are provided. These will enable business people to determine how well their programs measure up against accepted practices.

WHAT IS SALES PROMOTION?

Sales promotion is any special effort a business takes to improve its sales and hold on to its customers. In the broadest sense, it includes anything owners do to move goods out of their stores or to increase the level of services they are providing. It consists of those activities which make other sales efforts (such as advertising) more effective. It is a widely used tool of small business people, whether they are in retailing, distribution, service trades, or manufacturing. It may be directed toward consumers to motivate them to buy, toward other business people (by wholesalers or manufacturers) to convince them to handle certain goods or lines in preference to others, or toward salespeople to get them to sell more or to "push" certain lines of merchandise.

Sales promotion involves such things as creating special displays, offering premiums, running contests, distributing free samples, offering free introductory services, and demonstrating products. Frequently sales promotions are coupled with special advertising programs.

IF YOU'VE GOT THE "BEST GAME IN TOWN," WHY SPEND MONEY TO PROMOTE IT?

Having the better mousetrap offers no guarantee that the customer will buy your product. Owning a profitable business is no guarantee that it will still be profitable 5 years from now. You must assume that your competitors have a product as good as yours, and that they offer service and prices which are competitive. This premise puts everyone on the starting line with the same advantage. The winners in races of this sort will be the merchants who realize that they have to run fast just to stay even. If they want to get ahead and build volume, they have to offer something special—something better than their competitors' products. This will require the best creative imagination and ingenuity they can provide. They will soon learn that customers are fickle and that they respond to ideas rather than products. All new automobiles, for example, have basic similarities and all will "get you there" in varying degrees of comfort and economy. To sell them, automobile dealers know that certain ideas must be sold to the buying public, based on a knowledge of what the customer will be responsive to. Such basic ideas as smallness, economy, comfort, styling, resale value, and dependability have been used at various times to emphasize promotion drives and get customers to buy.

Statistics show that businesses lose about 25 percent of their customers each year. Based on 300 shopping days a year, a business with 1,200 customers would be "out of customers" in about 4 years unless it could find a way to add at least one new customer each business day. This fact alone should prevent you from becoming smug about success based only on sales. Unless you do a good job of promoting your product, your services, your business, and your prices, you will be left behind as an "also ran" by your competition. Sales promotion is an absolute necessity for survival in the business world. This is one place where yelling loudly pays off.

WHAT CAN YOU DO TO GET ON A CUSTOMER'S "FIRST-CHOICE" LIST AS A PLACE TO SHOP?

Most customers shop at many different stores, but surveys show that about 70 percent of all retail customers have a store of first choice. In order to get on such a list your store must stand for something concrete in the customer's mind. The image you project must be clear, recognizable, and pleasing to the customer.

The projection of an image is important because it will influence everything you do in sales promotion. The image can be related to your location, the kind of merchandise you handle, the service you provide, or some similar factor. A few images related to these categories are:

Location: Dining place of the stars (prestige)
Hollywood and Vine (excitement)
At the crossroads (easy to find)

Merchandise: The bargain spot (economy)
The smart shop (fashion)
Everything from A to Z (assortment)
Unconditional guarantee (quality)

Service: Free delivery anywhere
Use our easy credit
The friendly store

A store will probably associate itself with various characteristics of location, merchandise, and service. If you are a growing store you should select two or three features in which your business has the capacity to excel and place major emphasis on developing them. One mistake you can make is to try to cater to everybody. This approach will soon make you a nonentity so far as image is concerned. It can be a step toward failure. You have to offer so many services that none are performed well, and your store's image soon becomes blurred in the customer's mind. Table 19-1 shows a matrix of image-making features which is suggestive of the degree to which image can be pursued.

HOW DO YOU KNOW IF YOU'RE PROJECTING THE RIGHT IMAGE?

For your image to be acceptable to your customers, you should know something about the market you are trying to reach. This is a comparatively simple job but a necessary one. There are five major areas you need to explore before you attempt to establish an image:

1. *Who Are My Customers?* Where do they work? How much do they earn? Are they white- or blue-collar? What are their ages and social interests?

2. *Where Do They Come From?* Do they ride or walk? Do they make a special trip to shop or do they shop while going to and from work? Where do they live and how do they live (types of homes, apartments, etc.)?

3. *How Many Are There?* What is the population of the area served by your store? What is the family size? Are they considered permanent or transient? What share of this market can you expect to capture?

TABLE 19-1. THE STORE IMAGE

Quality	Uncontrolled.	Serviceable.	Tested.	Best market affords.
Standardization	Staples only.	Standardized goods.	Some exclusive.	Much exclusive.
Price range	Low.	Low to medium.	Medium to high.	High.
Price appeal	Bargains only.	Bargains on key items.	Market-par emphasis.	Mostly nonprice competition.
Timing—fashion	Late, after general acceptance.	Fashion-right emphasis.	Community leadership.	Much experimental fashions.
Continuity of lines and promotional emphasis	None, job lots only, heavily advertised.	Largely promotional goods, heavily advertised.	Semipromotional, some institutional emphasis.	Nonpromotional, mostly institutional advertising.
Variety of lines	One segment of a line.*	Single major line.†	Related lines.‡	One-stop shopping.
Breadth of assortments	Incomplete.	Best-sellers only.	Wide assortment.	Dominant assortments.
Brand emphasis	None.	National brands.	Both national and private.	Mainly private.
Personal service	None.	Minimal clerk service.	Fair salesmanship.	Well-trained customer advisers.
Nonpersonal service	Cash and carry.	Credit and delivery available.	Many services available.	Institutional center for community activities.
Atmosphere	Crude.	Functional only.	Pleasant and spacious.	Opulent.

*Example: a store that sells pants only or only tall girl's dresses and suits.
†A single major line would be a dress shop, an appliance store, or a grocery store.
‡Related lines refers to stores such as departmentized women's specialty stores, family shoe stores, and supermarkets selling meats and some nonfood items.

Source: Adapted from John Wingate and Seymour Helfant, *Small Store Planning for Growth*, Small Business Management Series, No. 33, U.S. Small Business Administration, Washington, 1966, p. 23.

---

4. *Competition.*   How does your store excel those of your competitors in the area? What do you have to offer that is unique or better than what your competitors can offer?

5. *Other Stores.*   What other shopping centers are in your area and what effect will they have on your store? Which stores do customers like? Why?

   Much of this information can be obtained from chambers of commerce, newspapers, and trade association literature, and from talking to people and salesclerks. Census data can provide helpful information about the family size, income level, and housing characteristics of the people in your community.

   Answers to these questions will prevent you from offering expensive lines to customers with limited incomes, or from entering fields where competition is very strong, unless you feel that customer merchandise and service requirements are not being satisfactorily met by your competition. The nature of your merchandise, the size of your market, the strength of your competition, and the capital you have available are all factors which will help shape your store's image.

HOW CAN YOU TELL WHAT TO PROMOTE?

Once you have decided on an image to promote and have defined your market, a decision regarding what to promote is needed. By now you will have an idea of the tastes and needs of your potential customers; this should guide you in selecting those things your customers want and *need*. If you have miscalculated this factor or have not adequately surveyed the market, you will be disappointed at the response your promotion brings. The income level of your potential customers will suggest a "right" *price* for the line of merchandise you intend to promote. Your customers must be willing and able to buy the merchandise you are offering, or they will be unable to respond. Selecting the "right" *time* for your promotional efforts means timing those efforts to coincide with the period during which the customer is ready and willing to buy the product. The sale of umbrellas, snow chains, rainwear, and ski clothing, for example, must be very carefully timed to the period of customer need. Finally, you should promote those items which have the *quality* suitable for the function to be performed. You will soon realize the shortsightedness of selling substandard merchandise which does not offer the degree of quality the customer has a right to expect.

Keep in mind the reasons why customers buy when you are trying to decide what to promote. Here are some typical reasons why customers buy and examples of items which might be purchased:

Reason for Buying	Examples of Items Purchased
Product fills a basic need	Furniture, clothing, food, pots and pans, transportation devices, insurance, health aids.
Product is desirable but not essential	Boats, television sets, sports equipment, tools, electric can openers, mixers, ice crushers, beauty aids, and air conditioners.
Maintaining status	Power lawn mowers, second car or television set, swimming pool, sports equipment, electric hedge trimmers.
Sentiment	Gifts and flowers for special occasions or anniversaries.
Safety/security	Fences, alarm devices, locks, firearms, and insurance.

Reason for Buying	Examples of Items Purchased
Purchase will add to buyer's wealth	Items used to make money (tools, typewriters, special equipment) or those which add to the value of one's property (fences, screens, lawns, awnings, paint, patio covers, and concrete walks and drives).

Keep in mind that products which have established customer acceptance through advertising usually move much better than those that are less well-known. Customers who have in mind a specific advertised product often refuse to take something "just as good."

IS THERE A "BEST" WAY TO PROMOTE A PRODUCT OR SERVICE?

Unfortunately not. There are dozens of methods which can be used, but there are no guarantees that any one method will show a precise dollar return on sales. It is possible, however, to measure the effectiveness of the various methods with some degree of accuracy and decide which method is best for your peculiar circumstances. Direct promotion methods which will be discussed in the remainder of this chapter are shown in the following table.

Direct Methods of Sales Promotion	Examples
Use of external advertising media	Newspapers, magazines, radio, direct mail, television, billboards, shoppers, directories, and transit cards.
Use of promotional events	Special sales, contests, celebrity visits, fashion shows, parades, coupons, premiums, and samples.
Use of internal media	Tear sheets, catalogs, copies of ads, manufacturers' literature, signs, posters, window displays, floor displays, tags, and labels.
Use of personal salesmanship	Suggestion selling, customer assistance, product knowledge, and cooperative friendly attitude.

The choice of media is dependent on many interrelated factors, such as the nature of the merchandise, the amount of merchandise available, the amount of money available, and the efficiency of the medium. No hard and fast rules can be made. The advantages and disadvantages of each method, if recognized, can help you decide on the one best suited to your needs.

Promotional events, if not overdone, can act as business stimulators during times when customer spending is normally "slow."

Internal promotion devices are helpful in clinching the sale after advertising has attracted the customer to the store.

Personal salesmanship is the final step in the sales promotion sequence. It is at this step that the customer is persuaded to buy. It is obvious that the effectiveness of the entire sales promotion depends upon well-trained, motivated salespeople who know how to respond to customer behavior and influence the customer's decision.

HOW IS PROMOTION DIFFERENT FROM ADVERTISING?

Promotion is a companion to advertising. Its purpose is to inform or persuade customers, to strengthen the image of the business and create goodwill, to attract customers, to introduce new products, or to increase a firm's share of the market.

Promotional effort is typified by holiday sales, "moonlight" sales, dollar days, 1-cent sales, opening sales, and back-to-school sales. It also includes special store features such as demonstrations, fashion shows, exhibits, and classes. Customer demand fluctuates during the year, reaching a peak for retail businesses in December. Table 19-2 shows that consumer buying habits are influenced by climatic conditions, established calendar events, and traditional activities which have been established by custom.

Promotions are often identified by special signs, badges, costumes, uniforms, wrapping paper, and shopping bags. Premiums such as "double trading stamps" and other giveaways are commonly used in promotional activities.

In-store promotional materials such as special displays, sales literature, and handouts are designed to trigger impulse purchases or to reinforce advertising by convincing those who came to look to buy.

WHAT IS THE FUNCTION OF ADVERTISING?

Advertising is designed to induce on the part of a reader or listener a favorable reaction to a product or service. Its purpose is to attract customers to your store by convincing them of the superiority of a product or service. Thus, an effective newspaper ad might cause potential customers to come to the store to examine merchandise firsthand. To turn customers into buyers, you depend on interior displays and personal salesmanship.

Money spent on advertising will be wasted unless your store can build repeat sales through good service, high quality, and fair prices. Keep in mind that advertising can bring only temporary success to an inferior product. If the service or the product does not live up to customers' expectations, they will not be likely to return. Even when no personal selling seems to be involved, as in self-service stores, other factors besides advertising usually enter into the final decision to buy. Among these are the product itself, the reputation of the maker or of the store, the package, and the price.

TABLE 19-2.   FACTORS WHICH AFFECT CONSUMER DEMAND

Month	Climatic	Calendar	Traditional
January	Clearance of winter merchandise, resort wear	Inventory clearance	White goods sales, drug sales
February	Advance showing of spring merchandise	Lincoln's birthday, Washington's birthday, Valentine's Day, Boy Scout Week, Lent*	Furniture, piece goods, housewares
March	Spring clothes	Girl Scout Week, Easter gifts,* St. Patrick's Day	Home furnishings*
April	Spring cleaning, garden supplies and outdoor furnishings, fur storage	Baseball season open, do-it-yourself week, baby week	Spring anniversary sales*
May	Spring clearance, summer sportswear, air conditioners	Mother's Day, camp wear	Bridal promotions
June	Summer wear	Graduation gifts, Father's Day, vacation needs, barbecue needs	Housewares, drug sales
July	Summer clearance	Fourth of July, inventory clearance	
August	Advance showing of fall merchandise	Back-to-school needs	Furniture,* piece goods, fur sale, housewares*
September	Fall clothes	Christmas-layaway promotion, back to school	China and glass, draperies and curtains
October	Fall clothes and accessories	Columbus Day	Fall anniversary sale,* woolen piece goods
November	Fall clothes and accessories	Election Day, Halloween, Christmas opening, toys	Linens, china and glass
December	Winter clothes, resort wear	Christmas gifts, evening wear	

*Subject to variations.

Source: Adapted from Bernard W. Smith, *Sales Promotion Pointers for Small Retailers,* Small Marketers Aids, No. 60, U.S. Small Business Administration, Washington, p. 3.

HOW DOES ADVERTISING HELP "MAKE" CUSTOMERS FOR THE BUSINESS?

Few of the purchases we make during a lifetime are one-time purchases. We tend to go back for repeat purchases to the stores where we have been satisfied, and we tend to purchase what has pleased us before. The aim of advertising should be to develop customers for repeat sales. People have to be reminded over and over again what you sell and why they should buy it from you. In addition to reminding old customers, advertising picks up new readers and listeners with each appearance. These new customers are needed just to hold your ground as old customers move out of your shopping area. If you want your business to grow, you have to do better than just hold the line on customer losses. This means that you have to attract customers from a wider market instead of merely from the immediate neighborhood. To do this, you need to advertise, especially by newspaper and radio.

Almost all businesses advertise or should advertise. The public expects them to. The ads of small business people are not as elaborate, or as costly, as the ads of national advertisers. Often a simple appeal based on price or quality or selection or good service is more effective for local merchants. But small business people who can capture the imagination of their own small segment of the public through advertising will see the results in increased sales in the same way big businesses do.

HOW MUCH SHOULD YOU SPEND FOR ADVERTISING?

Spending too much without getting results in extra sales can be costly. On the other hand, spending too little without getting adequate penetration of your potential market area is wasteful. Smart business people reserve a permanent place in their expense picture for advertising. They remember the practical business maxim "You've got to spend money to make money" and realize that nowhere is it more true than here. They know they cannot afford not to advertise. But, with the limited funds available, they must make every advertising dollar count.

Total yearly expenditures for advertising are usually expressed as a percentage of gross sales. If you had $100,000 in gross sales last year and spent $1,500 for advertising, your advertising ratio was 1.5 percent of sales. You can compare this level with other stores like yours locally and nationally. A survey made by the *Small Business Reporter* to determine the advertising experience of selected small businesses showed that respondents spent an average of 3.1 percent of gross sales on advertising.[1] Retailers reported an average expenditure of 2.5 percent and service firms 3.5 percent. United States retail hardware stores spent an average of 1.69 percent on advertising in 1974, with high-profit stores spending 1.49 percent and low-profit stores 1.83 percent. From the available statistics, it would appear that any amount less than 1.5 percent would be ineffective in producing significant improvements in sales. For some types of business, this amount would not even be sufficient to maintain the status quo.

---

[1]"Advertising," *Small Business Reporter* series, Vol. 9, No. 1, Bank of America, 1969, p. 3.

WHAT FACTORS OTHER THAN SALES ARE RELIABLE GUIDES TO HELP YOU DETERMINE ADVERTISING LEVELS?

The gross-sales method is not the only guide for establishing your advertising budget, although it is the one most commonly used and is most easily understood. The type of business you are in will affect your advertising expense. High-volume, low-cost items carried by stores selling highly promotional merchandise require heavier outlays for advertising than high-cost, low-volume items like automobiles, furniture, and major appliances. If your store is new, you will need to spend more in order to become known throughout your market area. If you advertise via radio and newspaper, media rates will be based on area coverage and circulation, even though many of the people reached by such media are outside your market area and are unlikely to become customers. Finally, you cannot ignore the amount of advertising your competitors do. Unless you want to be buried by them, your advertising will have to be aggressive and comparable to that of stores of your size. This could cost you more than you feel you can afford. The usual guidelines will have to be mofified in cases like this.

SHOULD SMALL BUSINESSES KEEP A RESERVE FUND FOR UNEXPECTED ADVERTISING OPPORTUNITIES?

Most large businesses set aside a nominal amount (5 percent) of their advertising budget for promotion of new products, "institutional" advertising (which primarily promotes the business image), or to serve as a cushion against the effects of economic downtrends, during which expenses must be reduced. Small businesses should set aside a modest reserve for such contingencies.

SHOULD YOU ALLOCATE YOUR ADVERTISING BUDGET BY MEDIA?

If you are using two or more media for your advertising, it is a good idea to plan your monthly expenditures for each medium and to record the information on a calendar. The monthly ad budget for each medium, the size of the ad, its cost, and the day on which it will run should be shown on the calendar. The items to be promoted are usually listed too. This plan enables you to see at a glance what is scheduled for the entire month. Then you can coordinate your buying and store activities to support the advertising campaign. Unless you do this, you will likely find yourself unprepared to take full advantage of the advertising because of uninformed salespeople, inadequate store displays, or stock which was ordered too late to arrive for the promotion.

Selecting an effective medium for advertising is not a simple job. Some well-known directories of advertising firms carry as many as 15,000 listings. Small business people can concentrate on utilizing the common ones shown in Table 19-3. A study of this chart will quickly show you the coverage, costs, advantages, and disadvantages of the various media.

Time and space costs are related to the following variables for newspaper and radio advertising:

1. Newspapers will probably quote their rates for local display advertising by column inches. If line rates are quoted, remember that there are 14 lines to the inch. The rates are almost always higher for national than for local advertisers. Most local newspaper rates are volume rates—as the amount of space you contract for increases, the cost per inch or line goes down.

2. If you ask to have your advertisement on a certain page of the paper or in a specific position on the page, the newspaper may grant your request as a matter of goodwill. However, you have no guarantee of position unless you pay a premium rate. The general practice is to charge premium rates for advertising on pages near the front of the paper, such as the second and third pages, and on special-interest sections, such as women's and sports pages. Premium rates are also charged for color.

3. Classified rates are quoted by lines. Occasional users pay "transient" rates, but a business user will usually qualify for "professional" rates, which are lower. These rates, whether for regular or display classified advertisements, are usually based on both frequency and volume. The frequency rate may be for consecutive days or for the total number of days, consecutive or otherwise.

4. Radio time is sold in 10, 30, or 60 second "spots." A useful buy is the "adjacency," which gives small business people a spot immediately preceding or following a popular feature (such as news, sports, or weather) but without the financial commitment of total sponsorship. If radio is the principal advertising medium you are going to use, 1-minute spots are usually preferable. If it supplements other media, you may get good results from shorter spots. The number of spots and when and where they are placed will be governed to a great extent on how many advertising dollars you can spend. As a general rule, the more spots the better. One of the strong points of radio advertising is the opportunity for frequent repetition.

5. Radio time is divided into several classes. The highest class, prime time, is the most expensive. Radio prime time corresponds to morning and evening drive times. As with other

TABLE 19-3. ADVERTISING MEDIA COMPARISON CHART

Medium	Market Coverage	Type of Audience	Sample Time/Space Costs*	Particular Suitability	Major Advantage	Major Disadvantage
DAILY NEWSPAPER	Single community or entire metro area. Zoned editions sometimes available.	General. Tends more toward men, older age group, slightly higher income and education.	Per agate line, weekday Circ. 10–20: $ .206 50–100: $ .52 300–400: $1.895	All general retailers.	Flexibility.	Nonselective audience.
WEEKLY NEWSPAPER	Single community usually; sometimes a metro area.	General. Usually residents of a smaller community.	Per agate line Circ. 1–5: $.133 5–10: $.261 10–20: $.31	Retailers serving a strictly local market.	Local identification.	Limited coverage.
SHOPPER	Most households in a single community. Chain shoppers can cover a metro area.	Consumer households.	Per agate line Circ. 6–10: $.166 31–40: $.32 51–100: $.492	Neighborhood retailers and service businesses.	Consumer orientation.	A giveaway and not always read.
DIRECTORIES	Geographic area or occupational field served by the directory.	Active shoppers for goods or services.	Yellow Pages: per half column per month Pop. 14–18: $15.00 110–135: $39.60 770–950: $82.30	Services, retailers of brand name items, highly specialized retailers.	Users are in the market for goods or services.	Limited to active shopper.
DIRECT MAIL	Controlled by the advertiser.	Controlled by the advertiser through use of demographic lists.	Mailing of 11" x 17" two-color, 4-page letter and business reply card in #10 envelope, label addressed, third-class mail: $.18 each	New and expanding businesses, ones using coupon returns or catalogs.	Personalized approach to an audience of good prospects.	Number of variables that can thwart success of a mailing.

	Market coverage	Audience	Typical cost	Businesses that use it	Advantages	Limitations
RADIO	Definable market surrounding the station's location.	Stations with a distinct programming format provide selected audiences.	Per 60-second AM morning drive time spot Pop. 16.7: $ 4.50 343.1: $ 17.00 3,151.2: $149.00	Business catering to identifiable groups: teens, commuters, housewives.	Market selectivity, reach and frequency.	Must be bought consistently to be of value.
TELEVISION	Definable market area surrounding the station's location.	Varies with the time of day. Tends toward younger age group, less print-oriented.	Per 30-second daytime spot, highest priority status Pop. 85.2: $ 25.00 443.9: $ 30.00 6,966.4: $267.00	Highly personal, owner-oriented businesses; and sellers' products or services with wide appeal.	Dramatic impact, wide market coverage.	Cost of time and complexity of ad production.
TRANSIT	Urban or metro community served by transit system; may be limited to a few transit routes.	Transit riders, especially wage earners and shoppers; pedestrians.	Per inside 11" x 28" card, 100 showing per month 25 buses: $ 70.20 104 buses: $182.00 300 buses: $780.00	Businesses along transit routes, especially those appealing to wage earners.	Repetition and length of exposure.	Limited audience.
OUTDOOR	Entire metro area or single neighborhood.	General, especially auto drivers.	Per 12' x 25' poster, 100 showing per month Pop. 5.6: $ 207.00 445.0: $ 5,696.00 9,799.7: $85,506.00	Amusements, tourist businesses, brand name retailers.	Dominant size, frequency of exposure.	Cost.
LOCAL MAGAZINE	Entire metro area or region. Zoned editions sometimes available.	General. Tends toward better educated, more affluent.	Per one-sixth page, black and white Circ. 25: $185.00 50: $245.00	Restaurants, entertainments, specialty shops, mail order businesses.	Delivery of a loyal, special interest audience.	Limited audience.

*Read circulation and population figures in thousands. All costs based on one-time rates exclusive of discounts.

Source: Adapted with permission from Bank of America, N.T. & S.A., copyright 1976, San Francisco, "Advertising," Vol. 13, No. 8, in the *Small Business Reporter* series.

media, rate structures vary according to the size of the audience a station can reach. Except on the smallest stations, time periods are classified for the purpose of setting rates in accordance with the following plan:

Class AA   Morning drive time—6 A.M. to 10 A.M.
Class B   Homemaker time—10 A.M. to 4 P.M.
Class A   Evening drive time—4 P.M. to 7 P.M.
Class C   Evening time—7 P.M. to 12 midnight
Class D   Night time—Midnight to 6 A.M.

A maximum classification would be AA, which claims the highest rate. Class D time is the lowest. The hours shown are not exactly the same for all stations.

WHAT GUIDELINES ARE AVAILABLE TO THOSE WHO WANT TO PREPARE THEIR OWN ADVERTISING COPY?

As a first step, the advertisers must know whom they are directing the ad to. Audiences composed primarily of homemakers, teenagers, pet owners, retirees, working women, students, boat owners, or professionals each requires a different kind of appeal. Each group has its own unique needs and your ad must capitalize on that fact. Trying to cover too large an audience with a "shotgun" approach will fail to attract anyone. If you have a clear idea of the type of customers that would patronize your business, you can prepare a sales message that appeals directly to their interests and desires.

Secondly, you need to decide which feature of the merchandise you want to stress. Will it be prestige, safety, convenience, price, or service? Or some other feature which has direct appeal to your intended audience? Items to advertise are those which will bring customers to the door. Best-sellers from past years, new products the public has been waiting for, items of special seasonal appeal, items whose price makes them an exceptionally good buy are all good choices. Brand-name items are an excellent choice because the advertiser gets a free ride on the manufacturer's national advertising. Because every piece of advertising serves to reinforce the total business image, the advertised item should be typical of the best merchandise the store handles. It must be stocked in sufficient quantity to cover response to the ad. It is poor public relations to advertise an item that cannot be produced when a customer comes into the store eager to buy.

In preparing your ad, you should use the same personal appeal and persuasiveness you would use if you were talking to prospective customers in person. Your ad should tell them what the product or service will do for them—fill some need, save them money, offer protection, increase their prestige, or improve their health. The fundamental components of a good newspaper display advertisement are shown in Table 19-4.

TABLE 19-4. CHECKLIST FOR NEWSPAPER PROMOTIONAL ADVERTISEMENT

*Merchandise	Does the ad offer merchandise having wide appeal, special features, price appeal, and timeliness?
Medium	Is a newspaper the best medium for the ad, or would another—direct mail, radio, television, or other—be more appropriate?
Location	Is the ad situated in the best spot (in both section and page location)?
Size	Is the ad large enough to do the job expected of it? Does it omit important details, or is it overcrowded with nonessential information?
*Headline	Does the headline express the major single idea about the merchandise advertised? The headline should usually be an informative statement and not simply a label. For example, "Sturdy shoes for active boys, specially priced at $6.95," is certainly better than "Boys' Shoes, $6.95."
Illustration	Does the illustration (if one is used) express the idea the headline conveys?
*Merchandise information	Does the copy give the basic facts about the goods, or does it leave out information that would be important to the reader? ("The more you tell, the more you sell.")
Layout	Does the arrangement of the parts of the ad and the use of white space make the ad easy to read? Does it stimulate the reader to look at all the contents of the ad?
Human interest	Does the ad—through illustration, headline, and copy—appeal to customers' wants and wishes?
*"You" attitude	Is the ad written and presented from the customer's point of view (with the customer's interests clearly in mind), or from the store's?
*Believability	To the objective, nonpartisan reader, does the ad ring true, or does it perhaps sound exaggerated or somewhat phony?
Type face	Does the ad use a distinctive typeface—different from those of competitors?
*Spur to action	Does the ad stimulate prompt action through devices such as use of a coupon, statement of limited quantities, announcement of a specific time period for the promotion or impending event?
*Sponsor identification	Does the ad use a specially prepared signature cut that is always associated with the store and that identifies it at a glance? Also, does it always include the following institutional details: Store location, hours open, telephone number, location of advertised goods, and whether phone and mail orders are accepted?

*The seven items starred are of chief importance to the smaller store.

Source: John W. Wingate and Seymour Helfant, *Small Store Planning for Growth*, Small Business Management Series, No. 33, U.S. Small Business Administration, Washington, 1966, p. 69.

Studies have shown that many merchants are careless in observing the fundamentals of good advertising. A study made by the American Newspaper Publishers' Association showed that only 53 percent of the ads studied carried informative headlines, 50 percent failed to include pertinent facts; only 52 percent gave the store's complete address; and only 44 percent gave its phone number. Almost 60 percent failed to give their hours of business.

WHAT ARE THE INGREDIENTS OF A GOOD AD?

An effective ad relies strongly on the following:

Originality: Use special type faces, unusual headlines, a catchy slogan, and a unique approach to the copy.

Simplicity: Stress one item, one sales pitch, and one point.

Strength: Make a definite claim. Be positive, forceful, and direct. Hedging shows lack of confidence and will affect the customer's attitude toward the ad.

Believability: Do not make extravagant claims; they might work once but can boomerang later. Consumers have a good memory for a bad deal.

Quality: Make your ad create a good image of you.

Restraint: Use as much space or air time as you need to make your point—and no more. Give your readers or listeners just what they need to make a decision. Their time is valuable too.

WHAT IS MEANT BY INSTITUTIONAL ADVERTISING?

Institutional advertising is that effort directed toward promoting the store's image. It selects certain special qualities to emphasize, such as outstanding personal service, high-quality merchandise, or broad assortments of goods. Occasional ads devoted to these institutional purposes do not bring in immediate traffic, but they do build for the future. Retailers should build their store image through institutional advertising over a period of time. They should remember that advertising not only stimulates short-term interest in specific items but also helps form a lasting impression in the customer's mind. Institutional advertising sells ideas while product advertising sells merchandise.

WHAT ADVERTISING APPROACHES CAN BE USED TO REINFORCE THE BUSINESS IMAGE?

The appearance or the sound of an advertisement contributes the most toward distinctiveness. The impression your advertising makes is the product of illustrations, type face, proportion, overall design, layout, and so on. By carefully selecting all the elements of the advertisement and combining them skillfully, you can make each project the image you wish.

Strive for balance, orderly arrangement, and attractiveness. Obtain a logo or trademark which can be used on your advertising to give it individuality. Use an individualized slogan or phrase which customers will associate with your store, or use distinctive artwork or layout which is easily recognized. Catchy radio jingles or musical identification is sometimes used effectively.

Some advertisers develop individuality in their advertising by presenting a regular column in which they describe in everyday language interesting sidelights about their business, unusual customers, hints on fashions, recipes, and similar topics. Such a column, signed at the bottom by the owner, represents the essence of individuality in advertising.

DO MANY SMALL BUSINESSES USE ADVERTISING AGENCIES?

Only a small percentage do. Franchise operators often have access to professionally prepared mats and similar advertising materials offered by the "home office" as a part of the package paid for by the franchise fee. By and large, most small business people prepare their own ads, using whatever talent, imagination, and free advertising aids available.

WHAT PROFESSIONAL ADVERTISING HELP IS AVAILABLE FOR THE BUSINESS PEOPLE WHO NEED IT?

If you decide you need help in preparing your advertising, you can find a lot of it among the professionals in the advertising industry.

You can expect help from most media because of the competition for your advertising dollars. Each medium is likely to try to make it easier for you to advertise there in order to get and keep your business. Not all of this help is free, but it may cost less than if you go elsewhere for it.

You can get mats for complete newspaper advertisements from companies whose branded products you sell. These ads come in a variety of column widths and inches. The newspaper inserts your name and business address, and the price if you wish. Copy for these advertisements is prepared by skilled professionals. The help you get from the newspapers themselves varies. They usually make mats or reproduction proofs of advertisements and illustrations available without charge. The mats and proofs are supplied by syndicated advertising services to which newspapers subscribe for the convenience of their advertisers. Some newspapers have staffs of copywriters and artists to prepare advertising. Often the service is free. But if you are going to use the advertisements they prepare in other newspapers too, there is almost certain to be a charge.

Help from directory publishers varies from practically nothing to complete preparation of the advertisement. For display advertising in the Yellow Pages, complete copy and layout is furnished without charge in many cities. Stock illustrations are also available.

Radio stations will give assistance in writing advertising. Or they will prepare taped commercials for a fee. Brand-name manufacturers often supply scripts and transcriptions or tapes for advertising their products on radio. These can be localized with your name and address and sometimes in other ways.

Car cards for the inside of public transportation vehicles and sign panels for the outside of buses and taxicabs are sometimes available from manufacturers of brand-name products. More often, they are made up locally. The transit company controlling the advertising space can be expected to help with the designing and printing.

Advertising media prefer to receive advertising from agencies rather than get involved in the preparation. They like to have the finished advertisement delivered ready for the press or for broadcasting. You might be ahead by having agency service even if it increases your advertising cost. At least, it would be worth your while to investigate what an agency can do for you.

HOW POPULAR IS NEWSPAPER ADVERTISING AMONG SMALL BUSINESS OWNERS?

Studies made by the Bank of America show that 82 percent of small businesses use one or more newspaper media and 31 percent use two or more. While more retailers (91 percent) use newspaper advertising than service firms (72 percent), all agree that newspaper advertising brings good results. Small businesses spend an average of 25 percent of their advertising budget in newspapers; one-fourth of them spend 50 percent.

Since most people read at least one newspaper each day, the market penetration of newspapers is usually good. The cost per potential customer reached makes the newspaper very attractive as an advertising medium.

Disadvantages of newspaper ads are their short life span (1 day) and the fact that your ad will be competing with many others for the attention of the reader. This makes layout, size, and position on the page critical.

ARE SHOPPERS EFFECTIVE ADVERTISING DEVICES?

Sometimes called shopping guides or community newspapers, shoppers have grown rapidly in popularity since World War II. They vary greatly in size, format, and in the amount of news they carry. Most are offered free to readers, who obtain them at racks in popular shopping locations. Although many have large circulations, their effectiveness in drawing customers is questionable since many of the copies are never read.

HOW DO THE YELLOW PAGES RATE AS AN ADVERTISING MEDIUM?

Advertising in the Yellow Pages of the telephone directory is a popular and effective method of advertising for small business people. It ranks second to newspapers in effectiveness despite the fact that small business advertisers spend more than half their budgets on Yellow Pages display advertising. One-line listings are free to business subscribers. Service firms spend more than retailers for this type of advertising. Many of them list under several different headings and often in the directories of surrounding towns.

The production staff of the regional Yellow Pages sales office can, for a charge, produce a finished ad from the advertiser's rough sketch. Or the advertiser may make up his or her own ad using stock illustrations available at Yellow Pages advertising offices.

DOES DIRECT-MAIL ADVERTISING COST MORE THAN NEWSPAPER ADVERTISING?

Direct mail generally costs more than any other form of advertising on a cost-per-impression basis. It is, however, an economical medium. Because small business people control their own circulation, direct mail can pinpoint the market more effectively than any other major medium. Very little of the circulation of a direct-mail piece need be waste circulation if you are selective in picking the addressees. The key to this selectivity is the mailing list. The list you use must be made up of people who can use what you sell and who will buy it or influence the purchase. Even those who do not respond to one mailing may be prospects later.

There are many companies that make a business of compiling mailing lists. These lists may contain many thousands of names or as few as 100. Compilers of mailing lists guarantee their lists to be current up to a specified percentage. They refund postage on pieces returned as undeliverable beyond the percentage allowed by the guarantee. For example, on a 95 percent guaranteed list, postage is refunded on returns above 5 percent of the list. A list purchased from one of these companies may be better than one you make up yourself, and it may even cost less in the end. It will certainly save you a lot of work.

The effectiveness of direct mail is rated third by small business owners, after newspapers and Yellow Pages.

WHAT KINDS OF DIRECT-MAIL ADVERTISEMENTS ARE COMMONLY USED?

Letters, catalogs, circulars, postcards, price lists, coupons, reprints, and order blanks are included in the direct-mail category.

Postcards can be handwritten and used to announce a special sale, thank a customer for his or her patronage, or announce a sales representative's call a few days in advance.

A self-mailer is a bulletin that is folded and mailed without an envelope. It can be used to describe your products. It should include information about prices and terms.

Pamphlets can be mimeographed sheets folded to make a booklet, or they can be commercially printed. Pamphlets do not normally carry pictures.

Brochures are similar to pamphlets but are usually printed commercially on a good grade of paper, often in color and with pictures. Brochures are ideal for announcing major events or major new products.

Special letters are very effective in reaching selected audiences. New parents, newlyweds, and new people in the neighborhood are groups you might wish to reach with a letter. Unusual store events, changes in store hours or services, or changes in your organization can be announced with special letters.

Coupon mailing is a powerful, short-term, special-event type of promotion often used for grand openings, remodelings, or the addition of a new department. It is a letter telling customers and prospects of the news and inviting them to visit your store. You add a coupon that offers something free—or at a reduced price—to bring the reader to your store. Coupon promotions can wear themselves out if overused. It is better to use them sparingly, with really good values each time, than to attempt to use them too often, with small values on the coupons.

WHAT ADVANTAGES ARE OFFERED BY RADIO ADVERTISING?

Radio advertising can be purchased at a relatively low cost per listener. It may reach some people newspapers miss (younger people and nonnewspaper readers). It is flexible, permitting last-minute changes right up to broadcast time. It can be heard almost anywhere and, while it is on the air, has no immediate competition from a more powerful advertiser.

Most merchants consider radio an ideal medium when teamed with outdoor and transit advertising. In order to get your radio message across you must advertise frequently. A spot aired once a week would probably be a waste of money.

Most small business owners consider radio advertising less effective than newspapers and Yellow Pages; hence, most of them spend 15 percent or less of their advertising budget for radio advertising.

ANY POINTERS ON SELECTING A RADIO STATION FOR ADVERTISING?

Radio stations are like people. Each has a personality of its own and a loyal following which usually listens to a particular station to the exclusion of practically all others. By selecting the station, the program, and the time, you can reach almost any group of buyers you want. Different programs attract different listeners. The time a program airs determines who is listening and the size of the audience.

In selecting a station, your selection should not be based on what you like to listen to but what your audience will be listening to. Most stations are strong on music, interspersed with weather reports, newscasts, and similar features. Each will probably feature a particular type of programming. Some will emphasize rock and roll, others will be entirely country and western, while many will feature middle-of-the-road selections, selections from Broadway musicals, or light classical music. Some stations are primarily talk stations, featuring interviews and discussions with guests covering a wide variety of subjects. Still others are known as news stations. They carry nothing but news, interspersed with spot advertisements. In larger metropolitan areas you can find stations devoted entirely to ethnic groups, featuring their music and performers. There are also many foreign language stations which have appeal for special segments of the general population.

The biggest problem in planning radio advertising is getting the time slots and programs you want. Since broadcast hours are limited, there is only so much time which can be made available to advertisers. If you are unable to get a slot you want, you might be better off to consider using other media.

HOW MANY SMALL BUSINESS PEOPLE ADVERTISE ON TELEVISION?

Not many small business people have tried television advertising, but most of them would like to. The medium is considered too expensive by most of them, being used by businesses with annual gross sales of $250,000 or more.

There is a definite trend toward use of the television medium by local advertisers. A number of national chains have invested increasing amounts of money in television advertising for their local retail branches. As the big retailers begin to find ways of making TV advertising pay off, thus breaking the retailer's traditional dependence on print media, smaller businesses will experiment with TV too, to the best of their ability to buy in.

Television is the closest of all advertising to personal selling. It is the only medium that combines sight, motion, and sound and comes right into the home. In it, you can explain and demonstrate what you are selling to thousands of homes simultaneously. You can show your product in realistic settings and reinforce your business image by injecting your personality into the advertising.

WHAT SPECIAL ADVERTISING NEED IS FILLED BY MAGAZINE ADVERTISING?

Magazines can reach special-interest groups such as hunters, bowlers, golfers, photographers, mechanics, collectors, and home decorators. The ability to preselect your audience can be an advantage.

Special-interest magazines outnumber the general magazines. Consumer magazines, both general and special-interest, have the advantage of a long reading life. People seldom read such a magazine from cover to cover at one sitting. They pick it up at intervals, and your advertising has a chance of being seen more than once.

How long the reading life of a magazine is and how often it will be picked up vary with its frequency and its editorial content. A magazine with general-interest content will attract more readers per copy than a special-interest magazine, but the latter has a better chance of being kept a long time and referred to from time to time.

The biggest problem with magazine advertising is the time lapse between the date you have to submit your complete advertisement and the publication date. This can amount to as long as 2 months—longer for color ads. Since longer time is needed for preparation of the ad, your planning must be done long before you can expect any response.

Few small business people use magazine advertising. Those that use it regularly do so to reach audiences that are difficult to reach by the other media.

WHAT OTHER ADVERTISING APPROACHES ARE EFFECTIVE?

The advertising value of an attractive sign over one's place of business is often overlooked. Since first impressions are lasting, this is one area where you should not try to economize.

Transit advertising takes a variety of forms. It is used mostly in the larger metropolitan areas. Car cards of standard sizes in buses, trains, and other public transportation vehicles are often sold as runs. A full run means a card in every vehicle in the transportation system. Half a run means a card in every other vehicle.

Small businesses often use handbills, giveaways such as book matches, calendars, pens and pencils, and similar items. Giveaways are popular advertising devices. Small businesses often spend as much as 20 percent of their advertising budget in this medium. Advertising novelties should be something unusual which can be related to your business or its objectives.

WHAT IS COOPERATIVE ADVERTISING?

Manufacturers advertise brand-name products nationally to persuade people *what* to buy. To tell people *where* to buy, they offer to share with retailers the cost of local advertising. This is cooperative advertising. Manufacturers get more advertising per dollar because local advertising rates are lower than national ones. For retailers, cooperative advertising is an incentive to stock and advertise brand-name products.

Cooperative advertising accounts for $1 of every $6 spent for advertising, according to one estimate. Exact figures are difficult to compile because much of the information is confidential. Many consumer products and some industrial products can be advertised under a cooperative plan. The most common ratio for sharing costs is 50-50, but other ratios are sometimes used.

Manufacturers set aside cooperative funds for the dealer according to a stated percent of dollar purchases or amount per unit of purchase. The amount accumulated in this fund sets the dollar limit on the manufacturer's share for that dealer.

Newspapers are used for 75 percent or more of cooperative advertising. Other media are permitted, however, in order to make the plan more flexible for small dealers.

To be reimbursed from a cooperative fund, the dealer must present proof of advertising and a copy of the receipted invoice. For newspaper advertising, a tear sheet of the page on which the advertisement appeared is required. For radio and TV, an affidavit that the advertising was broadcast is required.

SHOULD YOU EVER USE THE SAME ADVERTISEMENT MORE THAN ONCE?

If response to an ad is good, run it without change again. Studies have shown that an effective advertisement can be used up to four times before it loses its pulling power. Much advertising loses its effectiveness because the advertiser does not keep reminding people. Repetition helps increase knowledge of and interest in the product or service.

WHAT ADVANTAGES ARE OFFERED BY WINDOW DISPLAYS?

Window displays differ from conventional advertising in that they present the merchandise itself, not simply information about the merchandise.

When you first start your business, window displays might be your chief device for creating traffic. Even when you expand and start advertising in other media, a professional-looking window can increase the impact of your advertising message.

Window displays should be planned with the same care that you use in your newspaper advertising. Table 19-5 is a checklist for evaluating a window display.

In evaluating the effectiveness of a window display, try to determine, on a sampling basis, the following: (1) how many people pass the window, (2) how many passersby glance at the window, (3) how many stop to look, and (4) how many enter the store after looking at the window.

TABLE 19-5.   CHECKLIST FOR A WINDOW DISPLAY

I. Merchandise selected

 1. Is the merchandise timely?
 2. Is it representative of the stock assortment?
 3. Are the articles harmonious—in type, color, texture, use?
 4. Are the price lines of the merchandise suited to the interests of passersby?
 5. Is the quantity on display suitable (that is, neither overcrowded nor sparse)?

II. Setting

 1. Are glass, floor, props, and merchandise clean?
 2. Is the lighting adequate (so that reflection from the street is avoided)?
 3. Are spotlights used to highlight certain parts of the display?
 4. Is every piece of merchandise carefully draped, pinned, or arranged?
 5. Is the background suitable, enhancing the merchandise?
 6. Are the props well suited to the merchandise?
 7. Are window cards used, and are they neat and well placed?
 8. Is the entire composition balanced?
 9. Does the composition suggest rhythm and movement?

III. Selling power

 1. Does the window present a readily recognized central theme?
 2. Does the window exhibit power to stop passersby through the dramatic use of light, color, size, motion, composition, and/or item selection?
 3. Does the window arouse a desire to buy (as measured by shoppers entering the store)?

Source: John Wingate and Seymour Helfant, *Small Store Planning for Growth*, Small Business Management Series, No. 33, U.S. Small Business Administration, Washington, 1966, p. 77.

WHAT ARE THE AREAS TO WATCH FOR IN ADVERTISING AND PROMOTION?

Here is a checklist for retailers which will tell you whether you have weak points in your advertising and promotion program.[2]

This guide to self-appraisal will give you food for thought and assist you in isolating areas which need attention. The comments are not definitive answers to the questions they accompany. Instead, they give the "reasons why" for the questions.

ADVERTISING AND PROMOTION CHECKLIST

 1. Do you frequently supplement your routine day-by-day selling operations with special promotions?

[2]From John W. Wingate, *Management Audit for Small Retailers*, Small Business Management Series, No. 31, 2d ed., U.S. Small Business Administration, Washington, 1971, pp. 25–27. The comments have been abridged to capture the basic response.

Comment: Your customers expect you to offer timely specials periodically that are unusual and dramatic. The number and timing of these events should be geared to the type of customer you are trying to attract.

2. Do you advertise consistently in at least one appropriate medium: newspaper, direct mail, handbills, local television or radio?
Comment: Even if your store is small, you should not depend on passing traffic and satisfied customers' recommendations.

3. Do you approve all ads before they are released, reviewing their content and making sure that goods mentioned will be ready for selling?
Comment: Carelessness and error not only dissipate your investment in the ad but will lead to customer dissatisfaction.

4. Do you consistently choose items for advertising that are timely, have exceptional value or exclusive features, and help to build your store image?
Comment: If the items you advertise do not have these qualities, your advertising is wasteful and detracts from your store's image.

5. Do your ads tell a story, newsworthy and readable, rather than only trumpet a price appeal?
Comment: Customers buy, first, for what their purchase will do for them, and second, for price. Your advertising should be based on these considerations.

6. Are your advertisements factual, providing all pertinent details about the goods you are offering?
Comment: "The more you tell, the more you sell." As a small merchant you might well note the detailed descriptions and interesting reading to be found in a general mail-order catalog. Complete details are more likely to attract than vague generalities.

7. Does each of your ads specifically "sell" your store in addition to the merchandise advertised?
Comment: The greatest need of most stores is repeat patronage from customers who know and appreciate the kinds of assortments, values, and services offered. Advertising your store—as an institution—will help keep such customers coming back.

8. When you plan to advertise goods that are carried by your competitors or that are comparable to theirs, do you check their prices and assortments before releasing your ad?
Comment: Your store's reputation for good value is surely harmed if you advertise as a "bargain" what others are selling for less. Formal or informal comparison shopping is a "must" in planning your advertising as well as your merchandising.

9. Do you regularly and systematically familiarize your salespeople with your plans for advertised merchandise and promotions?
Comment: Regular weekly meetings are a good way to keep everyone informed. Advertising is only a means to an end—which is sales. The support of advertising by your salespeople is the only way to make it fully effective.

10. Do you keep records of your advertising which you use to improve your future ads?
Comment: Your records should contain a copy of the ad with notations on media used, date of insertion, cost, approximate sales results, weather, competitors' activity at the time, and comments. Use such information to write better ads, not simply to help repeat former successes.

We can summarize good and bad advertising practices in a list of "do's" and "don'ts" which should be observed if you are planning to run your own advertising program.

"Do's" In Advertising

1. Set sales goals by merchandising classifications at least 30 days ahead.

2. Budget the amount of advertising you will need to meet these goals.

3. Decide on the specific items you want to promote and schedule on specific days.

4. Set the tone of your ad to be persuasive without being forceful.

5. Advertise consistently. Several small ads spread over time are more effective than one large one.

6. Select the advertising medium for the type of buyer you want to reach. Using the wrong medium can be a waste of money.

7. If you are not knowledgeable about advertising techniques, seek professional advice.

"Don'ts" In Advertising

1. Don't try to cram material into every bit of available space in an advertisement. Plan the ad around one idea.

2. Don't indulge in advertising which is based on half-truths or which is misleading.

3. Don't expect advertising to do the entire selling job. It takes trained salespeople to close the deal.

4. Don't use ads that scream or pound the prospective customer. You can accomplish more with a "soft-sell" approach.

5. Don't drown your potential customer in a sea of words or pictures. If "brevity is the soul of wit," we can amplify Shakespeare's thought by adding that conciseness and clarity should be constant companions in planning a good advertisement.

HOW IMPORTANT IS PERSONAL SELLING TO AN ADVERTISING PROGRAM?

The entire program will depend on the ability of your salespeople to convince customers to buy after your advertising has attracted them to your store. If you have neglected the salesmanship aspect of your business operation, the best advertising you can afford will be ineffectual in helping you reach your sales goals.

Good personal selling is made up of more than a customer-centered attitude. It involves the conscious development of skills and techniques which successful salespeople everywhere have mastered. Special training in these skills is important:

1. Greeting customers sincerely and enthusiastically.

2. Asking customers the right questions: May I help you find something? Do you know about our gift wrap department? What is the price range you had in mind? Would you like to use our credit plan?

3. Using friendliness and courtesy to put customers in a good frame of mind.

4. Showing an interest in customers by remembering names or past purchases.

5. Using opinions as selling points. Customers are often more interested in a tactful opinion than an explanation of the physical characteristics of a product.

6. Supplying facts about a product the customer needs to make a decision, or answering their questions.

7. Meeting objections tactfully, without pointing out the shortcomings of other brands the customer has expressed an interest in.

8. Avoiding arguments and finding ways to agree with the customer.

9. Using "suggestion selling" to point out other products the customer might be interested in. Pointing out special sale items, "economy" sizes that will save the customer money, and similar approaches will help build sales volume. Additional sales with no more additional expense contribute to profits.

When you examine personal selling in your store, you will find that salespeople are often strong in some traits and weak in others. In trying to upgrade the selling talents of your people, a rating of their traits is helpful in pointing up those areas where training would help most. Figure 19-1 shows a rating scale designed for this purpose.

HOW CAN YOU TELL IF YOUR ADVERTISING IS GETTING RESULTS?

There is no precise way to relate cause and effect in measuring advertising effectiveness. Even when your sales volume has increased measurably after the insertion of an advertisement, it is difficult sometimes to determine which part of the advertising program provided the attraction, especially when you use more than one medium. Days of the week, climatic conditions, and competitors' activities can cause a poor response one week and a good one the following week, using the same ad. The biggest variable is customer behavior, which is influenced by a number of factors, some of which are beyond your control.

To rate one of your salespeople or yourself, check each trait listed below in the column you think applies most accurately to that person. Then put the number at the top of that column in the SCORE column. Finally, total the SCORE column. A score of 85 or above is excellent; 75 to 84, good; 55 to 74, average; and below 54, poor.

	Always (5)	Usually (4)	Half and Half (3)	Rarely (2)	Never (1)	SCORE
Objective						
Well-groomed						
Healthy						
Poised						
Correct speech						
Pleasant voice						
Enthusiastic						
Tactful						
Loyal						
Confident						
Courteous						
Friendly						
Emotionally mature						
Understanding						
Industrious						
Dependable						
Good memory						
Accurate						
Imaginative						
Knowledgeable						
Interested in job						
Total						

FIGURE 19-1. Rating traits needed in personal selling. (*Source:* Karen R. Gillespie, *Revitalize Personal Selling in Your Store*, Small Marketers Aids, No. 103, U.S. Small Business Administration, Washington.)

Despite these difficulties, it is important that records be kept which will enable you to get a feel for the effect of your advertising program. Here are some rule-of-thumb methods you can use:

Return of Coupons. Coupons brought in by customers represent immediate response to your ad. Record the number of returns during the first, second, and third weeks to determine what the response pattern is. If you offer coupons in two different newspapers, code them so that you can compare the responses.

Split Runs. Prepare two advertisements (different in some way you would like to test) and run them on the same day. When you place the ad, ask the newspaper to give you a "split run"—to print ad A in part of its press run, and ad B in the remainder of the run. Code them so that you can determine the response to each ad.

Number of Items Sold.   If you are advertising a specific product or item, keep track of the number sold each day or each week until the number sold per day is back to normal volume. You may need to make a judgment on how many sales came from personal selling to customers who did not see the ad.

Customer Traffic.   An important function of advertising is to get customers to come to your store. Studies show that many customers who are brought to a store by an ad for one item will buy a second one also, or will buy an item other than the one advertised. Customer interviews to determine which advertised item they bought, what other items they purchased besides the one advertised, and what they shopped for but did not buy can be helpful. These interviews are conducted by trained interviewers after the customer leaves the store.

Overall Sales Increase.   In a small store you can judge the overall effectiveness of an advertising program by looking at gross sales levels after insertion of the ad. Tally the sales for the 2 to 5 days immediately following the appearance of the ad because this is the period when you will expect the most sales. If your gross margin on increased sales pays for the advertising and provides additional profits, you can relate the ratio of net profit to sales during the test period to the ratio during periods when you are not advertising to determine how effective the advertising program was.

Customer Behavior.   Ask "first-time" customers if the advertisement was the cause of their visit to your store. You will find some attracted by your window display; others who were influenced by a friend to come in; and some who were attracted by the ad. By asking them, you will gain valuable information and also make a friend. Asking a person's opinion is a sincere form of flattery. Also ask your regular customers for opinions about your ads. These readership tests can sometimes be misleading because some customers will say they saw the ad when they did not and others will not remember having seen the ad when they did. Still others will have decided to buy the product even before seeing the ad. You will have to use some judgment in evaluating the responses.

Over a period of time your records and observations will enable you to identify high-response and low-response ads. By studying the medium used, the approach used, messages stressed, sizes of the ads, time of the month, and other variables, you will be able to identify those techniques your customers respond to.

Advertising that does not seem to increase sales immediately should not be dropped. Even good advertising does not always bring an immediate response. The ad may be laying the groundwork for future sales or it may be building your store's image. If poor results persists, you might have to reappraise your program. In this case money spent to have an advertising agency evaluate your program and make recommendations would be a good investment.

SELF-CHECK OF KEY CONCEPTS

This exercise is designed to test your understanding of the material presented in Chapter 19. Choose the response, *True* or *False*, which best fits each statement. Correct responses are presented in the back of the text.

1. A retail business with 1,200 customers would have to find one new customer each business day just to replace the ones who move away or change stores.
2. Most retail customers have a store of first choice where they normally shop.
3. A store's image is created primarily by price appeal.
4. A store should attempt to create an image which is "all things to all people."
5. If you know the reasons which prompt people to buy, you can conduct a more effective advertising program.
6. Customer demand reaches a peak in retail firms around mid-year.
7. Small businesses on the average spend around 3 percent of their gross sales for advertising.
8. Once you have built your business volume to an acceptable level, you can reduce advertising expenses because such expenditures are unnecessary.
9. What your competitors spend on advertising should have no effect on your advertising level.
10. A well-prepared advertisement will sell a single idea to a specific group of potential customers.
11. Newspaper advertising is the most widely used medium for promoting sales.
12. The effectiveness of direct-mail advertising can be seriously affected by using mailing lists which are not up-to-date.
13. Some small businesses spend as much as 20 percent of their advertising budget on giveaway items.
14. It is considered poor advertising practice to use the same ad more than once.

1. Make a list of special promotional events you would expect a candy store to plan during the year. Use Table 19-2 as a guide.
2. Design a form which could be used by small business people to compare their weekly dollar expenditures for advertising with those for the same week 1 year ago. Design the form so that weekly sales can also be shown and compared on the same basis.
3. Prepare the copy for an advertisement designed to reach customers who will be buying gifts for graduating seniors during the month of June. Assume that your newspaper can supply standard artwork mats (cap and gown, diploma, proud parents, etc.) to accompany the copy you prepare. Have the class score the ad using the criteria shown in Table 19-4.
4. Check the reference desk or special-collections section at your local library to find out which media directories they subscribe to. It is likely they will have one or more of the following directories, published by Standard Rate and Data Services, Inc., of Skokie, Illinois.

> *Business Publication Rates and Data*
> *Consumer Magazine and Farm Publication Rates and Data*
> *Direct Mail Lists Rates and Data*
> *Network Rates and Data*
> *Newspaper Circulation Analysis*
> *Newspaper Rates and Data*
> *Spot Radio Rates and Data*
> *Spot Television Rates and Data*
> *Transit Advertising Rates and Data*
> *Weekly Newspaper Rates and Data*

Select one of the directories and prepare a brief report to the class suggesting how it can be helpful to small business owners.
5. Select (a) a retail ad, (b) a service ad such as for insurance or cleaning, and (c) an automotive ad, each of which has a non-communicative headline. Rewrite the headline for each, adding strength by determining the goal of each ad and wording your headline accordingly.
6. Clip a half-dozen advertisements from your Sunday newspaper which illustrate the effective use of a business logo or trademark.
7. Find a series of ads with borders and clip them from the medium. Display them on a poster board and ask the class for opinions as to their effectiveness in selling the product.

HOW HOGUE'S WON THE BATTLE AND LOST THE WAR

Hogue's Department Store serves a population of 200,000 in a prosperous Midwest college town. It is a modern, up-to-date store, carrying quality merchandise reflecting the latest trends in consumer demand.

Ms. Allen, manager of the fine jewelry department at Hogue's, decided early in the fall to introduce a promotional program after Thanksgiving emphasizing wristwatches as ideal Christmas gifts. Her major advertising thrust would utilize a series of weekly newspaper ads featuring a different family of watches each week under the theme "We Have TIME for You." The copy would stress the wide assortments available (prices from $10.50 to $395), special features (electric, shockproof, water-resistant, digital-type, etc.), utility, and fashion.

The advertising program was well-planned. Stock was adequate, and traffic increased significantly after the promotion started. Two weeks before Christmas, Ms. Allen anticipated a record-breaking season in watch sales. She hired two extra college students to help handle the response.

One day Paul and Susan Blankenship came into the store to look at some of the watches they had seen advertised.

"I haven't bought a new watch in years," Paul said to Susan. "I guess I'll need some help in picking one out. The salesperson should be able to answer some questions about those new digital watches I've seen around."

A few feet away two salesmen were talking together. After waiting several minutes, Paul signaled to them, and one, looking annoyed, strolled over to the display case.

"Something you want?" the salesman mumbled.

"Yes," Paul said, "I want to buy a new watch. But I haven't kept up on the new models. Could you help me? These watches vary widely in price. What are the differences?"

"Well," said the salesman as he glanced into the showcase, "it all depends on how much you want to pay. The more you pay, the better watch you get."

Paul bent down to get a better look at the watches. The salesman leaned against the case and concentrated on a shapely female student passing by.

"In what ways are the more expensive watches better?" Paul finally asked with a puzzled look.

The salesman shrugged his shoulders. "That depends on your personal likes. They're all good." A long pause followed.

Finally, Paul looked at Susan disgustedly. "Guess I'd better stay with my old watch."

The salesman shrugged. "Okay," he said, and sauntered off to resume his conversation with his fellow salesman.

The Blankenships turned and walked out of the store.

1. What did Ms. Allen forget to cover in her promotional planning efforts?
2. What specific actions should she have taken to prevent a problem such as the one illustrated here from occurring?
3. Reconstruct this incident and indicate the correct approaches suggested for effective selling.

20

Special Problems in Employee Relations

PERFORMANCE OBJECTIVES

After reading this chapter you will gain a better appreciation of five managerial functions which are often given insufficient attention by the business owner because their value as profit contributors is not recognized. You should be able to discern the relationship which exists between these functions and to enumerate the problems which are likely to occur if the manager relegates them to the "unimportant" category and fails to include them in his or her planning. Specifically, you should be able to:

1. Explain why you will not be likely to get good employees without an active recruitment program.
2. Discuss some of the restrictions on preemployment inquiries which have been imposed by recent fair employment legislation and explain the logic behind the requirements.
3. Construct a job description sheet for a job with which you are familiar.
4. Demonstrate how a job breakdown sheet facilitates learning and helps the learner remember the things that are especially important.
5. Predict the effectiveness of training which is accomplished without a plan.
6. Outline a "model" program of communication for a small business operation.
7. Apply the concept of delegation to a business you are familiar with, pointing out tasks which can be delegated to competent workers and those which should not be delegated.

8. Classify the recognized barriers to effective communication into *speaker* and *listener* categories.
9. Defend the time spent by the manager in preparing written policies covering hiring and selection of employees, training, communication, delegation, and human relations.
10. Relate the absence of a positive, forward-looking human relations program to the profit-and-loss statement by showing the "cause-and-effect" relationship between dissatisfied workers and profits.

INTRODUCTION

This chapter discusses five problems faced by small business people in dealing effectively with their employees. These problems are: how to find good employees, how to develop employees through training, how to communicate effectively, how to make delegation help you accomplish more, and how to handle human relations.

These are areas small business people will usually handle themselves without the assistance of "specialists." It is the purpose of this chapter to explore each area in enough detail so that its importance to the success-ful operation of the business will become apparent. The result is a potpourri of practical suggestions stressing the "how to" approach to improving relationships with your employees.

Since all five topics are treated in depth in most textbooks on supervisory and management practices, no attempt has been made here to present an exhaustive discussion. The approach stresses those techniques which are simple enough to be utilized by small business owners within the time restraints under which they must work.

WHAT FACTORS DETERMINE THE NEED TO HIRE NEW EMPLOYEES?

Work load is the usual cause of additions to the work force. For retailers, this need will be reflected in their sales forecasts, requirements for handling peak loads during busy seasons, or the need for management types to relieve the owners of some of the routine responsibilities. For manufacturers, the need for additional people will result from customer orders and need dates as reflected in sales forecasts for the near-term future.

Owners should carefully consider their needs for new employees. Often there are other ways to get a job done without hiring additional workers. Temporary overloads can often be handled more economically by hiring temporary help from an agency or by working regular employees overtime until the emergency is over. Sometimes you can promote regular employees and assign them additional duties as a part of their new jobs. This technique will motivate other employees if they recognize your choice for the promotion as fair. This is important in preventing resentment among those who were passed over.

New methods of performing the necessary work will sometimes enable additional work to be done by the same number of workers. Thus, job improvement and work simplification can utilize the "work smarter" concept and save the expense of hiring additional workers.

The use of computer services can help reduce the work in the recordkeeping section by providing automated-payroll, inventory-control, accounts-payable, and accounts-receivable reports.

HOW CAN YOU TELL IF YOU CAN AFFORD TO HIRE MORE EMPLOYEES?

Business owners must be realistic about their expectations of business growth when they consider hiring new people. They will have to weigh the cost of compensating new employees against the profit these employees will help bring in. The percentage of expenses paid out in salaries varies with the type of business, with those firms stressing services rather than merchandise paying as much as 50 percent of their total expenses in salaries. In merchandising firms, total salaries often run less than 10 percent of expenses.

Your trade association can tell you what is typical for your kind of business. For example, the National Retail Hardware Association reports that 1974 operating ratios for retail hardware stores showed the following relationship of employee wages and benefits to net sales:

Income-Statement Data	Percent of Net Sales
Employee salaries	10.44
Federal and state payroll taxes	0.97
Group insurance	0.25
Benefit plans	0.35
	12.01

By relating such data to your projected income for the period ahead, you can get a good idea of how much more you can afford to spend for employee wages.

You will also want to consider seasonal trends in making staffing plans. Knowing where the above-average months are and where the slow periods normally occur can be helpful. Retail hardware experience in 1974 showed that nearly 11 percent of annual sales came in December, with the two following months averaging only half that amount.

Month	Percent of Sales	Month	Percent of Sales
January	5.4	July	9.1
February	5.4	August	8.4
March	7.3	September	8.1
April	9.0	October	8.9
May	9.6	November	8.7
June	9.4	December	10.7

There are also administrative expenses which you will have to consider—expenses involved in meeting payrolls, in keeping records, and in finding, selecting, and hiring new employees. You should be realistic in estimating what these costs will amount to.

HOW CAN YOU DESCRIBE THE KIND OF WORKER YOU NEED?

By knowing what the job requirements are for each job you want to fill. The best way to define these requirements is to write a job description. A written job description forces you to think of the specific requirements of the job and the type of employee you want to fill it. Such a description will greatly facilitate your task in placing a classified ad for an employee.

A good job description will do three things—describe the knowledge required, list the skills needed, and point out those personal characteristics which are desirable. Here is an example of a good job description:

Sample Job Description

Filling Station Attendant

Duties:

Greets and waits on customers at the pump. Services automobiles and checks oil level, water, and lights. Assists travelers with directions when required. May be required to perform light mechanical work such as changing light bulbs, replacing fuses, changing and repairing tires, and replacing windshield-wiper blades. Responsible for properly recording the transaction, completing the sales slip, and making change.

Responsible to:

Station manager.

Requirements:

Applicant should have a high school diploma. Minimum age 18 years. One year of high school auto mechanics or 1 year of previous work experience desirable. Must be available for night and weekend work. Must have a valid driver's license.

Personal:

Should be able to meet and communicate with the general public. Well-groomed appearance and courteous approach are essential. Initiative to assume more responsibility can lead to assistant station manager's position or assignment as part-time mechanic.

This job description leaves no doubt in the applicant's mind about the qualifications for the job. It will attract mechanically inclined young applicants who like the kind of work advertised.

Job descriptions for more complex jobs will contain more details about the use and operation of equipment, special schooling requirements, job responsibilities involving leadership, and physical and mental effort needed. They will also contain information about working conditions, including any hazards typical of the job.

You need to remain flexible about job specifications, keeping in mind that the "ideal" employee probably exists only in your mind. If you are too demanding, you might have to pay a higher salary or wait longer to find someone for the position. An adaptable employer can often spot compensating qualities in a person who does not meet all the standards. An inexperienced person with initiative and enthusiasm can often bring more to the job than a person who is knowledgeable but lacks interest and motivation.

HOW CAN YOU FIND QUALIFIED WORKERS?

It helps to locate your business in an area with an adequate labor supply. Experience indicates a direct relationship between the caliber of workers employed over a period of years and the number of prospects available for each job.

Employers usually do not wait for qualified workers to come to them. They will consider recommendations of their employees, consult with reputable employment agencies, run newspaper ads, or actively recruit on college campuses. Recruiting is not only the most difficult step in worker selection; it is indispensable to good selection. It requires effort, resourcefulness, and ingenuity. It involves a great deal more careful planning and hard work than luck or inspiration.

Table 20-1 shows the major sources of new employees and some notes pertaining to the relative costs, advantages, and disadvantages of each.

CAN YOU ASK POTENTIAL APPLICANTS FOR A BIRTH CERTIFICATE OR A PHOTOGRAPH BEFORE YOU INTERVIEW THEM?

Not any more. Many states have enacted legislation which provides guidelines to employers to help them comply with federal requirements related to hiring practices. For example, the state of California has a Fair Employment Practice Act administered by its Fair Employment Practice Commission. Its "Guide to Pre-Employment Inquiries" states that no *preemployment* inquiries or specifications, direct or indirect, may be made concerning a job applicant's race, religious creed, color, national origin, ancestry, age, sex, medical condition, or handicap. As a guide to employers, it lists acceptable and unacceptable questions which may be asked of potential applicants prior to hiring.

TABLE 20-1. WHERE TO FIND EMPLOYEES

Source and Cost:	Characteristics:
Classified Ads in the "help wanted" section of metropolitan newspapers, community "shoppers" and trade publications are well read by job seekers. Costs vary with readership, number of times ad is run, complexity of copy and artwork.	Employer can choose to have applicants reply by telephone or write to a box number: the latter method allows for confidential replies and application screening before scheduled interviews. Trade publications are especially advantageous in reaching a specific industry audience.
Private Employment Agencies match job seekers and employers and may specialize in clerical, manual, executive or other job classifications. A fee of 5% to 15% of the first year's salary may be paid by either the applicant or employer.	Agency pre-screens applicants with tests and interviews, ideally weeding out unsuitable candidates. The employer only pays fee if he hires the agency's applicant or, a temporary or reduced fee if the employee fails to stay a guaranteed length of time.
Temporary Agencies recruit, test and hire people in a number of job categories and place them with employers for limited periods of time. The employer pays a fee based on the number of hours the employee works. Rates vary depending on job classification.	Employer can obtain qualified people on short notice for emergency projects, seasonal relief. Hourly rates are more expensive than straight hire, although administrative costs are eliminated and the employer does not have to add another person to the payroll.
State Employment Agencies are under federal auspices with 2,000 offices throughout the U.S. Costs are paid for by taxes on payrolls, and services are free to both employers and employees.	A nationwide network of offices enables wide recruitment. In some areas, computer job banks match jobs with applicants. Service may be somewhat less personal than with a small private agency.
Unions may have an excellent referral system especially in metropolitan areas and in certain job categories. Referral services are free.	Referrals are usually experienced and have union approval, although some unions require that referrals be accepted sight unseen.
Schools: Trade, professional, vocational, local high schools and colleges may have a placement counselor or job bulletin board. Referral services are free.	While students may be inexperienced, they are often available part time, on holidays, and for emergencies, and are not looking for long-term employment or benefits programs.
Community Organizations, both private and public, are set up to improve local community conditions and often have job training programs. Referral services are free.	Applicants may lack previous experience and require special attention. Grants for training are sometimes available from the Department of Labor.

Source: Reprinted with permission from *Small Business Reporter*, Vol. 9, No. 8, "Personnel for the Small Business," Bank of America, © 1970.

The guide pertains only to inquiries, advertisements, and applications made prior to employment. Once applicants are on the payroll employers may, if they wish, enter otherwise prohibited information (such as birth certificates, photographs, etc.) in the applicants' personnel files, provided such information is not used for any subsequent discrimination as in upgrading or layoff. Employers may hire people subject to their ability to produce such proof on or after reporting for work.

In all situations, preemployment inquiries must be job-related.

HOW CAN YOU SAVE TIME IN INTERVIEWING PROSPECTIVE EMPLOYEES?

First, have a clear picture of the job for which the applicant is being interviewed—the duties, experience needed, physical requirements, working conditions, and similar factors. A job description will provide such a guide. Turnover is often traced to the fact that workers did not get a correct impression of their jobs at the time they were hired. Second, use a checklist of points to be covered in the interview. Include such items as schooling, number and kinds of previous jobs held, reasons for leaving them, present wage, whether free to move, skills possessed, and physical disabilities. Such a checklist will eliminate some applicants in the first few minutes and make it unnecessary to go into a detailed explanation of the job.

WHAT ARE SOME DANGER SIGNALS TO WATCH FOR IN INTERVIEWING?

These are the things you should be wary of in sizing up prospective employees:

☐ Workers who cannot give good reasons for leaving previous jobs.

☐ Workers whose earnings have been appreciably higher than what they are now willing to work for.

☐ Workers who have domestic difficulties.

☐ Workers who have had five or more jobs in the last 5 years.

☐ Applicants who have "reformed."

☐ Workers who have been less than 2 years at their longest previous job.

This does not mean that applicants should never be employed if they fall in any one of these categories. But such factors indicate potential problem areas since old work habits are not likely to change overnight.

DO TESTS HAVE ANY PRACTICAL VALUE IN SELECTING WORKERS?

One of the best ways to find out whether a test has any practical value is to check the relationship between test scores and actual performance on the job. For instance, if workers scoring in the top 25 percent of the ratings on a manual-dexterity test actually assemble significantly more units per day than workers who are in the bottom 25 percent, the test could be useful in weeding out low producers. However, you should remember that no matter how skillfully tests are used, they typically do not measure more than 20 percent of a worker's total qualifications. Therefore, any test ought to be used on an experimental basis until its value has been proved.

MAY PHYSICAL EXAMINATIONS BE USED AS PREEMPLOYMENT TOOLS?

No. Fair-employment laws prohibit inquiries about physical disabilities or general medical condition. You may inquire about an applicant's physical condition if the inquiry is directly related to the position applied for. You may also state that any offer made may be contingent on passing a physical examination.

HOW RELIABLE ARE REFERENCES IN SELECTING NEW EMPLOYEES?

References can save you a great deal of time and money by bringing to light pertinent information from former employers. Workers who have been problem employees in other jobs are likely to repeat their old patterns of behavior on the new job.

References from friends are considered of little value since most people can get three or four friends to write favorably about them. Those from former employers are quite a different thing. These should be obtained through a personal visit, or by telephone directly from the applicant's former supervisor if possible. Written reference forms should be used only as a last resort. Many companies have a rule against giving out unfavorable information in writing, but are willing to do so over the telephone. This practice provides reasonable assurance that what they say will not legally be held against them.

WHAT PROBLEMS CAN RESULT FROM HIRING UNQUALIFIED WORKERS?

Poor selection techniques can result in your taking on borderline workers, who turn out just enough to get by. These employees can be responsible for mediocre production, high labor turnover, material waste, and low morale. All these factors are costly. With today's labor cost amounting to such a large part of total costs, good employee selection and placement can save several dollars for each dollar spent.

Most of the discharges in industry are related to the personal shortcomings of the workers hired, not to their inability to do the work. Such things as dishonesty, laziness, excessive absenteeism and tardiness, poor health, hang-ups about working with women or minorities, and bad attitudes are characteristics you should look for when interviewing prospective new employees.

As much as you can. First impressions color people's attitudes toward the company and the job and can have a strong effect on their morale. Supplying new employees with all the information they need to feel that they "belong" to the organization is an important factor in their placement. It has been demonstrated that the dividends in goodwill, morale, and production efficiency greatly outweigh the cost involved in making a new worker feel at home. It is a common practice to place a new employee with an older trusted employee during the first days on the job. This facilitates training and the integration of the new employee into the work group.

WHAT IS THE PURPOSE OF A PROBATIONARY PERIOD FOR NEW EMPLOYEES?

Despite the thoroughness with which you approach the process of selecting new employees, the final decision to retain them should be predicated upon the successful completion of a probationary period. You can decide whether the new employees can do their jobs only after they have successfully discharged their duties for a long enough time to assure satisfactory performance. In a sense, both the employee and the employer are on trial during the probationary period. Each is evaluating the other and forming impressions which will affect the final decision.

The length of the probationary period depends upon the type of work involved and the length of time it takes the new employees to demonstrate that they can do their jobs the way you want them done. This could be as little as 4 weeks or as long as 12 weeks. Regardless of its length, a probationary period gives you a chance to observe new workers on the job. You should make regular observations, meeting frequently with them to discuss progress, answer questions, and coach them.

When you sit down to make the final decision, compare their observed performance with the job requirements as reflected on the job descriptions you have previously discussed with them. Some companies use a special merit-rating form for evaluating the performance of probationary employees. If there is any doubt about the employees' ability to do the job, they should not be retained. This decision should be arrived at fairly and discussed tactfully with the employees. When you keep unsuitable employees, you do them as well as your business a disservice. Weak employees cause morale problems for your good employees and affect your ability to operate profitably.

ISN'T A TRAINING PROGRAM A LUXURY MOST BUSINESSES CAN'T AFFORD?

Many writers have pointed out that a training program is one of the last things to be undertaken by management and one of the first to be eliminated when cost reduction becomes essential. This attitude is unfortunate. Studies have shown that more than half the customers who quit trading at a given store do so because of discourteous, unmotivated, untrained employees. That is a high price to pay for no training program. As customers, most of us can recall experiences where the actions and ineptness of clerks have caused us to decide not to shop again in that particular store. In retrospect, we have to conclude that proper training of employees is not a luxury, but a necessity if we are to operate efficiently. A modest program consisting of a planned approach to personnel training and development will result in competent employees who can grow as their jobs and the business expand. The reduction in labor turnover, improved quality of work, decreased cost of operation, and sound customer relations resulting from such a program will pay for its cost many times over.

WHAT SHOULD BE THE MAIN EMPHASIS OF A TRAINING PROGRAM?

The training provided for new employees should fill the gap between what the job requires and what the employee already knows. If you have done a thorough job of selecting new employees, you have a good idea of the areas where specific training needs exist. From this evaluation, you should tailor a training program for all your employees which will result in the acquisition of certain skills on a schedule basis. A training timetable is easy to make. It provides a substitute for memory and tells you the following things:

☐ How much the employees already know.

☐ Which skills they need to acquire.

☐ Those things they will not be required to know.

☐ The dates when you expect training in each phase of the job to be completed.

Figure 20-1 shows a typical training timetable for a group of retail salespeople.

This timetable reflects proposed training activities for two older employees who have already acquired many of the skills required but who will need some additional training in the operation of a new electronic cash register which is scheduled to be installed. Two employees are new and will require more training in basic skills. A well-planned timetable will assure adequate training in all the important phases of your operation, providing coverage in cases of illness, vacations, or terminations.

The type of training indicated in Figure 20-1 is called on-the-job or in-store training, as opposed to instruction in a classroom away from the job location. This type of instruction can be very effective if it is supplemented by charts, illustrations, and sample forms

Legend: √ Already trained — Training not required Skills Required	Taylor	Brown	Williams	Martinez
1. Techniques of greeting and assisting customers	√	√	7/6	9/3
2. Knowledge of products handled	√	√	8/15	10/10
3. Operating cash register; making change	6/18	6/18	7/6	9/3
4. Making out sales slips	√	√	7/6	9/3
5. Processing credit card sales	7/2	7/2	7/18	9/5
6. Handling returned merchandise	√	√	8/17	10/5
7. Stocking shelves	√	√	10/6	11/25
8. Pricing methods	√	√	8/18	10/12
9. Methods of delivering merchandise	√	√	—	—
10. Store opening and closing activities	√	√	—	—

FIGURE 20-1. A sample training timetable for retail salespeople.

posted near the employee's work station. Price lists, retail tax charts, instructions on the operation of equipment, manufacturers' literature, inventory lists, sample form letters, and special instructions relating to special activities such as credit sales are very useful instructional devices for new employees.

Product information booklets, often available from suppliers and distributors, can be used to acquaint employees with the product they are handling. A knowledge of fabrics, sizes, and special features of the product is often instrumental in helping to close a sale. Such extra effort is also impressive to customers who are accustomed to salespeople who "don't know" anything about the product.

Since most people usually learn a job best by doing it, new employees should be given a chance to try out their skills as soon as they can.

Once you have determined what the training needs are for your employees, you have to get down to the business of planning your training techniques. Fortunately, the principles of effective instruction developed over a number of years are available to guide you in translating your training plans into action. The need for quickly training thousands of employees during World War II led to the development of a tested method called *job instruction training*, which has been widely accepted and used by instructors in all kinds of businesses for training workers. The essential steps are condensed on a job instruction card shown in Figure 20-2. The logical sequence of steps

---

Job Instruction Training

How to Get Ready to Instruct:

1. Have a timetable.
   —How much skill you expect and when.
2. Break down the job.
   —List the important steps.
   —Pick out the key points.
3. Have everything ready.
   —The right equipment, material, and supplies.
4. Have the workplace properly arranged.
   —As you would expect the worker to maintain it.

How to Instruct

STEP 1: *Prepare the Worker*
a. Put the worker at ease.
b. Find out what he or she knows.
c. Arouse interest.
d. Place the worker correctly.
(Insure a learning situation.)

STEP 2: *Present the Operation*
a. Tell,
b. Show.
c. Explain.
d. Demonstrate.
(One point at a time. Stress key points.)

STEP 3: *Try Out Performance*
a. Have the worker perform the operation.
b. Have the worker explain the key points.
c. Correct errors.
d. Reinstruct as needed.
(Be sure he or she knows.)

STEP 4: *Follow-Up*
a. Put the worker on his own.
b. Encourage questioning.
c. Check frequently.
d. Taper off assistance.
(Practice—Key to Performance.)

FIGURE 20-2. The job instruction card. (*Source:* War Manpower Commission, *The Training Within Industry Report*, Government Printing Office, 1945.)

shown on these cards provides an effective approach to the business of training employees as simply and easily as possible. If you observe the instructions on the card, you will find that your training efforts will pay off in better satisfied workers. Remember that there is no shortcut to good training. It takes a lot of time, but it is worth it.

One of the tools often used in the process of "getting ready" is the job breakdown chart. This chart breaks any job down into its smallest components and shows how to perform each step in the order they will occur. Key points are provided as memory joggers to remind instructors that they should remember to mention things which will aid learning but which are perhaps "old hat" or obvious to them. A sample job breakdown sheet is shown in Table 20-2. The use of such a training tool virtually assures maximum effectiveness in teaching a skill to an inexperienced learner.

TABLE 20-2.   A JOB BREAKDOWN SHEET

Job: Tying a Fire Underwriter's Knot

Important Steps in the Operation*	Key Points†
1. Carefully separate the ends of a standard piece of two-strand electrical cord.	About 6 inches needed for this job.
2. Holding the wire in your left hand, make a right-hand loop with the right-hand strand.	Pass in *front* of the main strand. Hold in place with thumb and index finger of left hand.
3. Make a left-hand loop with the left-hand strand.	Pass in *front* of the stub protruding to the left. Pull the left-hand loop *under* the stub.
4. Pass the end of the left-hand loop through the right-hand loop.	Insert end through right-hand loop from back to front, with end of left-hand loop pointing toward you.
5. Pull end taut.	

*A logical segment of the operation when something happens to *advance* the work.
†Anything in a step that might make or break the job, injure the worker, or make the work easier to do. That is, a "knack," "trick," or special timing or information.

WHAT CAN YOU USE TO SUPPLEMENT THE LEARNING-BY-DOING APPROACH?

Informal meetings which are held periodically to discuss problems and policies are good supplementary training devices, especially if they feature question-and-answer periods. This two-way communication between management and employees improves morale.

Special assignments which allow employees to plan and carry out projects more complex than their regular duties provide a sense of accomplishment and positive identification with management's objectives. This concept is explored more fully in the discussion on delegation.

Job rotation is an effective means of achieving versatility in the work group. It also contributes to the employees' sense of achievement and worth to know that they are competent to perform several different jobs. Exchanging jobs will often develop a keener appreciation of the problems faced by coworkers in doing their jobs. This enhances cooperation within the work group.

Seminars and college courses can be valuable sources of information on new ideas, particularly those classes stressing techniques peculiar to small business. Employees should be encouraged to take job-related courses as well as training programs offered by trade associations, suppliers, and other groups.

Technical journals, trade publications, textbooks, and educational films can provide additional training. These tools are available from schools, libraries, suppliers, government agencies, trade associations, and film rental outlets.

An effective training program must be concerned with a means of measuring how well employees are measuring up to the requirements of the job. Periodic performance appraisals are good training devices if properly administered and constructively used.

WHAT'S ALL THE FUSS ABOUT COMMUNICATION?

It is true that people talk too much already. But some people do not say much when they talk, or they do not say things in such a way that listeners can understand them. It is somewhat like writing a letter in Chinese to someone who does not speak or read Chinese—a big waste of time for both parties. Besides, talking is only half the problem. Lazy listeners do not hear half of what is said, or they get so hung up on some of the "loaded" words used by the speaker that they do not hear the message at all. Communicating is hard work for both speakers and listeners. A lot of problems in business occur because people do not really hear each other.

This dilemma is aptly described by a sign on the wall of a fellow manager I visited recently, which said:

I know you believe you understand what you think I said . . . but I am not sure you realize that what you heard is not what I meant.

HOW MUCH OF A MANAGER'S DAY IS SPENT IN COMMUNICATING?

According to statistics reported by Bittel,[1] the average supervisor spends 43 percent of his or her time listening, 7 percent writing, and

[1]Lester R. Bittel, *What Every Supervisor Should Know*, 3d ed., McGraw-Hill Book Company, New York, 1974, p. 11.

3 percent showing—all activities related to communicating. Some authors place the percentage of working hours spent by executives in communicating with subordinates, superiors, and their peers at close to 70 percent. No matter how you look at it, more than half of a manager's day is spent communicating with customers, employees, suppliers, bankers, and others. The ability of managers to make themselves understood and to understand others will affect their businesses significantly. Mistakes in understanding can be costly.

In the course of a day we speak more words than we write and we hear more words than we read. It is important that we become effective speakers and good listeners.

WHAT ARE SOME OF THE BARRIERS TO GOOD COMMUNICATION IN BUSINESS?

The attitudes of the speaker and those of the listener often get in the way. Keeping an open mind and really listening to what the speaker is saying is sometimes difficult because you already know that what he or she is proposing will not work.

Negative thinkers (and listeners) are characterized by the widely circulated admonition. "Don't confuse me with facts. My mind's made up."

The relationship which exists between speakers and listeners can affect the way communication is received. If you have labeled some speakers as dishonest, untruthful, unreliable, deceitful, incompetent, or ineffective, you are not likely to take anything they say very seriously. A mental barrier tells you to discount most of what they say. Other manifestations of this problem are listeners who "know it all" and expect others to recognize their superiority and to act accordingly. This atmosphere causes speakers with ideas to withdraw and avoid communicating.

Physical barriers to good communication, such as stuttering, poor hearing, or impaired vision sometimes cause problems because of a lack of sensitivity about the impairment and the failure to make necessary personal adjustments which would enhance the sharing of ideas.

Educational and language differences make it difficult to communicate effectively. These lead to differences of interpretation, or to the inability to assimilate what is being said and understand its meaning. Because of their large Spanish-speaking population, some counties in the state of California now print ballots and instructions to voters in both English and Spanish, thereby eliminating language as a barrier to effective communication. Some businesses use bilingual contracts to prevent misunderstandings with customers.

The mechanics of speaking and listening make it easy for a listener to become distracted while someone is talking. The main reason for this is that the mind races ahead faster than the speaker can talk. Average speakers talk at a rate of 125 to 135 words a minute. People can think from 500 to 1,200 words a minute—or about ten times as fast. If your message is not of great interest to some listeners, they will have a tendency to miss a substantial part of what you say because of inattention.

WHAT CAN BUSINESS PEOPLE DO TO BECOME BETTER LISTENERS?

The first step is to estimate the amount of time you spend listening to others. If it is less than 25 percent of your time, you have room for improvement. An average of 50 percent is about right. The point is that to be a good listener you have to practice at it.

Second, analyze your listening skills against the following questions. If you can answer yes to most of them, your employees have probably already tagged you as a person they can really talk to.

- ☐ Do I always give the person speaking to me my undivided attention?
- ☐ Do I take steps to be sure that important conversations are not interrupted?
- ☐ Do I attempt to select a place free from noise and interruptions to talk to people?
- ☐ Do I look for the communicator's feelings and attitudes as well as the meaning of his words?
- ☐ Do I avoid interrupting the speaker or asking questions until she is finished?
- ☐ Do I restate the speaker's main thoughts in my own words to be sure I have understood him correctly?
- ☐ If I am unable to talk to a person who "drops in," do I set a definite time later to talk to her?
- ☐ Do I allow all the time needed for the speaker to finish without hurrying him?
- ☐ Do I keep an open mind, even when the speaker is voicing opinions contrary to my own?
- ☐ Do I encourage the free flow of communication by taking every opportunity to express appreciation for the thoughts and suggestions of others?

WHAT THINGS SHOULD YOU TALK TO YOUR EMPLOYEES ABOUT?

One of the best contributions you can make to employee morale is to share with them some of the problems and responsibilities related to the operation of the business. This not only means letting your workers know about your troubles but listening to them when they offer ideas and suggestions to improve operations. It means giving each worker a real voice in the affairs of the business and sharing the concern for its eventual success.

Here is a list of topics in which employees are interested:

1. Facts about the company:
    a. Its position in the industry
    b. Its organizational structure
    c. The financial position of the company
    d. Sales trends and order backlogs
    e. How good a job we are doing
2. Facts about company-employee relations:
    a. Wage and job classifications
    b. Employee benefits
    c. Personnel policies
    d. Opportunities for advancement
    e. Future employment prospects
3. Facts about future company plans:
    a. Public and community relations programs
    b. Expansion plans for the business
    c. Plans for new equipment, new products, or new methods

There is also a keen interest in personal news. Marriages, births, deaths, promotions, retirements, awards, and so on are subjects of interest to almost every employee. Simple mimeographed bulletins published once a month will satisfy this need in the small business.

WHAT ARE THE BEST WAYS OF COMMUNICATING WITH YOUR EMPLOYEES?

Nothing beats personal face-to-face contact for direct, effective communication. It is personal and instantaneous. Facial expressions and gestures speed the flow of information and add subtle meanings to the spoken word to convey the exact meaning you want the listener to receive. The listener has an opportunity to clarify questions on the spot and to explore the subject under discussion in detail if he or she desires. Meetings of owners with their employees or of managers with members of their departments are examples of such methods. In group meetings employees should feel free to make suggestions and should be heard. If grievances or potential problems are discussed openly within the business, there is a better chance of making the desired changes before more serious problems develop.

Many managers make it a point to contact each employee personally each day for informal face-to-face chats where questions are answered, problems are clarified, and rumors put to rest. This provides an excellent sounding board for detecting employee attitudes and measuring morale.

Nonverbal communication devices include bulletin boards, newsletters, newspapers, suggestion boxes, filmstrips, training films, safety posters, recorded telephone news "flashes," and announcements via public address systems. There are more than 25 different ways to exchange information between management and workers. Despite the versatility of such tools, they are, at best, limited substitutes for face-to-face communication.

TO THE BUSINESS OWNER, WHAT IS THE SIGNIFICANCE OF DELEGATION?

When businesses are small, it is physically possible for the owners to make most of the decisions, do all the planning, and keep their finger on everything that is going on. As their businesses grow, they will find that their responsibilities will become more numerous and that they will be unable to do everything themselves. Some owners attempt at this stage to "keep control" by working 80-hour weeks, developing ulcers, and ruining their health.

The background of most small business people is such that they feel an obligation to extend themselves to protect the business and keep close control. The thought of sharing their control with others is resisted by many who feel (often incorrectly) that no one can do the job as well as they can. Refusal to delegate responsibilities can limit the growth of a business and keep it small. If the business is to grow, delegation is an absolute prerequisite.

WHAT BENEFITS ARE DERIVED FROM DELEGATING?

The concept of delegation allows the manager to assign authority and responsibility to act or make decisions to someone else. Delegation is often temporary, with the delegated authority expiring upon completion of a specific assignment.

Managers benefit from delegation by freeing themselves from less important matters to spend more time on those areas of their businesses that can benefit from their attention. Long-range planning is one of the areas where most business people spend too little time. Delegating will provide the time to become more deeply involved in this important management function. Delegation allows owners freedom of action to conduct business away from the store because they know things will run efficiently in their absence.

Employees will benefit from completing delegated jobs through a heightened sense of responsibility and worth, through a broader understanding of the managerial function, and through the elimination of boredom and monotony. Delegation is a growth process which contributes to job satisfaction. Without it, employees simply take the path of least resistance and leave the headaches for owners to worry about.

WHAT KINDS OF THINGS CAN BE DELEGATED?

Some tasks can be delegated and some cannot. Some can be shared with others. Here are some examples of activities that can be delegated: maintenance of records, making reports, health and sanitation, care of tools and equipment, proper use and control of material, answering correspondence, escorting visitors, and keeping the workplace clean and orderly.

Tasks which may be shared with subordinates include: control of costs, control of quality, accident prevention, and training and indoctrination of new employees.

The following managerial responsibilities should not be delegated: administration of discipline, maintenance of morale among your workers, settlement of disputes among workers, confidential tasks or those personally delegated to you by your superiors, and technical jobs that only you can do. One thing to remember is that no matter how much you delegate, you are still responsible for the final results. Delegation is not abdication of responsibilities, it is just a sharing of responsibilities.

WHAT IF THE PERSON TO WHOM YOU DELEGATE GOOFS UP IN DOING THE ASSIGNMENT?

That is one of the hazards of delegating. Hardly anyone will do a delegated job the same way you would. You must accept the fact that some risk is involved when you delegate a job to another person. If you mourn the lack of people to whom you can delegate, remember that the best way to develop subordinates is to delegate responsibility to them. As you develop your subordinates, allow them to make a few mistakes and check your impulse to step in and take over when they do. If you have judged their potential correctly, they will learn from their mistakes—if you will let them.

Theodore Roosevelt once said: "The best executive is the one who has sense enough to pick good men to do what he wants done, and self-restraint enough to keep from meddling with them while they do it."

True delegation never assumes perfect results because you are dealing with people.

DO MOST SMALL BUSINESS OWNERS DO A GOOD JOB OF DELEGATING WORK?

For most owners, delegating work, responsibility, and authority is the hardest job they have to learn. Those owners who insist on handling every detail often work themselves into early graves. In many small businesses, the owners run them pretty much on their own. Even if they agree that delegation is a good thing, they often fail to appreciate its value, or they feel that with the time it takes to delegate they could do the job themselves. As a result, delegation in practice is pretty ineffectual. Most of what is called "delegation" is really not delegation at all, but a sporadic assignment of routine tasks, often without purpose and lacking the challenge that delegated tasks should offer.

IF DELEGATION IS SUCH A GOOD IDEA, WHY DON'T MORE MANAGERS DO IT?

Many managers do not know how to delegate. Delegation is a skill which requires a knowledge of what to do, how to do it, and when to do it. Like other learned skills, doing the correct things in the proper sequence is important. This lack of ability to direct subordinates in performing a delegated task is a real barrier to effective delegation.

Sometimes managers feel that they have no one who can do the job right. Subordinates' lack of maturity, questionable judgment, lack of initiative, and poor organizational ability are often cited as reasons for not delegating. If these shortcomings are found in all the subordinates of the managers, one must wonder about the criteria they use for choosing their subordinates. More often than not, these reasons are simply excuses for the managers who feel that they can do the job better themselves.

Fear is a positive barrier to effective delegation. Fear that they will lose control if they give some of their responsibilities to someone else; fear of taking a chance on someone who might goof up the job and get them in trouble; fear of loss of authority; fear of sharing credit with someone else—this hierarchy of fears forces managers into the least risky choice of all, that of doing the job themselves.

Since delegation is a two-way street, it often fails because subordinates do not want to assume the added responsibility of taking on a delegated job. Fear of failure, fear of criticism, lack of initiative, lack of self-confidence, and lack of positive incentives are all factors to be overcome when you attempt to convince your employees that they should assume delegated tasks.

WHAT CAN YOU DO TO BUILD THE RIGHT CLIMATE FOR DELEGATION?

Here are a few tips to help you use this important tool effectively:

1. Decide what you want to delegate. The objective is to save you as much time as possible for the big management tasks. Avoid delegating only dull, routine, or distasteful jobs. They will not help your employees grow. Above all, do not be guilty of delegating a "hot potato" just to get off the hook. It will not take your employees long to sense your motive for delegating.

2. Select the employees for delegated jobs carefully. Nothing will be gained if they lack the skill or motivation to do the jobs. Failure can cause embarrassment for you and bitterness on their part. If you have carefully evaluated their potential and have delegated jobs that are difficult enough to challenge them but

not too difficult to do, they will feel that they have personally improved when they successfully complete those jobs. This is important in keeping their sense of achievement intact.

3. Go over the details of the jobs carefully with them. Give them clear statements of what they are to do, what the objectives are, and when you want the jobs completed. Let them know the relative importance of the jobs, the prestige attached, and the needs they will fill. Tell them why you selected them. If your selection shows you have confidence in them, they will try hard to succeed. Tell them what the limits of their authority are. Then be sure those with whom they will have to deal know that they are authorized to do the delegated jobs for you. Make it clear to these employees that their cooperation is essential to the success of the jobs.

4. When all their questions have been answered, stand back and turn them loose. Let them know that you are there if they need you, but that they are free to do the jobs the way they feel is best. Encourage them to seek out the information they need, make the required decisions, and bring the jobs to a successful conclusion with a minimum of direction from you.

5. When you help your employees reach a high level of achievement through delegation, be sure your reward to them is big enough and well-timed. Nothing will discourage them as quickly as the feeling that they have been "used."

WHAT KINDS OF HUMAN RELATIONS PROBLEMS EXIST IN BUSINESS?

Industry and business activities are swarming with human relations problems. Many managers can confirm that the lion's share of their day involves them in "people problems." Here are some of the more prevalent ones:

Fitting People to Jobs.   Tests have consistently shown that many people are doing jobs they do not like. Good hiring practices and better job placement can minimize this problem. Remember that you cannot get maximum performance from a dissatisfied worker.

Job Satisfaction.   What satisfies each of us on the job is relative. Few of us are ever totally satisfied. Today's work force requires more than reasonable wages and an annual company picnic. Employees need intangible rewards as well—recognition, achievement, and a sense of belonging. If no attempt is made to fill these needs, apathy or hostility will result. Do not get booby-trapped into thinking that money is the answer. Most workers rate it far down the list of things they think are important on the job.

Communication Failures.   We have already stressed the need to listen for the real meaning in communicating with others. Many of our human relations problems happen because we talk past each other and succeed only in misunderstanding each other. This much neglected area of human relations contributes a lot to our inability to get along.

Performance Evaluation.   This area touches each of us since promotions, advancement, and wages help determine how well our needs for recognition and achievement are satisfied. Employees do not mind criticism for job performance if it is fair and constructive.

Fatigue and Boredom.   Both of these symptoms are related to morale and productivity. Absenteeism, dissatisfaction, and grievances result from jobs which fail to challenge workers and provide them a sense of worthwhileness.

The Work Environment.   Reactions of employees to lighting, ventilation, noise, sanitation, color, and similar factors can affect job performance significantly. When ignored, they can become costly in terms of grievances, slowdowns, and work stoppages.

WHAT CAN MANAGERS DO TO IMPROVE THEIR HUMAN RELATIONS SKILLS?

For a fresh view of the art of getting along with people, we could not do better than quote from an article on human relations published some time ago in the United States *Coast Guard Magazine.* Under the heading "Thirteen Mistakes," the Coast Guard raised warning flags above these thirteen pitfalls.

It's a mistake . . .

1.   To attempt to set up your own standard of right and wrong.
2.   To try to measure the enjoyment of others by your own.
3.   To expect uniformity of opinions in the world.
4.   To fail to make allowance for inexperience.
5.   To endeavor to mold all dispositions alike.
6.   Not to yield on unimportant trifles.
7.   To look for perfection in our own actions.
8.   To worry ourselves and others about what can't be remedied.
9.   Not to help everybody wherever, and whenever, we can.
10.   To consider impossible what we cannot ourselves perform.
11.   To believe only what our finite minds can grasp.
12.   Not to make allowances for the weakness of others.
13.   To estimate by some outside quality when it is that within which makes the man.

The reflective manager will accept this list as a negative guide to positive conduct, for it engages practically every principle which is vital to the growth of human relations.

Kaiser Industries of Oakland, California, is credited with the following widely circulated version of human relations which stresses the most important words to remember in our dealings with others:

HUMAN RELATIONS IN 15 WORDS

The *five* most important words—"I am proud of you."
The *four* most important words—"What do you think?"
The *three* most important words—"If you please."
The *two* most important words—"Thank you."
The *least* important word—"I."

This exercise is designed to test your understanding of the material presented in Chapter 20. Choose the response, *True* or *False*, which best fits each statement. Correct responses are presented in the back of the text.

1. An applicant's inability to satisfactorily explain reasons for leaving previous jobs should be considered a minus in the selection process.
2. Newspaper ads are considered an effective means of recruiting new employees.
3. Personal written references from a clergyman or a professional acquaintance are more useful in selecting an employee than telephone calls to former employers.
4. Most of the burden for effective verbal communication rests with the listener.
5. Training is more effective if it is spontaneous and does not follow a definite plan.
6. Nonverbal communication devices are more effective than face-to-face contacts because they offer more ways to transmit the message.
7. Consideration for the feelings of others underlies the practice of human relations.
8. The fact that all learners are alike makes it possible to apply the same training approaches to any training problem.
9. An employee who has developed the required skills will never require additional training.
10. In effective communication, we should show approval or disapproval as soon as a thought is expressed.

PERFORMANCE PROBLEMS AND PROJECTS

1. Prepare a job description for some job or position with which you are familiar, outlining the knowledge, responsibilities, and personal characteristics you would require for the job.
2. Make a job breakdown sheet for a simple four- or five-step manual operation like tying a four-in-hand tie, filling out a sales slip, or mixing a drink. Have the members of the class offer constructive comments.

3. Rewrite the following examples of foggy business writing in your own words, striving to improve the clarity, conciseness, and content wherever possible.

   a. "In potential problem solving, 20-20 hindsight in reverse is applied to identify future problems that may keep the plan from being successful."

   b. "The objective of this pilot study is to process transactions documents generated from these departments in a more rapid and accurate manner. The effort includes a substantial training process and major changes in the method by which documents flow. If this pilot effort is effective, there will be a major improvement in the speed with which transactions processing is completed."

MINICASES IN POINT

1. It was fall and the new model cars were in the dealers' showrooms. Sales were brisk and Bob Bradford, office manager for a large automobile agency, was 2 weeks behind with his paperwork. The agency owner had asked Bob to be sure to see what he could do to relieve the bottleneck since the agency had to pay interest to the distributor for every day the new cars were on the floor unsold. Interest stopped when the distributor received sales papers and payment indicating that a car had been sold.

   a. What alternatives are open to Bob to get the boss off his back?

   b. If you were Bob, what would you recommend? State the basis for your decision.

2. Pat Sanford is the manager of a notions department in a large department store, with six employees reporting to her. A month ago the store installed new electronic cash registers. The manufacturer had a special training session for the store's department heads to explain the features of the equipment and provide operating manuals for each manager to use for training his or her people. The business office has been auditing sales slips and has been complaining to Pat because her employees are making too many mistakes.

   "I had each of them read the manual," Pat explained, "and told them to see me if they had any trouble. I don't see what else I can do."

   a. What do you think of Pat's training program?

   b. What suggestions do you have for improving the performance of Pat's employees in using the new registers?

3. Jim Hodges had reported to work his first day as bookkeeper in a large accounting firm. He arrived at 8 A.M. and was introduced to his boss, Tim O'Leary, who greeted him with a big smile and a firm handshake.

   "Nice to have you on board," Tim said enthusiastically. "We have been looking for some time for someone with your background. I'm sure you'll find working with us challenging.

Right now I'm due at a weekly staff meeting which should last about an hour. While I'm gone browse through these departmental instructions and organization charts. You can make yourself at home in my office until I get back."

That was the last Jim saw of the boss until noon. By then, everyone in the office had gone to lunch. Jim had finished the instruction manuals around 9:30.

a. How do you think Jim felt about his first half day on the job?
b. What did Tim fail to do that would have improved Jim's initiation to the new job?

CHAPTER

21

Regulation and Taxation of Business

PERFORMANCE OBJECTIVES

After reading this chapter you should be able to classify, according to the purposes or objectives sought by the legislation, the various categories of federal legislation which affect small businesses. You should be able to give examples of local and state regulations and to explain their impact on small business owners. You should also be able to list the major taxes paid by business owners and explain their role as a debtor as well as an agent in managing their tax obligations. Specifically, you should be able to:

1. Assess the ability of the average small business owner to act as his or her own attorney in tax matters affecting the business.
2. Defend the concept of tax avoidance in business operations.
3. Develop some theories to explain why so many business owners over-pay their taxes.
4. Explain the method used to determine how much federal income tax will be withheld from an employee's wages.
5. Describe the limitations placed on the amount of wages on which social security taxes are withheld.
6. Describe the added responsibilities assumed by the business owner in complying with the provisions of the Truth in Lending Act.
7. Explain the objectives of the Fair Credit Reporting Act and tell how it benefits the consumer.
8. Predict the effects on small business of a repeal of the Clayton Act.

INTRODUCTION

According to an old adage, a man who attempts to be his own lawyer has a fool for his client. There is a great deal of truth in this statement. The purpose of this chapter is not to prepare you to become your own attorney in business matters but only to discuss some of the principles and laws which describe your legal rights and your obligations toward those with whom you do business. The ever-increasing number of laws and regulations affecting business and the various interpretations of these laws by the courts and regulatory agencies make business law very complex. It is an area where business people certainly need the assistance of professional, competent counsel.

Tax planning and tax management are areas fraught with anxiety and confusion for many small business owners. This chapter will explain your responsibilities as a debtor in managing your personal finances and paying those taxes you owe. In addition, your responsibilities as an agent in withholding taxes from the wages of your employees will be explored. The fact that many business people overpay their taxes and others get into trouble with the Internal Revenue Service at some time indicates a general lack of understanding of tax-management responsibilities. It will be one of the objectives of this chapter to help clear up the confusion surrounding the business owner's tax obligations.

WHAT ARE SOME OF THE SOURCES OF LEGAL PROBLEMS IN BUSINESS?

Once you decide to enter business, you will be subject to the provisions of a number of federal, state, and local laws and regulations. Hardly a business decision is made that does not have legal aspects. Purchasing agreements, sales arrangements, real estate transactions, licensing requirements, labor contracts, bank financing, and many other activities all involve decisions having legal implications.

As a business owner, you should understand the basic principles of law dealing with licenses, contracts, bills of sale, and mortgages so that you can carry on your business activities without breaking the law. You should be particularly aware of the legal implications of the following:

Type of business organization

Tax collections and payments

Real estate leases and purchases

Collection of delinquent accounts

Consumer protection and credit management

Insurance coverage and liabilities

Contracts and agreements

Reducing your exposure to liability in operating a business is not a do-it-yourself job. Even licensed attorneys are not always sure of certain provisions of the law and of the latest interpretations of the law by the courts. Some of the specific sources of legal problems are shown in Figure 21-1.

Acquisitions	Government—	Slander and libel
Advertising—copy	Federal, State,	Stock options
packaging	and local	Stock voting rights
Agents and brokers	Insurance contracts	Stockholders
Antitrust matters	Interstate	Taxes
Arbitration—role in	transportation	Tie-in sales
disputes	Inventions	Trade secrets
Bankruptcy	Labeling	Trademarks
Board of directors	Licenses	Unfair competition
Brand names	Mergers	Verbal agreements
Buying and	Misrepresentation	Wills
selling—terms	Multiple	Workmen's
and conditions	corporations	compensation
Checks—forgeries,	Negligence	Zoning
frauds	Negotiable	
Contracts and	instruments	
agreements	Order acknowledg-	
Competitors stealing	ment and	
employees	confirmation	
Corporate form	Patents	
Employer and	Permits	
employee	Price discrimination	
responsibilities	Profit sharing	
Employment	Product liability	
agreements	Records, legal	
Franchises	Retirement pensions	

FIGURE 21-1. Sources of legal problems. (*Source:* Harvey C. Krentzman, *Managing for Profits,* U.S. Small Business Administration, Washington, 1968, p. 165.)

HOW CAN YOU RECOGNIZE BUSINESS PROBLEMS WITH LEGAL IMPLICATIONS?

There will be little doubt in many business situations that legal aspects are involved. The nature of the transaction will tell you that legal responsibilities are inherent in the nature of the activity. Bank loans, real estate deals, bills of sale, contracts, and licensing transactions are of this type. Any situation involving large sums of money should alert you to the possibility of legal involvement, and you will probably want to seek legal assistance.

As a business owner, you will not want to consult an attorney every time you face a problem with legal overtones—even if you could afford to. One of the best ways to prepare yourself to handle the normal day-to-day legal problems is to take a course in business law. Almost all colleges and business schools offer such courses. In addition, watch for and read trade journals for your field which often contain articles on major legal changes that affect your industry or business. For major transactions, it is still a good idea to check with your lawyer to be sure that you are interpreting the law correctly and that you know about the latest changes in the law.

Most laws and regulations which will affect the way you do business may be grouped under the following headings:

Licensing regulations

Regulations for consumer protection

Laws encouraging competition

Labor relations legislation

Wage and hour laws

Fair employment legislation

Regulations on safety practices

There are dozens of laws touching on some aspect of these broad areas and they are constantly changing. We will cover the major provisions of the laws in a general way, stating the purpose of the legislation and showing how it can impact your way of doing business.

HOW DOES LICENSING AFFECT YOUR BUSINESS?

Many states have licensing regulations which restrict the entry of individuals into certain businesses. The objective of licensing is not to restrict business but to offer protection for the public's health, safety, and welfare. Licensing controls directly affect many small businesses. The degree of regulation will vary according to the type and location of the business. If your business is confined to your state, you will be affected by state and local licensing regulations. Among the businesses frequently subject to this kind of control are barbers, beauty shops, collection agencies, dentists, engineers, funeral directors, food establishments, plumbers, taxi firms, physicians and surgeons, veterinarians, and many others. The state of California lists 44 different occupations which are licensed by the State Department of Consumer Affairs. Many other occupations not listed are governed by independent departments. Real estate, banking, savings and loan companies, insurance firms, and housing are major business areas which are regulated by separate departments.

Retail stores devoted exclusively to handling merchandise may not be required to have a license, but they are subject to other regulations such as those dealing with fire, safety, and zoning restrictions.

Most licenses require the payment of fees and are usually issued on an annual basis. Ordinarily a written application is required. State, municipal, and county authorities can give you complete information on licensing requirements for your business.

WHAT HAS BEEN DONE TO PROTECT THE CONSUMER WHO BUYS ON CREDIT?

One of the most meaningful and far-reaching pieces of legislation in the field of consumer credit is the Consumer Credit Protection Act (commonly known as the Truth in Lending Act), which became effective on July 1, 1969. As a result of the law, extenders of credit began moving toward a uniform method of telling would-be debtors what they would owe in interest and other charges and what the annual percentage rate would be. The stated purpose of the legislation was to assure a meaningful disclosure of credit terms so that consumers would be able to compare more readily the various credit terms available to them. Such terms as "$4.50 per hundred on new car loans," "6 percent discount," and "6 percent add-on" can no longer be used to hide the real cost. Now lenders are required to tell the truth when lending money or extending credit, and must state the cost of credit in a uniform manner prescribed by law.

WHAT TYPES OF CREDIT ARE COVERED BY TRUTH IN LENDING?

Only credit to individuals for personal, family, household, or agricultural purposes which does not exceed $25,000. All real estate credit made to individuals for such purposes is covered, no matter what the amount.

WHO MUST COMPLY WITH TRUTH IN LENDING?

Any person or business which regularly extends or arranges for credit to individuals for personal, family, household, or agricultural purposes. This includes credit unions, banks, credit card companies, automobile dealers, consumer finance companies, mortgage bankers, and hospitals, doctors, dentists, plumbers, and electricians if they regularly extend or arrange credit.

DOES THE TRUTH IN LENDING ACT PROTECT A CONSUMER AGAINST GARNISHMENT OF WAGES?

The law only limits garnishments. Weekly garnishment cannot exceed the *lesser* of either 25 percent of the aftertax pay of the consumer or the aftertax pay minus 30 times the federal minimum hourly wage. This provision of the law went into effect on July 1, 1970.

HOW DOES THE FAIR CREDIT REPORTING ACT AFFECT YOU?

It requires you to disclose the source of credit information which you have used to deny credit to potential customers. This permits the applicants to pursue their rights under the law, to examine their files, and have erroneous or obsolete information corrected or removed. If you have collected credit information about applicants and later pass it along to another creditor evaluating the same applicants for credit, you would be regarded as a credit-reporting agency in the eyes of the law, subject to the same provisions as a credit bureau. For this reason, it is wise to report only your own factual information about customers and to leave the reporting of information from third parties to the credit bureaus.

The Fair Credit Reporting Act became law on April 25, 1971.

HOW IS COMPETITION AMONG BUSINESSES AFFECTED BY FEDERAL AND STATE LEGISLATION?

Some business practices are prohibited or restricted by federal and state laws in order to encourage competition. Federal laws govern dealings between states, while state legislation regulates transactions inside the states themselves. The broad body of federal legislation encouraging free private enterprise includes the Sherman Antitrust Act, the Clayton Act, and Federal Trade Commission acts.

The Sherman Antitrust Act of 1890 and the Clayton Act of 1914 were intended to outlaw monopolies, which tend to thwart competition. Unregulated businesses have historically shown tendencies to become monopolistic. Our antitrust laws were originally passed in an effort to curb the power of large trusts in oil, sugar, and whiskey in response to public pressures on the federal government and the states.

The Sherman Antitrust Act stated that "every contract, combination . . . or conspiracy in restraint of trade or commerce among the several states . . . is hereby declared to be illegal."

The Clayton Act later made it illegal for persons or firms engaged in interstate commerce to discriminate in price between purchasers if the effect was to decrease competition. Although the objectives of this legislation are beneficial to small business, there is a divergence of opinion concerning the extent to which the laws have achieved the objectives. The Clayton Act introduced a new approach to antitrust legislation by stressing control of practices such as price fixing, exclusive dealing, and tie-in contracts, which lead to monopolies.

In the same year that Congress enacted the Clayton Act, it created the Federal Trade Commission, with power to regulate unfair methods of competition. In an effort to provide guidelines to acceptable business practices, this agency has built a long list of unfair trade practices such as price cutting, boycotting, misbranding, false and misleading advertising, and secret rebates.

From time to time these statutes are amended, and new interpretations are made in the courts. Your lawyer, chamber of commerce, or business association should be a good source of guidance on how such laws or proposed changes might affect you.

The National Labor Relations Act, the Taft-Hartley Act, and the Labor Management Reporting and Disclosure Act are three major federal laws dealing with settlement of labor disputes. Business people who employ even a small labor force should familiarize themselves with the details of these acts.

The National Labor Relations Act, sometimes called the Wagner Act, guarantees the rights of workers to organize and to bargain collectively with their employers, or to refrain from all such activity. To enable employees to exercise these rights and to prevent labor disputes which may impede interstate commerce, the act places certain limits on the activities of employers and labor unions. The objectives of the act are to prevent obstacles to the free flow of interstate commerce by encouraging collective bargaining and by protecting workers in their right to organize and in their selection of a bargaining representative, and to protect the rights of the public in connection with labor disputes.

WHAT DID THE TAFT-HARTLEY ACT CONTRIBUTE TO LABOR RELATIONS?

It outlawed the closed shop. Under a closed shop, workers had to belong to a union before they could be hired. The law clarified and added to the list of unfair labor practices which could be charged against management. More significantly, it imposed upon unions certain controls over their organizing activities, their internal organizations, and their collective bargaining methods.

WHAT WAS THE PURPOSE OF THE DISCLOSURE ACT OF 1959?

The act was designed to eliminate or prevent improper practices, on the part of labor organizations, employers, labor relations consultants, and their officers and representatives, which distort and defeat the policies of the Labor Management Relations Act of 1947 and the Railway Labor Act.

The act compels a labor union to make a disclosure regarding the sources and disbursements of its funds, thereby preventing misuse of a union's funds by its leaders. It also requires employers to report payment to labor union officials, agents, or shop stewards for purposes other than payment for work. It further prohibits payments to employees for purposes of persuading other employees regarding their choice of a union or for purposes of influencing the latter's decision on other union matters. The act makes it illegal, during a labor dispute, to pay consultants for the purpose of getting information about either union employees or the union itself.

WHAT ARE YOUR LIABILITIES AS AN EMPLOYER IN REGARD TO WAGES, HOURS OF WORK, PAY, OVERTIME, AND CHILD LABOR?

Wages, hours, and working conditions are regulated by the Fair Labor Standards Act of 1938. Also known as the federal wage and hour law, it provides for minimum wages, maximum hours, overtime pay, recordkeeping to indicate compliance, and child labor limitations.

If your employees are covered under the act, you are required to do certain things. You must pay them a minimum wage established by law ($2.30 per hour in 1976); you must pay time and one-half for all hours worked over 40 in a week. The law restricts the employment of children over fourteen and under sixteen to nonmanufacturing and nonmining jobs, and it will not permit the employment of children between the ages of sixteen and eighteen in hazardous jobs or in helping a driver of a motor vehicle. The law does not require extra pay for Saturday, Sunday, or holiday work as such. It does not require vacation, holiday, or severance pay or a discharge notice. Nor does it set any limit on the number of hours of work for persons sixteen years of age or older. If you employ boys or girls, you should get age or employment certificates from the appropriate state agency.

WHO IS COVERED BY THE PROVISIONS OF THE FAIR LABOR STANDARDS ACT?

In 1976, there were 57.4 million workers covered by the act, including those employed by:

☐ Companies engaged in producing goods for interstate commerce.

☐ Retail or service enterprises with annual gross sales of at least $1 million and a $250,000 annual inflow of interstate goods.

☐ Local transit firms grossing at least $2 million a year.

☐ Construction firms grossing at least $350,000 annually.

☐ Other establishments with individually covered employees in enterprises with gross sales of at least $350,000 a year.

ARE ANY BUSINESSES OR WORKERS EXEMPT FROM THE MINIMUM WAGE AND OVERTIME PROVISIONS OF THE FAIR LABOR STANDARDS ACT?

Small retail and service establishments grossing less than $250,000 a year qualify for exemption, as do similar establishments with most of their sales within the state, such as motion-picture theaters, hotels, motels, restaurants, hospitals and nursing homes, schools, gasoline service stations, and recreational firms. True executive, administrative, and professional employees, and outside salespeople are exempt from the minimum wage and overtime provisions if they meet certain tests relative to their primary duty. There are certain employees who are exempt from the overtime provisions only. If you are in doubt about coverage for your employees, contact the nearest office of the Wage and Hour and Public Contracts Division, U.S. Department of Labor. There is an office near you.

DOES THE FAIR LABOR STANDARDS ACT SAY ANYTHING ABOUT EQUAL PAY?

The Fair Labor Standards Act provides for equal pay for equal work for employees who are subject to the minimum wage requirements. Employers cannot pay employees of one sex at rates lower than they pay employees of the opposite sex for the same work, that is, work on jobs which require equal skill, effort, and responsibility, and which are performed under similar working conditions. The act does not prohibit wage differentials based on seniority or on a system measuring earnings by quantity or quality of production. The only restriction is that any such system must be applied equally to men and women. The observance of state or local legal restrictions on hours, rest periods, and the like for women does not make otherwise equal work unequal. Nor does such observance justify unequal pay.

WHAT IS INCLUDED IN THE SO-CALLED "FAIR-EMPLOYMENT" LEGISLATION?

Fair-employment practices are established by the Federal Civil Rights Act, the Equal Opportunity clause, and the Equal Pay Act. This legislation makes it unlawful, as a condition of employment, to discriminate on the basis of race, religion, age, or sex. Many states have also enacted fair-employment-practice laws. As a small business owner, you will be concerned with observing the standards in selecting and hiring employees.

Title VII of the Civil Rights Act of 1964 was designed to prevent discrimination in employment practiced by employers and labor organizations. The act prohibits employers in interstate commerce from discrimination against job applicants because of race, color, sex, religion, or national origin except where these are bona fide qualifications necessary to normal operation of the business. Other restrictions prohibit separate lines of progression for men and women, advertisements which exclude consideration of an applicant because of sex, and separate seniority lists for men and women. The Civil Rights Act applies to all employers with more than 25 employees.

Executive Order No. 10925 requires each contracting agency of the federal government to obtain compliance with the Equal Opportunity clause which, the order states, must be included in all federal contracts. The clause provides that all government contractors and subcontractors will act affirmatively to ensure that employees and applicants for employment are treated without regard to race, creed, color, or national origin in the employment procedure. The clause also provides for penalties of contract termination or debarment for willful failure to comply.

In 1963, Congress amended the Fair Labor Standards Act by enacting the Equal Pay Act, which requires employers "to pay equal wages within an establishment to men and women doing equal work on jobs requiring equal skill, effort, and responsibility which are performed under similar working conditions." Wage differentials between male-female jobs are permissible only if there are demonstrable differences in job content.

WHAT SAFETY REGULATIONS DO EMPLOYERS HAVE TO COMPLY WITH?

You should be familiar with the provisions of the Occupational Safety and Health Act of 1970. Under this law, employers have the general duty to furnish each of their employees places of employment free from recognized hazards causing, or likely to cause, death or serious injury or physical harm. Although this responsibility is one which most employers have long accepted as a moral responsibility in the conduct of their business, the act places specific responsibilities on each employer and subjects the employer to heavy penalties if he or she fails to discharge them.

The act provides for mandatory penalties of up to $1,000 for each serious violation and for optional penalties of up to $1,000 for each nonserious violation. Penalties of up to $1,000 are required for each day during which an employer fails to correct a violation within the period set in the citation. Any employer who willfully or repeatedly violates the act can be assessed civil penalties of not more than $10,000 for each violation. Any willful violation resulting in the death of an employee, upon conviction, is punishable by a fine of not more than $10,000 or by imprisonment for not more than 6 months, or both.

WHAT IS THE UNIFORM COMMERCIAL CODE?

The code is an attempt to bring under one "umbrella" the legal aspects of business dealings in a wide variety of broad commercial areas such as sales, negotiable instruments, and contracts. These areas were previously covered in such legislation as the Uniform Negotiable Instruments Act, the Uniform Sales Act, and other "uniform laws" which were adopted by many of the states.

The need for one uniform "master" act which would encompass all commercial activities commonly found in business was met in the Uniform Commercial Code. The code was developed through the efforts of the American Law Institute and the National Conference of Commissioners on Uniform State Laws. Its adoption by the states began in the early 1950s; by now, all but a few states have adopted it.

The general principles of business law are best reflected in the types of legal transactions the small business people will likely become involved in. The Uniform Commercial Code treats these in several specific categories:

Transactions pertaining to sales

Commercial paper (negotiable instruments)

Bank deposits and collections

Letters of credit

Bulk transfers

Documents of title

Investment security

Sales of account, contract rights, and chattel paper

If your state has adopted the code, get a copy and read it carefully. In consultation with your attorney, you can quickly get "up to speed" on the many legal principles governing the operation of your business.

WHAT REGULATIONS GOVERN YOUR RELATIONSHIP WITH THE PUBLIC?

Many of your contacts with the public fall into the general areas of marketing or distribution. They involve your everyday dealings with people who buy from you and those transactions with others outside your business. Specific areas of concern are:

◻ Advertising

◻ Contracts

◻ Pricing

◻ Sales of real or personal property

◻ Warranties

We will examine each of these areas separately.

DOESN'T FREEDOM OF THE PRESS PROTECT YOUR RIGHT TO ADVERTISE AS YOU PLEASE?

Not if your advertising is false, misleading, deceptive, obscene, or libelous. The laws are particularly strict on those who advertise without assuming their social responsibilities of honesty and integrity. For example, if you advertise an article or service as "free," you must explain the conditions, obligations, and prerequisites for obtaining and keeping the "free" article. You are restricted in your use of deceptive, sound-alike, and copyrighted names, words, and phrases. You must comply with the advertising and labeling requirements of the Food, Drug, and Cosmetic Act and the regulations of the Federal Trade Commission regarding advertising of products which are injurious to the public or which do not possess the benefits claimed in the advertising. Good examples of enforcement practices in this area are the banning of cigarette ads on radio and television, and "cease and desist" orders related to misleading advertising of some patent medicines, sleep inducers, pain killers, and digestive aids.

Truthful advertising implies that you have stated all the facts, omitting none; that your claims are true and can be substantiated; that the nature of installment purchases are clearly spelled out; and that marked-down items showing a "former price" really were sold at that price for a period of time prior to the "sale."

Advertising which is defamatory or libelous in nature can get you involved in a lawsuit. If the material is used on radio or television by a newscaster, you will be held liable.

If you use "bait advertising" in an attempt to get customers into your store for the purpose of selling them something more expensive, you might be violating one of many state laws which deal specifically with this practice. You must also be careful about the use of such terms as *special, introductory, factory,* or *wholesale* prices unless you can prove that they are in fact unique or different from your regular prices. Misrepresentations of quality, purity, or of the ingredients in a product are common. They can cause real problems for you if you are asked to prove your statements.

Most states have laws which make it a misdemeanor to use a living person's name, portrait, or picture in commercial advertising without his or her express permission. This practice is not permitted even though the picture used was widely circulated for publicity purposes.

HOW CAN A PROPERLY EXECUTED CONTRACT HELP SMALL BUSINESS PEOPLE?

Almost every business act involves a promise of some kind made by someone, to perform in a certain way, or to buy or sell something, or pay for it in accordance with prescribed terms. Although not all agreements are contracts, all contracts represent an agreement or a meeting of the minds between two or more competent parties, acting in good faith, to consummate an agreement for a consideration. Although a contract does not have to be a written document, it is strongly suggested that business contracts be written, that the language be clear in regard to the intent of the parties involved, and that the amount of the consideration be clearly stated. Competent lawyers should be employed in drafting a contract where large sums of money are involved, or in cases where long-term contracts pose a great financial risk to the buyer or seller which could result from changing economic conditions such as a recession or depression.

The federal government and most states have enacted legislation which attempts to regulate price fixing, price control, and price cutting. Legal problems relative to pricing are usually associated with fair-trade pricing, selling below costs, or discriminatory pricing.

The federal antitrust laws make it illegal for businesses engaged in interstate commerce to conspire together to fix the prices of their products or to employ methods of achieving the same end result, such as discount agreements, methods of calculating markups, manipulation of delivery charges, and similar practices. If you engage in a price-fixing agreement or any conspiracy to fix prices or use price as a means to destroy a competitor, your actions are subject to the provisions of antitrust legislation.

Many of the states do not have antitrust laws, and as long as business people do not traffic in interstate commerce, they are free to establish any price they wish for their products or services in those states. In some states the prices of certain services or products are controlled by state boards. Common examples are the price of milk, taxi fares, and haircuts. Business people have no choice in these cases but to comply with the law.

Price control involves the setting of minimum retail prices by manufacturers in an effort to maintain fair price competition. Such fair-trade pricing is permitted in several states. There are, in addition, state laws which prevent merchants from selling below cost. Although cost is defined in different ways by the various states, a general approach has been to establish the selling price at cost plus some fixed markup over invoice cost, say 5 percent. The purpose of such legislation is to preserve competition by protecting small business people from the unfair price cutting of large chains and volume dealers. There is some question about the effectiveness of this legislation in accomplishing what it was designed to do. As a result of numerous court decisions and evasion of the laws through inflated trade-ins, unrecorded cash refunds, and tie-ins where customers are given free gifts or articles of merchandise when they buy the fair-traded items, many states have repealed their fair-trade laws.

Price cutting or discrimination by manufacturers and wholesalers in dealing with other business concerns was declared illegal by an amendment to the Clayton Act. The Robinson-Patman Act of 1936 makes it illegal to sell goods of like quality and grade to different buyers at different prices. The amendment allows quantity discounts to buyers only if the discounts can be justified by the seller on the basis of actual costs. The authors of this act also recognized some of the other methods of price discrimination and declared illegal excessive promotional and advertising allowances to certain customers, and brokerage fees collected from the seller when the "broker" was also acting with the buyer as principal.

IS THERE ANYTHING UNIQUE TO INSTALLMENT SELLING WHICH YOU SHOULD BE AWARE OF?

You should check the amount of interest you are allowed to charge and be sure you do not exceed the legal limit. Most states have laws which spell out the maximum you can charge. If you exceed this amount, whether deliberate or not, the penalties can be severe. You must also be sure you comply with the disclosure requirements of the Truth in Lending Act, discussed in Chapter 15.

TO WHAT EXTENT DO WARRANTIES AFFECT SMALL BUSINESS OWNERS?

All business transactions are conducted with some degree of warranty, either written or implied. If you sell at retail manufactured products which carry a manufacturer's warranty, the actual guarantor and the terms of the warranty should be clearly stated, with time limits specifically noted so that there is not doubt in the customer's mind concerning redress should the product turn out to be unsatisfactory. In the absence of any indication as to who is assuming responsibility to make good a warranty, the last person in the distribution chain is generally held responsible. Liabilities under warranty can best be handled by insurance. Your insurance agent can advise you on types of coverage, rates, and ways of reducing potential liability.

Legislation which became effective in 1976 made it legal for customers to withhold payments for defective products they purchased with credit cards or on installment terms if the merchants do not make a good-faith effort to repair or replace the defective items or render satisfaction to them. This legal protection of the consumer's basic right to fair treatment must be kept in mind when you establish policies regarding warranties.

WHAT LEGAL PROBLEMS ARE ASSOCIATED WITH OWNERSHIP OF REAL ESTATE?

Real estate is subject to the zoning ordinances established by local city planning groups, which control the use of real property located in certain areas. For this reason, zoning regulations should be carefully examined before business sites are purchased.

The condemnation of privately owned property for use by the government for highway construction, parks, or streets represents the exercise of the right of eminent domain, a well-known restriction business people should be aware of. Restrictions in deeds and mortgages regulating the owner's use of property should be understood and carefully checked by your lawyer. A reputable real estate broker can often offer valuable assistance in selecting plant sites which fit your needs without unnecessary restrictions and potential legal problems.

IS BANKRUPTCY THE ONLY ANSWER FOR BUSINESSES
WHICH ARE UNABLE TO PAY THEIR DEBTS?

If the reasons for insolvency are temporary and the owners can see a way to pay their bills and satisfy their creditors at a later date or to pay some pro rata share of their debts, there are open to them two voluntary settlement methods short of bankruptcy. To most creditors, forced settlement of claims through bankruptcy proceedings offers no guarantee of a quick or full settlement; therefore, any arrangement which would enable a firm to keep operating and permit it to make an out-of-court settlement is the more desirable alternative.

One or more creditors might agree to an *extension*, which postpones a debtor's obligation for some stipulated period of time. This method can succeed if the firm's cash problem is temporary and the possibility of later payment is good. Not all creditors have to agree to an extension, but if the major creditors agree, the debtor can often buy enough time to extricate himself or herself from his or her financial predicament, keeping the business intact.

The second type of voluntary settlement is known as a *composition*. Under this plan, the creditors must agree to accept a pro rata cash settlement—say, 30 cents on the dollar—as payment in full in lieu of instituting bankruptcy proceedings.

Either of the voluntary methods has the advantage of avoiding court costs. The difficulty lies in getting the creditors to agree to cooperate in carrying out the plan selected.

WHAT PLACE DOES TAX PLANNING OCCUPY IN THE
SMALL BUSINESS OWNER'S WORLD?

Tax laws are important factors in business planning. They affect both short- and long-range plans; the owner must, therefore, consider them as he or she plans current and future courses of action. Table 21-1 shows the tax aspects of some common business activities.

It is possible by intelligent planning to minimize the payment of taxes. It should be kept in mind that in a business making 5 percent profit on $100,000 of sales, a tax savings of $100 a year is equivalent to sales of $10,000 if profits are taxed at 20 percent.

Taxation is a technical, complex, and changing subject. It requires a lot of time to keep up-to-date on Treasury decisions, court decisions, and new federal, state, and local legislation. The services of a tax adviser or competent accountant will prevent costly mistakes and save you money.

ISN'T IT DISHONEST TO TRY TO AVOID PAYING TAXES?

Not at all. Taxpayers are not required to organize their businesses in a way that will create maximum revenues for the government. The government wants you to pay only your legal obligations—no more

TABLE 21-1.   TAX EFFECTS IN BUSINESS ACTIVITIES

Business Activity	Tax Considerations
Inventory	Taxes paid on inventories are based on the value of the inventory. Selection of fiscal year-ending to coincide with low inventory levels will save taxes. Method of valuing inventory will affect inventory amounts. Inventory-reduction programs prior to assessment dates are effective in reducing taxes.
Asset acquisition	Selection of the best depreciation method to be used can affect profits. Evaluation of the tax benefits of leasing compared with owning should be explored. Consider the tax benefits of using or buying secondhand or used equipment.
Employment/wages	Careful evaluation of how many workers are required will keep employer's contributions to social security taxes and unemployment taxes at a minimum. Tax effects of wage payment plans based on stock options and deferred payments of wages should be considered.
Profit planning	Legal form of business can offer tax advantages which increase profits. Maximizing legitimate tax deductions should be a major thrust of financial planning.
Capital gains and losses	Timing of transactions such as sale of assets, and acquisition of new assets or new businesses should consider the impact on taxes.

and no less. This fact has been best expressed by the late Judge Learned Hand[1] when he said:

Over and over again the courts have said that there is nothing sinister in arranging one's affairs to keep taxes as low as possible. Everybody does so, rich or poor; and all do right, for nobody owes any public duty to pay more than the law demands.

Tax avoidance is not the same thing as tax evasion, which is failure to pay taxes due. The latter is unlawful. Your job, and the job of your tax adviser, is to be sure that you pay no more taxes than the law requires.

HOW MANY DIFFERENT TAXES IS A BUSINESS LIABLE FOR?

Taxes affect almost every phase of business. More and more management decisions require the owner to have a broad knowledge of taxes. The continuing changes in tax laws force business owners to consider their effects in almost everything they plan. Table 21-2 shows the common kinds of business taxes grouped by taxing authority.

[1]William C. Greene, *Getting the Facts for Income Tax Reporting*, Small Marketers Aids, No. 144, U.S. Small Business Administration, Washington, 1974, p. 6.

TABLE 21-2.   KINDS OF BUSINESS TAXES

Federal	Individual income taxes
	Corporate income taxes
	Excise taxes—manufacturers, retailers
	Employment taxes
	Social security taxes
	Death taxes
	Stamp taxes
	Occupational taxes
	Customs
State (specific taxes vary in each state)	Individual income taxes
	Corporate income taxes
	Gross receipts and sales taxes
	Business real and personal property taxes
	Capital stock taxes
	Business automobile and truck licenses, inspection fees
	Death taxes
	Foreign-state business taxes
	Workmen's compensation insurance premiums
	Incorporation fees
	Employment taxes
Local	Individual income taxes
	Sales taxes
	City, school district, and county real and personal property taxes
	Business licenses
	Business real and personal property taxes

Source: Harvey C. Krentzman, *Managing for Profits*, U.S. Small Business Administration, Washington, 1968, p. 145.

WHAT CAN YOU DO TO MINIMIZE YOUR TAX LIABILITY?

Examine the records provided by your accounting system to determine what the profitability of your business is likely to be. You can make an estimate of annual income from a profit-and-loss statement prepared at the end of each quarter. From this you can make a sound estimate of taxable income for the year and plan the things you can do to minimize your taxes. The amount of taxes you pay will be determined by the way in which your business operates. The major areas subject to control on your part are business expenses and deductions, capital expenditures, travel and transportation expenses, and depreciation.

WHAT IS MEANT BY THE TERM *TAX MANAGEMENT*?

A well-managed business should never have any problems in meeting its tax obligations. Accounts payable are managed so that owners know what they owe, whether the funds to pay their bills are available, and where to turn to if they need assistance; the same management principles apply to planning and meeting your tax obligations. Tax management means that you must know the kinds of taxes that have to be paid, how much they amount to, and when they are due. It further suggests that your financial planning has provided for them so that you can pay them on time and avoid a penalty. Getting advice from accountants, lawyers, or tax advisers is a part of good tax management.

WHAT IS THERE ABOUT TAXES THAT GETS BUSINESS OWNERS IN TROUBLE?

Keeping track of taxes is a complicated job. As a business owner, you are not only responsible for paying your own taxes, but you are also liable for those taxes which you withhold from the wages of your employees. For example, each payday you deduct federal income taxes and social security taxes from your workers' wages. In some states you must also deduct state income taxes. In some localities you must deduct a local income tax. As if this were not enough, you also act as an agent for collecting state and local sales taxes and passing them along to the appropriate government agency.

The rules for withholding taxes and paying them vary according to the tax, so you must have accurate and complete records of all transactions regarding amounts withheld, the tax involved, and payments made. Payments must be made by certain deadlines, or else penalties are involved. If you have very many employees, accounting for taxes can be a big headache.

WHAT DO YOU NEED TO KNOW ABOUT FEDERAL INCOME TAXES?

In paying income taxes, you will be acting in a dual role—as agent for your employees in withholding taxes and making regular payments to the government and as an individual concerned with paying your own income taxes.

The law requires that every business owner with one or more employees withhold federal income taxes from wages paid.

The first step as an employer is to obtain an employer's identification number, required on employment tax returns, by filing Form SS-4 with the district director of Internal Revenue Service in your area. Upon application, you should request the "Mr. Businessman's Kit," which is filled with tax information useful in your business.

When you hire a new employee, and at the beginning of each year, you should furnish every employee with a Form W-4, the Employee's Withholding Exemption Certificate. The information on this form will enable you to tell how much to withhold from each paycheck. Use the information and tables in the *Employer's Tax Guide* to determine the proper amount to withhold.

If you are self-employed, you might be required to file a declaration of estimated taxes, even though a wage earner with the same income would not have to do so. This is because income taxes are not withheld from your wages, as they are in the case of a wage earner.

For the sole proprietor, filing an income tax return is relatively simple. You list all income and deductions on your individual income tax return, Form 1040, Schedule C.

A partnership's income is taxed as personal income to the partners, each partner reporting his or her distributive share on his or her individual income tax return. The partnership is not a taxable entity. However, its income must be determined and filed for information purposes under both federal and state laws. Form 1065 is used for the federal information return.

The corporate income tax return is filed on Form 1120. Estimated returns may be required. Form 1120-W details instructions for computing and paying the tax.

WHAT IS COVERED BY SOCIAL SECURITY TAXES?

Social security taxes, also known as FICA (Federal Insurance Contribution Act) taxes, was established to provide for the elderly, their survivors, disability, and hospitalization. The tax is deducted by employers from wages paid their employees and is matched by the employers in an equal amount.

Social security taxes are deducted at a rate stipulated in the law, based on maximum wages or salaries which are also set by law. For 1974, 1975, and 1976, these amounts were:

Year	Maximum Wages or Salary	Tax Rate, %	Maximum Annual Withholding
1974	$13,200	5.85	$772.20
1975	14,100	5.85	824.85
1976	15,300	5.85	895.05

The matching contribution from the employer places the total paid to the government at 11.70 (5.85 × 2) percent of the maximum wages for a given year. When business owners use social security for their own retirement, they must pay the tax for themselves.

If your type of business involves tips, such as restaurants, hotels, cocktail lounges, and similar businesses, employees receiving cash tips of $20 or more in a month while working for you must report these tips to you for income tax and social security purposes. On or before the tenth day of each month, tips received during the previous month must be reported. You then deduct the appropriate amount for your employees' social security and income taxes from wages due them. You are required to match only the deductions you made on your employees' wages. You need not match the social security taxes you deducted on tips your employees have received.

WHAT DO YOU DO WITH THE MONEY YOU WITHHOLD FROM EMPLOYEES' WAGES FOR FEDERAL TAXES?

First, you have to report the income and social security taxes you withheld from the employees' pay. You use tax return Form 941 to report the amounts due the government. The return is due for each calendar quarter on the last day of the month following the close of the quarter—April 30, July 31, October 31, and January 31.

In many cases remittances of taxes are required before the return is filed. The dates on which you are required to pay the taxes to the government depend on your situation. Generally, the smaller the amount of your tax liability, the less often you have to make a deposit. Table 21-3 gives the rules from Circular E, Employer's Tax Guide, published in April 1975.

TABLE 21-3. SUMMARY OF DEPOSIT RULES FOR WITHHELD INCOME TAX AND SOCIAL SECURITY TAXES

Deposit Rule	Deposit Due
1. If at the end of a quarter the total undeposited taxes are less than $200:	No deposit required. Pay balance directly to the Internal Revenue Service with your quarterly return, or make a deposit if you prefer.
2. If at the end of a quarter the total undeposited taxes are $200 or more:	On or before last day of next month. If $2,000 or more, see rule 4.
3. If at the end of any month (except the last month of a quarter), cumulative undeposited taxes for the quarter are $200 or more, but less than $2,000:	Within 15 days after end of month. (For the first 2 months of the quarter no deposit is required if you previously made a deposit for a quarter-monthly period that occurred during the month under the $2,000 rule in item 4, below.)
4. If at the end of any quarter-monthly period, cumulative undeposited taxes for the quarter are $2,000 or more:	Within 3 banking days after the quarter-monthly period ends.

Source: Circular E, Employer's Tax Guide, Internal Revenue Service Publication 15, Department of the Treasury, Washington, April 1975.

DO EMPLOYEES CONTRIBUTE TO UNEMPLOYMENT INSURANCE TAXES?

Not to federal unemployment taxes. Some states require an employee contribution to state plans. The employer pays the full amount of federal unemployment taxes. Every employer who has four or more employees on at least some portion of 1 day in each of 20 or more calendar weeks must pay unemployment taxes. The 20 weeks do not have to be consecutive. The rate in 1975 was 3.2 percent of total wages paid, with a limitation which applies to the first $4,200 of wages paid to each employee during the calendar year. You may receive credit for up to 2.7 percent of the wages for state unemployment taxes you pay, or for having received a favorable experience rate by the state. In this case your net federal unemployment tax liability would be 0.5 percent for taxable wages paid in 1975.

WHAT STATE AND LOCAL TAXES DO YOU HAVE TO WORRY ABOUT?

Three major state taxes are unemployment taxes, income taxes, and sales tax.

It is essential to know what taxes your state requires you to pay and what taxes it requires you to collect as an agent. In some states, business people who fail to remit state withheld taxes can be charged with embezzlement.

Each state has unemployment taxes. Since the requirements vary, find out what your state requires. In most cases, unemployment taxes are based on the taxable wage for a quarter. The rate of tax charged is usually determined by your unemployment experience, coupled with the unemployment experience of your state.

Several states have an income tax. In such cases, the employer deducts the tax from the employees' wages. State tax returns may be similar to the federal returns or they may be different. If state income tax requirements are different from federal requirements, be sure your records are kept in a manner that satisfies both.

Many states have sales taxes. The business owner acts as an agent in collecting the tax from customers and passing it along to the appropriate state agency. The method of collection, reporting, and paying sales tax is established by the state taxing authorities.

Local taxes consist largely of real estate taxes, personal property taxes, and taxes on gross receipts of businesses. Some larger cities also have an income tax.

WHAT HAPPENS IF THE INTERNAL REVENUE SERVICE FINDS A "DEFICIENCY" IN YOUR INCOME TAX RETURN?

Many small business people prepare their own tax returns without professional help; it is, therefore, not uncommon to find that some overpay their taxes and others underpay. If you do not agree with the district director's determination concerning an underpayment, you may appeal your case both in the Internal Revenue Service and in the United States courts.

The appeal procedure is characterized by a number of time-limiting documents such as the *30-day letter,* the *formal protest,* and the *90-day letter,* all of which serve as guidelines to the path you must follow in making an appeal. Your local IRS office can provide guidance in helping you decide what course of action to take.

A tax deficiency is not to be confused with errors in arithmetic. If an error in arithmetic involves underpayment, it is merely called to your attention and your remittance awaited. If it involves an overpayment, a check for the difference is mailed to you. Neither type of adjustment is subject to review by the courts.

This exercise is designed to test your understanding of the material presented in Chapter 21. Choose the response, *True* or *False*, which best fits each statement. Correct responses are presented in the back of the text.

SELF-CHECK OF KEY CONCEPTS

1. The Truth in Lending Act does not apply to loans for those homes whose value exceeds $25,000.
2. It is against the law for you to pass along to another creditor information about a customer's credit record with you.
3. If left unregulated, the proliferation of big business would thwart competition and force many smaller companies out of business.
4. The law does not require an employer to pay extra for work performed on a Saturday, Sunday, or holiday.
5. There is no limit imposed on the number of hours employees sixteen or older can work.
6. The Fair Labor Standards Act applies primarily to nonsupervisory employees working in businesses engaged in, or supplying material or services to businesses engaged in, interstate commerce.
7. The Civil Rights Act applies to all employers with more than 25 employees.
8. The Truth in Lending Act outlawed the garnishment of an employee's wages by creditors.
9. The Fair Labor Standards Act prohibits an employer from paying women less than men for the same work.
10. All the states now have fair-trade laws which regulate the price which may be charged for a product.

1. Obtain a copy of the Uniform Commercial Code at your local library or from the appropriate state agency in your state and prepare a 5-minute oral report for presentation to the class on warranties and how they affect business people.

2. Obtain a copy of the *Employer's Tax Guide, Circular E,* Publication 15, from the IRS office nearest you and find out how income tax withholding, social security taxes, and federal unemployment taxes are treated for the following special classes of unemployment:

Special Class	Treatment Under Different Employment Taxes		
	Income Tax Withholding	Social Security	Federal Unemployment
1. Son or daughter under 21 employed by parent.			
2. Parent employed by son or daughter.			
3. Household workers; domestic service in private home.			
4. Peace Corps volunteers (See federal employees).			
5. Students working for a private school, college or university, if enrolled and regularly attending classes.			

A
CASE
IN
POINT

A QUESTION OF FREE ENTERPRISE

Despite his lack of formal education, Jack Bourne was somewhat of an electronic wizard. All his life he had been fascinated by radio and its applications. During his early married years he spent much of his spare time tinkering with radios and other electronic gear in his garage workshop. In the process, he developed a unique electronic filter which he believed could have application in communications equipment. Upon advice of a friend, who was an attorney, he obtained a patent for the device.

During World War II, the Armed Forces found application for Jack's filter in some of its communication gear. Jack successfully bid on several small contracts and soon found that the demand for the filters far exceeded his ability to produce the quantities needed by assembling them in his garage with part-time help. Radio and television manufacturers had tested Jack's filters in their products and had indicated an interest in quantity prices and discussions of royalties.

In view of the potential business, Jack decided to borrow money and establish a modest manufacturing firm in his home town—a small Georgia community of 5,000 population. He leased an empty building which was suitable and solicited 35 employees through newspaper ads and personal interviews, paying them wages in accordance with their backgrounds and abilities. Since this was the biggest business in town, Jack had plenty of applicants who were willing to work. Based on his evaluation of each employee's "worth," Jack set up a salary scale which averaged $1.50 per hour or about $60 a week for 40 hours—more money than most of the workers had ever made from steady employment.

Most weeks it was necessary to work on Saturday to meet schedules for the filters. Straight-time rates were paid for such work, giving the average employee $72 a week in earnings. Since the community was in an economically depressed area, Jack hired only men who needed the work to support families. He took pride in the part his company played in keeping the community economically healthy.

The first hint of trouble came when some of his employees told Jack that they had been approached by union organizers from a nearby large town and had been told that the union could help them get higher wages, overtime pay, and a better "deal" for the workers. They hinted that Jack was not in compliance with federal laws in some of his hiring and pay practices.

At the same time, Jack got an invitation to bid on a very large government contract for electronic filters. As he read the conditions attached to the bid concerning wages and hours, payment for overtime, and equal opportunity, he exploded.

"Between the government and the unions telling you how to run your business, you can go broke. All this malarkey about minimum wages, overtime pay, and hiring women would add too much to the cost of our filters. With this kind of restriction on free enterprise, no wonder manufactured products cost so much."

Based on what you know now, answer the following questions:

1. What does Jack's concept of "free" enterprise seem to be?
2. Does Jack's firm come under the provision of the Fair Labor Standards Act? Explain your answer.
3. Is the business possibly in violation of the Federal Civil Rights Act of 1964?
4. What will Jack have to do to stay out of trouble with the law and save face with his workers?

Appendix

A. SMALL BUSINESS ADMINISTRATION FIELD OFFICE ADDRESSES

Boston	Massachusetts 02114, 150 Causeway Street
Holyoke	Massachusetts 01040, 326 Appleton Street
Augusta	Maine 04330, Federal Building, U.S. Post Office, 40 Western Avenue
Concord	New Hampshire 03301, 55 Pleasant Street
Hartford	Connecticut 06103, Federal Office Building, 450 Maine Street
Montpelier	Vermont 05602, Federal Building, Second Floor, 87 State Street
Providence	Rhode Island 02903, 702 Smith Building, 57 Eddy Street
New York	New York 10007, 26 Federal Plaza, Room 3100
Hato Rey	Puerto Rico 00919, 255 Ponce De Leon Avenue
Newark	New Jersey 07102, 970 Broad Street, Room 1635
Syracuse	New York 13202, Hunter Plaza, Fayette and Salina Streets
Buffalo	New York 14202, 111 West Huron Street
Albany	New York 12207, 99 Washington Avenue
Rochester	New York 14604, 55 St. Paul Street
Philadelphia	Bala Cynwyd, Pennsylvania 19004, 1 Decker Square
Harrisburg	Pennsylvania 17108, 7–11 Market Square
Wilkes-Barre	Pennsylvania 18703, 34 South Main Street
Baltimore	Towson, Maryland 21204, 7800 York Road
Wilmington	Delaware 19801, 901 Market Street
Clarksburg	West Virginia 26301, Lowndes Bank Building, 109 North Third Street
Charleston	West Virginia 25301, Charleston National Plaza, Suite 628
Pittsburgh	Pennsylvania 15222, Federal Building, 1000 Liberty Avenue
Richmond	Virginia 23240, Federal Building, 400 North Eighth Street
Washington	D.C. 20416, 1030 15th Street, N.W.
Atlanta	Georgia 30309, 1401 Peachtree Street, N.E.
Birmingham	Alabama 35205, 908 South 20th Street
Charlotte	North Carolina 28202, Addison Building, 222 South Church Street
Columbia	South Carolina 29201, 1801 Assembly Street
Jackson	Mississippi 39205, Petroleum Building, Pascagoula and Amite Streets
Gulfport	Mississippi 39501, Security Savings and Loan Building
Jacksonville	Florida, 32202, Federal Office Building, 400 West Bay Street
Louisville	Kentucky 40202, Federal Office Building, 600 Federal Place
Miami	Florida 33130, Federal Building, 51 Southwest First Avenue
Tampa	Florida 33607, Federal Building, 500 Zack Street
Nashville	Tennessee 37219, 500 Union Street
Knoxville	Tennessee 37902, 502 South Gay Street
Memphis	Tennessee 38103, Federal Building, 167 North Main Street
Chicago	Illinois 60604, Federal Office Building, 219 South Dearborn Street
Springfield	Illinois 62701, 502 East Monroe Street
Cleveland	Ohio 44199, 1240 East Ninth Street
Columbus	Ohio 43215, 34 North High Street

Cincinnati	Ohio 45202, Federal Building, 550 Main Street
Detroit	Michigan 48226, 1249 Washington Boulevard
Marquette	Michigan 49855, 201 McClellan Street
Indianapolis	Indiana 46204, 575 North Pennsylvania Street
Madison	Wisconsin 53703, 122 West Washington Avenue
Milwaukee	Wisconsin 53203, 735 West Wisconsin Avenue
Eau Claire	Wisconsin 54701, 500 South Barstow Street
Minneapolis	Minnesota 55402, 12 South Sixth Street
Dallas	Texas 75202, 1100 Commerce Street
Albuquerque	New Mexico 87110, 5000 Marble Avenue, N.E.
Houston	Texas 77002, 808 Travis Street
Little Rock	Arkansas 72201, 611 Gaines Street
Lubbock	Texas 79408, 1205 Texas Avenue
El Paso	Texas 79901, 109 North Oregon Street
Lower Rio Grande Valley	Harlingen, Texas 78550, 219 East Jackson Street
Corpus Christi	Texas 78408, 3105 Leopard Street
Marshall	Texas 75670, 505 East Travis Street
New Orleans	Louisiana 70113, 1001 Howard Avenue
Oklahoma City	Oklahoma 73118, 50 Penn Place
San Antonio	Texas 78205, 301 Broadway
Kansas City	Missouri 64106, 911 Walnut Street
Des Moines	Iowa 50309, New Federal Building, 210 Walnut Street
Omaha	Nebraska 68102, Federal Building, 215 North 17th Street
St. Louis	Missouri 63101, Federal Building, 210 North 12th Street
Wichita	Kansas 67202, 120 South Market Street
Denver	Colorado 80202, 721 19th Street, Room 426
Casper	Wyoming 82601, 100 East B Street
Fargo	North Dakota 58102, 653 Second Avenue, N.
Helena	Montana 59601, 613 Helena Avenue
Salt Lake City	Utah 84138, Federal Building, 125 South State Street
Sioux Falls	South Dakota 57102, National Bank Building, Eighth and Main Avenue
San Francisco	California 94102, Federal Building, 450 Golden Gate Avenue
Fresno	California 93721, Federal Building, 1130 O Street
Honolulu	Hawaii 96813, 1149 Bethel Street
Agana	Guam 96910, Ada Plaza Center Building
Los Angeles	California 90014, 849 South Broadway
Las Vegas	Nevada 89121, 301 East Stewart
Phoenix	Arizona 85004, 112 North Central Avenue
San Diego	California 92101, 110 West C Street
Seattle	Washington 98104, 710 Second Avenue
Anchorage	Alaska 99501, 1016 West Sixth Avenue
Fairbanks	Alaska 99701, 501½ Second Avenue
Boise	Idaho 83701, 216 North Eighth Street
Portland	Oregon 97205, 921 Southwest Washington Street
Spokane	Washington 99210, Courthouse Building, Room 651

Note: Telephone numbers of these offices may be obtained by finding the Small Business Administration office under "United States Government" in the appropriate city telephone directory.

B. SMALL BUSINESS ADMINISTRATION "FOR-SALE" PUBLICATIONS

These "for-sale" booklets may be ordered from the Superintendent of Documents, Government Printing Office, Washington, D.C. 20402. Payment may be made by check, money order, or document coupons. Do not send postage stamps or cash. These booklets are *not* sold by the Small Business Administration. Latest listings and prices are available on SBA Publications List 115-B, which may be obtained from your nearest SBA field office.

SMALL BUSINESS MANAGEMENT SERIES

The booklets in this series provide discussions of special management problems in small companies.

	Catalog No.	Pages
An Employee Suggestion System for Small Companies Explains the basic principles for starting and operating a suggestion system. It also warns of various pitfalls and gives examples of suggestions submitted by employees.	SBA 1.12:1	18
Human Relations in Small Business Discusses human relations as the subject involves finding and selecting employees, developing them, and motivating them.	SBA 1.12:3	68
Improving Material Handling in Small Business A discussion of the basics of the material handling function, the method of laying out workplaces, and other factors to setting up an efficient system.	SBA 1.12:4	42
Better Communications in Small Business Designed to help smaller manufacturers help themselves in winning cooperation by means of more skillful communications. It also seeks to explain how communications within the firm can improve operating efficiency and competitive strength.	SBA 1.12:7	37
Cost Accounting for Small Manufacturers Stresses the importance of determining and recording costs accurately. Designed for small manufacturers and their accountants. Diagrams, flow charts, and illustrations are included to make the material easier to use.	SBA 1.12:9	163
The Small Manufacturer and His Specialized Staff Stresses the necessity of building a competent staff through the use of staff specialist and outside professional advisers so that the small businessman can be relieved of routine work.	SBA 1.12:13	36

	Catalog No.	Pages

Handbook of Small Business Finance
Written for the small businessman who wants to improve his financial-management skills. Indicates the major areas of financial management and describes a few of the many techniques that can help the small businessman.

SBA 1.12:15 — 80

New Product Introduction for Small Business Owners
Provides basic information which will help the owners of small businesses to understand better what is involved in placing a new or improved product on the market.

SBA 1.12:17 — 69

Ratio Analysis for Small Business
Ratio analysis is the process of determining the relationships between certain financial or operating data of a business to provide a basis for managerial control. The purpose of the booklet is to help the owner/manager in detecting favorable or unfavorable trends in his business.

SBA 1.12:20 — 65

Profitable Small Plant Layout
Help for the small business owner who is in the predicament of rising costs on finished goods, decreasing net profits, and lowered production because of the lack of economical and orderly movement of production materials from one process to another throughout the shop.

SBA 1.12:21 — 48

Practical Business Use of Government Statistics
Illustrates some practical uses of federal government statistics, discusses what can be done with them, and describes major reference sources.

SBA 1.12:22 — Available Fall 1975

Guides for Profit Planning
Guides for computing and using the break-even point, the level of gross profit, and the rate of return on investment. Designed for readers who have no specialized training in accounting and economics.

SBA 1.12:25 — 52

Personnel Management Guides for Small Business
An introduction to the various aspects of personnel management as they apply to small firms.

SBA 1.12:26 — 79

Profitable Community Relations for Small Business
Practical information on how to build and maintain sound community relations by participation in community affairs.

SBA 1.12:27 — 36

	Catalog No.	Pages

Small Business and Government Research and Development
SBA 1.12:28   41
An introduction for owners of small research and development firms that seek government R and D contracts. Includes a discussion of the procedures necessary to locate and interest government markets.

Management Audit for Small Manufacturers
SBA 1.12:29   58
A series of questions which will indicate whether the owner/manager of a small manufacturing plant is planning, organizing, directing, and coordinating his business activities efficiently.

Insurance and Risk Management for Small Business
SBA 1.12:30   72
A discussion of what insurance is, the necessity of obtaining professional advice on buying insurance, and the main types of insurance a small business may need.

Management Audit for Small Retailers
SBA 1.12:31   50
Designed to meet the needs of the owner/manager of a small retail enterprise. 149 questions guide the owner/manager in an examination of himself and his business operation.

Financial Recordkeeping for Small Stores
SBA 1.12:32   131
Written primarily for the small store owner or prospective owner whose business doesn't justify hiring a full-time bookkeeper.

Small Store Planning for Growth
SBA 1.12:33   99
A discussion of the nature of growth, the management skills needed, and some techniques for use in promoting growth. Included is a consideration of merchandising, advertising and display, and checklists for increases in transactions and gross margins.

Selecting Advertising Media—A Guide for Small Business
SBA 1.12:34   120
Intended to aid the small businessman in deciding which medium to select for making his product, service, or store known to potential customers and how to best use his advertising money.

Franchise Index/Profile
SBA 1.12:35   56
Presents an evaluation process that may be used to investigate franchise opportunities. The Index tells what to look for in a franchise. The Profile is a worksheet for listing the data.

STARTING AND MANAGING SERIES

This series is designed to help small entrepreneurs in their effort "to look before they leap" into a business. The first volume in the series—*Starting and Managing a Small Business of Your Own*—deals with the subject in general terms. Each of the other volumes deals with one type of business in detail, and their titles are designed to inform of their contents. Available titles are listed below.

	Catalog No.	Pages
Starting and Managing a Small Business of Your Own	SBA 1.15:1	97
Starting and Managing a Service Station	SBA 1.15:3	80
Starting and Managing a Small Bookkeeping Service	SBA 1.15:4	64
Starting and Managing a Small Building Business	SBA 1.15:5	102
Starting and Managing a Small Restaurant	SBA 1.15:9	116
Starting and Managing a Small Retail Hardware Store	SBA 1.15:10	73
Starting and Managing a Small Retail Drugstore	SBA 1.15:11	103
Starting and Managing a Small Dry Cleaning Business	SBA 1.15:12	80
Starting and Managing a Small Automatic Vending Business	SBA 1.15:13	70
Starting and Managing a Carwash	SBA 1.15:14	76
Starting and Managing a Swap Shop or Consignment Sale Shop	SBA 1.15:15	78
Starting and Managing a Small Shoe Service Shop	SBA 1.15:16	86
Starting and Managing a Small Retail Camera Shop	SBA 1.15:17	86
Starting and Managing a Retail Flower Shop	SBA 1.15:18	121
Starting and Managing a Pet Shop	SBA 1.15:19	40
Starting and Managing a Small Retail Music Store	SBA 1.15:20	81
Starting and Managing a Small Retail Jewelry Store	SBA 1.15:21	78
Starting and Managing an Employment Agency	SBA 1.15:22	118
Starting and Managing a Small Drive-In Restaurant	SBA 1.15:23	65
Starting and Managing a Small Shoestore	SBA 1.15:24	104

SMALL BUSINESS RESEARCH SERIES

	Catalog No.	Pages
Cash Planning in Small Manufacturing Companies	SBA 1.20:1	276

This book reports on research that was done on cash planning for the small manufacturer. It is designed for owners of small firms and the specialists who study and aid them.

	Catalog No.	Pages

**The First Two Years: Problems of Small Firm
Growth and Survival**
SBA 1.20:2   233
This discussion is based on the detailed observation of 81 small retail and service firms over a
2-year period. The operations of each enterprise
was systematically followed from the time of
launching through the end of the second year.

NONSERIES PUBLICATIONS

	Catalog No.	Pages
Export Marketing for Small Firms	SBA 1.19:EX7/971	134

A manual for owner/managers of small firms
who seek sales in foreign markets.

U.S. Government Purchasing and Sales Directory   SBA 1.13/3:972   169
A directory for businesses that are interested in
selling to the U.S. government. Lists the purchasing needs of various agencies.

Managing for Profits   SBA 1.2:M31/11   170
Ten chapters on various aspects of small business
management, for example, marketing, production, and credit.

Buying and Selling a Small Business   SBA 1.2:B98   122
Deals with the problems that confront buyers and
sellers of small businesses. Discusses the buy/
sell transaction, sources of information for buyer/
seller decision, the buy/sell process, using financial statements in the buy/sell transaction, and
analyzing the market position of the company.

Strengthening Small Business Management   SBA 1.2:M31/14   158
Twenty-one chapters on small business manage-
ment. This collection reflects the experience
which the author gained in a lifetime of work with
the small business community.

C. SMALL BUSINESS ADMINISTRATION FREE MANAGEMENT-ASSISTANCE PUBLICATIONS

Single copies of Management Aids, Technical Aids, Small Marketers Aids, and
Small Business Bibliographies may be ordered from the nearest SBA field office
shown in Appendix A. There is no charge for this service. Since listings are
periodically updated, ask for a copy of SBA Publications List 115-A, which also
contains a convenient order form.

MANAGEMENT AIDS

These leaflets deal with functional problems in small manufacturing plants and concentrate on subjects of interest to administrative and operating personnel.

32. How Trade Associations Help Small Business
46. How to Analyze Your Own Business
49. Know Your Patenting Procedures
80. Choosing the Legal Structure for Your Firm
82. Reducing the Risks in Product Development
85. Analyzing Your Cost of Marketing
92. Wishing Won't Get Profitable New Products
111. Steps in Incorporating a Business
161. Proving Fidelity Losses
162. Keeping Machines and Operators Productive
169. Designing Small Plants for Economy and Flexibility
170. The ABC's of Borrowing
174. Is Your Cash Supply Adequate?
176. Financial Audits: A Tool for Better Management
177. Planning and Controlling Production for Efficiency
178. Effective Industrial Advertising for Small Plants
179. Breaking the Barriers to Small Business Planning
180. Guidelines for Building a New Plant
181. Numerical Control for the Smaller Manufacturer
182. Expanding Sales Through Franchising
185. Matching the Applicant to the Job
186. Checklist for Developing a Training Program
187. Using Census Data in Small Plant Marketing
188. Developing a List of Prospects
189. Should You Make or Buy Components?
190. Measuring the Performance of Salesmen
191. Delegating Work and Responsibility
192. Profile Your Customers to Expand Industrial Sales
193. What Is the Best Selling Price?
194. Marketing Planning Guidelines
195. Setting Pay for Your Management Jobs
196. Tips on Selecting Salesmen
197. Pointers on Preparing an Employee Handbook
198. How to Find a Likely Successor
199. Expand Overseas Sales With Commerce Department Help
200. Is the Independent Sales Agent for You?
201. Locating or Relocating Your Business
203. Are Your Products and Channels Producing Sales?
204. Pointers on Negotiating DOD Contracts
205. Pointers on Using Temporary-Help Services
206. Keep Pointed Toward Profit
207. Pointers on Scheduling Production
208. Problems in Managing a Family-Owned Business
209. Preventing Employee Pilferage
211. Termination of DOD Contracts for the Government's Convenience
212. The Equipment Replacement Decision
214. The Metric System and Small Business
215. How to Prepare for a Pre-Award Survey
216. Finding a New Product for Your Company
217. Reducing Air Pollution in Industry
218. Business Plan for Small Manufacturers
219. Solid Waste Management in Industry
220. Basic Budgets for Profit Planning
221. Business Plan for Small Construction Firms
222. Business Life Insurance

TECHNICAL AIDS

These leaflets are intended for top technical personnel in small concerns or for technical specialists who supervise the technical aspects of a company's operations.

73. Pointers in In-Plant Trucking
78. Controlling Quality in Defense Production
82. Inspection on Defense Contracts in Small Firms
86. PERT/CPM Management System for the Small Subcontractor
87. Value Analysis for Small Business
90. Welding and Flame-Cutting Processes and Practices
91. A Tested System for Achieving Quality Control
92. Using Adhesives in Small Plants

SMALL MARKETERS AIDS

These leaflets provide suggestions and management guidelines for small retail, whole-sale, and service firms.

SMALL BUSINESS BIBLIOGRAPHIES

These leaflets furnish reference sources for individual types of businesses.

D. NATIONAL TRADE ASSOCIATIONS

Trade associations publish a wealth of information on sales, operating expenses, profits, and financial performance of stores by geographical area. Data in summary form is often available for 5-year periods or longer. Many associations compile sales by department in order to enable the owners to compare the productivity of their departments with that of similar departments of stores located in other parts of the same geographical area. Compensation data on hours worked, salaries and wages paid, and number of persons employed are usually shown also. These statistics provide an excellent source of operating ratios.

Air-Conditioning & Refrigeration Wholesalers, 22371 Newman Avenue, Dearborn, Michigan 48124.

Air Transport Association of America, 1000 Connecticut Avenue, N.W., Washington, D.C. 20036.

American Bankers Association, 90 Park Avenue, New York, New York 10016.

American Book Publishers Council, One Park Avenue, New York, New York 10016.

American Booksellers Association, 175 Fifth Avenue, New York, New York 10010.

American Carpet Institute, 350 Fifth Avenue, New York, New York 10001.

American Institute of Laundering, Doris and Chicago Avenues, Joliet, Illinois 60433.

American Institute of Supply Associations, 1505 22d Street, N.W., Washington, D.C. 20037.

American Meat Institute, 59 East Van Buren Street, Chicago, Illinois 60605.

American Paper Institute, 260 Madison Avenue, New York, New York 10016.

American Society of Association Executives, 2000 K Street, N.W., Washington, D.C. 20006.

American Electric Association, 16223 Meyers Street, Detroit, Michigan 48235.

American Supply Association, 221 North LaSalle Street, Chicago, Illinois 60601.

Automotive Service Industry Association, 230 North Michigan Avenue, Chicago, Illinois 60601.

Bowling Proprietors' Association of America, Inc., West Higgins Road, Hoffman Estates, Illinois 60172.

Florists' Telegraph Delivery Association, 900 West Lafayette Boulevard, Detroit, Michigan 48226.

Food Service Equipment Industry, Inc., 332 South Michigan Avenue, Chicago, Illinois 60604.

Laundry and Cleaners Allied Trades Association, 1180 Raymond Boulevard, Newark, New Jersey 07102.

Material Handling Equipment Distributors Association, 20 North Wacker Drive, Chicago, Illinois 60616.

Mechanical Contractors Association of America, 666 Third Avenue, Suite 1464, New York, New York 10017.

Menswear Retailers of America, 390 National Press Building, Washington, D.C. 20004.

Motor and Equipment Manufacturers Association, 250 West 57th Street, New York, New York 10019.

National-American Wholesale Lumber Association, 180 Madison Avenue, New York, New York 10016.

National Appliance and Radio-TV Dealers Association, 1319 Merchandise Mart, Chicago, Illinois 60654.

National Association of Accountants, 525 Park Avenue, New York, New York 10022.

National Association of Building Owners and Managers, 134 South LaSalle Street, Chicago, Illinois 60603.

National Association of Electrical Distributors, 600 Madison Avenue, New York, New York 10022.

National Association of Food Chains, 1725 Eye Street, N.W., Washington, D.C. 20006.

National Association of Furniture Manufacturers, 666 North Lake Shore Drive, Chicago, Illinois 60611.

National Association of Insurance Agents, 96 Fulton Street, New York, New York 10038.

National Association of Music Merchants, Inc., 222 West Adams Street, Chicago, Illinois 60606.

National Association of Plastic Distributors, 2217 Tribune Tower, Chicago, Illinois 60611.

National Association of Retail Grocers of the United States, 360 North Michigan Avenue, Chicago, Illinois 60601.

National Association of Textile and Apparel Wholesalers, 350 Fifth Avenue, New York, New York 10001.

National Association of Tobacco Distributors, 360 Lexington Avenue, New York, New York 10017.

National Automatic Merchandising Association, 7 South Dearborn Street, Chicago, Illinois 60603.

National Beer Wholesalers' Association of America, 6310 North Cicero Avenue, Chicago, Illinois 60646.

National Builders' Hardware Association, 1290 Avenue of the Americas, New York, New York 10019.

National Electrical Contractors Association, 1200 18th Street, N.W., Washington, D.C. 20036.

National Electrical Manufacturers Association, 155 East 44th Street, New York, New York 10017.

National Farm and Power Equipment Dealers Association, 2340 Hampton Avene, St. Louis, Missouri 63130.

National Home Furnishing Association, 1150 Merchandise Mart, Chicago, Illinois 60654.

National Kitchen Cabinet Association, 918 Commonwealth Building, 674 South Fourth Street, Louisville, Kentucky 40204.

National Lumber and Building Material Dealers Association, Ring Building, Washington, D.C. 20036.

National Office Products Association, Investment Building, 1511 K Street, N.W., Washington, D.C. 20015.

National Machine Tool Builders Association, 2071 East 102d Street, Cleveland, Ohio 44106.

National Oil Jobbers Council, 1001 Connecticut Avenue, N.W., Washington, D.C. 20036.

National Paper Box Manufacturers Association, 121 North Bread Street, Suite 910, Philadelphia, Pennsylvania 19107.

National Paper Trade Association, 220 East 42d Street, New York, New York 10017.

National Parking Association, 1101 17th Street, N.W., Washington, D.C., 20036.

National Restaurant Association, 1530 North Lake Shore Drive, Chicago, Illinois 60610.

National Retail Furniture Association, 1150 Merchandise Mart Plaza, Chicago, Illinois 60654.

National Retail Hardware Association, 964 North Pennsylvania Avenue, Indianapolis, Indiana 46204.

National Retail Merchants Association, 100 West 31st Street, New York, New York 10001.

National Shoe Retailers Association, 200 Madison Avenue, New York, New York 10016.

National Sporting Goods Association, 23 East Jackson Boulevard, Chicago, Illinois 60604.

National Stationery and Office Equipment Association, Investment Building, 1511 K Street, N.W., Washington, D.C. 20005.

National Tire Dealers and Retreaders Association, 1343 L Street, N.W., Washington, D.C. 20005.

National Wholesale Druggists' Association, 220 East 42d Street, New York, New York 10017.

National Wholesale Jewelers Association, 1900 Arch Street, Philadelphia, Pennsylvania 19103.

National Wholesale Hardware Association, 1900 Arch Street, Philadelphia, Pennsylvania 19103.

Northamerican Heating & Airconditioning Wholesalers Association, 1200 West Fifth Avenue, Columbus, Ohio 43212.

Optical Wholesalers Association, 222 West Adams Street, Chicago, Illinois 60606.

Paint and Wallpaper Association of America, 7935 Clayton Road, St. Louis, Missouri 63117.

Petroleum Equipment Institute, 525 Dowell Building, Tulsa, Oklahoma 74114.

Printing Industries of America, 711 14th Street, N.W., Washington, D.C. 20005.

Robert Morris Associates, Philadelphia National Bank Building, Philadelphia, Pennsylvania 19107.

Scientific Apparatus Makers Associates, 20 North Wacker Drive, Chicago, Illinois 60606.

Shoe Service Institute of America, 222 West Adams Street, Chicago, Illinois 60606.

Super Market Institute, Inc., 200 East Ontario Street, Chicago, Illinois 60611.

United Fresh Fruit and Vegetable Association, 777 14th Street, N.W., Washington, D.C. 20005.

United States Wholesale Grocers' Association, 1511 K Street, N.W., Washington, D.C. 20005.

Urban Land Institute, 1200 18th Street, N.W., Washington, D.C. 20036.

Wine and Spirits Wholesalers of America, 319 North Fourth Street, St. Louis, Missouri 63102.

E. SMALL BUSINESS REPORTER PUBLICATION INDEX

These publications are compiled and published by Bank of America, Marketing Publications, Department 3120, P.O. Box 37000, San Francisco, California 94137. *Business Profiles* deal with specific businesses, discussing investment requirements and operational format. *Business Operations* describe and explain various aspects of business management and operations. They relate to problems encountered in all fields. *Professional Management* reports discuss the business side of medical practice for physicians, dentists, and veterinarians. Send for the *Small Business Reporter Publication Index* for an up-to-date listing since new topics are added from time to time.

BUSINESS PROFILES

Apparel Manufacturing
Vol. 10, No. 3, Pub. 1971

Apparel Retailing
Vol. 8, No. 3, Pub. 1968

Auto Parts and Accessory Stores
Vol. 8, No. 12, Pub. 1969.

Bars and Cocktail Lounges
Vol. 11, No. 9, Pub. 1973

Bicycle Shops
Vol. 12, No. 1, Pub. 1974

Bookstores
Vol. 11, No. 6, Pub. 1973

Building Contractors
Vol. 10, No. 1, Pub. 1971

Proprietary Day Care
Vol. 11, No. 8, Pub. 1973

Independent Drug Stores
Vol. 9, No. 12, Pub. 1970

Coin Operated Drycleaning
Vol. 8, No. 7, Pub. 1969

Equipment Rental Business
Vol. 10, No. 6, Pub. 1971

Convenience Food Stores
Vol. 9, No. 6, Pub. 1970

Home Furnishings Stores
Vol. 11, No. 1, Pub. 1972

Gift Stores
Vol. 9, No. 4, Pub. 1970

The Handcraft Business
Vol. 10, No. 8, Pub. 1972

Health Food Stores
Vol. 11, No. 2, Pub. 1973

Coin Operated Laundries
Vol. 8, No. 6, Pub. 1969

Liquor Stores
Vol. 11, No. 4, Pub. 1973

Mail Order Enterprises
Vol. 11, No. 7, Pub. 1973

Manufacturing
Vol. 9, No. 3, Pub. 1970

Mobile Home Parks
Vol. 9, No. 7, Pub. 1970

Mobile Home and Recreational Vehicle
Dealers
Vol. 9, No. 11, Pub. 1970

Retail Nurseries
Vol. 9, No. 10, Pub. 1970

Independent Pet Shops
Vol. 10, No. 2, Pub. 1971

Small Job Printing
Vol. 9, No. 5, Pub. 1970

Repair Services
Vol. 10, No. 9, Pub. 1972

Service Stations
Vol. 10, No. 7, Pub. 1971

Sewing and Needlecraft Centers
Vol. 11, No. 10, Pub. 1974

Independent Sporting Goods Stores
Vol. 10, No. 11, Pub. 1972

BUSINESS OPERATIONS

Advertising
Vol. 13, No. 8, Pub. 1976

Opening Your Own Business: A Personal
Appraisal
Vol. 7, No. 7, Pub. 1971

How to Buy or Sell a Business
Vol. 8, No. 11, Revised 1973

Understanding Financial Statements
Vol. 7, No. 11, Reissued 1971

Financing Small Business
Vol. 8, No. 5, Revised 1973

Franchising
Vol. 9, No. 9, Pub. 1970

Avoiding Management Pitfalls
Vol. 11, No. 5, Pub. 1973

Business Management Advice From
Consultants
Vol. 11, No. 3, Pub. 1973

Management Succession
Vol. 10, No. 12, Pub. 1972

Marketing a New Product
Vol. 10, No. 5, Pub. 1971

Personnel for the Small Business
Vol. 9, No. 8, Pub. 1970

Retail Financial Records
Vol. 10, No. 4, Pub. 1971

Steps to Starting a Business
Vol. 10, No. 10, Pub. 1972

PROFESSIONAL MANAGEMENT

Establishing a Dental Practice
Revised 1974

Establishing a Medical Practice
Pub. 1972

Establishing a Veterinary Practice
Revised 1974

Enrichment References

Baumbeck, Clifford M., et al., *How to Organize and Operate a Small Business,* 5th ed., Prentice-Hall, Inc., Englewood Cliffs, N.J., 1973.

Beckman, Theodore N., and Ronald S. Foster, *Credit and Collections: Management and Theory,* McGraw-Hill Book Company, New York, 1969.

Benton, Lewis R., *Supervision and Management,* McGraw-Hill Book Company, New York, 1972.

Bittel, Lester R., *What Every Supervisor Should Know,* 3d ed., McGraw-Hill Book Company, New York, 1974.

Boyd, Bradford B., *Management-Minded Supervision,* McGraw-Hill Book Company, New York, 1968.

Broom, H. N., and J. G. Longnecker, *Small Business Management,* 4th ed., South-Western Publishing Company, Incorporated, Cincinnati, 1975.

Brummett, R. Lee, and Jack C. Robertson, *Cost Accounting for Small Manufacturers,* Small Business Management Series, No. 9, 2d ed., U.S. Small Business Administration, Washington, 1972.

Bunn, Verne A., *Buying and Selling a Small Business,* U.S. Small Business Administration, Washington, 1969.

Carroll, Phil, *How to Control Production Costs,* McGraw-Hill Book Company, New York, 1962.

Carroll, Phil, *Profit Control: How to Plug Profit Leaks,* McGraw-Hill Book Company, New York, 1962.

Chapin, Albert F., and George E. Hassett, Jr., *Credit and Collection Principles and Practices,* McGraw-Hill Book Company, New York, 1960.

Cook, Harvey R., *Selecting Advertising Media—A Guide for Small Business,* Small Business Management Series, No. 34, U.S. Small Business Administration, Washington, 1969.

Dudick, Thomas S., *Cost Controls in Business,* Prentice-Hall, Inc., Englewood Cliffs, N.J., 1962.

Eccles, Robert W., et al., *Essentials of Management for First-Line Supervision,* John Wiley & Sons, Inc., New York, 1974.

Franchise Opportunities Handbook, U.S. Department of Commerce, Washington. (Order from Superintendent of Documents, Washington, D.C., 20402.)

Greene, Mark R., *Insurance and Risk Management for Small Business,* Small Business Management Series, No. 30, U.S. Small Business Administration, Washington, 1970.

Immer, John R., *Profitable Small Plant Layout,* Small Business Management Series, No. 21, 2d ed., U.S. Small Business Administration, Washington, 1964.

Krentzman, Harvey C., *Managing for Profit,* U.S. Small Business Administration, Washington, 1968.

Lewis, Herschell Gordon, *The Businessman's Guide to Advertising and Sales Promotion,* McGraw-Hill Book Company, New York, 1974.

Material Handling Institute, *Improving Material Handling in Small Business,* Small Business Series, No. 4, 3d ed., U.S. Small Business Administration, Washington, 1969.

Mayer, Kurt B., and Sidney Goldstein, *The First Two Years: Problems of Small Firm Growth and Survival,* U.S. Small Business Administration, Washington, 1961.

Metcalf, Wendell O., *Starting and Managing a Small Business of Your Own,* The Starting and Managing Series, Vol. 1, 3d ed., U.S. Small Business Administration, Washington, 1973.

Metz, Robert, *Franchising: How to Select a Business of Your Own,* Hawthorn Books, Inc., New York, 1969.

Moore, Franklin G., *Manufacturing Management,* Richard D. Irwin, Inc., Homewood, Ill., 1958.

Muther, Richard, *Practical Plant Layout,* McGraw-Hill Book Company, New York, 1956.

National Association of Credit Management, *Credit Management Handbook,* Richard D. Irwin, Inc., Homewood, Ill., 1965.

Ragan, Robert C., *Financial Recordkeeping for Small Stores,* U.S. Small Business Administration, Washington, 1966.

Sanzo, Richard, *Ratio Analysis for Small Business,* Small Business Management Series, No. 30, U.S. Small Business Administration, Washington, 1970.

Steinhoff, Dan, *Small Business Management Fundamentals,* McGraw-Hill Book Company, New York, 1974.

Steinmetz, Lawrence L., et al., *Managing the Small Business,* Richard D. Irwin, Inc., Homewood, Ill., 1968.

Zwick, Jack, *A Handbook of Small Business Finance,* Small Business Management Series, No. 15, U.S. Small Business Administration, Washington, 1965.

Key to Self-Checks

Chapter 1		Chapter 2		Chapter 3		Chapter 4	
1.	T	1.	F	1.	T	1.	T
2.	T	2.	T	2.	T	2.	F
3.	T	3.	T	3.	F	3.	T
4.	F	4.	T	4.	T	4.	T
5.	T	5.	T	5.	T	5.	T
6.	T	6.	F	6.	T	6.	F
7.	F	7.	T	7.	T	7.	F
8.	T	8.	F	8.	T	8.	T
9.	F	9.	F	9.	T	9.	F
10.	T	10.	T	10.	F	10.	T
		11.	T				
		12.	T				

Chapter 5		Chapter 6		Chapter 7		Chapter 8	
1.	T	1.	T	1.	T	1.	T
2.	T	2.	T	2.	T	2.	F
3.	F	3.	F	3.	T	3.	F
4.	T	4.	F	4.	F	4.	T
5.	T	5.	F	5.	F	5.	T
6.	F	6.	T	6.	F	6.	F
7.	T	7.	T	7.	T	7.	T
8.	T	8.	T	8.	T	8.	F
9.	F	9.	F	9.	T	9.	T
10.	T			10.	T	10.	F

Chapter 9		Chapter 10		Chapter 11		Chapter 12	
1.	T	1.	F	1.	F	1.	F
2.	T	2.	T	2.	T	2.	T
3.	F	3.	T	3.	T	3.	T
4.	T	4.	T	4.	T	4.	F
5.	F	5.	F	5.	F	5.	T
6.	F	6.	T	6.	T	6.	T
7.	T	7.	T	7.	F	7.	F
8.	T	8.	F	8.	T	8.	F
9.	T	9.	T	9.	F	9.	T
10.	F	10.	F	10.	T	10.	T
				11.	T		
				12.	T		
				13.	T		
				14.	T		
				15.	T		

Chapter 13

1. T
2. F
3. F
4. T
5. F
6. T
7. T
8. T
9. F
10. T

Chapter 14

1. F
2. T
3. T
4. T
5. F
6. T
7. F
8. T
9. T
10. T
11. T
12. T

Chapter 15

1. T
2. T
3. F
4. F
5. T
6. F
7. T
8. T
9. T
10. F

Chapter 16

1. T
2. T
3. F
4. T
5. F
6. T
7. F
8. T
9. T
10. F

Chapter 17

1. F
2. T
3. F
4. T
5. T
6. T
7. T
8. T
9. T
10. F

Chapter 18

1. F
2. F
3. T
4. T
5. T
6. T
7. T
8. F
9. F
10. T
11. T
12. F
13. T
14. T
15. F

Chapter 19

1. T
2. T
3. F
4. F
5. T
6. F
7. T
8. F
9. F
10. T
11. T
12. T
13. T
14. F

Chapter 20

1. T
2. T
3. F
4. F
5. F
6. F
7. T
8. F
9. F
10. F

Chapter 21

1. F
2. F
3. T
4. T
5. T
6. T
7. T
8. F
9. F
10. F

Index

Overhead costs (*continued*)
  in retailing and wholesaling, 226–229
Overhead rate, 235–237
Overtime
  high cost of, 362–364
  patterns of, 364–366
  point of no return in, 364

P

Parking as a site selection factor, 144
Partnerships
  administrative problems in, 97
  borrowing ability, 98
  characteristics, 94–95
  defined, 93–94
  ease of starting, 95–96
  liability of, 96
  tax advantages of, 98–100
Payroll record, 210–211
Personal selling, 454–455
Personal selling checklist, 456
Personnel acquisition
  applications, 465
  determining need for, 462–463
  finding qualified workers, 465, 468
  interviewing, 465–467
  sources of new employees, 465–466
  use of job descriptions, 464
  use of probationary periods, 469
  use of references, 468
Pilferage checklist, 376–377
Placement of merchandise (*see* Layout,
    placement of goods)
Planning
  and business success, 34
  nature of, 34–35
  obstacles to, 38
  steps in, 38–39
  time spent in, 36
  what to plan for, 36–37
Population data in market surveys, 394–
    396
Population requirements for small firms,
    140–141
Population statistics, sources of, 138
Price, meaning of, 407–408
Price lining, 420–421
Pricing
  to assure a profit, 274–275
  basic considerations, 409
  checklist, 424–425
  effect of competition on, 412–413

Pricing (*continued*)
  effect of fair-trade laws on, 413–414
  factors which influence, 409–410
  of new products, 415–416
  related to distribution costs, 414
  suggested retail prices, 414
Pricing policies
  in manufacturing, 422
  markdowns, 419–420
  markups, 416–419
  multiple pricing, 420
  price lining, 420–421
  in retailing, 421
  in service firms, 422–424
Process layout, 171–172
Product layout, 171
Profit
  eroded by rising costs, 265–266
  kinds of, 255–256
  leaks, 272–273
  planning for, 267
  related to price, 274–275
  related to return on investment, 269–
    270
  resulting from cost reduction, 266–267
  in selected lines, 74–75
  and volume, 273–274
Profit-and-loss statement
  illustrated, 250
  kinds of accounts in, 254–256
Profit planning, factors in, 263–265
Profitability ratios
  net profit, 268–269
  return-on-investment, 269–270
  return-on-owner's-equity, 269
Promotion, sales
  compared with advertising, 435
  defined, 429–430
  developing the store's image, 430–432
  direct methods of, 434
  what to promote, 433–434
Proprietorships
  administrative problems in, 97
  borrowing ability, 98
  characteristics, 94–95
  defined, 93–94
  ease of starting, 95–96
  liability of, 96
  tax advantages of, 98–100
Purchasing considerations
  contribution to profit, 379–383
  supplier evaluation, 382–383

Training of employees (continued)
    need for, 469–470
    timetables, use of, 470–471
    training devices, 473–474
Truth in Lending Act, 349–350
Turnover, inventory, 258–259
Turnover, labor
    cost of, 374
    defined, 373
    prevention of, 374–375
    rate of in United States, 374
Types of small business activity, 4–5

U

Unemployment insurance taxes, 506
Uniform Commercial Code, 495–499

V

Variable expenses (*see* Costs, variable)
Vehicle insurance, 324–325

W

Wage and hour legislation, 493–494
Warranties, effect on business, 499
Window display checklist, 452
Working capital
    and cash conservation, 118–119
    defined, 106
    sources of, 123–125

Y

Yellow Pages advertising, 447